D1393810

Advances in Economics and Econom

This is the first of three volumes containing edited versions of papers and commentaries presented at invited symposium sessions of the Eighth World Congress of the Econometric Society held in Seattle, WA, in August 2000. The papers summarize and interpret recent key developments, and they discuss future directions for a wide range of topics in economics and ʜ ʜ ʜ ʜ ʜ ics. The papers ʜ ʜ ver ʜ ʜ heory and applications. Written by leading ʜ ʜ ʜ ʜ in their fields ʜ ʜ ʜ provide a unique survey of progress in th ʜ ʜ cipline.

Mathias Dewatripont is Professor of Economics ʜ ʜ ʜ ʜ ʜ sité Libre de Bruxelles where he was the founding Director of the Europea.. Cc.:re for Advanced Research in Economics (ECARE). Since 1998, he has been Research Director of the London-based CEPR (Centre for Economic Policy Research) network. In 1998, he received the Francqui Prize, awarded each year to a Belgian scientist below the age of 50.

Lars Peter Hansen is Homer J. Livingston Distinguished Service Professor of Economics at the University of Chicago. He was a co-winner of the Frisch Prize Medal in 1984. He is also a member of the National Academy of Sciences.

Stephen J. Turnovsky is Castor Professor of Economics at the University of Washington and recently served as an Editor of the *Journal of Economic Dynamics and Control*. He is an Associate Editor and is on the Editorial Board of four other journals in economic theory and international economics.

Professors Dewatripont, Hansen, and Turnovsky are Fellows of the Econometric Society and were Program Co-Chairs of the Eighth World Congress of the Econometric Society, held in Seattle, WA, in August 2000.

Advances in Economics and Econometrics

Theory and Applications, Eighth World Congress, Volume I

Edited by

Mathias Dewatripont

*Université Libre de Bruxelles
and CEPR, London*

Lars Peter Hansen

University of Chicago

Stephen J. Turnovsky

University of Washington

CAMBRIDGE
UNIVERSITY PRESS

PUBLISHED BY THE PRESS SYNDICATE OF THE UNIVERSITY OF CAMBRIDGE
The Pitt Building, Trumpington Street, Cambridge, United Kingdom

CAMBRIDGE UNIVERSITY PRESS
The Edinburgh Building, Cambridge CB2 2RU, UK
40 West 20th Street, New York, NY 10011-4211, USA
477 Williamstown Road, Port Melbourne, VIC 3207, Australia
Ruiz de Alarcón 13, 28014 Madrid, Spain
Dock House, The Waterfront, Cape Town 8001, South Africa

http://www.cambridge.org

First published 2003

Printed in the United States of America

Typeface Times Roman 10/12 pt.   *System* LaTeX 2_ε [TB]

A catalog record for this book is available from the British Library.

Library of Congress Cataloging-in-Publication Data
Advances in economics and econometrics : theory and applications : eighth world
   Congress / edited by Mathias Dewatripont, Lars Peter Hansen, Stephen J. Turnovsky.
        p.   cm. – (Econometric Society monographs ; 2003.)
      ISBN 0-521-81872-9 (v.1) – ISBN 0-521-52411-3 (pb.) – ISBN 0-521-81873-7 (v.2) –
   ISBN 0-521-52412-1 (pb.) – ISBN 0-521-81874-5 (v.3) – ISBN 0-521-52413-X (pb.)
      1. Econometrics – Congresses.   2. Economics – Congresses.   I. Dewatripont, M.
   (Mathias)   II. Hansen, Lars Peter.   III. Turnovsky, Stephen J.   IV. Econometric
   Society. World Congress (7th : 1995 : Tokyo, Japan)   V. Series.
   HB139 .A35   2003
   330 – dc21   2002071258

ISBN 0 521 81872 9 hardback
ISBN 0 521 52411 3 paperback

Contents

Preface

These volumes contain the papers of the invited symposium sessions of the Eighth World Congress of the Econometric Society. The meetings were held at the University of Washington, Seattle, in August 2000; we served as Program Co-Chairs. The book also contains an invited address, the "Seattle Lecture," given by Eric Maskin. This address was in addition to other named lectures that are typically published in *Econometrica*. Symposium sessions had discussants, and about half of them wrote up their comments for publication. These remarks are included in the book after the session papers they comment on.

The book chapters explore and interpret recent developments in a variety of areas in economics and econometrics. Although we chose topics and authors to represent the broad interests of members of the Econometric Society, the selected areas were not meant to be exhaustive. We deliberately included some new active areas of research not covered in recent Congresses. For many chapters, we encouraged collaboration among experts in an area. Moreover, some sessions were designed to span the econometrics–theory separation that is sometimes evident in the Econometric Society. We followed the lead of our immediate predecessors, David Kreps and Ken Wallis, by including all of the contributions in a single book edited by the three of us. Because of the number of contributions, we have divided the book into three volumes; the topics are grouped in a manner that seemed appropriate to us.

We believe that the Eighth World Congress of the Econometric Society was very successful, and we hope that these books serve as suitable mementos of that event. We are grateful to the members of our Program Committee for their dedication and advice, and to Scott Parris at Cambridge University Press for his guidance and support during the preparation of these volumes. We also acknowledge support from the officers of the Society – Presidents Robert Lucas, Jean Tirole, Robert Wilson, Elhanan Helpman, and Avinash Dixit – as well as the Treasurer, Robert Gordon, and Secretary, Julie Gordon. Finally, we express our gratitude to the Co-Chairs of the Local Organizing Committee, Jacques Lawarree and Fahad Khalil, for a smoothly run operation.

CHAPTER 1

Auctions and Efficiency

Eric Maskin

1. INTRODUCTION

The allocation of resources is an all-pervasive theme in economics. Furthermore, the question of whether there exist mechanisms ensuring *efficient* allocation (i.e., mechanisms that ensure that resources end up in the hands of those who value them most) is of central importance in the discipline. Indeed, the very word "economics" connotes a preoccupation with the issue of efficiency.

But economists' interest in efficiency does not end with the question of existence. If efficient mechanisms can be constructed, we want to know what they look like and to what extent they might resemble institutions used in practice.

Understandably, the question of what will constitute an efficient mechanism has been a major concern of economic theorists going back to Adam Smith. But, the issue is far from just a theoretical one. It is also of considerable practical importance. This is particularly clear when it comes to *privatization*, the transfer of assets from the state to the private sector.

In the last 15 years or so, we have seen a remarkable flurry of privatizations in Eastern Europe, the former Soviet Union, China, and highly industrialized Western nations, such as the United States, the United Kingdom, and Germany. An important justification for these transfers has been the expectation that they will improve efficiency. But if efficiency is the rationale, an obvious leading question to ask is: "What sorts of transfer mechanisms will *best* advance this objective?"

One possible and, of course, familiar answer is "the Market." We know from the First Theorem of Welfare Economics (see Debreu, 1959) that, under certain conditions, the *competitive* mechanism (the uninhibited exchange and production of goods by buyers and sellers) results in an efficient allocation. A major constraint on the applicability of this result to the circumstances of privatization, however, is the theorem's hypothesis of *large numbers*. For the competitive mechanism to work properly – to avoid the exercise of monopoly power – there must be sufficiently many buyers and sellers so that no single agent has an appreciable effect on prices. But privatization often entails small numbers. In the recent U.S. "spectrum" auctions – the auctions in which the government sold rights (in the form of licenses) to use certain radio frequency bands for telecommunications – there were often only two or three serious bidders for a given license. The competitive model does not seem readily applicable to such a setting.

An interesting alternative possibility was raised by William Vickrey (1961) 40 years ago. Vickrey showed that, if a seller has a single indivisible good for sale, a *second-price* auction (see Section 2) is an efficient mechanism – i.e., the winner is the buyer whose valuation of the good is highest – in the case where buyers have *private values* ("private values" mean that no buyer's private information affects any other buyer's valuation). This finding is rendered even more significant by the fact that it can be readily extended to the sale of multiple goods,[1] as shown by Theodore Groves (1973) and Edward Clarke (1971). Unfortunately, once the assumption of private values is dropped and thus buyers' valuations *do* depend on other buyers' information (i.e., we are in the world of common[2] or interdependent values), the second-price auction is no longer efficient, as I will illustrate later by means of an example. Yet, the common-values case is the norm in practice. If, say, a telecommunications firm undertakes a market survey to forecast demand for cell phones in a given region, the results of the survey will surely be of interest to its competitors and thus turn the situation into one of common values.

Recently, a literature has developed on the design of efficient auctions in common-values settings. The time is not yet ripe for a survey; the area is currently evolving too rapidly for that. But I would like to take this opportunity to discuss a few of the ideas from this literature.

2. THE BASIC MODEL

Because it is particularly simple, I will begin with the case of a single indivisible good. Later, I will argue that much (but not all) of what holds in the one-good case extends to multiple goods.

Suppose that there are n potential buyers. It will be simplest to assume that they are risk-neutral (however, we can accommodate any other attitude toward risk if the model is specialized to the case in which there is no residual uncertainty about valuations when all buyers' information is pooled). Assume that each buyer i's private information about the good can be summarized by a *real-valued* signal. That is, buyer i's information is reducible to a one-dimensional parameter.[3] Formally, suppose that each buyer i's signal s_i lies in

---

[1] Vickrey himself also treated the case of multiple units of the same good.

[2] I am using "common values" in the *broad* sense to cover any instance where one agent's payoff depends on another's information. The term is sometimes used narrowly to mean that all agents share the same payoff.

[3] Later on, I will examine the case of multidimensional signals. As with multiple goods, much will generalize. As we will see, the most problematic case is that in which there are *both* multiple goods and multidimensional signals.

an interval $[\underline{s}_i, \bar{s}_i]$. The joint prior distribution of $(s_1, \ldots, s_n)$ is given by the c.d.f. $F(s_1, \ldots, s_n)$. Buyer i's valuation for the good (i.e., the most he would be willing to pay for it) is given by the function $v_i(s_1, \ldots, s_n)$. I shall suppose (with little loss of generality) that higher values of s_i correspond to higher valuations, i.e.,

$$\frac{\partial v_i}{\partial s_i} > 0. \tag{2.1}$$

Let us examine two illustrations of this model.

Example 2.1. *Suppose that*

$$v_i(s_1, \ldots, s_n) = s_i.$$

In this case, we are in the world of private values, not the interesting setting from the perspective of this lecture, but a valid special case.

A more pertinent example is:

Example 2.2. *Suppose that the* true *value of the good to buyer i is y_i, which, in turn, is the sum of a value component that is common to all buyers and a component that is peculiar to buyer i. That is,*

$$y_i = z + z_i,$$

where z is the common component and z_i is buyer i's idiosyncratic component. Suppose, however, that buyer i does not actually observe y_i, but only a noisy signal

$$s_i = y_i + \varepsilon_i, \tag{2.2}$$

where ε_i is the noise term, and all the random variables $-z$, the z_is, and the ε_is $-$ are independent. In this case, every buyer j's signal s_j provides information to buyer i about his valuation, because s_j is correlated [via (2.2)] with the common component z. Hence, we can express $v_i(s_1, \ldots, s_n)$ as

$$v_i(s_1, \ldots, s_n) = E[y_i | s_1, \ldots, s_n], \tag{2.3}$$

where the right-hand side of (2.3) denotes the expectation of y_i conditional on the signals $(s_1, \ldots, s_n)$.

This second example might be kept in mind as representative of the sort of scenario that the analysis is intended to apply to.

3. AUCTIONS

An *auction* in the model of Section 2 is a *mechanism* (alternatively termed a "game form" or "outcome function") that, on the basis of the bids submitted, determines (i) who wins (i.e., who – if anyone – is awarded the good), and

(ii) how much each buyer pays.[4] Let us call an auction *efficient* provided that, in equilibrium, buyer i is the winner if and only if

$$v_i(s_1, \ldots, s_n) \geq \max_{j \neq i} v_j(s_1, \ldots, s_n) \tag{3.1}$$

(this definition is slightly inaccurate because of the possibility of ties for highest valuation, an issue that I shall ignore). In other words, efficiency demands that, in an equilibrium of the auction, the winner be the buyer with the highest valuation, conditional on *all available information* (i.e., on all buyers' signals).

This notion of efficiency is sometimes called expost efficiency. It assumes implicitly that the social value of the good being sold equals the maximum of the potential buyers' individual valuations. This assumption would be justified if, for example, each buyer used the good (e.g., a spectrum license) to produce an output (e.g., telecommunication service) that is sold in a competitive market without significant externalities (market power or externalities might drive a wedge between individual and social values).

The reader may wonder why, even if one wants efficiency, it is necessary to insist that the auction itself be efficient. After all, the buyers could always retrade afterward if the auction resulted in a winner with less than the highest valuation. The problem with relying on postauction trade, however, is much the same as that plaguing competitive exchange in the first place: These mechanisms do not, in general, work efficiently when there are only a few traders. To see this, consider the following example:[5]

Example 3.1. *Suppose that there are two buyers. Assume that buyer 1 has won the auction and has a valuation of 1. If the auction is not guaranteed to be efficient, then there is some chance that buyer 2's valuation is higher. Suppose that, from buyer 1's perspective, buyer 2's valuation is distributed uniformly in the interval [0, 2]. Now, if there is to be further trade after the auction, someone has to initiate it. Let us assume that buyer 1 does so by proposing a trading price to buyer 2. Presumably, buyer 1 will propose a price p^* that maximizes his expected payoff, i.e., that solves*

$$\max_p \frac{1}{2}(2 - p)(p - 1). \tag{$*$}$$

[To understand $(*)$, note that $\frac{1}{2}(2 - p)$ is the probability that the proposal is accepted – since it is the probability that buyer 2's valuation is at least p – and that $p - 1$ is buyer 1's net gain in the event of acceptance.] But the solution to $(*)$ is $p^* = \frac{3}{2}$. Hence, if buyer 2's valuation lies between 1 and $\frac{3}{2}$, the allocation,

---

[4] For some purposes – e.g., dealing with risk-averse buyers (see Maskin and Riley, 1984), liquidity constraints (see Che and Gale, 1996, or Maskin, 2000) or allocative externalities (see Jehiel and Moldovanu (2001) – one must consider auctions in which buyers other than the winner also make payments. In this lecture, however, I will not have to deal with this possibility.

[5] In this example, buyers have private values, but, as Fieseler, Kittsteiner, and Moldavanu (2000) show, resale can become even more problematic when there are common values.

even after allowing for expost trade, will remain inefficient, because buyer 2 will reject 1's proposal.

I will first look at efficiency in the *second-price* auction. This auction form (often called the *Vickrey* auction) has the following rules: (i) each bidder i makes a (sealed) bid b_i, which is a nonnegative number; (ii) the winner is the bidder who has made the highest bid (again ignoring the issue of ties); (iii) the winner pays the second-highest bid, $\max_{j \neq i} b_j$. As I have already noted and will illustrate explicitly, in Section 6 this auction can readily be extended to multiple goods.

The Vickrey auction is efficient in the case of private values.[6] To see this, note first that it is optimal – in fact, a dominant strategy – for buyer i to set $b_i = v_i$ (i.e., to bid his true valuation). In particular, bidding below v_i does not affect buyer i's payment if he wins (because his bid does not depend on his own bid); it just reduces his chance of winning – and so is not a good strategy. Bidding above v_i raises buyer i's probability of winning, but the additional events in which he wins are precisely those in which someone else has bid higher than v_i. In such events, buyer i pays more than v_i, also not a desirable outcome. Thus, it is indeed optimal to bid $b_i = v_i$, which implies that the winner is the buyer with the highest valuation, the criterion for efficiency.

Unfortunately, the Vickrey auction does not remain efficient once we depart from private values. To see this, consider the following example.

Example 3.4. *Suppose that there are three buyers with valuation functions*

$$v_1(s_1, s_2, s_3) = s_1 + \frac{2}{3}s_2 + \frac{1}{3}s_3,$$

$$v_2(s_1, s_2, s_3) = s_2 + \frac{1}{3}s_1 + \frac{2}{3}s_3,$$

$$v_3(s_1, s_2, s_3) = s_3.$$

Notice that buyers 1 and 2 have common values (i.e., their valuations do not depend only on their own signals). Assume that it happens that $s_1 = s_2 = 1$ (of course, buyers 1 and 2 would not know that their signal values are equal, because signals are private information), and suppose that buyer 3's signal value is either slightly below or slightly above 1. In the former case, it is easy to see that

$$v_1 > v_2 > v_3,$$

and so, for efficiency, buyer 1 ought to win. However, in the latter case

$$v_2 > v_1 > v_3,$$

---

[6] It is easy to show that the "first-price" auction – the auction in which each buyer makes a bid, the high bidder wins, and the winner pays his bid – is a nonstarter as far as efficiency is concerned. Indeed, even in the case of private values, the first-price auction is never efficient, except when buyers' valuations are symmetrically distributed (see Maskin, 1992).

and so buyer 2 is the efficient winner. Thus, the efficient allocation between buyers 1 and 2 turns on whether s_3 is below or above 1. But, in a Vickrey auction, the bids made by buyers 1 and 2 cannot incorporate information about s_3, because that signal is private information to buyer 3. Thus, the outcome of the auction cannot in general be efficient.

4. AN EFFICIENT AUCTION

How should we respond to the shortcomings of the Vickrey auction as illustrated by Example 3.3? One possible reaction is to appeal to classical mechanism-design theory. Specifically, we could have each buyer i announce a signal value $\hat{s}_i$, award the good to the buyer i for whom $v_i(\hat{s}_1, \ldots, \hat{s}_n)$ is highest, and choose the winner's payment to evoke truth-telling in buyers (i.e., to induce each buyer j to set $\hat{s}_j$ equal to his true signal value s_j). This approach is taken in Crémer and McLean (1985) and Maskin (1992).

The problem with such a "direct revelation" mechanism is that it is utterly unworkable in practice. In particular, notice that it requires the mechanism designer to know the physical signal spaces $S_1, \ldots, S_n$, the functional forms $v_i(\cdot)$, and the prior distributions of the signals – an extraordinarily demanding constraint. Now, the mechanism designer could attempt to elicit this information from the buyers themselves using the methods of the implementation literature (see Palfrey, 1993). For example, to learn the signal spaces, he could have each buyer announce a vector $(\hat{S}_1, \ldots, \hat{S}_n)$ and assign suitable penalties if the announcements did not match up appropriately. A major difficulty with such a scheme, however, is that in all likelihood the signal spaces S_i are themselves *private* information. For analytic purposes, we model S_i as simply an interval of numbers. But, this abstracts from the reality that buyer i's signal corresponds to some *physical* entity – whatever it is that buyer i observes. Indeed, the signal may well be a sufficient statistic for data from a variety of different informational sources, and there is no reason why other buyers should know just what this array of sources is.

To avoid these complications, I shall concentrate on auction rules that do not make use of such details as signal spaces, functional forms, and distributions. Indeed, I will be interested in auctions that work well irrespective of these details; that is, I will adhere to the "Wilson Doctrine" (after Robert Wilson, who has been an eloquent proponent of the view that auction institutions should be "detail-free"). It turns out that a judicious modification of the Vickrey auction will do the trick.

Before turning to the modification, however, I need to introduce a restriction on valuation functions that is critical to the possibility of constructing efficient auctions. Let us assume that for all i and $j \neq i$ and all $(s_1, \ldots, s_n)$,

$$v_i(s_1, \ldots, s_n) = v_j(s_1, \ldots, s_n) \Rightarrow \frac{\partial v_i}{\partial s_i}(s_1, \ldots, s_n) > \frac{\partial v_j}{\partial s_i}(s_1, \ldots, s_n).^7 \quad (4.1)$$

---

[7] This condition was introduced by Gresik (1991).

In other words, condition (4.1) says that buyer i's signal has a greater marginal effect on his own valuation than on that of any other buyer j (at least at points where buyer i's and buyer j's valuations are equal).

Notice that, in view of (2.1), condition (4.1)[8] is automatically satisfied by Example 2.1 (the case of private values): the right-hand side of the inequality then simply vanishes. Condition (4.1) also holds for Example 2.2. This is because, in that example, s_i conveys relevant information to buyer j ($\neq i$) about the common component z, but tells buyer i not only about z but also his idiosyncratic component z_i. Thus, v_i will be more sensitive than v_j to variations in s_i.

But whether or not condition (4.1) is likely to be satisfied, it is, in any event, essential for efficiency. To see what can go wrong without it, consider the following example.

Example 4.5. *Suppose that the owner of a tract of land wishes to sell off the rights to drill for oil on her property. There are two potential drillers who are competing for this right. Driller 1's fixed cost of drilling is 1, whereas his marginal cost is 2. In contrast, driller 2 has fixed and marginal costs of 2 and 1, respectively. Assume that driller 1 observes how much oil is underground. That is, s_1 equals the quantity of oil. Driller 2 obtains no private information. Then, if the price of oil is 4, we have*

$$v_1(s_1) = (4-2)s_1 - 1 = 2s_1 - 1,$$
$$v_2(s_1) = (4-1)s_1 - 2 = 3s_1 - 2.$$

Observe that $v_1(s_1) > v_2(s_1)$ if and only if $s_1 < 1$. Thus, for efficiency, driller 1 should be awarded drilling rights provided that $\frac{1}{2} < s_1 < 1$ (for $s_1 < \frac{1}{2}$, there is not enough oil to justify drilling at all). Driller 2, by contrast, should get the rights when $s_1 > 1$.

In this example, there is no way (either through a modified Vickrey auction or otherwise) of inducing driller 1 to reveal the true value s_1 to allocate drilling rights efficiently. To see this, consider, without loss of generality, a direct revelation mechanism and let $t_1(\hat{s}_1)$ be a monetary transfer (possibly negative) to driller 1 if he announces signal value $\hat{s}_1$. Let s_1' and s_1'' be signal values such that

$$\frac{1}{2} < s_1' < 1 < s_1''. \tag{4.2}$$

Then, for driller 1 to have the incentive to announce truthfully when $s_1 = s_1''$, we must have

$$t_1(s_1'') \geq 2s_1'' - 1 + t_1(s_1') \tag{4.3}$$

---

[8] Notice that the strictness of the inequality in (4.1) rules out the case of "pure common values," where all buyers share the same valuation. However, in that case, the issue of who wins does not matter for efficiency.

version of (4.1):

$$\frac{\partial v_i}{\partial s_i} > \frac{\partial v_j}{\partial s_i}. \tag{4.12}$$

Let us suppose that buyer 2 is truthful, i.e., he bids $b_2(\cdot)$ satisfying (4.9). I must show that it is optimal for buyer 1 to bid $b_1(\cdot)$ satisfying (4.8).

Notice first that if buyer 1 wins, his payoff is

$$v_1(s_1, s_2) - v_1^*, \quad \text{where} \quad v_1^* = b_2(v_1^*), \tag{4.13}$$

regardless of how he bids (because neither his valuation nor his payment depends on his bid). I claim that if buyer 1 bids truthfully, then he wins if and only if (4.13) is positive. Observe that if this claim is established, then I will in fact have shown that truthful bidding is optimal; because buyer 1's bid does not affect (4.13), the most he can possibly hope for is to win precisely in those cases where the net payoff from winning is positive.

To see that the claim holds, let us first differentiate (4.9) with respect to s_1' to obtain

$$\frac{db_2}{dv_1}(v_1(s_1', s_2))\frac{\partial v_1}{\partial s_1}(s_1', s_2) = \frac{\partial v_2}{\partial s_1}(s_1', s_2) \quad \text{for all} \quad s_1'.$$

This identity, together with (2.1) and (4.12), implies that

$$\frac{db_2}{dv_1}(v_1) < 1, \quad \text{for all} \quad v_1. \tag{4.14}$$

But, from (4.14), (4.13) is positive if and only if

$$v_1(s_1, s_2) - v_1^* > \frac{db_2}{dv_1}(v_1')(v_1(s_1, s_2) - v_1^*) \quad \text{for all} \quad v_1'. \tag{4.15}$$

Now, from the intermediate value theorem, there exists $v_1' \in [v_1^*, v_1(s_1, s_2)]$ such that

$$b_2(v_1(s_1, s_2)) - b_2(v_1^*) = \frac{db_2}{dv_1}(v_1')(v_1(s_1, s_2) - v_1^*).$$

Hence (4.13) is positive if and only if

$$v_1(s_1, s_2) - v_1^* > b_2(v_1(s_1, s_2)) - b_2(v_1^*), \tag{4.16}$$

which, because $v_1^* = b_2(v_1^*)$, is equivalent to

$$v_1(s_1, s_2) > v_2(s_1, s_2). \tag{4.17}$$

Now suppose that buyer 1 is truthful. Because $(v_1(s_1, s_2), v_2(s_1, s_2))$ is then a fixed point, 1 wins if and only if (4.17) holds. So, we can conclude that, when buyer 1 is truthful, his net payoff from winning is positive [i.e., (4.13) is positive] if and only if he wins, which is what I claimed. That is, the modified Vickrey auction is efficient. (This analysis ignores the possible costs to buyers of aquiring signals; once such costs are incorporated the modified Vickrey auction is no longer efficient in general – see Maskin, 1992 and Bergeman and Välimäki, 2000.)

An attractive feature of the Vickrey auction in the case of private values is that bidding one's true valuation is optimal *regardless* of the behavior of other buyers (i.e., it is a *dominant strategy*). Once we abandon private values, however, there is no hope of finding an efficient mechanism with dominant strategies (this is because, if my payoff depends on your signal, then my optimal strategy necessarily depends on the way that your strategy reflects your signal value, and so is not independent of what you do). Nevertheless, equilibrium in our modified Vickery auction has a strong robustness property. In particular, notice that although, technically, truthful bidding constitutes only a Bayesian (rather than dominant-strategy) equilibrium, equilibrium strategies are *independent* of the prior distribution of signals F. That is, regardless of buyers' prior beliefs about signals, they will behave the same way in equilibrium. In particular, this means that the modified Vickrey auction will be efficient even in the case in which buyers' signals are believed to be independent of one another.[11] It also means that truthful bidding will remain an equilibrium even after buyers learn one another's signal values; i.e., truthful bidding constitutes an ex post Nash equilibrium. Finally Chung and Ely (2001) show that, at least in the two-buyer case, the modified Vickrey auction is dominant solvable.

One might complain that having a buyer make his bid a function of the other buyer's valuation imposes a heavy informational burden on him – what if he does not know anything about the connection between the other's valuation and his own? I would argue, however, that the modified Vickrey auction should be viewed as giving buyers an additional *opportunity* rather than as setting an onerous requirement. After all, the degree to which a buyer makes his bid contingent is entirely up to him. In particular, he always has the option of bidding entirely *uncontingently* (i.e., of submitting a constant function). Thus, contingency is *optional* (but, of course, the degree to which the modified Vickrey auction will be more efficient than the ordinary Vickrey will turn on the extent to which buyers are prepared to bid contingently).

I have explicitly illustrated how the modified Vickrey auction works only in the case of two bidders, but the logic extends immediately to larger numbers. For the case of n buyers, the rules become:

1. Each buyer i submits a contingent bid schedule $\hat{b}_i(\cdot)$, which is a function of v_{-i}, the vector of valuations excluding that of buyer i.
2. The auctioneer computes a fixed point $(v_1^o, \ldots, v_n^o)$, where $v_i^o = \hat{b}_i(v_{-i}^o)$ for all i.
3. The winner is the buyer i for whom $v_i^o \geq v_j^o$ for all $j \neq i$.

---

[11] Crémer and McLean (1985) exhibit a mechanism that attains efficiency if the joint distribution of signals is common knowledge (including to the auction designer) and exhibits correlation. R. McLean and A. Postlewaite (2001) show how this sort of mechanism can be generalized to the case where the auction designer himself does not know the joint distribution.

4. The winner pays $\max_{j \neq i} \hat{b}_j(v^*_{-j})$, where, for all $j \neq i$, v^*_j satisfies $v^*_j = \hat{b}_j(v^*_{-j})$.

Under conditions (2.1) and (4.1), an argument similar to the two-buyer demonstration establishes that it is an equilibrium in this auction for each buyer to bid truthfully (see Dasgupta and Maskin, 2000).[12] That is, if buyer i's signal value is s_i, he should set $\hat{b}_i(\cdot) = b_i(\cdot)$ such that

$$b_i(v_{-i}(s_i, s'_{-i})) = v_i(s_i, s'_{-i}) \quad \text{for all} \quad s'_{-i}.^{13} \tag{4.18}$$

Furthermore, it is easy to see that, if buyers bid truthfully, the auction results in an efficient allocation.

One drawback of the modified Vickrey auction that I have exhibited is that a buyer must report quite a bit of information (this is an issue distinct from that of the buyer's having to *know* a great deal, discussed previously) – a bid for each possible vector of valuations that others may have. Perry and Reny (1999a) have devised an alternative modification of the Vickrey auction that considerably reduces the complexity of the buyer's report.

Specifically, the Perry–Reny auction consists of two rounds of bidding. This means that a buyer can make his second-round bid depend on whatever he learned about other buyers' valuations from their first-round bids, and so the auction avoids the need to report bid schedules. In the first round, each buyer i submits a bid $b_i \geq 0$. In the second round, each buyer i submits a bid b_i^j for each buyer $j \neq i$. If some buyer submits a bid of zero in the first round, then the Vickrey rules apply: the winner is the high bidder, and he pays the second-highest bid. If all first-round bids are strictly positive, then the second-round bids determine the outcome. In particular, if there exists a buyer i such that

$$b_i^j \geq b_j^i \quad \text{for all} \quad j \neq i, \tag{4.19}$$

then buyer i wins and pays $\max_{j \neq i} b_j^i$. If there exists no i satisfying (4.19), then the good is allocated at random.

Perry and Reny show that, under conditions (2.1) and (4.1) and provided that the probability a buyer has a zero valuation is zero, there exists an efficient

---

[12] The reader may wonder whether, when (4.1) is not satisfied and so an efficient auction may not be possible, the efficiency of the final outcome could be enhanced by allowing buyers to retrade after the auction is over. However, any postauction trading episode could alternatively be viewed as part of a single mechanism that embraces both it and the auction proper. That is, in our search for efficient auctions, we need not consider postauction trade, because such activity could always be folded into the auction itself. Indeed, permitting trade after an auction can, in principle, distort buyers' bidding in the same way that the prospect of renegotiation can distort parties' behavior in the execution of a contract (see Dewatripont, 1989). Ausubel and Cramton (1999) argue that only an efficient auction is exempt from such distortion.

[13] It is conceivable – although unlikely – that for a given vector v_{-i} there could exist two different signal vectors s'_{-i} and s''_{-i}, such that $v_{-i}(s_i, s'_{-i}) = v_{-i}(s_i, s''_{-i}) = v_{-i}$, but $v_i(s_i, s'_{-i}) \neq v_i(s_i, s''_{-i})$, in which case (4.18) is not well defined. To see how to handle that possibility, see Dasgupta and Maskin (2000).

equilibrium of this auction. They also demonstrate that the auction can be readily extended to the case in which multiple identical goods are sold, provided that a buyer's marginal utility from additional units is declining.

5. THE ENGLISH AUCTION

The reader may wonder why, in my discussion of efficiency, I have not brought up the *English auction*, the familiar open format in which (i) buyers call out bids publicly (with the proviso that each successive bid exceed the one before), (ii) the winner is the last buyer to make a bid, and (iii) the winner pays his bid. After all, the opportunity to observe other buyers' bids in the English auction would seem to allow a buyer to make a conditional bid in the same way that the modified Vickrey auction does.

However, as shown in Maskin (1992), Eso and Maskin (2000b), and Krishna (2000), the English auction is not efficient in as wide a class of cases as the modified Vickrey auction. To see this, let us consider a variant of the English auction, sometimes called the "Japanese" auction (see Milgrom and Weber, 1982), which is particularly convenient analytically:

1. All buyers are initially in the auction.
2. The auctioneer raises the price continuously starting from zero.
3. A buyer can drop out (publicly) at any time.
4. The last buyer remaining wins.
5. The winner pays the price prevailing when the penultimate buyer dropped out.

Now, in this auction, a buyer can indeed condition his drop-out point according to when other buyers have dropped out, allowing bids in effect to be conditional on other buyers' valuations. However, a buyer can condition only on buyers who have already dropped out. Thus, for efficiency, buyers must drop out in the "right" order in the equilibrium. That this might not happen is illustrated by the following example from Eso and Maskin (2000a):

Example 5.6. *Suppose there are two buyers, where*

$$v_1(s_1, s_2) = 2 + s_1 - 2s_2,$$

and

$$v_2(s_1, s_2) = 2 + s_2 - 2s_1$$

and s_1 and s_2 are distributed uniformly on [0, 1]. Notice first that conditions (2.1) and (4.1) hold, so that the modified Vickrey auction results in an efficient equilibrium allocation. Indeed, buyers' equilibrium contingent bids are

$$b_1(v_2) = 6 - 3s_1 - 2v_2,$$

and

$$b_2(v_1) = 6 - 3s_2 - 2v_1.$$

Now, consider the English auction. For $i = 1, 2$, let $p_i(s_i)$ be the price at which buyer i drops out if his signal value is s_i. If the English auction were efficient, then we would have

$$s_1 > s_2 \quad \text{if and only if} \quad p_1(s_1) > p_2(s_2). \qquad (\blacklozenge)$$

From symmetry,

$$\text{if } s_1 = s_2 = s, \text{ then } p_1(s_1) = p_2(s_2). \qquad (\blacklozenge\blacklozenge)$$

But from ($\blacklozenge$) and ($\blacklozenge\blacklozenge$), $p_i(s + \Delta s) > p_i(s)$ and so

$$p_i(\cdot) \text{ is strictly increasing in } s_i. \qquad (\blacklozenge\blacklozenge\blacklozenge)$$

Thus,

$$p_1(s) = v_1(s, s)$$

and

$$p_2(s) = v_2(s, s)$$

[if $v_1(s, s) > p_1(s)$ and $s_1 = s_2 = s$, then buyer 1 drops out before the price reaches his valuation and so would do better to stay in a bit longer; if $v_1(s, s) < p_1(s)$, then buyer 1 stays in for prices above his valuation, and so would do better to drop out earlier]. But,

$$v_1(s, s) = 2 + s - 2s = 2 - s,$$

which is decreasing in s, violating our finding that $p_1(\cdot)$ is increasing. In short, efficiency demands that a buyer with a lower signal value drop out first. But, if buyer i's signal value is s, he has the incentive to drop out when the price equals $v_1(s, s)$, and this function is decreasing in s. So, in equilibrium, buyers will not drop out in the right order. We conclude that the English auction does not have an efficient equilibrium in this example.

In Example 5.6, each buyer's valuation is decreasing in the other buyer's signal. Indeed, this feature is important: as Maskin (1992) shows, the English and Vickrey auctions are efficient in the case $n = 2$ when valuations are non-decreasing functions of signals [and conditions (2.1) and (4.1) hold]. However, examples due to Perry and Reny (1999b), Krishna (2000), and Eso and Maskin (2000b) demonstrate that this result does not extend to more than two buyers. Nevertheless, Krishna (2000) provides some interesting conditions [considerably stronger than the juxtaposition of (2.1) and (4.1)] under which the English auction is efficient with three or more buyers (see also Eso and Maskin, 2000b). Moreover, Izmalkov (2001) shows that these conditions can be relaxed considerably when reentry in the English auction is permitted. Finally Perry and Reny (1999b) shows that the English auction can be modified [in a way analogous to their (1999a) alteration of the Vickrey auction] that renders it efficient under the same conditions as the modified Vickrey auction. In fact, this modified English auction extends to multiple (identical) units, as long as buyers' marginal valuations are decreasing in the number of units consumed [in the multiunit case, the Perry–Reny auction is actually a modification of the Ausubel (1997) generalization of the English auction].

6. MULTIPLE GOODS

In the same way that the ordinary Vickrey auction extends to multiple goods via the Groves–Clarke mechanism, so our modified Vickrey auction can be extended to handle more than one good. It is simplest to consider the case of two buyers, 1 and 2, and two goods, A and B. If there were private values, the pertinent information about buyer i would consist of three numbers $(v_{iA}, v_{iB},$ and $v_{iAB})$, his valuations, respectively, for good A, good B, and both goods together. Efficiency would then mean allocating the goods to maximize the sum of valuations. For example, it would be efficient to allocate both goods to buyer 1 provided that

$$v_{1AB} \geq \max\{v_{1A} + v_{2B}, v_{1B} + v_{2A}, v_{2AB}\}.$$

The Groves–Clarke mechanism is the natural generalization of the Vickrey auction to a multigood setting. In this mechanism, buyers submit valuations (in our two-good, private-values model, each buyer i submits $\hat{v}_{iA}, \hat{v}_{iB},$ and $\hat{v}_{iAB}$); the goods are allocated in the way that maximizes the sum of the submitted valuations; and each buyer makes a payment equal to his marginal impact on the other buyers (as measured by their submitted valuations). Thus, in the private-values model, if buyer 1 is allocated good A, then he should pay

$$\hat{v}_{2AB} - \hat{v}_{2B}, \tag{6.1}$$

because $\hat{v}_{2AB}$ would be buyer 2's payoff were buyer 1 absent, $\hat{v}_{2B}$ is his payoff given buyer 1's presence, and so the difference between the two – i.e., (6.1) – is buyer 1's marginal effect on buyer 2.

Given private values, bidding one's true valuation is a dominant strategy in the Vickrey auction, and the same is true in the Groves–Clarke mechanism. Hence, in view of its allocative rule, the mechanism is efficient in the case of private values. But, as with the Vickrey auction, the Groves–Clarke mechanism is not efficient when there are common values. Hence, I shall examine a modification of Groves–Clarke analogous to that for Vickrey.

As in the one-good case, assume that each buyer i ($i = 1, 2$) observes a private real-valued signal s_i. Buyer i's valuations are functions of the two signals:

$$v_{iA}(s_1, s_2), \ v_{iB}(s_1, s_2), v_{iAB}(s_1, s_2).$$

The appropriate counterpart to condition (2.1) is the requirement that if H and H' are two bundles of goods for which, given (s_1, s_2), buyer i prefers H, then the intensity of that preference rises with s_i. That is, for all $i = 1, 2$ and for any two bundles, H, $H' = \phi$, A, B, AB,

$$v_{iH}(s_1, s_2) - v_{iH'}(s_1, s_2) > 0 \Rightarrow \frac{\partial}{\partial s_i}(v_{iH}(s_1, s_2) - v_{iH'}(s_1, s_2)) > 0.$$

(6.2)

Notice that if, in particular, $H = A$ and $H' = \phi$, then (6.2) just reduces to the requirement that if $v_{iA}(s_1, s_2) > 0$, then $\partial v_{iA}/\partial s_i(s_1, s_2) > 0$, i.e., to (2.1).

Similarly, the proper generalization of (4.1) is the requirement that if, for given signal values, two allocations of goods are equally efficient (i.e., give rise to the same sum of valuations), then an increase in s_i leads to the allocation that buyer i prefers to become the more efficient. That is, for all $i = 1, 2$, and any two allocations (H_1, H_2), (H_1', H_2'),

if $\displaystyle\sum_{j=1}^{2} v_{jH_j}(s_1, s_2) = \sum_{j=1}^{2} v_{jH_j'}(s_1, s_2)$ and $v_{iH_i}(s_1, s_2) > v_{iH_i'}(s_1, s_2)$,

(6.3)

then $\displaystyle\frac{\partial}{\partial s_i} \sum_{j=1}^{2} v_{jH_j}(s_1, s_2) > \frac{\partial}{\partial s_i} \sum_{j=1}^{2} v_{jH_j'}(s_1, s_2).$

Notice that, if just one good A was being allocated and the two allocations were $(H_1, H_2) = (A, \phi)$ and $(H_1', H_2') = (\phi, A)$, then, when $i = 1$, condition (6.3) would reduce to the requirement

if $v_{1A}(s_1, s_2) = v_{2A}(s_1, s_2)$ and $v_{1A}(s_1, s_2) > 0,$

(6.4)

then $\displaystyle\frac{\partial v_{1A}}{\partial s_1}(s_1, s_2) > \frac{\partial v_{2A}}{\partial s_1}(s_1, s_2),$

which is just (4.1).

An auction is efficient in this setting if, for all (s_1, s_2), the equilibrium allocation (H_1^o, H_2^o) solves

$$\max_{(H_1, H_2)} \sum_{i=1}^{2} v_{iH_i}(s_1, s_2).$$

Under assumptions (6.2) and (6.3), the following rules constitute an efficient auction:

    1. Buyer i submits schedules $\hat{b}_{iA}(\cdot)$, $\hat{b}_{iB}(\cdot)$, $\hat{b}_{iAB}(\cdot)$, where for all $H = A$, B, AB and all v_j,

$$\hat{b}_{iH}(v_j) = \text{buyer } i\text{'s bid for } H \text{ if buyer } j\text{'s } (j \neq i)$$
$$\text{valuations are } v_j = (v_{jA}, v_{jB}, v_{jAB}).$$

2. The auctioneer computes a fixed point (v_1^o, v_2^o) such that, for all i and H,

$$v_{iH}^o = \hat{b}_{iH}(v_j^o).$$

3. Goods are divided according to allocation (H_1^o, H_2^o), where

$$(H_1^o, H_2^o) = \arg \max_{(H_1, H_2)} \sum_{i=1}^{2} v_{iH_i}^o.$$

4. Suppose that buyer 1 is allocated good A (i.e., $H_1^o = A$); if (i) there exists v_1^* such that

$$v_{1A}^* + \hat{b}_{2B}(v_1^*) = \hat{b}_{2AB}(v_1^*), \tag{6.5}$$

then buyer 1 pays

$$\hat{b}_{2AB}(v_1^*) - \hat{b}_{2B}(v_1^*); \tag{6.6}$$

if instead of (6.5), (ii) there exist $\hat{v}_1^*$ (with $\hat{v}_{1A}^* < v_{1A}^0$) and v_1^{**} such that

$$\hat{v}_{1A}^* + \hat{b}_{2B}(\hat{v}_1^*) = \hat{v}_{1B}^* + \hat{b}_{2A}(\hat{v}_1^*)$$

and

$$v_{1B}^{**} + \hat{b}_{2A}(v_1^{**}) = \hat{b}_{2AB}(v_1^{**}),$$

then buyer 1 pays

$$(\hat{b}_{2A}(\hat{v}_1^*) - \hat{b}_{2B}(\hat{v}_1^*)) + (\hat{b}_{2AB}(v_1^{**}) - \hat{b}_{2A}(v_1^{**})). \tag{6.7}$$

5. If buyer 1 is allocated good B, then his payment is completely analogous to that of 4.
6. If buyer 1 is allocated goods A and B, then see the Appendix for his payment.
7. Buyer 2's payments are completely analogous to those of buyer 1.

Rules 1–3 so closely mirror rules 1–3 of the modified Vickrey auction in Section 4 that they do not require further comment. Let us, therefore, focus on rule 4. If A was the only good being allocated, then to compute buyer 1's payment, we would reduce v_{1A} from v_{1A}^o to the point v_{1A}^*, where it is no longer uniquely efficient to allocate buyer 1 good A (i.e., it becomes equally efficient to allocate A to buyer 2) and have him pay his marginal impact at v_1^* on buyer 2: the difference between buyer 2's payoff from getting A and that from getting nothing:

$$\hat{b}_{2A}(v_{1A}^*) - 0 = \hat{b}_{2A}(v_{1A}^*),$$

which is payment rule (4.10). Using this same principle in the two-good setting, let us reduce v_{1A} from v_{1A}^o to the first point, where it is no longer uniquely efficient to allocate A to buyer 1 and B to buyer 2. There are two possible cases. In case (i), at this first switching point, it becomes efficient to allocate *both* goods to buyer 2. Let us denote the switching point in this case by v_{1A}^* [choose v_{1B}^* and v_{1AB}^* to conform with v_{1A}^*, i.e., choose them so that $v_1^* = (v_{1A}^*, v_{1B}^*, v_{1AB}^*)$ lies in the domain of $(\hat{b}_{2A}(\cdot), \hat{b}_{2B}(\cdot), \hat{b}_{2AB}(\cdot))$]. Hence, at v_{1A}^*, buyer 1's marginal impact on buyer 2 is the difference between 2's payoff from getting both goods, $\hat{b}_{2AB}(v_1^*)$, and that from getting just B, $\hat{b}_{2B}(v_1^*)$, i.e., (6.6). In case (ii), it becomes efficient at the first switching point $\hat{v}_{1A}^*$ (choose $\hat{v}_{1B}^*$ and $\hat{v}_{1AB}^*$ to conform with $\hat{v}_{1A}^*$) to allocate A to buyer 2 but B to buyer 1. Hence, at $\hat{v}_{1A}^*$, buyer 1's marginal impact on buyer 2 from being allocated A rather than B is the difference between buyer 2's payoff from A and that from B:

$$\hat{b}_{2A}(\hat{v}_1^*) - \hat{b}_{2B}(\hat{v}_1^*). \tag{6.8}$$

But (6.8) does not represent buyer 1's full marginal impact on buyer 2 because it compares buyer 2's payoff from B with that from good A, rather than from both A and B. To obtain the latter comparison, reduce v_{1B} from $\hat{v}_{1B}^*$ to the point v_{1B}^{**}, where it just becomes efficient to allocate both A and B to buyer 2. The marginal impact on buyer 2 at v_{1B}^{**} (choose v_{1A}^{**} and v_{1AB}^{**} to conform with v_{1B}^{**}) is

$$\hat{b}_{2AB}(v_1^{**}) - \hat{b}_{2A}(v_1^{**}). \tag{6.9}$$

Adding (6.8) and (6.9), we obtain buyer 1's full marginal impact on buyer 2, viz. (6.7). Notice that, in the case of private values, where $\hat{b}_{2A}(v_1^{**}) = \hat{b}_{2A}(\hat{v}_1^*)$, (6.7) reduces to $\hat{b}_{2AB} - \hat{b}_{2B}$, which is buyer 1's payment for good A in the ordinary Groves–Clarke mechanism.

It can be shown (see Dasgupta and Maskin, 2000) that it is an equilibrium for buyers to bid truthfully in the above auction [i.e., for each i and bundle of goods $H = A, B, AB$, buyer i should set $\hat{b}_{iH}(\cdot) = b_{iH}(\cdot)$], where

$$b_{iH}(v_{jH}(s_i, s_j')) = v_{iH}(s_i, s_j') \quad \text{for all} \quad s_j'$$

if buyer i's signal value is s_i. Notice that if, in fact, buyers are truthful, the auction results in an efficient equilibrium.

7. MULTIDIMENSIONAL SIGNALS

Up until now, the results I have quoted on efficient auctions with common values have assumed that buyers' signals are one-dimensional. This is for good reason – the results are simply not true otherwise. Indeed, with multidimensional signals, efficiency in the sense I have defined it is generally unattainable with any mechanism (a point found in Maskin, 1992, and Jehiel and Moldovanu, 2001). To see this, consider the following example:

Example 7.7. *Suppose that there are two buyers and one good. Assume that buyer 2's signal s_2 is, as usual, one-dimensional but that buyer 1's signal s_1 has two components: $s_1 = (s_{11}, s_{12})$.*
    Let

$$v_1(s_{11}, s_{12}, s_2) = s_{11} + s_{12} + \alpha s_2$$

and

$$v_2(s_{11}, s_{12}, s_2) = s_2 + \beta s_{11} + \gamma s_{12}.$$

Because of independence, buyer 1's objective function is the same for any pairs (s_{11}, s_{12}) *that add up to the same constant, and thus, he will behave the same way for any such pairs. In particular, if* (s'_{11}, s'_{12}) *and* (s''_{11}, s''_{12}) *are pairs such that* $s'_{11} + s'_{12} = s''_{11} + s''_{12}$, *then, in any auction, the equilibrium outcome must be identical for the two pairs. But, unless* $\beta = \gamma$, *the efficient allocation may turn on which pair obtains – specifically, given* s_2, *we might have*

$$s'_{11} + s'_{12} + \alpha s_2 > s_2 + \beta s'_{11} + \gamma s'_{12} \tag{7.1}$$

but

$$s''_1 + s''_2 + \alpha s_2 < s_2 + \beta s''_{11} + \gamma s''_{12}, \tag{7.2}$$

so that, with $(s_{11}, s_{12}) = (s'_{11}, s'_{12})$, *the good should be allocated to buyer 1 and, with* $(s_{11}, s_{12}) = (s''_{11}, s''_{12})$, *it should be allocated to buyer 2 [if* $\beta = \gamma$, *this conflict does not arise; the directions of the inequalities in (7.1) and (7.2) must be the same]. Hence, an efficient auction is impossible when* $\beta \neq \gamma$.

However, because buyer 1 cares only about the sum $s_{11} + s_{12}$, *it is natural to define*

$$r_1 = s_{11} + s_{12}$$

and set

$$w_1(r_1, s_2) = r_1 + \alpha s_2$$

and

$$w_2(r_1, s_2) = E_{s_{11}, s_{12}}[s_2 + \beta s_{11} + \gamma s_{12} | s_{11} + s_{12} = r_1].$$

Notice that we have reduced the two-dimensional signal s_1 *to the one-dimensional signal* r_1. *Furthermore, provided that* α, β, *and* γ *are all less than 1 [so that condition (4.1) holds], our modified Vickrey auction is efficient with respect to the "reduced" valuation functions* $w_1(\cdot)$ *and* $w_2(\cdot)$ *(because all the analysis of Section 4 applies). Hence, a moment's reflection should convince the reader that, although full efficiency is impossible for the valuation functions* $v_1(\cdot)$ *and* $v_2(\cdot)$, *the modified Vickrey auction is* constrained *efficient, where "constrained" refers to the requirement that buyer 1 must behave the same way for any pair* (s_{11}, s_{12}) *summing to the same* r_1 *(in the terminology of Holmstrom and Myerson, 1983, the auction is "incentive efficient").*

Unfortunately, as Jehiel and Moldovanu (2001) show in their important paper, this trick of reducing a multidimensional signal to one dimension no longer works in general if there are multiple goods. To see the problem, suppose that, as in Section 5, there are two goods, A and B, but that now a buyer i ($i = 1, 2, 3$) receives *two* signals – one for each good. Specifically, let s_{1A} and s_{1B}

References

Ausubel, L. (1997), An Efficient Ascending-Bid Auction for Multiple Objects, mimeo.

Ausubel, L. and P. Cramton (1999), The Optimality of Being Efficient, mimeo.

Che, Y. K. and I. Gale (1996), Expected Revenue of the All-Pay Auctions and First-Price Sealed-Bid Auctions with Budget Constraints, *Economics Letters*, 50, 373–380.

Chung, K.-C. and J. Ely (2001), Efficient and Dominant Solvable Auction with Interdependent Valuations, mimeo.

Clarke, E. (1971), Multipart Pricing of Public Goods, *Public Choice*, 11, 17–33.

Crémer, J. and R. McLean (1985), Optimal Selling Strategies Under Uncertainty for a Discriminating Monopolist When Demands Are Interdependent, *Econometrica*, 53, 345–362.

Dasgupta, P. and E. Maskin (2000), Efficient Auctions, *Quarterly Journal of Economics*, 115, 341–388.

Bergemann, D. and J. Välinäki (2001), Information Acquisition and Efficient Mechanism Design, mimeo.

Debreu, G. (1959), *Theory of Value*, New Haven, CT: Yale University Press.

Dewatripont, M. (1989), Renegotiation and Information Revelation Over Time: The Case of Optimal Labor Contracts, *Quarterly Journal of Economics*, 104, 589–619.

Eso, P. and E. Maskin (2000a), Multi-Good Efficient Auctions with Multidimensional Information, mimeo.

Eso, P. and E. Maskin (2000b), Notes on the English Auction, mimeo.

Fiesler, K. T. Kittsteiner, and B. Moldovanu (2000), Partnerships, Lemons, and Efficient Trade, mimeo.

Gresik, T. (1991), Ex Ante Incentive Efficient Trading Mechanisms without the Private Valuation Restriction, *Journal of Economic Theory*, 55, 41–63.

Groves, T. (1973), Incentives in Teams, *Econometrica*, 41, 617–631.

Holmstrom, B. and R. Myerson (1983), Efficient and Durable Decision Rules with Incomplete Information, *Econometrica*, 51, 1799–1819.

Izmalkov, S. (2001), English Auctions with Reentry, mimeo.

Jehiel, P. and B. Moldovanu (2001), Efficient Design with Interdependent Values, *Econometrica*, 69, 1237–1260.

Krishna, V. (2000), Asymmetric English Auctions, mimeo.

McLean, R., and A. Postlewaite (2001), Efficient Auction Mechanisms with Interdependent Signals, mimeo.

Maskin, E. (1992), Auctions and Privatization, in *Privatization* (ed. by H. Siebert), Tübingen: J. C. B. Mohr, 115–136.

Maskin, E. (2000), Auctions, Development and Privatization: Efficient Auctions with Liquidity-Constrained Buyers, *European Economic Review*, 44(4–6), 667–681.

Maskin, E. and J. Riley (1984), Optimal Auctions with Risk-Averse Buyers, *Econometrica*, 52, 1473–1518.

Milgrom, P. and R. Weber (1982), A Theory of Auctions and Competitive Bidding, *Econometrica*, 50, 1081–1122.

Palfrey, T. (1993), Implementation in Bayesian Equilibrium, in *Advances in Economic Theory* (ed. by J. J. Laffont), Cambridge, U.K.: Cambridge University Press.

Perry, M. and P. Reny (1999a), An Ex Post Efficient Auction, mimeo.

Perry, M. and P. Reny (1999b), An Ex Post Efficient Ascending Auction, mimeo.

Vickrey, W. (1961), Counterspeculation, Auctions, and Competitive Sealed Tenders, *Journal of Finance*, 16, 8–37.

CHAPTER 2

Why Every Economist Should Learn Some Auction Theory

Paul Klemperer

Figure 2.1. *Disclaimer*: We don't contend that the following ideas are all as important as the one illustrated, merely that those who haven't imbibed auction theory are missing out on a potent brew!

    This chapter discusses the strong connections between auction theory and "standard" economic theory; we show that situations that do not at first sight look like auctions can be recast to use auction-theoretic techniques; and we argue that auction-theoretic tools and intuitions can provide useful arguments and insights in a broad range of mainstream economic settings. We also discuss some more obvious applications, especially to industrial organization.

1. INTRODUCTION

Auction theory has attracted enormous attention in the last few years.[1] It has been increasingly applied in practice, and this has generated a new burst of theory. It has also been extensively used, both experimentally and empirically, as a testing ground for game theory.[2] Furthermore, by carefully analyzing very simple trading models, auction theory is developing the fundamental building blocks for our understanding of more complex environments. But some people still see auction theory as a rather specialized field, distinct from the main body of economic theory, and as an endeavor for management scientists and operations researchers rather than as a part of mainstream economics. This paper aims to counter that view.

This view may have arisen in part because auction theory was substantially developed by operational researchers, or in operations research journals,[3] and using technical mathematical arguments rather than standard economic intuitions. But it need not have been this way. This paper argues that the connections between auction theory and "standard" economic theory run deeper than many people realize; that auction-theoretic tools provide useful arguments in a broad range of contexts; and that a good understanding of auction theory is valuable in developing intuitions and insights that can inform the analysis of many mainstream economic questions. In short, auction theory is central to economics.

We pursue this agenda in the context of some of the main themes of auction theory: the revenue equivalence theorem, marginal revenues, and ascending vs. (first-price) sealed-bid auctions. To show how auction-theoretic tools can be applied elsewhere in economics, Section 2 exploits the revenue equivalence theorem to analyze a wide range of applications that are not, at first sight, auctions, including litigation systems, financial crashes, queues, and wars of attrition. To illustrate how looser analogies can usefully be made between auction theory and economics, Section 3 applies some intuitions from the comparison of ascending and sealed-bid auctions to other economic settings, such as rationing and e-commerce. To demonstrate the deeper connections between auction theory and economics, Section 4 discusses and applies the close parallel between the optimal auction problem and that of the discriminating monopolist; both are about maximizing marginal revenues.

Furthermore, auction-theoretic ways of thinking are also underutilized in more obvious areas of application, for instance, price-setting oligopolies we

---

[1] See Klemperer (1999a) for a review of auction theory; many of the most important contributions are collected in Klemperer (2000). See Figure 2.1.

[2] Kagel (1995) and Laffont (1997) are excellent recent surveys of the experimental and empirical work, respectively. Section 6 of this paper and Klemperer (2002a) discuss practical applications.

[3] The earliest studies appear in the operations research literature, for example, Friedman (1956). Myerson's (1981) breakthrough article appeared in *Mathematics of Operations Research*, and Rothkopf's (1969) and Wilson's (1967, 1969) classic early papers appeared in *Management Science*. Ortega's (1968) pathbreaking models of auctions, including a model of signaling that significantly predated Spence (1972), remain relatively little known by economists, perhaps because they formed an operations research Ph.D. thesis.

discuss in Section 5.[4] Few non-auction theorists know, for example, that marginal-cost pricing is *not* always the only equilibrium when identical firms with constant marginal costs set prices, or know the interesting implications of this fact. Section 6 briefly discusses direct applications of auction theory to markets that are literally auction markets, including electricity markets, treasury auctions, spectrum auctions, and internet markets, and we conclude in Section 7.

2. USING AUCTION-THEORETIC TOOLS IN ECONOMICS: THE REVENUE EQUIVALENCE THEOREM

Auction theory's most celebrated theorem, the Revenue Equivalence Theorem (RET), states conditions under which different auction forms yield the same expected revenue, and also allows revenue rankings of auctions to be developed when these conditions are violated.[5] Our purpose here, however, is to apply it in contexts where the use of an auction model might not seem obvious.

Revenue Equivalence Theorem. *Assume each of a given number of risk-neutral potential buyers has a privately known valuation independently drawn from a strictly increasing atomless distribution, and that no buyer wants more than one of the k identical indivisible prizes.*

Then, any mechanism in which (i) the prizes always go to the k buyers with the highest valuations and (ii) any bidder with the lowest feasible valuation expects zero surplus, yields the same expected revenue (and results in each bidder making the same expected payment as a function of her valuation).[6]

More general statements are possible, but are not needed for the current purpose.

Our first example is very close to a pure auction.

2.1. Comparing Litigation Systems

In 1991, U.S. Vice President Dan Quayle suggested reforming the U.S. legal system in the hope, in particular, of reducing legal expenditures. One of his

---

[4] Of course, standard auction models form the basic building blocks of models in many contexts. See, for example, Stevens' (1994, 2000) models of wage determination in oligopsonistic labor markets, Bernheim and Whinston (1986), Feddersen and Pesendorfer (1996, 1998), Persico (2000) and many others' political economy models, and many models in finance (including, of course, takeover battles, to which we give an application in Section 4). Another major area we do not develop here is the application of auction theorists' understanding of the winner's curse to adverse selection more generally.

[5] For example, Klemperer's (1999a) survey develops a series of revenue rankings starting from the RET.

[6] See Klemperer (1999a, Appendix A) for more general statements and an elementary proof. The theorem was first derived in an elementary form by Vickrey (1961, 1962) and subsequently extended to greater generality by Myerson (1981), Riley and Samuelson (1981), and others.

proposals was to augment the current rule according to which parties pay their own legal expenses, by a rule requiring the losing party to pay the winner an amount equal to the loser's own expenses. Quayle's intuition was that if spending an extra $1 on a lawsuit might end up costing you $2, then less would be spent. Was he correct?[7]

A simple starting point is to assume each party has a privately known value of winning the lawsuit relative to losing, independently drawn from a common, strictly increasing, atomless distribution;[8] that the parties independently and simultaneously choose how much money to spend on legal expenses; and that the party who spends the most money wins the "prize" (the lawsuit).[9] It is not too hard to see that both the existing U.S. system and the Quayle system satisfy the assumptions of the RET, so the two systems result in the same expected total payments on lawyers.[10] Thus Quayle was wrong (as usual); his argument is precisely offset by the fact that the value of winning the lawsuit is greater when you win your opponent's expenses.[11]

Ah, Quayle might say, but this calculation has taken as given the set of lawsuits that are contested. Introducing the Quayle scheme will change the "bidding functions," that is, change the amount any given party spends on litigation, and also change who decides to bring suits. Wrong again, Dan! Although it is correct that the bidding functions change, the RET also tells us (in its parenthetical remark) that any given party's *expected* payoffs from the lawsuit are unchanged, so the incentives to bring lawsuits are unchanged.

What about other systems, such as the typical European system in which the loser pays a fraction of the winner's expenses? This is a trick question: It is no longer true that a party with the lowest possible valuation can spend nothing and lose nothing. In this case, this party always loses in equilibrium and

---

[7] This question was raised and analyzed (although not by invoking the RET) by Baye, Kovenock, and de Vries (1997). The ideas in this section, except for the method of analysis, are drawn from them. See also Baye, Kovenock, and de Vries (1998).

[8] For example, a suit about which party has the right to a patent might fit this model. The results extend easily to common-value settings, e.g., contexts in which the issue is the amount of damages that should be transferred from one party to another.

[9] American seminar audiences typically think this is a natural assumption, but non-Americans often regard it as unduly jaundiced. Of course, we use it as a benchmark only, to develop insight and intuition (just as the lowest price does not win the whole market in most real "Bertrand" markets, but making the extreme assumption is a common and useful starting point). Extensions are possible to cases in which with probability $(1 - \lambda)$ the "most deserving" party wins, but with probability $\lambda > 0$, the biggest spender wins.

[10] The fact that no single "auctioneer" collects the players' payments as revenues, but that they are instead dissipated in legal expenses in competing for the single available prize (victory in the lawsuit), is of course irrelevant to the result. Formally, checking our claims requires confirming that there are equilibria of the games that satisfy the RET's assumptions. The assumption we made that the parties make a one-shot choice of legal expenses is not necessary, but makes confirming this relatively easy. See Baye, Kovenock, and de Vries (1997) for explicit solutions.

[11] Some readers might argue they could have inferred the effectiveness of the proposal from the name of the proponent, without need of further analysis. In fact, however, this was one of Dan Quayle's policy interventions that was not subject to immediate popular derision.

must pay a fraction of the winner's expenses, and so makes negative expected surplus. Thus, condition (ii) of the RET now fails. Thinking through the logic of the proof of the RET makes clear that all the players are worse off than under the previous systems.[12] Thus, legal bills are higher under the European rule. The reason is that the incentives to win are greater than in the U.S. system, and there is no offsetting effect. Here, of course, the issue of who brings lawsuits is important because low-valuation parties would do better not to contest suits in this kind of system; consistent with our theory, there is empirical evidence (e.g., Hughes and Snyder, 1995) that the American system leads to more trials than, for example, the British system.

This last extension demonstrates that even where the RET in its simplest form fails, it is often possible to see how the result is modified; Appendix 1 shows how to use the RET to solve for the relative merits of a much broader class of systems in which those we have discussed are special cases. We also show there that a system that might be thought of as the exact opposite of Quayle's system is optimal in this model. Of course, many factors are ignored (e.g., asymmetries); the basic model should be regarded as no more than a starting point for analysis.

2.2.   The War of Attrition

Consider a war of attrition in which N players compete for a prize. For example, N firms compete to be the unique survivor in a natural monopoly market, or N firms each hold out for the industry to adopt the standard they prefer.[13] Each player pays costs of 1 per unit time until she quits the game. When just one player remains, that player also stops paying costs and wins the prize. There is no discounting. The two-player case, where just one quit is needed to end the game, has been well analyzed.[14] Does the many-player case yield anything of additional interest?

Assume players' values of winning are independently drawn from a common, strictly increasing, atomless distribution, and the game has an equilibrium satisfying the other conditions of the RET. Then the RET tells us that, in expectation,

---

[12] As Appendix 1 discusses, every type's surplus is determined by reference to the lowest valuation type's surplus [see, also, Klemperer (1999a, Appendix A)], and the lowest type is worse off in the European system. Again, our argument depends on condition (i) of the RET applying. See Appendix 1 and Baye et al. (1997).

[13] Another related example analyzed by Bulow and Klemperer (1999) is that of N politicians, each delaying in the hope of being able to avoid publicly supporting a necessary but unpopular policy that requires the support of $N - 1$ to be adopted.

[14] See, for example, Maynard Smith (1974) and Riley (1980) who discuss biological competition, Fudenberg and Tirole (1986) who discuss industrial competition, Abreu and Gul (2000), Kambe (1999), and others who analyze bargaining, and Bliss and Nalebuff (1984) who give a variety of amusing examples. Bliss and Nalebuff note that extending to $K + 1$ players competing for K prizes does not change the analysis in any important way, because it remains true that just one quit is needed to end the game.

the total resources spent by the players in the war of attrition equal those paid by the players in any other mechanism satisfying the RET's conditions – e.g., a standard ascending auction in which the price rises continuously until just one player remains and (only) the winner pays the final price. This final price will equal the second-highest actual valuation, so the expected total resources dissipated in the war of attrition are the expectation of this quantity.

Now imagine the war of attrition has been under way long enough that just the two highest-valuation players remain. What are the expected resources that will be dissipated by the remaining two players, starting from this time on? The RET tells us that they equal the auctioneer's expected revenue if the war of attrition was halted at this point and the objects sold to the remaining players by an ascending auction, that is, the expected second-highest valuation of these two remaining players. This is the same quantity, on average, as before![15] Thus the expected resources dissipated, and hence the total time taken until just two players remain must be zero; all but the two highest-valuation players must have quit at once.

Of course, this conclusion is, strictly speaking, impossible; the lowest-valuation players cannot identify who they are in zero time. However, the conclusion is correct in spirit, in that it is the limit point of the unique symmetric equilibria of a sequence of games that approaches this game arbitrarily closely (and there is no symmetric equilibrium of the limit game).[16] Here, therefore, the role of the RET is less to perform the ultimate analysis than it is to show that there is an interesting and simple result to be obtained.[17] Of course by developing intuition about what the result must be, the RET also makes proving it much

---

[15] Of course, the expectation of the second-highest valuation of the last two players is computed when just these two players remain, rather than at the beginning of the war of attrition as before. But, on average, these two expectations must be the same.

[16] Bulow and Klemperer (1999) analyze games in which each player pays costs at rate 1 before quitting, but must continue to pay costs even after quitting at rate c per unit time until the whole game ends. The limit $c \to 0$ corresponds to the war of attrition discussed here. (The case $c = 1$ corresponds, for example, to "standards battles" or political negotiations in which all players bear costs equally until *all* have agreed on the same standard or outcome; this game also has interesting properties; see Bulow and Klemperer.) Other series of games, for example games in which being kth to last to quit earns a prize of ε^{k-1} times one's valuation, with $\varepsilon \to 0$, or games in which players can quit only at the discrete times $0, \varepsilon, 2\varepsilon, \ldots$, with $\varepsilon \to 0$, also yield the same outcome in the limit.

[17] It was the RET that showed Bulow and Klemperer that there was an analysis worth doing. Many people, and some literature, had assumed the many-player case would look like the two-player case, but with more complicated expressions, although Fudenberg and Kreps (1987) and Haigh and Cannings (1989) observed a similar result to ours in games without any private information and in which all players' values are equal. However, an alternative way to see the result in our war of attrition is to imagine the converse, but that a player is within ε of her planned quit time when $n > 1$ other players remain. Then, the player's cost of waiting as planned is of the order ε, but her benefit is of the order ε^n, because only when all n other players are within ε of giving up will she ultimately win. So, for small ε, she will prefer to quit now rather than wait; but, in this case, she should, of course, have quit ε earlier, and so on. So, only when $n = 1$ is delay possible.

easier. Furthermore, the RET was also useful in the actual analysis of the more complex games that Bulow and Klemperer (1999) used to approximate this game. In addition, anyone armed with a knowledge of the RET can simplify the analysis of the basic two-player war of attrition.

2.3.   Queueing and Other "All-Pay" Applications

The preceding applications have both been variants of "all-pay" auctions. As another elementary example of this kind, consider different queueing systems (e.g., for tickets to a sporting event). Under not unreasonable assumptions, a variety of different rules of queue management (e.g., making the queue more or less comfortable, informing or not informing people whether the number queueing exceeds the number who will receive a ticket, etc.) will make no difference to the social cost of the queueing mechanism. As in our litigation example (Section 2.1), we think of these results as a starting point for analysis rather than as final conclusions.[18]

Many other issues – such as lobbying battles, political campaigns,[19] tournaments in firms, contributions to public goods,[20] patent races, and some kinds of price-setting oligopoly (see Section 5.2) – can be modeled as all-pay auctions and may provide similar applications.

2.4.   Solving for Equilibrium Behavior: Market Crashes and Trading "Frenzies"

The examples thus far have all proceeded by computing the expected total payments made by all players. But, the RET also states that each individual's expected payment must be equal across mechanisms satisfying the assumptions. This fact can be used to infer what players' equilibrium actions must be in games that would be too complex to solve by any direct method of computing optimal behavior.[21]

Consider the following model. The aim is to represent, for example, a financial or housing market and show that trading "frenzies" and price "crashes"

---

[18] Holt and Sherman (1982) compute equilibrium behavior and hence obtain these results without using the RET.

[19] See, especially, Persico (2000).

[20] Menezes, Monteiro, and Temimi (2000) use the RET in this context.

[21] The same approach is also an economical method of computing equilibrium bids in many standard auctions. For example, in an ascending auction for a single unit, the expected payment of a bidder equals her probability of winning times the expected second-highest valuation among all the bidders conditional on her value being higher. So, the RET implies that her equilibrium bid in a standard all-pay auction equals this quantity. Similarly, the RET implies that her equilibrium bid in a first-price, sealed-bid auction equals the expected second-highest valuation among all the bidders, conditional on her value being higher. See Klemperer (1999a, Appendix A) for more details and discussion.

are the inevitable outcome of rational strategic behavior in a market that clears through a sequence of sales rather than through a Walrasian auctioneer. There are N potential buyers, each of whom is interested in securing one of K available units. Without fully modeling the selling side of the market, we assume it generates a single asking price at each instant of time according to some given function of buyer behavior to date. Each potential buyer observes all prices and all past offers to trade, and can accept the current asking price at any instant, in which case, supply permitting, the buyer trades at that price.

Thus traders have to decide both whether *and when* to offer to buy, all the while conditioning their strategies on the information that has been revealed in the market to date. Regarding the function generating the asking prices, we specify only that (i) if there is no demand at a price, then the next asking price is lower, and (ii) if demand exceeds remaining supply at any instant, then no trade actually takes place at that time but the next asking price is higher and only those who attempted to trade are allowed to buy subsequently.[22] Note, however, that even if we did restrict attention to a specific price-setting process, the direct approach of computing buyers' optimal behavior using first-order conditions as a function of all prior behavior to solve a dynamic program would generally be completely intractable.

To use the RET, we must first ensure that the appropriate assumptions are satisfied. We assume, of course, that buyers' valuations are independently drawn from a common, strictly increasing, atomless distribution, and that there is no discounting during the time the mechanism takes. Furthermore, the objects do eventually go to the highest-valuation buyers, and the lowest-possible-valuation buyer makes zero surplus in equilibrium, because of our assumption that if demand ever exceeds remaining supply, then no trade takes place and nondemanders are henceforth excluded. So, the RET applies, and it also applies to any subgame of the whole game.[23]

Under our assumptions, then, starting from any point of the process, the remainder of the game is revenue equivalent to what would result if the game were halted at that point and the remaining k objects were sold to the remaining buyers using a standard ascending auction [which sells all k objects at the $(k + 1)$st-highest valuation among the remaining buyers]. At any point of our game, therefore, we know the expected payment of any buyer in the remainder of our game, and therefore also the buyer's expected payment conditional on

---

[22] Additional technical assumptions are required to ensure that all units are sold in finite time. See Bulow and Klemperer (1994) for full details.

[23] If, instead, excess demand resulted in random rationing, the highest-valuation buyers might not win, violating the requirements of the RET; so, even if we thought this was more natural, it would make sense to begin with our assumption to be able to analyze and understand the process using the RET. The effects of the alternative assumption could then be analyzed with the benefit of the intuitions developed using the RET. Bulow and Klemperer (1994) proceed in exactly this way.

winning.[24] But any potential buyer whose expected payment conditional on winning equals or exceeds the current asking price will attempt to buy at the current price.[25] This allows us to completely characterize buyer behavior, so fully characterizes the price path for any given rule generating the asking prices.

It is now straightforward to show (see Bulow and Klemperer, 1994) that potential buyers are extremely sensitive to the new information that the price process reveals. It follows that almost any seller behavior – e.g., starting at a very high price and slowly lowering the price continuously until all the units are sold or there is excess demand – will result in "frenzies" of trading activity in which many buyers bid simultaneously, even though there is zero probability that two buyers have the same valuation.[26] Furthermore, these frenzies will sometimes lead to "crashes" in which it becomes common knowledge that the market price must fall a substantial distance before any further trade will take place.[27] Bulow and Klemperer also show that natural extensions to the model (e.g., "common values," the possibility of resale, or an elastic supply of units) tend to accentuate frenzies and crashes. Frenzies and crashes arise precisely because buyers are rational and strategic; by contrast, buyer irrationality might lead to "smoother" market behavior.

Of course, our main point here is not the details of the process, but rather that the RET permits the solution and analysis of the dynamic price path of a market that would otherwise seem completely intractable to solve for.

---

[24] Specifically, if k objects remain, the buyer's expected payment conditional on winning will be the expected $(k + 1)$st-highest valuation remaining conditional on the buyer having a valuation among the k-highest remaining, and conditional on all the information revealed to date. This is exactly the buyer's expected payment conditional on winning an object in the ascending auction, because in both cases only winners pay and the probability of a bidder winning is the same.

[25] The marginal potential buyer, who is just indifferent about bidding now, either will win now or will never win an object. (If bidding now results in excess demand, this bidder will lose to inframarginal current bidders, because there is probability zero that two bidders have the same valuation.) So, conditional on winning, this bidder's actual payment is the current price. Inframarginal bidders, whose expected payment conditional on winning exceeds the current price, may eventually end up winning an object at above the current price.

[26] To see why a frenzy must arise if the price is lowered continuously, note that, for it to be rational for any potential buyer to jump in and bid first, there must be positive probability that there will be a frenzy large enough to create excess demand immediately after the first bid. Otherwise, the strategy of waiting to bid until another player has bid first would guarantee a lower price. For more general seller behavior, the point is that while buyers' valuations may be very dispersed, higher-valuation buyers are all almost certainly inframarginal in terms of whether to buy and are therefore all solving virtually identical optimization problems of when to buy. So, a small change in asking price, or a small change in market conditions (such as the information revealed by a single trade) at a given price, can make a large number of buyers change from being unwilling to trade to wanting to trade. The only selling process that can surely avoid a frenzy is a repeated Dutch auction.

[27] The price process is also extremely sensitive to buyer valuations; an arbitrarily small change in one buyer's value can discontinuously and substantially change all subsequent trading prices.

3. TRANSLATING LOOSER ANALOGIES FROM AUCTIONS INTO ECONOMICS: ASCENDING VS. (FIRST-PRICE) SEALED-BID AUCTIONS

A major focus of auction theory has been contrasting the revenue and efficiency properties of "ascending" and "sealed-bid" auctions.[28] Ideas and intuitions developed in these comparisons have wide applicability.

3.1.   Internet Sales vs. Dealer Sales

There is massive interest in the implications of e-commerce and internet sales. For example, the advent of internet sales in the automobile industry as a partial replacement for traditional methods of selling through dealers has been widely welcomed in Europe;[29] the organization of the European automobile market is currently a major policy concern in both official circles and the popular press, and the internet sales are seen as increasing "transparency." But is transparency a good thing?

Auction theory shows that internet sales need *not* be good for consumers. Clearly, transparent prices benefit consumers if they reduce consumers' search costs so that, in effect, there are more competitors for every consumer,[30] and internet sales may also lower prices by cutting out the fixed costs of dealerships, albeit by also cutting out the additional services that dealers provide. But, transparency also makes internet sales more like ascending auctions, by contrast with dealer sales that are more like (first-price) sealed-bid auctions, and we will show this is probably *bad* for consumers.

Transparent internet prices are readily observable by a firm's competitors and therefore result, in effect, in an "ascending" auction; a firm knows if and when its offers are being beaten and can rapidly respond to its competitors' offers if it wishes. Viewing each car sale as a separate auction, the price any consumer faces falls until all but one firm quits bidding to sell to him. (The price is, of course, descending because firms are competing to sell, but the process corresponds exactly to the standard ascending auction among bidders competing to buy an object, and we therefore maintain the standard "ascending" terminology.)

On the other hand, shopping to buy a car from one of the competing dealers is very much like procuring in a (first-price) "sealed-bid" auction. It is typically impossible to credibly communicate one dealer's offer to another. (Car dealers

---

[28] By "sealed-bid," we mean standard, first-price, sealed-bid auctions. "Ascending" auctions have similar properties to second-price, sealed-bid auctions. See Klemperer (1999a) for an introduction to the different types of auctions.

[29] See, for example, "May the Net Be with You," *Financial Times*, October 21, 1999, p. 22. In the UK, Vauxhaul began selling a limited number of special models over the Internet late in 1999, while Ford began a pilot project in Finland.

[30] There may be both a direct effect (that consumers can observe more firms) and an indirect effect (that new entry is facilitated). See Baye and Morgan (2001) and Kühn and Vives (1994) for more discussion.

often deliberately make this hard by refusing to put an offer in writing.) From the buyer's perspective, it is as if sellers were independently making sealed-bid offers in ignorance of the competition.

Of course, the analogies are imperfect,[31] but they serve as a starting point for analysis. What, therefore, does auction theory suggest?

Because, under the conditions of the revenue equivalence theorem, there is no difference between the auction forms for either consumer or producer welfare, we consider the implications of the most important violations of the conditions.

First, market demand is downward sloping, not inelastic.[32] Hansen (1988) showed that this means consumers always prefer the sealed-bid setting, and firms may prefer it also; the sum of producer and consumer surpluses is always higher in a sealed-bid auction.[33] The intuition is that, in an "ascending" auction, the sales price equals the runner-up's cost, and is therefore less reflective of the winner's cost than is the sealed-bid price. So, the sealed-bid auction is more productively efficient (the quantity traded better reflects the winner's cost) and provides greater incentive for aggressive bidding (a more aggressive sealed bid not only increases the probability of winning, but also increases the quantity traded contingent on winning).

Second, we need to consider the possibilities for collusion, implicit or explicit. The general conclusion is that ascending auctions are more susceptible to collusion, and this is particularly the case when, as in our example, many auctions of different car models and different consumers are taking place simultaneously.[34] As has been observed in the United States and German auctions of radiospectrum, for example, bidders may be able to tacitly coordinate on dividing up the spoils in a simultaneous ascending auction. Bidders can use the early rounds when prices are still low[35] to signal their views about who should win which objects, and then, when consensus has been reached, tacitly agree

---

[31] The analogies are less good for many other products. For lower-value products than cars, internet sales are less like an "ascending" auction because search costs will allow price dispersion, while traditional sales through posted prices in high-street stores are more like "ascending" auctions than are dealer sales of cars. Note also that the outcomes of the two auction types differ most when competitors have private information about their costs, which is more likely when competitors are original manufacturers than when competitors are retailers selling goods bought at identical prices from the same wholesaler.

[32] For an individual consumer, demand might be inelastic for a single car up to a reservation price. From the point of view of the sellers who do not know the consumer's reservation price, the expected market demand is downward sloping.

[33] Of course, Hansen is maintaining the other important assumptions of the revenue equivalence theorem.

[34] See Robinson (1985) and Milgrom (1987) for discussion of the single-unit case. See Ausubel and Schwartz (1999), Brusco and Lopomo (1999), Cramton and Schwartz (2000), Engelbrecht-Wiggans and Kahn (1998), Menezes (1996), and Weber (1997), for the multi-unit case. Klemperer (2002a) reviews these arguments and gives many examples.

[35] Bidders are competing to buy rather than sell spectrum, so prices are ascending rather than descending.

to stop pushing prices up.[36] The same coordination cannot readily be achieved in simultaneous sealed-bid auctions, in which there is neither the opportunity to signal, nor the ability to retaliate against a bidder who fails to cooperate.[37] The conclusion is less stark when there are many repetitions over time, but it probably remains true that coordination is easier in ascending auctions. Furthermore, as is already well understood in the industrial organization literature,[38] this conclusion is strengthened by the different observabilities of internet and dealer sale prices that make mutual understanding of firms' strategies, including defections from "agreements," far greater in the internet case. Thus selling over the internet probably makes it easier for firms to collude.

A third important issue is that bidders may be asymmetric. Then "ascending" auctions are generally more efficient (because the lowest-cost bidders win[39]), but sealed-bid auctions typically yield lower consumer prices.[40] In this case economists generally favor ascending auctions, but competition-policy practitioners should usually prefer sealed-bid auctions because most competition regimes concentrate on consumer welfare.

Furthermore, this analysis ignores the impact of auction type on new entry in the presence of asymmetries. Because an "ascending" auction is generally efficient, a potential competitor with even a slightly higher cost (or lower quality) than an incumbent will see no point in entering the auction. However, the same competitor might enter a sealed-bid auction, which gives a weaker bidder a shot

---

[36] For example, in a 1999 German spectrum auction, Mannesman bid a low price for half the licenses and a slightly lower price for the other half. Here is what one of T-Mobil's managers said: "There were no agreements with Mannesman. But [T-Mobil] interpreted Mannesman's first bid as an offer." T-Mobil understood that it could raise the bid on the other half of the licenses slightly, and that the two companies would then "live and let live," with neither company challenging the other on "their" half. Just that happened. The auction closed after just two rounds, with each of the bidders having half the licenses for the same low price. See Jehiel and Moldovanu (2000) and Grimm et al. (2001). In U.S. FCC auctions, bidders have used the final three digits of multimillion dollar bids to signal the market id codes of the areas they coveted, and a 1997 auction that was expected to raise $1,800 million raised less than $14 million. See Cramton and Schwartz (2001), and "Learning to Play the Game," *The Economist*, May 17, 1997, p. 120. Klemperer (2002a) gives many more examples.

[37] The low prices in the ascending auction are supported by the threat that, if a bidder overbids a competitor anywhere, then the competitor will retaliate by overbidding the first bidder on markets where the first bidder has the high bids.

[38] At least since Stigler (1964).

[39] To the extent that the auctions for individual consumers are independent single-unit auctions, an ascending auction is efficient under a broad class of assumptions if bidders' private signals are single-dimensional, even with asymmetries among bidders and common-value components to valuations. See Maskin (1992).

[40] A price-minimizing auction allocates the object to the bidder with the lowest "virtual cost," rather than to the one with the lowest actual cost. (See Section 4; virtual cost is the analogous concept to marginal revenue for an auction to buy an object.) Compared with an ascending auction, a sealed-bid auction discriminates in favor of selling to "weaker" bidders, whose costs are drawn from higher distributions, because they bid more aggressively (closer to their actual costs) than stronger ones. But, for a given cost, a weaker bidder has a lower virtual cost than a stronger one. So, the sealed-bid auction often, but not always, yields lower prices. See Section 7.1 of Klemperer (1999a).

at winning. The extra competition may lower prices substantially. Of course, the entry of the weaker competitor may also slightly reduce efficiency, but if competition is desirable per se, or if competition itself improves efficiency, or if the objective is consumer welfare rather than efficiency, then the case for sealed-bid auctions is very strong (see next subsection and Klemperer, 2002a).

Although there are other dimensions in which our setting fails the revenue equivalence assumptions, they seem less important.[41] It follows that the transparency induced between firms that makes internet sales more like ascending auctions than sealed-bid auctions is probably bad for consumers. Although gains from lower consumer search costs and dealer costs could certainly reverse this conclusion, auction-theoretic considerations mount a strong case against "transparent" internet sales.[42]

In another application of auction-theoretic insights to e-commerce, Bulow and Klemperer (2002b) apply Milgrom and Weber's (1982) celebrated *linkage principle* to show when the price discrimination that internet markets make possible *helps* consumers.

3.2. Anglo-Dutch Auctions, a Theory of Rationing, and Patent Races

The last disadvantage of ascending auctions discussed earlier – the dampening effect on entry – has been very important in practical auction contexts (see Klemperer 2002a). For example, in the main (1995) auction of U.S. mobile-phone licenses, some large potential bidders such as MCI, the U.S.'s third-largest phone company, failed to enter at all, and many other bidders were deterred from competing seriously for particular licenses such as the Los Angeles and New York licenses, which therefore sold at very low prices.[43] Entry was therefore a prominent concern when the UK planned an auction of four UMTS "third-generation" mobile-phone licenses in 1998 for a market in which four companies operated mobile telephone services and therefore had clear advantages over any new entrant.[44]

In this case, the design chosen was an "Anglo-Dutch" auction as first proposed in Klemperer (1998):[45] in an Anglo-Dutch auction for four licenses, the

---

[41] Other violations of the revenue equivalence assumptions may include buyer and seller risk aversion that both favor sealed-bid auctions and affiliation of costs that favors ascending auctions.

[42] Empirical evidence is limited. Lee (1998) and Lee et al. (1999) find electronic markets yield higher prices than conventional markets for cars. Scott Morton et al. (2001) find that California customers get lower prices if they use automobile internet sites, but this is unsurprising because these sites merely refer customers to dealers for price quotes, so behave more like traditional dealers than like the "transparent" sites that we have described and that are being promised in Europe.

[43] See Klemperer and Pagnozzi (2002) for econometric evidence of these kinds of problems in U.S. spectrum auctions, Bulow and Klemperer (2000) and Klemperer (1998) for extensive discussion, and Bulow, Huang, and Klemperer (1999) for related modeling.

[44] Bidders could not be allowed to win more than one license each.

[45] See Klemperer (1998, 2002a) and Radiocommunications Agency (1998a, 1998b) for more details and for variants on the basic design. (The Agency was advised by Binmore, Klemperer, and others.)

price rises continuously until five bidders remain (the "English" stage), after which the five survivors make sealed bids (required to be no lower than the current price level) and the four winners pay the fourth-highest bid (the "Dutch" stage). Weak bidders have an incentive to enter such an auction because they know they have a chance of winning at the sealed-bid stage if they can survive to be among the five finalists. The design accepts some risk of an ex post inefficient allocation to increase the chance of attracting the additional bidders that are necessary for a successful auction and reasonable revenues.[46,47]

Translating this idea into a more traditional economics context suggests a theory of why firms might ration their output at prices in which there is excess demand as, for example, microprocessor manufacturers routinely do after the introduction of a new chip. Raising the price to clear the market would correspond to running an ascending auction. It would be ex post efficient and ex post profit maximizing, but would give poor incentives for weaker potential customers who fear being priced out of the market to make the investments necessary to enter the market (such as the product design necessary to use the new chip). Committing to rationing at a fixed price at which demand exceeds supply is ex post inefficient,[48] but may encourage more entry into the market and so improve ex ante profits. Details and more examples are in Gilbert and Klemperer (2000).

A similar point is that a weaker firm may not be willing to enter a patent race in which all parties can observe others' progress. Such a race is akin to an ascending auction in which a stronger rival can always observe and overtake a weaker firm, which therefore has no chance of winning.[49] A race in which rivals' progress cannot be monitored is more akin to a sealed-bid auction and may attract more entry.

---

[46] The additional bidders might yield a higher price even after the English stage, let alone after the final stage, than in a pure ascending auction.

[47] The design performed very successfully in laboratory testing, but the auction was delayed until 2000, and technological advances made it possible to offer five licenses, albeit of different sizes. The additional license resolved the problem of attracting new entrants, and because collusion was not a serious problem in this case (bidders were not allowed to win more than one license each), it was decided to switch to a simultaneous ascending design. The actual UK auction was very successful, but the wisdom of the UK decision not to run an ascending auction when the number of strong bidders equaled the number of licences was confirmed when the Netherlands did just this three months later, and raised little more than one-quarter of the per capita revenue raised by the UK In large part, the Netherlands' problem was that their ascending auction deterred entry, Denmark also had the same number of strong bidders as licences, and (successfully) used a sealed-bid auction for similar reasons that the UK would have run an Anglo-Dutch auction in this context. (In Denmark it was clear that there were too few potential bidders to make an Anglo stage worthwhile.) See Klemperer (2002a, 2002b, 2002c) for more detail.

[48] We assume any resale is inefficient. But see Cramton, Gibbons, and Klemperer (1987).

[49] Of course, this point is closely related to the idea of "ε-preemption" in R&D races with observability that has already been well discussed in the standard industrial organization literature (Fudenberg et al. 1983).

These analogies illustrate how an insight that is routine in auction theory may help develop ideas in economics more broadly.

4. EXPLOITING DEEPER CONNECTIONS BETWEEN AUCTIONS AND ECONOMICS: MARGINAL REVENUES

The previous sections showed how a variety of economic problems can be thought of in auction-theoretic terms, allowing us to use tools such as the revenue equivalence theorem and intuitions such as those from the comparison of ascending and sealed-bid auctions. This section explains that the connections between auction theory and standard economic theory run much deeper.

Much of the analysis of optimal auctions can be phrased, like the analysis of monopoly, in terms of "marginal revenues." Imagine a firm whose demand curve is constructed from an arbitrarily large number of bidders whose values are independently drawn from a bidder's value distribution. When bidders have independent private values, a bidder's "marginal revenue" is defined as the marginal revenue of this firm at the price that equals the bidder's actual value (see Figure 2.2).[50]

Although it had been hinted at before,[51] the key point was first explicitly drawn out by Bulow and Roberts (1989), who showed that under the assumptions of the revenue equivalence theorem *the expected revenue from an auction equals the expected marginal revenue of the winning bidder(s)*. The new results in the article were few – the paper largely mimicked Myerson (1981), while renaming Myerson's concept of "virtual utility" as "marginal revenue"[52,53] – but their contribution was nevertheless important. Once the connection had been made, it was possible to take ways of thinking that are second nature to economists from the standard theory of monopoly pricing and apply them to auction theory.

---

[50] The point of this construction is particularly clear when a seller faces a single bidder whose private value is distributed according to $F(v)$. Then, setting a take-it-or-leave-it price of v yields expected sales, or "demand," $1 - F(v)$, expected revenue of $v(1 - F(v))$, and expected marginal revenue $d(qv)/dq = v - (1 - F(v))/f(v)$. See Appendix B of Klemperer (1999a).

[51] For example, Mussa and Rosen's (1978) analysis of monopoly and product quality contained expressions for "marginal revenue" that look like Myerson's (1981) analysis of optimal auctions.

[52] Myerson's results initially seemed unfamiliar to economists, in part because his basic analysis (although not all his expressions) expressed virtual utilities as a function of bidders' values, which correspond to *prices*, and so computed revenues by integrating along the vertical axis, whereas we usually solve monopoly problems by expressing marginal revenues as functions of *quantities* and integrating along the horizontal axis of the standard (for monopoly) picture.

[53] Bulow and Roberts emphasize the close parallel between a monopolist third-degree price-discriminating across markets with different demand curves, and an auctioneer selling to bidders whose valuations are drawn from different distributions. For the { $\begin{smallmatrix}\text{monopolist}\\\text{auctioneer}\end{smallmatrix}$ }, { $\begin{smallmatrix}\text{revenue}\\\text{expected revenue}\end{smallmatrix}$ } is maximized by selling to the { $\begin{smallmatrix}\text{consumers}\\\text{bidder}\end{smallmatrix}$ } with the highest marginal revenue(s), *not* necessarily the highest value(s), subject to never selling to a { $\begin{smallmatrix}\text{consumer}\\\text{bidder}\end{smallmatrix}$ } with marginal revenue less than the { $\begin{smallmatrix}\text{monopolist's marginal cost}\\\text{auctioneer's own valuation}\end{smallmatrix}$ }, assuming (i) resale can be prohibited, (ii) credible commitment can be made to { $\begin{smallmatrix}\text{no future sales}\\\text{sticking to any reserve price}\end{smallmatrix}$ }, and (iii) { $\begin{smallmatrix}\text{marginal revenue curves are all downward sloping}\\\text{higher "types" of any bidder have higher marginal revenues than lower "types"}\\\text{of the same bidder}\end{smallmatrix}$ }, etc.

Value, v

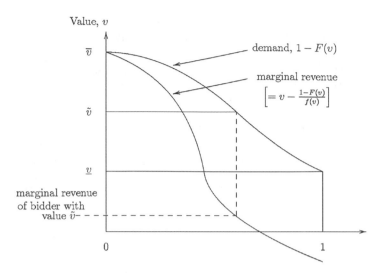

demand, $1 - F(v)$

marginal revenue
$$\left[= v - \frac{1-F(v)}{f(v)} \right]$$

$\bar{v}$

$\tilde{v}$

$\underline{v}$

marginal revenue
of bidder with
value $\tilde{v}$-----

0

1

Figure 2.2. Construction of marginal revenue of bidder with value $\tilde{v}$ drawn from distribution $F(v)$ on $[\underline{v}, \bar{v}]$.

For example, once the basic result (that an auction's expected revenue equals the winning bidder's expected marginal revenue) was seen, Bulow and Klemperer (1996) were able to use a simple monopoly diagram to derive it more simply and under a broader class of assumptions than had previously been done by Myerson or Bulow and Roberts.[54] Bulow and Klemperer also used standard monopoly intuition to derive additional results in auction theory.

The main benefits from the marginal-revenue connection come from translating ideas from monopoly analysis into auction analysis, because most economists' intuition for and understanding of monopoly is much more highly developed than for auctions. But, it is possible to go in the other direction, too, from auction theory to monopoly theory.

Consider, for example, the main result of Bulow and Klemperer (1996):

Proposition 4.1 (Auction-Theoretic Version). *An optimal auction of K units to Q bidders earns less profit than a simple ascending auction (without a reserve price) of K units to Q + K bidders, assuming (a) bidders are symmetric, (b) bidders are serious (i.e., their lowest possible valuations exceed the seller's supply cost), and (c) bidders with higher valuations have higher marginal revenues.*[55]

Proof. See Bulow and Klemperer (1996).   ∎

---

[54] See Appendix B of Klemperer (1999a) for an exposition.

[55] See Bulow and Klemperer (1996) for a precise statement. We do not require bidders' valuations to be private, but do place some restrictions on the class of possible mechanisms from which the "optimal" one is selected, if bidders are not risk neutral or their signals are not independent. We assume bidders demand a single unit each.

Application. One application is to selling a firm (so, $K = 1$). Because the seller can always resort to an ascending auction, attracting a single additional bidder is worth more than any amount of negotiating skill or bargaining power against an existing bidder or bidders, under reasonable assumptions. Thus, there is little justification for, for example, accepting a "lock-up" bid for a company without fully exploring the interest of alternative possible purchasers.

The optimal auction translates, for large Q and K, to the monopolist's optimum. An ascending auction translates to the competitive outcome, in which price-taking firms make positive profits only because of the fixed supply of units. (An ascending auction yields the $K + 1st$-highest value among the bidders; in a perfectly competitive market, an inelastic supply of K units is in equilibrium with demand at any price between the Kth and $K + 1st$-highest value, but the distinction is unimportant for large K.) So, one way of expressing the result in the market context is:

Proposition 4.2 (Monopoly-Theoretic Version). *A perfectly competitive industry with (fixed) capacity K and Q consumers would gain less by fully cartelizing the industry (and charging the monopoly price) than it would gain by attracting K new potential customers into the industry with no change in the intensity of competition, assuming (a') the K new potential consumers have the same distribution of valuations as the existing consumers, (b') all consumers' valuations for the product exceed sellers' supply costs (up to sellers' capacity), and (c') the marginal-revenue curve constructed from the market-demand curve is downward sloping.*[56]

Proof. No proof is required – the proposition is implied by the auction-theoretic version – but once we know the result we are looking for and the necessary assumptions, it is very simple to prove it directly using introductory undergraduate economics. We do this in a brief Appendix 2. ∎

Application. One application is that this provides conditions under which a joint-marketing agency does better to focus on actually marketing rather than (as some of the industrial organization literature suggests) on facilitating collusive practices.[57]

5. APPLYING AUCTION THEORY TO PRICE-SETTING OLIGOPOLIES

We have stressed the applications of auction theory to contexts that might not be thought of as auctions, but even though price-setting oligopolies are obviously

---

[56] We are measuring capacity in units such that each consumer demands a single unit of output. Appendix 2 makes it clear how the result generalizes.

[57] Of course, the agency may wish to pursue both strategies in practice.

auctions, the insights that can be obtained by thinking of them in this way are often passed by.

5.1.   Marginal-Cost Pricing Is *Not* the Unique Bertrand Equilibrium

One of the most famous results in economics is the "Bertrand paradox," that with just two firms with constant and equal marginal costs in a homogeneous products industry, the unique equilibrium is for both firms to set price equal to marginal cost and firms earn zero profit. This "theorem" is widely quoted in standard texts. But, it is *false*. There are other equilibria with large profits, for some standard demand curves, a fact that seems until recently to have been known only to a few auction theorists.[58]

Auction theorists are familiar with the fact that a boundary condition is necessary to solve a sealed-bid auction. Usually, this is imposed by assuming no bidder can bid less than any bidder's lowest possible valuation, but there are generally a continuum of equilibria if arbitrarily negative bids are permitted.[59] Exactly conversely, with perfectly inelastic demand for one unit and, for example, two risk-neutral sellers with zero costs, it is a mixed-strategy equilibrium for each firm to bid above any price p with probability k/p, for any fixed k. (Each firm therefore faces expected residual demand of constant elasticity -1, and is therefore indifferent about mixing in this way; profits are k per firm.)

It is not hard to see that a similar construction is possible with downward-sloping demand, for example, standard constant-elasticity demand, provided that monopoly profits are unbounded. [See, especially, Baye and Morgan (1999a) and Kaplan and Wettstein (2000).] One point of view is that the nonuniqueness of the "Bertrand paradox" equilibrium is a merely technical point, because it requires "unreasonable" (even though often assumed[60]) demand. However, the construction immediately suggests another more important result: quite generally (including for demand which becomes zero at some finite choke price), there are very profitable mixed-strategy ε-equilibria to the Bertrand game, even though there are no pure-strategy ε-equilibria. That is, there are mixed strategies that are very different from marginal-cost pricing

---

[58] We assume firms can choose any prices. It is well known that if prices can be quoted only in whole pennies, there is an equilibrium with positive (but small) profits in which each firm charges one penny above cost. (With perfectly inelastic demand, there is also an equilibrium in which each firm charges two pennies above cost.)

[59] For example, if each of two risk-neutral bidders' private values is independently drawn from a uniform distribution on the open interval $(0, 1)$, then for any nonnegative k there is an equilibrium in which a player with value v bids $v/2 - k/v$. If it is common knowledge that both bidders have value zero, there is an equilibrium in which each player bids below any price $-p$ with probability k/p, for any fixed nonnegative k.

[60] This demand can, for example, yield unique and finite-profit Cournot equilibrium.

in which no player can gain more than a very small amount, ε, by deviating from the strategies.[61] (There are also "quantal response" equilibria with a similar flavor.) Experimental evidence suggests that these strategies may be empirically relevant (see Baye and Morgan, 1999b).[62]

5.2. The Value of New Consumers

The revenue equivalence theorem (RET) can, of course, be applied to price-setting oligopolies.[63]

For example: what is the value of new consumers in a market with strong brand loyalty? If firms can price discriminate between new uncommitted consumers and old "locked-in" consumers, Bertrand competition for the former will mean their value is low, but, what if price discrimination is impossible?

In particular, it is often argued that new youth smokers are very valuable to the tobacco industry because brand loyalty (as well as loyalty to the product) is very high (only about 10 percent of smokers switch brands in any year), so price-cost margins on all consumers are very high. Is there any truth to this view?

The answer, of course, under appropriate assumptions, is that the RET implies that the ability to price discriminate is irrelevant to the value of the new consumers (see the discussion in Section 2). With price discrimination, we can model the oligopolists as acting as monopolists against their old customers, and as being in an "ascending"[64] price auction for the uncommitted consumers with the firm that is prepared to price the lowest selling to all these consumers at the cost of the runner-up firm. Alternatively, we can model the oligopolists as making sealed bids for the uncommitted consumers, with the lowest bidder selling to these consumers at its asking price. The expected profits are the same under the RET assumptions. Absent price discrimination, a natural model is the latter one, but in addition each oligopolist must discount its price to its own locked-in customers down to the price it bids for the uncommitted consumers. The RET tells us that the total cost to the industry of these "discounts" to old consumers will, on average, precisely compensate the higher

---

[61] Of course, the concept of mixed-strategy ε-equilibrium used here is even more contentious than either mixed-strategy (Nash) equilibria or (pure-strategy) ε-equilibrium. The best defense for it may be its practical usefulness.

[62] Spulber (1995) uses the analogy with a sealed-bid auction to analyze a price-setting oligopoly in which, by contrast with our discussion, firms do not know their rivals' costs. For a related application of auction theory to price-setting oligopoly, see Athey et al. (2000).

[63] As another example, Vives (1999) uses the revenue equivalence theorem to compare price-setting oligopoly equilibria with incomplete and complete (or shared) information about firms' constant marginal costs, and so shows information sharing is socially undesirable in this context.

[64] The price is descending because the oligopolists are competing to sell rather than buy, but it corresponds to an ascending auction in which firms are competing to buy, and we stick with this terminology as in Section 3.1.

sale price achieved on new consumers.[65] That is, the net value to the industry of the new consumers is exactly as if there was Bertrand competition for them, even when the inability to price discriminate prevents this.

Thus, Bulow and Klemperer (1998) argue that the economic importance to the tobacco companies of the youth market is actually very tiny, even though from an accounting perspective new consumers appear as valuable as any others.[66]

Similarly, applying the same logic to an international trade question, the value of a free-trading market to firms, each of which has a protected home market, is independent (under appropriate assumptions) of whether the firms can price discriminate between markets.[67]

Section 3.1's discussion of oligopolistic e-competition develops this kind of analysis further by considering implications of failures of the RET.

5.3.   Information Aggregation in Perfect Competition

Although the examples cited previously, and in Section 3,[68] suggest auction theory has been underused in analyzing oligopolistic competition, it has been very important in influencing economists' ideas about the limit as the number of firms becomes large.

An important strand of the auction literature has focused on the properties of pure-common-value auctions as the number of bidders becomes large, and asked: does the sale price converge to the true value, thus fully aggregating all of the economy's information even though each bidder has only partial information? Milgrom (1979) and Wilson (1977) showed assumptions under which the answer is "yes" for a first-price, sealed-bid auction. Milgrom (1981) obtained similar results for a second-price auction [or for a $(k + 1)$th-price auction for k objects].[69] These models justify some of our ideas about perfect competition.

---

[65] Specifically let n "old" consumers be attached to each firm i, and firms' costs c_i be independently drawn from a common, strictly increasing, atomless distribution. There are m "new" consumers who will buy from the cheapest firm. All consumers have reservation price r. Think of firms competing for the prize of selling to the new consumers, worth $m(r - c_i)$ to firm i. Firms set prices $p_i = r - d_i$ to "new" consumers; equivalently, they set "discounts" d_i to consumers' reservation prices. If price discrimination is feasible, the winner pays md_i for the prize and all firms sell to their old consumers at r. Absent price discrimination, the prices p_i apply to all firms' sales, so relative to selling just to old consumers at price r, the winner pays $(m + n)d_i$ for the prize and the losers pay nd_i each. For the usual reasons, the two sets of payment rules are revenue equivalent. For more discussion of this result, including its robustness to multiperiod contexts, see Bulow and Klemperer (1998); if the total demand of new consumers is more elastic, their economic value will be somewhat less than our model suggests; for a fuller discussion of the effects of "brand loyalty" or "switching costs" in oligopoly, see, especially, Beggs and Klemperer (1992) and Klemperer (1987a, 1987b, 1995).

[66] If industry executives seem to value the youth segment, it is probably due more to concern for their own future jobs than concern for their shareholders.

[67] See also Rosenthal (1980).

[68] Bulow and Klemperer (2002b) provides an additional example.

[69] Matthews (1984), on the other hand, showed that the (first-price) sale price does not in general converge to the true value when each bidder can acquire information at a cost. Pesendorfer and

6. APPLYING AUCTION THEORY (AND ECONOMICS) TO AUCTION MARKETS

Finally, although it has not always been grasped by practitioners, some markets are literally auctions. The increasing recognition that many real markets are best understood through the lens of auction theory has stimulated a burst of new theorizing,[70] and created the new subject of market design that stands in similar relation to auction theory as engineering does to physics.

6.1. Important Auction Markets

It was not initially well understood that deregulated *electricity markets*, such as in the United Kingdom, are best described and analyzed as auctions of infinitely divisible quantities of homogeneous units.[71] Although much of the early analysis of the UK market was based on Klemperer and Meyer (1989), which explicitly followed Wilson's (1979) seminal contribution to multiunit auctions, the Klemperer and Meyer model was not thought of as an "auctions" paper, and only recently received much attention among auction theorists.[72] Indeed, von der Fehr and Harbord (1993) were seen as rather novel in pointing out that the new electricity markets could be viewed as auctions. Now, however, it is uncontroversial that these markets are best understood through auction theory, and electricity market design has become the province of leading auction theorists, such as Wilson, who have been very influential.

Treasury bill auctions, like electricity markets, trade a divisible homogeneous good; but, although treasury auctions have always been clearly understood to be "auctions," and the existing auction theory is probably even more relevant to treasury markets than to electricity markets,[73] auction theorists have never been as influential as they are now in energy markets. In part, this is

Swinkels (1997) recently breathed new life into this literature, by showing convergence under weaker assumptions than previously if the number of objects for sale, as well as the number of bidders, becomes large. See also Kremer (2000), Swinkels (2001), and Pesendorfer and Swinkels (2000).

[70] Especially on multiunit auctions in which bidders are not restricted to winning a single unit each, because most markets are of this kind.

[71] von der Fehr and Harbord (1998) provide a useful overview of electricity markets.

[72] Klemperer and Meyer (1989) was couched as a traditional industrial organization study of the question of whether competition is more like Bertrand or Cournot, following Klemperer and Meyer (1986).

[73] Non-auction-theoretic issues that limit the direct application of auction theory to electricity markets include the very high frequency of repetition among market participants who have stable and predictable requirements, which makes the theory of collusion in repeated games also very relevant; the nature of the game the major electricity suppliers are playing with the industry regulator who may step in and attempt to change the rules (again) if the companies are perceived to be making excessive profits; the conditions for new entry; and the effects of vertical integration of industry participants. On the other hand, the interaction of a treasury auction with the financial markets for trading the bills both before and after the auction complicates the analysis of that auction.

because the treasury auctions predated any relevant theory,[74] and the auctions did not seem to have serious problems. In part it may be because no clear view has emerged about the best form of auction to use; indeed, one possibility is that the differences between the main types of auction may not be too important in this context – see Klemperer (2002a).[75]

Academics were involved at all stages of the *radiospectrum auctions*, from suggesting the original designs to advising bidders on their strategies. The original U.S. proponents of an auction format saw it as a complex environment that needed academic input, and a pattern of using academic consultants was set in the U.S. and spread to other countries.[76]

Many other new auction markets are currently being created using the *internet*, such as the online consumer auctions run by eBay, Amazon, and others that have more than 10 million customers, and the business-to-business auto parts auctions being planned by General Motors, Ford, and Daimler-Chrysler that are expected to handle $250 million in transactions a year. Here, too, auction theorists have been in heavy demand, and there is considerable ongoing

---

[74] By contrast, the current U.K. government sales of gold are a new development, and government agencies have now consulted auction theorists (including myself) about the sale method.

[75] In a further interesting contrast, the U.K. electricity market – the first major market in the world to be deregulated and run as an auction – was set up as a uniform price auction, but its perceived poor performance has led to a planned switch to an exchange market, followed by a discriminatory auction (see Klemperer 2002a; Office of Gas and Electricity Markets 1999; Newbery 1998, Wolfram 1998, 1999). Meanwhile, the vast majority of the world's treasury bill markets have until recently been run as discriminatory auctions (see Bartolini and Cottarelli 1997), but the U.S. switched to uniform price auctions in late 1998, and several other countries have been experimenting with these. In fact, it seems unlikely that either form of auction is best either for all electricity markets or for all treasury markets (see, e.g., Klemperer 1999b, Federico and Rahman 2000, McAdams 1998, Nyborg and Sundaresan 1996).

[76] Evan Kwerel was especially important in promoting the use of auctions. The dominant design has been the simultaneous ascending auction sketched by Vickrey (1976), and proposed and developed by McAfee, Milgrom, and Wilson for the U.S. auctions. (See McMillan 1994, McAfee and McMillan 1996, and especially Milgrom forthcoming.) Although some problems have emerged, primarily its susceptibility to collusion and its inhospitability to entry (see Section 3.2), it has generally been considered a success in most of its applications (see, e.g., Board 1999, Cramton 1997, Plott 1997, Salant 1997, Weber 1997, and Zheng 1999). A large part of the motivation for the U.S. design was the possibility of complementarities between licenses (see Ausubel et al. 1997), although it is unproven either that the design was especially helpful in allowing bidders to aggregate efficient packages, or that it would work well if complementarities had been very significant. Ironically, the simultaneous ascending auction is most attractive when each of an exogenously fixed number of bidders has a privately known value for each of a collection of heterogeneous objects, but (contrary to the U.S. case) is restricted to buying at most a single license. In this case, entry is not an issue, collusion is very unlikely, and the outcome is efficient. For this reason a version of the simultaneous ascending auction was designed by Binmore and Klemperer for the U.K. 3G auction (in which each bidder was restricted to a single license) after concerns about entry had been laid to rest. A sealed-bid design was recently used very successfully in Denmark where attracting entry was a serious concern. See Section 3.2, see Binmore and Klemperer (2002) for discussion of the U.K. auction, and see Klemperer (2002a, 2002b, 2002c, 2002d, 2002e) for a discussion of the recent European spectrum auctions.

experimentation with different auctions forms.[77] Furthermore, we have already argued that internet markets that are not usually thought of as auctions can be illuminated by auction theory [see Section 3.1 and Bulow and Klemperer (2002b)].

6.2.   Applying Economics to Auction Design

Although many economic markets are now fruitfully analyzed as auctions, the most significant problems in auction markets and auction design are probably those with which industry regulators and competition authorities have traditionally been concerned – discouraging collusive, predatory, and entry-deterring behavior, and analyzing the merits of mergers or other changes to market structure.

This contrasts with most of the auction literature that focuses on Nash equilibria in one-shot games with a fixed number of bidders, and emphasizes issues such as the effects of risk aversion, correlation of information, budget constraints, complementarities, asymmetries, etc. Certainly these are also important topics – and auction theorists have made important progress on them that other economic theory can learn from – but they are probably not the main issues.

Although the relative thinness of the auction-theoretic literature on collusion and entry deterrence may be defensible to the extent general economic principles apply, there is a real danger that auction theorists will underemphasize these problems in applications. In particular, ascending, second-price, and uniform-price auction forms, although attractive in many auction theorists' models, are more vulnerable to collusive and predatory behavior than (first-price) sealed-bid and hybrid forms, such as the Anglo-Dutch auction described in Section 3.2. Klemperer (2002a) provides an extensive discussion of these issues.

Although auction theorists are justly proud of how much they can teach economics, they must not forget that the classical lessons of economics continue to apply.

7.   CONCLUSIONS

Auction theory is a central part of economics and should be a part of every economist's armory; auction theorists' ways of thinking shed light on a whole range of economic topics.

We have shown that many economic questions that do not at first sight seem related to auctions can be recast to be solvable using auction-theoretic techniques, such as the revenue equivalence theorem. The close parallels between auction theory and standard price theory – such as those between the theories of optimal auctions and of price discrimination – mean ideas can be arbitraged

---

[77] See, e.g., Hall (2001). The UK government recently used the internet to run the world's first auction for greenhouse gas emissions reductions. (Peter Cramton, Eric Maskin, and I advised on the design, and Larry Ausubel and Jeremy Bulow also helped with the implementation.)

from auction theory to standard economics, and vice versa. The insights and intuitions that auction theorists have developed in comparing different auction forms can find fertile application in many other contexts.

Furthermore, although standard auction theory models already provide the basis of much work in labor economics, political economy, finance, and industrial organization, we have used the example of price-setting oligopoly to show that a much greater application of auction-theoretic thinking may be possible in these more obvious fields.

"Heineken refreshes the parts other beers cannot reach" was recently voted one of the top advertising campaigns of all time, worldwide. The moral of this paper is that, "Auction theory refreshes the parts other economics cannot reach." Like Heineken, auction theory is a potent brew that we should all imbibe.

ACKNOWLEDGMENTS

Susan Athey was an excellent discussant of this paper. I have also received extremely helpful comments and advice from many other friends and colleagues, including Larry Ausubel, Mike Baye, Alan Beggs, Simon Board, Jeremy Bulow, Peter Cramton, Joe Farrell, Giulio Federico, Nils Hendrik von der Fehr, Dan Kovenock, David McAdams, Peter McAfee, Flavio Menezes, Meg Meyer, Jonathan Mirrlees-Black, John Morgan, Marco Pagnozzi, Nicola Persico, Eric Rasmussen, David Salant, Margaret Stevens, Rebecca Stone, Lucy White, Mark Williams, Xavier Vives, Caspar de Vries, and Charles Zheng.

APPENDIX 1:   COMPARING LITIGATION SYSTEMS

Assume that after transfers between the parties, the loser ends up paying fraction $\alpha \geq 0$ of his own expenses and fraction $\beta \leq 1$ of his opponent's. (The winner pays the remainder.)[78] The American system is $\alpha = 1, \beta = 0$; the British system is $\alpha = \beta = 1$; the Netherlands system is, roughly, $\alpha = 1, 0 < \beta < 1$; and Quayle's is $\alpha = 2, \beta = 0$. It is also interesting to consider a "reverse-Quayle" rule $\alpha = 1, \beta < 0$ in which both parties pay their own expenses, but the winner transfers an amount proportional to her own expenses to the loser. Let L be the average legal expenses spent per player.

The following slight generalization of the RET is the key: assuming the conditions of the RET all hold except for assumption (ii) (i.e., the expected surplus of a bidder with the lowest feasible valuation, say $\underline{S}$, may not be zero), it remains true that the expected surplus of any other types of bidder is a fixed amount above $\underline{S}$. [See, e.g., Klemperer (1999a; Appendix A); the fixed amount

---

[78] As in the main text, we assume a symmetric equilibrium with strictly increasing bidding functions. For extreme values of α and β, this may not exist (and we cannot then use the RET directly). See Baye, Kovenock, and de Vries (1997) for explicit solutions for the equilibria for different α and β.

depends on the distribution of the parties' valuations, but unlike $\underline{S}$ and L does not depend on the mechanism $\{\alpha, \beta\}$.]

It follows that the average bidder surplus is $\underline{S}$ plus a constant. But the average bidder surplus equals the average lawsuit winnings (expectation of {probability of winning} $\times$ {valuation}) minus L, equals a constant minus L by assumption (i) of the RET. So, $\underline{S} = K - L$ in which K is a constant independent of α and β. Because the lowest valuation type always loses in equilibrium [by assumption (i) of the RET], she bids zero so $\underline{S} = -\beta L$, because in a one-shot game her opponent, on average, incurs expenses of L. Solving, $L = K/(1 - \beta)$ and the expected surplus of any given party is a constant minus $\beta K/(1 - \beta)$.

It follows that both expected total expenses and any party's expected payoff are invariant to α; hence the remarks in the text about the Quayle proposal. But legal expenses are increasing in β, indeed become unbounded in the limit corresponding to the British system. The mechanism that minimizes legal expenses taking the set of lawsuits as given is the reverse Quayle. The intuition is that it both increases the marginal cost of spending on a lawsuit and reduces the value of winning the suit. On the other hand, of course, bringing lawsuits becomes more attractive as β falls.

APPENDIX 2:   DIRECT PROOF OF MONOPOLY-THEORETIC VERSION OF PROPOSITION IN SECTION 4

The proof rests precisely on the assumptions (a'), (b'), and (c'). Without loss of generality, let firms' marginal costs be flat up to capacity,[79] and consider what would be the marginal revenue curve for the market if the K new consumers were attracted into it (see Figure 2.3).

A monopolist on this (expanded) market would earn area A in profits (i.e., the area between the marginal revenue and marginal cost curves up to the monopoly point, M). The perfectly competitive industry in the same (expanded) market would earn $\Pi^c = A - B$, that is, the integral of marginal revenue less marginal cost up to industry capacity, K. By assumption (a'), a monopolist (or fully cartelized industry) in the original market would earn $\Pi^M = [Q/(Q + K)]A$. Now, the average marginal revenue up to quantity $Q + K$ equals the price at demand $Q + K$ (because total marginal revenue = price $\times$ quantity), which exceeds marginal cost by assumption (b'), so $B + C \leq A$. Furthermore, by assumption (c') and elementary geometry, $B \leq [(K - M)/((Q + K) - M)](B + C)$. So, $B \leq [(K - M)/(Q + K - M)]A$, and therefore $\Pi^c = A - B \geq [Q/(Q + K - M)]A \geq \Pi^M$, as required.

---

[79] If the industry cost curve is not flat up to the capacity, then use the argument in the text to prove the result for a cost curve that is flat and everywhere weakly above the actual cost curve. A fortiori, this proves the result for the actual curve, because a monopoly saves less from a lower cost curve than a competitive industry saves from the lower cost curve.

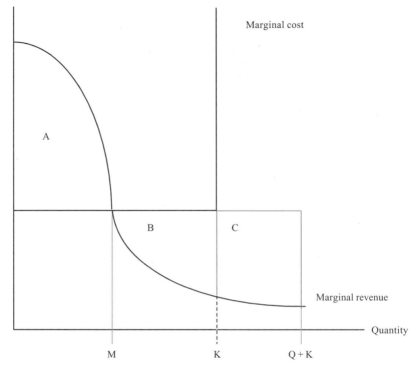

Figure 2.3. Marginal revenue if demand is expanded.

References

Abreu, D. and F. Gul (2000), "Bargaining and Reputation," *Econometrica*, 68, 85–117.
Athey, S., K. Bagwell, and C. Sanchirico (2000), "Collusion and Price Rigidity," mimeo, MIT.
Ausubel, L. M., P. Cramton, R. P. McAfee, and J. McMillan (1997), "Synergies in Wireless Telephony: Evidence from the Broadband PCS Auctions," *Journal of Economics and Management Strategy,* 6, 497–527.
Ausubel, L. M. and J. A. Schwartz (1999), "The Ascending Auction Paradox," Working Paper, University of Maryland.
Bartolini, L. and C. Cottarelli (1997), "Designing Effective Auctions for Treasury Securities," *Current Issues in Economics and Finance*, 3, 1–6.
Baye, M. R., D. Kovenock, and C. de Vries (1997), "Fee Allocation of Lawyer Services in Litigation," mimeo, Indiana University, Purdue University, and Tinbergen Institute, Erasmus University.
Baye, M. R., D. Kovenock, and C. de Vries (1998, February), "A General Linear Model of Contests," Working Paper, Indiana University, Purdue University, and Tinbergen Institute, Erasmus University.
Baye, M. R. and J. Morgan (1999a), "A Folk Theorem for One-Shot Bertrand Games," *Economics Letters,* 65, 59–65.

Baye, M. R. and J. Morgan (1999b), "Bounded Rationality in Homogeneous Product Pricing Games," Working Paper, Indiana University and Princeton University.

Baye, M. R. and J. Morgan (2001), "Information Gatekeepers on the Internet and the Competitiveness of Homogeneous Product Markets," *American Economic Review*, 91, 454–474.

Beggs, A. W. and P. D. Klemperer (1992), "Multi-Period Competition with Switching Costs," *Econometrica*, 60(3), 651–666.

Bernheim, B. D. and M. D. Whinston (1986), "Menu Auctions, Resource Allocation, and Economic Influence," *Quarterly Journal of Economics*, 101, 1–31.

Binmore, K. and P. D. Klemperer (2002), "The Biggest Auction Ever: The Sale of the British 3G Telecom Licenses," *Economic Journal*, 112(478), C74–C96.

Bliss, C. and B. Nalebuff (1984), "Dragon-Slaying and Ballroom Dancing: The Private Supply of a Public Good," *Journal of Public Economics*, 25, 1–12.

Board, S. A. (1999), "Commitment in Auctions," M. Phil. Thesis, Nuffield College, Oxford University.

Brusco, S. and G. Lopomo (1999), "Collusion via Signalling in Open Ascending Auctions with Multiple Objects and Complementarities," Working Paper, Stern School of Business, New York University.

Bulow, J. I., M. Huang, and P. D. Klemperer (1999), "Toeholds and Takeovers," *Journal of Political Economy*, 107, 427–454.

Bulow, J. I. and P. D. Klemperer (1994), "Rational Frenzies and Crashes," *Journal of Political Economy*, 102, 1–23.

Bulow, J. I. and P. D. Klemperer (1996), "Auctions vs. Negotiations," *American Economic Review*, 86, 180–194.

Bulow, J. I. and P. D. Klemperer (1998), "The Tobacco Deal," *Brookings Papers on Economic Activity (Microeconomics)*, 323–394.

Bulow, J. I. and P. D. Klemperer (1999), "The Generalized War of Attrition," *American Economic Review*, 89, 175–189.

Bulow, J. I. and P. D. Klemperer (2002a), "Prices and the Winner's Curse," *Rand Journal of Economics*, 33(1), 1–21.

Bulow, J. I. and P. D. Klemperer (2002b), "Privacy and Prices," Nuffield College, Oxford University Discussion Paper, available at www.paulklemperer.org.

Bulow, J. I. and D. J. Roberts (1989), "The Simple Economics of Optimal Auctions," *Journal of Political Economy*, 97, 1060–1090.

Cramton, P. (1997), "The FCC Spectrum Auctions: An Early Assessment," *Journal of Economics and Management Strategy*, 6(3), 431–495.

Cramton, P., R. Gibbons, and P. D. Klemperer (1987), "Dissolving a Partnership Efficiently," *Econometrica*, 55(3), 615–632.

Cramton, P. and J. A. Schwartz (2001), "Collusive Bidding: Lessons from the FCC Spectrum Auctions," *Journal of Regulatory Economics,* 18, 187–205.

Engelbrecht-Wiggans, R. and C. M. Kahn (1998), "Low Revenue Equilibria in Simultaneous Auctions," Working Paper, University of Illinois.

Feddersen, T. J. and W. Pesendorfer (1996), "The Swing Voter's Curse," *American Economic Review*, 86(3), 408–424.

Feddersen, T. J. and W. Pesendorfer (1998), "Convicting the Innocent: The Inferiority of Unanimous Jury Verdicts under Strategic Voting," *American Political Science Review,* 92(1), 23–35.

Federico, G. and D. Rahman (2000), "Bidding in an Electricity Pay-as-Bid Auction," Working Paper, Nuffield College.

von der Fehr, N.-H. and D. Harbord (1993), "Spot Market Competition in the UK Electricity Industry," *Economic Journal*, 103, 531–546.

von der Fehr, N.-H. and D. Harbord (1998), "Competition in Electricity Spot Markets: Economic Theory and International Experience," Memorandum No. 5/1998, Department of Economics, University of Oslo.

Friedman, L. (1956), "A Competitive Bidding Strategy," *Operations Research*, 4, 104–112.

Fudenberg, D., and D. M. Kreps (1987), "Reputation in the Simultaneous Play of Multiple Opponents," *Review of Economic Studies*, 54, 541–568.

Fudenberg, D. and J. Tirole (1986), "A Theory of Exit in Duopoly," *Econometrica*, 54, 943–960.

Fudenberg, D., R. Gilbert, J. Stiglitz and J. Tirole (1983), "Preemption, Leapfrogging, and Competition in Patent Races," *European Economic Review*, 22, 3–31.

Gilbert, R. and P. D. Klemperer, (2000), "An Equilibrium Theory of Rationing," *Rand Journal of Economics,* 31(1), 1–21.

Grimm, V., F. Riedel, and E. Wolfstetter (2001), "Low Price Equilibrium in Multi-Unit Auctions: The GSM Spectrum Auction in Germany," Working Paper, Humboldt Universität zu Berlin.

Haigh, J. and C. Cannings, (1989), "The *n*-Person War of Attrition," *Acta Applicandae Mathematicae*, 14, 59–74.

Hall, R. E. (2001), *Digital Dealing*. New York: W. W. Norton.

Hansen, R. G. (1988), "Auctions with Endogenous Quantity," *Rand Journal of Economics*, 19, 44–58.

Holt, C. A. Jr. and R. Sherman (1982), "Waiting-Line Auctions." *Journal of Political Economy*, 90, 280–294.

Hughes, J. W. and E. A. Snyder (1995), "Litigation and Settlement under the English and American Rules: Theory and Evidence." *Journal of Law and Economics,* 38, 225–250.

Jehiel, P. and B. Moldovanu (2000), "A Critique of the Planned Rules for the German UMTS/IMT-2000 License Auction," Working Paper, University College London and University of Mannheim.

Kagel, J. H. (1995), "Auctions: A Survey of Experimental Research," in *The Handbook of Experimental Economics* (ed. by J. H. Kagel and A. E. Roth), Princeton, NJ: Princeton University Press, 501–586.

Kambe, S. (1999), "Bargaining with Imperfect Commitment," *Games and Economic Behavior*, 28(2), 217–237.

Kaplan, T. and D. Wettstein (2000), "The Possibility of Mixed-Strategy Equilibria with Constant-Returns-to-Scale Technology under Bertrand Competition," *Spanish Economic Review*, 2(1), 65–71.

Klemperer, P. D. (1987a), "Markets with Consumer Switching Costs," *Quarterly Journal of Economics*, 102(2), 375–394.

Klemperer, P. D. (1987b), "The Competitiveness of Markets with Switching Costs," *Rand Journal of Economics*, 18(1), 138–150.

Klemperer, P. D. (1995), "Competition When Consumers Have Switching Costs: An Overview with Applications to Industrial Organization, Macroeconomics, and International Trade," *Review of Economic Studies*, 62(4), 515–539.

Klemperer, P. D. (1998), "Auctions with Almost Common Values," *European Economic Review*, 42, 757–769.

Klemperer, P. D. (1999a), "Auction Theory: A Guide to the Literature," *Journal of*

Economic Surveys, 13(3), 227–286. [Also reprinted in *The Current State of Economic Science*, 2, 711–766, (ed. by S. Dahiya), 1999.]

Klemperer, P. D. (1999b), "Applying Auction Theory to Economics," Working Paper, Nuffield College Oxford.

Klemperer, P. D. (Ed.) (2000), *The Economic Theory of Auctions*. Cheltenham, UK: Edward Elgar.

Klemperer, P. D. (2002a), "What Really Matters in Auction Design," *Journal of Economic Perspectives*, 16(1), 169–189.

Klemperer, P. D. (2002b), "How (Not) to Run Auctions: The European 3G Telecom Auctions," *European Economic Review*, 46(4–5), 829–845.

Klemperer, P. D. (2002c), "Using and Abusing Economic Theory," 2002 Marshall Lecture to the European Economic Association. Forthcoming at www.paulklemperer. org.

Klemperer, P. D. (2002d), "Some Observations on the British 3G Telecom Auction," *ifo Studien*, 48(1), forthcoming, and at www.paulklemperer.org

Klemperer, P. D. (2002e), "Some Observations on the German 3G Telecom Auction." *ifo Studien*, 48(1), forthcoming, and at www.paulklemperer.org

Klemperer, P. D. and M. A. Meyer (1986), "Price Competition vs. Quantity Competition: The Role of Uncertainty," *Rand Journal of Economics*, 17(4), 618–638.

Klemperer, P. D. and M. A. Meyer (1989), "Supply Function Equilibria in Oligopoly under Uncertainty," *Econometrica*, 57, 1243–1277.

Klemperer, P. D. and M. Pagnozzi (2002), "Advantaged Bidders and Spectrum Prices: An Empirical Analysis," Discussion Paper, Nuffield College, Oxford University, available at www.paulklempcrer.org

Kremer, I. (2000), "Information Aggregation in Common Value Auctions," Working Paper, Northwestern University.

Kühn, K.-U. and X. Vives (1994), "Information Exchanges among Firms and Their Impact on Competition," Working Paper, Institut d'Anàlisi Econòmica (CSIC) Barcelona.

Laffont, J.-J. (1997), "Game Theory and Empirical Economics: The Case of Auction Data," *European Economic Review*, 41, 1–35.

Lee, H. G. (1998), "Do Electronic Marketplaces Lower the Price of Goods?" *Communications of the ACM*, 41, 73–80.

Lee, H. G., J. C. Westland, and S. Hong (1999), "The Impact of Electronic Marketplaces on Product Prices: An Empirical Study of AUCNET," *International Journal of Electronic Commerce*, 4-2, 45–60.

Maskin, E. S. (1992), "Auctions and Privatization," in *Privatization: Symposium in Honour of Herbert Giersch* (ed. by H. Siebert), Tübingen: Mohr, 115–136.

Matthews, S. A. (1984), "Information Acquisition in Discriminatory Auctions," in *Bayesian Models in Economic Theory* (ed. by M. Boyer and R. E. Kihlstrom), New York: North-Holland, 181–207.

Maynard Smith, J. (1974), "The Theory of Games and the Evolution of Animal Conflicts," *Journal of Theoretical Biology*, 47, 209–219.

McAdams, D. (1998), "Adjustable Supply and "Collusive-Seeming Equilibria" in The *Uniform-Price Share Auction*, Working Paper, Stanford University.

McAfee, R. P. and J. McMillan (1996), "Analyzing the Airwaves Auction," *Journal of Economic Perspectives*, 10, 159–175.

McMillan, J. (1994), "Selling Spectrum Rights," *Journal of Economic Perspectives*, 8, 145–162.

Menezes, F. (1996), "Multiple-Unit English Auctions," *European Journal of Political Economy*, 12, 671–684.

Menezes, F., P. K. Monteiro, and A. Temimi (2000), "Discrete Public Goods with Incomplete Information," Working Paper, EPGE/FGV.

Milgrom, P. R. (1979), "A Convergence Theorem for Competitive Bidding with Differential Information," *Econometrica*, 47, 679–688.

Milgrom, P. R. (1981), "Rational Expectations, Information Acquisition, and Competitive Bidding," *Econometrica*, 49, 921–943.

Milgrom, P. R. (1985), "The Economics of Competitive Bidding: A Selective Survey," in *Social Goals and Social Organization: Essays in Memory of Elisha Pazner*, (ed. by L. Hurwicz, D. Schmeidler, and H. Sonnenschein), Cambridge: Cambridge University Press.

Milgrom, P. R. (1987), "Auction Theory," in *Advances in Economic Theory–Fifth World Congress*, (ed. by T. F. Bewley), Cambridge:Cambridge University Press.

Milgrom, P. R. (forthcoming), *Putting Auction Theory to Work*. Cambridge:Cambridge University Press.

Milgrom, P. R. and R. J. Weber (1982), "A Theory of Auctions and Competitive Bidding," *Econometrica*, 50, 1089–1122.

Mussa, M. and S. Rosen (1978), "Monopoly and Product Quality," *Journal of Economic Theory*, 18, 301–317.

Myerson, R. B. (1981), "Optimal Auction Design," *Mathematics of Operations Research*, 6, 58–73.

Newbery, D. M. (1998), "Competition, Contracts, and Entry in the Electricity Spot Market," *Rand Journal of Economics*, 29(4), 726–749.

Nyborg, K. and S. Sundaresan (1996), "Discriminatory Versus Uniform Treasury Auctions: Evidence from When-Issued Transactions," *Journal of Financial Economics*, 42, 63–104.

Office of Gas and Electricity Markets (1999), *The New Electricity Trading Arrangements*, July, available at www.open.gov.uk/offer/reta.htm.

Ortega-Reichert, A. (1968), *Models for Competitive Bidding under Uncertainty*. Stanford University Ph.D. Thesis (and Technical Report No. 8, Department of Operations Research, Stanford University). [Chapter 8 reprinted with foreword by S. A. Board and P. D. Klemperer, in P. D. Klemperer (Ed.) (2000), *The Economic Theory of Auctions*, Cheltenham, UK: Edward Elgar.]

Persico, N. (2000), "Games of Redistribution Politics are Equivalent to All-Pay Auctions with Consolation Prizes," Working Paper, University of Pennsylvania.

Pesendorfer, W. and J. M. Swinkels (1997), "The Loser's Curse and Information Aggregation in Common Value Auctions," *Econometrica*, 65, 1247–1281.

Pesendorfer, W. and J. M. Swinkels (2000), "Efficiency and Information Aggregation in Auctions," *American Economic Review*, 90(3), 499–525.

Plott, C. (1997), "Laboratory Experimental Testbeds: Application to the PCS Auction," *Journal of Economics and Management Strategy*, 6(3), 605–638.

Radiocommunications Agency (1998a), "UMTS Auction Design." *UMTS Auction Consultative Group Report*, 98, 14, available at www.spectrumauctions.gov.uk.

Radiocommunications Agency. (1998b), "UMTS Auction Design 2." *UMTS Auction Consultative Group Report*, 98, 16, available at www.spectrumauctions.gov.uk.

Riley, J. G. (1980), "Strong Evolutionary Equilibrium and the War of Attrition," *Journal of Theoretical Biology*, 82, 383–400.

Riley, J. G. and W. F. Samuelson (1981), "Optimal Auctions," *American Economic Review*, 71, 381–392.

Robinson, M. S. (1985), "Collusion and the Choice of Auction," *Rand Journal of Economics*, 16, 141–145.

Rosenthal, R. W. (1980), "A Model in Which an Increase in the Number of Sellers Leads to a Higher Price," *Econometrica*, 48(6), 1575–1579.

Rothkopf, M. H. (1969), "A Model of Rational Competitive Bidding," *Management Science*, 15, 362–373.

Salant, D. (1997), "Up in the Air: GTE's Experience in the MTA Auction for Personal Communication Services Licenses," *Journal of Economics and Management Strategy*, 6(3), 549–572.

Scott Morton, F., F. Zettelmeyer, and J. Silva Risso (2001), "Internet Car Retailing," Working Paper, Yale University.

Spence, M. A. (1972), "Market Signalling: The Informational Structure of Job Markets and Related Phenomena," Ph.D. Thesis, Harvard University.

Spulber, D. F. (1995), "Bertrand Competition When Rivals' Costs Are Unknown," *Journal of Industrial Economics*, 43, 1–12.

Stevens, M. (1994), "Labour Contracts and Efficiency in On-the-Job Training," *Economic Journal*, March, 104(423), 408–419.

Stevens, M. (2000), "Reconciling Theoretical and Empirical Human Capital Earnings Functions," Working Paper, Nuffield College, Oxford University.

Stigler, G. J. (1964), "A Theory of Oligopoly," *Journal of Political Economy*, 72, 44–61.

Swinkels, J. M. (2001), "Efficiency of Large Private Value Auctions," *Econometrica*, 69 37–68.

Vickrey, W. (1961), "Counterspeculation, Auctions, and Competitive Sealed Tenders," *Journal of Finance*, 16, 8–37.

Vickrey, W. (1962), "Auction and Bidding Games," in *Recent Advances in Game Theory*, Princeton, NJ: The Princeton University Conference, 15–27.

Vickrey, W. (1976), "Auctions Markets and Optimum Allocations," in *Bidding and Auctioning for Procurement and Allocation: Studies in Game Theory and Mathematical Economics*, (ed. by Y. Amihud), New York: New York University Press, 13–20.

Vives, X. (1999), "Information Aggregation, Strategic Behavior, and Efficiency in Cournot Markets," Discussion Paper, Institut d'Anàlisi Econòmica (CSIC, Barcelona).

Weber, R. J. (1997), "Making More from Less: Strategic Demand Reduction in the FCC Spectrum Auctions," *Journal of Economics and Management Strategy,* 6(3), 529–548.

Wilson, R. (1967), "Competitive Bidding with Asymmetric Information," *Management Science*, 13, A816–A820.

Wilson, R. (1969), "Competitive Bidding with Disparate Information," *Management Science*, 15, 446–448.

Wilson, R. (1977), "A Bidding Model of Perfect Competition," *Review of Economic Studies,* 44, 511–518.

Wilson, R. (1979), "Auctions of Shares," *Quarterly Journal of Economics*, 93, 675–689.

Wolfram, C. D. (1998), "Strategic Bidding in a Multiunit Auction: An Empirical Analysis of Bids to Supply Electricity in England and Wales," *Rand Journal of Economics*, 29(4), 703–725.

Wolfram, C. D. (1999), "Measuring Duopoly Power in the British Electricity Spot Market," *American Economic Review*, 89, 805–826.

Zheng, C. (1999), "High Bids and Broke Winners," mimeo, University of Minnesota.

CHAPTER 3

Global Games: Theory and Applications
Stephen Morris and Hyun Song Shin

1. INTRODUCTION

Many economic problems are naturally modeled as a game of incomplete information, where a player's payoff depends on his own action, the actions of others, and some unknown economic fundamentals. For example, many accounts of currency attacks, bank runs, and liquidity crises give a central role to players' uncertainty about other players' actions. Because other players' actions in such situations are motivated by their beliefs, the decision maker must take account of the beliefs held by other players. We know from the classic contribution of Harsanyi (1967–1968) that rational behavior in such environments not only depends on economic agents' beliefs about economic fundamentals, but also depends on beliefs of higher-order – i.e., players' beliefs about other players' beliefs, players' beliefs about other players' beliefs about other players' beliefs, and so on. Indeed, Mertens and Zamir (1985) have shown how one can give a complete description of the "type" of a player in an incomplete information game in terms of a full hierarchy of beliefs at all levels.

In principle, optimal strategic behavior should be analyzed in the space of all possible infinite hierarchies of beliefs; however, such analysis is highly complex for players and analysts alike and is likely to prove intractable in general. It is therefore useful to identify strategic environments with incomplete information that are rich enough to capture the important role of higher-order beliefs in economic settings, but simple enough to allow tractable analysis. Global games, first studied by Carlsson and van Damme (1993a), represent one such environment. Uncertain economic fundamentals are summarized by a state θ and each player observes a different signal of the state with a small amount of noise. Assuming that the noise technology is common knowledge among the players, each player's signal generates beliefs about fundamentals, beliefs about other players' beliefs about fundamentals, and so on. Our purpose in this paper is to describe how such models work, how global game reasoning can be applied to economic problems, and how this analysis relates to more general analysis of higher-order beliefs in strategic settings.

One theme that emerges is that taking higher-order beliefs seriously does not require extremely sophisticated reasoning on the part of players. In Section 2, we present a benchmark result for binary action continuum player games with strategic complementarities where each player has the same payoff function. In a global games setting, there is a unique equilibrium where each player chooses the action that is a best response to a uniform belief over the proportion of his opponents choosing each action. Thus, when faced with some information concerning the underlying state of the world, the prescription for each player is to hypothesize that the proportion of other players who will opt for a particular action is a random variable that is uniformly distributed over the unit interval and choose the best action under these circumstances. We dub such beliefs (and the actions that they elicit) as being *Laplacian*, following Laplace's (1824) suggestion that one should apply a uniform prior to unknown events from the "principle of insufficient reason."

A striking feature of this conclusion is that it reconciles Harsanyi's fully rational view of optimal behavior in incomplete information settings with the dissenting view of Kadane and Larkey (1982) and others that rational behavior in games should imply only that each player chooses an optimal action in the light of his subjective beliefs about others' behavior, without deducing his subjective beliefs as part of the theory. If we let those subjective beliefs be the agnostic Laplacian prior, then there is no contradiction with Harsanyi's view that players should *deduce* rational beliefs about others' behavior in incomplete information settings.

The importance of such analysis is not that we have an adequate account of the subtle reasoning undertaken by the players in the game; it clearly does not do justice to the reasoning inherent in the Harsanyi program. Rather, its importance lies in the fact that we have access to a form of short-cut, or heuristic device, that allows the economist to identify the actual *outcomes* in such games, and thereby open up the possibility of systematic analysis of economic questions that may otherwise appear to be intractable.

One instance of this can be found in the debate concerning self-fulfilling beliefs and multiple equilibria. If one set of beliefs motivates actions that bring about the state of affairs envisaged in those beliefs, while another set of self-fulfilling beliefs bring about quite different outcomes, then there is an apparent indeterminacy in the theory. In both cases, the beliefs are logically coherent, consistent with the known features of the economy, and are borne out by subsequent events. However, we do not have any guidance on which outcome will transpire without an account of how the initial beliefs are determined. We have argued elsewhere (Morris and Shin, 2000) that the apparent indeterminacy of beliefs in many models with multiple equilibria can be seen as the consequence of two modeling assumptions introduced to simplify the theory. First, the economic fundamentals are assumed to be common knowledge. Second, economic agents are assumed to be certain about others' behavior in equilibrium. Both assumptions are made for the sake of tractability, but they do much more besides.

They allow agents' actions and beliefs to be perfectly coordinated in a way that invites multiplicity of equilibria. In contrast, global games allow theorists to model information in a more realistic way, and thereby escape this strait-jacket. More importantly, through the heuristic device of Laplacian actions, global games allow modelers to pin down which set of self-fulfilling beliefs will prevail in equilibrium.

As well as any theoretical satisfaction at identifying a unique outcome in a game, there are more substantial issues at stake. Global games allow us to capture the idea that economic agents may be pushed into taking a particular action because of their belief that others are taking such actions. Thus, ineffi-cient outcomes may be forced on the agents by the external circumstances even though they would all be better off if everyone refrained from such actions. Bank runs and financial crises are prime examples of such cases. We can draw the important distinction between whether there can be inefficient equilibrium outcomes and whether there is a unique outcome in equilibrium. Global games, therefore, are of more than purely theoretical interest. They allow more en-lightened debate on substantial economic questions. In Section 2.3, we discuss applications that model economic problems using global games.

Global games open up other interesting avenues of investigation. One of them is the importance of public information in contexts where there is an element of coordination between the players. There is plentiful anecdotal ev-idence from a variety of contexts that public information has an apparently disproportionate impact relative to private information. Financial markets ap-parently "overreact" to announcements from central bankers that merely state the obvious, or reaffirm widely known policy stances. But a closer look at this phenomenon with the benefit of the insights given by global games makes such instances less mysterious. If market participants are concerned about the reac-tion of other participants to the news, the public nature of the news conveys more information than simply the "face value" of the announcement. It conveys im-portant strategic information on the likely beliefs of other market participants. In this case, the "overreaction" would be entirely rational and determined by the type of equilibrium logic inherent in a game of incomplete information. In Section 3, these issues are developed more systematically.

Global games can be seen as a particular instance of equilibrium selection though perturbations. The set of perturbations is especially rich because it turns out that they allow for a rich structure of higher-order beliefs. In Section 4, we delve somewhat deeper into the properties of general global games – not merely those whose action sets are binary. We discuss how global games are related to other notions of equilibrium refinements and what is the nature of the perturbation implicit in global games. The general framework allows us to disentangle two properties of global games. The first property is that a unique outcome is selected in the game. A second, more subtle, question is how such a unique outcome depends on the underlying information structure and the noise in the players' signals. Although in some cases the outcome is sensitive to the details of the information structure, there are cases where a particular outcome is selected and where this outcome turns out to be robust to the form of the noise in the players' signals. The theory of "robustness to incomplete information" as developed by Kajii and Morris (1997) holds the key to this property. We also discuss a larger theoretical literature on higher-order beliefs and the relation to global games.

In Section 5, we show how recent work on local interaction games and dynamic games with payoff shocks use a similar logic to global games in reaching unique predictions.

2. SYMMETRIC BINARY ACTION GLOBAL GAMES

2.1. Linear Example

Let us begin with the following example taken from Carlsson and van Damme (1993a). Two players are deciding whether to invest. There is a safe action (not invest); there is a risky action (invest) that gives a higher payoff if the other player invests. Payoffs are given in Table 3.1:

Table 3.1. *Payoffs of leading example*

	Invest	NotInvest
Invest	θ, θ	$\theta - 1, 0$
NotInvest	$0, \theta - 1$	$0, 0$

(2.1)

If there was complete information about θ, there would be three cases to consider:

- If $\theta > 1$, each player has a dominant strategy to invest.
- If $\theta \in [0, 1]$, there are two pure strategy Nash equilibria: both invest and both not invest.
- If $\theta < 0$, each player has a dominant strategy not to invest.

But there is incomplete information about θ. Player i observes a private signal $x_i = \theta + \varepsilon_i$. Each ε_i is independently normally distributed with mean 0 and standard deviation σ. We assume that θ is randomly drawn from the real line, with each realization equally likely. This implies that a player observing signal x considers θ to be distributed normally with mean x and standard deviation σ. This in turn implies that he thinks his opponent's signal x' is normally distributed with mean x and standard deviation $\sqrt{2}\sigma$. The assumption that θ is uniformly distributed on the real line is nonstandard, but presents no technical difficulties. Such "improper priors" (with an infinite mass) are well behaved, as long as we are concerned only with conditional beliefs. See Hartigan (1983) for a discussion of improper priors. We will also see later that an improper

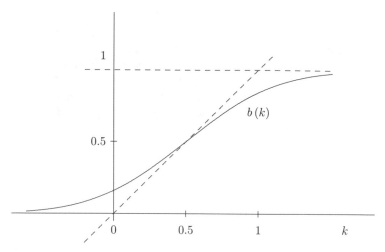

Figure 3.1. Function $b(k)$.

prior can be seen as a limiting case *either* as the prior distribution of θ becomes diffuse *or* as the standard deviation of the noise σ becomes small.

A strategy is a function specifying an action for each possible private signal; a natural kind of strategy we might consider is one where a player takes the risky action only if he observes a private signal above some cutoff point, k:

$$s(x) = \begin{cases} \text{Invest}, & \text{if } x > k \\ \text{NotInvest}, & \text{if } x \leq k. \end{cases}$$

We will refer to this strategy as the switching strategy around k. Now suppose that a player observed signal x and thought that his opponent was following such a "switching" strategy with cutoff point k. His expectation of θ will be x. He will assign probability $\Phi(1/\sqrt{2}\sigma(k-x))$ to his opponent observing a signal less than k [where $\Phi(\cdot)$ is the c.d.f. of the standard normal distribution]. In particular, if he has observed a signal equal to the cutoff point of his opponent ($x = k$), he will assign probability $\frac{1}{2}$ to his opponent investing. Thus, there will be an equilibrium where both players follow switching strategies with cutoff $\frac{1}{2}$.

In fact, a switching strategy with cutoff $\frac{1}{2}$ is the unique strategy surviving iterated deletion of strictly interim-dominated strategies. To see why,[1] first define $b(k)$ to be the unique value of x solving the equation

$$x - \Phi\left(\frac{k-x}{\sqrt{2}\sigma}\right) = 0. \tag{2.2}$$

The function $b(\cdot)$ is plotted in Figure 3.1. There is a unique such value because the left-hand side is strictly increasing in x and strictly decreasing in k. These

---

[1] An alternative argument follows Milgrom and Roberts (1990): if a symmetric game with strategic complementarities has a unique symmetric Nash equilibrium, then the strategy played in that unique Nash equilibrium is also the unique strategy surviving iterated deletion of strictly dominated strategies.

properties also imply that $b(\cdot)$ is strictly increasing. So, if your opponent is following a switching strategy with cutoff k, your best response is to follow a switching strategy with cutoff $b(k)$. We will argue that if a strategy s survives n rounds of iterated deletion of strictly dominated strategies, then

$$s(x) = \begin{cases} \text{Invest}, & \text{if } x > b^{n-1}(1) \\ \text{NotInvest}, & \text{if } x < b^{n-1}(0). \end{cases} \tag{2.3}$$

We argue the second clause by induction (the argument for the first clause is symmetric). The claim is true for $n = 1$, because as we noted previously, NotInvest is a dominant strategy if the expected value of θ is less than 0. Now, suppose the claim is true for arbitrary n. If a player knew that his opponent would choose action NotInvest if he had observed a signal less than $b^{n-1}(1)$, his best response would always be to choose action NotInvest if his signal was less than $b(b^{n-1}(1))$. Because $b(\cdot)$ is strictly increasing and has a unique fixed point at $\frac{1}{2}$, $b^n(0)$ and $b^n(1)$ both tend to $\frac{1}{2}$ as $n \to \infty$.

The unique equilibrium has both players investing only if they observe a signal greater than $\frac{1}{2}$. In the underlying symmetric payoff complete information game, investing is a risk dominant action (Harsanyi and Selten, 1988), exactly if $\theta \geq \frac{1}{2}$; not investing is a risk dominant action exactly if $\theta \leq \frac{1}{2}$. The striking feature of this result is that no matter how small σ is, players' behavior is influenced by the existence of the ex ante possibility that their opponent has a dominant strategy to choose each action.[2] The probability that either individual invests is

$$\Phi\left(\frac{\frac{1}{2} - \theta}{\sigma}\right);$$

Conditional on θ, their investment decisions are independent.

The previous example and analysis are due to Carlsson and van Damme (1993a). There is a many-players analog of this game, whose solution is no more difficult to arrive at. A continuum of players are deciding whether to invest. The payoff to not investing is 0. The payoff to investing is $\theta - 1 + l$, where l is the proportion of other players choosing to invest. The information structure is as before, with each player i observing a private signal $x_i = \theta + \varepsilon_i$, where the ε_i are normally distributed in the population with mean 0 and standard deviation σ. Also in this case, the unique strategy surviving iterated deletion of strictly dominated strategies has each player investing if they observe a signal above $\frac{1}{2}$ and not investing if they observe a signal below $\frac{1}{2}$. We will briefly sketch why this is the case.

Consider a player who has observed signal x and thinks that *all his opponents* are following the "switching" strategy with cutoff point k. As before, his expectation of θ will be x. As before, he will assign probability $\Phi((k - x)/\sqrt{2}\sigma))$ to

---

[2] Thus, a "grain of doubt" concerning the opponent's behavior has large consequences. This element has been linked by van Damme (1997) to the classic analysis of surprise attacks of Schelling (1960), Chapter 9.

any given opponent observing a signal less than k. But, because the realization of the signals are independent conditional on θ, his expectation of the proportion of players who observe a signal less than k will be exactly equal to the probability he assigns to any one opponent observing a signal less than k. Thus, his expected payoff to investing will be $x - \Phi((k - x)/\sqrt{2}\sigma)$, as before, and all the previous arguments go through.

This argument shows the importance of keeping track of the layers of beliefs across players, and as such may seem rather daunting from the point of view of an individual player. However, the equilibrium outcome is also consistent with a procedure that places far less demands on the capacity of the players, and that seems to be far removed from equilibrium of any kind. This procedure has the following three steps.

- Estimate θ from the signal x.
- Postulate that l is distributed uniformly on the unit interval $[0, 1]$.
- Take the optimal action.

Because the expectation of θ conditional on x is simply x itself, the expected payoff to investing if l is uniformly distributed is $x - \frac{1}{2}$, whereas the expected payoff to not investing is zero. Thus, a player following this procedure will choose to invest or not depending on whether x is greater or smaller than $\frac{1}{2}$, which is identical to the unique equilibrium strategy previously outlined. The belief summarized in the second bullet point is *Laplacian* in the sense introduced in the introductory section. It represents a "diffuse" or "agnostic" view on the actions of other players in the game. We see that an apparently naive and simplistic strategy coincides with the equilibrium strategy. This is not an accident. There are good reasons why the Laplacian action is the correct one in this game, and why it turns out to be an approximately optimal action in many binary action global games. The key to understanding this feature is to consider the following question asked by a player in this game.

"My signal has realization x. What is the probability that proportion less than z of my opponents have a signal higher than mine?"

The answer to this question would be especially important if everyone is using the switching strategy around x, since the proportion of players who invest is equal to the proportion whose signal is above x. If the true state is θ, the proportion of players who receive a signal higher than x is given by $1 - \Phi((\psi - \theta)/\sigma)$. So, this proportion is less than z if the state θ is such that $1 - \Phi((\psi - \theta)/\sigma) \leq z$. That is, when

$$\theta \leq x - \sigma \Phi^{-1}(1 - z). \tag{2.4}$$

The probability of this event conditional on x is

$$\Phi\left(\frac{x - \sigma \Phi^{-1}(1 - z) - x}{\sigma}\right) = z.$$

In other words, the cumulative distribution function of z is the identity function, implying that the density of z is uniform over the unit interval. If x is to serve as the switching point of an equilibrium switching strategy, a player must be indifferent between choosing to invest and not to invest given that the proportion who invest is uniformly distributed on $[0, 1]$.

More importantly, even away from the switching point, the optimal action motivated by this belief coincides with the equilibrium action, even though the (Laplacian) belief may not be correct. Away from the switching point, the density of the random variable representing the proportion of players who invest will not be uniform. However, as long as the payoff advantage to investing is increasing in θ, the Laplacian action coincides with the equilibrium action. Thus, the apparently naive procedure outlined by the three bulleted points gives the correct prediction as to what the equilibrium action will be. In the next section, we will show that the lessons drawn from this simple example extend to cover a wide class of binary action global games.

We will focus on the continuum player case in most of this paper. However, as suggested by this example, the qualitative analysis is very similar irrespective of the number of players. In particular, the analysis of the continuum player game with linear payoffs applies equally well to any finite number of players (where each player observes a signal with an independent normal noise term). Independent of the number of players, the cutoff signal in the unique equilibrium is $\frac{1}{2}$. However, a distinctive implication of the infinite player case is that the outcome is a deterministic function of the realized state. In particular, once we know the realization of θ, we can calculate exactly the proportion of players who will invest. It is

$$\widehat{\xi}(\theta) = 1 - \Phi\left(\frac{\frac{1}{2} - \theta}{\sigma}\right).$$

With a finite number of players (I), we write $\xi_{\lambda,I}(\theta)$ for the probability that at least proportion λ out of the I players invest when the realized state is θ:

$$\xi_{\lambda,I}(\theta) = \sum_{n \geq \lambda I} \binom{I}{n} \left[\Phi\left(\frac{\frac{1}{2} - \theta}{\sigma}\right)\right]^{I-n} \left[1 - \Phi\left(\frac{\frac{1}{2} - \theta}{\sigma}\right)\right]^{n}.$$

Observe, however, that the many finite player case converges naturally to the continuum model: by the law of large numbers, as $I \to \infty$,

$$\xi_{\lambda,I}(\theta) \to 1 \quad \text{if} \quad \lambda < \widehat{\xi}(\theta)$$

and

$$\xi_{\lambda,I}(\theta) \to 0 \quad \text{if} \quad \lambda > \widehat{\xi}(\theta).$$

2.2. Symmetric Binary Action Global Games: A General Approach

Let us now take one step in making the argument more general. We deal first with the case where there is a uniform prior on the initial state, and each player's signal is a sufficient statistic for how much they care about the state (we call this the private values case). In this case, the analysis is especially clean, and it is possible to prove a uniqueness result and characterize the unique equilibrium independent of both the structure and size of the noise in players' signals. We then show that the analysis can be extended to deal with general priors and payoffs that depend on the realized state.

2.2.1. Continuum Players: Uniform Prior and Private Values

There is a continuum of players. Each player has to choose an action $a \in \{0, 1\}$. All players have the same payoff function, $u : \{0, 1\} \times [0, 1] \times \mathbb{R} \to \mathbb{R}$, where $u(a, l, x)$ is a player's payoff if he chooses action a, proportion l of his opponents choose action 1, and his "private signal" is x. Thus, we assume that his payoff is independent of which of his opponents choose action 1. To analyze best responses, it is enough to know the payoff gain from choosing one action rather than the other. Thus, the utility function is parameterized by a function $\pi : [0, 1] \times \mathbb{R} \to \mathbb{R}$ with

$$\pi(l, x) \equiv u(1, l, x) - u(0, l, x).$$

Formally, we say that an action is the *Laplacian* action if it is a best response to a uniform prior over the opponents' choice of action. Thus, action 1 is the *Laplacian* action at x if

$$\int_{l=0}^{1} u(1, l, x)dl > \int_{l=0}^{1} u(0, l, x)dl,$$

or, equivalently,

$$\int_{l=0}^{1} \pi(l, x)dl > 0;$$

action 0 is the *Laplacian* action at x if

$$\int_{l=0}^{1} \pi(l, x)dl < 0.$$

Generically, a continuum player, symmetric payoff, two-action game will have exactly one Laplacian action.

A state $\theta \in \mathbb{R}$ is drawn according to the (improper) uniform density on the real line. Player i observes a private signal $x_i = \theta + \sigma \varepsilon_i$, where $\sigma > 0$. The noise terms ε_i are distributed in the population with continuous density $f(\cdot)$, with support on the real line.[3] We note that this density need not be symmetric around the mean, nor even have zero mean. The uniform prior on the real line is "improper" (i.e., has infinite probability mass), but the conditional probabilities are well defined: a player observing signal x_i puts density $(1/\sigma)f((x_i - \theta)/\sigma)$ on state θ (see Hartigan 1983). The example of the previous section fits this setting, where $f(\cdot)$ is the standard normal distribution and $\pi(l, x) = x + l - 1$.

We will initially impose five properties on the payoffs:

>   A1: **Action Monotonicity**: $\pi(l, \theta)$ is nondecreasing in l.
>
>   A2: **State Monotonicity**: $\pi(l, \theta)$ is nondecreasing in θ.
>
>   A3: **Strict Laplacian State Monotonicity**: There exists a unique θ^* solving $\int_{l=0}^{1} \pi(l, \theta^*)dl = 0$.
>
>   A4: **Limit Dominance**: There exist $\underline{\theta} \in \mathbb{R}$ and $\overline{\theta} \in \mathbb{R}$, such that [1] $\pi(l, x) < 0$ for all $l \in [0, 1]$ and $x \le \underline{\theta}$; and [2] $\pi(l, x) > 0$ for all $l \in [0, 1]$ and $x \ge \overline{\theta}$.
>
>   A5: **Continuity**: $\int_{l=0}^{1} g(l) \pi(l, x)dl$ is continuous with respect to signal x and density g.

Condition A1 states that the incentive to choose action 1 is increasing in the proportion of other players' actions who use action 1; thus there are *strategic complementarities* between players' actions (Bulow, Geanakoplos, and Klemperer, 1985). Condition A2 states that the incentive to choose action 1 is increasing in the state; thus a player's optimal action will be increasing in the state, given the opponents' actions. Condition A3 introduces a further strengthening of A2 to ensure that there is at most one crossing for a player with Laplacian beliefs. Condition A4 requires that action 0 is a dominant strategy for sufficiently low signals, and action 1 is a dominant strategy for sufficiently high signals. Condition A5 is a weak continuity property, where continuity in g is with respect to the weak topology. Note that this condition allows for some discontinuities in payoffs. For example,

$$\pi(l, x) = \begin{cases} 0, & \text{if} \quad l \le x \\ 1, & \text{if} \quad l > x \end{cases}$$

satisfies A5 as for any given x, it is discontinuous at only one value of l.

We denote by $G^*(\sigma)$ this incomplete information game – with the uniform prior and satisfying A1 through A5. A strategy for a player in the incomplete information game is a function $s : \mathbb{R} \to \{0, 1\}$, where $s(x)$ is the action chosen if a player observes signal x. We will be interested in strategy profiles, $\mathbf{s} = (s_i)_{i \in [0,1]}$, that form a Bayesian Nash equilibrium of $G^*(\sigma)$. We will show not merely that there is a unique Bayesian Nash equilibrium of the game, but that a unique strategy profile survives iterated deletion of strictly (interim) dominated strategies.

---

[3] With small changes in terminology, the argument will extend to the case where $f(\cdot)$ has support on some bounded interval of the real line.

Proposition 2.1. *Let θ^* be defined as in (A3). The essentially unique strategy surviving iterated deletion of strictly dominated strategies in $G^*(\sigma)$ satisfies $s(x) = 0$ for all $x < \theta^*$ and $s(x) = 1$ for all $x > \theta^*$.*

The "essential" qualification arises because either action may be played if the private signal is exactly equal to θ^*. The key idea of the proof is that, with a uniform prior on θ, observing x_i gives no information to a player on his ranking within the population of signals. Thus, he will have a uniform prior belief over the proportion of players who will observe higher signals.

Proof. Write $\pi_\sigma^*(x, k)$ for the expected payoff gain to choosing action 1 for a player who has observed a signal x and knows that all other players will choose action 0 if they observe signals less than k:

$$\pi_\sigma^*(x, k) \equiv \int_{\theta=-\infty}^{\infty} \frac{1}{\sigma} f\left(\frac{x - \theta}{\sigma}\right) \pi\left(1 - F\left(\frac{k - \theta}{\sigma}\right), x\right) d\theta.$$

First, observe that $\pi_\sigma^*(x, k)$ is continuous in x and k, increasing in x, and decreasing in k, $\pi_\sigma^*(x, k) < 0$ if $x \le \underline{\theta}$ and $\pi_\sigma^*(x, k) > 0$ if $x \ge \bar{\theta}$. We will argue by induction that a strategy survives n rounds of iterated deletion of strictly interim dominated strategies if and only if

$$s(x) = \begin{cases} 0, & \text{if} \quad x < \underline{\xi}_n \\ 1, & \text{if} \quad x > \bar{\xi}_n, \end{cases}$$

where $\underline{\xi}_0 = -\infty$ and $\bar{\xi}_0 = +\infty$, and $\underline{\xi}_n$ and $\bar{\xi}_n$ are defined inductively by

$$\underline{\xi}_{n+1} = \min\{x : \pi_\sigma^*(x, \underline{\xi}_n) = 0\}$$

and

$$\bar{\xi}_{n+1} = \max\{x : \pi_\sigma^*(x, \bar{\xi}_n) = 0\}.$$

Suppose the claim was true for n. By strategic complementarities, if action 1 were ever to be a best response to a strategy surviving n rounds, it must be a best response to the switching strategy with cutoff $\underline{\xi}_n$; $\underline{\xi}_{n+1}$ is defined to be the lowest signal where this occurs. Similarly, if action 0 were ever to be a best response to a strategy surviving n rounds, it must be a best response to the switching strategy with cutoff $\bar{\xi}_n$; $\bar{\xi}_{n+1}$ is defined to be the highest signal where this occurs.

Now note that $\underline{\xi}_n$ and $\bar{\xi}_n$ are increasing and decreasing sequences, respectively, because $\underline{\xi}_0 = -\infty < \underline{\theta} < \underline{\xi}_1$, $\bar{\xi}_0 = \infty > \bar{\theta} > \bar{\xi}_1$, and $\pi_\sigma^*(x, k)$ is increasing in x and decreasing in k. Thus, $\underline{\xi}_n \to \underline{\xi}$ and $\bar{\xi}_n \to \bar{\xi}$ as $n \to \infty$. The continuity of π_σ^* and the construction of $\underline{\xi}$ and $\bar{\xi}$ imply that we must have $\pi_\sigma^*(\underline{\xi}, \underline{\xi}) = 0$ and $\pi_\sigma^*(\bar{\xi}, \bar{\xi}) = 0$. Thus, the second step of our proof is to show that θ^* is the unique solution to the equation $\pi_\sigma^*(x, x) = 0$.

To see this second step, write $\Psi_\sigma^*(l; x, k)$ for the probability that a player assigns to proportion less than l of the other players observing a signal greater than k, if he has observed signal x. Observe that if the true state is θ, the proportion of players observing a signal greater than k is $1 - F((k - \theta)/\sigma)$. This proportion is less than l if $\theta \leq k - \sigma F^{-1}(1 - l)$. So,

$$
\Psi_\sigma^*(l; x, k) = \int_{\theta=-\infty}^{k-\sigma F^{-1}(1-l)} \frac{1}{\sigma} f\left(\frac{x - \theta}{\sigma}\right) d\theta
$$

$$
= \int_{z=\frac{x-k}{\sigma}+F^{-1}(1-l)}^{\infty} f(z)\, dz, \quad \text{changing variables to} \quad z = \frac{x - \theta}{\sigma}
$$

$$
= 1 - F\left(\frac{x - k}{\sigma} + F^{-1}(1 - l)\right). \tag{2.6}
$$

Also observe that if $x = k$, then $\Psi_\sigma^*(\cdot; x, k)$ is the identity function [i.e., $\Psi_\sigma^*(l; x, k) = l$], so it is the cumulative distribution function of the uniform density. Thus,

$$
\pi_\sigma^*(x, x) = \int_{l=0}^{1} \pi(l, x)\, dl.
$$

Now by A3, $\pi_\sigma^*(x, x) = 0$ implies $x = \theta^*$. ∎

2.2.2. *Continuum Players: General Prior and Common Values*

Now suppose instead that θ is drawn from a continuously differentiable strictly positive density $p(\cdot)$ on the real line and that a player's utility depends on the realized state θ, not his signal of θ. Thus, $u(a, l, \theta)$ is his payoff if he chooses action a, proportion l of his opponents choose action 1, *and the state is θ,* and as before, $\pi(l, \theta) \equiv u(1, l, \theta) - u(0, l, \theta)$. We must also impose two extra technical assumptions.

A4*: **Uniform Limit Dominance:** There exist $\underline{\theta} \in \mathbb{R}$, $\overline{\theta} \in \mathbb{R}$, and $\varepsilon \in \mathbb{R}_{++}$, such that [1] $\pi(l, \theta) \leq -\varepsilon$ for all $l \in [0, 1]$ and $\theta \leq \underline{\theta}$; and [2] there exists $\overline{\theta}$ such that $\pi(l, \theta) > \varepsilon$ for all $l \in [0, 1]$ and $\theta \geq \overline{\theta}$.

Property A4* strengthens property A4 by requiring that the payoff gain to choosing action 0 is *uniformly* positive for sufficiently low values of θ, and the payoff gain to choosing action 1 is *uniformly* positive for sufficiently high values of θ.

A6: **Finite Expectations of Signals:** $\int_{z=-\infty}^{\infty} z f(z) dz$ is well defined.

Property A6 requires that the distribution of noise is integrable.

We will denote by $G(\sigma)$ this incomplete information game, with prior $p(\cdot)$ and satisfying A1, A2, A3, A4*, A5, and A6.

Proposition 2.2. *Let θ^* be defined as in A3. For any $\delta > 0$, there exists $\overline{\sigma} > 0$ such that for all $\sigma < \overline{\sigma}$, if strategy s survives iterated deletion of strictly dominated strategies in the game $G(\sigma)$, then $s(x) = 0$ for all $x \leq \theta^* - \delta$, and $s(x) = 1$ for all $x \geq \theta^* + \delta$.*

We will sketch here why this general prior, common values, game $G(\sigma)$ becomes like the uniform prior, private values, game $G^*(\sigma)$ as σ becomes small. A more formal proof is relegated to Appendix A. Consider $\Psi_\sigma(l; x, k)$, the probability that a player assigns to proportion less than or equal to l of the other players observing a signal greater than or equal to k, if he has observed signal x:

$$
\begin{aligned}
\Psi_\sigma(l; x, k) &= \frac{\int_{\theta=-\infty}^{k-\sigma F^{-1}(1-l)} p(\theta) f(\frac{x-\theta}{\sigma}) \, d\theta}{\int_{\theta=-\infty}^{\infty} p(\theta) f(\frac{x-\theta}{\sigma}) \, d\theta} \\
&= \frac{\int_{z=\frac{x-k}{\sigma}+F^{-1}(1-l)}^{\infty} p(x-\sigma z) f(z) \, dz}{\int_{z=-\infty}^{\infty} p(x-\sigma z) f(z) \, dz},
\end{aligned}
$$

$$
\text{changing variables to} \quad z = \frac{x-\theta}{\sigma}.
$$

For small σ, the shape of the prior will not matter and the posterior beliefs over l will depend only on $(x-k)/\sigma$, the normalized difference between the x and k. Formally, setting $\kappa = (x-k)/\sigma$, we have

$$
\Psi_\sigma^*(l; x, x-\sigma\kappa) = \frac{\int_{z=\kappa+F^{-1}(1-l)}^{\infty} p(x-\sigma z) f(z) \, dz}{\int_{z=-\infty}^{\infty} p(x-\sigma z) f(z) \, dz},
$$

so that as $\sigma \to 0$,

$$
\begin{aligned}
\Psi_\sigma^*(l; x, x-\sigma\kappa) &\to \int_{z=\kappa+F^{-1}(1-l)}^{\infty} f(z) \, dz \\
&= 1 - F(\kappa + F^{-1}(1-l)). \quad (2.7)
\end{aligned}
$$

In other words, for small σ, posterior beliefs concerning the proportion of opponents choosing each action are almost the same as under a uniform prior. The formal proof of proposition 2.2 presented in Appendix A consists of showing, first, that convergence of posterior beliefs described previously is uniform; and, second, that the small amount of uncertainty about payoffs in the common value case does not affect the analysis sufficiently to matter.

2.2.3.   Discussion

The proofs of propositions 2.1 and 2.2 follow the logic of Carlsson and van Damme (1993) and generalize arguments presented in Morris and Shin (1998). The technique of analyzing the uniform prior private values game, and then showing continuity with respect to the general prior, common values game, follows Frankel, Morris, and Pauzner (2000). (This paper is discussed further in Section 4.1.) Carlsson and van Damme (1993b) showed a version of the uniform prior result (proposition 2.1) in the finite player case (see also Kim, 1996). We briefly discuss the relation to the finite player case in Appendix B.

How do these propositions make use of the underlying assumptions? First, note that assumptions A1 and A2 represent very strong monotonicity assumptions: A1 requires that each player's utility function is supermodular in the action profile, whereas A2 requires that each player's utility function is supermodular in his own action and the state. Vives (1990) showed that the supermodularity property A2 of complete information game payoffs is inherited by the incomplete information game. Thus, the existence of a largest and smallest strategy profile surviving iterated deletion of dominated strategies when payoffs are supermodular, noted by Milgrom and Roberts (1990), can be applied also to the incomplete information game. The first step in the proof of proposition 2.1 is a special case of this reasoning, with the state monotonicity assumption A2 implying, in addition, that the largest and smallest equilibria consist of strategies that are monotonic with respect to type (i.e., switching strategies). Once we know that we are interested in monotonic strategies, the very weak assumption A3 is sufficient to ensure the equivalence of the largest and smallest equilibria and thus the uniqueness of equilibrium.

Can one dispense with the full force of the supermodular payoffs assumption A1? Unfortunately, as long as A1 is not satisfied at the cutoff point θ^* [i.e., $\pi(l, \theta^*)$ is decreasing in l over some range], then one can find a problematic noise distribution $f(\cdot)$ such that the symmetric switching strategy profile with cutoff point θ^* is *not* an equilibrium, and thus there is no switching strategy equilibrium. To obtain positive results, one must either impose additional restrictions on the noise distribution or relax A1 only away from the cutoff point. We discuss both approaches in turn.

Athey (2002) provides a general description of how monotone comparative static results can be preserved in stochastic optimization problems, when supermodular payoff conditions are weakened to single crossing properties, but signals are assumed to be sufficiently well behaved (i.e., satisfy a monotone likelihood ratio property). Athey (2001) has used such techniques to prove existence of monotonic pure strategy equilibria in a general class of incomplete information games, using weaker properties on payoffs, but substituting stronger restrictions on signal distribution. We can apply her results to our setting as follows. Consider the following two new assumptions.

> A1*: **Action Single Crossing**: For each $\theta \in \mathbb{R}$, there exists $l^* \in \mathbb{R} \cup \{-\infty, \infty\}$ such that $\pi(l, \theta) < 0$ if $l < l^*$ and $\pi(l, \theta) > 0$ if $l > l^*$.
> A7: **Monotone Likelihood Ratio Property**: If $\overline{x} > \underline{x}$, then $f(\overline{x} - \theta)/f(\underline{x} - \theta)$ is increasing in θ.

Assumption A1* is a significant weakening of assumption A1 to a single crossing property. Assumption A7 is a new restriction on the distribution of the noise. Recall that we earlier made no assumptions on the distribution of the noise. Denote by $\tilde{G}(\sigma)$ the incomplete information game with a uniform prior satisfying A1*, A2, A3, A4, A5, and A7.

Lemma 2.3. *Let θ^* be defined as in A3. The game $\widetilde{G}(\sigma)$ has a unique (symmetric) switching strategy equilibrium, with $s(x) = 0$ for all $x < \theta^*$ and $s(x) = 1$ for all $x > \theta^*$.*

The proof is in Appendix C. An analog of proposition 2.2 could be similarly constructed. Notice that this result does not show the nonexistence of other, nonmonotonic, equilibria. Additional arguments are required to rule out nonmonotonic equilibria. For example, in Goldstein and Pauzner (2000a) – an application to bank runs discussed in the next section – noise is uniformly distributed (and thus satisfies A7) and payoffs satisfy assumption A1*. They show that (1) there is a unique symmetric switching strategy equilibrium and that (2) there is no other equilibrium. Lemma 2.3 could be used to extend the former result to all noise distributions satisfying the MLRP (assumption A7), but we do not know if the latter result extends beyond the uniform noise distribution.

Proposition 2.1 can also be weakened by allowing assumption A1 to fail away from θ^*. We will report one weakening that is sufficient. Let $g(\cdot)$ and $h(\cdot)$ be densities on the interval $[0, 1]$; g *stochastically dominates* h ($g \succeq h$) if $\int_{z=0}^{l} g(z)\,dz \le \int_{z=0}^{l} h(z)\,dz$ for all $l \in [0, 1]$. We write $\overline{g}(\cdot)$ for the uniform density on $[0, 1]$, i.e., $\overline{g}(l) = 1$ for all $l \in [0, 1]$. Now consider

> A8: There exists θ^* which solves $\int_{l=0}^{1} \pi(l, \theta^*)dl = 0$ such that [1] $\int_{l=0}^{1} g(l)\,\pi(l, x)dl \ge 0$ for all $x \ge \theta^*$ and $g \succeq \overline{g}$, with strict inequality if $x > \theta^*$; and [2] $\int_{l=0}^{1} g(l)\pi(l, x)dl \le 0$ for all $x \le \theta^*$ and $g \preceq \overline{g}$, with strict inequality if $x < \theta^*$.

We can replace A1–A3 with A8 in propositions 2.1 and 2.2, and all the arguments and results go through. Observe that A1–A3 straightforwardly imply A8. Also, observe that A8 implies that $\pi(l, \theta^*)$ be nondecreasing in l [suppose that $l > l'$ and $\pi(l, \theta^*) < \pi(l', \theta^*)$; now start with the uniform distribution $\overline{g}$ and shift mass from l' to l]. But, A8 allows some failure of A1 away from θ^*.

Propositions 2.1 and 2.2 deliver strong negative conclusions about the efficiency of noncooperative outcomes in global games. In the limit, all players will be choosing action 1 when the state is θ if $\int_{l=0}^{1} \pi(l, \theta)dl > 0$. However, it is *efficient* to choose action 1 at state θ if $u(1, 1, \theta) > u(0, 0, \theta)$. These conditions will not coincide in general. For example, in the investment example, we had $u(1, l, \theta) = \theta + l - 1$, $u(0, l, \theta) = 0$ and thus $\pi(l, \theta) = \theta + l - 1$. So in the limiting equilibrium, both players will be investing if the state θ is at least $\frac{1}{2}$, although it is efficient for them to be investing if the state is at least 0.

The analysis of the unique noncooperative equilibrium serves as a benchmark describing what will happen in the absence of other considerations. In practice, repeated play or other institutions will often allow players to do better. We will briefly consider what happens in the game if players were allowed to make cheap talk statements about the signals that they have observed in the investment example (for this exercise, it is most natural to consider a finite player case; we consider the two-player case). The arguments here follow Baliga and Morris (2000). The investment example as formulated has a nongeneric feature, which is that if a player plans not to invest, he is exactly indifferent about which action his opponent will take. To make the problem more interesting, let us perturb the payoffs to remove this tie:

Table 3.2. *Payoffs for cheap talk example*

	Invest	NotInvest
Invest	$\theta + \delta, \theta + \delta$	$\theta - 1, \delta$
NotInvest	$\delta, \theta - 1$	$0, 0$

Thus, each player receives a small payoff δ (which may be positive or negative) if the other player invests, independent of his own action. This change does not influence each player's best responses, and the analysis of this game in the absence of cheap talk is unchanged by the payoff change. But, observe that if $\delta \leq 0$, there is an equilibrium of the game with cheap talk, where each player truthfully announces his signal, and invests if the (common) expectation of θ conditional on both announcements is greater than $-\delta$ (this gives the efficient outcome). On the other hand, if $\delta > 0$, then each player would like to convince the other to invest even if he does not plan to do so. In this case, there cannot be a truth-telling equilibrium where the efficient equilibrium is achieved, although there may be equilibria with some partially revealing cheap talk that improves on the no cheap talk outcome.

2.3. Applications

We now turn to applications of these results and describe models of pricing debt (Morris and Shin, 1999b), currency crises (Morris and Shin, 1998), and bank runs (Goldstein and Pauzner, 2000a).[4] Each of these papers makes specific assumptions about the distribution of payoffs and signals. But, if one is interested only in analyzing the limiting behavior as noise about θ becomes

---

[4] See Fukao (1994) for an early argument in favor of using global game reasoning in applied settings. Other applications include Karp's (2000) noisy version of Krugman's (1991) multiple equilibrium model of sectoral shifts; Scaramozzino and Vulkan's (1999) noisy model of Shleifer's (1986) multiple equilibrium model of implementation cycles; and Dönges and Heinemann's (2000) model of competition between dealer markets and crossing networks in financial markets.

small, the results of the previous section imply that we can identify the limiting behavior independently of the prior beliefs and the shape of the noise.[5] In each example, we describe one comparative static exercise changing the payoffs of the game, illustrating how changing payoffs has a direct effect on outcomes and an indirect, strategic effect via the impact on the cutoff point of the unique equilibrium. We emphasize that it is also interesting in the applications to study behavior away from the limit; indeed, the focus of the analysis in Morris and Shin (1999b) is on comparative statics away from the limit. More assumptions on the shape of the prior and noise are required in this case. We study behavior away from the limit in Section 3.

2.3.1. *Pricing Debt*

In Morris and Shin (1999b), we consider a simple model of debt pricing. In period 1, a continuum of investors hold collateralized debt that will pay 1 in period 2 if it is rolled over and if an underlying investment project is successful; the debt will pay 0 in period 2 if the project is not successful. If an investor does not roll over his debt, he receives the value of the collateral, $\kappa \in (0, 1)$. The success of the project depends on the proportion of investors who do not roll over and the state of the economy, θ. Specifically, the project is successful if the proportion of investors not rolling over is less than θ/z. Writing 1 for the action "roll over" and 0 for the action "do not roll over," payoffs can be described as follows:

$$u(1, l, \theta) = \begin{cases} 1, & \text{if} \quad z(1-l) \leq \theta \\ 0, & \text{if} \quad z(1-l) > \theta, \end{cases}$$

$$u(0, l, \theta) = \kappa.$$

So

$$\begin{aligned} \pi(l, \theta) &\equiv u(1, l, \theta) - u(0, l, \theta) \\ &= \begin{cases} 1 - \kappa, & \text{if} \quad z(1-l) \leq \theta \\ -\kappa, & \text{if} \quad z(1-l) > \theta. \end{cases} \end{aligned}$$

Now

$$\int_{l=0}^{1} \pi(l, \theta) \, dl = \begin{cases} -\kappa, & \text{if} \quad \theta \leq 0 \\ \dfrac{\theta}{z} - \kappa, & \text{if} \quad 0 \leq \theta \leq z \\ 1 - \kappa, & \text{if} \quad z \leq \theta. \end{cases}$$

---

[5] The model in Goldstein and Pauzner (2000a) fails the action monotonicity property (A1) of the previous section, but they are nonetheless able to prove the uniqueness of a symmetric switching equilibrium, exploiting their assumption that noise terms are distributed uniformly. However, their game satisfies assumptions A1* and A2, and therefore whenever there is a unique equilibrium, it must satisfy the Laplacian characterization with the cutoff point θ^* defined as in A3.

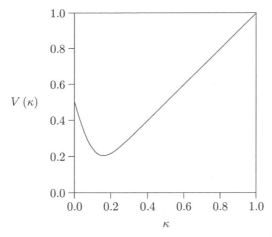

Figure 3.2. Function $V(\kappa)$.

Thus, $\theta^* = z\kappa$. In other words, if private information about θ among the investors is sufficiently accurate, the project will collapse exactly if $\theta \leq z\kappa$. We can now ask how debt would be priced ex ante in this model (before anyone observed private signals about θ). Recalling that $p(\cdot)$ is the density of the prior on θ, and writing $P(\cdot)$ for the corresponding cdf, the value of the collateralized debt will be

$$V(\kappa) \equiv \kappa P(z\kappa) + 1 - P(z\kappa)$$
$$= 1 - (1 - \kappa)P(z\kappa),$$

and

$$\frac{dV}{d\kappa} = P(z\kappa) - z(1 - \kappa)p(z\kappa).$$

Thus, increasing the value of collateral has two effects: first, it increases the value of debt in the event of default (the direct effect). But, second, it increases the range of θ at which default occurs (the strategic effect). For small κ, the strategic effect outweighs the direct effect, whereas for large κ, the direct effect outweighs the strategic effect. Figure 3.2 plots $V(\cdot)$ for the case where $z = 10$ and $p(\cdot)$ is the standard normal density.

Morris and Shin (1999b) study the model away from the limit and argue that taking the strategic, or liquidity, effect into account in debt pricing can help explain anomalies in empirical implementation of the standard debt pricing theory of Merton (1974). Brunner and Krahnen (2000) present evidence of the importance of debtor coordination in distressed lending relationships in Germany [see also Chui, Gai, and Haldane (2000) and Hubert and Schäfer (2000)].

2.3.2. *Currency Crises*

In Morris and Shin (1998), a continuum of speculators must decide whether to attack a fixed–exchange rate regime by selling the currency short. Each speculator may short only a unit amount. The current value of the currency is e^*; if the monetary authority does not defend the currency, the currency will float to the shadow rate $\zeta(\theta)$, where θ is the state of fundamentals. There is a fixed transaction cost t of attacking. This can be interpreted as an actual transaction cost or as the interest rate differential between currencies. The monetary authority defends the currency if the cost of doing so is not too large. Assuming that the costs of defending the currency are increasing in the proportion of speculators who attack and decreasing in the state of fundamentals, there will be some critical proportion of speculators, $a(\theta)$, increasing in θ, who must attack in order for a devaluation to occur. Thus, writing 1 for the action "not attack" and 0 for the action "attack," payoffs can be described as follows:

$$u(1, l, \theta) = 0,$$
$$u(0, l, \theta) = \begin{cases} e^* - \zeta(\theta) - t, & \text{if } l \leq 1 - a(\theta) \\ -t, & \text{if } l > 1 - a(\theta), \end{cases}$$

where $\zeta(\cdot)$ and $a(\cdot)$ are increasing functions, with $\zeta(\theta) \leq e^* - t$ for all θ. Now

$$\pi(l, \theta) = \begin{cases} \zeta(\theta) + t - e^*, & \text{if } l \leq 1 - a(\theta) \\ t, & \text{if } l > 1 - a(\theta). \end{cases}$$

If θ were common knowledge, there would be three ranges of parameters. If $\theta < a^{-1}(0)$, each player has a dominant strategy to attack. If $a^{-1}(0) \leq \theta \leq a^{-1}(1)$, then there is an equilibrium where all speculators attack and another equilibrium where all speculators do not attack. If $\theta > a^{-1}(1)$, each player has a dominant strategy to attack. This tripartite division of fundamentals arises in a range of models in the literature on currency crises (see Obstfeld, 1996).

However, if θ is observed with noise, we can apply the results of the previous section, because $\pi(l, \theta)$ is weakly increasing in l, and weakly increasing in θ:

$$\int_{l=0}^{1} \pi(l, \theta)\, dl = (1 - a(\theta))(\zeta(\theta) + t - e^*) + a(\theta)t$$
$$= t - (1 - a(\theta))(e^* - \zeta(\theta)).$$

Thus, θ^* is implicitly defined by

$$(1 - a(\theta))(e^* - \zeta(\theta)) = t.$$

Theorem 2 in Morris and Shin (1998) gave an incorrect statement of this condition. We are grateful to Heinemann (2000) for pointing out the error and giving a correct characterization.

Again, we will describe one simple comparative statics exercise. Consider a costly ex ante action R for the monetary authority that lowered their costs of defending the currency. For example, R might represent the value of foreign currency reserves or (as in the recent case of Argentina) a line of credit with foreign banks to provide credit in the event of a crisis. Thus, the critical proportion of speculators for which an attack occurs becomes $a(\theta, R)$, where $a(\cdot)$ is increasing in R. Now, write $\theta^*(R)$ for the unique value of θ solving

$$(1 - a(\theta, R))(e^* - \zeta(\theta)) = t.$$

The ex ante probability that the currency will collapse is

$$P(\theta^*(R)).$$

So, the reduction in the probability of collapse resulting from a marginal increase in R is

$$-p(\theta^*(R))\frac{d\theta^*}{dR} = p(\theta^*(R))\frac{\frac{\partial a}{\partial R}}{\frac{\partial a}{\partial \theta} + \frac{1-a(\theta,R)}{e^*-\zeta(\theta)}\frac{d\zeta}{d\theta}}.$$

This comparative static refers to the limit (as noise becomes very small), and the effect is entirely strategic [i.e., the increased value of R reduces the probability of attack *only* because it influences speculators' equilibrium strategies ("builds confidence") and not because the increase in R actually prevents an attack in any relevant contingency].

In Section 4.1, we very briefly discuss Corsetti, Dasgupta, Morris, and Shin (2000), an extension of this model of currency attacks where a large speculator is added to the continuum of small traders [see also Chan and Chiu (2000), Goldstein and Pauzner (2000b), Heinemann and Illing (2000), Hellwig (2000), Marx (2000), Metz (2000), and Morris and Shin (1999a)].

2.3.3.   Bank Runs

We describe a model of Goldstein and Pauzner (2000a), who add noise to the classic bank runs model of Diamond and Dybvig (1983). A continuum of depositors (with total deposits normalized to 1) must decide whether to withdraw their money from a bank or not. If the depositors withdraw their money in period 1, they will receive $r > 1$ (if there are not enough resources to fund all those who try to withdraw, then the remaining cash is divided equally among early withdrawers). Any remaining money earns a total return $R(\theta) > 0$ in period 2 and is divided equally among those who chose to wait until period 2 to withdraw their money. Proportion λ of depositors will have consumption needs only in period 1 and will thus have a dominant strategy to withdraw. We will be concerned with the game among the proportion $1 - \lambda$ of depositors who have consumption needs in period 2. Consumers have utility $U(y)$ from consumption y, where the relative risk aversion coefficient of U is strictly greater than 1. They note that if $R(\theta)$ was greater than 1 and θ were common knowledge, the ex ante optimal choice of r maximizing

$$\lambda U(r) + (1 - \lambda)U\left(\frac{1 - \lambda r}{1 - \lambda}R(\theta)\right)$$

would be strictly greater than 1. But, if θ is not common knowledge, we have a global game. Writing 1 for the action "withdraw in period 2" and 0 for the action "withdraw in period 1," and l for the proportion of late consumers who do not withdraw early, the money payoffs in this game can be summarized in Table 3.3:

Table 3.3. *Payoffs in bank run game*

	$l \leq \frac{r-1}{r(1-\lambda)}$	$l \geq \frac{r-1}{r(1-\lambda)}$
Early Withdrawal	0	$\frac{1-\lambda r}{(1-\lambda)(1-l)r}$	r
Late Withdrawal	1	0	$\left(r - \frac{r-1}{l(1-\lambda)}\right) R(\theta)$

Observe that, if θ is sufficiently small [and so $R(\theta)$ is sufficiently small], all players have a dominant strategy to withdraw early. Goldstein and Pauzner assume that, if θ is sufficiently large, all players have a dominant strategy to withdraw late (a number of natural economic stories could justify this variation in the payoffs).

Thus, the payoffs in the game among late consumers are

$$u(1, l, \theta) = \begin{cases} U(0), & \text{if } l \leq \frac{r-1}{r(1-\lambda)}, \\ U\left(\left(r - \frac{r-1}{l(1-\lambda)}\right) R(\theta)\right), & \text{if } l \geq \frac{r-1}{r(1-\lambda)}, \end{cases}$$

$$u(0, l, \theta) = \begin{cases} U\left(\frac{1}{1-l(1-\lambda)}\right), & \text{if } l \leq \frac{r-1}{r(1-\lambda)} \\ U(r), & \text{if } l \geq \frac{r-1}{r(1-\lambda)} \end{cases}$$

so that

$$\pi(l, \theta) = \begin{cases} U(0) - U\left(\frac{1}{1-l(1-\lambda)}\right), & \text{if } l \leq \frac{r-1}{r(1-\lambda)} \\ U\left(\left(r - \frac{r-1}{l(1-\lambda)}\right) R(\theta)\right) - U(r), & \text{if } l \geq \frac{r-1}{r(1-\lambda)}. \end{cases}$$

The threshold state θ^* is implicitly defined by

$$\int_{l=0}^{\frac{r-1}{r(1-\lambda)}} U(0) - U\left(\frac{1}{1-l(1-\lambda)}\right) dl$$
$$+ \int_{l=\frac{r-1}{r(1-\lambda)}}^{1} U\left(\left(r - \frac{r-1}{l(1-\lambda)}\right) R(\theta)\right) - U(r) dl = 0.$$

The ex ante welfare of consumers as a function of r (as noise goes to zero) is

$$W(r) = P(\theta^*(r))U(1)$$
$$+ \int_{\theta=\theta^*(r)}^{\infty} p(\theta)\left(\lambda U(r) + (1-\lambda)U\left(\frac{1-\lambda r}{1-\lambda}R(\theta)\right)\right).$$

There are two effects of increasing r: the direct effect on welfare is the increased value of insurance in the case where there is not a bank run. But, there is also the strategic effect that an increase in r will lower $\theta^*(r)$.

Morris and Shin (2000) examine a stripped down version of this model, where alternative assumptions on the investment technology and utility functions imply that payoffs reduce to those of the linear example in Section 2.1 [see also Boonprakaikawe and Ghosal (2000), Dasgupta (2000b), Goldstein (2000), and Rochet and Vives (2000)].

3. PUBLIC VERSUS PRIVATE INFORMATION

The analysis so far has all been concerned with behavior when either there is a uniform prior or the noise is very small. In this section, we look at the behavior of the model with large noise and nonuniform priors. There are three reasons for doing this. First, we want to understand how extreme the assumptions required for uniqueness are. We will provide sufficient conditions for uniqueness depending on the relative accuracy of private and public (or prior) signals. Second, away from the limit, prior beliefs play an important role in determining outcomes. In particular, we will see how even with a continuum of players and a unique equilibrium, public information contained in the prior beliefs plays a significant role in determining outcomes, *even controlling for beliefs concerning the fundamentals.* Finally, by seeing how and when the model jumps from having one equilibrium to multiple equilibria, it is possible to develop a better intuition for what is driving results.

We return to the linear example of Section 2.1: there is a continuum of players, the payoff to not investing is 0, and the payoff to investing is $\theta + l - 1$, where θ is the state and l is the proportion of the population investing. It may help in following in the analysis to recall that, with linear payoffs, the exact number of players is irrelevant in identifying symmetric equilibrium strategies (and we will see that symmetric equilibrium strategies will naturally arise). Thus, the analysis applies equally to a two-player game.

Now assume that θ is normally distributed with mean y and standard deviation τ. The mean y is publicly observed. As before, each player observes a private signal $x_i = \theta + \varepsilon_i$, where the ε_i are distributed normally in the population with mean 0 and standard deviation σ. Thus, each player i observes a public signal $y \in \mathbb{R}$ and a private signal $x_i \in \mathbb{R}$. To analyze the equilibria of this game, first fix the public signal y. Suppose that a player observed private signal x. His expectation of θ is

$$\bar{\theta} = \frac{\sigma^2 y + \tau^2 x}{\sigma^2 + \tau^2}.$$

It is useful to conduct analysis in terms of these posterior expectations of θ. In particular, we may consider a switching strategy of the following form:

$$s(\bar{\theta}) = \begin{cases} \text{Invest,} & \text{if } \bar{\theta} > \kappa \\ \text{NotInvest,} & \text{if } \bar{\theta} \leq \kappa. \end{cases}$$

If the standard deviation of players' private signals is sufficiently small relative to the standard deviation of the public signal in the prior, then there is a strategy surviving iterated deletion of strictly dominated strategies. Specifically, let

$$\gamma \equiv \tilde{\gamma}(\sigma, \tau) \equiv \frac{\sigma^2}{\tau^4} \left(\frac{\sigma^2 + \tau^2}{\sigma^2 + 2\tau^2} \right).$$

Now we have

Proposition 3.1. *The game has a symmetric switching strategy equilibrium with cutoff κ if κ solves the equation*

$$\kappa = \Phi(\sqrt{\gamma}(\kappa - y)); \tag{3.1}$$

if $\tilde{\gamma}(\sigma, \tau) \leq 2\pi$, then there is a unique value of κ solving (3.1) and the strategy with that trigger is the essentially unique strategy surviving iterated deletion of strictly dominated strategies; if $\tilde{\gamma}(\sigma, \tau) > 2\pi$, then (for some values of y) there are multiple values of κ solving (3.1) and multiple symmetric switching strategy equilibria.

Figure 3.3 plots the regions in $\sigma^2 - \tau^2$ space, where uniqueness holds.

In Morris and Shin (2000), we gave a detailed version of the uniqueness part of this result in Appendix A. Here, we sketch the idea. Consider a player who has observed private signal x. By standard properties of the normal distribution

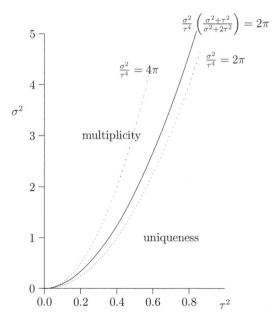

Figure 3.3. Parameter range for unique equilibrium.

(see DeGroot, 1970), his posterior beliefs about θ would be normal with mean

$$\bar{\theta} = \frac{\sigma^2 y + \tau^2 x}{\sigma^2 + \tau^2}$$

and standard deviation

$$\sqrt{\frac{\sigma^2 \tau^2}{\sigma^2 + \tau^2}}.$$

He knows that any other player's signal, x', is equal to θ plus a noise term with mean 0 and standard deviation σ. Thus, he believes that x' is distributed normally with mean $\bar{\theta}$ and standard deviation

$$\sqrt{\frac{2\sigma^2 \tau^2 + \sigma^4}{\sigma^2 + \tau^2}}.$$

Now suppose he believed that all other players will invest exactly if their expectation of θ is at least κ [i.e., if their private signals x' satisfy $(\sigma^2 y + \tau^2 x')/(\sigma^2 + \tau^2) \geq \kappa$, or $x' \geq \kappa + (\sigma^2/\tau^2)(\kappa - y)$]. Thus, he assigns probability

$$1 - \Phi\left(\frac{\kappa - \bar{\theta} + \frac{\sigma^2}{\tau^2}(\kappa - y)}{\sqrt{\frac{2\sigma^2 \tau^2 + \sigma^4}{\sigma^2 + \tau^2}}}\right) \tag{3.2}$$

to any particular opponent investing. But his expectation of the proportion of his opponents investing must be equal to the probability he assigns to any one opponent investing. Thus, (3.2) is also equal to his expectation of the proportion of his opponents investing. Because his payoff to investing is $\theta + l - 1$, his expected payoff to investing is $\bar{\theta}$ plus expression (3.2) minus one, i.e.,

$$v(\bar{\theta}, \kappa) \equiv \bar{\theta} - \Phi\left(\frac{\kappa - \bar{\theta} + \frac{\sigma^2}{\tau^2}(\kappa - y)}{\sqrt{\frac{2\sigma^2 \tau^2 + \sigma^4}{\sigma^2 + \tau^2}}}\right).$$

His payoff to not investing is 0. Because $v(\bar{\theta}, \kappa)$ is increasing in $\bar{\theta}$, we have that there is a symmetric equilibrium with switching point κ exactly if $v^*(\kappa) \equiv v(\kappa, \kappa) = 0$. But

$$v^*(\kappa) \equiv v(\kappa, \kappa)$$

$$= \kappa - \Phi\left(\frac{\sigma^2(\kappa - y)}{\tau^2 \sqrt{\frac{2\sigma^2 \tau^2 + \sigma^4}{\sigma^2 + \tau^2}}}\right)$$

$$= \kappa - \Phi(\sqrt{\gamma}(\kappa - y)).$$

Figure 3.4 plots the function $v^*(\kappa)$ for $y = \frac{1}{2}$ and $\gamma = 1,000, 10, 5$, and 0.1, respectively.

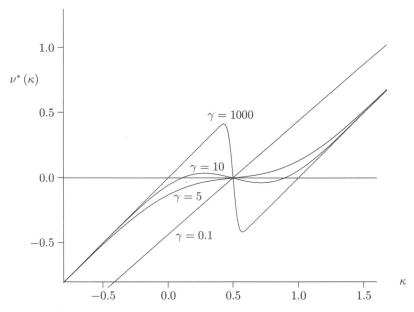

Figure 3.4. Function $v^*(\kappa)$.

The intuition for these graphs is the following. If public information is relatively large (i.e., $\sigma \gg \tau$ and thus γ is large), then players with posterior expectation κ less than $y = \frac{1}{2}$ confidently expect that their opponent will have observed a higher signal, and therefore will be investing. Thus, his expected utility is (about) κ. But, as κ moves above $y = \frac{1}{2}$, he rapidly becomes confident that his opponent has observed a lower signal and will not be investing. Thus, his expected utility drops rapidly, around y, to (about) $\kappa - 1$. But, if public information is relatively small (i.e., $\sigma \ll \tau$ and γ is small), then players with κ not too far above or below $y = \frac{1}{2}$ attach probability (about) $\frac{1}{2}$ to their opponent observing a higher signal. Thus, his expected utility is (about) $\kappa - \frac{1}{2}$.

We can identify analytically when there is a unique solution: Observe that

$$\frac{dv^*}{d\kappa} = 1 - \sqrt{\gamma}\phi(\sqrt{\gamma}\,(\kappa - y)).$$

Recall that $\phi(x)$, the density of the standard normal, attains its maximum of $1/\sqrt{2\pi}$ at $x = 0$. Thus, if $\gamma \le 2\pi$, $dv^*/d\kappa$ is greater than or equal to zero always, and strictly greater than zero, except when $\kappa = y$. So, (3.1) has a unique solution. But, if $\gamma > 2\pi$ and $y = \frac{1}{2}$, then setting $\kappa = \frac{1}{2}$ solves (3.1), but $dv^*/d\kappa|_{\kappa=\frac{1}{2}} < 0$, so (3.1) has two other solutions.

Throughout the remainder of this section, we assume that there is a unique equilibrium [i.e., that $\tilde{\gamma}(\alpha, \beta) \le 2\pi$]. Under this assumption, we can invert the equilibrium condition (3.1) to show in $(\bar{\theta}, y)$ space what the unique equilibrium

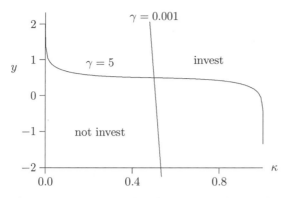

Figure 3.5. Investment takes place above and to the right of the line.

looks like:

$$y = h_\gamma(\bar\theta) = \bar\theta - \frac{1}{\sqrt{\gamma}}\Phi^{-1}(\bar\theta). \tag{3.3}$$

Figure 3.5 plots this for $\gamma = 5$ and $\gamma = 1/1{,}000$.

The picture has an elementary intuition. If $\bar\theta < 0$, it is optimal to not invest (independent of the public signal). If $\bar\theta > 1$, it is optimal to invest (independent of the public signal). But, if $0 < \bar\theta < 1$, there is a trade-off. The higher y is (for a given $\bar\theta$), the more likely it is that the other player will invest. Thus, if $0 < \bar\theta < 1$, the player will always invest for sufficiently high y, and not invest for sufficiently low y. This implies in particular that changing y has a larger impact on a player's action than changing his private signal (controlling for the informativeness of the signals). We next turn to examining this "publicity" effect.

3.1. The Publicity Multiplier

To explore the strategic impact of public information, we examine how much a player's private signal must adjust to compensate for a given change in the public signal. Equation (3.1) can be written as

$$\frac{\sigma^2 y + \tau^2 x}{\sigma^2 + \tau^2} - \Phi\left(\sqrt{\gamma}\left(\frac{\sigma^2 y + \tau^2 x}{\sigma^2 + \tau^2} - y\right)\right) = 0.$$

Totally differentiating with respect to y gives

$$\frac{dx}{dy} = -\frac{\frac{\sigma^2}{\tau^2} + \sqrt{\gamma}\phi(\cdot)}{1 - \sqrt{\gamma}\phi(\cdot)}.$$

This measures how much the private signal would have to change to compensate for a change in the public signal (and still leave the player indifferent between investing or not investing). We can similarly see how much the private signal would have to change to compensate for a change in the public signal, if there was no strategic effect. Totally differentiating

$$\bar{\theta} = \frac{\sigma^2 y + \tau^2 x}{\sigma^2 + \tau^2} = k,$$

we obtain

$$\frac{dx}{dy} = -\frac{\sigma^2}{\tau^2}.$$

Define the *publicity multiplier* as the ratio of these two:

$$\zeta = \frac{1 + \frac{\tau^2}{\sigma^2}\sqrt{\gamma}\phi(\cdot)}{1 - \sqrt{\gamma}\phi(\cdot)}.$$

Thus, suppose a player's expectation of θ is $\bar{\theta}$ and he has observed the public signal that makes him indifferent between investing and not investing $[y = \bar{\theta} - (1/\sqrt{\gamma})\Phi^{-1}(\bar{\theta})]$; the publicity multiplier evaluated at this point will be:

$$\zeta = \frac{1 + \frac{\tau^2}{\sigma^2}\sqrt{\gamma}\phi(\Phi^{-1}(\bar{\theta}))}{1 - \sqrt{\gamma}\phi((\Phi^{-1}(\bar{\theta})))}.$$

Notice that (for any given σ and τ) the publicity multiplier is maximized when $\bar{\theta} = \frac{1}{2}$, and thus the critical public signal $y = \frac{1}{2}$. Thus, it is precisely when there is no conflict between private and public signals that the multiplier has its biggest effect. Here, the publicity multiplier equals

$$\zeta^* = \frac{1 + \frac{\tau^2}{\sigma^2}\sqrt{\frac{\gamma}{2\pi}}}{1 - \sqrt{\frac{\gamma}{2\pi}}}.$$

Notice that, when γ is small (i.e., σ/τ^2 is small), the publicity multiplier is very small. The multiplier is biggest just before we hit the multiplicity zone of the parameter space (i.e., when $\gamma \approx 2\pi$).

There is plentiful anecdotal evidence that in settings where coordination is important, public signals play a role in coordinating outcomes that exceed the information content of those announcements. For example, financial markets apparently "overreact" to announcements from the Federal Reserve Board and public announcements in general. If market participants are concerned about the reaction of other participants to the news, the "overreaction" may be rational and determined by the type of equilibrium logic of our example. Further evidence for this is briefings on market conditions by key players in financial markets using conference calls with hundreds of participants. Such public briefings have a larger impact on the market than bilateral briefings with the same information, because they automatically convey to participants not only information about market conditions, but also valuable information about the beliefs of the other participants.

Urban renewal also has a coordination aspect. Private firms' incentives to invest in a run-down neighborhood depend partly on exogenous characteristics of the neighborhood, but they also depend to a great extent on whether other firms are investing. A well-publicized investment in the neighborhood might be expected to have an apparently disproportionate effect on the probability of ending in the good equilibrium. The willingness of public authorities to subsidize football stadiums and conference centers is consistent with this view.

An indirect econometric test of the publicity effect is performed by Chwe (1998). Chwe observes that the per viewer price of advertising during the Super Bowl is exceptionally high (i.e., the price of advertising increases more than linearly in the number of viewers). The premium price is explained by the fact that any information conveyed by those advertisements becomes not merely known to the wide audience, but also common knowledge among them. The value of this common knowledge to advertisers should depend on whether there is a significant coordination problem in consumers' decisions whether to purchase the product. Chwe makes some plausible ex ante guesses about when coordination is an important issue because of network externalities (e.g., the Apple Macintosh) or social consumption (e.g., beer) and when it is not (e.g., batteries). He then confirms econometrically that it is the advertisers of coordination goods who pay a premium for large audiences.

In Morris and Shin (1999b), we use the publicity effect to explain an anomaly in the pricing of debt. Empirically, the option pricing model of debt due to Merton (1974) underestimates the yield on debt (i.e., underestimates the empirical default rate). This deviation from theory is largest for low-grade (high-risk) bonds. A deterioration in public signals for low-grade bonds generates a large publicity effect: the deterioration makes investors more pessimistic about default for any given strategies of the other players, but, more importantly, the deterioration makes investors more pessimistic about other players' strategies.

3.2.   Limiting Behavior

If we increase the precision of public signals, while holding the precision of private signals fixed (i.e., let $\tau \to 0$ for fixed σ), then we clearly exit the unique equilibrium zone.[6] If we increase the precision of private signals, while holding the precision of public signals fixed (i.e., let $\sigma \to 0$ for fixed τ), then we return to the uniform prior setting of Section 2.1. But, we can also examine what happens to the unique equilibrium as the precision of both signals increases in such a way that uniqueness is maintained. Specifically, let $\tau \to 0$ and let

---

[6] For sufficiently small τ, either action is rationalizable as long as $y \in (0, 1)$ and $\bar{\theta} \in (0, 1)$. If either $\bar{\theta} \geq 1$ or $\bar{\theta} > 0$ and $y \geq 1$, then only investing is rationalizable. If either $\bar{\theta} \leq 0$ or $\bar{\theta} < 1$ and $y \leq 0$, then only not investing is rationalizable.

$\sigma^2 \to c\tau^4$, where $c < 4\pi$. In this case,

$$\begin{aligned}
\widetilde{\gamma}(\sigma, \tau) &= \frac{\sigma^2}{\tau^4}\left(\frac{\sigma^2 + \tau^2}{\sigma^2 + 2\tau^2}\right) \\
&\to \frac{c\tau^4}{\tau^4}\left(\frac{c\tau^4 + \tau^2}{c\tau^4 + 2\tau^2}\right) \\
&\to \frac{c}{2} \\
&< 2\pi.
\end{aligned}$$

Thus

$$h_{\widetilde{\gamma}(\sigma,\tau)}(\overline{\theta}) \to \overline{\theta} - \left(\sqrt{\frac{2}{c}}\right)\Phi^{-1}\left(\overline{\theta}\right).$$

This result says that, *even though the public signal becomes irrelevant to a player's expected value of* θ *in the limit*, it continues to have a large impact on the outcome. For example, suppose $c = 1$ and $y = \frac{1}{3}$ (i.e., public information looks bad). Each player will invest only if $\overline{\theta} \geq 0.7$ (i.e., they will be very conservative). This is true even as they ignore y (i.e., $\overline{\theta} \to x$).

The intuition for this result is the following. Suppose public information looks bad ($y < \frac{1}{2}$). If each player's private information is much more accurate than the public signal, each player will mostly ignore the public signal in forming his own expectation of θ. But, each will nonetheless expect the other to have observed a somewhat worse signal than themselves. This pessimism about the other's signal makes it very hard to support an investment equilibrium.

3.3.   Sufficient Conditions for Uniqueness

We derived a very simple necessary and sufficient condition for uniqueness in the linear example, depending only on the precision of public and private signals. In this section, we briefly demonstrate that a similar sufficient condition works for general payoff functions. In particular, we will show that there is always a unique equilibrium if σ^2/τ^4 is sufficiently small.[7]

We will show this in a simple setting, although the argument can be extended. We maintain the normal distribution assumptions on the prior and signals, but let the payoffs be as in Section 2.2, so that $\pi(l, \theta)$ is the payoff gain from choosing action 1 instead of action 0. Furthermore, we will focus on the continuum players case, where $\pi(l, \theta)$ is differentiable and strictly increasing in l and θ, with $d\pi/dl(l, \theta) \leq K$ and $d\pi/d\theta(l, \theta) \geq \varepsilon$ for all l and θ.

Under these assumptions, we may look at the expected gain to choosing action 1 rather than action 0 if your expectation of θ is $\overline{\theta}$ and you think that

---

[7] Hellwig (2000) performs a related exercise in a version of our currency attacks model (Morris and Shin, 1998).

others follow a switching strategy at κ:

$$V(\bar{\theta}, \kappa) = \int_{\theta=-\infty}^{\infty} \sqrt{\frac{\sigma^2 \tau^2}{\sigma^2 + \tau^2}} \phi\left(\frac{\theta - \bar{\theta}}{\sqrt{\frac{\sigma^2 \tau^2}{\sigma^2 + \tau^2}}}\right)$$

$$\times \pi\left(1 - \Phi\left(\frac{\kappa - \theta + \frac{\sigma^2}{\tau^2}(\kappa - y)}{\sigma}\right), \theta\right) d\theta$$

$$= \int_{\theta'=-\infty}^{\infty} \sqrt{\frac{\sigma^2 \tau^2}{\sigma^2 + \tau^2}} \phi\left(\frac{\theta'}{\sqrt{\frac{\sigma^2 \tau^2}{\sigma^2 + \tau^2}}}\right)$$

$$\times \pi\left(1 - \Phi\left(\frac{-\theta' + \kappa - \bar{\theta} + \frac{\sigma^2}{\tau^2}(\kappa - y)}{\sigma}\right), \theta' + \bar{\theta}\right) d\theta'.$$

Now to apply our earlier argument for uniqueness, it is enough to show that expression is increasing in $\bar{\theta}$ and $V(\kappa, \kappa) = 0$ has a unique solution. The former is clearly true; to show the latter, observe that

$$V(\kappa, \kappa) = \int_{\theta'=-\infty}^{\infty} \sqrt{\frac{\sigma^2 \tau^2}{\sigma^2 + \tau^2}} \phi\left(\frac{\theta'}{\sqrt{\frac{\sigma^2 \tau^2}{\sigma^2 + \tau^2}}}\right)$$

$$\times \pi\left(1 - \Phi\left(\frac{-\theta' + \frac{\sigma^2}{\tau^2}(\kappa - y)}{\sigma}\right), \theta' + \kappa\right) d\theta',$$

so

$$\frac{dV(\kappa, \kappa)}{d\kappa} = \int_{\theta'=-\infty}^{\infty} \sqrt{\frac{\sigma^2 \tau^2}{\sigma^2 + \tau^2}} \phi\left(\frac{\theta'}{\sqrt{\frac{\sigma^2 \tau^2}{\sigma^2 + \tau^2}}}\right) \left[\frac{d\pi(\cdot)}{d\theta} - \frac{d\pi(\cdot)}{dl} \phi(\cdot) \frac{\sigma}{\tau^2}\right] d\theta'$$

$$= \int_{\theta'=-\infty}^{\infty} \sqrt{\frac{\sigma^2 \tau^2}{\sigma^2 + \tau^2}} \phi\left(\frac{\theta'}{\sqrt{\frac{\sigma^2 \tau^2}{\sigma^2 + \tau^2}}}\right) \frac{d\pi(\cdot)}{d\theta} \left[1 - \frac{\frac{d\pi(\cdot)}{dl}}{\frac{d\pi(\cdot)}{d\theta}} \phi(\cdot) \frac{\sigma}{\tau^2}\right] d\theta'.$$

$$(3.4)$$

If this expression is always positive, then there is a unique value of κ solving $V(\kappa, \kappa) = 0$, and the unique strategy surviving iterated deletion of strictly dominated strategies is the switching strategy with that cutoff. Because $\phi(\cdot)$ is at most $1/\sqrt{2\pi}$, the expression in square brackets within equation (3.4) is positive as long as

$$\frac{\frac{d\pi(\cdot)}{dl}}{\frac{d\pi(\cdot)}{d\theta}} < \frac{\tau^2 \sqrt{2\pi}}{\sigma};$$

since

$$\frac{\dfrac{d\pi(\cdot)}{dl}}{\dfrac{d\pi(\cdot)}{d\theta}} \leq \frac{K}{\varepsilon};$$

this will be true as long as

$$\frac{K}{\varepsilon} < \frac{\tau^2 \sqrt{2\pi}}{\sigma},$$

i.e.,

$$\frac{\sigma^2}{\tau^4} < 2\pi \left(\frac{\varepsilon}{K} \right)^2.$$

4. THEORETICAL UNDERPINNINGS

4.1.   General Global Games

All the analysis thus far has dealt with symmetric payoff games. The analysis of Carlsson and van Damme (1993a) in fact provided a remarkably general result for two-player, two-action games, even with asymmetric payoffs. Let the payoffs of a two-player, two-action game be given by Table 3.4:

Table 3.4. *Payoffs for general* 2×2 *global game*

	1	0
1	θ_1, θ_2	θ_3, θ_4
0	θ_5, θ_6	θ_7, θ_8

Thus, a vector $\theta \in \mathbb{R}^8$ describes the payoffs of the game. Each player i observes a signal $x_i = \theta + \sigma \varepsilon_i$, where the ε_i are eight-dimensional noise terms. This setup describes an incomplete information game parameterized by σ. Under mild technical assumptions,[8] as $\sigma \to 0$, any sequence of strategy profiles surviving iterated deletion of strictly dominated strategies converges to a unique limit. Moreover, that limit is independent of the distribution of the noise and has the unique Nash equilibrium of the underlying complete information game being played (if there is one), and has the risk-dominant Nash equilibrium played (if there are two strict Nash equilibria).

To understand if and when this remarkable result might extend to many players and many action games, it is useful to first observe that there are two

---

[8] The following technical conditions are sufficient (Carlsson and van Damme's actual setup is a little more general): payoff vector θ is drawn according to a strictly positive, continuously differentiable, bounded density on $\mathbb{R}^8$; and the noise terms $(\varepsilon_1, \varepsilon_2)$ are drawn according to a continuous density with bounded support, independently of θ.

independent things being proved here. First, there is a *limit uniqueness* result. As the noise goes to zero, there is a unique strategy profile surviving iterated deletion of strictly dominated strategies. Given that with no noise we know that there are multiple equilibria, this is a striking result by itself. Second, there is a *noise-independent selection* result. We can characterize behavior in that unique limit as a function of the complete information payoffs in the limit, and thus independently of the shape of the prior beliefs on θ and the distribution of noise. Thus, Carlsson and van Damme's two-player, two-action analysis combines separate limit uniqueness and noise-independent selection results. Similarly, the results in Section 2 for continuum player, symmetric binary action games simultaneously showed that there was a unique strategy surviving iterated deletion of strictly dominated strategies in the limit (a limit uniqueness result) and characterized behavior in the limit (the Laplacian action) independent of the structure of the noise (a noise-independent selection result).

Frankel, Morris, and Pauzner (2000) (hereafter, FMP) examine global games with many players, asymmetric payoffs, and many actions. They show that a limit uniqueness result holds quite generally, as long as some monotonicity properties are satisfied. They consider the following environment. Each player has an ordered set of actions (finite or continuum); his payoff depends on the action profile played and a payoff parameter $\theta \in \mathbb{R}$; he observes a signal $x_i = \theta + \sigma \varepsilon_i$, where $\sigma > 0$, and ε_i is an independently distributed noise term. For sufficiently low values of θ, each player has a dominant strategy to choose his lowest action, and that for sufficiently high values of θ, each player has a dominant strategy to choose his highest action. Each player's payoffs are supermodular in the action profile, implying that each player's best response is increasing in others actions (for any θ). Each player's payoffs are supermodular in his own action and the state, implying that his best response is increasing in the payoff parameter θ (for any given actions of his opponents). Under these substantive assumptions, and additional technical assumptions,[9] FMP show a limit uniqueness result. The proof uses the technique, also followed in Section 2.2, of first analyzing the uniform prior, private values game and showing a uniqueness result independent of the size of the noise; and then showing that, if the noise is small, all equilibria of the game with a general prior and common values are close to the unique equilibrium of the uniform prior, private values game. The limit uniqueness result of FMP provides a natural many-player, many-action generalization of Carlsson and van Damme (1993a). It is true that Carlsson and van Damme required no strategic complementarity and other monotonicity properties. But, when a two-player, two-action game has multiple Nash equilibria (the interesting case for Carlsson and van Damme's analysis), there are automatically strategic complementarities. FMP's limit uniqueness

---

[9] Payoffs are continuous with respect to actions and θ, and there is a Lipschitz bound on the sensitivity of payoffs to changes in own and others' actions. The state is drawn according to a continuous and positive density, and signals are drawn according to a continuous and positive density with bounded support.

results could presumably be extended straightforwardly to many-dimensional payoff parameters and signals, if the relevant monotonicity conditions were suitably adjusted.[10]

Within this class of monotonic global games where limit uniqueness holds, FMP also provide sufficient conditions for noise-independent selection. They generalize the notion of a potential maximizing action, due to Monderer and Shapley (1996). We will discuss these generalized potential conditions in more detail in Section 4.4, because they are also sufficient for the (more demanding) property of being *robust to incomplete information*. The sufficient conditions for noise-independent selection encompass two classes of games already discussed in this survey: many-player, two-action, symmetric payoff games (where the Laplacian action is played); and two-player, two-action games, with possibly asymmetric payoffs (where the risk dominant equilibrium is played). They also encompass two-player, three-action games with symmetric payoffs. They encompass the minimum effort game of Bryant (1983).[11]

FMP also provide an example of a two-player, four-action, symmetric payoff game where noise-independent selection fails. Thus, there is a unique limit as the noise goes to zero, but the nature of the limit depends on the exact distribution of the noise. Carlsson (1989) gave a three-player, two-action example in which noise-independent selection failed. Corsetti, Dasgupta, Morris, and Shin (2000) describe a global games model of currency crises, where there is a continuum of small traders and a single large trader. This is thus a many-player, two-action game with *asymmetric* payoffs. We show that the equilibrium selected as noise goes to zero depends on the relative informativeness of the large and small traders' signals. This is thus an application where noise-independent selection fails.

We conclude this brief summary by noting one consequence of FMP for the earlier analysis in this paper. In Section 2.2, it was shown that the Laplacian action was selected in symmetric binary action global games. The argument exploited the fact that players observed signals with iid noise in that class of games. But, FMP show noise-independent selection of the Laplacian action *independent of the distribution of noise*. If the distribution of noise is very different for different players, we surely cannot guarantee that each player has a uniform belief over the proportion of his opponents taking each action. Nonetheless, the Laplacian action must be played in the limit. We can illustrate this implication with a simple example. Consider a three-player game, with binary action set $\{0, 1\}$. The payoff to action 1 is θ if both of the other players choose action 1, $\theta - z$ if one other player chooses action 1, and $\theta - 1$ if neither

---

[10] The conditions for limit uniqueness in FMP conditions could also presumably be weakened in a number of directions. For example, with additional restrictions on the noise structure, one could perhaps use the monotone comparative statics under uncertainty techniques of Athey (2001, 2002), as in lemma 2.3.

[11] Carlsson and Ganslandt (1998) show the potential maximizing action is selected in the minimum effort game when players' continuous actions are perturbed.

player chooses action 1 (where $0 < z < 1$). The payoff to action 0 is zero. State θ is uniformly distributed on the real line. Observe that the Laplacian action is 1 if $\frac{1}{3}\theta + \frac{1}{3}(\theta - z) + \frac{1}{3}(\theta - 1) > 0$ [i.e., $\theta > \frac{1}{3}(z + 1)$]. Let ε_1, ε_2, and ε_3 be i.i.d. with symmetric c.d.f. $F(\cdot)$, let δ be a very small positive number, and let σ be a parameter describing the size of the noise. The players' signals x_1, x_2, and x_3 are given by

$$x_1 = \theta + \sigma\delta\varepsilon_1,$$
$$x_2 = \theta + \sigma\delta\varepsilon_2,$$
$$x_3 = \theta + \sigma\varepsilon_3.$$

Thus, 1 and 2 observe much more informative signals. We will look for a switching strategy equilibrium, where players 1 and 2 use cutoff $\overline{x}_\sigma$ and player 3 uses cutoff $\widetilde{x}_\sigma$. Let

$$\lambda_\sigma = F\left(\frac{\widetilde{x}_\sigma - \overline{x}_\sigma}{\sigma}\right).$$

We are interested in what happens in the limit as first we take $\delta \to 0$, and then take the limit as $\sigma \to 0$. As δ becomes very small, if player 1 or 2 observes signal $\overline{x}_\sigma$, he will assign probability (about) $\frac{1}{2}(1 - \lambda_\sigma)$ to both players choosing action 1, probability (about) $\frac{1}{2}$ to one player choosing action 1, and probability (about) $\frac{1}{2}\lambda_\sigma$ to neither player choosing action 1; although, if player 3 observes signal $\widetilde{x}_\sigma$, he will assign probability λ_σ to both players choosing action 1, probability 0 to one player choosing action 1, and probability $1 - \lambda_\sigma$ to neither player choosing action 1.

Thus, we must have:

$$\frac{1}{2}(1 - \lambda_\sigma)\overline{x}_\sigma + \frac{1}{2}(\overline{x}_\sigma - z) + \frac{1}{2}\lambda_\sigma(\overline{x}_\sigma - 1) = 0,$$
$$\lambda_\sigma\widetilde{x}_\sigma + 0(\widetilde{x}_\sigma - z) + (1 - \lambda_\sigma)(\widetilde{x}_\sigma - 1) = 0.$$

Rearranging gives:

$$\overline{x}_\sigma = \frac{1}{2}z + \frac{1}{2}\lambda_\sigma,$$
$$\widetilde{x}_\sigma = 1 - \lambda_\sigma.$$

As $\sigma \to 0$, we must have $\overline{x}_\sigma \to \widetilde{x}_\sigma$ and thus $\lambda_\sigma \to \frac{2}{3}(1 - \frac{1}{2}z)$ [so, $(\widetilde{x}_\sigma - \overline{x}_\sigma)/\sigma \longrightarrow F^{-1}(\lambda_\sigma)$]. Thus, $\overline{x}_\sigma$ and $\widetilde{x}_\sigma$ must both converge to $\frac{1}{3}(z + 1)$. But this gives the result that the Laplacian action is played by all players in the limit, independent of the shape of F.

4.2. Higher-Order Beliefs

In global games, the importance of the noisy observation of the underlying state lies in the fact that it generates *strategic uncertainty*, that is, uncertainty about others' behavior in equilibrium. That strategic uncertainty is generated by players' uncertainty about other players' payoffs. Thus, understanding global games involves understanding how equilibria depend on players' uncertainty about other players' payoffs. But, clearly, it is not going to be enough to know each player's beliefs about other players' payoffs. We must also take into account each player's beliefs about other players' beliefs about his payoffs, and further such *higher-order beliefs*. Players' payoffs and higher-order beliefs about payoffs are the true primitives of a game of incomplete information, not the asymmetric information structure. In earlier sections, we told an asymmetric information story about how there is a true state of fundamentals θ drawn from some prior and each player observes a signal of θ generated by some technology. But, our analysis of the resulting game implicitly assumes that there is common knowledge of the prior distribution of θ and the signaling technologies. It is hard to defend this assumption literally when the original purpose was to get away from the unrealistic assumption that there is common knowledge of the realization of θ. The classic arguments of Harsanyi (1967–1968) and Mertens and Zamir (1985) tell us that we can assume common knowledge of *some* state space without loss of generality. But such a common knowledge state space makes sense with an incomplete information interpretation (a player's "type" is a description of his higher-order beliefs about payoffs), but not with an asymmetric information interpretation (a player's "type" is a signal drawn according to some ex ante fixed distribution); see Battigalli (1999) and Dekel and Gul (1996) for forceful defenses of this position. Thus, we believe that the noise structures analyzed in global games are interesting because they represent a tractable way of generating a rich structure of higher-order beliefs. The analysis of global games represents a natural vehicle to illustrate the power of higher-order beliefs at work in applications.[12] But, then, the natural way to understand the "trick" to global games analysis is to go back and understand what is going on in terms of higher-order beliefs.

Even if one is uninterested in the philosophical distinction between incomplete information and asymmetric information, there is a second reason why the higher-order beliefs literature may contribute to our understanding of global games. Even keeping a pure asymmetric information interpretation, we can calculate (from the prior distribution over θ and the signal technologies) the players' higher-order beliefs about payoffs. Statements about higher-order beliefs about payoffs turn out to represent a natural mathematical way of characterizing which properties of the prior distribution and signal technologies matter for the results.

The pedagogical risk of emphasizing higher-order beliefs is that readers may conclude that playing in the uniquely rational way in a global game requires fancy powers of reasoning, some kind of hyperrationality that allows them to reason to an arbitrarily high number of levels. We emphasize that the fact that either the analyst or a player expresses information about the game in terms

---

[12] For work on higher-order beliefs not using the global games technology, see Townsend (1983); Allen, Morris, and Postlewaite (1993); Shin (1996); and the discussion of Section 4.1 of Allen and Morris (2000).

of higher-order beliefs does not make standard equilibrium concepts any less compelling and does not suggest any particular view about how equilibrium behavior might be arrived at. In particular, recall that there is a very simple heuristic that will generate equilibrium behavior in symmetric binary action games. If there is not common knowledge of the environment you are in, you should hold diffuse beliefs about others' behavior. In particular, if you are on the margin between your two actions, it seems reasonable to take the agnostic view that you are equally likely to hold any rank in the population concerning your evaluation of the desirability of the two actions. Thus, if other people behave like you, you should make your decision on the assumption that the proportion of other players choosing each action is uniformly distributed. This reasoning sound naive, but actually generates a very simple heuristic for behavior that is consistent with the unique rational behavior.

In the remainder of this section, we first informally discuss the role of higher-order beliefs in a global game example. Then, we review briefly the theoretical literature on higher-order beliefs in games.[13] Finally, we show how results from that literature can be taken back to the analysis of global games.

Monderer and Samet (1989) introduced a natural language for characterizing players' higher-order beliefs. Fix a probability $p \in (0, 1]$. Let Ω be a set of possible states, and let E be any subset of Ω. The event E is *p-believed* at state ω among some fixed group of individuals if everyone believes that it is true with probability at least p (and we write $B^p E$ for the set of states where event E is p-believed). The event E is *common p-belief* at state ω if it is p-believed, it is p-believed that it is p-believed, and so on, up to an arbitrary number of levels [and we write $C^p(E)$ for the set of states where event E is common p-belief]. The event E is *p-evident* if whenever it is true, it is p-believed (i.e., $E \subseteq B^p E$). Monderer and Samet proved the following result:

Proposition 4.1. *Event E is common p-belief at ω [i.e., $\omega \in C^p(E)$] if and only if there exists a p-evident event F such that $\omega \in F \subseteq B^p E$.*

This result provides a fixed-point characterization (i.e., using the p-evident property) of an iterative definition of common p-belief. It thus generalizes Aumann's classic characterization of *common knowledge* (Aumann, 1976).

We will illustrate these properties of higher-order beliefs in the global games setting.[14] So, consider again the two-player example of Section 2.1: θ is drawn uniformly from the real line and players $i = 1, 2$ each observe a signal

---

[13] Our review of this literature is much abbreviated and highly selective. See Fudenberg and Tirole (1991) Chapter 14; Osborne and Rubinstein (1994) Chapter 5; Geanakoplos (1994); and Dekel and Gul (1996) for more background on this material. Morris and Shin (1997) survey the higher-order beliefs in game theory literature with a focus on the relationship to related literatures in philosophy and computer science. Kajii and Morris (1997c) survey this literature with a focus on the relation to the standard *refinements* literature in game theory.

[14] Monderer and Samet (1989) characterized common p-belief for discrete state spaces, but Kajii and Morris (1997b) show the straightforward extension to continuum state spaces.

$x_i = \theta + \varepsilon_i$, where ε_i is distributed normally with mean 0 and standard deviation σ. Thus, the relevant state space is $\mathbb{R}^3$, with typical element (θ, x_1, x_2). Fix the payoff relevant event $E_k = \{(\theta, x_1, x_2) : \theta \geq k\}$; this is the set of states where the true θ is at least k. If player i observes signal x_i, he will assign probability $\Phi(x_i - k/\sigma)$ to the event E_k being true. Thus, he will assign probability at least p to the event E_k exactly if $x_i \geq k + \sigma \Phi^{-1}(p) \geq k$. Thus

$$B^p E_k = \{(\theta, x_1, x_2) : x_i \geq k + \sigma \Phi^{-1}(p), \quad \text{for} \quad i = 1, 2\}.$$

Now, if player i observes x_i, he assigns probability $\Phi(x_i - \kappa)/\sqrt{2}\sigma$ to player j observing a signal above κ, and he assigns probability at least p to that event exactly if $x_i \geq \kappa + \sqrt{2}\sigma \Phi^{-1}(p)$. In addition, player i knows for sure whether x_i is greater than κ. Thus

$$\begin{aligned} B^p B^p E_k = \{(\theta, x_1, x_2) : x_i &\geq k + \sigma \Phi^{-1}(p) \\ &+ \max\{0, \sqrt{2}\sigma \Phi^{-1}(p)\}, \quad \text{for} \quad i = 1, 2\} \end{aligned}$$

and, by induction,

$$\begin{aligned} [B^p]^n E_k = \{(\theta, x_1, x_2) : x_i &\geq k + \sigma \Phi^{-1}(p) \\ &+ (n-1)\max\{0, \sqrt{2}\sigma \Phi^{-1}(p)\}, \quad \text{for} \quad i = 1, 2\}. \quad (4.1) \end{aligned}$$

So

$$\begin{aligned} C^p E_k &= \bigcap_{n \geq 1} [B^p]^n E \\ &= \begin{cases} \emptyset, & \text{if } p > \frac{1}{2} \\ \{(\theta, x_1, x_2) : x_i \geq k + \sigma \Phi^{-1}(p), \quad \text{for} \quad i = 1, 2\}, & \text{if } p \leq \frac{1}{2}. \end{cases} \end{aligned}$$

Thus, a remarkable feature of this simple example is that for *any* $p > \frac{1}{2}$, there is never common p-belief that θ is greater than k, for *any* k. We could also have shown this using the characterization of common p-belief described in proposition 4.1. For any k, event E_k is p-evident only if $p \leq \frac{1}{2}$. This is because a player observing signal k will always assign probability $\frac{1}{2}$ to his opponent observing a signal less than k. A key property of global games is that they fail to deliver nontrivial common p-belief and p-evident events (for high p). As we will see, the existence of such events is key to supporting multiple equilibria in incomplete information games.

Combining this information structure with the payoffs from the two-player example of Section 2.1, we can illustrate the extreme sensitivity of strategic outcomes to players' higher-order beliefs. Recall that each player had to choose between not investing (with payoff 0) and investing (with payoff θ if the other player invests, and payoff $\theta - 1$ otherwise). The unique equilibrium involved each player i investing if his signal x_i was greater than $\frac{1}{2}$ and not otherwise. This result was independent of σ (the scale variable of the noise). Now observe that if

$$\sigma \leq \frac{1}{5(1 + (n-1)\sqrt{2})\Phi^{-1}(p)},$$

then [by equation (4.1)] for all θ,

$$\left(\theta, \frac{2}{5}, \frac{2}{5}\right) \in [B^p]^n E_{\frac{1}{5}}.$$

In words, suppose that each player observed signal $\frac{2}{5}$. If we fix *any* integer n and *any* $p < 1$, we may choose σ sufficiently small such that it is p-believed that it is p-believed that (n times) ... that θ is greater than $\frac{1}{5}$. If it was common knowledge that θ was greater than $\frac{1}{5}$, it would clearly be rational for both players to invest. But, the unique rational behavior has each player not investing.

Rubinstein (1989) used his *electronic mail game* to illustrate this sensitivity of strategic outcomes to common knowledge. Monderer and Samet (1989) showed why n levels of p-belief or even knowledge was not enough to approximate common knowledge in strategic settings, and common p-belief (i.e., an infinite number of levels) is required. The idea behind this observation is illustrated in the next section. Morris, Rob, and Shin (1995) showed why only some Nash equilibria (e.g., risk-dominated equilibria) were sensitive to higher-order beliefs and not others, and provided a characterization – related to the lack of common p-belief events – of which (discrete state) information systems displayed an extreme sensitivity to higher-order beliefs (see also Sorin, 1998). Kajii and Morris (1997a) introduced a notion of robustness to incomplete information to characterize equilibria that are not sensitive to higher-order beliefs. This work is reviewed and related back to global games in Sections 4.4 and 4.5.

4.3.   Common *p*-Belief and Game Theory

Fix a finite set of players $1, \ldots, I$ and a finite action set A_i for each player i. A *complete information game* is then a vector of payoff functions, $g \equiv (g_1, \ldots, g_I)$, where each $g_i : A \to \mathbb{R}$. A (discrete state) *incomplete information game* is then a collection $\{\Omega, \pi, (\mathcal{P}_i)_{i=1}^I, (u_i)_{i=1}^I\}$, where Ω is a countable state space, $\pi \in \Delta(\Omega)$ is a prior probability on that state space, $\mathcal{P}_i$ is the partition of the state space of player i; and $u_i : A \times \Omega \to \mathbb{R}$ is the payoff function of player i.

For any given incomplete information game $\{\Omega, \pi, (\mathcal{P}_i)_{i=1}^I, (u_i)_{i=1}^I\}$, we may write $|g|$ for the set of states in the incomplete information game where payoffs are given by g. Thus,

$$|g| = \{\omega \in \Omega \mid u_i(a, \omega) = g_i(a) \quad \text{for all} \quad a \in A \text{ and } i = 1, \ldots, I\}.$$

Using this language, we can summarize some key observations from the theoretical literature on higher-order beliefs in game theory. A pure strategy Nash equilibrium a^* of a complete information game, g, is said to be a *p-dominant* equilibrium (Morris, Rob, and Shin, 1995) if each player's action is a best response whenever he assigns probability at least p to his opponents choosing according to a^*, i.e.,

$$\sum_{a_{-i} \in A_i} \lambda(a_{-i}) g_i(a_i^*, a_{-i}) \geq \sum_{a_{-i} \in A_i} \lambda(a_{-i}) g_i(a_i, a_{-i})$$

for all $i = 1, \ldots, I$, $a_i \in A_i$ and $\lambda \in \Delta(A_{-i})$, such that $\lambda(a_{-i}^*) \geq p$.

Lemma 4.2. *If a^* is a p-dominant equilibrium of complete information game g, then every incomplete information game $\{\Omega, \pi, (\mathcal{P}_i)_{i=1}^I, (u_i)_{i=1}^I\}$ has an equilibrium where a^* is played with probability 1 on the event $C^p(|g|)$.*

The proof of this result is straightforward. The event $C^p(|g|)$ is itself a p-evident event. Consider the modified incomplete information game where each player is constrained to choose according to a^* when he p-believes the event $C^p(|g|)$. Find an equilibrium of that modified game. By construction, a^* is played with probability 1 on the event $C^p(|g|)$. But, the equilibrium of the modified game is also an equilibrium of the original game. If a player i p-believes the event $C^p(|g|)$, then he p-believes that other players are choosing a_{-i}^*. But, because his payoffs are given by g and a^* is a p-dominant equilibrium, a_i^* must be a best response for player i.

Because every strict Nash equilibrium is a p-dominant equilibrium for some $p < 1$, we immediately have:

Corollary 4.3. *If a^* is a strict Nash equilibrium of complete information game g, then there exists $p < 1$, such that every incomplete information game $\{\Omega, \pi, (\mathcal{P}_i)_{i=1}^I, (u_i)_{i=1}^I\}$ has an equilibrium where a^* is played on the event $C^p(|g|)$.*

Thus, if we took a sequence of incomplete information games where in the limit payoffs are common knowledge, and close to the limit they are common p-belief (with p close to 1) with ex ante probability close to 1, then payoffs from equilibria of that sequence of incomplete information games must converge to payoffs in the limit game. Monderer and Samet (1989) proved such a lower hemicontinuity result. One can also ask a converse question: what is the relevant topology on information systems, such that information systems close to common knowledge information systems deliver outcomes that are close to common knowledge outcomes. Monderer and Samet (1996) and Kajii and Morris (1998) characterize such topologies (for different kinds of information system).

4.4.   Robustness to Incomplete Information

Let a^* be a pure strategy Nash equilibrium of complete information game g; a^* is *robust to incomplete information* if every incomplete information game where payoffs are almost always given by g has an equilibrium where players almost always choose a^* [Kajii and Morris (KM), 1997a)].[15] More precisely, a^* is robust to incomplete information if, for all $\delta > 0$, there exists $\varepsilon > 0$, such that every incomplete information game where $\pi(|g|) \geq 1 - \varepsilon$ has an equilibrium where a^* is played by all players on an event with probability at least $1 - \delta$.

Robustness (to incomplete information) can be seen as a very strong refinement of Nash equilibrium. Kajii and Morris (1997b) provide a detailed account of the relation between robustness and the existing refinements literature, which we briefly summarize here. The refinements literature examines what happens to a given Nash equilibrium in perturbed versions of the complete information game. A weak class of refinements requires only that the Nash equilibrium continues to be equilibrium in *some* nearby perturbed game [Selten's (1975) notion of *perfect equilibrium* is the leading example of this class]; a stronger class requires that the Nash equilibrium continues to be played in *all* perturbed nearby games [Kohlberg and Mertens' (1986) notion of *stable equilibria* is the leading example of this class]. Robustness belongs to the latter, stronger class of refinements. Moreover, robustness to incomplete information allows an extremely rich set of "perturbed games." In particular, while Kohlberg and Mertens allow only independent action trembles across players, the definition of robustness leads to highly correlated trembles and thus an even stronger refinement. Indeed, KM construct an example in the spirit of Rubinstein (1989) to show that even a game with a unique Nash equilibrium, which is strict, may fail to have any robust equilibrium.

Yet it turns out that a large set of games do have robust equilibria. KM provided two sufficient conditions. The first is that if a^* is the unique correlated equilibrium of g, then a^* is robust. The second sufficient condition comes from a generalization of the notion of p-dominance. Fix a vector of probabilities, $\mathbf{p} = (p_1, \ldots, p_I)$, one for each player. Action profile a^* is a $\mathbf{p}$-*dominant* equilibrium if each player i's action is a best response whenever he assigns probability at least p_i to his opponents choosing according to a^*, i.e.,

$$\sum_{a_{-i} \in A_i} \lambda(a_{-i}) g_i(a_i^*, a_{-i}) \geq \sum_{a_{-i} \in A_i} \lambda(a_{-i}) g_i(a_i, a_{-i})$$

for all $i = 1, \ldots, I$, $a_i \in A_i$, and $\lambda \in \Delta(A_{-i})$ such that $\lambda(a_{-i}^*) \geq p_i$. If a^* is a $\mathbf{p}$-dominant equilibrium for some $\mathbf{p}$ with $\sum_{i=1}^{I} p_i \leq 1$, then a^* is robust to incomplete information. This property is a many-player, many-action generalization of risk dominance. KM proved this result by showing a surprising property of higher-order beliefs. Say that an event is $\mathbf{p}$-believed (for some vector of probabilities $\mathbf{p}$) if each player i believes it with probability at least p_i; and the event is common $\mathbf{p}$-belief if it is $\mathbf{p}$-believed, it is $\mathbf{p}$-believed that it is $\mathbf{p}$-believed, etc. KM show that if vector $\mathbf{p}$ satisfies $\sum_{i=1}^{I} p_i \leq 1$, and an event

---

[15] KM define the property of robustness to incomplete information for mixed strategy equilibria also, but most of the sufficient conditions described previously apply only to pure strategy profiles. For this reason, we focus on pure strategy profiles in the discussion that follows.

has a high probability, then with high probability that event is common **p**-belief. A generalization of lemma 4.2 then proves the robustness result.

Further sufficient conditions for robustness exploit the idea of potential games due to Monderer and Shapley (1996). A function $v : A \to \mathbb{R}$ is a *potential function* for complete information game g, if

$$v(a_i, a_{-i}) - v(a_i', a_{-i}) = g_i(a_i, a_{-i}) - g_i(a_i', a_{-i})$$

for all $i = 1, \ldots, I$, $a_i, a_i' \in A_i$, and $a_{-i} \in A_{-i}$. This property implies that the game g has identical mixed strategy best response correspondences to the common interest game with common payoff function v. Observe that a^* is thus a Nash equilibrium of g if it is a local maximizer of v (i.e., it is not possible to increase v by changing one player's action). Monderer and Shapley suggested if a game has multiple Nash equilibria, the global maximizer of v (which must of course be a local maximizer and thus a Nash equilibrium) is a natural candidate for selection. If action profile a^* is the strict maximum of a potential function v for complete information game g, we say that a^* is potential maximizer of g. Ui (2001) shows that a potential maximizing action profile is necessarily robust to incomplete information.[16] Many-player, two-action, symmetric payoff games are potential games, so this result provides a proof that the strategy profile where all players choose the Laplacian action is robust to incomplete information.[17]

The p-dominance sufficient conditions and potential game sufficient conditions for robustness can be unified and generalized. We very briefly sketch the main ideas and refer the reader to Morris (1999) for more details. Action profile a^* is a *characteristic potential maximizer* of the complete information game g if there exists a function $v : 2^{\{1,\ldots,I\}} \to \mathbb{R}$ with $v(\{1,\ldots,I\}) > v(S)$ for all $S \neq \{1,\ldots,I\}$, and $\mu_i : A_i \to \mathbb{R}_+$ such that for all i, $a_i \in A_i$, and $a_{-i} \in A_{-i}$,

$$v(\{j : a_j = a_j^*\}) - v(\{j : a_j = a_j^*\} \cup \{i\}) \geq \mu_i(a_i)(g_i(a_i, a_{-i})$$
$$- g_i(a_i^*, a_{-i})).$$

Here, $v(\cdot)$ is a potential function that depends only on the set of players choosing according to a^*. In this sense, the characteristic potential maximizer condition strengthens the potential maximizer condition. But, the earlier equalities are replaced with inequalities, and the constants μ_i also add extra degrees of freedom. So, the characteristic potential maximizer condition neither implies nor is implied by the potential maximizer condition. Any characteristic potential maximizing action profile is robust to incomplete information. One can use duality arguments to show that if a^* is a **p**-dominant equilibrium for some **p** with $\sum_{i=1}^{I} p_i \leq 1$, then a^* is a characteristic potential maximizer.[18]

---

[16] Ui uses a slightly weaker version of robustness to incomplete information, where all types in the perturbed game *either* have payoffs given exactly by the complete information game g *or* have a dominant strategy to choose some action.

[17] Morris (1997) previously provided an independent argument showing the robustness of the Laplacian strategy profile.

[18] Ui (2000) extends these ideas with a set-based notion of robustness to incomplete information.

Let the actions of each player be ordered, and for any action $a_i \in A_i$, write a_i^- for the action below a_i and a_i^+ for the action above a_i. Action profile a^* is a *local potential maximizer* of the complete information game g if there exists a local potential function $v : A \to \mathbb{R}$ with $v(a^*) > v(a)$ for all $a \neq a^*$ and, for each i, $\mu_i : A_i \to \mathbb{R}_+$, such that for all $i = 1, \ldots, I$ and $a_{-i} \in A_{-i}$,

$$v(a_i, a_{-i}) - v(a_i^-, a_{-i}) \geq \mu_i(a_i) \begin{bmatrix} g_i(a_i, a_{-i}) \\ -g_i(a_i^-, a_{-i}) \end{bmatrix} \quad \text{if} \quad a_i > a_i^*$$

(4.2)

and

$$v(a_i, a_{-i}) - v(a_i^+, a_{-i}) \geq \mu_i(a_i) \begin{bmatrix} g_i(a_i, a_{-i}) \\ -g_i(a_i^+, a_{-i}) \end{bmatrix} \quad \text{if} \quad a_i < a_i^*.$$

One can show that if a^* is a local potential maximizer, then a^* is both a potential maximizer and a characteristic potential maximizer. Thus, it generalizes both conditions. If a^* is a local potential maximizer of g, and g satisfies strategic complementarities and each $g_i(a_i, a_{-i})$ is concave with respect to a_i, then a^* is robust to incomplete information. The following two-player, three-action, symmetric payoff game satisfies the strategic complementarity and concavity conditions, and one can show that $(0, 0)$ is the local potential maximizer and thus robust (the earlier conditions do not help to characterize robustness in this example; see Table 3.5):

Table 3.5. *Payoffs in three-action example*

	0	1	2
0	4, 4	0, 0	−6, −3
1	0, 0	1, 1	0, 0
2	−3, −6	0, 0	2, 2

In fact, the local potential maximizer condition can be used to characterize the unique robust equilibrium in generic two-player, three-action, symmetric payoff games.

4.5. Noise-Independent Selection

If an action profile is robust to incomplete information, we know that – roughly speaking – any way that a "small" amount of incomplete information is added cannot prevent that action profile being played in equilibrium. This observation has important implications for global games. Consider a global game where payoffs depend continuously on a random parameter θ (which could be multidimensional), and each player observes a noisy signal $x_i = \theta + \sigma \varepsilon_i$. If a^* is a robust equilibrium of the game being played at θ^*, then there will always be an equilibrium of the global game (for small σ) where action profile a^* is almost always played whenever all players observe signals close to θ^*. In other words, there will be no way of adding noise that will prevent action profile a^* being played in the neighborhood of θ^* in some equilibrium. Thus, *if* there is limit uniqueness [say, because there are strategic complementarities and the other assumptions of Frankel, Morris, and Pauzner (2000) are satisfied], then a^* must be played in the unique limit for *every* noise distribution. In the language of Section 4.1, a^* must be the noise-independent selection.

Here is a heuristic argument for this claim. Fix θ^* and let a^* be a Nash equilibrium of the complete information game at θ^* that is robust to incomplete information. By definition, if a^* is robust to incomplete information in game $u(\cdot, \theta^*)$, every incomplete information game where payoffs are almost always given by $u(\cdot, \theta^*)$ has an equilibrium where a^* is almost always played. Generically, it will also be true that every incomplete information game where payoffs are almost always *close to* $u(\cdot, \theta^*)$ will have an equilibrium where a^* is almost always played. But now consider an incomplete information where some types of each player have payoffs close to $u(\cdot, \theta^*)$ ("sane" types), although some types may have very different payoffs ("crazy" types). Suppose that conditional on any player being sane, with probability close to 1, he assigns probability close to 1 to all other players being sane. Now, the robustness arguments described previously could be adapted to show that this incomplete information game has an equilibrium where, conditional on all players being sane, a^* is almost always played.

Now, return to the global game and write $B(\theta^*, \delta)$ for a δ ball around θ^* (i.e., the set of θ within Euclidean distance δ of θ^*). For a generic choice of θ^*, a^* will remain robust to incomplete information close to θ^* [i.e., at all $\theta \in B(\theta^*, \delta)$ for some sufficiently small $\delta > 0$]. Now, consider a sequence of global games where we let the noise go to zero (i.e., $\sigma \to 0$). For fixed δ and fixed $q < 1$, we can choose σ sufficiently small such that conditional on a player observing a signal in $B(\theta^*, \delta)$, with probability at least q, he will assign probability at least q to all other players observing signals within $B(\theta^*, \delta)$. Labeling the types who observe signals in $B(\theta^*, \delta)$ "sane" and types who observe signals not in $B(\theta^*, \delta)$ "crazy," this argument shows that there is an equilibrium where a^* is almost always played in a neighborhood of θ^*.[19]

5. RELATED MODELS: LOCAL HETEROGENEITY AND UNIQUENESS

There are a number of ways that adding local heterogeneity to a population of players can remove multiplicity. In this section, we will attempt to give some intuition for a general logic at work. We start with a familiar example.

---

[19] There is a technical problem formalizing this argument. The robustness analysis described in Section 4.4 was carried out in discrete state spaces, where existence of equilibrium in incomplete information games is never a problem. In the uncountable state space setting of global games, it would be necessary to impose extra assumptions to ensure existence.

There are two players, 1 and 2, and each player i has a payoff parameter x_i. Expected payoffs are given by Table 3.6 :

Table 3.6. *Payoffs in private value example*

	Invest	NotInvest
Invest	x_1, x_2	$x_1 - 1, 0$
NotInvest	$0, x_2 - 1$	$0, 0$

If there was common knowledge that $x_1 = x_2 = x \in (0, 1)$, then there would be multiple strict Nash equilibria of the complete information game. Because both pure strategy equilibria are strict, they seem quite stable. It seems surprising that an apparently "small" perturbation could remove either equilibrium.

But, now let x be a publicly observed random variable and let $x_1 = x_2 = x$. Let players be restricted to switching strategies, so that player i will invest if his payoff parameter exceeds some cutoff k_i and not invest otherwise. Thus, player i's strategy is parameterized by a number k_i. Because the game is symmetric, we can write $b^*(k)$ to the optimal cutoff of any player if he expects his opponent to choose cutoff k. Clearly, we have

$$b^*(k) = \begin{cases} 0, & \text{if } k \le 0 \\ k, & \text{if } 0 \le k \le 1 \\ 1, & \text{if } 1 \le k. \end{cases}$$

This function is plotted in Figure 3.6.

Symmetric equilibria will exist when this best response function crosses the 45° line. So, there are a continuum of equilibria: for any $x \in [0, 1]$, there is an equilibrium where each player follows a switching strategy with cutoff x.

If we perturb this best response function, we would expect there to be a finite number of equilibria (i.e., a finite number of points where the function b^* crosses the 45° line). Given the shape of the best response function, it does not

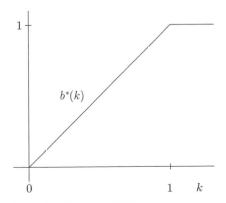

Figure 3.6. Function $b^*(k)$.

seem surprising that there might be natural ways of perturbing the best response function so that there is a unique equilibrium.

The two-player example of Section 2.1 represented one way of carrying out such a perturbation. There, it was assumed that there was a payoff parameter θ, and each player i observed a noisy signal $x_i = \theta + \sigma \varepsilon_i$. The payoffs in Table 3.6 then represent the *expected* payoffs of the players, given their signals. Recall that a player observing signal x_i will believe that his opponent's signal x_j is distributed normally with mean x_i and standard deviation $\sqrt{2}\sigma$. If $\sigma = 0$ in that example, so there is no noise in the signal, we have exactly the scenario described previously with best response function b^*. But, if $\sigma > 0$, then the best response function rotates clockwise a little bit and crosses the $45°$ line only at $\frac{1}{2}$ (see Figure 3.1) and there is a unique equilibrium.

However, this argument does not really rely on the incomplete information interpretation. The important feature of the argument is the *local heterogeneity* in payoffs: a player with payoff parameter x_i knows that he is interacting with other player(s) who have some perhaps different, but nearby, payoff parameters; and he knows that those other player(s) in turn know that they are interacting with other player(s) who have some perhaps different, but nearby, payoff parameters. In the remainder of this section, we will see how a similar logic to the global game argument can arise when players are interacting not with unknown types of an opponent, but with (known) opponents at different locations or at different points in time.[20,21]

5.1.   Local Interaction Games

A continuum of players are evenly distributed on the real line. If a player does not invest, his payoff is 0. If he invests, his payoff is $x + l - 1$, where x is his location and l is a *weighted* average of the proportion of his neighbors investing. In particular, let $f(\cdot)$ be the density of a standard normal distribution with mean 0 and standard deviation $\sqrt{2}\sigma$; a player puts weight $f(z)$ on the actions of players at location $x + z$.

This setup describes a game among a continuum of players. The analysis of this game is identical to the analysis of the continuum player example of Section 2.1. In particular, players at locations less than $\frac{1}{2}$ will not invest, and

[20] This logic also emerges in the the models of Carlsson (1991) and Carlsson and Ganslandt (1998), where players' continuous action choice is subject to a small heterogeneous tremble. The exact connection to global games is not known.

[21] A distinctive feature of these arguments relying on *local* heterogeneity is that a very small amount of heterogeneity is sufficient to imply unique equilibrium in environments where there are multiple strict equilibria without heterogeneity. One can also sometimes obtain uniqueness results assuming global, not local, heterogeneity (i.e. assuming that each player or type has the same, but sufficiently diffuse, beliefs about other players or types' payoff parameters). Such global heterogeneity uniqueness arguments rely on the existence of a sufficiently *large* amount of heterogeneity. See Baliga and Sjöström (2001) in an incomplete information context (where global heterogeneity corresponds to independent types); Herrendorf, Valentinyi, and Waldmann (2000) and Glaeser and Scheinkman (2000) in models of large population interactions; and Frankel (2000b) in the context of a dynamic model with payoff shocks.

players at locations above $\frac{1}{2}$ will invest. This is despite the fact that, if players were interacting only with people at the exact same location (i.e., $\sigma = 0$), there would be multiple equilibria at all locations between 0 and 1.

This rather stylized game illustrates the possibility that in local interaction games, play at some locations may be influenced by play at distant locations via the structure of local interaction. A literature on local interaction games has examined this type of effect.[22] To understand the connection a little better, imagine a local interaction game where payoffs depend in a nonlinear way on location. Thus, let the payoff to investing be $\psi(x) + l - 1$ (instead of $x + l - 1$). Furthermore, suppose that $\psi(x) < \frac{1}{2}$ for all x and that $\psi(x) < 0$ for some open interval of values of x. For small σ, this game will have a unique equilibrium where no player ever invests. To see why, note that for sufficiently small σ, players inside the open interval where $\psi(x) < 0$ will have a dominant strategy to not invest. But, now players close to the edge of that interval will have about $\frac{1}{2}$ their neighbors within that interval, and thus [since $\psi(x) < \frac{1}{2}$ always] will not invest in equilibrium. This argument will iterate to ensure that no investment takes place anywhere.

This argument has very much the flavor of the contagion argument developed by Ellison (1993) and others. There, a population with constant payoffs interacts with near neighbors on a line. Players choose best responses to some average behavior of their neighbors. But, a low rate of mutations ensures small neighborhoods where each action is played with periodically arise randomly. Once a risk-dominant action is played in a small neighborhood, it will tend to spread to the whole population under the best response dynamics. The initial mutant region where the risk-dominant action is played plays much the same role as the dominant strategy region in the story described previously. In this setting with strategic complementarities, best response dynamics mimic iterated deletion of strictly dominated strategies. Morris (1997) describes more formally an exact relationship between a version of Rubinstein's (1989) e-mail game and a version of Ellison's contagion effect, and describes more generally an exact equivalence between games of incomplete information and local interaction games.[23]

The connection between games of incomplete information and local interaction games can be exploited. In evolutionary models, local interaction leads to much faster convergence to stochastically stable states than global interaction, because of the contagious dynamics. But, there is a very close connection between which action will spread contagiously in a local interaction game and which action will be played in the limit in a global game. In particular, recall from Section 4.1 that some games have a noise-independent selection (i.e., an action profile played in the limit of a global game, independent of the noise

---

[22] For example, Blume (1995), Ellison (1993), and Young (1998). See Glaeser and Scheinkman (2000) for a recent survey.

[23] Hofbauer (1998, 1999) introduces an approach to equilibrium selection in a local interaction environment. His "spatially dominant equilibria" seem to coincide with those that are robust to incomplete information.

structure); whereas in other games, the action played in the limit depends on the noise structure. Translated to a local interaction setting, this result implies that some games that have the same action tend to spread contagiously, independent of the structure of interaction, whereas in other games fine details of the local interaction structure will determine which action is contagious [see Morris (1999) for details]. Thus, local interaction may not just speed up convergence to stochastically stable states, but may change the stochastically stable states in subtle ways.[24]

5.2.   Dynamic Games

5.2.1.   Dynamic Payoff Shocks

A continuum of players each live for an instant of time. If a player does not invest, his payoff is 0. If he invests, his payoff is $x + l - 1$, where x is the date at which he lives and l is a *weighted* average of the proportion of players investing at other points in time. In particular, let $f(\cdot)$ be the density of a standard normal distribution with mean 0 and standard deviation $\sqrt{2}\sigma$; a player puts weight $f(z)$ on the actions of players living at date $x + z$.

This setup describes a game among a continuum of players. The analysis of this game is identical to the analysis of the continuum player example of Section 2.1 and thus also the local interaction example of the previous section. In particular, players will not invest before date $\frac{1}{2}$ and will invest after date $\frac{1}{2}$. This is despite the fact that, if players were interacting only with people making contemporaneous choices (i.e., $\sigma = 0$), there would be multiple equilibria at all dates between 0 and 1.

This was a very stylized example. But, the logic is quite general. In many dynamic strategic environments where choices are made at different points in time, a player's payoff may depend not only on contemporaneous choices, but also on choices made by other players at other times. Payoff conditions may be varying through time. Thus, players' optimal choices may depend indirectly on environments, where payoffs are very different from what they are now. These features may allow us to identify a unique equilibrium. We discuss two approaches that exploit this logic.[25]

One approach has been developed recently in Burdzy, Frankel, and Pauzner (2001), Frankel and Pauzner (1999), and Frankel (2000a).[26] A continuum of players are periodically randomly matched in a two-player, two-action game.

---

[24] Morris (2000) also exploits techniques from the higher-order beliefs literature to prove new results about local interaction.

[25] Morris (1995) describes a third approach. Suppose that players are deciding whether to invest or not invest at different points in time, but they make their decisions in private and their watches are not synchronized. Thus, each player will believe that the time on any other player's watch is close to his own, but not identical. Risk-dominant play may result even when perfect synchronization would have allowed multiple equilibria.

[26] See also Frankel and Pauzner (2000) and Levin (2000a) for applications following this approach.

For simplicity, we can think of them playing the investment game described in matrix (2.1). But assume that the publicly observed common payoff parameter θ evolves through time according to some random process [a random walk in Burdzy, Frankel, and Pauzner (2001), a continuous Brownian motion in Frankel and Pauzner (1999)]. Furthermore, suppose that each player can only occasionally alter his behavior: Revision opportunities arrive according to a Poisson process and arrive slowly relative to changes in the game's payoffs. Under certain conditions on the noise process (roughly equivalent to the sufficiently uniform prior conditions in global games), there is a unique equilibrium where each player invests when θ exceeds $\frac{1}{2}$ and not when θ is less than $\frac{1}{2}$.

This description considerably oversimplifies the analysis. For example, it is natural to assume that players observe the public evolution of θ, so they will be able to infer at any point in time (even if they cannot observe) the proportion of players taking each action. This creates an extra state variable (relative to the global games analysis), and the resulting asymmetry between the past and future complicates the analysis. Nonetheless, the logic is similar to the stylized example previously described. In particular, note how the friction in revision opportunities exactly ensures that a player making a choice given some publicly observed θ will take into account the choices that others will make at different times with different publicly observed θ.[27]

Levin (2000a) describes another approach that is closer to the stylized example previously described. At discrete time t, player t chooses an action. His payoff may depend on the actions of players choosing before him or the player choosing after him, but also depends on a payoff parameter θ. The payoff parameter is publicly observed and evolves according to a random walk. If players act as if they cannot influence or do not care about the action of the decision maker in the next period, then under weak monotonicity conditions (a player's best response is increasing in others' actions and the payoff parameter) and limit dominance conditions [the highest (lowest) action is a dominant strategy for sufficiently high (low) values of θ], there is a unique equilibrium. The no influence assumption makes sense if there are in fact a continuum of players at each date or if actions are observed only with a sufficiently long lag. In Matsui's (1999) currency crisis model, there are overlapping generations of players, but there is a natural reason why players do not care about the actions of players preceding them.[28]

---

[27] Matsui and Matsuyama (1995) earlier analyzed a model with Poisson revision opportunities. However, they assumed that the same game was being played through time (i.e., θ was constant), but examined the stability of different population states. The state where the whole population plays the risk-dominant action can be reached in equilibrium from the state where the whole population plays the risk-dominated action, but not vice versa. Hofbauer and Sorger (1999) show that the potential maximizing action of (many-action) symmetric potential games tends to be played in the Matsui-Matsuyama environment. Oyama (2000) shows that the $\frac{1}{2}$-dominant equilibrium is selected in this context. In a private communication, Hofbauer has reported that it also selects the "local potential maximizing action" (see Section 4.4) in two-player, three-action games with strategic complementarities and symmetric payoffs.

[28] See also Frankel (2000b) on the relationship between some of these models.

5.2.2.   Recurring Incomplete Information

Let θ_t follow a random walk, with $\theta_t = \theta_{t-1} + \eta_t$, where each η_t is independently normally distributed with mean 0 and standard deviation τ. In period t, θ_{t-1} is publicly observed, but θ_t is observed only with noise. In particular, each player i observes $x_{it} = \theta_t + \varepsilon_{it}$, where each ε_{it} is independently normally distributed with mean 0 and standard deviation σ. In each period, a continuum of players decide whether to invest with linear payoffs depending on θ_t (the payoff to not investing is 0, and the payoff to investing is $\theta_t + l - 1$, where l is the proportion of the population investing).

This dynamic game represents a crude way of embedding the static global games analysis in a dynamic setting. In particular, each period's play of this dynamic game can be analyzed independently and is exactly equivalent to the public signals model of Section 3. In particular, θ_{t-1} is the public signal about θ_t, whereas x_{it} is player i's private signal. A unique equilibrium will exist in this dynamic game exactly if $\tilde{\gamma}(\sigma, \tau) \leq 2\pi$ (i.e., σ is small relative to τ). In Morris and Shin (2000), we sketch a continuous time version of this recurring incomplete information model and derive the continuous time sufficient conditions for uniqueness.

In Morris and Shin (1999a), we discuss such a recurring incomplete information model of currency crises. One distinctive implication of that analysis is that by the publicity effect, the previous period's fundamentals may be expected to have a disproportionate influence on current outcomes. Thus, for any given actual level of fundamentals, an attack on the exchange rate is more likely when the fundamentals have just risen.

Chamley (1999) considers a richer global game model with recurring incomplete information. A large population of players play a coordination game in each period, but each player has a private cost of taking a risky action that evolves through time. There is correlation in private costs and dominance regions, so that each period's coordination game has the structure of a global game. But past actions convey information about other players' private costs and thus (because of persistence) their current costs. Chamley identifies sufficient conditions for uniqueness in all periods and discusses a variety of applications.

5.2.3.   Herding

In the herding models of Banerjee (1992) and Bikhchandani, Hirshleifer, and Welch (1992), players sequentially make some discrete choice. Players do not care about each other's actions directly, but players have private information, and so each player may partially learn the information of players who choose before him. But, if a number of early-moving players happen to observe signals favoring one action, late-moving players may start ignoring their own private information, leading to inefficient herding because of the negative informational externality.

Herding models share with global game models the feature that outcomes are highly sensitive to fine details of the information structure. However, it is important to note that the mechanisms are quite different. The global games analysis is driven by strategic complementarities and the highly correlated signals generated by the noisy observations technology. However, sensitivity to the information structure arises in a purely static setting. The herding stories have no payoff complementarities and simple information structures, but rely on sequential choice.

Dasgupta (2000a) analyzes a simple model where it is possible to see both kinds of effects at work. A finite set of players decide sequentially (in an exogenous order) whether to invest or not. Investment conditions are either bad (when each player has a dominant strategy to not invest) or good (in which case it pays to invest *if all other players invest*). Each player observes a signal from a continuum, with high signals implying a higher probability that investment conditions are good. All equilibria in this model are switching equilibria: each player invests only if all previous players invested *and* his private signal exceeds some cutoff. Such equilibria encompass herding effects: previous players' decisions to invest convey positive information to later players and make it more likely that they will invest. They also encompass higher-order belief effects: an increase in a player's signal makes it more likely that he will invest both because he thinks it more likely that investment conditions are good *and* because he thinks it more likely that later players will observe high signals and choose to invest.[29]

6. CONCLUSIONS

Global games rest on the premise that the information received by economic agents is informative, but not so informative so as to achieve common knowledge of the underlying fundamentals. Indeed, as the information concerning the fundamentals become more and more accurate, the actions elicited in equilibrium resemble behavior when the uncertainty concerning the actions of other agents becomes more and more diffuse. This points to the potential pitfalls if we rely too much on our intuitions that are based on complete information games that allow perfectly coordinated switching of beliefs and actions. Decentralized decision making in market environments cannot be relied on to rule out inefficient outcomes, so that there may be room for policies that mitigate the inefficiencies. The analysis of economic problems using the methods from global games is in its infancy, but the method seems promising.

Global games also present a "user-friendly" face of games with incomplete information in the tradition of Harsanyi. The potentially daunting task of forming an infinite hierachy of beliefs over the actions of all players in the game can be given a representation in terms of beliefs (and the behavior that they elicit) that are simple to the point of being naive. Global games go some

---

[29] For other models combining elements of payoff complementarities and herding, see Chari and Kehoe (2000), Corsetti, Dasgupta, Morris, and Shin (2000), Jeitshcko and Taylor (2001), and Marx (2000).

way to bridging the gap between those who believe that rigorous game theory has a role in economics (as we do) and those who insist on tractable and usable tools for applied economic analysis.

ACKNOWLEDGMENTS

This study was supported by the National Science Foundation Grant 9709601(to S.M.). Section 3 incorporates work circulated earlier under the title "Private Versus Public Information in Coordination Problems." We thank Hans Carlsson, David Frankel, Josef Hofbauer, Jonathan Levin, and Ady Pauzner for valuable comments on this paper, and Susan Athey for her insightful remarks. Morris would like to record an important intellectual debt in this area to Atsushi Kajii, through joint research and long discussions.

APPENDIX A: PROOF OF PROPOSITION 2.2

We will prove the first half of the result [$s(x) = 0$ for all $x \leq \theta^* - \delta$]. The second half [$s(x) = 0$ for all $x \leq \theta^* - \delta$] follows by a symmetric argument. For any given strategy profile $\mathbf{s} = \{s_i\}_{i \in [0,1]}$, we write $\zeta(x)$ for the proportion of players observing signal x who choose action 1; $\zeta(\cdot)$ will always be a continuous function of x.

Write $\pi_\sigma(x, k)$ for the highest possible expected payoff gain to choosing action 1 for a player who has observed a signal x and knows that all other players will choose action 0 if they observe signals less than k:

$$\pi_\sigma(x, k) \equiv \max_{\{\zeta : \zeta(x) = 0 \text{ for all } x < k\}}$$

$$\frac{\int_{\theta = -\infty}^{\infty} p(\theta) f\left(\frac{x-\theta}{\sigma}\right) \pi\left(1 - F\left(\frac{k-\theta}{\sigma}\right), \theta\right) d\theta}{\int_{\theta = -\infty}^{\infty} p(\theta) f\left(\frac{x-\theta}{\sigma}\right) d\theta}. \tag{A.1}$$

Lemma 6.1. *There exists $\underline{x} \in \mathbb{R}$ and $\overline{\sigma}_1 \in \mathbb{R}_{++}$ such that $\pi_\sigma(x, k) < 0$ for all $\sigma \leq \overline{\sigma}_1, x \leq \underline{x}$, and $k \in \mathbb{R}$.*

Proof. By property A4*, we can choose $\underline{x} < \theta$ and a continuously differentiable function $\overline{\pi} : \mathbb{R} \to \mathbb{R}$ with $\overline{\pi}'(\theta) = 0$ and $\overline{\pi}(\theta) = -\varepsilon$ for all $\theta \leq \underline{x}$ such that

$$\pi(l, \theta) \leq \overline{\pi}(\theta) \leq -\varepsilon$$

for all $l \in [0, 1]$ and $\theta \in \mathbb{R}$. Now let

$$\overline{\pi}_\sigma(x) \equiv \frac{\int_{\theta = -\infty}^{\infty} p(\theta) f\left(\frac{x-\theta}{\sigma}\right) \overline{\pi}(\theta) d\theta}{\int_{\theta = -\infty}^{\infty} p(\theta) f\left(\frac{x-\theta}{\sigma}\right) d\theta}$$

$$= \frac{\int_{z = -\infty}^{\infty} p(x + \sigma z) f(-z) \overline{\pi}(x + \sigma z) dz}{\int_{z = -\infty}^{\infty} p(x + \sigma z) f(-z) dz},$$

changing variables to $z = \dfrac{\theta - x}{\sigma}$.

Clearly, $\overline{\pi}_\sigma(x)$ is an upper bound on $\pi_\sigma(x, k)$ for all k. Observe that $\overline{\pi}_\sigma(x)$ is continuous in σ; also, $\overline{\pi}_0(x) = \overline{\pi}(x)$ so $\overline{\pi}_0(x) = -\varepsilon$ for all $x \leq \underline{x}$. Also observe that

$$
\left. \frac{d\overline{\pi}_\sigma}{d\sigma}(x) \right|_{\sigma=0}
$$

$$
\begin{aligned}
= & \left. \frac{\left[\int_{z=-\infty}^{\infty} p(x+\sigma z)f(-z)dz\right]\left[\int_{z=-\infty}^{\infty} zf(-z)\left(p'(x+\sigma z)\overline{\pi}(x+\sigma z)+p(x+\sigma z)\overline{\pi}'(x+\sigma z)\right)dz\right]}{\left[\int_{z=-\infty}^{\infty} p(x+\sigma z)f(-z)dz\right]^2} \right. \\
& \left. - \frac{\left[\int_{z=-\infty}^{\infty} zf(-z)p'(x+\sigma z)dz\right]\left[\int_{z=-\infty}^{\infty} p(x+\sigma z)f(-z)\overline{\pi}(x+\sigma z)dz\right]}{\left[\int_{z=-\infty}^{\infty} p(x+\sigma z)f(-z)dz\right]^2} \right|_{\sigma=0}
\end{aligned}
$$

$$
= \left[\int_{z=-\infty}^{\infty} zf(-z)\,dz \right] \frac{\overline{\pi}'(x)}{p(x)}.
$$

Thus, by A6, $d\overline{\pi}_\sigma/d\sigma(x) = 0$ for all $x \leq \underline{x}$. Thus, there exists $\overline{\sigma} \in \mathbb{R}_{++}$ such that $\overline{\pi}_\sigma(x) < 0$ for all $\sigma \leq \overline{\sigma}$ and $x \leq \underline{x}$. ∎

Lemma 6.2. *There exists $\overline{\sigma}_2 \in \mathbb{R}_{++}$ such that $\pi_\sigma(x, k) < 0$ for all $\sigma \leq \overline{\sigma}_2$, $\underline{x} \leq x < \theta^*$, and $x \leq k \leq \theta^*$:*

$$
\pi_\sigma(x, k) = \frac{\int_{\theta=-\infty}^{\infty} p(\theta) f\left(\frac{x-\theta}{\sigma}\right) \pi\left(1 - F\left(\frac{k-\theta}{\sigma}\right), \theta\right) d\theta}{\int_{\theta=-\infty}^{\infty} p(\theta) f\left(\frac{x-\theta}{\sigma}\right) d\theta}
$$

$$
= \int_{l=0}^{1} \psi_\sigma(l; x, k) \pi\left(l, k - \sigma F^{-1}(l)\right) dl,
$$

where $\psi_\sigma(l; x, k)$ is the density with cdf

$$
\Psi_\sigma(l; x, k) = \frac{\int_{\theta=-\infty}^{k-\sigma F^{-1}(1-l)} p(\theta) f\left(\frac{x-\theta}{\sigma}\right) d\theta}{\int_{\theta=-\infty}^{\infty} p(\theta) f\left(\frac{x-\theta}{\sigma}\right) d\theta}
$$

$$
= \frac{\int_{z=\frac{x-k}{\sigma}+F^{-1}(1-l)}^{\infty} p(x - \sigma z) f(z)\,dz}{\int_{z=-\infty}^{\infty} p(x - \sigma z) f(z)\,dz},
$$

changing variables to $z = \dfrac{x - \theta}{\sigma}$.

Thus, as $\sigma \to 0$, $\Psi_\sigma(l; x, x - \sigma\xi) \to 1 - F(\xi + F^{-1}(1 - l))$. Thus, as $\sigma \to 0$, $\pi_\sigma(x, x - \sigma\xi) \to \pi_\sigma^*(x, x - \sigma\xi)$ continuously (where π_σ^* is the variable corresponding to a uniform prior derived in the text). We know that $\pi_\sigma^*(x, x - \sigma\xi) > 0$ for the required values of x and ξ. Because we are interested in values of x in the closed interval $[\overline{x}, \theta^*]$ and because varying ξ generates a compact set of distributions over l, covergence is uniform. ∎

APPENDIX B: THE FINITE PLAYER CASE

As we noted in the linear example of Section 2.1, analysis of the continuum and finite players can follow similar methods. Here, we briefly note how to extend the uniform prior private values analysis of proposition 2.1 to the finite player case. The extension of the general prior common values analysis of proposition 2.2 is then straightforward.

The setting is as in Section 2.2.1, except that there are now $I \geq 2$ players, and the noise terms in the private signals are identically and independently distributed according to the density $f(\cdot)$. As before, $\pi(l, x)$ is the payoff gain to choosing action 1 rather than action 0, if you have observed signal x and proportion l of your opponents choose action 1. Of course, now (because you have $I - 1$ opponents) l will always be an element of the set $\{0, 1/(I - 1), 2/(I - 1), \ldots, 1\}$. Property A3 becomes:

A3(I): I-**Player Single Crossing**: There exists a unique θ_I^* solving $\sum_{k=0}^{I-1}(1/I)\pi(k/(I - 1), \theta_I^*) = 0$.

Observe that, as $I \to \infty$, $\theta_I^* \to \theta^*$ (i.e., the θ^* of assumption A3). In the special case where $I = 2$, this reduces to $\frac{1}{2}\pi(0, \theta_2^*) + \frac{1}{2}\pi(1, \theta_2^*) = 0$; in other words, θ_2^* is the point where the *risk-dominant* action (Harsanyi and Selten 1988) switches from 0 to 1. Proposition 2.1 remains true as stated for the finite player game, with θ_I^* replacing θ^*. This was essentially shown by Carlsson and van Damme (1993b). The key step in the proof is showing that, in a symmetric strategy profile, each player has uniform beliefs over the proportion of players observing a higher signal. To see why this is true, note that the probability that a player observing signal x assigns to exactly proportion $n(I - 1)$ of his opponents signal greater than k is

$$\int_{\theta=-\infty}^{\infty} \frac{1}{\sigma} f\left(\frac{x - \theta}{\sigma}\right) \binom{I - 1}{I - 1 - n} \left[F\left(\frac{k - \theta}{\sigma}\right)\right]^{I-1-n}$$
$$\times \left[1 - F\left(\frac{k - \theta}{\sigma}\right)\right]^n d\theta,$$

where $F(\cdot)$ is the c.d.f. of $f(\cdot)$. Letting $x = k - \sigma z$ and carrying out the change of variables $\xi = (k - \theta)/\sigma$, this expression becomes

$$\int_{\xi=-\infty}^{\infty} f(\xi - z)\binom{I - 1}{I - 1 - n}[F(\xi)]^{I-1-n}[1 - F(\xi)]^n d\xi.$$

This expression is now independent of σ and k, so we may denote this expression by $\psi^I(n/(I - 1); z)$. For the same argument to work as in the continuum case, it is enough to show that $\psi^I(\cdot; 0)$ is the uniform distribution. But, integration by parts gives

$$\psi'\left(\frac{n}{I-1};0\right) = \binom{I-1}{I-1-n}\int_{\xi=-\infty}^{\infty} f(\xi)\,[F(\xi)]^{I-1-n}\,[1-F(\xi)]^n\,d\xi$$

$$= \binom{I-1}{I-n}\int_{\xi=-\infty}^{\infty} f(\xi)\,[F(\xi)]^{I-n}\,[1-F(\xi)]^{n-1}\,d\xi$$

$$= \cdots$$

$$= \int_{\xi=-\infty}^{\infty} f(\xi)\,[F(\xi)]^{I-1}\,d\xi$$

$$= \frac{1}{I}.$$

APPENDIX C: PROOF OF LEMMA 2.3

Recall the following expression for a player's expected payoff gain to choosing action 1 for a player who has observed a signal x and knows that all other players will choose action 0 if they observe signals less than k:

$$\pi_\sigma^*(x,k) \equiv \int_{\theta=-\infty}^{\infty} \frac{1}{\sigma} f\left(\frac{x-\theta}{\sigma}\right)\pi\left(1-F\left(\frac{k-\theta}{\sigma}\right),x\right)d\theta.$$

With a change of variables [setting $z = (\theta - k)/\sigma$], this expression becomes

$$\pi_\sigma^*(x,k) = \int_{z=-\infty}^{\infty} f\left(\frac{x-k}{\sigma}-z\right)\pi(1-F(-z),x)\,dz.$$

We can rewrite this expression as

$$\pi_\sigma^*(x,k) = h(x,k,x),$$

where

$$h(x,k,x') \equiv \int_{z=-\infty}^{\infty} \widetilde{f}(x,z)g(z,x')\,dz,$$

$$\widetilde{f}(x,z) \equiv f\left(\frac{x-k}{\sigma}-z\right),$$

and

$$g(z,x') \equiv \pi(1-F(-z),x').$$

Now observe that, by A7, $\widetilde{f}(x,z)$ satisfies a monotone likelihood ratio property [i.e., if $\overline{x} > \underline{x}$, then $\widetilde{f}(\overline{x},z)/\widetilde{f}(\underline{x},z)$ is increasing in z]; also observe that, by A1*, $g(\cdot,x')$ satisfies a single crossing property: there exists $z^* \in \mathbb{R} \cup \{-\infty, \infty\}$ such that $g(z,x') < 0$ if $z < z^*$ and $g(z,x') > 0$ if $z > z^*$. Now lemma 5 in Athey (2000b) implies that $h(\cdot,k,x')$ satisfies a single crossing property: there exists $x^*(k,x')$ such that $h(x,k,x') < 0$ for all $x < x^*(k,x')$, and $h(x,k,x') > 0$ for all $x > x^*(k,x')$. But by A2, we know that $h(x,k,x')$ is strictly increasing in x'.

Now suppose $h(x, k, x) = 0$. If $x' < x$, then

$$h(x', k, x') < h(x', k, x), \quad \text{by} \quad A2$$
$$< h(x, k, x), \quad \text{by the single crossing property of } h.$$

By a symmetric argument, we have $x' > x \Rightarrow h(x', k, x') > h(x, k, x)$. Thus, there exists $\beta : \mathbb{R} \to \mathbb{R}$ such that

$$\pi_\sigma^*(x, k) < 0 \quad \text{if} \quad x < \beta(k)$$
$$\pi_\sigma^*(x, k) = 0 \quad \text{if} \quad x = \beta(k)$$
$$\pi_\sigma^*(x, k) > 0 \quad \text{if} \quad x > \beta(k).$$

Thus, if a player thinks that others are following a strategy with cutoff k, a player's best response is to follow a switching strategy with cutoff $\beta(k)$. But, by A3, we know that there exists exactly one value of k such that

$$\pi_\sigma^*(k, k) = \int_{l=0}^1 \pi(l, k) dl = 0.$$

Thus, there is a unique symmetric switching strategy equilibrium.

References

Allen, F. and S. Morris (2001), "Finance Applications of Game Theory," in *Advances in Business Applications of Game Theory*, (ed. by K. Chatterjee and W. Samuelson), Boston, MA: Kluwer Academic Press.

Allen, F., S. Morris, and A. Postlewaite (1993), "Finite Bubbles with Short Sales Constraints and Asymmetric Information," *Journal of Economic Theory*, 61, 209–229.

Athey, S. (2001), "Single Crossing Properties and the Existence of Pure Strategy Equilibria in Games of Incomplete Information," *Econometrica*, 69, 861–889.

Athey, S. (2002), "Monotone Comparative Statics under Uncertainty," *Quarterly Journal of Economics,* 117(1), 187–223.

Aumann, R. (1976), "Agreeing to Disagree," *Annals of Statistics*, 4, 1236–1239.

Baliga, S. and S. Morris (2000), "Coordination, Spillovers and Cheap Talk," *Journal of Economic Theory*.

Baliga, S. and T. Sjöström (2001), "Arms Races and Negotiations," Northwestern University.

Banerjee, A. (1992), "A Simple Model of Herd Behavior," *Quarterly Journal of Economics*, 107, 797–818.

Battigalli, P. (1999), "Rationalizability in Incomplete Information Games," available at http://www.iue.it/Personal/Battigalli.

Bikhchandani, S., D. Hirshleifer, and I. Welch (1992), "A Theory of Fads, Fashion, Custom, and Cultural Change as Informational Cascades," *Journal of Political Economy*, 100, 992–1026.

Blume, L. (1995), "The Statistical Mechanics of Best-Response Strategy Revision," *Games and Economic Behavior*, 11, 111–145.

Boonprakaikawe, J. and S. Ghosal (2000), "Bank Runs and Noisy Signals," University of Warwick.

Brunner, A. and J. Krahnen (2000), "Corporate Debt Restructuring: Evidence on Coordination Risk in Financial Distress," Center for Financial Studies, Frankfurt.

Bryant, J. (1983), "A Simple Rational Expectations Keynes Type Model," *Quarterly Journal of Economics*, 98, 525–529.

Bulow, J., J. Geanakoplos, and P. Klemperer (1985), "Multimarket Oligopoly: Strategic Substitutes and Complements," *Journal of Political Economy*, 93, 488–511.

Burdzy, K., D. Frankel, and A. Pauzner (2001), "Fast Equilibrium Selection by Rational Players Living in a Changing World," *Econometrica*, 69, 163–189.

Carlsson, H. (1989), "Global Games and the Risk Dominance Criterion," University of Lund.

Carlsson, H. (1991), "A Bargaining Model where Parties Make Errors," *Econometrica*, 59, 1487–1496.

Carlsson, H. and E. van Damme (1993a), "Global Games and Equilibrium Selection," *Econometrica*, 61, 989–1018.

Carlsson, H. and E. van Damme (1993b), "Equilibrium Selection in Stag Hunt Games," in *Frontiers of Game Theory*, (ed. by K. Binmore, A. Kirman, and A. Tani), Cambridge, MA: MIT Press.

Carlsson, H. and M. Ganslandt (1998), "Noisy Equilibrium Selection in Coordination Games," *Economics Letters*, 60, 23–34.

Chamley, C. (1999), "Coordinating Regime Switches," *Quarterly Journal of Economics*, 114, 817–868.

Chan, K. and Y. Chiu (2000), "The Role of (Non)Transparency in a Currency Crisis Model," McMaster University.

Chari, V. and P. Kehoe (2000), "Financial Crises as Herd Behavior," Working Paper 600, Federal Reserve Bank of Minneapolis.

Chui, M., P. Gai, and A. Haldane (2000), "Sovereign Liquidity Crises: Analytics and Implications for Public Policy," International Finance Division, Bank of England.

Chwe, M. (1998), "Believe the Hype: Solving Coordination Problems with Television Advertising," available at http://chwe.net/michael.

Corsetti, G., A. Dasgupta, S. Morris, and H. S. Shin (2000), "Does One Soros Make a Difference? The Role of a Large Trader in Currency Crises," *Review of Economic Studies*.

Dasgupta, A. (2000a), "Social Learning and Payoff Complementarities," available at http://aida.econ.yale.edu/~amil.

Dasgupta, A. (2000b), "Financial Contagion Through Capital Connections: A Model of the Origin and Spread of Bank Panics," available at http://aida.econ.yale.edu/~amil.

DeGroot, M. (1970), *Optimal Statistical Decisions*. New York: McGraw-Hill.

Dekel, E. and F. Gul (1996), "Rationality and Knowledge in Game Theory," in *Advances in Economic Theory–Seventh World Congress of the Econometric Society*, (ed. by D. Kreps and K. Wallace), Cambridge: Cambridge University Press.

Diamond, D. and P. Dybvig (1983), "Bank Runs, Deposit Insurance, and Liquidity," *Journal of Political Economy*, 91, 401–419.

Dönges, J. and F. Heinemann (2000), "Competition for Order Flow as a Coordination Game," Center for Financial Studies, Frankfurt, Germany.

Ellison, G. (1993), "Learning, Local Interaction, and Coordination," *Econometrica*, 61, 1047–1071.

Frankel, D. (2000a), "Determinacy in Models of Divergent Development and Business Cycles," available at www.tau.ac.il/~dfrankel.

Frankel, D. (2000b), "Noise versus Shocks," seminar notes, University of Tel Aviv.

Morris, S. and H. S. Shin (1998), "Unique Equilibrium in a Model of Self-Fulfilling Currency Attacks," *American Economic Review*, 88, 587–597.

Morris, S. and H. S. Shin (1999a), "A Theory of the Onset of Currency Attacks," in *Asian Financial Crisis: Causes, Contagion and Consequences*, (ed. by P.-R. Agenor, D. Vines, and A. Weber), Cambridge: Cambridge University Press.

Morris, S. and H. S. Shin (1999b), "Coordination Risk and the Price of Debt," available at http://www.econ.yale.edu/~smorris.

Morris, S. and H. S. Shin (2000), "Rethinking Multiple Equilibria in Macroeconomic Modelling," *NBER Macroeconomics Annual 2000*, (ed. by B. Bernanke and K. Rogoff) Cambridge, MA: MIT Press.

Obstfeld, M. (1996), "Models of Currency Crises with Self-Fulfilling Features," *European Economic Review*, 40, 1037–1047.

Osborne, M. and A. Rubinstein (1994), *A Course in Game Theory*. Cambridge, MA: MIT Press.

Oyama, D. (2000), "*p*-Dominance and Equilibrium Selection under Perfect Foresight Dynamics," University of Tokyo, Tokyo, Japan.

Rochet, J.-C. and X. Vives (2000), "Coordination Failures and the Lender of Last Resort: Was Bagehot Right after All?" Universitat Autonoma de Barcelona.

Rubinstein, A. (1989), "The Electronic Mail Game: Strategic Behavior under Almost Common Knowledge," *American Economic Review*, 79, 385–391.

Scaramozzino, S. and N. Vulkan (1999), "Noisy Implementation Cycles and the Informational Role of Policy," University of Bristol.

Schelling, T. (1960), *Strategy of Conflict*. Cambridge, MA: Harvard University Press.

Selten, R. (1975), "Reexamination of the Perfectness Concept for Equilibrium Points in Extensive Games," *International Journal of Game Theory*, 4, 25–55.

Shin, H. S. (1996), "Comparing the Robustness of Trading Systems to Higher Order Uncertainty," *Review of Economic Studies*, 63, 39–60.

Shleifer, A. (1986), "Implementation Cycles," *Journal of Political Economy*, 94, 1163–1190.

Sorin, S. (1998), "On the Impact of an Event," *International Journal of Game Theory*, 27, 315–330.

Townsend, R. (1983), "Forecasting the Forecasts of Others," *Journal of Political Economy*, 91, 546–588.

Ui, T. (2000), "Generalized Potentials and Robust Sets of Equilibria," University of Tsukuba.

Ui, T. (2001), "Robust Equilibria of Potential Games," *Econometrica*, 69, 1373–1380.

van Damme, E. (1997), "Equilibrium Selection in Team Games," in *Understanding Strategic Interaction: Essays in Honor of Reinhard Selten*, (ed. by W. Albers et al.), New York: Springer-Verlag.

Vives, X. (1990), "Nash Equilibrium with Strategic Complementarities," *Journal of Mathematical Economics*, 19, 305–321.

Young, P. (1998), "Individual Strategy and Social Structure," Princeton, NJ: Princeton University Press.

CHAPTER 4

Testing Contract Theory: A Survey of Some Recent Work

Pierre-Andre Chiappori and Bernard Salanié

1. INTRODUCTION

> It is a capital mistake to theorise before one has data.
> Arthur Conan Doyle, *A Scandal in Bohemia.*

Since the early seventies, the development of the theoretical literature on contracts has been nothing short of explosive. The study of more and more sophisticated abstract models has gone hand in hand with the use of the tools of the theory to better understand many fields of economics, such as industrial organization, labor economics, taxation, insurance markets, or the economics of banking. However, it is only fair to say that the empirical validation of the theory has long lagged behind the theoretical work. Many papers consist of theoretical analyses only, with little attention to the facts. Others state so-called stylized facts often based on fragile anecdotal evidence and go on to study a model from which these stylized facts can be derived. Until the beginning of the eighties, empirical tests using actual data and econometric methods were very rare, even though the theoretical literature had by then given birth to a large number of interesting testable predictions.

Although such a long lag is not untypical in economics, it is clearly unfortunate, especially when one compares our practice to that of other scientists. Even without fully sharing the somewhat extreme methodological views expressed above by Sherlock Holmes, one can hardly dispute that interactions between theory and reality are at the core of any scientific approach. To give only one example, the models of insurance markets under asymmetric information developed at the beginning of the seventies were extensively tested (and found to lack empirical support) only in the middle of the nineties. If this had been done earlier, the 20-year period could have been used to devise better models.

Fortunately, a number of empirical researchers have turned their attention to the theory of contracts in recent years, so that such long lags should become less common. This survey will present a panorama of this burgeoning literature. Because new papers are appearing every week in this field, we cannot claim to be exhaustive. We just hope that we can convey to the reader both a sense of excitement at these recent developments and an understanding of the specific econometric problems involved in taking contract theory to the data.

A unifying theme of our survey is the necessity of controlling adequately for unobserved heterogeneity in this literature. If it is not done properly, then the combination of unobserved heterogeneity and endogenous matching of agents to contracts is bound to create selection biases on the parameters of interest. This is given a striking illustration in a recent contribution by Ackerberg and Botticini (2002). They consider the choice between sharecropping and fixed-rent contracts in a tenant–landlord relationship. Standard moral hazard models stress the trade-off between incentives and risk-sharing in the determination of contractual forms. Fixed-rent contracts are very efficient from the incentives viewpoint, since the tenant is both the main decision maker and the residual claimant. However, they also generate a very inefficient allocation of risk, in which all the risk is borne by one agent, the tenant, who is presumably more risk averse. When uncertainty is small, risk-sharing matters less, and fixed-rent contracts are more likely to be adopted. On the contrary, in a very uncertain environment, risk-sharing is paramount, and sharecropping is the natural contractual form. This prediction can readily be tested from data on existing contracts, provided that a proxy for the level of risk is available. For instance, if some crops are known to be more risky than others, the theory predicts that these crops are more likely to be associated with sharecropping contracts.

A number of papers have tested this prediction by regressing contract choice on crop riskiness. The underlying argument, however, has an obvious weakness: it takes contracts as exogenously given, and disregards any possible endogeneity in the matching of agents to contracts. In other words, the theoretical prediction described holds only for *given* characteristics of the landlord and the agents. It can be taken to the data only to the extent that this "everything equal" assumption is satisfied, so that agents facing different contracts do not differ by some otherwise relevant characteristic. Assume, on the contrary, that agents exhibit ex ante heterogeneous degrees of risk aversion. To keep things simple, assume that a fraction of the agents are risk neutral, whereas the rest are risk averse. Different agents will be drawn to different crops; efficiency suggests that risk-neutral agents should specialize in the more risky crops. But, note that risk-neutral agents should also be proposed fixed-rent contracts, because risk-sharing is not an issue for them. Thus, given heterogeneous risk aversions, fixed-rent contracts are associated with the more risky crops, and the standard prediction is reversed.

Clearly, the core of the difficulty lies in the fact that, although risk aversion plays a crucial role in the story, it is not directly observable. *Conditional on risk aversion*, the initial theoretical argument remains valid: more risk makes fixed-rent contracts look less attractive. This prediction can in principle be tested, but it requires that differences in risk aversion be controlled for in the estimation or that the resulting endogeneity bias be corrected in some way.

The paper is divided in two parts. In Section 2, we study the effect of contractual forms on behavior. This obviously comprises the measure of the so-called "incentive effect" (i.e., the increase in productivity generated by moving to a higher-powered incentive contract), but we adopt a more general approach here. Thus, we consider that the decision to participate in a relationship and the choice of a contract in a menu of contracts all are effects of contractual forms on behavior. Section 3 turns to the optimality of observed contracts. The central question here can be stated as follows: does the theory predict well the contractual forms that we actually observe? Section 4 provides a brief conclusion.

Contract theory encompasses a very large body of literature, and we had to make choices to keep a manageable length for this survey. First, we consider only situations in which contracts are explicit and the details of the contractual agreement are available to the econometrician. In particular, we do not cover the literature on optimal risk-sharing within a group, which has rapidly developed since the initial contributions of Cochrane (1991) and Townsend (1994).[1] There are also areas where excellent surveys of the empirical literature have been written recently. Thus, we will not mention any work on auctions in this survey, and we refer the reader to Laffont (1997). Similarly, we will only briefly touch on the provision of incentives in firms, which is discussed by Gibbons and Waldman (1998) and Prendergast (1999).

2.   CONTRACTS AND BEHAVIOR

> Circumstantial evidence is a very tricky thing.
> Arthur Conan Doyle, *The Boscombe Valley Mystery.*

Several papers aim at analyzing the links between the form of existing contracts and observed behavior. A recurrent problem of this literature is related to selection issues. Empirical observation provides direct evidence of *correlations* between contracts and behavior. Theoretical predictions, on the other hand, are concerned with *causality* relationships. Assessing causality from correlations is an old problem in economics, and indeed in all of science; but the issue is particularly important in our context. Typically, one can observe that different contracts are associated with different behaviors, as documented by a large number of contributions. But, the interpretation of the observed correlations is not straightforward. One explanation is that contracts *induce* the corresponding behavior through their underlying incentive structure; this defines the so-called incentive effect of contracts. However, an alternative, and often just as convincing, story is that differences in behavior simply reflect some unobserved heterogeneity across agents and that this heterogeneity is also responsible for the variation in contract choices.

Interestingly enough, this distinction is familiar to both theorists and econometricians, although the vocabulary may differ. Econometricians have for a long time stressed the importance of endogenous selection. In the presence of unobserved heterogeneity, the matching of agents to contracts must be studied with care. If the outcome of the matching process is related to the unobserved heterogeneity variable (as one can expect), then the choice of the contract is

---

[1] See the contribution by Attanasio and Rios-Rull in this volume.

endogenous. In particular, any empirical analysis taking contracts as given will be biased.

Contract theory, on the other hand, systematically emphasizes the distinction between adverse selection (whereby unobserved heterogeneity preexists the contractual relationship and constrains its form) and moral hazard (whereby behavior directly responds to the incentive structure created by the contract). As an illustration, consider the literature on automobile insurance contracts. The idea, here, is to test a standard prediction of the theory: Everything being equal, people who face contracts entailing more comprehensive coverage should exhibit a larger accident probability. Such a pattern, if observed, can however be given two different interpretations. One is the classical adverse selection effect à la Rothschild–Stiglitz: high-risk agents, knowing they are more likely to have an accident, self-select by choosing contracts entailing a more comprehensive coverage. Alternatively, one can evoke moral hazard. If some agents, for *exogenous* reasons (say, picking up the insurance company located down the corner), end up facing a contract with only partial coverage, they will be highly motivated to adopt a more cautious behavior, which may result in lower accident rates. In practice, the distinction between adverse selection and moral hazard may be crucial, especially from a normative viewpoint.[2] But it is also very difficult to implement empirically, especially on cross-sectional data.

Most empirical papers relating contracts and behavior face, at least implicitly, a selection problem of this kind. Various strategies can be adopted to address it. Some papers explicitly recognize the problem and merely test for the presence of asymmetric information without trying to be specific about its nature. In other cases, however, available data allow to disentangle selection and incentives. Such is the case, in particular, when the allocation of agents to contracts is exogenous, either because it results from explicit randomization or because some "natural experiment" has modified the incentive structure without changing the composition of the population. In some cases, an explicit modelization of the economic and/or econometric structure at stake leads to simultaneous estimation of selection and incentives effects. Finally, a promising direction relies on the use of panel data, the underlying intuition being that the dynamics of behavior exhibit specific features under moral hazard.

2.1.   Testing for Asymmetric Information

Several papers have recently been devoted to the empirical analysis of insurance contracts and insurees' behavior.[3] Following initial contributions by Dahlby

---

[2] One of the most debated issues regarding health insurance is the impact of deductible on consumption. It is a well-established fact that, in cross-sectional data, better coverage is correlated with higher expenditure levels. But the welfare implications are not straightforward. If incentives are the main explanation, deductibles or copayments are likely to be useful, because they reduce overconsumption. However, should selection be the main driving force, then limits on the coverage level can only reduce the insurance available to risk averse agents with no gain in terms of expenditure. The result is an unambiguous welfare loss.

[3] See Chiappori (2000) for a recent overview.

(1983), Boyer and Dionne (1987), and Puelz and Snow (1994), a (nonexhaustive) list includes Chiappori and Salanié (1997, 2000), Gouriéroux (1999), Bach (1998), Cawley and Philipson (1999), Dionne, Gouriéroux, and Vanasse (2001), and Richaudeau (1999).[4] In most cases, the nature of the test is straightforward: conditionally on all information that is available to the insurance company, is the choice of a particular contract correlated to risk, as proxied ex post by the occurrence of an accident?

This idea can be given a very simple illustration. Consider an automobile insurance context, where insurees choose between two types of coverage (say, comprehensive versus liability only). Then they may or may not have an accident during the subsequent period. The simplest representation of this framework relies on two probit equations. One describes the choice of a contract, and takes the form

$$y_i = I \left[X_i \beta + \varepsilon_i > 0 \right], \tag{2.1}$$

where $y_i = 1$ when the insuree chose the full coverage contract at the beginning of the period, 0 otherwise; here, the X_i are exogenous covariates that control for all the information available to the insurer, and β is a vector of parameters to be estimated. The second equation relates to the occurrence of an accident:

$$z_i = I \left[X_i \gamma + \eta_i > 0 \right], \tag{2.2}$$

where $z_i = 1$ when the insuree had an accident during the period contract, 0 otherwise, and γ is a vector of parameters to be estimated.[5] In this context, asymmetric information should result in a positive correlation between y_i and z_i conditional on X_i, which is equivalent to a positive correlation between ε_i and η_i. This can be tested in a number of ways; for instance, Chiappori and Salanié (2000) propose two parametric tests and a nonparametric test.[6] Interestingly enough, none of these tests can reject the null hypothesis of zero correlation (corresponding to the absence of asymmetric information).

These results are confirmed by most studies on automobile insurance[7]; similarly, Cawley and Philipson (1997) find no evidence of asymmetric information in life insurance. However, Bach (1998), analyzing mortgage-related unemployment insurance contracts, finds that insurees who choose contracts with

---

[4] A related reference is Toivanen and Cressy (1998), who consider credit contracts.

[5] An additional problem is that, typically, claims, not accidents, are observed. The decision to fill a claim is obviously influenced by many factors, including the form of the contract, which may induce spurious correlations. For that reason, most studies concentrate on accidents involving several vehicles and/or bodily injuries. See Dionne and Gagné (2001) for a careful investigation of these issues.

[6] One parametric test is based on a computation of generalized residuals from independent estimations of the two probits, whereas the other requires a simultaneous estimation of the two probits using a general covariance matrix for the residuals. The nonparametric approach relies on the construction of "cells" of identical profiles, followed by a series of χ^2 tests.

[7] One notable exception is the initial paper by Puelz and Snow (1994). However, subsequent studies strongly suggest that their result may be due to a misspecification of the model [see Chiappori and Salanié (2000) and Dionne et al. (2001)].

better (in her case earlier) coverage are more likely to become unemployed. Evidence of adverse selection has also been repeatedly found in annuity markets. Following earlier work by Friedman and Warshawski (1990) and Brugiavini (1993) shows that, controlling for age and gender (the two variables used for pricing), annuity buyers have a longer life expectancy than the rest of the population. Recently, Finkelstein and Poterba (2000) have studied the annuity policies sold by a large UK insurance company since the early 1980s. Again, the systematic and significant relationships they find between ex post mortality and some relevant characteristics of the policies suggest that adverse selection may play an important role in that market. For instance, individuals who buy more backloaded annuities are found to be longer lived, whereas policies involving payment to the estate in the event of an early death are preferred by customers with shorter life expectancy.

This empirical literature on asymmetric information in insurance suggests a few general insights. One is that asymmetric information may be an important issue in some insurance markets, but not in others. Ultimately, this is an empirical question, and the last word should be given to empirical analysis instead of theoretical speculations. From a more methodological perspective, the treatment of the information available to both the insuree and the insurer appears as a key issue. Correctly controlling for this information is a crucial, but quite delicate, task. It may be, for instance, that the linear forms used are not flexible enough, in the sense that they omit relevant nonlinearities or cross-effects.[8] Should this be the case, then the resulting, omitted variable bias will result in a spurious correlation between contract choices and risk that could mistakenly be interpreted as evidence of asymmetric information. A last conclusion is that static models may miss important dimensions of the problem. In automobile insurance, for instance, experience rating is known to play an important role. Insurers typically observe past driving records; these are highly informative on accident probabilities, and, as such, are used for pricing. Again, omitting history in the probit regressions will generate a bias toward overestimating the importance of asymmetric information. However, in the presence of unobserved heterogeneity, the introduction of variables reflecting past behavior raises complex endogeneity problems. In many cases, an explicit model of the dynamics of the relationship will be required.

2.2. Experiments

The most natural way to overcome selection problems is to make sure that the allocation of people to contracts is fully exogenous. Assume that different people are assigned to different contracts in a purely random way; then differences in observed behavior can safely be analyzed as responses to the different

---

[8] Chiappori and Salanié argue that the use of simple, linear functional forms (such as logit or probit) should be restricted to homogeneous populations, such as "young" drivers. An additional advantage of this approach is that it avoids the problems raised by experience rating.

incentive structures at stake. Random assignment may be seen as an ideal situation, a kind of "first-best" context for testing contract theory. Such situations, although infrequent, can however be found; their analysis generates some of the most interesting and robust conclusions of the literature.

The best example of a random experiment of this kind certainly is the celebrated Rand Health Insurance Experiment (HIE).[9] Between November, 1974 and February 1977, the HIE enrolled families in six sites in the United States. Families participating in the experiment were randomly assigned to one of 14 different insurance plans, involving different coinsurance rates and different upper limits on annual out-of-pocket expenses. In addition, lump-sum payments were introduced to guarantee that no family would lose by participating in the experiment.

The HIE has provided extremely valuable information about the sensitivity of the demand for health services to out-of-pocket expenditures under a number of different schemes. The use of medical services was found to respond to changes in the amount paid by the insuree. The largest decrease in the use of outpatient services occurs between a free plan and a plan involving a 25% copayment rate; larger rates did not significantly affect expenditures. The impact of the various features of the different plans could be estimated, as well as their interaction with such family characteristics as income or number of children. Also, it is possible, using the regressions results, to estimate "pure coinsurance elasticities" (i.e., the elasticity of expenditures to coinsurance rates in the absence of ceilings on out-of-pocket expenses).

It is fair to say that the results of the HIE study have been extremely influential in the subsequent discussions on health plan reforms. The HIE will probably remain as one of the best empirical studies ever made in that field, a "Rolls Royce" of empirical contract theory. However, quality comes at a cost. That of the HIE (130 million 1984 dollars) may not be totally prohibitive, but is high enough to severely hamper the repetition of such experiments in the future.

Fortunately, not only academics (or government agencies) are willing to run experiments of this kind. Knowledge about the incentive effects of contractual forms is valuable for firms as well; as a consequence, they may be eager to invest in acquiring such relevant information, in particular through experiments. In a recent contribution, Shearer (1999) studies the case of a tree-planting firm that randomly allocated workers to plant under piece rate and fixed-wage contracts under a subset of planting conditions. Daily productivities were recorded for each worker and are used to measure the percentage difference in average productivity under both types of payment. A simple analysis of variance analysis suggests an incentive effect of piece wages of about 20 percent. In addition, Shearer estimates a structural econometric model of worker behavior. This enables him to take into account nonexperimental data as well, to impose nonlinear restrictions on the analysis of variance model, and finally to extend

---

[9] See Manning et al. (1987).

his conclusions to a larger set of planting conditions. The estimates appear to be very robust: Shearer finds a lower bound of 17 percent for the incentive effect.

Ausubel (1999) analyzes the market for bank credit cards. A substantial portion of bank credit card marketing today is done via direct-mailed preapproved solicitations; furthermore, several card issuers decide on the terms of the solicitations by conducting large-scale randomized trials. Ausubel uses the outcomes of such a trial to test for a standard prediction of adverse selection theory, namely that high-risk agents are more willing to accept less favorable deals.[10] The trial is conducted by generating a mailing list of 600,000 customer names and randomly assigning them among equal market cells. The market cells are mailed solicitations that vary in the introductory interest rate, in the duration of the introductory offer, and in the postintroductory interest rate. Three tests can be conducted on these data. The first test relates to a "winner's curse" prediction: respondents should be worse borrowers than nonrespondents. Ausubel indeed finds that respondents have on average shorter credit histories, inferior credit rating, and are more borrowed-up than nonrespondents. Second, respondents to inferior offers (i.e., offers displaying a higher introductory interest rate, a shorter duration of the introductory period, or a higher postintroductory interest rate) are also worse borrowers on average, in the sense that they exhibit lower incomes, inferior credit records, lower balances on other credit cards, and higher utilization rates of credit lines on other credit cards. Note, however, that these two tests involve characteristics that are observable by the bank and hence do not correspond to adverse selection in the usual sense. On the other hand, a third test looks for hidden information by checking whether, even after controlling for the observable characteristics of respondents to inferior offers, the latter still yield a customer pool that is more likely to default. The answer is an unambiguous yes, which provides very convincing evidence supporting the existence of adverse selection on the credit card market.

2.3.   Natural Experiments

Selection issues arise naturally in a cross-sectional context: if different people are involved in different contracts, the mechanism that allocates contracts to people deserves close scrutiny. Assume, however, that the *same* people successively face different contracts. Then, selection is no longer a problem; in particular, any resulting change of behavior can safely be attributed to the variation of incentives, at least to the extent that no other significant factor has changed during the same period. This is the basic insight of natural experiments: incentive effects are easier to assess when they stem from some *exogenous* change in the incentive structure.

---

[10] Technically, the market for credit card exhibits nonexclusive contracts. In particular, the relevant theoretical reference is Stiglitz and Weiss (1981) rather than Rothschild and Stiglitz (1976) as in automobile insurance. Also, Ausubel (1999) focuses on testing for adverse selection, but he argues that moral hazard cannot explain his findings.

Changes in regulations constitute an obvious source of natural experiments. For instance, the automobile insurance regulation in Québec was modified in 1978 by the introduction of a "no fault" system, which in turn was deeply restructured in 1992. Dionne and Vanasse (1996) provide a careful investigation of the effects of these changes. They show in particular that the average accident frequency dropped significantly after strong incentives to increase prevention efforts were reinstated in 1992. They conclude that changes in agents' behavior, as triggered by new incentives, did have a significant effect on accident probabilities.[11] Another illustration is provided by the study of tenancy reform in West Bengal by Banerjee, Gertler, and Ghatak (2002). The reform, which took place in 1976, entitled tenants, upon registration with the Department of Land-Revenue, to permanent and inheritable tenure on the land they sharecropped so long as they paid the landlord at least 25 percent of output as rent. The incentive impact of the reform is rather complex, because it changes the respective bargaining powers of the parties and the tenant's incentives to invest while reducing the set of incentive devices available for the landlord. To test for the impact of the reform, the authors use two methods. One is to use neighboring Bangladesh as a control; the fact that the reform was implemented in West Bengal, but not in Bangladesh, the authors argue, was to a large extent due to an exogenous political shock. The second method compares changes in productivity across districts with different registration rates. Again, endogeneity might be a problem here; the authors carefully discuss this issue. They find that the reform significantly increased productivity.

Regulation is not the only cause of changes in incentive structures. Periodically, firms modify their incentive schemes, introduce new rewards, or restructure their wage schedules. Natural experiments of this kind have been repeatedly analyzed. To take only one example, Lazear (2000) uses data from a large auto glass company that changed its compensation structure from hourly wages to piece rates. He finds that, in accordance with the theoretical predictions, the productivity increases sharply, half of which can be attributed to existing workers producing more.

A first potential limitation of any work of this kind is that, strictly speaking, it establishes a simultaneity rather than a causality. What the studies by Dionne and Vanasse or Lazear show is that, on a given period, outcomes have changed significantly, and that this evolution immediately followed a structural change in incentives. But, the two phenomena might stem from simultaneous and independent (or correlated) causes. The lower rate of accidents following the 1992 Québec reform may be due, say, to milder climatic conditions. Such a "coincidence" may be more or less plausible, but it is difficult to discard totally. A second and related problem is that the change in the incentive structure may well fail to be exogenous. This is particularly true for firms, which are supposed to adopt optimal contracts. If the switch from fixed wages to piece rates

---

[11] See Browne and Puelz (1999) for a similar study on U.S. data.

indicates that, for some reason, fixed wages were the best scheme before the reform but ceased to be by the time the reform was implemented, then a direct regression will provide biased estimates, at least to the extent that the factors affecting the efficiency of fixed wages had an impact on productivity Again, this type of explanation may be difficult to discard.[12]

The "coincidence" problem can be overcome when the experiment provides a "control" sample that is not affected by the change, so that the effects can be estimated in differences (or more precisely differences of differences). In two recent papers, Chiappori, Durand, and Geoffard (1998) and Chiappori, Geoffard, and Kyriazidou (2000) use such data on health insurance. Following a change in regulation in 1993, French health insurance companies modified the coverage offered by their contracts in a nonuniform way. Some of them increased the level of deductible, whereas others did not. The tests use a panel of clients belonging to different companies, who were faced with different changes in coverage, and whose demand for health services is observed before and after the change in regulation. To concentrate on those decisions that are essentially made by consumers themselves (as opposed to those partially induced by the physician), the authors study the number of physician visits, distinguishing between general practitioner office visits, general practitioner home visits, and specialist visits. They find that the number of home visits significantly decreased for the "treatment" group (i.e., agents who experienced a change of coverage), but not for the "control" group (for which the coverage remained constant). They argue that this difference is unlikely to result from selection, because the two populations are employed by similar firms, they display similar characteristics, and participation in the health insurance scheme was mandatory.

A paper by Dionne and St.-Michel (1991) provides another illustration of these ideas. They study the impact of a regulatory variation of the coinsurance level in the Québec public insurance plan on the demand for days of compensation. The main methodological contribution of the paper is to introduce a distinction between injuries, based on the type of diagnosis; it reflects the fact that it is much easier for a physician to detect a fracture than, say, lower back pain. In the first case, moral hazard (interpreted, in the ex post sense, as the tendency to cheat on the true severity of the accident) can play only a minor role, whereas it may be prevalent when the diagnosis is more difficult. In a sense, the easy diagnoses play the role of a control group, although in a specific way: they represent situations where the moral hazard problem does not exist. Theory predicts that the regulatory change will have more significant effects on the number of days of compensation for those cases where the diagnosis is more problematic. This prediction is clearly confirmed by empirical evidence. A more generous insurance coverage, resulting from an exogenous regulatory change,

---

[12] This remark illustrates a general phenomenon: if contracts are always optimal, then contract changes should always be taken as endogenous. In real life, however, (at least temporarily) inefficient contracts can hardly be assumed away, which, paradoxically, may simplify a lot the task of the econometrician!

is found to increase the number of days on compensation, but only for the cases of difficult diagnoses. Note that the effect thus identified is ex post moral hazard. The reform is unlikely to have triggered significant changes in prevention; and, in any case, such changes would have affected all types of accidents.

Another natural experiment based on reforms of public programs is studied by Fortin, Lanoie, and Laporte (1995), who examine how the Canadian Worker's Compensation (WC) and the Unemployment Insurance (UI) programs interact to influence the duration of workplace accidents. They show that an increase in the generosity of WC in Québec leads to an increase in the duration of accidents. In addition, a reduction in the generosity of UI is, as in Dionne and St.-Michel, associated with an increase in the duration of accidents that are difficult to diagnose. The underlying intuition is that worker's compensation can be used as a substitute to UI. When a worker goes back to the labor market, he may be unemployed and entitled to UI payments for a certain period. Whenever worker's compensation is more generous than UI, there will be strong incentives to delay the return to the market. In particular, the authors show that the hazard of leaving WC is 27 percent lower when an accident occurs at the end of the construction season, when unemployment is seasonally maximum.[13]

Finally, an interesting situation is when the changes in the incentive structure are random but endogenous. Take the example of mutual fund managers, as studied by Chevalier and Ellison (1997). The basic assumption of the paper is that fund companies have an incentive to increase the inflow of investments. That, in turn, depends on the fund's performance in an implicit contract between fund companies and their customers. The authors estimate the shape of the flow–performance relationship for a sample of funds observed over the 1982–1992 period, and find that it is highly nonlinear. Such a nonlinear shape, in turn, creates incentives for fund managers to alter the riskiness of their portfolios, and these incentives vary with time and past performance. Examining portfolio holdings, the authors find that risk levels are changed toward the end of the year in a manner consistent with these incentives. For instance, the flow performance is convex for funds that are ahead of the market; and, as expected, these tend to gamble so as to increase their expected inflow of investment.[14] In a similar vein, Oyer (1998) remarks that compensation contracts for salespersons and executives are typically nonlinear in firm revenues, which creates incentives for these agents to manipulate prices, vary effort, and influence the timing of customer purchases. Using an extensive data set (gathering firm revenue and cost of goods sold for 31,936 quarterly observations covering 981 manufacturers), Oyer finds evidence of business seasonality patterns that fully support the theoretical predictions.

---

[13] See also Fortin and Lanoie (1992), Bolduc et al. (1997), and the survey by Fortin and Lanoie (1998).

[14] Chevalier and Ellison (1999) extend this approach to study the impact of career concerns on the investment decisions of mutual fund managers. For another, recent work on the incentive impact of managerial contracts, see Lemmon, Schallheim, and Zender (2000).

2.4.   Explicit Modeling

2.4.1.   *Econometric Tools*

In the absence of (natural) experiments, the endogenous matching problem is pervasive. Adequate theoretical tools may, however, allow it to be tackled in a satisfactory way. From the econometric perspective, much attention has been devoted to exogeneity tests, which find a natural application in our context. An illustration is provided by Laffont and Matoussi (1995), who study a model of sharecropping with moral hazard. The main prediction of this class of models is that production increases with the share of the product kept by the tenant. Laffont and Matoussi use data collected in 1986 on contracts and production in a Tunisian village to test that sharecropping indeed reduces production. To do this, they estimate augmented Cobb–Douglas production functions, adding contract dummy variables as explanatory variables. They find that moving from a sharecropping contract to a rental contract increases production by 50 percent on average. However, longer-term sharecropping relationships, which allow for delayed retaliation, tend to be much more efficient, as one would expect from the repeated moral hazard literature in a context of missing credit markets (see Chiappori, Macho, Rey, and Salanié, 1994).

As presented, the Laffont–Matoussi approach seems very sensitive to the criticism of selection bias: if they find higher production in plots with rental contracts, it may simply be that rental contracts are more often adopted for more fertile plots. Their answer to this criticism is to test for exogeneity of the contract-type variables in production functions. This they do, and they do not reject exogeneity, which validates their approach. One problem with exogeneity tests is that they may not be very powerful. As we will see, another solution to the selection bias problem is to use instruments. In fact, the exogeneity test used by Laffont–Matoussi assumes that some variables (such that the tenant's age, his wealth, and working capital) are valid instruments for the contract variables in the production function.

2.4.2.   *Structural Models of Regulation under Adverse Selection*

Often, however, identification requires a full-grown structural model. Wolak (1994) pioneered the estimation of structural models with adverse selection. His paper is set within the context of the regulator–utility relationship for California water companies. However, it is simpler to present it for a price discriminating monopoly (the principal) facing consumers (agents) with an unknown taste θ for the good. Let X be the vector of exogenous variables that are observed by both parties and by the econometrician, α be the vector of parameters we want to estimate, and let q be the quantity traded as per the contract. The observational status of θ depends on our assumptions. First, consider model S (for symmetric information), in which both Principal and Agent observe θ. Then, we obtain by maximizing the total surplus[15] a likelihood function $l^S(q, X, \alpha; \theta)$. Note that this is conditional on θ.

Now consider the more interesting model A (for asymmetric information) in which only the Agent knows θ and the Principal has a prior given by a probability distribution function f and a cumulative distribution function F. In that case, we know from the theoretical literature that under the appropriate hazard rate condition, the solution is given by maximizing the virtual surplus, which generates a likelihood function

$$l^A(q, X, \alpha; \theta, (1 - F(\theta))/f(\theta)).$$

Note that the latter is conditional both on θ and on $(1 - F(\theta))/f(\theta)$.

Assume that we have data on n relationships between Principals and Agents that are identical except for the exogenous variables X, so that our sample is $(q_i, X_i)_{i=1}^n$. The difficulty here is that we do not know θ or f, even in model S, in which both parties observe θ. In econometric terms, θ is an unobserved heterogeneity parameter and we must integrate over it. To do this, we must find a functional form for f that is flexible enough, given that we have very little idea of what the Principal's prior may look like. Let (f_γ) be such a parameterized family.

We can now estimate all parameters of model S by maximizing over α and γ the log-likelihood

$$\sum_{i=1}^n \log \int l^S(q_i, X_i, \alpha; \theta) f_\gamma(\theta) \, d\theta.$$

To estimate model A, we must first integrate f_γ to get F_γ; then, we maximize

$$\sum_{i=1}^n \log \int l^A\left(q_i, X_i, \alpha; \theta, \frac{1 - F_\gamma(\theta)}{f_\gamma(\theta)}\right) f_\gamma(\theta) \, d\theta.$$

These log-likelihood functions are obviously highly nonlinear and also require a numerical integration in both models; however, modern computers make it quite feasible to maximize them.

As pointed out before, Wolak (1994) introduced this approach to study the regulation of water utilities in California in the eighties. He found that nonnested tests à la Vuong (1989) favor model A over model S, indicating that asymmetric information is relevant in this regulation problem. Wolak also noted that using model S instead of model A may lead the analyst to conclude wrongly that returns are increasing, whereas they are estimated to be constant in model A. Finally, he was able to evaluate the underproduction that is characteristic of adverse selection models to about 10 percent in the middle of the θ range.

One difficulty with Wolak's method is that the econometrician observes only the conditional distribution of q, given X; thus, identification of the preferred

---

[15] Assuming that utilities are quasilinear.

model heavily relies on functional form assumptions. Without them, it is easy to find examples in which model S with parameters (α, F) yields exactly the same likelihood function as model A with parameters (α', F'), so that there is no way to discriminate between these two models on the basis of data. Of course, this problem is not specific to Wolak's model; it is just the usual identification problem in structural models, with the new twist that the parameter F is really infinite-dimensional.[16]

Ivaldi and Martimort (1994) have used a similar approach in a model that has both market power and asymmetric information. They study competition through supply schedules in an oligopoly, where two suppliers of differentiated goods do not know the consumers' valuations for the two goods. They model this situation as a multiprincipals game where the suppliers are the principals and the consumers are the agents. Assuming supply schedules to be quadratic, they derive the perfect Bayesian equilibrium in supply schedules and the corresponding segmentation of the market according to the valuations of consumers for the two goods.

Ivaldi and Martimort apply this theoretical model to study energy supply to the French dairy industry. The first supplier is the public sector monopoly on gas and electricity, EDF-GDF. The second supplier consists of oil firms, who are assumed to act as a cartel. Oil firms maximize profit, but EDF-GDF maximizes social welfare. The authors use pseudo–maximum likelihood (Gouriéroux, Monfort, and Trognon, 1984) to estimate the structural equations derived from their theoretical model. They find that the estimated variance of suppliers' priors on the valuations of consumers is significantly positive, so that there is evidence of asymmetric information in this market. Obviously, our remark on identification in Wolak's model also applies here.[17]

2.4.3.   *Structural Models Involving Moral Hazard and Selection*

Structural models can be used in a more specific way to disentangle selection from incentive effects. Paarsch and Shearer (2000) analyze data from a tree-planting firm, where some workers receive a piece rate, whereas others are paid a fixed wage. In their model, the decision to adopt a piece rate or a fixed wage is modeled as resulting from the observation of the planting conditions by the firm. The endogeneity problem arises from the fact that neither the planting conditions nor the individual-specific cost of effort is observed by the econometrician. According to the structural model developed in the paper,

---

[16] Wolak also assumes that the regulator maximizes social welfare. Timmins (2000) relaxes this assumption and estimates the relative weights of consumers' surplus and firms' profits in the regulator's objective function. Gagnepain and Ivaldi (2001) take the existing regulatory framework as given; they estimate the structural parameters of supply and demand and use them to simulate the optimal contracts.

[17] See also Lavergne and Thomas (2000).

fixed wages are efficient under poor planting conditions and for less productive employees, whereas piece rates work well in more favorable contexts. A direct comparison of observed productivities under each type of contract thus is biased, because the estimated difference results partly from the incentive effect of piece rates and partly from the selection effect. Hence observed discrepancies in productivity provide an upper bound of the incentive effect. Conversely, differences in real earnings provide a lower bound for the incentive effect. This simple idea can be taken to the data quite easily; the authors find an upper (respectively lower) bound of 60 percent (respectively 8 percent). Finally, a parametric version of the structural model is estimated. The authors conclude that about half of the difference in productivity is due to incentive effects and half to selection. Interestingly enough, these nonexperimental findings are fully compatible with the experimental results in Shearer (1999).[18]

A related approach is adopted by Cardon and Hendel (2001), who consider employer-provided health insurance. As argued here, a contract that involves a larger copayment rate is likely to correspond to smaller health expenditures, either because of the incentive impact of the copayment rate or because high-risk agents self-select by choosing contracts entailing more coverage. The main identifying assumption used by Cardon and Hendel is that agents do not choose their employer on the basis of the health insurance coverage. A consequence is that whereas the allocation of individuals among the various options *of a given plan* typically reflects adverse selection, the differences in behavior *across plans* must be from incentive effects. Again, a structural model is needed to disentangle the two effects; the authors find that selection effects are negligible, whereas incentives matter.[19]

2.5. Using Behavioral Dynamics

If selection and moral hazard are difficult to disentangle in a static context, a natural response is to turn to dynamic data.[20] Adverse selection and moral hazard indeed induce *different behavioral dynamics,* which provides a new source for identification. An illustration of this line of research is provided by a recent work by Chiappori, Abbring, Heckman, and Pinquet (2001). They consider a French data base provided by an automobile insurer. A particular feature of automobile insurance in France is that pricing relies on experience rating (i.e., the premium associated to any particular contract depends, among other things, on the

---

[18] Paarsch and Shearer (1999) use a similar model, where the firm, having observed the planting conditions, chooses a specific piece rate. Again, the structural model allows the endogeneity of the rate to be taken into account.

[19] Other references include, among others, Holly et al. (1998) and Ferrall and Shearer (1999).

[20] A different but related idea is that the use of panel data allows control of unobserved heterogeneity and selection issues in a much more satisfactory way than in cross-sectional analysis. See, for instance, MacLeod and Parent (1999).

past history of the relationship), but the particular form experience rating may take is strongly regulated. All companies must apply the same "bonus/malus" system, according to which the premium is decomposed as the product of a "basis" premium, freely set by the insurer but independent of past history, and a bonus coefficient, the dynamics of which is imposed by law. Specifically, the coefficient is decreased by a factor $\mu < 1$ after each year without an accident but increased by a factor $\lambda > 1$ after each year with an accident.[21] The authors show that this scheme has a very general property, namely that each accident increases the *marginal cost* of (future) accidents. Under moral hazard, any accident thus increases prevention efforts and reduces accident probability. The conclusion is that for any given individual, moral hazard induces a **negative contagion** phenomenon: the occurrence of an accident in the past reduces accident probability in the future. The tricky part, however, is that this prediction holds only *conditional on individual characteristics*, whether observable or unobservable. As is well known, unobserved heterogeneity induces an opposite, **positive contagion** mechanism: past accidents are typical of bad drivers, hence are a good predictor of a higher accident rate in the future. The problem thus is to control for unobserved heterogeneity. This problem is fairly similar to an old issue of the empirical literature on dynamic data, namely the distinction between pure heterogeneity and state dependence. The authors show that nonparametric identification can actually be achieved under mild identifying restrictions, even when the history available to the econometrician about each driver consists only of the number of years of presence and the total number of accidents during this period. Using a proportional hazard duration model on French data, they cannot reject the null of no moral hazard.

3.   ARE CONTRACTS OPTIMAL?

We now turn to tests of contract optimality. The papers we are going to survey all focus on the same question: do observed contracts have the properties predicted by contract theory? There is a sense in which the answer is always positive: given any contract, a theorist with enough ingenuity may be able to build an ad hoc theory that "explains" it. The operative word here is "ad hoc." Clearly, there is no precise definition of what constitutes an ad hoc assumption, but there may be accepted standards. So, we can rephrase the optimality question thus: do the properties of observed contracts correspond to those that the currently standard models of contract theory predict? This new formulation makes it clear that a negative answer may be only temporary, as better models with new predictions are developed (ideally, in response to such rejections of currently standard models).

---

[21] Currently, $\mu = .95$ and $\lambda = 1.25$. In addition, the coefficient at any time is capped and floored (at 3.5 and .5, respectively). Note that the strict regulation avoids selection problems, because the insuree cannot choose between menus involving different bonus/malus coefficients, as is often the case in other countries.

3.1.   Static, Complete Contracts

3.1.1.   Managerial Pay

The standard model of moral hazard implies that managers' pay should be sensitive to their firms' performance. The "pay-performance sensitivity" has been estimated by many papers [for a recent survey of the evidence, see Murphy (1999)]. The seminal contribution is that of Jensen and Murphy (1990); using data on CEOs of U.S. firms from 1969 to 1983, they obtained what seemed to be very low estimates of the elasticity of executive compensation to firm performance. Their oft-quoted result was that when the firm's value increases by $1,000, the (mean) manager's wealth increases only by $3.25.

The early reaction to Jensen and Murphy's result was that they indicated inefficiently low incentives for top management (see, e.g., Rosen 1992). However, Haubrich (1994) showed that even fairly low levels of manager's risk aversion (such as a relative index of risk aversion of about 5) were consistent with this empirical result. The intuition is that for large companies, changes in firm value can be very large and imply large swings in CEO wealth even for such lowish pay-performance sensitivity levels. Moreover, more recent estimates point to much higher elasticities. Thus, Hall and Liebman (1998) use a more recent data set (1980–1994). They show that the spectacular increase in the stock options component of managers' pay has made their pay much more sensitive to firm performance. Their mean (respectively median) estimate of the change in CEO wealth (salary, bonus, and the change in value of stocks and stock options) linked to a $1,000 increase in firm value indeed is about $25 (respectively $5.3). Much of it is due to the change in value of stocks and stock options.

Another testable implication of the moral hazard model is that pay-performance sensitivity should be inversely related to the variance of the measure of performance used (typically firm value for managers). Aggarwal and Samwick (1999) show that, indeed, CEO pay is much less sensitive to performance for firms whose stock returns are less volatile.[22] This result, however, may itself be sensitive to the choice of covariates.[23] This illustrates a problem frequently encountered by this literature. Theory predicts the form of optimal contracts within simplified models, where comparative statics are easy to work out (one can change the level of uncertainty within a moral hazard model by varying one parameter). Taking such predictions to data typically requires some very strong "everything equal" qualification. In practice, firms differ by the uncertainty they face, but also by their size, market share, relationship to the clients, technology, internal organization and others – all of which may be

---

[22] Aggarwal and Samwick use panel data and include fixed CEO effects that allow them to control for CEO risk aversion.

[23] For instance, Core and Guay (2000) find that the sign of the relationship is reversed when controlling for firm size.

correlated, moreover, in various ways. In this context, sorting out one particular type of causality is a difficult task indeed.

Other models relate the use of a particular form of compensation to the characteristics of the task to be performed. Using various data sets, MacLeod and Parent (1999) find, for instance, that jobs using high-power incentives are associated with more autonomy on the job, and that a high local rate of unemployment results in less discretion in pay or promotion, confirming standard conclusions of incomplete contract theory.

Finally, one empirical puzzle in this literature is that firms do not seem to use relative performance evaluation of managers very much.[24] The theory indeed predicts that managers should not be paid for performance that is due to "observable luck," such as a favorable industrywide exchange rate shock or a change in input prices. Bertrand and Mullainathan (2001) revisit this issue of "pay for luck"; they find that manager pay in fact reacts about as much to performance changes that are predictable from observable luck measures as to unpredictable changes in performance. This clearly contradicts the theoretical prediction. However, Bertrand and Mullainathan also find that better-governed firms (such as those with large shareholders) give less pay for luck, as one would expect.

3.1.2. Sharecropping

Many papers have tested the moral hazard model of sharecropping, and we will quote only a few recent examples.[25] Ackerberg and Botticini (2002) regress the type of contract (rental or sharecropping) on crop riskiness and tenant's wealth. As explained previously, theory predicts that more risky crops are more likely to be grown under sharecropping contracts. If wealth is taken to be a proxy for risk aversion, we would also expect that richer (and presumably less risk averse) tenants are more likely to be under a rental contract. Now wealth is only an imperfect proxy for risk aversion, and as explained earlier, the unobserved component of risk aversion is likely to be correlated with crop riskiness. This implies that the error in the contract choice equation is correlated with one of the explanatory variables, and the estimators of such a naive regression are biased. To remedy this endogenous matching problem, Ackerberg and Botticini instrument the crop riskiness variable, using geographical variables as instruments. They find that the results are more compatible with theory than a naive regression would suggest. Moreover, the implicit bias in the naive estimators goes in the direction implied by a matching of more risk-averse tenants with less risky crops: it leads to overestimating the effect of crop risk and underestimating the effect of wealth.[26]

---

[24] Gibbons and Murphy (1990) argue that they do.

[25] Other recent works include, in particular, a series of papers by Allen and Lueck (1992, 1993, 1998, 1999).

[26] An alternative strategy used by Dubois (2000a, 2000b) is to independently estimate individual risk aversion (as a function of the available covariates) from panel data on consumptions (in the line of the consumption smoothing literature), then include the estimated parameter of risk aversion within the explanatory variables for the contract choice equation.

Laffont and Matoussi (1995) test a different variant of the moral hazard sharecropping model. In their story, tenants are risk neutral; but they are facing financial constraints that limit how much risk they may take. This model predicts that tenants with less working capital tend to work under sharecropping or even wage contracts. They find that their Tunisian data support this prediction.

In either of these variants, the theory used is drastically simplified. Empirical work must often extend the theory to take into account features of real-world applications. Dubois (1999) makes a step in that direction by taking into account landlords' concerns that tenant effort may exhaust the soil and reduce future land fertility and hence future profits. This is a problem because contracts are incomplete: they cannot be made contingent on land fertility. Moreover, many contracts extend over only one season and so long-term contracts are not feasible. Then, sharecropping may be optimal even with risk-neutral tenants, as it improves future land fertility by reducing tenant effort. This "extended model" of sharecropping has some predictions that differentiate it from the "canonical model" of Stiglitz (1974) and that seem to fit Dubois' Philippines data set better. For instance, the data show that incentives are higher powered for more valuable plots of land. This is incompatible with most versions of the canonical model; on the other hand, it is quite possible under the extended model. Moreover, observed incentives are lower powered for crops such as corn that tend to exhaust the soil, as the extended model predicts.

The theory also predicts that a technological shock that makes the effort of the tenant less crucial should increase the share of the landlord at the optimal contract. Hanssen (2001) argues that this is exactly what happened in the movie industry with the coming of sound in 1927. When films were silent, the exhibitor was expected to provide musical background and other live acts. With sound films, all of this was incorporated in the movie itself, making the receipts less sensitive to the exhibitor's effort. Hanssen shows that, as we would expect, contracts between film companies and exhibitors rapidly moved from flat-fee rentals to the revenue-sharing agreements that now dominate the industry.

Finally, when long-term contracts are available, they are effective in providing incentives for noncontractible investment. If incentive provision is costly because of information rents, long-term contracts will be used only when maintenance benefits are large enough. This idea is exploited by Bandiera (2001) in her study of agricultural contracts in nineteenth century Sicily. She finds that long-term contracts were indeed used for crops requiring higher maintenance efforts.

There are still some features of sharecropping contracts that are harder to explain. One of them is that the share of output that goes to the tenant is not as responsive to economic fundamentals as theory predicts it should be. Young and Burke (2001) show that, in their sample of Illinois farms, almost all contracts have the same tenant share for all types of crops, and this share is one-half for 80 percent of the contracts. They argue that such inflexible terms are due to local custom: whereas shares do vary across regions, they are almost constant within regions. Young and Burke put this down to fairness concerns.

3.2.   Multitasking

Both the managerial pay and the sharecropping literature test traditional versions of the moral hazard model; but, more recent variants have also been tested. Slade (1996) tests the multitask agency model of Holmstrom and Milgrom (1991) on contracts between oil firms and their service stations in the Vancouver area. Service stations do not only deliver gasoline, but also may act as convenience stores and/or repair cars. In multitask models, the form of the optimal contract crucially depends on complementarity patterns between tasks: incentives should be lower powered when tasks are more complementary. Slade argues that the convenience store task is likely to be more complementary to the gasoline task than the repairs task. Thus, the theory predicts that service stations that also do repairs should face higher-powered incentives than those that run convenience stores. Slade tests this prediction by running probits for contract type: service station operators may be lessee dealers (with high-powered incentives) or commissioned agents (with low-powered incentives). She finds that, as predicted by the theory, doing repairs increases the probability of running a lessee dealership, while having a convenience store reduces it.

3.3.   Incomplete Contracts/Transaction Costs

The formal literature on incomplete contracts is still rather young, and to the best of our knowledge, it has not been submitted yet to econometric testing.[27] On the other hand, a number of papers have tested the main intuitions from the transactions cost literature as developed by Williamson (1975, 1985, 1996). We will give only a few examples; the reader can refer to more detailed surveys such as in Shelanski and Klein (1995).

Perhaps the best-known result from the transactions cost literature, following Williamson, is that, when relationship-specific investments matter more, contracts will have a longer duration (so as to avoid hold-up problems). This has been tested by Joskow (1987). He studies the relationship between coal suppliers and electric plants that burn coal in the United States in 1979.

Williamson distinguishes four types of specificity. Joskow uses three of them to construct testable predictions:

- site specificity: some electric plants are "mine-mouth" (i.e., located close to the coal mine that supplies them)
- physical asset specificity: electric plants are designed to burn a specific type of coal (but not necessarily from a specific supplier); Joskow argues that this consideration matters most in the West, less in the Midwest, and least in the East
- dedicated asset specificity: this holds when large annual quantities are contracted for

---

[27] We will discuss a descriptive study of Kaplan and Strömberg (1999).

Thus, transaction cost theory predicts that contracts should have longer duration when they involve mine-mouth plants, when the firms are in the West, and when large annual quantities are contracted for. Joskow runs a simple regression of contract duration on the three specificity variables and finds that all three hypotheses are robustly validated by the data.

Crocker and Masten (1988) also test whether the determinants of contract duration conform to what transactions cost theory predicts, with one interesting twist. This goes back to the difficulty for the analyst to know whether actual contracts optimally maintain incentives for efficient adaptation, while minimizing need for costly enforcement. Crocker and Masten argue that sometimes there is external interference from courts or government that makes contract terms deviate from the optimal trade-off in predictable ways, and this can be used by the econometrician. They use the example of natural gas, where wellhead regulation at times imposed price ceilings at the producer level. When such a price ceiling is binding, contracts should stipulate higher damages or take-or-pay rates to protect producers. Then, the contract is less efficient, and the contract duration will be shorter – unless the seller fears that the next renegotiation will lead to much lower prices. Crocker and Masten indeed find that when the price ceiling is much lower than the notional price (estimated as the latent variable in a probit model), contracts have a shorter duration. This effect is highly significant and matters a lot: price regulation may have shortened contract duration by half.

Crocker and Reynolds (1993) look at the determinants of the degree of contract incompleteness itself. They argue that this results from a trade-off between the ex ante costs of crafting more detailed arrangements and the ex post costs of inefficiencies. Because the former increase with uncertainty and complexity and the latter increase with the likelihood of opportunistic behavior, one expects that contracts will be less complete when the environment is more uncertain and complex and when opportunistic behavior is less likely. Crocker and Reynolds test these predictions on a sample of U.S. Air Force procurement contracts. They run an ordered probit for the type of the contract on variables that proxy for uncertainty and the reputation of the supplier for opportunistic behavior. Their results support the theoretical prediction.

Transactions cost theory also predicts that when quasi-rents are large, sometimes even long-term contracts will not suffice, and vertical integration will take place. A number of papers have tested this prediction and generally found good support for it. An early example is Monteverdi and Teece (1982). They looked at the "make-or-buy" decision in the automobile industry: should components be produced in-house or should they be obtained from outside suppliers? They argued that the answer depends on whether making a particular component involves much or little engineering-specific knowledge. Then, they ran a probit of the make-or-buy decision on a set of variables that included a measure of engineering-specific knowledge provided to them by an independent engineer. They found that, as predicted by the theory, components tend to be made in-house when they involve more specific knowledge.

Some less obvious results from transactions cost theory have also been tested. Thus, Crocker and Masten (1991) look at the provisions for adjusting prices during the lifetime of contracts. Some contracts rely on "redetermination provisions": price adjustment is predetermined through a more or less contingent price adjustment formula. Others emphasize renegotiation provisions, which more or less structure the process of renegotiating prices. Crocker and Masten argue that renegotiations provisions are more useful when the environment is more uncertain or the contract has a longer duration. To test this, they examine a 1982 sample of natural gas contracts in the United States. The observed price adjustment provisions are very diverse, but a probit model for renegotiation vs. redetermination validates the predictions of the theory.

Transactions cost theory has also been tested against other theories. For instance, Hubbard and Weiner (1991) use natural gas contracts in the United States in the fifties to examine whether considerations of market power or efficient contracting matter most. Market power is often invoked in this market, because switching contracting parties is difficult and thus there is an element of bilateral monopoly. A linear regression for contract prices (paid by the pipeline to the gas producer) indeed appears to show some evidence for pipeline monopsony power: prices are higher in regions with more pipelines. However, Hubbard and Weiner show that this is due to a spurious correlation: growing markets have more pipelines, but they also exhibit larger quasi-rents. The existence of these quasi-rents motivates the use of a most-favored-nation clause according to which a pipeline that has a contract with producer A and signs a new contract with producer B at a higher price must grant that new price to producer A. Because the most-favored-nation clause tends to be associated with higher prices, this generates the positive correlation between prices and the number of pipelines. That correlation thus appears to be due to efficient contracting considerations and not to market power on either side.

Most of the empirical tests of transactions cost theory have been implemented on data from relatively thin markets, where quasi-rents are large. An interesting question is whether these intuitions extend to thicker markets. This has been studied by Hubbard (1999) for the trucking industry. This is an industry in which assets are not very specific, even less so when local markets are thick. Still, there is some variation on how thick local markets are, and transactions cost theory then predicts that spot arrangements should be more likely when the local market is thicker. Hubbard runs an ordered logit on the various contractual forms in the industry that confirms this prediction.

It is fair to say that most of the empirical literature has been supportive of the basic ideas of transactions cost theory. Nevertheless, it is hard to feel completely satisfied with the methodology of these studies. One first problem is a consequence of the somewhat vague character of some of the concepts in the theory: because quasi-rents and uncertainty are such broad categories, it is very difficult to find good proxies for them. Besides, it is not always clear what the observability/verifiability status of these variables is. Consider uncertainty, for instance; in this literature, it is often proxied by the volatility of a price index. But, this is certainly verifiable information, so one still has to explain why the contract is not made contingent on the value of that price index.

A second problem with this literature is that it usually does not control for the possible endogeneity of right-hand-side variables. Consider, for instance, Joskow's (1987) study. One of the right-hand-side variables is a dummy variable for a mine-mouth location. But, we are not given any evidence on the determinants of the decision to site a plant mine-mouth; and that may certainly depend on unobserved factors that also influence contract duration, making the mine-mouth variable endogenous in the regression of contract duration. Because Joskow does not attempt to correct for endogeneity or to test for it, the estimates may be biased. A related point is that Joskow does not condition on the fact that these firms are not vertically integrated,[28] whereas the decision to not vertically integrate again may be correlated with contract duration. Clearly, these two points exemplify the endogenous matching problem that we mentioned repeatedly: regressions of contract variables on characteristics of the parties are fraught with selection bias and endogeneity problems.

Finally, what does this tell us about the more recent theory of incomplete contracts, as exposited in Hart's (1995) book? Because many of the underlying ideas started with transactions cost theory, one might think that the relative empirical success of the older theory somehow validates the newer one. However, this would certainly be premature, as argued by Whinston (2000) for theories of vertical integration. One first point is that, because incomplete contracts theory is more formalized, it has a much richer set of predictions than transactions cost theory does. By implication, it exposes itself more to empirical refutation. A second point is that testing incomplete contracts theory is bound to be a much more demanding task. Although we have argued that transactions cost theory relies on quasi-rents that may be difficult to proxy properly, the situation is even worse for incomplete contracts theory, because predictions rather precisely depend on how the marginal returns to noncontractible investments are distributed among the parties. Measuring these marginal returns reliably enough to test the predictions of the theory will require much more highly detailed information on contracting environments than is usually present in our data sets.[29]

Of course, one may forgo econometrics for the moment and take a more descriptive look at the data. A first attempt to do this is the work by Kaplan and Strömberg (1999), who analyze a large number of venture capital contracts. The authors argue that venture capitalists (VCs) are real-world entities who most closely approximate the investors of the theory; hence, relating theoretical predictions to real-life VC contracts will provide precious insights about the relevance of theory. Indeed, some of their findings tend to support standard predictions of the incomplete contract literature. Separate allocation of cash flow

---

[28] In a separate paper, Joskow (1985) explores the determinants of vertical integration for this same sample; but what we would want is a joint modeling of contract duration and the decision to integrate vertically.

[29] Whinston (2001) and Baker and Hubbard (2001) also discuss this issue.

and control rights is a standard feature of VC contracts. The allocation of rights is contingent on observed measures of financial and nonfinancial performance, especially at early stages of the relationship. Existing contracts are consistent with a basic prediction of the theory, namely that control should be left to the manager in case of success (then the VC keeps cash flow rights only), whereas it shifts to the VC when the firm's performance is poor. Finally, the importance of noncompete and vesting provisions suggests that imperfect commitment and hold-up problems are indeed an important aspect of VC contracts. However, some theories seem to fare less well than others. "Stealing" theories à la Hart and Moore (1998) or Gale and Hellwig (1982), for instance, rely on the impossibility of making contracts contingent on profits (or other measures of financial performance), an assumption that is not supported by the data. Finally, several problems are left open by the empirical investigation. For instance, existing theories cannot explain why we observe in these contracts that control rights are allocated across a number of dimensions, such as voting rights, board rights, or liquidation rights. Similarly, the variety and the complexity of the financial tools used to allocate rights – convertible securities (with specific strikes), common and preferred stocks, . . . – go well beyond the simple settings (typically, debt vs. equity) considered so far.

Finally, some recent studies usefully remind us that there may be more to incomplete contracting than transactions cost theory or the more recent approach. Banerjee and Duflo (1999) focus on the Indian-customized software industry, which writes specialized software for (usually) foreign clients. In this industry, the product is very difficult to describe ex ante; the client writes a vague description of what he wants, software firms bid by announcing a price and a time schedule, and the client chooses whom he will contract with. Much of the process of describing the functions of the software is interactive and takes place after the contract is signed. Therefore, the contracts are highly incomplete and cost overruns are frequent: Three-quarters of the contracts have cost overruns, of 25 percent of planned costs on average. Because the initial description of the software is so vague, it would be impossible for a court to decide in what proportions the overruns are due to the firm or to the client. In practice, the contracts are often renegotiated in case of cost overruns to increase the price the software firm is paid. Banerjee and Duflo find that the client is more generous in these renegotiations when he faces an older firm, especially if he has already contracted with that firm in the past. Banerjee and Duflo put it down to reputation effects: they argue that older firms have shown in the past that they were reliable, all the more so if the client has already dealt with them. They show that alternative explanations fit the data less well.[30]

McMillan and Woodruff (1999) use a survey of private firms in Vietnam to investigate the determinants of trade credit. Vietnam does not have a reliable

---

[30] In particular, this cannot be due to optimal risk-sharing, because younger firms tend to be smaller than older firms.

legal system, so trust matters a great deal. McMillan and Woodruff indeed find that a firm tends to grant more trade credit to its customers when these have no alternative supplier, when the supplier has more information about the customer's reliability, and when the supplier belongs to a business or social network that makes information available and/or makes it easier to enforce sanctions.

Baker and Hubbard (2000a) investigate the impact on asset ownership of technological changes that modify the contractibility of actions. They consider the U.S. trucking industry, where the introduction, in the late 1980s, of on-board computers (OBCs) allowed contracts to be made contingent on various operating parameters of trucks (speed, etc.). Because of the exogenous enlargement of the space of feasible contracts, suboptimal behavior becomes monitorable, and the need for powerful incentive schemes (such as ownership by drivers) is reduced. Using a survey of the U.S. trucking fleet, they actually find that OBC adoption leads to less driver ownership. All OBCs are not equal, however: some improve the monitoring of drivers and others improve the coordination of the fleets. Baker and Hubbard (2000b) argue that this distinction is relevant to the make-or-buy decision (whether the shipper should use an internal or an external fleet): equipments that improve monitoring (respectively coordination) should lead to more (respectively less) integration. Using the same survey, they find supporting evidence for this prediction.

3.4.   Dynamics of Contracts

Finally, a few papers have tried to take the predictions of dynamic contract theory to data. This is a difficult task, if only because the theory is often inconclusive or relies on very strong assumptions that are difficult to maintain within an applied framework.[31] Still, interesting insights have emerged from this line of work.

Three types of models have been considered in the literature. One is the pure model of repeated adverse selection; a second one considers repeated moral hazard; finally, a couple of papers have recently been devoted to empirical testing of models entailing symmetric learning.

3.4.1.   Dynamic Models of Asymmetric Information

An important contribution is due to Dionne and Doherty (1994), whose model of repeated adverse selection with one-sided commitment transposes previous

---

[31] For instance, most papers in the field assume that agents cannot freely save or borrow, so that the dynamics of their consumption can be fully monitored by the principal (whether the latter is an employer, a landlord, or an insurance company). When this assumption is relaxed, the models typically use very specific preferences (such as constant absolute risk aversion with monetary cost of effort) to guarantee that income effects do not matter. For a detailed discussion in a moral hazard context, see Chiappori et al. (1994).

work by Laffont and Tirole (1990) to a competitive framework. The key testable prediction is that, in a repeated adverse selection framework of this kind, whenever commitment is possible for the insurer, then optimal contracts entail experience rating and exhibit a "highballing" property (i.e., the insurance company makes positive profits in the first period, compensated by low, below-cost second-period prices). Dionne and Doherty test this property on Californian automobile insurance data. According to the theory, when contracts with and without commitment (from the insurer) are simultaneously available, contracts entailing commitments will typically attract low-risk agents. The presence of highballing is empirically characterized by the fact that the loss to premium ratio should rise with the cohort age. If insurance companies are classified according to their average loss per vehicle (which reflects the "quality" of their portfolio of insurees), one expects the premium growth to be negative for the best-quality portfolios; in addition, the corresponding slope should be larger for firms with higher average loss ratios. This prediction is confirmed by the data. Insurance companies are classified into three subgroups. The slope coefficient is negative and significant for the first group (with lowest average loss), positive and significant for the third group, and nonsignificant for the intermediate group. Dionne and Doherty conclude that the "highballing" prediction is not rejected.

In a recent contribution, Margiotta and Miller (2000) analyze a dynamic model of managerial compensation under moral hazard. Their framework is reminiscent of that introduced by Fudenberg, Holmstrom, and Milgrom (1990): the manager's utility function exhibits constant absolute risk aversion, so that wealth effects do not make the analysis untractable. They estimate the model from longitudinal data on returns to firms and managerial compensations. Obviously, the dynamic nature of the data introduces more robustness into the estimations, compared with simple cross-sectional analysis. In particular, it allows mitigation of an obvious selection problem with cross-sectional data: the level of incentives provided by the manager's contract should be endogenous to the firm's situation, and the latter may impact the outcome in a nonobservable way. The conclusions drawn by Margiotta and Miller are particularly interesting in view of the Jensen–Murphy controversy. They find that, although the benefits of providing incentives are large, the costs are small, in the sense that even a relatively small fraction of the firm's shares is generally sufficient to induce the required level of effort.

3.4.2.   Symmetric Learning

Finally, several works test a model of symmetric but incomplete information and learning. The basic reference, here, is the labor contract paper by Harris and Holmstrom (1992), in which the employer and the employee have identical priors about the employee's ability and learn at the same pace from the employee's performance. This setting has been applied with success to labor contracts, but also to long-term insurance relationships.

An application to internal labor markets is proposed by Chiappori, Salanié, and Valentin (1999). Their model borrows the two main ingredients of the Harris and Holmstrom framework, namely symmetric learning and downward rigidity of wages (the latter being explained either by risk-sharing considerations as in the initial model or by hold-up problems and contractual incompleteness). They show that optimal contracts should then exhibit a "late beginner" effect: if two agents, A and B, are at the same wage level at date 0 and at date 2, but A's wage at date 1 was higher, then B has better future prospects for date 3 and later. They test this prediction on data on contracts and careers within a French public firm. Interestingly enough, careers, in this context, must be analyzed as sequences of discrete promotions – a feature that requires specific econometric tools. The results very strongly confirm the predictions: the "late beginner" effect seems like a crucial feature of careers in the context under consideration.

Recently, the same type of model has been applied to life insurance contracts by Hendel and Lizzeri (2000). They exploit an interesting database of contracts that includes information on the entire profile of future premiums. Some contracts involve commitment from the insurer, in the sense that the evolution of premia will not be contingent on the insuree's health status, whereas under the other contracts future premiums are increased if the insuree's health condition deteriorates. According to the theory, commitment implies front loading (initial premiums should be higher than without commitment, because they include an insurance premium against the reclassification risk) and a lower lapsation rate (a fraction of the agents whose health has actually deteriorated would be *strictly* worse off if they were to change company). These predictions are satisfied by existing contracts. Even more interesting is the fact that this confirmation obtains only for general life insurance. Accidental death contracts exhibit none of these features, as one would expect, given that learning considerations are much less prominent.

Finally, in such a context, any friction that limits the agent's mobility between contracts is welfare-improving, because the precommitment of insurees to stay in the pool helps mitigate the uninsurability of the reclassification risk. This idea is exploited by Crocker and Moran (1997) in a study of employer-provided health insurance contracts, for which precommitment is proxied by the difficulty for workers of switching jobs. They show that when employers must offer the same contract to all of their workers, then the optimal contract exhibits a coverage limitation that is inversely proportional to the degree of employee job lock. If, on the other hand, employers are able to offer multiple contracts that experience-rate the insurees, then the optimal contract exhibits full coverage of medical expenditures, albeit at second-period premiums that partially reflect each individual's observable health status. Crocker and Moran confirm these predictions on data with insurance coverages using proxies for job lock: the insurance contracts associated with firms who offer a single policy exhibit coverage limitations that are decreasing in the amount of employee job lock, and those firms offering multiple plans to their workforce have higher levels of coverage that are insensitive to the degree of job lock.

4. CONCLUSIONS

"Data! data! data!" he cried impatiently. "I can't make bricks without clay."
Arthur Conan Doyle, *The Adventure of the Copper Beeches.*

We hope this survey has shown that the econometrics of contracts is a very promising and burgeoning field. Although empirical testing of the theory of contracts started in the eighties, most of the papers we have surveyed were indeed written in the last 5 years. For a long time, econometricians could be heard echoing Sherlock Holmes's complaint about lack of data on contracts. It is true that some researchers have gone far to find their data [as far as Renaissance Tuscany for Ackerberg and Botticini (2002)]. Still, it has proven much less difficult than expected to find data amenable to econometric techniques. In fact, we draw the impression from Bresnahan's (1997) earlier World Congress survey that the situation is somewhat worse in industrial organization.

It is still true that many papers in this field use similar data and/or focus on similar problems, as shown by the number of papers on sharecropping or natural gas we surveyed. We would certainly want to see wider-ranging empirical work in the future. Insurance data are very promising in that respect, because they are fairly standardized, come in large data sets, and can be used to test many different theories. It can also be hoped that, in the future, firms will be less averse to opening their personnel data to researchers, as they did to Baker, Gibbs, and Holmstrom (1994a, 1994b).

Our conclusion on the importance of incentive effects echoes that of Prendergast (1999) for incentives in firms: the recent literature, as surveyed in Section 2, provides very strong evidence that contractual forms have large effects on behavior. As the notion that "incentives matter" is one of the central tenets of economists of every persuasion, this should be comforting to the community. On the other hand, it raises an old puzzle: if contractual form matters so much, why do we observe such a prevalence of fairly simple contracts? More generally, the question asked in Section 3 is whether observed contracts take the form predicted by the theory. As we have seen, the evidence is more mixed in that regard. However, it is reassuring to see that papers that control adequately for selection and endogeneity bias have generally been more supportive of the theory.

Throughout this survey, we emphasized the crucial role of the selection, matching, and contract endogeneity issues. These problems are prevalent in the two approaches we distinguish (i.e., whether one is testing for the optimality of contracts or for the behavioral impact of given contractual forms). It can be argued that selection issues are probably even more difficult to address in the first case, because our theoretical understanding of situations involving "realistic" forms of unobserved heterogeneity is often very incomplete. To take but one example, Rothchild and Stiglitz's (1976) celebrated model of insurance under adverse selection assumes identical preferences across agents. Should risk aversion differ across insurees as well, then the shape of the equilibrium contract is not fully known for the moment.[32] It is safe, however, to predict that where the theory cannot be reconciled with the facts, new and improved models will emerge. Thus we hope that some econometricians will be inspired by this survey to contribute to the growing literature on testing of contract theory, while negative empirical findings may prompt some theorists to improve the theory itself. As an example of this potentially fruitful dialog between theorists and econometricians, the empirical findings by Chiappori and Salanié (1997, 2000) and others that the standard models of insurance do not fit the data well in some insurance markets has led Chassagnon and Chiappori (1997), Jullien, Salanié, and Salanié (2000), and de Meza and Webb (2001) to propose new models of insurance that are based on a combination of moral hazard and adverse selection. Similarly, new tools have recently been developed that allow tackling the possible coexistence of several types of unobserved heterogeneity.[33] We hope to see more of this interplay between theory and testing in the future.

ACKNOWLEDGMENTS

We thank our discussant Patrick Legros and Jeff Campbell, Pierre Dubois, Phillippe Gagnepain, Lars Hansen, Jim Heckman, Patrick Legros, Bruce Shearer, Steve Tadelis, and Rob Townsend for their comments. This paper was written while Salanié was visiting the University of Chicago, which he thanks for its hospitality.

References

Ackerberg, D. and M. Botticini (2002), "Endogenous Matching and the Empirical Determinants of Contract Form," *Journal of Political Economy*, 110(3), 564–91

Aggarwal, R. and A. Samwick (1999), "The Other Side of the Trade-off: The Impact of Risk on Executive Compensation," *Journal of Political Economy*, 107, 65–105.

Akerlof, G. (1970), "The Market for 'Lemons': Quality Uncertainty and the Market Mechanism," *Quarterly Journal of Economics*, 84, 488–500.

Allen, D. W. and D. Lueck (1992), "Contract Choice in Modern Agriculture: Cash Rent Versus Cropshare," *Journal of Law and Economics*, 35, 397–426.

Allen, D. W. and D. Lueck (1993), "Transaction Costs and the Design of Cropshare Contracts," *Rand Journal of Economics*, 24(1), 78–100.

Allen, D. W. and D. Lueck (1998), "The Nature of the Farm," *Journal of Law and Economics*, 41, 343–386.

Allen, D. W. and D. Lueck (1999), "The Role of Risk in Contract Choice," *Journal of Law, Economics and Organization*, 15(3), 704–736.

Ausubel, L. (1999), "Adverse Selection in the Credit Card Market," mimeo, University of Maryland.

---

[32] See Landsberger and Meilijson (1999).
[33] See Rochet and Stole in this volume (pp. 150–197).

Bach, K. (1998), *Negativauslese und Tarifdifferenzierung im Versicherungs-sektor.* DUV, Schesslitz.

Baker, G., M. Gibbs, and B. Holmstrom (1994a), "The Internal Economics of the Firm: Evidence from Personnel Data," *Quarterly Journal of Economics*, 109, 881–919.

Baker, G., M. Gibbs, and B. Holmstrom (1994b), "The Wage Policy of a Firm," *Quarterly Journal of Economics*, 109, 921–955.

Baker, G. and T. Hubbard (2000a), "Contractibility and Asset Ownership: On-Board Computers and Governance in U.S. Trucking," NBER Working Paper 7634.

Baker, G. and T. Hubbard (2000b), "Make vs. Buy in Trucking: Asset Ownership, Job Design, and Information," mimeo, Harvard University.

Baker, G. and T. Hubbard (2001), "Empirical Strategies in Contract Economics: Information and the Boundary of the Firm," *American Economic Review*, 91, 189–194.

Bandiera, O. (2001), "On the Structure of, Tenancy Contracts: Theory and Evidence from 19th Century Rural Sicily," CEPR Working Paper 3032.

Banerjee, A. and E. Duflo (1999), "Reputation Effects and the Limits of Contracting: A Study of the Indian Software Industry," mimeo, MIT.

Banerjee, A., P. Gertler, and M. Ghatak (2002), "Empowerment and Efficiency: Tenancy Reform in West Bengal," *Journal of Political Economy*, 110, 239–280.

Bertrand, M. and S. Mullainathan (2001), "Are CEOs Rewarded for Luck? The Ones without Principals are," *Quarterly Journal of Economics*, 116, 901–932.

Bolduc, D., B. Fortin, F. Labrecque, and P. Lanoie (1997), "Workers' Compensation, Moral Hazard and the Composition of Workplace Injuries," mimeo, HEC, Montreal.

Boyer, M. and G. Dionne (1989), "An Empirical Analysis of Moral Hazard and Experience Rating," *Review of Economics and Statistics*, 71, 128–134.

Bresnahan, T. (1997), "Testing and Measurement in Competition Models," in *Advances in Economics and Econometrics–Theory and Applications, Volume 3*, (ed. by D. Kreps and K. Wallis), Econometric Society Monographs, 28, Cambridge University Press, pp. 61–81.

Browne, M., and R. Puelz (1999), "The Effect of Legal Rules on the Value of Economic and Non-Economic Damages and the Decision to File," *Journal of Risk and Uncertainty*, 18, 189–213.

Brugiavini, A. (1993), "Uncertainty Resolution and the Timing of Annuity Purchase," *Journal of Public Economics*, 50, 31–62.

Cardon, J. and I. Hendel (2001), "Asymmetric Information in Health Insurance: Evidence from the National Health Expenditure Survey," *Rand Journal of Economics*, 32, 408–427.

Cawley, J. and T. Philipson (1999), "An Empirical Examination of Information Barriers to Trade in Insurance," *American Economic Review*, 89, 827–846.

Chevalier, J. and G. Ellison (1997), "Risk Taking by Mutual Funds as a Response to Incentives," *Journal of Political Economy*, 105, 1167–1200.

Chevalier, J. and G. Ellison (1999), "Career Concerns of Mutual Fund Managers," *Quarterly Journal of Economics*, 114, 389–432.

Chassagnon, A. and P. A. Chiappori (1997), "Insurance under Moral Hazard and Adverse Selection: The Competitive Case," mimeo, DELTA.

Chiappori, P. A. (2000), "Econometric Models of Insurance under Asymmetric Information," *Handbook of Insurance*, (ed. by G. Dionne), Amsterdam: North-Holland.

Chiappori, P. A., J. Abbring, J. Heckman, and J. Pinquet (2001), "Testing for Adverse Selection Versus Moral Hazard from Dynamic Data," mimeo, University of Chicago.

Chiappori, P. A., F. Durand, and P. Y. Geoffard (1998), "Moral Hazard and the Demand for Physician Services: First Lessons from a French Natural Experiment," *European Economic Review*, 42, 499–511.

Chiappori, P. A., P. Y. Geoffard, and E. Kyriazidou (2000), "Cost of Time, Moral Hazard, and the Demand for Physician Services," mimeo, University of Chicago.

Chiappori, P. A., I. Macho, P. Rey, and B. Salanié (1994), "Repeated Moral Hazard: The Role of Memory and Commitment, and the Access to Credit Markets," *European Economic Review*, 38, 1527–1553.

Chiappori, P. A. and B. Salanié (1997), "Empirical Contract Theory: The Case of Insurance Data," *European Economic Review*, 41, 943–950.

Chiappori, P. A. and B. Salanié (2000), "Testing for Asymmetric Information in Insurance Markets," *Journal of Political Economy*, 108, 56–78.

Chiappori, P. A., B. Salanié, and J. Valentin (1999), "Early Starters versus Late Beginners." *Journal of Political Economy*, 107, 731–760.

Cochrane, J. (1991), "A Simple Test of Consumption Insurance," *Journal of Political Economy*, 99, 957–976.

Core, J. and W. Guay (2000), "The Other Side of the Trade-off: The Impact of Risk on Executive Compensation: a Comment," mimeo, Wharton School.

Crocker, K. and S. Masten (1988), "Mitigating Contractual Hazards: Unilateral Options and Contract Length," *Rand Journal of Economics*, 19, 327–343.

Crocker, K. and S. Masten (1991), "Pretia Ex Machina? Prices and Process in Long-Term Contracts," *Journal of Law and Economics*, 34, 69–99.

Crocker, K. and J. Moran (1997), "Commitment and the Design of Optimal Agreements: Evidence from Employment-Based Health Insurance Contract," mimeo, University of Michigan.

Crocker, K. and K. Reynolds (1993), "The Efficiency of Incomplete Contracts: An Empirical Analysis of Air Force Engine Procurement," *Rand Journal of Economics*, 24, 126–146.

Dahlby, B. (1983), "Adverse Selection and Statistical Discrimination: An Analysis of Canadian Automobile Insurance," *Journal of Public Economics*, 20, 121–130.

de Meza, D. and D. Webb (2001), "Advantageous Selection in Insurance Markets," *Rand Journal of Economics*, 32, 249–262.

Dionne, G. and N. Doherty (1994), "Adverse Selection, Commitment and Renegotiation: Extension to and Evidence from Insurance Markets," *Journal of Political Economy*, 102(2), 210–235.

Dionne, G. and R. Gagné (2001), "Deductible Contracts against Fraudulent Claims: Evidence from Automobile Insurance," *Review of Economics and Statistics*, 83, 290–301.

Dionne, G., C. Gouriéroux, and C. Vanasse (2001), "Testing for Adverse Selection in the Automobile Insurance Market: A Comment," *Journal of Political Economy*, 109, 444–453.

Dionne, G, and P. St-Michel (1991), "Worker's Compensation and Moral Hazard," *Review of Economics and Statistics*, 73, 236–244.

Dionne, G., and C. Vanasse (1996), "Une évaluation empirique de la nouvelle tarification de l'assurance automobile au Québec," mimeo, Montreal.

Dubois, P. (1999), "Moral Hazard, Land Fertility, and Sharecropping in a Rural Area of the Philippines," CREST Working Paper 9930.

Dubois, P. (2000a), "Assurance complète, hétérogénéité des préférences et métayage au Pakistan," *Annales d'Économie et de Statistiques*, 59, 1–36.

Dubois, P. (2000b), "Consumption Insurance with Heterogeneous Preferences: Can Sharecropping Help Complete Markets?," mimeo, INRA, Toulouse.

Ferrall, C. and B. Shearer (1999), "Incentives and Transactions Cost within the Firm: Estimating an Agency Model Using Payroll Records," *Review of Economic Studies*, 66, 309–338.

Finkelstein, A. and J. Poterba (2000), "Adverse Selection in Insurance Markets: Policy-holder Evidence from the U.K. Annuity Market," NBER Working Paper W8045.

Fortin, B. and P. Lanoie (1992), "Substitution between Unemployment Insurance and Workers' Compensation," *Journal of Public Economics*, 49, 287–312.

Fortin, B. and P. Lanoie (1998), "Effects of Workers' Compensation: A Survey," *CIRANO Scientific Series*, Montréal, 98s–104s.

Fortin, B., P. Lanoie, and C. Laporte (1995), "Is Workers' Compensation Disguised Unemployment Insurance?" *CIRANO Scientific Series*, Montréal, 95s-148s.

Friedman, B. M. and M. J. Warshawski (1990), "The Cost of Annuities: Implications for Savings Behavior and Bequests," *Quarterly Journal of Economics*, 105, 135–154.

Fudenberg, D., B. Holmstrom, and P. Milgrom (1990), "Short-Term Contracts and Long-Term Agency Relationships," *Journal of Economic Theory*, 51, 1–31.

Gagnepain, P. and M. Ivaldi (2001), "Incentive Regulatory Policies: The Case of Public Transit Systems in France," mimeo.

Gale, D. and M. Hellwig (1985), "Incentive-Compatible Debt Contracts: The One-Period Problem," *Review of Economic Studies*, 52, 647–663.

Gibbons, R. and K. Murphy (1990), "Relative Performance Evaluation of Chief Executive Officers," *Industrial and Labor Relations Review*, 43, S30–S51.

Gibbons, R. and M. Waldman (1999), "Careers in Organizations: Theory and Evidence, *Handbook of Labor Economics*," Volume 3b (ed. by O. Ashenfelter and D. Card): North-Holland, Amsterdam, 2373–2437

Gouriéroux, C. (1999), "The Econometrics of Risk Classification in Insurance," *Geneva Papers on Risk and Insurance Theory*, 24, 119–139.

Gouriéroux, C., A. Monfort, and A. Trognon (1984), "Pseudo-Maximum Likelihood Methods: Theory," *Econometrica*, 52, 681–700.

Hall, J. and J. Liebman (1998), "Are CEOs Really Paid Like Bureaucrats?" *Quarterly Journal of Economics*, 113, 653–691.

Hanssen, R. (2001), "The Effect of a Technological Shock on Contract Form: Revenue Sharing in Movie Exhibition and the Coming of Sound," mimeo.

Harris, M. and B. Holmstrom (1982), "A Theory of Wage Dynamics," *Review of Economic Studies*, 49, 315–333.

Hart, O. (1995), *Firms, Contracts, and Financial Structure*. London: Oxford University Press.

Hart, O. and J. Tirole (1988), "Contract Renegotiation and Coasian Dynamics," *Review of Economic Studies*, 55, 509–540.

Haubrich, J. (1994), "Risk Aversion, Performance Pay, and the Principal-Agent Model," *Journal of Political Economy*, 102, 258–276.

Hendel, I. and A. Lizzeri (2000), "The Role of Commitment in Dynamic Contracts: Evidence from Life Insurance," Working Paper, Princeton University.

Holly, A., L. Gardiol, G. Domenighetti, and B. Bisig (1998), "An Econometric Model of Health Care Utilization and Health Insurance in Switzerland," *European Economic Review*, 42, 513–522.

Holmstrom, B. and P. Milgrom (1991), "Multitask Principal-Agent Analyses: Incentive

Contracts, Asset Ownership and Job Design," *Journal of Law, Economics and Organization*, 7, 24–51.

Hubbard, T. (1999), "How Wide Is the Scope of Hold-Up-Based Theories? Contractual Form and Market Thickness in Trucking," mimeo, UCLA .

Hubbard, R. and R. Weiner (1991), "Efficient Contracting and Market Power: Evidence from the U.S. Natural Gas Industry," *Journal of Law and Economics*, 34, 25–67.

Ivaldi, M. and D. Martimort (1994), "Competition under Nonlinear Pricing," *Annales d'Economie et de Statistiques*, 34, 72–114.

Jensen, M. and K. Murphy (1990), "Performance Pay and Top-Management Incentives," *Journal of Political Economy*, 98, 225–264.

Joskow, P. (1985), "Vertical Integration and Long-Term Contracts: The Case of Coal-Burning Electric Generation Plants," *Journal of Law, Economics, and Organization*, 1, 33–80.

Joskow, P. (1987)," Contract Duration and Relationship-Specific Investments: Empirical Evidence from Coal Markets," *American Economic Review*, 77, 168–185.

Jullien, B., B. Salanié, and F. Salanié (2000), "Screening Risk-Averse Agents under Moral Hazard," mimeo.

Kaplan, S. and P. Strömberg (1999), "Financial Contracting Theory Meets the Real World: Evidence from Venture Capital Contracts," mimeo.

Laffont, J. J. (1997), "Game Theory and Empirical Economics: The Case of Auction Data," *European Economic Review*, 41, 1–35.

Laffont, J.-J. and M. Matoussi (1995), "Moral Hazard, Financial Constraints and Share-cropping in El Oulja," *Review of Economic Studies*, 62, 381–399.

Laffont, J.-J. and J. Tirole (1990), "Adverse Selection and Renegotiation in Procurement," *Review of Economic Studies*, 57(4), 597–625.

Landsberger, M. and I. Meilijson (1999), "A General Model of Insurance under Adverse Selection," *Economic Theory*, 14, 331–352.

Lavergne, P., and A. Thomas (2000), "Semiparametric Estimation and Testing in a Model of Environmental Regulation with Adverse Selection," mimeo, INSEE, Paris.

Lazear, E. (2000), "Performance Pay and Productivity," *American Economic Review*, 90, 1346–1361.

Lemmon, M., J. Schallheim, and J. Zender (2000), "Do Incentives Matter? Managerial Contracts for Dual-Purpose Funds," *Journal of Political Economy*, 108, 273–299.

MacLeod, B., and D. Parent (1999), "Job Characteristics and the Form of Compensation," *Research in Labor Economics*, 18, 177–242.

Manning, W., J. Newhouse, N. Duan, E. Keeler, and A. Leibowitz (1987), "Health Insurance and the Demand for Medical Care: Evidence from a Randomized Experiment," *American Economic Review*, 77, 251–277.

Margiotta, M. and R. Miller (2000), "Managerial Compensation and the Cost of Moral Hazard," *International Economic Review*, 41, 669–719.

Masten, S. and K. Crocker (1985), "Efficient Adaptation in Long-Term Contracts: Take-or-Pay Provisions for Natural Gas," *American Economic Review*, 75, 1083–1093.

McMillan, J. and C. Woodruff (1999), "Interfirm Relationships and Informal Credit in Vietnam," *Quarterly Journal of Economics*, 114, 1285–1320.

Monteverdi, K. and D. Teece (1982), "Supplier Switching Costs and Vertical Integration in the Automobile Industry," *Bell Journal of Economics*, 13, 206–213.

Murphy, K. (1999), "Executive Compensation," in *Handbook of Labor Economics,* Vol. 3, (ed. by O. Ashenfelter and D. Card), Amsterdam: North-Holland.

Oyer, P. (1998), "Fiscal Year End and Nonlinear Incentive Contracts: The Effect on Business Seasonality," *Quarterly Journal of Economics,* 113, 149–185.

Paarsch, H. and B. Shearer (1999), "The Response of Worker Effort to Piece Rates: Evidence from the British Columbia Tree-Planting Industry," *Journal of Human Resources,* 34, 643–667.

Paarsch, H. and B. Shearer (2000), "Piece Rates, Fixed Wages, and Incentive Effects: Statistical Evidence from Payroll Records," *International Economic Review,* 41, 59–92.

Prendergast, C. (1999), "The Provision of Incentives in Firms," *Journal of Economic Literature,* 37, 7–63.

Puelz, R. and A. Snow (1994), "Evidence on Adverse Selection: Equilibrium Signaling and Cross-Subsidization in the Insurance Market," *Journal of Political Economy,* 102, 236–257.

Richaudeau, D. (1999), "Automobile Insurance Contracts and Risk of Accident: An Empirical Test Using French Individual Data," *Geneva Papers on Risk and Insurance Theory,* 24, 97–114.

Rosen, S. (1992), "Contracts and the Market for Executives," in *Contract Economics,* (ed. by L. Werin and H. Wijkander), Oxford, UK: Basil Blackwell.

Rothschild, M. and J. Stiglitz (1976), "Equilibrium in Competitive Insurance Markets," *Quarterly Journal of Economics,* 90, 629–649.

Shearer, B. (1999), "Piece Rates, Fixed Wages and Incentives: Evidence from a Field Experiment," mimeo, Laval University.

Shelanski, H. and P. Klein (1995), "Empirical Research in Transaction Cost Economics: A Review and Assessment," *Journal of Law, Economics and Organization,* 11, 335–361.

Slade, M. (1996), "Multitask Agency and Contract Choice: An Empirical Exploration," *International Economic Review,* 37, 465–486.

Stiglitz, J. (1974), "Incentives and Risk Sharing in Sharecropping," *Review of Economic Studies,* 41, 219–255.

Stiglitz, J. and A. Weiss (1981), "Credit Rationing in Markets with Imperfect Information," *American Economic Review,* 71, 393–410.

Timmins, C. (2002), "Measuring the Dynamic Efficiency Costs of Regulators' Preferences: Municipal Water Utilities in the Arid West," *Econometrica* 70(2), 603–29.

Toivanen, O. and R. Cressy (1998), "Is There Adverse Selection on the Credit Market?" mimeo, Warwick.

Townsend, R. (1994), "Risk and Insurance in Village India," *Econometrica,* 62, 539–591.

Vuong, Q. (1989), "Likelihood Ratio Tests for Model Selection and Non-Nested Hypotheses," *Econometrica,* 57, 307–334.

Whinston, M. (2000), "On the Transaction Cost Determinants of Vertical Integration," mimeo, Northwestern University.

Whinston, M. (2001), "Assessing the Property Rights and Transaction Cost Theories of Firm Scope," *American Economic Review,* 91, 184–188.

Williamson, O. (1975), *Markets and Hierarchies: Analysis and Antitrust Implications.* New York: The Free Press.

Williamson, O. (1985), *The Economic Institutions of Capitalism: Firms, Markets, Relational Contracting.* New York: The Free Press.

Williamson, O. (1996), *The Mechanisms of Governance*. London: Oxford University Press.

Wolak, F. (1994), "An Econometric Analysis of the Asymmetric Information, Regulator-Utility Interaction," *Annales d'Economie et de Statistiques*, 34, 13–69.

Young, P. and M. Burke (2001), "Competition and Custom in Economic Contracts: A Case Study of Illinois Agriculture," *American Economic Review*, 91, 559–573.

CHAPTER 5

The Economics of Multidimensional Screening
Jean-Charles Rochet and Lars A. Stole

1. MOTIVATION AND INTRODUCTION

Since the late 1970s, the theory of optimal screening contracts has received considerable attention. The analysis has been usefully applied to such topics as optimal taxation, public good provision, nonlinear pricing, imperfect competition in differentiated industries, regulation with information asymmetries, government procurement, and auctions, to name a few prominent examples.[1] The majority of these applications have made the assumption that preferences can be ordered by a single dimension of private information, largely to facilitate finding the optimal solution of the design problem. However, in most cases that we can think of, a multidimensional preference parameterization seems critical to capturing the basic economics of the environment. For example, consider the case of duopolists in a market where each firm competes with nonlinear pricing over its product line. In many examples of nonlinear pricing (e.g., Mussa and Rosen 1978 and Maskin and Riley 1984), it is natural to think of consumers' preferences being ordered by the willingness to pay for additional units of quantity or quality. But, if we believe that competition between duopolists is imperfect in the horizontal dimension as suggested, for example, by models such as Hotelling's (1929), then we need to introduce a form of horizontal heterogeneity as well. As a consequence, a minimally accurate model of imperfect competition between duopolists suggests including *two* dimensions of heterogeneity – vertical and horizontal.

There are several additional economic applications that naturally lend themselves to multidimensional heterogeneity.

- General models of pricing. In some instances, a firm may offer a single product over which the preferences of the consumer may depend

---

[1] Among the seminal contributions, we can cite Mirrlees (1971, 1976) for optimal taxation, Green and Laffont (1977) for public good provision, Spence (1980) and Goldman, Leland, and Sibley (1984) for nonlinear pricing, Mussa and Rosen (1978) for imperfect competition in differentiated industries, Baron and Myerson (1982), Baron and Besanko (1984), McAfee and McMillan (1987), and Laffont and Tirole (1986, 1993) for regulation, and Myerson (1981) for auctions.

importantly on several dimensions of uncertainty (e.g., tastes, marginal utility of income, etc.). In other instances, a firm may be selling an array of distinct products, of which consumers may desire any subset of the total bundle of goods. In this latter case, the dimension of heterogeneity of consumers' preferences for the firm's products will be at least as large as the number of distinct products.

- Regulation under richer asymmetries of information. As noted in the seminal article by Baron and Myerson (1982) on regulation under private information, at least two dimensions of private cost information naturally arise – fixed and marginal costs. Another example is studied by Lewis and Sappington (1988) in which the regulator is simultaneously uncertain about cost and demand. If we wish to take the normative consequences of asymmetric information models of regulation seriously, we should check the robustness of the results to such reasonable bidimensional private information.

- Income effects and related phenomena. Many times it makes sense to think of two-dimensional information when privately known budget constraints or other forms of limited liability are present. For example, how should a seller design a price schedule when customers have random valuations and simultaneously random budget constraints?

- Auctions. Similar to the aforementioned problem, we may suppose that multiple buyers bid for a single item, but their preferences depend on a privately known budget constraint in addition to a private valuation for the good (as in Che and Gale, 1998, 1999, 2000). Or in another important auction setting, suppose (as in Jehiel, Moldovanu, and Stacchetti 1999) that a buyer's preferences depend not only on his own valuation of the good, but also on the privately known externality from someone else getting the good instead (e.g., two downstream firms bid for an exclusive franchise and the loser must compete against the winner with an inferior product). Although in this paper, we do not consider the auction literature in depth, the techniques of optimal contract design in multidimensional environments are clearly relevant.[2]

Unfortunately, the techniques for confronting multidimensional settings are far less straightforward as in the one-dimensional paradigm. This difficulty has meant that the bulk of applied theory papers in the self-selection literature are based on one-dimensional models of heterogeneity. As a consequence, the results of these economic applications remain uncomfortably restrictive and possibly inaccurate (or at least nonrobust) in their conclusions. In this sense, we have been searching under the proverbial street lamp, looking for our lost keys, not because that is where we believe them to lie, but because it is apparently the only place where we can see. This survey is an attempt to catalog and

---

[2] Other multidimensional auctions problems are studied by Gal, Landsberger, and Nemirovski (1999) and Zheng (2000).

explain the terrain that has been discovered in the brief forays away from the one-dimensional street lamp – indicating both what we have learned and how light or dark the night sky actually is.

In Section 2, we review the one-dimensional paradigm, emphasizing those aspects that will generate problems as we extend the analysis to multiple dimensions. In Section 3, the general multidimensional paradigm is explained for both the discrete and continuous settings. We illustrate the concepts in a simple two-type "multidimensional" model, explaining how the multidimensionality of types introduces new economic and mathematical aspects of the screening problem. In Sections 4–9, we specialize our discussion to specific classes of multidimensional models that have proven successful in the applied literature. Section 4 presents results on separation and aggregation that greatly simplify multidimensional screening. Section 5 considers environments in which there is a single, nonmonetary contracting variable, but multiple dimensions of type – a scenario that also frequently gives rise to explicit solutions. Section 6 looks at a further specialized subset of models (from Section 5) that are economically important and mathematically tractable: bidimensional private information settings in which one dimension of information enters the agent's utility function additively. Section 7 considers a series of multidimensional models that have been successfully applied to competitive environments. Section 8 considers a distinct set of multidimensional environments in which information is revealed over time. Finally, Section 9 considers the more subtle problems inherent in general models of multiple instruments and multidimensional preferences; here, most papers written to date have considered the scenario of multiproduct monopoly bundling, so we study this model in some detail. Section 10 concludes.

2. A REVIEW OF THE ONE-DIMENSIONAL PREFERENCE MODEL

Although it is often recognized that agents typically have several characteristics and that principals typically have several instruments, the screening problem has most of the time been examined under the assumption of a single characteristic and a single instrument (in addition to monetary transfers). In this case, several qualitative results can be obtained with some generality:

1. When the single-crossing condition is satisfied, only local (first- and second-order) incentive compatibility constraints can be binding.
2. In most problems, the second-order (local) incentive compatibility constraints can be ignored, provided that the distribution of types is not too irregular.
3. If bunching is ruled out, then the principal's optimal mechanism is found in two steps:
    (a) First, compute the minimum expected rent of the agent as a function of the allocation of (nonmonetary) goods.

(b) Second, find the allocation of goods that maximizes the surplus
of the principal, net of the expected rent computed in (a).

To understand the difficulties inherent in designing optimal screening contracts when preferences are multidimensional, it is useful to first review this
basic one-dimensional paradigm. This will serve both as a building block for
the multidimensional extensions and as an illustration of how one-dimensional
preferences generate simplicity and recursion in the optimization program.

We will use a simple nonlinear pricing framework similar to Mussa and
Rosen (1978) as our basic screening environment, elaborating as appropriate.
Suppose that a monopolist sells its products using a nonlinear tariff, $P(q)$, where
q is the amount of quantity chosen by the consumer and $P(q)$ is the associated
price. The population of potential consumers of the firm's good have preferences
that can be indexed by a single-dimensional parameter, $\theta \in \Theta \equiv [\underline{\theta}, \overline{\theta}]$, and is
distributed in the population according to the absolutely continuous distribution
function $F(\theta)$, where $f(\theta) \equiv F'(\theta)$ represents the associated density. Let each
consumer's preferences for consuming $q \in \mathcal{Q} \equiv [0, \bar{q}]$ for a price of P be given
by

$$u = v(q, \theta) - P.$$

Note that preferences are linear in money. To place some additional structure on the effect of θ, we assume the well-known, single-crossing property
that $v_{q\theta}$ has a constant sign; in this paper, we will associate higher types
with higher marginal valuations of consumption; hence, $v_{q\theta} > 0$. This condition makes the one-dimensional assumption restrictive.[3] It is worth noting
that this condition has two equivalent implications: (i) the indifference curves
of any two types of consumers cross at most once in price-quantity space, and
(ii) the associated demand curves do not intersect and are completely ordered as
a family of curves given by $p = v_q(q, \theta)$. We will begin our focus on the even
simpler linear-quadratic setting in which $v(q, \theta) = \theta q - \frac{1}{2}q^2$. In this case, the
associated demand curves are parallel lines, $p = \theta - q$.

There are two methodologies used to solve one-dimensional screening
problems – what we refer to as the parametric-utility approach and the demand-
profile approach. The former has been more commonly used in the applied theory literature, but the latter provides useful conceptual insights, particularly in
the multidimensional context, that are easily overlooked in the former methodology. For completeness, we will briefly present both here.[4]

---

[3] In a discrete setting, for example, multidimensional types can always be reassigned to a one-
dimensional parameter, but the single-crossing property is not always preserved.

[4] Most recent methodological treatments of the screening problem use the parametric-utility
approach, referred to by Wilson (1993a) as the "disaggregated-type" approach. See, for example, the article by Guesnerie and Laffont (1984), and the relevant sections in Fudenberg and
Tirole (1991), Myerson (1991), Mas-Colell, Whinston, and Green (1995), and Stole (1997). The
demand-profile approach is thoroughly expounded in Wilson (1993a). Brown and Sibley (1986)
and Wilson (1993a) discuss both approaches.

2.1.   The Parametric-Utility Approach

The basic methodology we follow here was initially developed by Mirrlees (1971), and applied to nonlinear pricing by Mussa and Rosen (1978). The firm in our setting cares only about expected profit and so seeks to maximize

$$E[\pi] = \int_{\underline{\theta}}^{\overline{\theta}} [P(q(\theta)) - cq(\theta)] \, dF(\theta),$$

where $q(\theta)$ is a parametric representation of the choice of type θ consumers, and c is the constant marginal cost of producing q units for a given consumer.

Suppose that our monopolist offers a nonlinear, lower-semi-continuous pricing schedule $P(q)$ defined over the compact domain $\mathcal{Q}$. Then, we can define a type θ consumer's indirect utility under this scheme as

$$u(\theta) \equiv \max_{q \in \mathcal{Q}} \{v(q, \theta) - P(q)\}.$$

Provided that the derivatives of v are bounded, $u(\theta)$ is absolutely continuous.

Applying the revelation principle, we can reparameterize our problem and focus on maximizing expected profits over all incentive-compatible and individually rational mechanisms, $\{p(\theta), q(\theta)\}_{\theta \in \Theta}$. As is well known, a mechanism in this context is incentive-compatible if and only if, for almost all θ, we have $\dot{u}(\theta) = v_\theta(q(\theta), \theta)$ and $q(\theta)$ is nondecreasing.[5] The former condition is equivalent to the local first-order condition and arises as a natural analog of the envelope condition in Roy's identity; the latter is equivalent to the local second-order condition. When preferences satisfy the single-crossing property, the local second-order condition implies a global condition as well. Hence, our monopolist firm can maximize expected profits subject to $\dot{u}(\theta) = v_\theta(q(\theta), \theta)$ and the monotonicity of q.

Given our incentive compatibility conditions are stated in terms of u and q, it is useful to transform our monopolist's program from price-quantity space to the utility-quantity space. Because $S(q, \theta) \equiv v(q, \theta) - cq$ represents joint surplus from producing q units of output to be consumed by a type θ consumer, the firm's expected profit can be restated as

$$E[\pi] = \int_{\underline{\theta}}^{\overline{\theta}} [S(q(\theta), \theta) - u(\theta)] \, dF(\theta). \tag{2.1}$$

Hence, the monopolist maximizes (2.1) over $\{q(\theta), u(\theta)\}_{\theta \in \Theta}$ subject to $\dot{u}(\theta) = v_\theta(q(\theta), \theta)$, $q(\theta)$ nondecreasing and subject to individual rationality. Note that this program is entirely defined by the social surplus function $S(q, \theta)$ and the partial derivative of the consumer's utility function with respect to θ. For example, the setting in which utility over quantity is $v(q, \theta) = \theta q - \frac{1}{2}q^2$ and cost is cq is formally equivalent to the setting in which a monopolist sells a

---

[5] Throughout, we use the notation $\dot{x}(y)$ to represent the derivative of x with respect to y.

product line with various qualities, in which the consumer's value of consuming one unit of quality q is given by $\tilde{v}(q, \tilde{\theta}) = \tilde{\theta}q$ and the cost of producing such a unit is $\frac{1}{2}q^2$, where $\tilde{\theta} = \theta - c$. Both settings give rise to identical surplus functions and partial derivatives with respect to type, and hence have identical optimal price schedules. In this sense, there is little to distinguish the use of quality [as in Mussa and Rosen's (1978) seminal paper] from quantity [as in Maskin and Riley's (1984) generalization of this model]. Fortunately, in both cases, the operative instruments begin with the letter q and, as a pleasant historical accident, we can refer to this second-best allocation as the MR allocation. We will nonetheless focus our attention on the quantity variation of this model.

As a technical simplification, we use the local first-order condition for truth-telling to replace u in the firm's objective via integration by parts. The result is an objective function that is maximized over $\{\{q(\theta)\}_{\theta\in\Theta}, u(\underline{\theta})\}$ subject to q nondecreasing and the individual rationality constraint:

$$E[\pi] = \int_{\underline{\theta}}^{\overline{\theta}} \left(S(q(\theta), \theta) - \frac{1 - F(\theta)}{f(\theta)} v_\theta(q(\theta), \theta) - u(\underline{\theta}) \right) dF(\theta).$$

This objective function has been usefully termed the monopolist's "virtual surplus" function by Myerson (1991); it includes the total surplus generated by the monopolist's production less the information rents that must be left to the consumers as a function of their type.

Because $\dot{u}(\theta) = v_\theta(q, \theta) \geq 0$, individual rationality is equivalent to requiring $u(\underline{\theta}) \geq 0$. Thus, we choose $u(\underline{\theta}) = 0$ as a *corner solution* in this program, guaranteeing participation at the least possible cost. Note that, in this simple program, it is never profitable to leave excess rents to consumers. Hence, we are left with an objective function that can be maximized pointwise in $q(\theta)$ if we ignore the monotonicity condition. Providing that the virtual surplus

$$\Lambda(q, \theta) \equiv S(q, \theta) - \frac{1 - F(\theta)}{f(\theta)} v_\theta(q, \theta)$$

is quasi-concave in q and satisfies a cross-partial condition, $\Lambda_{q\theta} \geq 0$, the solution $\{q(\theta)\}_{\theta\in\Theta}$, which is defined by the pointwise first-order condition $\Lambda_q(q(\theta), \theta) = 0$, maximizes expected profit and is nondecreasing as required. This solution satisfies

$$S_q(q(\theta), \theta) = \frac{1 - F(\theta)}{f(\theta)} v_\theta(q(\theta), \theta) \geq 0.$$

Hence, we have the familiar result that $q(\theta)$ is distorted downward relative to the social optimum, everywhere but at the "top" (i.e., at $\theta = \overline{\theta}$). If $\Lambda_{q\theta}$ is not everywhere nonnegative, it is possible that an ironing procedure needs to be used to constrain $q(\theta)$ to be nondecreasing.[6] Such a procedure typically requires that we utilize more general control-theoretic techniques and depart from our

---

[6] See, for example, Fudenberg and Tirole (1991) for details.

simple pointwise maximization program. However, in the single-dimensional setting, a mild set of regularity conditions on v and F guarantees us the simple case.[7]

Note that because profit per customer, $\pi = S - u$, is linear in utility, we are able to use integration by parts to eliminate the utility function from the objective function, except for the requirement that $u(\underline{\theta}) \geq 0$. This allows us to maximize profits pointwise in q; i.e., we do not have to concern ourselves simultaneously with the value of $u(\theta)$. In this sense, the program is block recursive: first the optimum can be found for each $q(\theta)$ and for $u(\underline{\theta})$ in isolation; then using the resulting function $q(\theta)$ and $u(\underline{\theta})$, $u(\theta)$ can be determined via integration. The resulting utility schedule can then be combined with $q(\theta)$ to determine the total type-specific transfer, $p(\theta) = v(q(\theta), \theta) - u(\theta)$. Given $\{p(\theta), q(\theta)\}_{\theta \in \Theta}$, the price schedule can be constructed by inverting the function $q(\theta)$: $P(q) = p(\theta^{-1}(q))$.

A second inherent simplicity in the one-dimensional model is that the incentive compatibility conditions are determined by a simple differential equation and a monotonicity condition. Whether we use integration by parts or the maximum principle to solve the program, in both instances we made important use of this fact: without it, we also lose the recursive nature of the problem. In the multidimensional setting, if we are uncertain as to which constraints bind, we will generally be forced to maximize profits subject to a far larger set of global constraints.

To this end, it is useful to briefly consider the discrete setting. Suppose that θ is distributed discretely on $\underline{\theta} = \theta_1 < \theta_2 < \cdots < \theta_I = \overline{\theta}$, with respective probabilities $f_i > 0$, $i = 1, \ldots, I$ and cumulative distribution function $F_k \equiv \sum_{i=1}^{k} f_i$. A direct mechanism is a menu of I price-quantity pairs, where the ith indexed pair is given to consumers who report that they are of the ith type: $\{q_i, p_i\}_{i=1,\ldots,I}$. Given that the single-crossing property is satisfied, it is straightforward to show that, if adjacent incentive compatibility constraints are satisfied, then global incentive compatibility is satisfied. The adjacent constraints are typically referred to as the *downward local* and *upward local* incentive constraints:

$$v(q_i, \theta_i) - p_i \geq v(q_{i-1}, \theta_i) - p_{i-1}, \quad \text{for} \quad i = 2, \ldots, I, \qquad (\text{IC}_{i,i-1})$$

$$v(q_i, \theta_i) - p_i \geq v(q_{i+1}, \theta_i) - p_{i+1}, \quad \text{for} \quad i = 1, \ldots, I-1. \qquad (\text{IC}_{i,i+1})$$

Furthermore, assuming that it is always profitable to transfer rents from the consumer to the firm, one can easily demonstrate that the downward constraints are binding. In addition, providing that the resulting quantity allocation, $\{q_i\}_{i=1,\ldots,I}$, is monotonic, one can show that the upward constraints must be slack and consequently incentive compatibility is global. This set of results is typically used to solve the relaxed program with only the downward constraints. In this sense, the sequence of binding downward-local incentive constraints (and the difference

---

[7] The commonly made assumptions that preferences are quadratic, and θ has a log-concave distribution are sufficient for $\Lambda_{q\theta} \geq 0$.

equation that they imply) are analogous to the ordinary differential equation $\dot{u}(\theta) = v_\theta(q(\theta), \theta)$ in the continuous setting. Not surprisingly, the solution to the relaxed program (ignoring monotonicity constraints) satisfies an analogous condition:

$$S_q(q_i, \theta_i) = \left(\frac{1 - F_i}{f_i} \right) \{v_q(q_i, \theta_{i+1}) - v_q(q_i, \theta_i)\},$$

$$i = 1, \ldots, I - 1.$$

In the discrete setting case, it is perhaps easier to see the importance of focusing on the local constraints, and in particular on the downward-local constraints. Without such a simplification, we would have to introduce a Lagrange multiplier for every type-report pair, (i, j), resulting in $I(I - 1)$ total constraints rather than simply $I - 1$. Not only does the single-crossing property in tandem with a one-dimensional type space allow us to reduce the set of potential constraints by a factor of I, it also renders these local constraints in an tractable fashion: a simple first-order difference equation. The absence of such a convenient ordering is the source of much difficulty in the multiple-dimension setting.

2.2. The Demand-Profile Approach

An alternative approach to modeling optimal screening contracts in parametric-utility space is to work with a less primitive and perhaps more economically salient structure – demand curves ordered by type and then aggregated into a demand profile.[8] Because demand curves entirely capture consumers' preferences, there is no informational loss from restricting our attention to demand profiles. Given that they are generally easier to estimate empirically, this primitive has arguably more practical appeal. For our purposes, however, the demand profile approach is useful also in that this method more clearly illustrates the simplicity and recursiveness of the single-type framework, and also underscores the aspects of the multiple-type framework that will lead to genuine economic difficulties rather than merely technical concerns.

Consider first the continuous parameterization of demand curves that we will index by θ: an individual of type θ has a demand curve given by

$$p = v_q(q, \theta).$$

The single-crossing property is equivalent to the requirement that these demand curves do not intersect. In the parametric-utility approach where $v(q, \theta) = \theta q - \frac{1}{2}q^2$, this generates a simple family of parallel demand curves: $p = \theta - q$. The primitive object on which we will work, however, is the aggregate demand profile generated by calculating the measure of consumers who consume q or

---

[8] An interested reader is urged to consult Wilson (1993a) for a wealth of examples and insights into this approach. Wilson (1993a) builds on the work of Brown and Sibley (1986), who provide an earlier treatment of this approach.

more units of output with a price schedule, $P(q)$. Formally, we characterize this "cumulative" aggregate demand functional as

$$M[P(\cdot), q] = \text{Prob}[\theta \in \Theta \mid \arg \max_x \{v(x, \theta) - P(x)\} \geq q].$$

If the consumer's program is quasi-concave [which is equivalent to the requirement that the marginal price schedule, $p(q) \equiv P'(q)$, intersects the consumer's demand curve once from below], then consumer θ will demand q or more units if and only if $v_q(q, \theta)$ is not less than the marginal price, $p(q)$, which implies that the cumulative aggregative demand functional has a very simple form:

$$M[P(\cdot), q] = \text{Prob}\,[v_q(q, \theta) \geq p(q)] \equiv N(p(q), q).$$

In this case, the problem is fully decomposable: The seller's program is to choose optimal marginal prices, $p(q)$, to maximize

$$N(p, q)[p - c]$$

pointwise for each q. Assuming that the monopolist's local first-order necessary condition is also sufficient, we can characterize the solution by

$$N(p(q), q) + \frac{\partial N(p(q), q)}{\partial p}[p(q) - c] = 0,$$

or in a more familiar inverse-elasticity formula

$$\frac{p(q) - c}{p(q)} = \frac{1}{\eta(p(q), q)}, \quad \text{where} \quad \eta(p, q) \equiv \frac{-p}{N} \frac{\partial N}{\partial p}.$$

Providing that the resulting marginal price schedule, $p(q)$, cuts each parameterized demand curve only once from below, this solution to the relaxed program will satisfy the agent's global incentive compatibility constraints. The resulting nonlinear price schedule in this case is $P(q) = P(0) + \int_0^q p(s)\,ds$, where the fixed fee is chosen optimally to induce participation for all consumers who generate nonnegative virtual surplus.

When the monopolist's program is not quasi-concave over p for all q, the solution is still given by the maximization over p of $N(p, q)(p - c)$, but the resulting marginal price schedule $p(q)$ may fail to be continuous in q, which gives rise to kinks in the price function P. This situation corresponds to the cases where $\Lambda_{\theta q} < 0$ and $q(\theta)$ is not strictly monotonic (bunching arises). Notice that in this case, also the demand profile approach is less difficult than the parametric-utility approach, which must resort to an ironing procedure.

The demand profile approach does not work well when the resulting price schedule cuts some demand curve twice. In this case the expression of the aggregated demand function M cannot be simplified, because it depends on the whole function P. As an illustration, consider the following numerical example. Suppose that there are three types of consumers with demand curves for the quantities given in the first three numeric columns (we normalize

Table 5.1. *The demand-profile approach: a numerical example*

Unit	θ_1	θ_2	θ_3	$p(q)$	$N(p(q), q)$	$R(q)$
1st	7	9	11	7	3	21
2nd	5	7	9	5	3	15
3rd	3	5	7	5	2	10
4th	1	3	5	3	2	6
5th	0	1	3	3	1	3
6th	0	0	1	1	1	1
Total						56

marginal cost to zero; see Table 5.1): The fourth numeric column represents the pointwise optimal price $p(q)$, obtained by maximizing revenue $pN(p, q)$ for the qth unit. The fifth column is the number of consumers purchasing that quantity (we have normalized the population to an average of one consumer of each type), and the final column represents the revenue attributed to the particular quantity level. Total revenue using nonlinear pricing is equal to 56, whereas a uniform-pricing monopolist would choose a price of 5 per unit, sell 9 units, and make a total revenue of 45. The simplicity of this method for finding the optimal price schedule is worth noting.

The local demand-profile representation sometimes falls short, however. If the zeros in the θ_1 type's demand curve were replaced by $1 - 2\varepsilon$, and the zero in the θ_2 type's demand curve was replaced by $1 - \varepsilon$, the maximum revenue for the 6th unit would be obtained by selling to all types, whereas it would still be optimal to sell the 5th unit only to θ_3 types. Thus, we would generate gaps in consumption choices for types θ_1 and θ_2 when we maximized $p(q)$ pointwise by q. Specifically, types θ_1 and θ_2 would each be directed to choose only units 1–4 and unit 6 (but to skip unit 5), which is not feasible. This candidate solution represents the failure of the local representation; specifically, the marginal demand profile $N(p, q)$ does not capture the consumer's true preferences, which are instead characterized by the full demand profile, $M[P(\cdot), q]$.

3. THE GENERAL MULTIDIMENSIONAL SCREENING PROGRAM

3.1. A General Discrete Formulation

We begin with the discrete setting, because it is perhaps most easiest to follow, relying on simple techniques of summation and optimization for the characterization of an optimum, unlike its continuous-type counterpart that makes use of more complex techniques in vector calculus and differential forms. Nonetheless, both approaches are closely related, and the conditions in the discrete setting have smooth analogs in the continuous setting. More importantly for the purposes of this survey, the rough equivalence between the two settings allows us to understand what is difficult about "multiple dimensions." To be precise, the problems arise not because of multiple dimensionality itself, but because of a commonly associated lack of exogenous type-ordering in multiple-dimensional environments. This source of the problem is clearest in the discrete setting, where it makes no sense to speak about dimensionality without simultaneously imposing structure on preferences.[9]

Let us consider now a more general version of the discrete model, where there are I distinct consumer types, and the monopolist produces n different goods: $q \in \mathbb{R}^n$. Hence, we can speak of there being n available instruments (i.e., varieties of goods exchanged for money). We make no assumptions on preferences, except for linearity in money. For the sake of consistency with the rest of the paper, we still parameterize gross utilities in the form $v(q, \theta_i)$ (where θ_i is the consumer type $i = 1, \ldots, I$), but we make no assumption on v. By convention, $q = 0$ represents "no consumption," and we normalize utility such that $v(0, \theta) = 0$ for all θ. We denote the allocation for consumer θ_i by the vector $q_i = q(\theta_i)$ and the associated utility by the scalar $u_i = u(\theta_i)$. We will use $\mathbf{q}$ to denote the $n \times I$ matrix $(q_1, \ldots, q_I)$, and $\mathbf{u}$ to denote the I-length row vector $(u_1, \ldots, u_I)$.

Using the parametric-utility approach, we represent the firm's expected profit as

$$E[\pi] = \sum_{i=1}^{I} f_i \{ S(q_i, \theta_i) - u_i \},$$

to be maximized under the discrete incentive compatibility constraints, $\mathrm{IC}_{i,j}$, as defined previously in the one-dimensional case, and individual rationality constraints:

$$\forall i \quad u_i \equiv v(q_i, \theta_i) - P(q_i) \geq 0. \tag{IR$_i$}$$

The individual rationality constraints can be considered as a particular case of incentive compatibility constraints by defining a "dummy"-type θ_0, such that $v(q, \theta_0) \equiv 0$, which implies that it will always be optimal to choose $q_0 = 0$ and $P(0) = 0$.[10] The firm's problem is thus to maximize its expected profit under implementability (i.e., IC and IR) constraints:

$$\forall i, j \in \{0, \ldots, I\}, \quad u_i \geq v(q_j, \theta_i) - P(q_j),$$

or, equivalently,

$$\forall i, j \in \{0, \ldots, I\}, \quad u_i - u_j \geq v(q_j, \theta_i) - v(q_j, \theta_j). \tag{IC$_{ij}$}$$

---

[9] For example, whether we index preferences using two dimensions, $v(q, \theta_{1i}, \theta_{2j})$ where $i, j = 1, \ldots, I/2$, or a single dimension, $v(q, \theta_k)$ with $k = 1, \ldots, I$, is immaterial by itself. Fundamentally, any difficulty in extending single-dimensional models to multidimensional models must arise from a lack of ordering among the types rather than any primitive notions of dimensionality.

[10] This is just a convention. It is compatible with fixed fees, because P can be discontinuous in 0.

Following Spence (1980), it is natural to decompose the firm's problem in two subproblems:

1. Minimize expected utility for fixed $\mathbf{q} = (q_1, \ldots, q_I)$.
2. Choose $\mathbf{q}$ to maximize expected surplus minus expected utility.

It is remarkable that the first subproblem has a general solution that can be found by a relatively simple algorithm. Let us denote by $\mathcal{U}(\mathbf{q})$ the set of utility vectors that implement $\mathbf{q}$. That is,

$$\mathcal{U}(\mathbf{q}) = \{(u_1, \ldots, u_I) \text{such that IC}_{ij} \text{ is satisfied}$$
$$\text{for all } i, j = 0, \ldots, I \text{ and } u_0 = 0\}.$$

In what follows, it will be useful to consider arbitrary paths in the set $\Theta = \{\theta_1, \ldots, \theta_I\}$. We will denote such a path from type θ_i to θ_j by the function γ. We denote the "length" of γ by ℓ; i.e., ℓ is the number of segments used to connect $\theta_i = \gamma(0)$ to $\theta_j = \gamma(\ell)$. Hence, γ is a mapping, $\gamma : \{0, 1, \ldots, \ell\} \to \Theta$. Finally, we say that a path of length ℓ is "closed" if $\gamma(0) = \gamma(\ell)$. With this notation for discrete paths, the following characterization of $\mathcal{U}(\mathbf{q})$ can be stated. A proof is found in Rochet (1987).

Lemma 3.1. $\mathcal{U}(\mathbf{q})$ *is nonempty if and only if for every closed ℓ-length path* γ

$$\sum_{k=0}^{\ell-1} v(q_{\gamma(k)}, \theta_{\gamma(k+1)}) - v(q_{\gamma(k)}, \theta_{\gamma(k)}) \leq 0. \tag{3.1}$$

To provide an intuition for condition (3.1), define the *incremental utility* between type i and type j as the difference between the utility of type i and the utility of type j when consuming the bundle assigned to type j. Condition (3.1) means that, for all closed paths γ in the set of types, the sum of incremental utilities along γ is nonpositive. Consider, for example, a closed path of length k. Incentive compatibility requires

$$u_{\gamma(k+1)} - u_{\gamma(k)} \geq v(q_{\gamma(k)}, \theta_{\gamma(k+1)}) - v(q_{\gamma(k)}, \theta_{\gamma(k)}).$$

By summing over these inequalities, we see that condition (3.1) is implied by incentive compatibility for any closed path. Lemma 3.1 says that the converse is true: condition (3.1) implies incentive compatibility, as well.[11] The proof is constructive: Lemma 3.2 gives an algorithm for constructing the minimal element of $\mathcal{U}(\mathbf{q})$.

---

[11] The reader versed in vector calculus will recognize this as a discrete variation of the requirement that $v_\theta(q(\theta), \theta)$ is a conservative field, where $\mathcal{C}$ represents an arbitrary closed path in Θ:

$$\oint_{\mathcal{C}} v_\theta(q(\theta), \theta) \, d\theta = 0.$$

Lemma 3.2. *When (3.1) is satisfied, $\mathcal{U}(\mathbf{q})$ has a unique minimal element, $\underline{\mathbf{u}}$, characterized for $i = 0, \ldots, I$ by*

$$\underline{u}_i \equiv \sup_{\gamma} \sum_{k=0}^{\ell-1} v(q_{\gamma(k)}, \theta_{\gamma(k+1)}) - v(q_{\gamma(k)}, \theta_{\gamma(k)}), \tag{3.2}$$

where the sup *is taken over all* **open** *paths from 0 to i, and $\underline{u}_0 \equiv 0$.*

Condition (3.2) means that agent i is guaranteed a utility level, $\underline{u}_i$, equal to the sum of the incremental utilities along any path connecting θ_0 to θ_i. We will refer to this ith element of the minimum of $\mathcal{U}(\mathbf{q})$ as the *informational rent* of agent i. Note that this rent does not depend on the frequencies $\{f_1, \ldots, f_I\}$ of the distribution of types, but only on the support, $\Theta = \{\theta_1, \ldots, \theta_I\}$, of this distribution. Formula (3.2) shows that the informational rent of each agent can be computed by a recursive algorithm. Intuitively, it is as if each type i chooses the path from θ_0 to θ_i that maximizes the sum of incremental utilities. Denote by u_i^{ℓ} the maximum of formula (3.2) over all paths of length *less than or equal to* ℓ from 0 to i. u_i^{ℓ} can be computed recursively by the Bellman-type formula:

$$u_i^{\ell+1} = \max_j \left\{ u_j^{\ell} + v(q_j, \theta_i) - v(q_j, \theta_j) \right\}.$$

Condition (3.1) implies that this algorithm has no cycles. The set of types being finite, u_i^{ℓ} converges to the rent of agent i in a finite number of steps as ℓ is increased to I.

For any allocation $\mathbf{q}$, the dynamic programming principle implies that if j belongs to the optimal path γ from 0 to i, the truncation of γ to the path between 0 and j defines the optimal path from 0 to j.

This allows us to define a partial ordering $\prec$ on types:

$$j \prec i \iff j \text{ belongs to one of the optimal paths from 0 to } i.$$

For generic[12] allocations, there is a unique optimal path γ [with $\gamma(0) = 0$ and $\gamma(\ell) = i$] from 0 to i, and the rent of i is easily computed:

$$u_i(\mathbf{q}, \prec) = \sum_{k=1}^{\ell-1} [v(q_{\gamma(k)}, \theta_{\gamma(k+1)}) - v(q_{\gamma(k)}, \theta_{\gamma(k)})].$$

Graphically, the collection of optimal paths comprises a "tree" (i.e., a connected graph without cycles such that, from the "root" vertex 0, there is a unique path to any other point in the graph); we use Γ to represent such a tree. We can therefore represent the binding incentive constraints by such a tree emanating from the type, θ_0. One can also define for all i, j, such that $i \prec j$, the "immediate successor" $s(i, j)$ of i in the direction of j by the formula

$$s(i, j) = \min\{k \mid i \prec k \prec j, k \neq i\}.$$

---

[12] However, the optimal allocation $\mathbf{q}$ may be such that there are several optimal paths. We give an example of such a case in Section 3.3.

Then, it is easy to see that the agent's expected rent can be written as[13]

$$\text{ER}(\mathbf{q}, \prec) = \sum_{i=1}^{I} \sum_{j \succ i} f_j [v(q_i, \theta_{s(i,j)}) - v(q_i, \theta_i)].$$

In the classic one-dimensional case when the single-crossing holds, condition (3.1) reduces to the well-known monotonicity condition $q_1 \leq q_2 \leq \cdots \leq q_I$ and $\prec$ always consists of the complete ordering: $\theta_1 < \theta_2 < \cdots < \theta_I$; the associated tree is a single connected branch. In this case

$$\text{ER}(\mathbf{q}, \prec) = \sum_{i=1}^{I} (1 - F_i) [v(q_i, \theta_{i+1}) - v(q_i, \theta_i)],$$

and as previously shown in Section 2, subproblem 2 is easily solved by maximizing the virtual surplus

$$\Lambda(q_i, \theta_i) = S(q_i, \theta_i) - \frac{1 - F_i}{f_i} [v(q_i, \theta_{i+1}) - v(q_i, \theta_i)].$$

In the general case, the binding IC constraints (corresponding to the agent's optimal paths defining the tree Γ) depend on the allocation $\mathbf{q}$, which means that the virtual surplus does not have in general a simple expression. As will be illustrated later, the virtual surplus approach works only when one can anticipate a priori the optimal paths $\gamma \in \Gamma$: i.e., which IC constraints will be binding.

To summarize, from this discussion of the general discrete formulation, two conclusions emerge that are inherent in all multidimensional problems. First, and most significantly, multiple-dimension models are difficult precisely when they give rise to an endogenous ordering over the types of Θ (i.e., the set of binding IC constraints is endogenous to the choice of $\mathbf{q}$). Second, and closely related, the incentive compatibility conditions are frequently binding not only among local types, and hence the discrete analog of the first-order approach is not generally valid and a form of an integrability condition, (3.1), must necessarily be satisfied. We will see a similar structure in the continuous-type setting.

3.2. The Continuous Case

In the continuous case, the implementability condition (3.1) translates into two necessary conditions. The first is an integrability condition that requires, for every closed path $\gamma : [0, 1] \to \Theta$, that

$$\int_0^1 v_\theta(q(\gamma(s)), \gamma(s)) \, d\gamma(s) = 0. \tag{3.3'}$$

---

[13] When i is a maximal element, the set $\{j \mid j \succ i\}$ is empty and ER does not depend on q_i.

This is equivalent to saying that $v_\theta(q(\theta), \theta)$ is the gradient[14] of some function $u(\theta)$. The second condition is a set of inequalities:

$$\forall \theta \quad D^2 u(\theta) \geq v_{\theta\theta}(q(\theta), \theta), \tag{3.3''}$$

where $D^2 u$ is the Hessian matrix of any function u such that $\nabla u = v_\theta$ and the inequality is taken in the sense of matrices (i.e., $D^2 u - v_{\theta\theta}$ is positive semidefinite).

The trouble is that these conditions are not sufficient, except when $v_{\theta\theta} \equiv 0$ (the linear parameterization) in which case (3.3′) and (3.3″) are necessary and sufficient for implementability by Fenchel's duality theorem[15] (Rochet, 1987).

The continuous equivalent of Lemma 3.2 is somewhat trivial. This is because the integrability condition (3.3′) implies that, for **any** path γ connecting $\gamma(0) = \theta_0$ to $\gamma(1) = \theta$, we have

$$u(\theta) = \int_0^1 v_\theta(q(\gamma(s)), \gamma(s)) \, d\gamma(s).$$

Expected surplus can be computed using the divergence theorem:[16]

$$\int_\Theta u(\theta) f(\theta) \, d\theta = \int_\Theta \lambda(\theta) \cdot v_\theta(q(\theta), \theta) f(\theta) \, d\theta$$
$$- \int_{\partial\Theta} \lambda(\theta) \cdot n(\theta) f(\theta) u(\theta) \, d\sigma(\theta),$$

where λ is any solution of the partial-differential equation:

$$\mathrm{div}\,(\lambda(\theta) f(\theta)) + f(\theta) = 0, \tag{3.4}$$

where $n(\theta)$ is the outward normal to the boundary $\partial\Theta$ of Θ, and the notation $\int_{\partial\Theta} W(\theta) \, d\sigma(\theta)$ represents the integral of some function W along the boundary $\partial\Theta$.

---

[14] As noticed by several authors, this is also equivalent to a set of partial differential equations reminiscent of Slutsky equations:

$$\forall n, m \quad \frac{\partial}{\partial\theta_n}\left(\frac{\partial v}{\partial\theta_m}(q(\theta), \theta)\right) = \frac{\partial}{\partial\theta_m}\left(\frac{\partial v}{\partial\theta_n}(q(\theta), \theta)\right).$$

[15] McAfee and McMillan (1988) define a Generalized Single-Crossing condition that slightly generalizes the linear case: it amounts to assuming that, for any nonlinear price, the set of types who choose the same allocation is a linear subspace. They use it to generalize the results of Laffont, Maskin, and Rochet (1987). They also find a necessary and sufficient condition for implementability.

[16] The divergence theorem is the multidimensional analog of the integration-by-parts formula. It asserts that, under regularity conditions,

$$- \int_\Theta u(\theta)\mathrm{div}[\lambda(\theta) f(\theta)] \, d\theta = \int_\Theta \lambda(\theta) \cdot \nabla u(\theta) f(\theta) \, d\theta - \int_{\partial\Theta} \lambda(\theta) \cdot n(\theta) u(\theta) f(\theta) \, d\sigma(\theta).$$

Now, the expected profit of the firm can be written as

$$E[\pi] = \int_{\Theta} \{S(q(\theta), \theta) - \lambda(\theta)v_{\theta}(q(\theta), \theta)\} f(\theta) \, d\theta$$
$$+ \int_{\partial\Theta} \lambda(\theta) \cdot n(\theta) u(\theta) f(\theta) \, d\sigma(\theta),$$

which has to be maximized under the implementability conditions (3.3′) and (3.3″). When these constraints are not binding, this problem can, in principle, be solved by point-wise maximization of virtual surplus:

$$\Lambda(q, \theta) = S(q, \theta) - \lambda(\theta)v_{\theta}(q, \theta).$$

The trouble is that, like in the discrete case, λ is not known explicitly. It is defined as the unique solution of partial differential equation (3.4) that satisfies the boundary condition

$$u(\theta)[\lambda(\theta) \cdot n(\theta)] = 0 \quad \text{for all} \quad \theta \text{ on } \partial\Theta.$$

It can be proved that the general solution to equation (3.4) can be computed by integrating the density, f, along arbitrary paths γ:

$$\lambda(\theta) = \int_{\gamma^{-1}(\theta)}^{1} f(\gamma(s)) \, d\gamma(s).$$

Therefore, the optimal u is characterized by two objects:

- A partition of the boundary of Θ into two regions: the "lower boundary" $\partial_0\Theta$, where the participation constraint is binding $[u(\theta) = 0]$ and the "upper boundary" $\partial_1\Theta$, where $\lambda(\theta) \cdot n(\theta) = 0$, which means that there is no distortion along the normal to the boundary;
- A family of paths connecting the lower boundary [where $u(\theta) = 0$] to the upper boundary (where there is no distortion). This is the continuous equivalent of the pattern found in the discrete case: a partial ordering of types along paths connecting the region where the participation constraint binds to the region where there is no distortion.

As in the discrete setting, again two ideas emerge that are distinct to the multidimensional case: (i) the set of paths connecting the lower and upper boundaries of Θ are endogenous to the choice of allocation $\{q(\theta)\}_{\theta \in \Theta}$, and (ii) an integrability condition must necessarily be satisfied.

3.3.   Tractable Discrete Models

To illustrate the different patterns that can arise in multidimensional screening models and how our conclusions affect our results, we consider here a very simple example of nonlinear pricing problems, inspired by Sibley and Srinagesh

(1997) and Armstrong and Rochet (1999).[17] In those examples, a monopolist firm produces two goods $j = 1, 2$ at a constant marginal cost (normalized to zero). There are two types of consumers, characterized by independent linear inverse demands

$$p_{ij}(q_{ij}) = \theta_{ij} - q_{ij}, \quad j = 1, 2, \quad i = 1, 2.$$

Thus types are bidimensional $\theta_i = (\theta_{i1}, \theta_{i2}), i = 1, 2$. Linear demands are equivalent to quadratic utilities:

$$v(\theta_i, q_i) = \sum_{j=1}^{2} \left\{ \theta_{ij} q_{ij} - \frac{1}{2} q_{ij}^2 \right\},$$

where q_i is the vector $q_i = (q_{i1}, q_{i2})$. The first-best efficient allocation is characterized by the vector $q_i^* = \theta_i$ and surplus by the scalar $S_i^* = \frac{1}{2}(\theta_{i1}^2 + \theta_{i2}^2)$.

Following lemma 3.1, the implementability condition reduces to[18]

$$(\theta_1 - \theta_2) \cdot q_2 + (\theta_2 - \theta_1) \cdot q_1 \leq 0. \tag{3.5}$$

Providing this condition is satisfied, lemma 3.2 implies that, at the optimum, the rents to the types are given by

$$u_1 = \max(0, (\theta_1 - \theta_2) \cdot q_2),$$
$$u_2 = \max(0, (\theta_2 - \theta_1) \cdot q_1).$$

The implementability condition then implies that either u_1 or u_2 equals 0 (i.e., the IR constraint binds somewhere). To fix ideas, we assume that $S_1^* < S_2^*$. By analogy with the unidimensional case, one may conjecture that the second-best allocation is then characterized by $u_1 = 0$ (binding IR "at the bottom") and $q_2 = q_2^*$ (efficiency "at the top"). This is indeed one possible regime, illustrated by Figure 5.1.

In this first case,

$$u_2 = (\theta_2 - \theta_1) \cdot q_1$$

and

$$q_1 = \theta_1 - \frac{f_2}{f_1}(\theta_2 - \theta_1).$$

This allocation can be implemented by a menu of two-part tariffs: tariff 1 has a low fixed fee $T_1 = \frac{1}{2} q_1^2$ and a unit price vector $p_1 = f_2/f_1(\theta_2 - \theta_1)$; tariff 2 has a high fixed fee $T_2 = S_2^* - u_2$ and a zero unit price vector. Note that unit prices are not necessarily above marginal costs (which have been normalized to zero), because we did not assume[19] $\theta_2 > \theta_1$. Apart from this feature the completely

---

[17] Dana (1992) and Armstrong (1999a) also provide related examples of tractable discrete-type models.

[18] The only relevant closed path to consider is the cycle from θ_1 to θ_2.

[19] The case $\theta_2 > \theta_1$ corresponds to what Sibley and Srinagesh (1997) have called uniformly ordered demands.

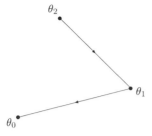

Figure 5.1. First-regime – the completely ordered case. Arrows indicate the direction of the binding incentive constraints; e.g., an arrow from θ_2 to θ_1 represents type θ_2's indifference between their own allocation and that meant for θ_1.

ordered case is analogous to the unidimensional case. It corresponds to the solution of the monopoly problem whenever

$$u_2 = (\theta_2 - \theta_1) \cdot q_1 \geq 0 = u_1 \geq (\theta_1 - \theta_2) \cdot q_2.$$

The second inequality is implied by the first, given the implementability condition in (3.5), whereas the first inequality is equivalent to

$$f_1(\theta_2 - \theta_1) \cdot \theta_1 \geq f_2(\theta_2 - \theta_1)^2,$$

or

$$\theta_1 \cdot \theta_2 \geq \frac{\theta_1^2 + f_2\theta_2^2}{1 + f_2}. \tag{3.6}$$

When this condition is not satisfied, a second possible regime corresponds to the case where there is no interaction between types; we call it the separable case (see Figure 5.2).

In this second case, there are no distortions:

$$q_1 = \theta_1 \quad \text{and} \quad q_2 = \theta_2,$$

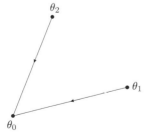

Figure 5.2. Second regime – the separable case.

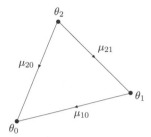

Figure 5.3. Third regime – the mixed case.

and all the surplus is captured by the seller:

$$u_1 = u_2 = 0.$$

Following (3.5), this allocation is implementable if and only if

$$(\theta_2 - \theta_1) \cdot \theta_1 \leq 0, \qquad (\theta_1 - \theta_2) \cdot \theta_2 \leq 0.$$

Given our assumption that $\theta_1^2 \leq \theta_2^2$, this is equivalent to

$$\theta_1 \cdot \theta_2 \geq \theta_1^2. \tag{3.7}$$

Finally, when neither (3.6) nor (3.7) is satisfied, there is an intermediate case that combines the features of the two regimes (see Figure 5.3).

In this third and final case, the firm is still able to capture all the surplus, but this is at the cost of a distortion on q_1, designed in such a way that type θ_2 is just indifferent between the efficient bundle $q_2 = \theta_2$ at a total tariff $T_2 = S_2^*$ and bundle q_1 at tariff $T_1 = \frac{1}{2}q_1^2$. Notice that there are two optimal paths connecting θ_2 to θ_0, corresponding to two different trees, Γ_1 and Γ_2. The weight μ_{21} put on this second path is determined by this indifference condition:

$$u_2 = 0 = (\theta_2 - \theta_1)q_1,$$

where

$$q_1 = \theta_1 - \frac{\mu_{21}}{f_1}(\theta_2 - \theta_1).$$

This gives

$$\mu_{21} = f_1 \frac{(\theta_2 - \theta_1) \cdot \theta_1}{(\theta_2 - \theta_1)^2},$$

which has to be between 0 and f_2. These conditions determine the boundary of this regime in the parameter space:

$$0 \leq (\theta_2 - \theta_1) \cdot \theta_1 \leq f_2(\theta_2 - \theta_1) \cdot \theta_2,$$

or

$$\theta_1^2 \leq \theta_1 \cdot \theta_2 \leq \frac{\theta_1^2 + f_2 \theta_2^2}{1 + f_2}.$$

Notice that, in this case, we have that $u_1 = u_2 = 0$ but $q_1 \neq q_2$, which cannot arise in dimension 1.

The three cases (completely ordered, separable, and mixed) illustrate the three settings that generally arise in multidimensional models. When we place significant restrictions on preferences and heterogeneity, we can frequently obtain simpler solutions that correspond to the first two cases. We discuss these in the following section, and then consider variations on these themes in Sections 5–8. The mixed case corresponds to the more general and difficult setting we discuss in Section 9.

4. AGGREGATION AND SEPARABILITY

In this section, we explore two cases where multidimensional problems can be effectively reduced to unidimensional problems: the case of **aggregation**, where a one-dimensional sufficient statistic can be found for representing unobservable preference heterogeneity, and the case of **separability**, where the set of types can be partitioned a priori into one-dimensional subsets. In the former setting, the binding IC constraints necessarily lie in a completely ordered graph, which is known a priori and corresponds to the completely ordered case, discussed in the previous section. In the latter setting, the incentive constraints can be partitioned into an exogenously given tree that is known a priori, which corresponds to the separable case.

4.1.   Aggregation

A family of multidimensional screening problems that effectively reduces to one-dimensional problems are characterized by the existence of a sufficient statistic of dimension 1 that summarizes all relevant information on unobservable heterogeneity of types and that has an *exogenously* given distribution. Let us start with a trivial example where the sufficient statistics can be found immediately. Suppose that only one good is sold ($n = 1$), but types are bidimensional ($m = 2$) and social surplus is given by

$$ S(\theta, q) = (\theta_1 + \theta_2)q - \frac{1}{2}q^2. $$

It is then obvious that $\hat{\theta} \equiv \theta_1 + \theta_2$ is a one-dimensional sufficient statistic for the consumer's preferences, and the monopolist's can be solved by applying the usual techniques to the distribution of $\hat{\theta}$.

Even in this simple transformable setting, however, we can see that everything is not the same as in the canonical one-dimensional model. The primary difference is the exclusion property discovered by Armstrong (1996). Suppose, indeed, that $\theta = (\theta_1, \theta_2)$ has a bounded density on $\mathbb{R}_+^2$, or on a rectangle $[\underline{\theta}_1, \bar{\theta}_1] \times [\underline{\theta}_2, \bar{\theta}_2]$ (or any domain with a "southwest" corner). Then, it is easy to see that the density of $\hat{\theta}$, obtained by convolution of the marginals[20] of θ_1 and θ_2 tends to zero when $\hat{\theta}$ tends to the lower bound of its support. As a result, the inverse hazard rate tends to infinity, which implies the existence of an exclusion region at the bottom that would not necessarily emerge if either θ_1 or θ_2 was observable and contractible. There is an associated intuition that relates to the envelope theorem: raising prices by ε raises revenues from infra-marginal buyers by a first-order amount at a loss of a second-order measure of consumers in the southwest corner of the support of types, ε^2. We will see this insight extends to more general settings; for example, Armstrong (1996) originally demonstrates this result for the separable setting discussed in the following section.[21]

It is worth noting that, whereas the aggregation technique appears trivial in our toy example, it is often more subtle and arises from a property of the market setting. For example, Biais, Martimort, and Rochet (2000) consider a market maker who sells a risky asset to a population of potential investors, characterized by two dimensions of adverse selection, $\theta = (\theta_1, \theta_2)$ (using our notation): θ_1 corresponds to the investor's fundamental information; i.e., his evaluation of the asset's liquidation value [the true liquidation value is $\theta_1 + \tilde{\varepsilon}$, where $\tilde{\varepsilon}$ is $N(0, \sigma^2)$ and independent of θ_2]; θ_2 corresponds to a sort of personal taste variable – namely, the initial position of the investor in the risky asset (his hedging needs). If he buys q units of the asset for a total price $P(q)$, the investor's final wealth is

$$\tilde{W}(q) = W_0 - P(q) + (\theta_1 + \tilde{\varepsilon})(\theta_2 + q),$$

where W_0 denotes his initial endowment of money. Assuming that the investor has constant absolute risk aversion preferences [$u(W) = -e^{-\rho W}$], the certainty equivalent of trading q units is

$$V(q) = W_0 - P(q) + \theta_1(\theta_2 + q) - \frac{1}{2}\rho\sigma^2(\theta_2 + q)^2.$$

Thus, the net utility of trading q is given by

$$U = V(q) - V(0) = (\theta_1 - \sigma^2\theta_2)q - \frac{1}{2}\rho\sigma^2 q^2 - P(q).$$

Even though the initial screening problem is bidimensional, the simplified

---

[20] As noticed by Miravete (1996), the monotone hazard-rate property is preserved by convolution.

[21] Armstrong (1996) shows that the exclusion property is also true when Θ is strictly convex. However, suppose that θ is uniformly distributed on a rectangle that has been rotated 45 degrees:

$$\Theta = \{\theta \in \mathbb{R}^2, \underline{\theta} \geq \theta_1 + \theta_2 \geq \bar{\theta}, -d \leq \theta_1 - \theta_2 \leq d\}.$$

Then, it is easy to see that $\hat{\theta}$ has a uniform distribution on $[\underline{\theta}, \bar{\theta}]$, which implies that $q^*(\theta) = 2\hat{\theta} - \bar{\theta}$ and that the exclusion region vanishes when $2\underline{\theta} > \bar{\theta}$. This shows that the exclusion property discovered by Armstrong (1996) is not intrinsically related to multidimensionality, but rather to the properties of the distribution of types.

version of the problem reduces to a one-dimensional screening problem with a sufficient statistic $\hat{\theta} = \theta_1 - \rho \sigma^2 \theta_2$ that aggregates the two motives for trade.

Other examples of this sort appear in Laffont and Tirole (1993) and Ivaldi and Martimort (1994). Ivaldi and Martimort (1994) study a model of competition with two dimensions of preference heterogeneity, which, given their assumptions about distributions and preferences, aggregates into a model with a one-dimensional statistic. Laffont and Tirole (1993) study regulation of multidimensional firms in a model combining adverse selection and moral hazard. By assuming that costs are observable to the regulator, they effectively transform their problem into a pure screening model, amenable to the technique presented here. In particular, when the unobservable technological parameters of the firms (their "types") are multidimensional, Laffont and Tirole find conditions, inspired by the aggregation theorems of Blackorby and Schworm (1984), under which the type vectors can be aggregated into a single number.

4.2.   Separability

Wilson (1993a, 1993b) and Armstrong (1996) were the first to provide closed-form solutions to multidimensional screening models. These solutions are all of the separable type. An illustration can be given in our framework by assuming linear parametrization of surplus with respect to types $S(\theta, q) = \theta \cdot q - W(q)$, where W is convex such that $\nabla W(0) = 0$, and a density f of types that depends only on $\|\theta\|$. Consider, for example, the case where there are two goods ($m = 2$), and f is the density of a truncated normal on a quarter of a circle of center 0 and radius $R > 1$.

Wilson (1993a) and Armstrong (1996) find conditions under which the solution to the monopolist problem depends only on the distribution of types along the "rays" (i.e., the straight lines through the origin). In other words, they look for cases where the only binding IC constraints are "radial" (see the Figure 5.4).

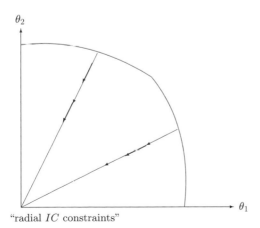

"radial IC constraints"

Figure 5.4. Radial incentive compatibility constraints.

If this is the case, the solution can be determined by computing the conditional distribution of types along the rays. This is done by introducing the change of variable $\theta = t\left(\begin{smallmatrix} \cos \alpha \\ \sin \alpha \end{smallmatrix}\right)$, with $t \in [0, R]$ and $\alpha \in [0, \pi/2]$. The change of variable formula for multivariate densities gives the conditional density along the rays:

$$g(t) = t \exp -\frac{t^2}{2},$$

which does not depend on α. The virtual surplus is easily computed as

$$\Lambda(\theta, q) = S(\theta, q) - \frac{1 - G(t)}{g(t)} \frac{\theta}{\|\theta\|} \cdot q,$$

which gives, after easy computations:

$$\Lambda(\theta, q) = \left(1 - \frac{1}{\|\theta\|^2}\right) \theta q - W(q).$$

This virtual surplus is maximized for $q^*(\theta)$ defined implicitly by $\nabla W(q) = (1 - 1/\|\theta\|^2)\theta$ for $\|\theta\| \geq 1$, and $q = 0$ for $\|\theta\| < 1$. If we use the indirect surplus function $S^*(\theta) = \max_q \{\theta \cdot q - W(q)\}$, this is equivalent to: $q^*(\theta) = \nabla S^*([1 - 1/\|\theta\|^2]_+ \cdot \theta)$, where $[x]_+$ denotes $\max(0, x)$.

We now have to check whether this function q^* satisfies the necessary conditions of the monopoly problem, namely boundary conditions and implementability conditions. The boundary conditions require that the boundary of $\Theta = \mathbb{R}_+^2$ be partitioned into two regions:

- $\partial_0 \Theta$, where $u(\theta) \equiv 0$ (no rent)
- $\partial_1 \Theta$, where the gradient of the surplus is tangent to the boundary (no distortion at the boundary).

These two regions are represented in Figure 5.5.

Notice that the boundary condition is satisfied in $\partial_1 \Theta$ only because the extreme rays are tangent to the boundary. This property would not be satisfied if the support of θ was shifted by an arbitrarily small vector. This more complex case is discussed in Section 9.2. On the other hand, Armstrong (1996) discovered a robust property of the solution, namely the existence of an exclusion region (where $u \equiv 0$): in our example, it corresponds to the region $\|\theta\| \leq 1$. This is explained by the fact that, for "regular" distributions on $\mathbb{R}_+^2$ (similar properties hold for many other domains), the conditional densities along the rays tend to zero when $\|\theta\|$ tends to zero, which implies that inverse hazard rates tend to infinity, as discussed in Section 4.1.

It remains to check that implementability conditions are satisfied. Due to the linearity of preferences with respect to θ, these implementability conditions are equivalent to saying that q^* is the gradient of a convex function (i.e., that Dq^* is a symmetric, positive definite matrix). Easy computations show that symmetry is equivalent to saying that $S^*(\theta)$ depends only on $\|\theta\|$; that is, it possesses the same type of symmetry as the density of types. If this property is satisfied, the

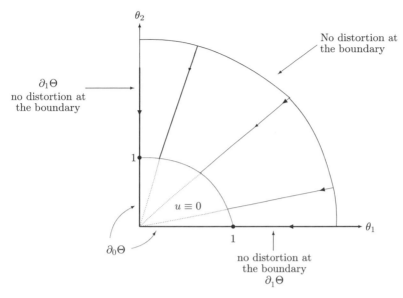

Figure 5.5. Exclusion region and boundaries.

second-order conditions for implementability (i.e., the fact that Dq^* is positive definite) will be automatically satisfied. When this is not the case, the solution is much more complex to characterize, because bunching necessarily appears. We study such an example in Section 9.2.

5. ENVIRONMENTS WITH ONE-DIMENSIONAL INSTRUMENTS

In many multidimensional screening problems, there are more dimensions of heterogeneity than instruments available to the principal ($n < m$). Here, we turn attention to the case of screening problems with one instrument ($n = 1$), but several parameters of adverse selection ($m > 1$) in which, even though a univariate sufficient statistic exists, its distribution is *endogenous*, depending on the pricing schedule chosen by the firm.

Typically, the set of instruments may be limited either by exogenous reasons [see, e.g., the justifications given by Rochet and Stole (2002) for ruling out stochastic contracts] or because the principal restricts herself to a subclass of all possible instruments. For example, Armstrong (1996) focuses on cost-based tariffs in his search of optimal nonlinear prices for a monopolist.[22] Using our notation, the monopolist problem in Armstrong (1996) can then be simplified

---

[22] Similarly, several authors e.g., Zheng (2000) and Che and Gale (1996a, 1996b), have studied score auctions, a particular subclass of multidimensional auctions in which the auctioneer aggregates bids using a prespecified scoring rule. As another example, Armstrong and Vickers (2000) consider price-cap regulation under the restriction of no lump-sum transfers.

by computing indirect utilities

$$V(y, \theta) = \max_q \{v(q, \theta) \mid C(q) \le y\}$$

representing the maximum utility attained by a consumer of type θ who gets a bundle of total cost less than or equal to y. The problem reduces then to find the best one-dimensional schedule $T(y)$ $(n = 1)$ for screening a multidimensional distribution of buyers $(m > 1)$.

As in the one-dimensional case, there are two approaches available for this class of problems: the parametric-utility approach and the demand-profile approach. The demand-profile approach is typically far easier to implement, provided that the consumer's preferences can be accurately summarized by a demand profile that depends only on the marginal prices.

Laffont, Maskin, and Rochet (1987) solved such a problem using the parametric-utility approach. Consider the scenario in which a monopolist sells only one good $(n = 1)$ to buyers differing by two characteristics: the intercept θ_1 and the slope $-\theta_2$ of their (individual) inverse demand curves. This corresponds to the following parameterization of preferences:

$$v(q, \theta) = \theta_1 q - \frac{1}{2} \theta_2 q^2.$$

If we want to apply the parametric-utility methodology, we are confronted with the problem that implementability of an indirect utility function $u(\cdot)$ is more complex to characterize. Indeed, let $P(q)$ be a given price schedule. The corresponding indirect utility u and allocation rule q satisfy

$$u(\theta) = \max_q \left\{ \theta_1 q - \frac{1}{2} \theta_2 q^2 - P(q) \right\},$$

where the maximum is attained for $q = q(\theta)$. By the envelope principle, we have that u is again a convex function such that

$$\nabla u(\theta) = \begin{pmatrix} q(\theta) \\ -\frac{1}{2} q^2(\theta) \end{pmatrix} \quad \text{for} \quad \text{a.e. } \theta.$$

This shows that u necessarily satisfies a nonlinear partial-differential equation

$$\frac{\partial u}{\partial \theta_2} + \frac{1}{2} \left(\frac{\partial u}{\partial \theta_1} \right)^2 = 0. \tag{5.1}$$

The monopolist's problem can then be transformed as before into a calculus of variations problem in u and ∇u, but with the additional constraint (5.1) that makes the program difficult.

Interestingly, Wilson's demand-profile approach works very well in this case. Let us define the demand profile for quantity q at marginal price p as

$$N(p, q) = \text{Prob}[v_q(q, \theta) \ge p] = \text{Prob}[\theta_1 - \theta_2 q \ge p].$$

Assuming a constant marginal cost c, the optimal marginal price $p(q) = P'(q)$ can be obtained by maximizing $(p - c)N(p, q)$ with respect to p. If θ_1

and θ_2 are distributed independently according to cumulative distributions F_1 and F_2 (and densities f_1 and f_2), we obtain

$$N(p,q) = \int_0^{+\infty} \{1 - F_1(p + \theta_2 q)\} f_2(\theta_2)\, d\theta_2.$$

The optimal marginal price is defined implicitly by

$$p(q) = c - \frac{N(p(q), q)}{N_p(p(q), q)} = c + \frac{\displaystyle\int_0^{+\infty} \{1 - F_1(p(q) + \theta_2 q)\} f_2(\theta_2)\, d\theta_2}{\displaystyle\int_0^{+\infty} f_1(p(q) + \theta_2 q) f_2(\theta_2)\, d\theta_2},$$

which generalizes the classical formula obtained when θ_2 is nonstochastic:

$$p(q) = c + \frac{1 - F_1}{f_1}(p(q) + \theta_2 q).$$

For example, when θ_1 is exponentially distributed (i.e., $f_1(\theta_1) = \lambda_1 e^{-\lambda_1 \theta_1}$), the mark-up is constant and the two formulas coincide: $p(q) = c + 1/\lambda_1$.

Notice also that $\hat{\theta} = \theta_1 - \theta_2 q(\theta)$ is a univariate sufficient statistic, but unlike the case considered in Section 4.1, its distribution depends on $q(\theta)$ and thus on the price schedule chosen by the monopolist.

We now turn to a subset of these models with a single instrument, in which one dimension of type enters utilities additively.

6. ENVIRONMENTS WITH RANDOM PARTICIPATION

6.1. A General Framework

We consider a class of environments in which $n = 1$, but in which a particular additivity assumption provides sufficient structure to produce some general economic conclusions. Specifically, suppose that $n = 1$ and $m = 2$, but utility of the agent is restricted to the form

$$u = v(q, \theta_1) - \theta_2 - P,$$

where $\Theta_1 = [\underline{\theta}_1, \overline{\theta}_1]$ and $\Theta_2 = \mathbb{R}_+$.

Several interesting economic settings can be studied within this model. First, we can think of the θ_2 parameter as capturing a type-dependent participation constraint. Previous work on type-dependent participation has assumed that θ_2 is a deterministic function of θ_1 (e.g., they are perfectly correlated).[23] In this sense, the framework generalizes the previous one-dimensional literature, although many of the more interesting results rely on independent distributions of θ_1 and θ_2.

---

[23] See, for example, Maggi and Rodriguez-Clare (1995), Lewis and Sappington (1989a, 1989b), and Jullien (2000).

Second, one can think of θ_2 as capturing a "locational cost" in a discrete-choice model of consumer behavior.[24] This allows one to extend the nonlinear pricing model of Mussa and Rosen (1978) to a more general setting, which may be important to obtain a more realistic model of consumer behavior. As an illustration, consider the predicted consumer behavior of the standard, one-dimensional model following a uniform price increase from $P(q)$ to $P(q) + \delta$: the units sold at every quality level except the lowest should remain unchanged. This is because a shift in $P(q)$ has no effect on any of the incentive compatibility conditions, since the shift occurs on both sides of the constraints. By adding the stochastic utility effect of θ_2, predicted market shares would smoothly change for all types, although perhaps more dramatically for lower types.

Third, consider the regulatory setting first discussed in Baron and Myerson (1982). There, a regulator designs an optimal mechanism for regulating a monopoly with unknown marginal cost. Suppose that, in addition, fixed costs are also private information: i.e., $C(q) = \theta_1 q + \theta_2$. Profit for the regulated firm that receives $T(q)$ as a transfer from the regulator for producing q units is $\pi = T(q) - \theta_1 q + \theta_2$, that has a one-to-one correspondence with the previous monopoly setting.[25]

Other closely related examples that we discuss in more detail include selling to liquidity-constrained buyers, where θ_2 captures the buyer's available budget, regulation of a firm in an environment with demand and cost heterogeneity, competition between oligopolists selling differentiated products with nonlinear pricing, and competition among sellers providing goods via auctions.

The key simplifications in all of these settings are twofold. First, one dimension of information enters additively. As such, q is unavailable for direct screening on this additive attribute. Second, attention is limited to deterministic[26] price schedules, $P(q)$.

---

[24] See Anderson, de Palma, and Thisse (1992) for a review of this large literature, and Berry, Levinsohn, and Pakes (1995) for an econometric justification of the additive specification.

[25] Rochet (1984) first solved this problem on an example with general mechanisms that rely on randomization. Applying Rochet and Stole's (2002) results to this context is appropriate in the restricted setting in which the price schedule is deterministic. In this case, Rochet and Stole (2002) show that the presence of uncertainty over fixed costs causes the optimal regulation to reduce the extent of the production distortion.

[26] Given the relevance of deterministic contracts, this may seem a reasonable restriction, a priori. In general, however, the principal may be able to do better by introducing a second screening instrument, ϕ, which represents the probability that the agent is turned away with $q = 0$. In this case, utility becomes $\phi(v(q, \theta_1) - \theta_2 - P)$ and ϕ can be used to screen different values of θ_2. On the other hand, it is without loss of generality to rule out such random mechanisms when either (i) the value θ_2 is lost by participating in the mechanism (i.e., even if $\phi = 0$), which eliminates the possibility to screen over θ_2; alternatively, (ii) if the agent can anonymously return to the principal until $\phi = 1$ is realized, the problem is stationary and the agent will continue to return until $q > 0$, and so there is no benefit to the randomization. We leave the discussion of stochastic mechanisms unresolved and simply restrict attention to deterministic price schedules remaining agnostic about the reasons.

We take the joint density to be $f(\theta_1, \theta_2) > 0$ on $\Theta_1 \times \Theta_2$, the marginal distribution of θ_1 as $f_1(\theta_1)$, and the conditional cumulative distribution function for θ_2 as $G(\theta_2 \mid \theta_1) \equiv \int_{\underline{\theta}_2}^{\theta_2} f(\theta_1, t) \, dt$. Define the indirect utility function

$$u(\theta_1) \equiv \max_{q \in Q} \; v(q, \theta_1) - P(q).$$

This indirect utility is independent of the additive component, θ_2, because it does not affect the optimal choice of q, conditional on $q > 0$. Net utility is given by $u(\theta_1) - \theta_2$. Note that the agent's participation contains an additional random component: i.e., the agent participates iff $u(\theta_1) \geq \theta_2$. Hence, an agent with type θ_1 participates with probability $G(u(\theta_1) \mid \theta_1)$, and the expected profit of a mechanism that generates $\{q(\theta_1), u(\theta_1)\}$ for all participating agents is

$$\int_{\Theta_1} G(u(\theta_1) \mid \theta_1) \, (S(q(\theta_1), \theta_1) - u(\theta_1)) \, f(\theta_1) \, d\theta_1.$$

This is maximized subject to the standard one-dimensional incentive compatibility conditions: $\dot{u}(\theta_1) = v_{\theta_1}(q(\theta_1), \theta_1)$ and $q(\theta_1)$ nondecreasing. In short, we have removed the typical corner condition that would require the utility of the lowest type – which we denote $\underline{u} \equiv u(\underline{\theta}_1)$ – to be zero, and instead introduced an endogenous determination of $\underline{u}$.

The endogeneity of $\underline{u}$ poses some difficulties that were not present in the one-dimensional setting. First and foremost, part of the block-recursive structure is now lost: There is a nonrecursive aspect to the problem as the entire function $q(\theta_1)$ and the initial condition $u(\underline{\theta}_1)$ must be *jointly* determined. Given that a purchasing consumer's preferences are ordered by a single-crossing property in (θ_1, q), the general problem of global vs. local incentive constraints is not present; incentive constraints are still recursive in their structure, although we may have to restrict q to a nondecreasing allocation. The problem is that the first-order condition determining the optimal utility for the lowest-type $\underline{u}$ depends on the optimal quantity schedule, $\{q(\theta_1)\}_{\theta_1 \in \Theta_1}$, and the first-order equation for the latter (specifically, the Euler equation) depends on the value of the former. Thus, although the resulting system of equations is not a system of partial differential equations as is common in the general multidimensional continuous type setting, but rather a second-order boundary-value problem, it is still more complicated than the standard initial-value first-order problem that arises in the canonical class of one-dimensional models.

Finding general characteristics of the solution is difficult without imposing some additional structure. A convenient restriction used in Rochet and Stole (2002) is to focus attention on independent distributions of θ_1 and θ_2, requiring that the former is distributed uniformly on Θ_1 and that the latter have a log-concave conditional cumulative distribution function.[27] Even with these distributional simplifications, the additional effect on market share still

---

[27] In Rochet and Stole (2002), some general results are nonetheless available in the two-type setting, providing that $G(\theta_2 \mid \theta_1)$ is log-concave in θ_2.

provides substantial difficulty. The primary cause of the difficulties is that the relaxed program (without monotonicity imposed) frequently generates nonmonotonic solutions. Hence, pooling occurs even with nonpathological distributions. Nonetheless, as a first result, one can show that if pooling occurs, it occurs only for a lower interval on Θ_1 and that otherwise efficiency occurs on the boundaries of Θ_1. This already is a substantial departure from the one-dimensional setting, and shares many similarities with the work of Rochet and Choné (1998) (see Section 9.2), especially the general presence of bunching and the efficiency on the boundaries.

Several results emerge beyond pooling or efficiency at the bottom. First, as the distribution on Θ_2 converges to an atom at $\theta_2 = 0$, the optimal allocation converges to that of the standard one-dimensional setting. Second, one can demonstrate that the optimal solution is always bounded above by the first-best allocation and below by the MR allocation. This last result has a clear economic intuition behind it. Under the standard one-dimensional setting, there is no reason not to extract the maximal amount of rent from the agents. This is the reason for distorting output downward; it allows the principal to extract greater rents from the higher types without completely shutting off the lower types from the market. When participation depends monotonically on the amount of rent left to the agent, it seems natural to leave more rents to the agent on the margin, and therefore to reduce the magnitude of the distortions. The argument is a bit more involved than this, because the presence of pooling eliminates these simple envelope-style arguments.

These results can be illustrated with a numerical example. Suppose that $\Theta_1 = [4, 5]$ and $G(\theta_2) = 1 - e^{-\theta_2/\sigma}$. Here, we use σ as a crude measure of the amount of noise in the participation constraint. As σ goes to zero, the exponential distribution converges to an atom on zero. In the example, as σ becomes small, the optimal allocation converges pointwise to the MR allocation, although pooling emerges at the bottom. For σ sufficiently large, the allocation becomes efficient on the boundaries of Θ_1 (see Figure 5.6).

Returning to our previous discussion of other applications, it should be clear that these results immediately extend to the regulatory environment of Baron and Myerson (1982), where marginal and fixed costs are represented by θ_1 and θ_2, respectively, and the regulator is restricted to offering a deterministic, nonlinear transfer schedule.

Other settings fit into this class of models in a less obvious manner. For example, consider the papers of Lewis and Sappington (1988) and Armstrong (1999a), which look at regulation of a firm in an environment of two-dimensional private information: demand is $q = x - p$, marginal cost is c, and the firm's private information is (x, c). The regulator observes only the price of the firm's output and offers a transfer that depends on price, $T(p)$. The firm's payoff is $u = (x - p)(p - c) + T(p)$; the regulator maximizes consumer surplus less transfer, $W = \frac{1}{2}(x - p)^2 - T(p)$.

Redefine the private information as $\theta_1 = x + c$ and $\theta_2 = xc$. Following similar arguments as previously described after substituting for the demand function,

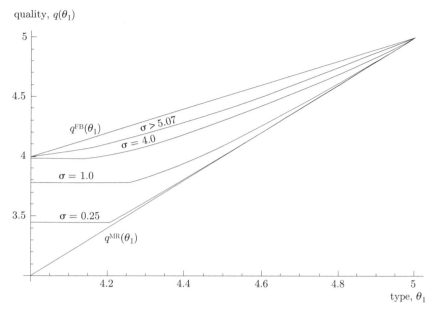

quality, $q(\theta_1)$

Figure 5.6. The monopoly solution with a uniform distribution of θ_1 on $[4, 5]$ and an exponential distribution of θ_2: $G(u) = 1 - e^{-u}$.

we can define $u(\theta_1) \equiv \max_p \theta_1 p - p^2 + T(p)$ and $p(\theta_1)$ to be the corresponding maximizer. Note that the local IC constraint requires that $\dot{u}(\theta_1) = p(\theta_1) \geq 0$; second-order conditions require that u is convex in θ_1 (i.e., p is nondecreasing in θ_1). The firm will participate if and only if $u(\theta_1) \geq \theta_2$. The regulator's program can then be written as

$$\max_{\{p(\theta_1), u(\theta_1)\}} \int_{\Theta_1} G(u(\theta_1) \mid \theta_1)$$

$$\times \left[\gamma_1(\theta_1, u(\theta_1)) + p(\theta_1)\gamma_2(\theta_1, u(\theta_1)) - \frac{1}{2} p(\theta_1)^2 - u(\theta_1) \right] d\theta_1,$$

subject to $\dot{u}(\theta_1) = p(\theta_1)$ and $\ddot{u}(\theta_1) \geq 0$, where $\gamma_1(\theta_1, \theta_2) = E[\frac{1}{2}x^2 \mid \theta_1, \tilde{\theta}_2 \leq \theta_2]$ and $\gamma_2(\theta_1, \theta_2) = E[c \mid \theta_1, \tilde{\theta}_2 \leq \theta_2]$.

As another example, the work on optimal taxation is frequently concerned about leaving rents to agents that is characterized as part of the principal's objective function. Here, there is a natural connection to this class of models.

As a last example, it is worth noting the recent work of Che and Gale (2000) on two-dimensional screening when one of the dimensions is the budget constraint of the buyer. In their framework, the monopolist is selling a good to a consumer with preferences $u = \theta_1 q - P$, but with a budget constraint given by θ_2. Hence, the indirect utility function is necessarily two-dimensional:

$$u(\theta_1, \theta_2) \equiv \max_{\{q \mid P(q) \leq \theta_2\}} \theta_1 q - P(q).$$

This is a departure from the basic model presented in that θ_2 does not enter utility linearly, and monetary payments can be directly informative about the buyer's budget θ_2, because a buyer cannot pay more than he has available. Although this problem looks more complicated than the previous setting, the authors demonstrate that an optimal nonlinear pricing schedule is increasing, convex, and goes through the origin. This pins down the utility of the lowest type, $\underline{u}$; efficiency at the top determines the other boundary. Although the resulting Euler equation generates a second-order differential equation, the solution can be found analytically in many simple examples. Formally, this setting differs from the previous in that the variable θ_2 represents dissipated surplus in the case of Rochet and Stole (2002), but θ_2 represents a constraint on how much money can be transferred to the principal in Che and Gale (2000). This minor difference nonetheless translates into a significant effect on the nature of the solution: in Rochet and Stole (2002) the determination of the participation region is more difficult than in Che and Gale's (2000) setting, where the latter are able to demonstrate that the optimal tariff goes through the origin and generates full participation, albeit with distorted consumption.[28]

Finally, it is worth pointing out that the general class of problems contained in this section are closely related to models of nonlinear pricing with income effects. As Wilson (1993a) has noted in his discussion of income effects (i.e., in models in which the marginal utility of money is not constant, but varies either with wealth levels or with some related parameterization), in general the Euler conditions for optimality will consist of second-order differential equations (rather than first-order in the canonical case) and fixed fees may be part of an optimal pricing schedule. Using the demand-profile approach, suppose that the income effect is modeled by a nonlinearity in money:

$$N[P, p, q] = \text{Prob}[\theta \in \Theta \mid \text{MRS}(q, I - P(q), \theta) \geq p(q)].$$

---

[28] One may be tempted to solve the budget-constrained class of problems in Che and Gale (2000) by appealing to the aggregation results presented earlier. In particular, a natural candidate for a sufficient statistic when there are unit demands, $q \in [0, 1]$, is $\theta = \min\{\theta_1, \theta_2\}$. This line of reasoning is flawed because $\min\{\theta_1, \theta_2\}$ is not a sufficient statistic for the consumer's marginal rate of substitution between money and q. A simple example from Che and Gale (2000) demonstrates this most clearly. Suppose first that the consumer's valuation for the good is distributed uniformly on $\Theta_1 = [0, 1]$ and the consumer's wealth is nonstochastic and equal to $\theta_2 = 2$. The revenue-maximizing unit price is $P(1) = \frac{1}{2}$ and expected revenues are $\frac{1}{4}$. Utilizing a price-quantity schedule cannot further increase revenues. Now, suppose instead that the consumer's valuation is fixed at $\theta_1 = 2$, but wealth is a random variable distributed uniformly on $\Theta_2 = [0, 1]$. In this case, $\min\{\theta_1, \theta_2\}$ is identical as in the former setting, but now the monopolist can raise expected revenues by charging the price schedule $P(q) = 2q$ for $q \in [0, 1]$. Each consumer of type θ_2 purchases the fraction $q = \theta_2/2$, and expected revenues are $\frac{1}{2}$. Aggregation fails because the marginal rates of substitution differ across the two settings and are not functions of the same aggregate statistic. In the first, the marginal rate of substitution of q for money is θ_1 if the total purchase price is less than or equal to 2 and 0 if the total price is greater than 2. In the second setting, the marginal rate of substitution is 2 if the total price is less than or equal to θ_2, and 0 otherwise.

Here, I represents income and the demand profile depends on the marginal price, $p(q)$, and the total price level, $P(q)$, since the latter affects the marginal rate of substitution of q for money. The Euler equation is

$$\frac{\partial N}{\partial P}[p(q) - C'(q)] - \frac{d}{dq}\left\{N + \frac{\partial N}{\partial p}[p(q) - C'(q)]\right\} = 0.$$

Because the second component is totally differentiated by q, a second-order differential equation arises.

The problem loses much of its tractability because N now depends on the total price level P as well as marginal price, p. Economically, the problem is complicated because the choice of a marginal price for some q will shift the consumer's demand curve via an income effect, which will affect the optimality of other marginal prices. Hence, the program is no longer block-recursive in structure as in Rochet and Stole (2002). As one raises the marginal price of a given level of output, one also lowers the participation rate for all consumers who consume that margin or greater. It is not a coincidence that, in some models of self-selection, private information over income, and exponential utility, the nature of the optimal allocation resembles that of the allocations in the nonlinear pricing context with random participation, as in Salanié (1990) and Laffont and Rochet (1998).

7. COMPETITIVE ENVIRONMENTS

This section builds on the previous sections by applying various models to study the effects of competition on the design of screening contracts. There have been some limited attempts to model imperfect competition between firms competing with nonlinear prices within a one-dimensional framework. This, for example, is the approach taken in the papers by Spulber (1989), Ivaldi and Martimort (1994), and Stole (1995). Similarly, in most work on common agency in screening environments (e.g., Stole 1991 and Martimort 1992, 1996), the agent's private information is of one dimension. Unfortunately, as argued previously, competitive models naturally suggest at least two dimensions of heterogeneity; so, the robustness of these approaches may be called into question.

Several papers have considered competitive nonlinear pricing using a variety of methodologies. We briefly survey a few papers using the demand-profile methodology with some limited success. We then present a specific form of bidimensional heterogeneity that has been successful in applied work.

7.1. A Variety of Demand-Profile Approaches

Wilson (1993a, Chapter 12) surveys the basic economics of firms competing with nonlinear prices, outlining two general classes of models. The first category supposes that there is some product differentiation between the firms. As before, an aggregate demand profile can be constructed that measures the proportion of consumers who buy from firm i at least q units when the marginal price is p;

this demand profile obviously depends on the nonlinear price schedules offered by the other firms. The first-order conditions for optimality now include terms capturing the flux of consumer purchases on the boundaries, but also isolate a competitive externality. Wilson numerically solves two models of this sort.

A second category of models discussed by Wilson (1993a) assumes that products are homogeneous. Now, to avoid the outcome of zero-profit, marginal-cost pricing between the competing firms, one has to assume some sort of extensive form game (e.g., a Cournot game where output is brought to market and then is subsequently priced with nonlinear price schedules, etc.). Several games are considered with a variety of strategic restrictions and results in Oren, Smith, and Wilson (1982) using the demand-profile approach.

7.2.   A Specific Approach: Location Models (Hotelling Type)

The third, more recent, approach has been to model competition in multidimensional environments in which simple aggregation is not available by introducing one dimension of uncertainty to handle the differentiation between firms (e.g., brand location and, more generally, "horizontal" heterogeneity) and another dimension to capture important characteristics of consumer tastes that may be similar in effect across all firms (e.g., marginal willingness to pay for quantity/quality and, more generally, "vertical" heterogeneity). Recent papers that take this approach include Armstrong and Vickers (1999), Biglaiser and Mezzetti (1999), Rochet and Stole (2002), and Schmidt-Mohr and Villas-Boas (1999), among others. We briefly survey the model and results in Rochet and Stole (1997, 2002) before remarking on the similar treatments by other authors.

As we suggest, this framework for modeling oligopoly markets is quite general; we need only posit some distribution of horizontal preferences.[29] What is fundamental is that our proposed model affords both a vertical preference parameter along the lines of Mussa and Rosen (1978), while also incorporating a measure of imperfect competition by allowing for distinct horizontal preferences.[30]

For simplicity, consider the case of two firms competing on either ends of a market with unit length and transportation cost σ. We will let $\theta_2^L \equiv \theta_2$ denote the distance from a consumer located at θ_2 to the left firm and $\theta_2^R \equiv 1 - \theta_2$ denote the distance from the same consumer to the right firm. Preferences are as before: For a consumer of type (θ_1, θ_2) consuming from firm j, an amount q_j at a price

---

[29] Such a framework has been usefully employed recently by Laffont, Rey, and Tirole (1998a, 1998b) and Dessein (1999) for studying competition between telecommunications networks.

[30] This modeling of competition is in the spirit of some recent empirical work on price discrimination. Leslie (1999), for example, in his study of Broadway theater ticket pricing finds it useful to incorporate heterogeneous valuations of outside alternatives to capture the presence of competing firms while maintaining a distinct form of vertical heterogeneity (in this case, income) to capture variation in preferences over quality. Because Leslie (1999) takes the quality of theater seats as fixed, he does not solve for the optimal quality-price schedule. Similarly, Ginsburgh and Weber (1996) use a Hotelling-type model to study price discrimination in the European car market.

of P_j, the consumer obtains utility of $\theta_1 q_j - \theta_2^j - P_j$. We further assume that θ_1 is distributed independently of θ_2, with $F(\theta_1)$ and $G(\theta_2)$ representing the distribution of types, respectively. Each firm simultaneously posts a publicly observable price schedule, $P_i(q_i)$, after which each consumer decides which firm (if any) to visit and which price-quality pair to select. The market share of firm j among consumers of type (θ_1, θ_2) can be computed easily:

$$M_j(u_j, u_k) = G_j \left(\min \left\{ \frac{u_j}{\sigma}, \frac{1}{2} + \frac{u_j - u_k}{2\sigma} \right\} \right). \tag{7.1}$$

This comes from the fact that the marginal consumer of firm j is located at a distance that is the minimum of $u_j(\theta_1)/\sigma$ (which occurs when the total market shares are less than one – the *local monopoly* regime) and $\frac{1}{2} + (u_j - u_k)/2\sigma$ (which occurs when all the market is served – the *competitive* regime). Again, using the dual approach, we can write the total expected profit of firm i as a functional involving the consumers' rents $u_i(\cdot)$ and $u_j(\cdot)$ taken as the strategic variables of the two firms:

$$u_j(\theta_1) \equiv \max_q \ \theta_1 q - P_j(q),$$

where P_j is the price schedule chosen by firm j. We obtain

$$B_j(u_j, u_k) = \int_{\underline{\theta}_1}^{\bar{\theta}_1} \{S(t, q_j(t)) - u_j(t)\} M_j(u_j(t), u_k(t)) \, dt, \tag{7.2}$$

where q_i is again related to u_i by the first-order differential equation $\dot{u}_j(\theta_1) = q_j(\theta_1)$.

We now look for a Nash equilibrium of the normal form game defined by (7.1) and (7.2), where the strategy spaces of the firms have been restricted to u_i consistent with nondecreasing quality allocations. This turns out to be a difficult task in general, because of the monotonicity conditions [remember that $q_L(\cdot)$ and $q_R(\cdot)$ have to be nondecreasing]. However, if we neglect these monotonicity conditions (which can be checked ex post), competitive nonlinear prices can be characterized by a straightforward set of Hamiltonian equations.

A numerical example is illustrative. Consider, for example, the case when θ_1 is uniformly distributed on $[4, 5]$, which is shown in Figure 5.7. For σ sufficiently large (i.e., $\sigma > 14.8$), the market shares of the two firms do not adjoin: each firm is in a (local) monopoly situation and the quality allocation is exactly the same as in our previously analyzed monopoly setting.[31] Interestingly, when the market shares are adjoining for high θ_1 (i.e., $u_L(\bar{\theta}_1) + u_R(\bar{\theta}_1) \geq \sigma$), but not all θ_1 (i.e, $u_L(\underline{\theta}_1) + u_R(\underline{\theta}_1) < \sigma$), the qualitative pattern of the solution remains identical (cf. Figure 5.7 below for $\sigma = 10$). However, when $u_L(\underline{\theta}_1) + u_R(\underline{\theta}_1) \geq \sigma$ (the fully competitive regime), it turns out that quality distortions disappear completely (cf. Figure 5.7 below, $\sigma < 16/3$). In this particular case, the equilibrium pricing schedules are cost-plus-fee schedules.

---

[31] It can be proved that this local monopoly solution involves full separation.

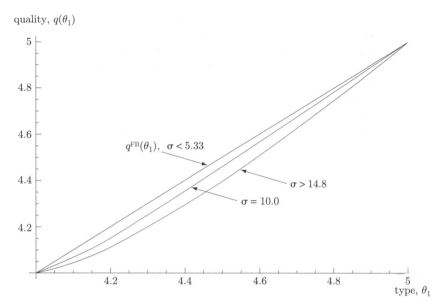

quality, $q(\theta_1)$

Figure 5.7. Quality choices in the oligopoly equilibrium for three regimes: fully competitive ($\sigma < 16/3$), mixed ($\sigma = 10$), and local monopoly ($\sigma > 14.8$). We assume that θ_2 is uniform on $[0, 1]$; θ_1 is uniform on $[4, 5]$.

As demonstrated by Armstrong and Vickers (1999) and Rochet and Stole (2002), the result that efficiency in q emerges for a fully covered market is somewhat general, extending well beyond this simple example. Formally, if σ is sufficiently small so as to guarantee that every consumer in $\Theta_1 \times \Theta_2$ purchases, in equilibrium each firm offers a cost-plus-fee pricing schedule, $P_j(q) = C(q) + F_j$, and each customer consumes the efficient allocation $q^{fb}(t)$ from one of the two firms.

Fundamentally, this result relies on full coverage and the requirement that the inverse hazard rate is constant over θ_1 in equilibrium for each firm. More generally, we could think about an N-firm oligopoly with a joint distribution of $(\theta_2^1, \ldots, \theta_2^N)$. Formally, let $G_i(u_1, \ldots, u_N) \equiv \text{Prob}[u_i - \theta_2^i \geq \max_{j \neq i} (u_j - \theta_2^j)]$, and let the inverse hazard rate be given by

$$H_i(u_1, \ldots, u_N) = \frac{G_i(u_1, \ldots, u_N)}{\frac{\partial}{\partial u_i} G_i(u_1, \ldots, u_N)}.$$

Then, if $d/du H_i(u, \ldots, u) = 0$, for each i, cost-plus-fixed-fee pricing is an equilibrium outcome.

Biglaiser and Mezzetti (1999), in a different context, consider the case of auctions for incentive contracts of a restricted form. Because sellers have heterogeneity over their ability to provide quality, each seller's objective function takes a similar form as in Armstrong and Vickers (1999) and Rochet and Stole

(2002). Nonetheless, because of the structure of preferences and contracts, efficient cost-based pricing emerges only in the limit as preferences become homogeneous.

8. SEQUENTIAL SCREENING MODELS

A common setting in which multidimensional screening is particularly important is when information evolves over time. For example, an important paper by Baron and Besanko (1984) considers the environment in which a regulated firm learns information about its marginal cost over time, and the regulator sets prices over time as a function of the firm's sequential choices.[32] As another example, consider the problem of refund pricing studied by Courty and Li (2000). Here, a consumer purchases an airline ticket knowing that, with some probability, the value of the trip may change. The initial purchase price may depend on the refund price, particularly when marginal return to the ticket may be positively correlated with the likelihood of a change in plans or a high second-period valuation. As a third important example, Clay, Sibley, and Srinagesh (1992) and Miravete (1997) provide convincing evidence that individuals choose a variety of purchase plans, such as telephone services and electricity, which turns out ex post to be suboptimal, suggesting that the consumer is uncertain about his final needs at the time of contracting. Miravete (1997) goes on to analyze this optimal two-stage tariff problem theoretically.

In these settings, the agent learns at $t = 1$ an initial one-dimensional type parameter, θ_1, distributed according to $F_1(\theta_1)$ on Θ_1, and enters into a contractual relationship with this private information. Making an appeal to the revelation principle, without loss of generality it is assumed that the firm offers a menu of nonlinear price schedules, $\{P(q, \hat{\theta}_1)\}_{\theta_1 \in \Theta_1}$, which we index by first-period report, $\hat{\theta}_1$. Later, at $t = 2$, additional information is revealed to the agent that is economically relevant and that affects the agent's marginal utility of the contractual activity in the final period. We denote this second-period information as θ_2, which is conditionally distributed according to $F_2(\theta_2 \mid \theta_1)$ on Θ_2 with density $f(\theta_2 \mid \theta_1)$. After the realization of θ_2, the consumer chooses a particular quantity from the schedule. Assume that the consumer's final utility is given by[33]

$$u = \theta_2 q - \frac{1}{2} q^2 - P.$$

---

[32] Baron and Besanko (1984) also address issues of moral hazard and optimal production choice over time in the context of their model.

[33] Note that θ_2 can directly depend on θ_1 in this setting. For example, it can be the case that $\theta_2 = \theta_1 + x$, where x is independently distributed from θ_1 and is learned at $t = 2$; this is the setting studied in Miravete (1996). For conciseness, we do, however, require that the support Θ_2 is independent of θ_1.

Given the specific utility of the agent in this setting, we know that θ_2 would be a sufficient statistic for the agent's preferences, and therefore at date $t = 2$, in absence of a prior contract, there would be a simple one-dimensional problem to solve – θ_1 is payoff irrelevant conditional on θ_2.[34]

This class of models differs from previous formulations of the multidimensional problem in that the sequential nature of the information revelation restricts the agent's ability to lie. Nonetheless, the recurring theme of this survey – that multidimensional models generally pose difficulties in determining the "tree" of binding incentive constraints – reappears in the sequential context as the single-crossing property is once again endogenous. Although the papers written to date on sequential screening have typically imposed sufficient conditions to guarantee a complete ordering (i.e., the single-crossing condition), the source of the problem is still the familiar one.

To see this clearly, consider the second stage of the relationship: incentive compatibility for any given schedule chosen at $t = 1$ is guaranteed by the standard methods. Specifically, defining second-period indirect utility and optimal choice by

$$u(\hat{\theta}_1, \theta_2) \equiv \max_{q \in Q} \; \theta_2 q - \frac{1}{2}q^2 - P(q \mid \hat{\theta}_1),$$

$$q(\hat{\theta}_1, \theta_2) \equiv \arg\max_{q \in Q} \; \theta_2 q - \frac{1}{2}q^2 - P(q \mid \hat{\theta}_1),$$

second-period incentive compatibility is equivalent to $\partial u(\theta_1, \theta_2)/\partial \theta_2 = q(\theta_1, \theta_2)$ and $q(\theta_1, \theta_2)$ nondecreasing in θ_2. The approach is standard because preferences satisfy a single-crossing property in the second period. First-period incentive compatibility is more difficult to address because single crossing in (q, θ_1) is not exogenously given. Assuming second-period incentive compatibility, first-period indirect utility as a function of true type θ_1 and reported type $\hat{\theta}_1$ can be defined as

$$\tilde{u}(\hat{\theta}_1 \mid \theta_1) \equiv \int_{\underline{\theta}_2}^{\overline{\theta}_2} u(\hat{\theta}_1, \theta_2) f_2(\theta_2 \mid \theta_1) \, d\theta_2.$$

The relevant first-order local condition for truth-telling at $t = 1$ requires that

$$\frac{d}{d\theta_1}\tilde{u}(\theta_1 \mid \theta_1) = \int_{\underline{\theta}_2}^{\overline{\theta}_2} u(\hat{\theta}_1, \theta_2) \frac{\partial f_2(\theta_2 \mid \theta_1)}{\partial \theta_1} \, d\theta_2.$$

In the standard setting, the *local* second-order condition $\partial^2 \tilde{u}(\theta_1 \mid \theta_1)/\partial \theta_1 \partial \hat{\theta}_1 \geq 0$, in tandem with a monotonicity condition, yields a sufficient condition for

---

[34] With more general preferences, however, we could remove the presence of a one-dimensional aggregate and still find that the sequential mechanism restricts the manner in which the agent can misreport, thereby simplifying the set of binding incentive constraints.

global incentive compatibility – the global single-crossing property:

$$\partial^2 \tilde{u}(\theta_1 \mid \hat{\theta}_1)/\partial \theta_1 \partial \hat{\theta}_1 \geq 0 \quad \forall \theta_1, \hat{\theta}_1 \in \Theta_1. \tag{scp}$$

In the present setting, this argument is not available. Instead, the focus is on maximizing the relaxed program (i.e., the program with only local first-order incentive conditions imposed), and then checking ex post that the second-order conditions are satisfied.

Substituting the agent's first-order condition into the principal's program and integrating by parts twice, we obtain the following virtual surplus for the sequential design program:

$$\Lambda(q, \theta_1, \theta_2) = \theta_2 q - \frac{1}{2} q^2 + \alpha(\theta_1, \theta_2)q - \tilde{u}(\underline{\theta}_1 \mid \underline{\theta}_1),$$

where

$$\alpha(\theta_1, \theta_2) \equiv \left(\frac{\partial F_2(\theta_2 \mid \theta_1)/\partial \theta_1}{f_2(\theta_2 \mid \theta_1)} \right) \left(\frac{1 - F_1(\theta_1)}{f_1(\theta_1)} \right).$$

Given that expected profit is $E_{\theta_1, \theta_2}[\Lambda(q, \theta_1, \theta_2)]$ and the IR constraint binds only for the lowest type $\theta_1 = \underline{\theta}_1$, profit is maximized by choosing q to maximize $\Lambda(q, \theta_1, \theta_2)$ pointwise over $\Theta_1 \times \Theta_2$. In general, the nature of the distortion will depend on the nature of the conditional distribution, $F_2(\theta_2 \mid \theta_1)$.

Baron and Besanko (1984) and Courty and Li (2000) consider the case of first-order stochastic dominance (FSD): i.e., θ_1 represents a first-order FSD shift in the distribution of θ_2. Both demonstrate that, under FSD, the IR constraint will bind for the lowest type because: (i) utility in the second period is nondecreasing in θ_2, and (ii) θ_1 shifts the distribution toward higher types. Hence, this relaxed program is cast in the appropriate form, and the principal will choose $\tilde{u}(\underline{\theta}_1, \underline{\theta}_1) = 0$. Examining the relaxed program, we see that in the FSD case, $\alpha < 0$, and the distortion in q is downward, away from the full-information solution. The intuition is by now familiar: By distorting consumption downward by a small amount, Δq, only a second-order loss in surplus arises, but a first-order gain in rent reduction is obtained as captured by $-\alpha \Delta q$. The difference in the sequential screening FSD model is that the dependence of future rents on θ_1 depends on the informativeness function, α. Baron and Besanko (1984) note the importance of commitment in this context, because the second-period allocation will be constrained efficient only if $\alpha(\theta_1, \theta_2)$ happens to equal $1 - F_2(\theta_2 \mid \theta_1)/f_2(\theta_2 \mid \theta_1)$.

When are the global incentive constraints satisfied by the q that solves the relaxed program? Baron and Besanko (1984) are silent on the sufficient conditions for global incentive compatibility, providing instead an example in which the global constraints are satisfied. Courty and Li (2000) demonstrate that if the resulting $q(\theta_1, \theta_2)$ allocation is nondecreasing in *both* arguments, then a price schedule exists that implements the allocation and satisfies global incentive compatibility.[35]

Courty and Li (2000) also consider the case in which θ_1 parameterizes the distribution of θ_2 in terms of a mean-preserving spread. Again, they demonstrate that the IR constraint will bind only for the lowest type, so the relaxed program is appropriate.[36] Global incentive compatibility in the first stage is again difficult to assess, but Courty and Li provide a useful sufficient condition to this end.[37] Interestingly, this incentive problem shares many similarities with the one-dimensional problem in which the sign of the cross-partial of expected utility with respect to q and θ_1 changes sign as one varies $(q, \theta_1) \in \mathcal{Q} \times \Theta_1$; see Araujo and Moreira (2000) for a discussion.[38] Taking the distributional assumption of Courty and Li, the solution to the relaxed program has a simple economic description. For all stage-one types, $\theta_1 < \bar{\theta}_1$, the principal introduces a *distortion in the second-period adjustment*. One can think of the final price as a markup over cost that depends on the difference between the final consumption and its expected value. The lower the initial type (i.e., the lower the noise in the second-stage marginal utility of consumption), the less valuable is the option to change consumption plans in the future. Note that variability creates higher value in expected consumption (which is why the IR constraint binds only for the lowest type, θ_1) and hence the monopolist will offer a lower price to this less consumption-valuing segment. The high types have high variability and also

---

[35] This follows immediately from the global sufficient condition for incentive compatibility,

$$\frac{\partial^2 \bar{u}(\theta_1 \mid \hat{\theta}_1)}{\partial \theta_1 \partial \hat{\theta}_1} = \int_{\underline{\theta}_2}^{\bar{\theta}_2} \frac{\partial u(\hat{\theta}_1, \theta_2)}{\partial \hat{\theta}_1} \frac{\partial f_2(\theta_2 \mid \theta_1)}{\partial \theta_1} \, d\theta_2 \geq 0.$$

Given that $q(\theta_1, \theta_2)$ is nondecreasing in the first argument, the first term in the integrand is a nondecreasing function of θ_2. Because θ_1 represents an FSD improvement in θ_2, this integral must be nonnegative. Moreover, the fact that $q(\theta_1, \theta_2)$ is nondecreasing in its second argument guarantees second-period global incentive compatibility. Because global incentive compatibility does not require that $q(\theta_1, \theta_2)$ be nondecreasing in the first argument, when the relaxed solution is neither monotone nor globally incentive compatible, the solution to the unrelaxed program is more complex than simply using an ironing procedure on q in the relaxed program.

[36] This follows from the necessary condition for second-stage incentive compatibility: $q(\theta_1, \theta_2)$ is nondecreasing in θ_2. This (with the local first-order condition) implies that $u(\theta_1, \theta_2)$ is convex in θ_2, and hence a mean-preserving spread must increase utility; hence the IR constraint can bind only for the lowest type, θ_1.

[37] One useful simplifying assumption used by Courty and Li is that the class of distribution functions passes through the same point $\theta_2 = z$ for all θ_1. This assumption guarantees that $\alpha(\theta_1, \theta_2)$ is negative (positive) for all $\theta_2 < z$ (resp., $\theta_2 > z$). Providing that the resulting allocation $q(\theta_1, \theta_2)$ from the relaxed program is nondecreasing in each argument, global incentive compatibility is satisfied at both stages. This will be the case, for example, whenever $(\partial F_2/\partial \theta_1)/f_2$ does not vary much in θ_1.

[38] Araujo and Moreira (2000) study a one-dimensional screening model where the single-crossing condition is relaxed. As a result, nonlocal incentive constraints can be binding. They derive optimal contracts within the set of piecewise continuous contracts, and apply their techniques to bidimensional models with (perfect) negative correlation between the two dimensions of individual heterogeneity.

high option value from altering future consumption. Hence, the firm can screen these customers from the low types by charging a premium for the initial ticket, but allowing a low-cost variation in the level of final consumption. It is also the case that *any* θ_1 *type* that draws $\theta_2 = z$ in the second period will consume the efficient allocation; in our present setting, this is $q = \theta_2 = z$. The actual allocation will rotate through this point, departing from the first-best allocation $q = \theta_2$ increasingly as θ_1 decreases. Although the final allocation may have some individuals consuming above the first-best level of output, this should not be considered an *upward* distortion. Rather, the distortion is in the amount of allowed stage-two adjustment; the principal optimally distorts this adjustment downward from the efficient level.[39]

9. PRODUCT BUNDLING

In the previous discussions, we have largely focused on a variety of models that are tractable at some expense in generality. Providing, for example, that either simple aggregation or separability exists, the type space is small and discrete, or $n = 1$, we can deal with multidimensional environments with some success. We now turn to a set of models in which multidimensional screening poses the most difficult problems: $n > 1$ and $m > 1$ with nonseparable and nonaggregatable preferences. The most well-studied version of this problem is the problem of commodity bundling by a multiproduct monopolist. We will consider the papers in the literature in this context.

9.1.   Some Simple Bundling Environments

We begin with the simplest linear n-product monopolist bundling environment, where $m = n$. Consumer preferences are given by

$$ u = \sum_{i=1}^{n} \theta_i q_i - P, $$

where each θ_i is independently and identically distributed according to the distribution function $F(\theta_i)$ on Θ_i. (Below, we extend this model to quadratic preferences.) The cost of production is assumed to be zero, but demands are for at most one unit of each product; hence without loss of generality $q_i \in [0, 1]$.

The monopolist's space of contracts is assumed to be a price schedule $P(q_1, \ldots, q_n)$ defined on the domain $[0, 1]^n$. Given that preferences are linear in money and consumption, we can think of $q_i \in (0, 1)$ as representing either a lottery over unit consumption or partial (but deterministic) consumption. We seek to find the optimal price schedule. Nonetheless, even in this simplified setting, we are still looking for a collection of $2^n - 1$ prices.

---

[39] This effect is similar to that which arises in signaling models in which agents desire to signal variance to the market. See, e.g., Prendergast and Stole (1996).

Unlike the full one-dimensional ($n = m = 1$) setting in which the economics of the downward distortion is well understood, it is difficult to see the economics behind the optimal screening contract in multidimensional environments. This is in part because the multidimensional bundling environment is mathematically more complex, but also because there are at least two distinct economic effects. The first is a familiar sorting effect in which consumption is distorted downward to reduce the rents to "higher" types; the second effect arises because if demand parameters are independently distributed, a law-of-large-numbers argument shows that multigoods have a "homogenizing" effect on consumer heterogeneity. To illustrate these effects, we will present two extreme forms of this model: when $n = 2$ and when $n \to \infty$.

9.1.1.   The Case of $n = m = 2$: Similarities with the One-Dimensional Paradigm

When $n = 2$, given the symmetry of the problem, we are looking for two marginal prices, $p(1)$ and $p(2)$; i.e., the price for one good, and the price for a second good, having already purchased the first good. The key insight is that even though the marginal values are independently distributed, the *order statistics are positively correlated*. This positive correlation makes the bundling environment akin to the classic one-dimensional paradigm. In short, provided that the first-order statistic of one consumer is greater than the first-order statistic of another, it is more likely than not that the second-order statistics are similarly ordered. Hence, it is probable that the two-good demand curves of any two consumers are nested. In this sense, a single-crossing property is present in a stochastic fashion.

To demonstrate this more precisely, denote consumer θ's first- and second-order statistics as $\theta^{(1)}$ and $\theta^{(2)}$, and refer to the corresponding first and second units of consumption as $q^{(1)}$ and $q^{(2)}$. Considering that it is physically possible to consume the second unit only after having consumed the first unit, the firm could think of this as a simple one-dimensional problem and construct the demand profile as follows:

$$N(p, q^{(i)}) = \text{Prob}[\theta^{(i)} \geq p].$$

One could then apply the one-dimensional paradigm for the demand profile to this function to obtain the optimal marginal prices. This procedure, although possibly profitable, will not obtain the maximum possible revenue. The reason why it may work in a crude sense is that a large subset of the type space will have nested demand curves (hence the one-dimensional single-crossing property will hold). Because not all types are so ordered, however, this procedure will fail to maximize revenue.

To return to the intuition for why a large subset of types are ordered as if they had one dimension, think about two consumers, where consumer A has a higher first-order statistic than consumer B. Conditional on this fact, it is also likely that consumer A will have a higher second-order statistic than B. In the case of uniformly distributed types on $\Theta_i = [0, 1]$, there is a three-fourths probability that such a nesting of demand curves will emerge between any two consumers. If the types were perfectly positively correlated, then demand curves over $\{q^{(1)}, q^{(2)}\}$ would always be nested, and we would be in the equivalent of a one-dimensional world. Because some types will have nonnested demand, a one-dimensional single-crossing property will not hold, and hence the simple demand-profile procedure will not maximize profits. Mathematically, the firm needs to account for the possibility of nonnested curves, and this alters the optimal price. A firm following the simple demand-profile procedure incorrectly perceives its profit to be

$$\pi = p(1)\text{Prob}[\theta^{(1)} \geq p^{(1)}] + p(2)\text{Prob}[\theta^{(2)} \geq p^{(2)}],$$

when in fact its profit is given by

$$\pi = p(1)(\text{Prob}[\theta^{(1)} \geq p^{(1)}] + \text{Prob}[\theta^{(1)} < p^{(1)} \ \& \ \theta^{(1)}$$
$$+ \theta^{(2)} > p^{(1)} + p^{(2)}]) + p(2)(\text{Prob}[\theta^{(2)} \geq p^{(2)}]$$
$$- \text{Prob}[\theta^{(2)} \geq p^{(2)} \ \& \ \theta^{(1)} + \theta^{(2)} < p^{(1)} + p^{(2)}]).$$

There is an adjustment that must be made to the demand for each product that is not noted by the naive seller. Nonetheless, to the extent that these second terms are small, the naive one-dimensional screening approach does well in approximating the optimal solution.

This simple example makes two points. First, the well-known economic principle behind nonlinear pricing in the one-dimensional model is still present in the two-dimensional model, albeit obscured. Second, as n becomes large, the likelihood that any two consumers will have ordered demand curves decreases to zero, suggesting that the one-dimensional intuition begins to wane as n increases. Although it is difficult to make this second idea precise, we will see that a homogenizing effect along the lines of the law of large numbers removes most of the value for sorting as n increases, suggesting that the one-dimensional intuition is less appropriate for larger n.

9.1.2. The Case of $n = m \rightarrow \infty$: The Homogenizing Effect of the Law of Large Numbers

It has been noted in a few papers that an increase in n with independently distributed types has the effect of allowing a firm to capture most of the consumer surplus.[40] The idea is simple: selling a single aggregate bundle (again assuming marginal cost is zero) can extract most of the consumer's rents, because as n becomes large the per-unit value of this bundle converges to the sample mean. Using the argument in Armstrong (1999b), let $s_i(\theta_i) \equiv \theta_i q_i^*(\theta_i) - C(q_i^*(\theta_i))$ represent the social surplus generated by a consumer of type θ who consumes the full-information efficient allocation, $q_i^*(\theta_i)$. Suppose that the distribution of $s_i(\theta_i)$ [derived from $F(\theta_i)$] has mean μ and standard deviation σ. Then, a firm that offers cost-plus-fee pricing, $P(\mathbf{q}) = (1 - \varepsilon)\mu + C(\mathbf{q})$, where

---

[40] Schmalensee (1984), Armstrong (1999b), and Bakos and Brynjolfsson (1996).

$\varepsilon = 2^{\frac{1}{3}} (\sigma/\mu)^{\frac{2}{3}}$, will obtain expected profits that converge to the full-information profit level as n approaches infinity.[41] Armstrong demonstrates that this result easily extends to a setting with a particular form of positive correlation:

$$u = \theta_0 \sum_{i=1}^{n} \theta_i q_i - P.$$

Now, θ_0 is a multiplicative shock, common to all n products, but independently distributed across consumers. Armstrong shows that as n increases, the firm's profit approaches that of a monopolist with uncertainty *only* over the common component.

9.2.   General Results on Product Bundling

In this section [based on Rochet and Choné (1998)], we generalize the bundling model presented to allow for multiple units demands. We come back to the general framework of nonlinear pricing by a multiproduct monopolist already studied by Wilson (1993a, 1993b) and Armstrong (1996) and presented in our Section 3.2. However, we do not assume the particular homogeneity properties of costs and types distributions that have allowed these authors to find explicit solutions using the separability property. In other words, we consider the most general multidimensional screening model in which binding IC constraints are unknown a priori. For simplicity, we assume linear-quadratic preferences:

$$u = \sum_{i=1}^{n} \left\{ \theta_i q_i - \frac{1}{2} q_i^2 \right\} - P.$$

Like before, production costs are assumed to be constant and normalized to zero, but contrary to the simple bundling model presented previously, demands for each good are not restricted to be 0 or 1. Types θ are distributed on some convex domain Θ, in accord with a continuous and positive density $f(\theta)$. Building on our previous discussions, we want to characterize the optimal pricing policy of a monopolist, using the parametric-utility approach. The problem is thus to find the function u^* that maximizes expected profit

$$E[\pi] = \int \{ S(\theta, \nabla u(\theta)) - u(\theta) \} f(\theta) \, d\theta,$$

over all convex, nonnegative functions u.

When the second-order condition is not binding (i.e., when u^* is strictly convex), we already saw that u^* is characterized by two elements:

1. a partition of the boundary $\partial \Theta$ of Θ into two subsets:
   - $\partial_0 \Theta$, where $u^* = 0$ (binding participation constraint), and

---

[41] More specifically, as shown in Armstrong (1999b), let π^* be the full-information expected profit level and let $\tilde{\pi}$ be the expected profit from the cost-plus-fee price schedule. Then, $\tilde{\pi}/\pi^*$ converges to 1 at speed $n^{-1/3}$.

- $\partial_1 \Theta$, where $\partial / \partial q \, S(\theta, \nabla u(\theta))$ is orthogonal to the boundary of Θ (no distortion along the boundary)
2. a set of paths γ connecting $\partial_0 \Theta$ to $\partial_1 \Theta$, along which u^* is computed by integrating $q^*(\theta) = \nabla u^*(\theta)$.

As proved by Armstrong (1996), the nonparticipation region Θ_0 (where $u^* = 0$) typically has a nonempty interior, and u^* can be computed numerically by solving a free-boundary problem; that is, finding the curve Ψ_0 that partitions Θ into two regions: Θ_0 (where $u^* = 0$), and Θ_1, where $u^* > 0$, and, in the latter region, u^* satisfies the Euler equation:

$$\operatorname{div}\left[\frac{\partial}{\partial q} S(\theta, \nabla u(\theta) \cdot f(\theta)\right] = -f(\theta),$$

together with the boundary condition stated previously.

The problem is that, for most distributions of types [for details, see Rochet and Choné (1998)], the solution of this free-boundary problem violates the second-order conditions. The economic intuition behind this result is the presence of a strong conflict between the desire of the monopolist to limit the nonparticipation region (by pushing Ψ_0 toward the lower boundary of Θ) and "transverse" incentive compatibility constraints (that force Θ_0 and thus Ψ_0 to be convex). By trading off these two effects, the typical shape of Ψ_0 will be linear, which means that, in the region immediately above it, u^* will depend only on a linear combination of θ_1 and θ_2.

This is a robust property of multidimensional screening problems: even with log concave distributions of types, bunching cannot be ruled out, and typically occurs in the "southwest" part of Θ (i.e., for consumers with low valuations in all dimensions). From an economic viewpoint, it means that "pure bundling" (i.e., an inefficient limitation of the choice set of consumers with low valuations) is a general pattern. Rochet and Choné (1998) consider, for example, the case where θ is exponentially distributed on $[a, +\infty)^2$: with $f(\theta) = \exp(2a - \theta_1 - \theta_2)$ and $a > 1$. Because θ_1 and θ_2 are independently distributed and demands are separable, a natural candidate for the optimal price schedule is the best separable price, which can easily be computed:

$$P(q_1, q_2) = q_1 + q_2 + (a - 1)^2,$$

giving rise to demands $q_i(\theta) = \theta_i - 1, i = 1, 2$.

However, this *cannot* be the solution, because the nonparticipation region would be empty. In fact, the true solution has the characteristic pattern of multidimensional screening models, whereby Θ is partitioned into three regions:

- the nonparticipation region Θ_0, delimited by a first boundary Ψ_0 (of equation $\theta_1 + \theta_2 = \tau_0$) in which $u^* = 0$,
- the pure bundling region Θ_1, delimited by a second boundary Ψ_1 (of equation $\theta_1 + \theta_2 = \tau_1$) in which consumers are forced to buy a bundle with identical quantities of the two goods (thus u^* is not strictly convex, because it depends only on $\theta_1 + \theta_2$), and finally

- the fully separating region, where consumers have a complete choice and u^* can only be determined numerically.

Rochet and Choné (1998) design a specific technique, the sweeping procedure, which generalizes the ironing procedure of Mussa and Rosen (1978) for dealing with this new form of bunching, that is specific to multidimensional screening problems.

10. CONCLUDING REMARKS

In this survey, we have emphasized one general theme – that in models with multidimensional heterogeneity over preferences, the ordering of the binding incentive constraints is endogenous. Because the resulting endogenous ordering also is a source of our economic predictions, the difficulty in finding general, tractable mathematical models is particularly significant.

Notwithstanding this pessimistic appraisal, we have also emphasized in these pages that several solutions to this problem of endogenous ordering exist, all of which shed light on this issue. The simple discrete model we presented, together with a sketch of the algorithm for determining the endogenous ordering and a solution for the simple two-type case, is helpful in illustrating the economic multidimensional screening contracts – one of our primary goals in this paper. In addition, we present a variety of classes of restricted models that make the modeling tractable although still allowing sufficient theoretical degrees of freedom for interesting economics to come out of the analysis. We are particularly heartened by the recent results applied to auctions, bundling, and other rich economic settings, especially competitive environments.

ACKNOWLEDGMENTS

We are grateful to Mark Armstrong and Patrick Legros for helpful comments. The first author thanks CNRS for financial support. The second author thanks the National Science Foundation for financial support through the PFF Program. Any errors are our own.

References

Anderson, S., A. de Palma, and J.-F. Thisse (1992), *Discrete Choice Theory of Product Differentiation*. Cambridge, MA: MIT Press.

Araujo, A. and H. Moreira (2000), "Adverse Selection Problems without the Spence-Mirrlees Condition," mimeo, IMPA, Rio de Janeiro, Brazil.

Armstrong, M. (1996), "Multiproduct Nonlinear Pricing," *Econometrica*, 64(1), 51–75.

Armstrong, M. (1999a), "Optimal Regulation with Unknown Demand and Cost Functions," *Journal of Economic Theory*, 84(2), 196–215.

Armstrong, M. (1999b), "Price Discrimination by a Many-Product Firm," *Review of Economic Studies*, 66(1), 151–168.

Armstrong, M. and J.-C. Rochet (1999), "Multi-dimensional Screening: A User's Guide," *European Economic Review*, 43(4–6), 959–979.

Armstrong, M. and J. Vickers (1999), "Competitive Price Discrimination," mimeo.

Armstrong, M. and J. Vickers (2000), "Multiproduct Price Regulation under Asymmetric Information," *Journal of Industrial Economics*, 48(2), 137–159.

Bakos, Y. and E. Brynjolfsson (1996), "Bundling Information Goods: Pricing, Profits and Efficiency," Discussion Paper, MIT.

Baron, D. P. and D. Besanko (1984), "Regulation and Information in a Continuing Relationship," *Information Economics and Policy*, 1(3), 267–302.

Baron, D. and R. Myerson (1982), "Regulating a Monopolist with Unknown Costs," *Econometrica*, 50(4), 911–930.

Berry, S., J. Levinsohn, and A. Pakes (1995), "Automobile Prices in Market Equilibrium," *Econometrica* 63(4), 841–890.

Biais, B., D. Martimort, and J.-C. Rochet (2000), "Competing Mechanisms in a Common Value Environment," *Econometrica*, 68(4), 799–838.

Biglaiser, G. and C. Mezzetti (1999), "Incentive Auctions and Information Revelation," mimeo, University of North Carolina.

Blackorby, C. and W. Schworm (1984), "The Structure of Economies with Aggregate Measures of Capital: A Complete Characterization," *Review of Economic Studies*, 51, 633–650.

Brown, S. and D. Sibley (1986), *The Theory of Public Utility Pricing*. New York: Cambridge University Press.

Che, Y.-K. and I. Gale (1996a), "Expected Revenue of All-Pay Auctions and First-Price Sealed-Bid Auctions with Budget Constraints," *Economics Letters*, 50(3), 373–379.

Che, Y.-K. and I. Gale (1996b), "Financial Constraints in Auctions: Effects and Antidotes," in *Advances in Applied Microeconomics, Volume 6: Auctions*, (ed. by M. R. Baye), Greenwich, CT: JAI Press, 97–120.

Che, Y.-K. and I. Gale (1998), "Standard Auctions with Financially Constrained Bidders," *Review of Economic Studies*, 65(1), 1–21.

Che, Y.-K. and I. Gale (1999), "Mechanism Design with a Liquidity Constrained Buyer: The 2×2 Case," *European Economic Review*, 43(4–6), 947–957.

Che, Y.-K. and I. Gale (2000), "The Optimal Mechanism for Selling to a Budget-Constrained Buyer," *Journal of Economic Theory*, 92(2), 198–233.

Clay, K., D. Sibley, and P. Srinagesh (1992), "Ex Post vs. Ex Ante Pricing: Optional Calling Plans and Tapered Tariffs," *Journal of Regulatory Economics*, 4(2), 115–138.

Courty, P. and H. Li (2000), "Sequential Screening," *Review of Economic Studies*, 67(4), 697–718.

Dana, J. (1993), "The Organization and Scope of Agents: Regulating Multiproduct Industries," *Journal of Economic Theory*, 59(2), 288–310.

Dessein, W. (1999), "Network Competition in Nonlinear Pricing," mimeo, ECARE, Brussels.

Fudenberg, D. and J. Tirole (1991), *Game Theory*. Cambridge, MA: MIT Press, Chapter 7.

Gal, S., M. Landsberger and A. Nemirouski (1999), "Costly Bids, Rebates and a Competitive Environment," mimeo, University of Haifa.

Ginsburgh, V. and S. Weber (1996), "Product Lines and Price Discrimination in the European Car Market," mimeo.

Goldman, M. B., H. Leland, and D. Sibley (1984), "Optimal Nonuniform Prices," *Review of Economic Studies*, 51, 305–319.

Green, J. and J.-J. Laffont (1977), "Characterization of Satisfactory Mechanisms for the Revelation of Preferences for Public Goods," *Econometrica*, 45, 427–438.

Guesnerie, R. and J.-J. Laffont (1984), "A Complete Solution to a Class of Principal-Agent Problems with an Application to the Control of a Self-Managed Firm," *Journal of Public Economics*, 25, 329–369.

Hotelling, H. (1929), "Stability in Competition," *Economic Journal*, 39, 41–57.

Ivaldi, M. and D. Martimort (1994), "Competition under Nonlinear Pricing," *Annales d'Economie et de Statistique*, 34, 71–114.

Jehiel, P., B. Moldovanu, and E. Stacchetti (1999), "Multidimensional Mechanism Design for Auctions with Externalities," *Journal of Economic Theory*, 85(2), 258–293.

Jullien, B. (2000), "Participation Constraints in Adverse Selection Models," *Journal of Economic Theory*, 93(1), 1–47.

Laffont, J.-J., E. Maskin, and J.-C. Rochet (1987), "Optimal Nonlinear Pricing with Two-Dimensional Characteristics," in *Information, Incentives, and Economic Mechanisms.*, (ed. by T. Groves, R. Radner, and S. Reiter), Minneapolis MN: University of Minnesota Press.

Laffont, J.-J., P. Rey, and J. Tirole (1998a), "Network Competition: Overview and Nondiscriminatory Pricing," *Rand Journal of Economics*, 29(1), 1–37.

Laffont, J.-J., P. Rey, and J. Tirole (1998b), "Network Competition: Price Discrimination," *Rand Journal of Economics*, 29(1), 38–56.

Laffont, J.-J. and J.-C. Rochet (1998), "Regulation of a Risk-Averse Firm," *Games and Economic Behavior*, 25, 149–173.

Laffont, J.-J. and J. Tirole (1986), "Using Cost Observation to Regulate Firms," *Journal of Political Economy*, 94, 614–641.

Laffont, J.-J. and J. Tirole (1993), *A Theory of Incentives in Regulation and Procurement.* Cambridge, MA: MIT Press.

Leslie, P. (1999), "Price Discrimination in Broadway Theatre," mimeo, UCLA.

Lewis, T. and D. Sappington (1988), "Regulating a Monopolist with Unknown Demand and Cost Functions," *Rand Journal of Economics*, 19(3), 438–457.

Lewis, T. and D. Sappington (1989a), "Inflexible Rules in Incentive Problems," *American Economic Review*, 79(1), 69–84.

Lewis, T. and D. Sappington (1989b), "Countervailing Incentives in Agency Problems," *Journal of Economic Theory*, 49, 294–313.

Maggi, G. and A. Rodriguez-Clare (1995), "On Countervailing Incentives," *Journal of Economic Theory*, 66(1), 238–263.

Martimort, D. (1992), "Multi-principaux avec Anti-selection," *Annales d'Economie et de Statistique*, 28, 1–37.

Martimort, D. (1996), "Exclusive Dealing, Common Agency, and Multiprincipals Incentive Theory," *Rand Journal of Economics*, 27(1), 1–31.

Mas-Colell, A., M. Whinston and J. Green (1995), *Microeconomic Theory*. New York: Oxford University Press.

Maskin, E. and J. Riley (1984), "Monopoly with Incomplete Information," *Rand Journal of Economics*, 15, 171–196.

McAfee, R. P. and J. McMillan (1987), "Competition for Agency Contracts," *Rand Journal of Economics*, 18(2), 296–307.

McAfee, R. P. and J. McMillan (1988), "Multidimensional Incentive Compatibility and Mechanism Design," *Journal of Economic Theory*, 46(2), 335–354.

Miravete, E. (1996), "Screening Consumers Through Alternative Pricing Mechanisms," *Journal of Regulatory Economics*, 9(2), 111–132.

Miravete, E. (1997), "Estimating Demand for Local Telephone Service with Asymmetric Information and Optimal Calling Plans," Working Paper, INSEAD.

Mirrlees, J. (1971), "An Exploration in the Theory of Optimum Income Taxation," *Review of Economic Studies*, 38(114), 175–208.

Mirrlees, J. (1976), "Optimal Tax Theory: A Synthesis," *Journal of Public Economics*, 6(4), 327–358.

Mussa, M. and S. Rosen (1978), "Monopoly and Product Quality," *Journal of Economic Theory*, 18, 301–317.

Myerson, R. (1981), "Optimal Auction Design," *Mathematics of Operations Research*, 6, 58–73.

Myerson, R. (1991), *Game Theory*. Cambridge, MA: Harvard University Press.

Oren, S., S. Smith, and R. Wilson (1983), "Competitive Nonlinear Tariffs," *Journal of Economic Theory*, 29(1), 49–71.

Prendergast, C. and L. Stole (1996), "Impetuous Youngsters and Jaded Oldtimers: Acquiring a Reputation for Learning," *Journal of Political Economy*, 104(6), 1105–1134.

Rochet, J.-C. (1984), "Monopoly Regulation with Two Dimensional Uncertainty," mimeo, Université Paris 9.

Rochet, J.-C. (1987), "A Necessary and Sufficient Condition for Rationalizability in a Quasi-linear Context," *Journal of Mathematical Economics*, 16(2), 191–200.

Rochet, J.-C. and P. Choné (1998), "Ironing, Sweeping, and Multidimensional Screening," *Econometrica*, 66(4), 783–826.

Rochet, J.-C. and L. Stole (1997), "Competitive Nonlinear Pricing," mimeo.

Rochet, J.-C. and L. Stole (2000), "Nonlinear Pricing with Random Participation," *Review of Economic Studies* 69(1), 277–311.

Salanié, B. (1990), "Selection Adverse et Aversion pour le Risque," *Annales d'Economie et de Statistique*, 18, 131–149.

Schmalensee, R. (1984), "Gaussian Demand and Commodity Bundling," *Journal of Business*, 57(1), Part 2, S211–S230.

Schmidt-Mohr, U. and M. Villas-Boas (1999), "Oligopoly with Asymmetric Information: Differentiation in Credit Markets," *Rand Journal of Economics*, 30(3), 375–396.

Sibley, D. and P. Srinagesh (1997), "Multiproduct Nonlinear Pricing with Multiple Taste Characteristics," *Rand Journal of Economics*, 28(4), 684–707.

Spence, M. (1980), "Multi-Product Quantity Dependent Prices and Profitability Constraints," *Review of Economic Studies*, 47, 821–841.

Spulber, D. (1989), "Product Variety and Competitive Discounts," *Journal of Economic Theory*, 48, 510–525.

Stole, L. (1991), "Mechanism Design and Common Agency," mimeo, MIT.

Stole, L. (1995), "Nonlinear Pricing and Oligopoly," *Journal of Economics and Management Strategy*, 4(4), 529–562.

Stole, L. (1997), "Lectures on the Theory of Contracts", mimeo, University of Chicago.

Wilson, R. (1993a), *Nonlinear Pricing*. Oxford, UK: Oxford University Press.

Wilson, R. (1993b), "Design of Efficient Trading Procedures," in *The Double Auction Market: Institutions, Theories and Evidence*, Chapter 5, Santa Fe Institute Studies, Volume 14, (ed. by D. Friedman and J. Rust), Reading, MA: Addison Wesley, 125–152.

Wilson, R. (1996), "Nonlinear Pricing and Mechanism Design," in *Handbook of Computational Economics. Volume 1. Handbooks in Economics, Volume 13*, (ed. by H. Amman, D. Kendricks, and J. Rust), New York: Elsevier Science, 253–293.

Zheng, C. G. (2000), "Optimal Auction in a Multidimensional World," Discussion Paper, Northwestern University.

A Discussion of the Papers by Pierre-Andre Chiappori and Bernard Salanié and by Jean Charles Rochet and Lars A. Stole

Patrick Legros

Each of these surveys is a "must read": anyone who wants to analyze multi-dimensional screening models should start by reading Rochet and Stole (RS), and anyone who wants to do empirical work on contracts should begin with Chiappori and Salanié (CS). I will start this discussion (Section 1) by what I perceived to be the main message of each survey. Although the two papers are quite different in nature and in focus, they both remind us why we should be interested in contracts and organizations: when markets are incomplete or imperfect, contracts and organizations are the relevant allocation devices and are not neutral from an "efficiency" point of view. Therefore, if we want to understand the effects of economic policies, macroeconomic shocks, techno-logical shocks on the performance of firms, or the economy, we are bound first to answer two questions.

1. What are the effects of contractual and organizational choices on be-havior and economic performance?
2. What are the determinants of contractual choices?

RS and CS show how answers to these questions can be enhanced by the-oretical and empirical work in contract theory. Reading these surveys and the literature, it seems fair to acknowledge two tendencies: first, that empirical work has been an active consumer of theory, but that theory has been a more timid consumer of empirical work and, second, that we seem to have many answers to (1), but fewer answers to (2). I will therefore develop two themes in my discussion: the necessity of a *constructive dialogue* between theory and empirical work, and the necessity to provide theoretical models that will more accurately capture market forces. Although the first theme is clearly present in RS and CS, the second theme is less present in these surveys, but is a logical consequence of the agendas described in RS and CS. Section 2 develops the two themes, and Section 3 illustrates these themes with some examples taken from CS.

1. ROCHET-STOLE AND CHIAPPORI-SALANIÉ

1.1. RS: Multidimensional Screening

The difficulty in multidimensional screening models is the lack of a natural order on types. The problem is not so much one of feasibility, because RS show an algorithm by which the solution can be computed. The problem is rather the possibility to obtain robust qualitative results (similar, e.g., to the "no ineffi-ciency at the top" result in the one dimension). RS provide a useful classification of the multidimensional models into three categories. They show that, for two of them (aggregation and separability), such robust results can be obtained.

The properties of the solution in the aggregation case (i.e., when the mul-tidimensionality can be reduced to one dimension by using an aggregator) are (obviously) related to the distribution of the aggregator. RS footnote 21 nicely illustrates this point. More important differences arise in the separability case (when transversality conditions can be ignored): bundling at the bottom and the possibility of efficiency at the top *and* at the bottom when one looks at one dimension only. RS convincingly show that a rich new set of economic prob-lems can be studied by going from one to two (or more) dimensions. Budgetary constraints, sequential screening, and multiple product purchase are naturally modeled as multidimensional screening problems that can be analyzed at times as simply as in the one-dimensional case.

Because in practice not all dimensions can be quantified or instrumented, a challenge faced by theory is to provide results like those in Figure 5.6 of RS (i.e., to establish a relationship between the endogenous variable and the quantifiable dimension). Figure 5.6 summarizes the relationship between the noise in the distribution of outside options and the quantity schedule contingent on the first dimension in a parametric example. Because outside options are not observable, the relevant exogenous variable in a regression would indeed be the first dimension only (the residual would then be the noise in outside options). We observe that all solutions are increasing in the first dimension, and that the schedule becomes "flatter" as the noise in outside options becomes larger. Note also that there is a U-shaped relationship between the noise and the size of the bundling region at the bottom. The comparative static results in Figure 5.6 are therefore quite useful from a theoretical perspective, since they tell us how noise in outside options yields different quality-price schedules than the fixed (and uniform) outside option case.

However, it is not clear how easy it will be to identify these results. For instance, a change in the flatness of the optimal schedule could be obtained in the one-dimensional case by changing the distribution function (since the flatness is related to the hazard rate). It is not clear at this point how one can empirically distinguish a multidimensional model in which the second dimension is a (random) outside option from a one-dimensional model. There is a sense, however, in which this difficulty is also a strength, because the interpretation of the residual as unobserved outside options might be more satisfying than the interpretation in terms of measurement error.

1.2.   CS: Capturing (Endogenous) Heterogeneity

CS's survey covers a lot of ground. They identify early on the main challenge that empirical work must face: controlling for heterogeneity and endogeneity of the contractual relationships. If agents self-select into firms or contracting relationships, the outcome of the relation, as well as the contract itself, are explained by the characteristics of the agents, whereas the modeler would be tempted to see the contract as the endogenous variable and the characteristics of the agents in the relationship as the exogenous variables. Their warning should also echo to theorists.

CS show that it is possible to create or find good data sets to test a variety of important questions: incentive effects of compensation schemes, relative importance of adverse selection and moral hazard to explain behavior in markets, role of reputation, and effects of contractual instruments (e.g., insurance deductible, technology that make contracts more complete). At the same time CS make clear the difficulties in meeting their challenge: controlling for the selection effect, distinguishing between the available theoretical models, and controlling for quasi-rents.

The task of identifying the incentive effect is already daunting. Trying to identify whether the *form* of contracting is "optimal," as they set to do in their Section 3, is certainly even more daunting. For instance, principal-agent theory simply tells that, for a *given* outside option of the agent, there exists a second-best optimal contract that maximizes the level of utility of the principal. Changing the outside option might – and often will – also change the *form* of the second-best contract. Hence, unless there is a good way to proxy for the outside option, or for the market forces that affect this outside option, it is not clear how one can answer the question, "Are contracts optimal?" This problem is even more severe when other organizational instruments such as monitoring, auditing, size of the hierarchy, etc. define the form of the contract.

2.   TOWARD A CONSTRUCTIVE DIALOGUE

2.1.   More Theory or More Facts? Necessity of a Dialogue

Research in contract theory has proceeded like most other scientific endeavors: one step at a time. It has isolated sources of imperfections and has analyzed the consequences of these imperfections for contracts, prices, or organizations. This literature has generated a large "toolbox" consisting of a host of models (e.g., adverse selection, moral hazard, multitasks, teams, principal-agent, principal-agents, principals-agent, principals-agents, additive noise, multiplicative noise, complete contracting, incomplete contracting, dynamic contracting, career concerns). Do we now have an embarrassment of riches? To paraphrase the title of a recent paper,[1] is contract theory plagued by too many theories and too few facts? I will argue in fact that we need more facts *and* more theory.

A dialogue between theory and empirical work is necessary to identify the relevant *omitted variables* in theoretical and empirical research. Omitted variables are usually associated with econometric analysis. Theory is useful because it helps the econometrician pinpoint the relevant omitted variables, and how these variables affect the observed outcome. Here, the "embarrassment of riches" becomes the solution. Less appreciated perhaps is the fact that theoretical work also faces (by nature?) a problem of omitted variables. An analysis based on a moral hazard model will fail if the essence of the imperfection is adverse selection. If *both* moral hazard and adverse selection are important, a new model combining the two effects might be necessary if one expects new effects to emerge when the two imperfections are taken simultaneously into account. Here, empirical work helps by providing a "sanity check" on the relevance of a model in a given situation and by suggesting new avenues for research.

Now, it is easy to make a model "more general": generalize some assumptions. Ignoring issues of tractability, such generalizations seem to be useful for the dialogue with empirical work if they yield robust theoretical results that are qualitatively different from the simpler case *and* if these differences can be identified in empirical work. CS and RS are excellent illustrations of the benefits of such a dialogue between theory and empirical work. The main focus of RS is on finding robust theoretical results and the main focus of CS is on identifying theoretical results in the data.

However, and this is another theme of this discussion, while existing theoretical and empirical work can generate a dialogue to answer (1) – do incentives matter and how? – the theoretical literature uses a modeling paradigm that will eventually limit the possibility to pursue the dialogue successfully and answer (2) – what determines contracts? This modeling paradigm is the use of outside options for capturing market effects (i.e., forces external to the contract or the organization). Outside options capture the underlying market forces at play in the economy. The question is then *which* outside options correctly capture market forces. As I argue in the next section, there is a need for theoretical constructs that "bypass" the outside options and that capture directly the relationship between observable data and market forces. This would facilitate, for instance, the identification of the effects in the random outside options model of RS, or the completion of the agenda set forth in Section 3 of CS.

---

[1] Baker and Holmström (1995).

to accept to bear all risk (i.e., we should observe rental contracts for risky crops and sharecropping for less risky crops, which is consistent with stylized facts, but is the opposite to what a model with homogeneous workers would predict). Hence, theory omits both an "internal variable" – the heterogeneity in workers' risk attitude – and an "external variable" – the competitive determination of the assignment of workers to crops. Here, "facts" force theory to identify relevant omitted variables.

However, this is not the end of the dialogue. Imagine that workers indeed have the same risk attitude and that crops have different riskiness. Can theory still make sense of "the facts"? If yes, what are the relevant omitted variables? We can follow here an early work of Rao (1971).[5] Because the ability to contract on output is linked to its verifiability, riskier crops prevent the use of output contingent contracts – absent technologies that make output verifiable. Hence, a profit-maximizing land owner who can allocate resources between technologies that make input verifiable and technologies that make output verifiable will tend to favor output monitoring when crops are risky and to favor input monitoring when crops are less risky. Now, if there is input monitoring, it is easier to contract directly on the worker effort, and the contract should reflect first-best risk-sharing arrangements, whereas if there is output monitoring, incentives will be created by having the worker bear more risk. Here, again, we obtain a negative correlation between riskiness of crop and sharecropping, absent heterogeneity in risk attitudes. Theory therefore points out an omitted internal variable – the ability to monitor (or measure) input and output[6] – and emphasizes the trade-off between rent extraction and incentives.

3.2.   From Fixed Wages to Piece Rates

3.2.1.   Incentives Matter

CS cite the papers by Lazear (1999) and by Paarsch and Shearer (1999), who show how going from fixed wage to piece rates will generate (large) productivity gains. For those of us who are interested in incentive theory, this is good news indeed. In the case of Paarsch and Shearer, the firm uses both piece rate and wage contracts, whereas in the case of Lazear there was a change in management that coincided with a change of compensation scheme from fixed wage to piece rate. In the first case, the observed productivity reflects both the contractual terms and

---

[5] See, also, Allen and Lueck (1995), Newman (1999), and Prendergast (2000). Leffler and Rucker (1991) show also that contractual choices are best explained by variables like enforcement costs or measurement costs rather than differences in risk attitudes. Interestingly, Ackerberg and Botticini (2000) conclude that there is no empirical support for the risk-sharing hypothesis, but that there is empiricial support for the moral hazard and the imperfect capital market hypotheses.

[6] A corollary of this story is that riskier crops should also be correlated with more delegation of authority to the worker. See Rao (1971) or Prendergast (2000).

the land condition (piece rate is associated with good planting conditions).[7] In the second case the observed productivity *seems* to reflect only the contractual change.

Both studies are related to question (1). Paarsch and Shearer also partially answer question (2) because they see as a possible source of contractual choice the quality of the land. Lazear is more silent on (2). For both situations, outside options are not taken into account. This raises a natural question in the case of Lazear: Why did we observe the contractual change following the change of management? There are at least three possible answers.

- Is it because there was some type of organizational innovation? This is not likely given the prevalence of piece-rate contracts elsewhere.
- Is it because the previous management did not realize the productivity benefits of using piece rates? Possibly (and could explain why the previous management was replaced). In this case, the contractual change generates sorting effects: high types are paid more and therefore will tend to "flow" toward the firm more than before.[8]
- Or is it because the change of management coincided with a change in outside options (or other market conditions) of the workers?[9] In this case, sorting effects generate the contractual change. It is because high types have a relatively larger outside option than low types that the contract must be piece-rate in order to minimize the cost to the firm of giving each type of agent his outside option. Here the omitted variable is external.

3.2.2. Outside Options Matter

In the work cited by RS and by CS, moral hazard or asymmetric information was key to explaining the performance and nature of the contracts. As I have argued, external variables are also important. Here, I would like to propose a simple example showing how external variables could be sufficient to explain, for instance, the choice of piece-rate versus wage contracts.

Consider a risk-neutral principal *who has limited liability* (this is the first "market variable"; there is a missing insurance market) and who contracts with a risk-averse worker. Assume that output is verifiable *and that effort is contractable*. To simplify, assume that there is a unique level of effort consistent

---

[7] Note the parallel with the previous explanation for correlation between sharecropping and riskiness of crop.

[8] This is the observation of Lazear (1999)

[9] Think of a situation in which the type of a worker affects his private cost of production, but not the level of production. It is easy to show that, if there is any cost to implementing menu contracts, we will observe for relatively equal outside options a unique wage-effort contract, although if the outside options are more unequal, we will observe a menu contract that can be implemented by a piece-rate contract.

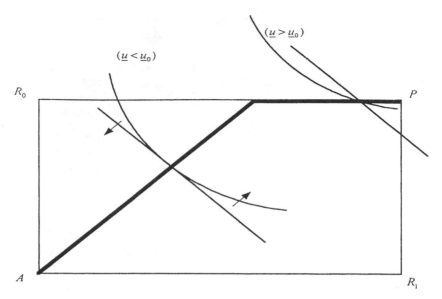

Figure 1. Piece-rate contracts are optimal when outside option is large.

with production and that there is an equal probability that a low output R_0 and a high output R_1 are realized.

The principal will therefore choose a contingent contract (w_0, w_1) that minimizes the expected wage bill subject to two constraints: (i) the limited liability constraint that wages cannot exceed available output and (ii) the participation constraint that the expected utility of the agent is greater than his outside option $\underline{u}$ (this is our second "market variable"). The principal solves the problem

$$\begin{cases} \min w_0 + w_1 \\ u(w_0) + u(w_1) \geq 2\underline{u} \\ w_i \in [0, R_i], \ i = 0, 1. \end{cases}$$

It is straightforward to show that the cost-minimizing schedule is of the form $w_1 = w_0 + b(R_1 - R_0)$ and that there exists a cutoff level $\underline{u}_0 = u(R_0)$ such that when the outside option is smaller than $\underline{u}_0$, the optimal b is equal to zero (wage contract) and when the outside option is greater than $\underline{u}_0$, the optimal b is positive and increases in the outside option (piece-rate contract). This is also simply illustrated in the Edgeworth box diagram (Figure 1) where the contract curve corresponding to the previous problem is the thick line.

For low values of the outside option, the contract curve is the full insurance line. For high values of the outside option, the limited liability constraint of the principal binds and prevents full insurance. A change from wage contracting to piece-rate contracting is therefore directly due to an increase in outside options, absent any agency problem.

References

Ackerberg, D. and M. Botticini (2002), "Endogenous Matching and the Empiricial Determinants of Contract Form," *Journal of Political Economy*, 110(3), 564–591.

Ackerberg, D. and M. Botticini (2000), "The Choice of Agrarian Contracts in Early Renaissance Tuscany: Risk Sharing, Moral Hazard, or Capital Market Imperfections?" *Explorations in Economics History*, 37(3), 241–257.

Aghion, P., M. Dewatripont, and P. Rey (1999), "Competition, Financial Discipline and Growth," *Review of Economic Studies*, 66, 825–852.

Allen, D. W. and D. Lueck (1995), "Risk Preferences and the Economics of Contracts," *American Economic Review*, 85, 447–451.

Baker, G. and B. Holmström (1995), "Internal Labor Markets: Too Many Theories, Too Few Facts," *American Economic Review*, 85(2), 255–259.

Fershtman, C. and K. Judd (1987), "Equilibrium Incentives in Oligopoly," *American Economic Review*, 77, 927–940.

Lazear, E. (1999), "Performance Pay and Productivity," mimeo (revised version of NBER W5672, 1996, with the same title).

Leffler, K. B. and R. R. Rucker (1991), "Transaction Costs and the Organization of Production: Evidence from Timber Sales Contracts," *Journal of Political Economy*, 99(5), 1060–1087.

Legros, P. and A. Newman (1996), "Wealth Effects, Distribution and the Theory of Organization," *Journal of Economic Theory*, 70, 312–341.

Newman, A. (1999), "Risk-Bearing, Entrepreneurship and the Theory of Moral Hazard," mimeo.

Prendergast, C. (2000), "Uncertainty and Incentives," mimeo.

Rao, C. H. H. (1971), "Uncertainty, Entrepreneurship, and Sharecropping in India," *Journal of Political Economy*, 79(3), 578–595.

Schmidt, K. (1997), "Managerial Incentives and Product Market Competition," *Review of Economic Studies*, 64, 191–213.

CHAPTER 6

Theories of Fairness and Reciprocity: Evidence and Economic Applications

Ernst Fehr and Klaus M. Schmidt

1. INTRODUCTION

Most economic models are based on the *self-interest hypothesis* that assumes that *all* people are *exclusively* motivated by their material self-interest. Many influential economists – including Adam Smith (1759), Gary Becker (1974), Kenneth Arrow (1981), Paul Samuelson (1993), and Amartya Sen (1995) – pointed out that people often do care for the well-being of others and that this may have important economic consequences. Yet, so far, these opinions have not had much of an impact on mainstream economics. In recent years, experimental economists have gathered overwhelming evidence that systematically refutes the self-interest hypothesis. The evidence suggests that many people are strongly motivated by other-regarding preferences, and that concerns for fairness and reciprocity cannot be ignored in social interactions. Moreover, several theoretical papers have been written showing that the observed phenomena can be explained in a rigorous and tractable manner. Some of these models shed new light on problems that have puzzled economists for a long time (e.g., the persistence of noncompetitive wage premia, the incompleteness of contracts, the allocation of property rights, the conditions for successful collective action, and the optimal design of institutions). These theories in turn induced a new wave of experimental research offering additional exciting insights into the nature of preferences and into the relative performance of competing theories of fairness. The purpose of this paper is to review these recent developments, to point out open questions, and to suggest avenues for future research. Furthermore, we will argue that it is not only necessary, but also very promising for mainstream economics to take the presence of other-regarding preferences into account.

Why are economists so reluctant to give up the self-interest hypothesis? One reason is that this hypothesis has been quite successful in providing accurate predictions in some economic domains. For example, models based on the self-interest hypothesis make very good predictions for competitive markets with standardized goods. This has been shown in many carefully conducted market experiments. However, a large amount of economic activity is taking place outside of competitive markets – in markets with a small number of traders, in markets with informational frictions, in firms and organizations, and under incompletely specified and incompletely enforceable contracts. In these environments, models based on the self-interest assumption frequently make very misleading predictions. An important insight provided by some of the newly developed fairness models is that they show why, in competitive environments with standardized goods, the self-interest model is so successful and why, in other environments, it is refuted. In this way, the new models provide fresh and experimentally confirmed insights into important phenomena (e.g., nonclearing markets or the widespread use of incomplete contracts).

We consider it important to stress that the available experimental evidence also suggests that many subjects behave quite selfishly even when they are given a chance to affect other peoples' well-being at a relatively small cost. However, there are also many people who are strongly motivated by fairness and reciprocity and who are willing to reward or punish other people at a considerable cost to themselves. One of the exciting insights of some of the newly developed theoretical models is that the interaction between fair and selfish individuals is key to the understanding of the observed behavior in strategic settings. These models explain why, in some strategic settings, almost all people behave as if they are completely selfish, whereas in others the same people will behave as if they are driven by fairness.

A second reason for the reluctance to give up the self-interest hypothesis is methodological. There is a strong convention in economics of not explaining puzzling observations by changing assumptions on preferences. Changing preferences is said to open Pandora's box, because everything can be explained by assuming the "right" preferences. We believe that this convention made sense in the past when economists did not have sophisticated tools to examine the nature of preferences in a scientifically rigorous way. However, because of the development of experimental techniques, this is no longer true. In fact, one purpose of this paper is to show that much progress and fascinating new insights into the nature of fairness preferences have been made in the past decade. Although there is still much to be done, this research clearly shows that it is possible to discriminate between theories based on different preference assumptions. Therefore, in view of the facts, the new theoretical developments, the importance of fairness concerns in many economic domains, and in view of the existence of rigorous experimental techniques that allow us to examine hitherto unsolvable problems in a scientific manner, we believe that it is time to recognize that a substantial fraction of the people is also motivated by fairness concerns. People do not differ only in their tastes for chocolate and bananas, but also along a more fundamental dimension. They differ with regard to how selfish or fair-minded they are, and this does have important economic consequences.

The rest of this paper is organized as follows. Section 2 provides many real-life examples indicating the relevance of fairness considerations and reviews the experimental evidence. It shows that the self-interest model is refuted in many important situations and that a substantial number of people seem to be strongly concerned about fairness and behave reciprocally. Section 3 surveys different theoretical approaches that try to explain the observed phenomena. In the meantime, there is also a large and growing literature on the evolutionary origins of reciprocity (see, e.g., Bowles and Gintis 1999; Gintis 2000; Sethi and Somananthan 2000, 2001). We do not discuss and review this literature in our paper. Section 4 discusses the wave of new experiments that have been conducted to discriminate between these theories. Section 5 explores the implications of fairness-driven behavior in various economic applications and offers some directions for future research. Section 6 concludes. In view of the length of our paper, it is also possible to read the paper selectively. For example, readers who are already familiar with the basic evidence and the different fairness theories may go directly to the new evidence in Section 4 and the economic applications in Section 5.

2.   EMPIRICAL FOUNDATIONS OF FAIRNESS AND RECIPROCITY

2.1.   Where Does Fairness Matter?

The notion of fairness is frequently invoked in families, at the workplace, and in people's interactions with neighbors, friends, and even strangers. For instance, our spouse becomes sour if we do not bear a fair share of family responsibilities. Our children are extremely unhappy and envious if they receive less attention and gifts than their brothers and sisters. We do not like those among our colleagues who persistently escape doing their share of important, yet inconvenient, departmental activities.

Fairness considerations are, however, not restricted to our personal interactions with others. They shape the behavior of people in important economic domains. For example, employee theft and the general work morale of employees are affected by the perceived fairness of the firm's policy (Greenberg, 1990 and Bewley, 1999). The impact of fairness and equity norms may render direct wage cuts unprofitable (Kahneman, Knetsch, and Thaler 1986, Agell and Lundborg, 1995). Firms may, therefore, be forced to cut wages in indirect ways (e.g., by outsourcing activities). Fairness concerns may thus influence decisions about the degree of vertical integration. They may also severely affect the hold-up problem as demonstrated by Ellingsen and Johannesson (2000). Debates about the appropriate income tax schedule are strongly affected by notions of merit and fairness (Seidl and Traub, 1999). The amount of tax evasion is likely to be affected by the perceived fairness of the tax system (Frey and Weck-Hanneman, 1984, Alm, Sanchez, and de Juan 1995, Andreoni, Erard, and Feinstein 1998). Public support for the regulation of private industries depends on the perceived fairness of the firms' policies (Zajac, 1995). Compliance with contractual obligations, with organizational rules, and with the law in general is strongly shaped by the perceived fairness of the allocation of material benefits and by issues of procedural justice (Lind and Tyler, 1988, Fehr, Gächter, and Kirchsteiger, 1997). The functioning of incentive-compatible mechanisms has been shown to depend on fairness considerations (Andreoni and Varian, 1999). The solution of collective action problems (e.g., rules regulating the access to common pool resources) critically depends on the fairness of the allocation of the costs and benefits of the rules (Ostrom 1990, 2000, Falk, Fehr, and Fischbacher, 2000c). The erosion of public support for the welfare state in the United States in the last two decades probably has much to do with deeply entrenched notions of reciprocal fairness (Bowles and Gintis, 2000). Many people cease to support public programs that help the poor if they have the impression that the poor do not attempt to bear their share of a society's obligations.

Thus, real-world examples in which fairness concerns are likely to matter abound. Nevertheless, in the following, we concentrate on clean experimental studies, because in most real-life situations, it is impossible to unambiguously isolate the impact of fairness motives. A skeptic may always argue that the notion of fairness is used only for rhetorical purposes that disguises purely self-interested behavior in an equilibrium of a repeated game. Therefore, we rely on experimental evidence of human decision making. In these experiments, real subjects make decisions with real monetary consequences in carefully controlled laboratory settings. In particular, the experimenter can implement one-shot interactions between the subjects so that long-term self-interest can be ruled out as an explanation for what we observe. As we will see, in some experiments, the monetary stakes involved are quite high – amounting up to the income of three months' work. In the experiments reviewed, subjects do not know each others' identity, they interact anonymously, and, sometimes, even the experimenter cannot observe their *individual* choices.

2.2.   Experimental Evidence

In hindsight, it is a bit ironic that experiments have proved to be critical for the discovery and the understanding of fairness-driven behavior, because for several decades, experimental economists were firmly convinced that fairness motives would not matter much. At best, fair behavior was viewed as a temporary deviation from the strong forces of self-interest. In the 1950s, Vernon Smith discovered that, under relatively weak conditions, experimental markets quickly converge to the competitive equilibrium.[1] Since then, the remarkable convergence properties of experimental markets have been confirmed by hundreds of experiments (see, e.g., Davis and Holt, 1993). For these experiments, the equilibrium is computed under the assumption that *all* players are

---

[1] Smith's results were eventually published in 1962 in the *Journal of Political Economy* after time-consuming debates with the referees. It is also ironic that Smith's initial aim was "to do a more credible job of rejecting competitive price theory" than Chamberlin (1948).

exclusively self-interested. Therefore, the quick convergence to equilibrium has been interpreted as a confirmation of the self-interest hypothesis. We will see later in this paper that this conclusion was premature because, as the newly developed models of fairness show (see Section 3 and Section 5.1), convergence to standard competitive predictions can occur even if agents are very strongly concerned about fairness.

This strong commitment to the self-interest hypothesis slowly weakened in the 1980s when experimental economists started to study bilateral bargaining games and interactions in small groups in controlled laboratory settings (see, e.g., Roth, Malouf, and Murningham, 1981, Güth et al., 1982). One of the important experimental games that ultimately led many people to realize that the self-interest hypothesis is problematic was the so-called Ultimatum Game (UG) invented by Güth, Schmittberger, and Schwarze (1982). In addition, the Gift Exchange Game (GEG), the Trust Game (TG), the Dictator Game (DG), and Public Good Games (PGGs) played an important role in weakening the exclusive reliance on the self-interest hypothesis. All these games share the feature of simplicity. Because they are so simple, they are easy to understand for the experimental subjects, and this makes inferences about subjects' motives more convincing.

In the UG, a pair of subjects has to agree on the division of a fixed sum of money. Person A, the Proposer, can make one proposal of how to divide the amount. Person B, the Responder, can accept or reject the proposed division. In the case of rejection, both receive nothing; in the case of acceptance, the proposal is implemented. Under the standard assumptions that (i) both the Proposer and the Responder are rational *and* care only about how much money they get and (ii) that the Proposer knows that the Responder is rational and selfish, the subgame perfect equilibrium prescribes a rather extreme outcome: The Responder accepts *any* positive amount of money and, hence, the Proposer gives the Responder the smallest money unit, ε, and keeps the rest.

A robust result in the UG, across hundreds of experiments, is that proposals offering the Responder less than 20 percent of the available surplus are rejected with probability 0.4–0.6. In addition, the probability of rejection is decreasing in the size of the offer (see, e.g., Güth et al., 1982, Camerer and Thaler, 1995; Roth, 1995, and the references therein). Apparently, many Responders do not behave in a self-interest maximizing manner. In general, the motive indicated for the rejection of positive, yet "low," offers is that subjects view them as unfair. A further robust result is that many Proposers seem to anticipate that low offers will be rejected with a high probability. This is suggested, for example, by the comparison of the results of DGs and UGs. In a DG, the Responder's option to reject is removed – the Responder must accept any proposal. Forsythe et al. (1994) were the first who compared the offers in UGs and DGs. They report that offers are substantially higher in the UG, which suggests that many Proposers do apply backward induction. This interpretation is also supported by the surprising observation of Roth, Prasnikar, Okuno-Fujiwara, and Zamir

(1991), who showed that the modal offer in the UG tends to maximize the expected income of the Proposer.[2]

The UG shows that a sizeable fraction of Responders is willing to punish behavior that is perceived as unfair. In contrast, the GEG indicates that a substantial fraction of the Responders is willing to reward actions that are perceived as generous or fair. The first GEG has been conducted by Fehr, Kirchsteiger, and Riedl (1993). In the GEG, the Proposer offers an amount of money $w \in [\underline{w}, \overline{w}]$, $\underline{w} \geq 0$, which can be interpreted as a wage payment, to the Responder. The Responder can accept or reject w. In case of a rejection, both players receive zero payoff; in case of acceptance, the Responder has to make a costly "effort" choice $e \in [\underline{e}, \overline{e}]$, $\underline{e} > 0$. The monetary payoff for the Proposer is $x^P = ve - w$, whereas the Responder's payoff is $x^R = w - c(e)$, where v denotes the marginal value of effort for the Proposer and $c(e)$ the strictly increasing effort cost schedule.[3] Under the standard assumptions (i) and (ii), the Responder will always choose the lowest feasible effort level $\underline{e}$ and will, in equilibrium, never reject any w. Therefore, the subgame perfect proposal is the lowest feasible wage level $\underline{w}$.

The GEG captures a principal–agent relation with highly incomplete contracts in a stylized way. Variants of the GEG have been conducted by several authors.[4] All of these studies report that the mean effort is, in general, positively related to the offered wage that is consistent with the interpretation that the Responders, on average, reward generous wage offers with generous effort choices. However, as in the case of the UG, there are considerable individual differences among the Responders. Although there typically is a sizeable fraction of Responders (frequently roughly 40 percent, sometimes more than 50 percent) who exhibit a reciprocal effort pattern, there is also a substantial fraction of Responders who always make purely selfish effort choices or whose choices seem to deviate randomly from the self-interested action. Despite the presence of selfish Responders, the relation between average effort and wages is in general sufficiently steep to render a high wage policy profitable. This induces Proposers to pay wages far above $\underline{w}$. Evidence for this interpretation comes from Fehr, Kirchsteiger, and Riedl, who embedded the GEG into an experimental market.

---

[2] Suleiman (1996) reports the results of UGs with varying degrees of veto power. In these games, a rejection meant that λ percent of the cake was destroyed. For example, if $\lambda = 0.8$, and the Proposer offered a 9:1 division of $10, a rejection implied that the Proposer received $1.8, whereas the Responder received $0.2. Suleiman reports that Proposers' offers are strongly increasing in λ.

[3] In some applications of this game, the Proposer's payoff was given by $x^P = (v - w)e$. This formulation rules out that Proposers can make losses when they offer generously high wages. Likewise, in some applications of the GEG, the Responder did not have the option to reject w. Thus, the Proposer just sent w, whereas the Responder choose an effort level. Under the standard assumptions of rationality and selfishness, the subgame perfect equilibrium is, however, not affected by these differences.

[4] See, e.g., Fehr, Kirchsteiger, and Riedl (1993, 1998), Charness (1996, 2000), Brandts and Charness (1999), Falk, Gächter, and Kovacs (1999), Fehr and Falk, (1999), Gächter and Falk (1999), and Hannan, Kagel, and Moser (1999).

In addition to the embedded GEG, there was a control condition in which the effort level was exogenously fixed by the experimenter. Note that, in the control condition, the Responders can no longer reward generous wages with high effort levels. It turns out that the average wage is substantially reduced when the effort is exogenously fixed.

Another important game that did much to change the exclusive reliance on the self-interest hypothesis was the TG, first studied by Berg, Dickhaut, and McCabe (1995). In a TG, a Proposer receives an amount of money y from the experimenter, and then can send between zero and y to the Responder. The experimenter then triples the amount sent, which we term z, so that the Responder has $3z$. The Responder is then free to return anything between zero and $3z$ to the Proposer. It turns out that many Proposers send money and that many Responders give back some money. Moreover, there is frequently a strong correlation between z and the amount sent back at the individual, as well as at the aggregate, level (see, e.g., Miller 1997, Cox 2000, Fahr and Irlenbusch, 2000).

Finally, we briefly consider the evidence on PGGs. Like the GEG, the PGG is important because it not only provides interesting insights into the nature of nonpecuniary motivations, but it also captures the essence of numerous real-world situations. There is by now a huge experimental literature on PGGs (see, for surveys, Dawes and Thaler, 1988, Ledyard, 1995). In the typical experiment, there are n players who simultaneously decide how much of their endowment to contribute to a public good. Player i's monetary payoff is given by $x_i = y_i - g_i + m \sum g_j$, where y_i is player i's endowment, g_i her contribution, m the monetary payoff per unit of the public good, and $\sum g_j$ the amount of the public good provided by all players. The unit payoff m obeys $m < 1 < nm$. This ensures that it is a dominant strategy to contribute nothing to the public good, although the total surplus would be maximized if all players contributed their whole endowment.[5] In many experiments, the PGG is repeated for about 10 periods, in which in each period the group composition changes randomly. If we restrict attention to behavior in the final period (to abstract from repeated games or learning effects), it turns out that roughly 75 percent of all subjects contribute nothing to the public good and the rest contributes very little.[6]

If one adds to the PGG the opportunity to punish other group members, the contribution pattern changes radically (Fehr and Gächter 2000). In a PGG with a punishment option, there are two stages. Stage 1 is identical to the previously described PGG. At stage 2, after every player in the group has been informed

---

[5] Typically, endowments are identical and $n \leq 10$, but there are also experiments with a group size of 40 and 100 (Isaac, Walker, and Williams, 1994).

[6] At the beginning of a repeated PGG, subjects contribute on average between 40 and 60 percent of their endowment; but, toward the end, contributions are typically very low. This pattern may be due to repeated game effects. Another plausible reason for the decay of cooperation is that many subjects are conditional cooperators, as shown by Croson (1999), Fischbacher, Gächter, and Fehr (1999), and Sonnemans, Schram, and Offerman (1999). Conditional cooperators cease to cooperate once they notice that selfish subjects take advantage of their cooperation.

about the contributions of each group member, each player can assign up to
ten punishment points to each of the other players. The assignment of one punishment point reduces the first-stage income of the punished subject by three
points on average, but it also reduces the income of the punisher according to a
strictly increasing and convex cost schedule. Note that because punishment is
costly for the punisher, the self-interest hypothesis predicts zero punishment.
Moreover, because rational players will anticipate this, the self-interest hypothesis predicts that nobody will contribute (i.e., there should be no difference in
the contribution behavior between the usual PGG and a PGG with a punishment
opportunity). The experimental evidence is, however, completely at odds with
this prediction. Although, in the usual PGG, cooperation is close to zero in the
final period, the punishment opportunity causes, on average, stable cooperation
rates around 75 percent of subjects' endowment.[7] The reason for these huge
differences in contribution behavior is that in the punishment condition many
cooperators punish the free riders. The more a subject deviates from the average contribution of the other group members, the more it is punished. Thus, the
willingness to punish "unfair" behavior is not restricted to the UG.

The above-mentioned facts in the UG, the GEG, the TG, and the PGG are
now well established, and there is little disagreement about them. But there are,
of course, questions about which factors change the behavior in these games.
For example, a question that routinely comes up in discussions with economists
is whether a rise in the stake level will eventually induce subjects to behave
in a self-interested manner. There are several papers examining this question
(Hoffman, McCabe, and Smith 1996; Fehr and Tougareva 1995; Slonim and
Roth 1998; Cameron 1999). The surprising answer is that relatively large increases in the monetary stakes did nothing or little to change behavior. Hoffman
et al. could not detect any effect of the stake level in their UGs. Fehr and
Tougareva conducted GEGs (embedded in a competitive exerimental market)
in Moscow. In one condition, the subjects earned, on average, the equivalent
amount of the income of 1 week in the experiment. In another condition, they
earned the equivalent of 10 weeks' income. Despite this large difference in the
stake size, there are no significant differences across conditions in the behavior
of both the Proposers and the Responders. Slonim and Roth conducted UGs
in Slovakia. They found a small interaction effect between experience and the
stake level. In the final period of a series of one-shot UGs, the Responders
in the high-stake condition (with a tenfold increase in the stake level relative
to the low-stake condition) seem to be willing to reject a bit less frequently.
Fehr and Tougareva also allowed subjects to repeat the game (with randomly
matched partners). They found no such interaction effects. Cameron conducted
UGs in Indonesia and – in the high-stake condition – subjects could earn

---

[7] If the same subjects are allowed to stay together for 10 periods, the cooperation rate even climbs
to 90 percent of subjects' endowments *in the final period*. In Fehr and Gächter (2000), the group
size was $n = 4$. Recently, Carpenter (2000) showed that, with a group size of $n = 10$, subjects
achieve almost *full* cooperation, even with a random group composition over time.

the equivalent of three months' income in her experiment. She observed no effect of the stake level on Proposers' behavior and a slight reduction of the rejection probability when stakes were high.

Of course, it is still possible that, in the presence of extremely high stakes, there may be a shift toward more selfish behavior. However, for large segments of the population, this is not the economically relevant question. For almost all people, the vast majority of their decisions involves stake levels well below three months' income. Thus, even if fairness-driven behavior would play no role at all at stake levels above that size, fairness concerns would still play a major role in many economically important domains.

2.3.   Interpretation of the Evidence

Although there is now little disagreement regarding the facts, there is still disagreement about the interpretation of these facts. In Section 3, we will describe several recently developed theories of fairness that maintain the rationality assumption, but change the assumption of purely selfish preferences. Some researchers have, however, reservations about changes in the motivational assumptions and prefer, instead, to interpret the behavior in these games as elementary forms of bounded rationality. For example, Binmore, Gale, and Samuelson (1995) and Roth and Erev (1995) try to explain the presence of fair offers and rejections of low offers in the UG by learning models that are based on purely pecuniary preferences. These models are based on the idea that the rejection of low offers is not very costly for the Responder and, therefore, the Responders learn only very slowly not to reject such offers. The rejection of offers is, however, quite costly for the Proposers. Therefore, Proposers learn more quickly that it does not pay to make low offers. Moreover, because Proposers quickly learn to make fair offers, the pressure on the Responders to learn accepting low offers is greatly reduced. This gives rise to very slow convergence to the subgame perfect equilibrium – if there is convergence at all. The simulations of Binmore et al. and Roth and Erev show that it often takes thousands of iterations until play comes close to the standard prediction.

In our view, there can be little doubt that learning processes are important in real life, as well as in laboratory experiments. There are numerous examples where the behavior of subjects changes over time, and it seems clear that learning models are prime candidates to explain such dynamic patterns. We believe, however, that attempts to explain the basic facts in such simple games as the UG, the GEG, and the TG in terms of learning models that assume completely selfish preferences are misplaced. The decisions of the Responders, in particular, are so simple in these games that it is difficult to believe that they make systematic mistakes and reject money or reward generous offers, although their true preferences would require them not to do so. Moreover, the previously cited evidence from Roth et al. (1991), Forsythe et al. (1994), Suleiman (1996), and Fehr et al. (1998) suggests that many Proposers do anticipate Responders' actions surprisingly well. Thus, at least in these simple two-stage games, many Proposers seem to be quite rational and forward-looking.

Sometimes it is also argued that the behavior in these games is because of a social norm (see, e.g., Binmore 1998). In real life, so the argument goes, experimental subjects make the bulk of their decisions in repeated interactions. It is well known that, in repeated interactions, the rejection of unfair offers or the rewarding of generous offers can be sustained as an equilibrium. According to this argument, notions of fairness perform the function of selecting a particular equilibrium among the infinitely many equilibria that typically exist in long-term interactions. Subjects' behavior is, therefore, adapted to repeated interactions, and they tend to apply behavioral rules that are appropriate in the context of repeated interactions erroneously to laboratory one-shot games. This argument essentially boils down to the claim that subjects cannot rationally distinguish between one-shot and repeated interactions. One problem with this argument – apart from claiming that subjects make systematic mistakes – is that it cannot explain the huge behavioral variations across one-shot games. Why do, in Forsythe et al. (1994), the Proposers give so much less in the DG compared with the UG? Why do the Proposers in the control condition with exogenously fixed effort (Fehr et al., 1998) make so low wage offers? Why is there so much defection in the final round of PGGs, whereas in the presence of a punishment opportunity, a high level of cooperation can be achieved? Invoking some kind of social norm cannot explain this behavior unless one is willing to assume that different social norms apply to these different situations. A second problem with this argument is that there is compelling evidence that, in repeated interactions, experimental subjects do behave very differently compared with one-shot situations. In Gächter and Falk (1999), it is shown that the Responders in GEGs put forward much higher effort levels if they can stay together with the same Proposer.[8] In fact, experimental subjects who participate in one-shot GEGs frequently complain after the experiment that the experimenter ruled out repeated interactions because that would have enabled them, so the subjects' claim, to develop a much more trustful and efficient relation with their partner. All this indicates that experimental subjects are well aware of the difference between one-shot interactions and repeated interactions.

These arguments suggest that an approach that combines bounded rationality with purely selfish preferences does not provide a satisfactory explanation of the facts observed in UGs, GEGs, TGs, and PGGs. In our view, there remain two plausible approaches to account for the facts. One approach is to maintain the assumption of rationality at least for the analysis of these simple games and to assume, in addition, that some players are not only motivated by pecuniary forces. The other approach is to combine models of learning with models that take into account nonselfish motives. In the following we focus on the first

---

[8] Andreoni and Miller (1993) also report that, in prisoner's dilemmas, increases in the probability of staying together or meeting the same partner again increase cooperation rates.

approach because there has been much progress in this area in recent years, whereas the second approach is still in its infancy.[9]

3. THEORIES OF FAIRNESS AND RECIPROCITY

This section surveys the most prominent recent attempts to explain the experimental evidence sketched in Section 2 within a rational choice framework. Two main approaches can be distinguished. The first approach assumes that at least some agents have "social preferences" (i.e., the utility function of these agents depends not only on the own material payoff, but also on how much the other players receive). Given these social preferences, all agents are assumed to behave perfectly rational, and the well-known concepts of traditional utility and game theory can be applied to analyze optimal behavior and to characterize equilibrium outcomes in experimental games. The second approach focuses on "intention-based reciprocity." This approach assumes that a player cares about the intentions of her opponent. If she feels treated kindly, she wants to return the favor and be nice to her opponent. If she feels treated badly, she wants to hurt her opponent. Thus, in this approach, it is crucial how a player interprets the behavior of the other players. This cannot be captured by traditional game theory but requires the framework of psychological game theory.

The starting point of both of these approaches is to make rather specific assumptions on the utility functions of the players. Alternatively, one could start from a general preference relation and ask what kind of axioms are necessary and sufficient to generate utility functions with certain properties. Axiomatic approaches are discussed at the end of this section.

3.1.   Social Preferences

Classical utility theory assumes that a decision maker has preferences over allocations of material outcomes (e.g., goods) and that these preferences satisfy some "rationality" or "consistency" requirements, such as completeness and transitivity. However, in almost all applications, this fairly general framework is interpreted much more narrowly by implicitly assuming that the decision maker cares about only one aspect of an allocation, namely the material resources that are allocated to her. Models of social preferences assume, in contrast, that the decision maker may also care about how much material resources are allocated to others.

Somewhat more formally, let $\{1, 2, \ldots, N\}$ denote a set of individuals and $x = (x_1, x_2, \ldots, x_N)$ denote an allocation of physical resources out of some set X of feasible allocations, where x_i denotes the material resources allocated to person i. The self-interest hypothesis says that the utility of individual i

---

[9] An exemption is the recent paper by Cooper and Stockman (1999), which combines reenforcement learning with a model of social preferences, and the paper by Costa-Gomes and Zauner (1999).

depends on x_i only. We will say that individual i has *social preferences* if for any given x_i person i's utility is affected by variations of x_j, $j \neq i$. Of course, simply assuming that the utility of individual i may be any function of the total allocation is too general, because it does not yield any empirically testable restrictions on observed behavior. In the following, we will discuss several models of social preferences, each of which assumes that the preferences of an individual depend on x_j, $j \neq i$, in a different way.

3.1.1. Altruism

A person is altruistic if the first partial derivatives of $u(x_1, \ldots, x_N)$ with respect to $x_1, \ldots, x_N$ are strictly positive (i.e., if her utility increases with the well-being of other people).[10] The hypothesis that people are altruistic has a long tradition in economics and has been used to explain charitable donations and the voluntary provision of public goods (see, e.g., Becker, 1974).

Clearly, the simplest game to elicit altruistic preferences is the DG. Adreoni and Miller (2000) conducted a series of DG experiments in which one agent could allocate "tokens" between herself and another agent for a series of different budgets. The tokens were exchanged into money at different rates for the two agents and the different budgets. Let $U_i(x_1, x_2)$ denote subject i's utility function representing her preferences over monetary allocations (x_1, x_2).

In a first step, Adreoni and Miller check for violations of the General Axiom of Revealed Preference and find that almost all subjects behaved consistently and passed this basic rationality check. Then they classify the subjects into three main groups. They find that about 30 percent of the subjects give tokens to the other party in a fashion that equalizes the monetary payoffs between players. The behavior of 20 percent of the subjects can be explained by a utility function in which x_1 and x_2 are perfect substitutes [i.e., these subjects seem to have maximized the (weighted) sum of the monetary payoffs]. However, there are also almost 50 percent of the subjects who behaved "selfishly" and did not give any significant amounts to the other party. Andreoni and Miller (2000, p. 23) conclude that altruistic behavior exists and that it is consistent with rationality, but also that individuals are heterogeneous.

Charness and Rabin (2000) consider a specific form of altruism that they call *quasi-maximin preferences*. They start from a "disinterested social welfare function," which is a convex combination of Rawls' maximin criterion and a utilitarian welfare function:

$$W(x_1, x_2, \ldots, x_N) = \delta \cdot \min\{x_1, \ldots, x_N\} + (1 - \delta) \cdot (x_1 + \cdots + x_N),$$

---

[10] *The Encyclopaedia Britannica* (1998, 15th edition) defines an altruistic agent as someone who feels the obligation "to further the pleasures and alleviate the pains of other people." Note that our definition of altruism differs somewhat from the definition used in moral philosophy, where "altruism" requires a moral agent to be concerned *only* about the welfare of others and not about his own happiness.

where $\delta \in (0, 1)$ is a parameter reflecting the weight that is put on the maximin criterion. The utility function of an individual is then given by a convex combination of his own monetary payoff and the above social welfare function:[11]

$$U_i(x_1, x_2, \ldots, x_N) = (1 - \gamma)x_1 + \gamma[\delta \cdot \min\{x_1, \ldots, x_N\}$$
$$+ (1 - \delta) \cdot (x_1 + \cdots + x_N)].$$

In the two-player case, this boils down to

$$U_i(x_1, x_2) = \begin{cases} x_i + \gamma(1 - \delta)x_j & \text{if} \quad x_i < x_j \\ (1 - \gamma\delta)x_i + \gamma x_j & \text{if} \quad x_i \geq x_j. \end{cases}$$

Note that the marginal rate of substitution between x_i and x_j is smaller if $x_i < x_j$. Hence, the decision maker cares about the well-being of the other person, but less so if the other person is better off than she is.

Altruism in general and quasi-maximin preferences, in particular, can explain positive acts to other players, such as giving in DGs, voluntary contributions in PGGs, and the kind behavior of Responders in TGs and GEGs[12]; but, it is clearly inconsistent with the fact that, in some experiments, subjects try to retaliate and hurt other subjects, even if this is costly for them (as in the UG or a PGG with punishments). This is why Charness and Rabin augment quasi-maximin preferences by incorporating reciprocity (see Section 3.2.3).

3.1.2.   Relative Income and Envy

An alternative hypothesis is that subjects are concerned not only about the absolute amount of money they receive, but also about their relative standing compared with others. This "relative income hypothesis" has a long tradition in economics and goes back at least to Veblen (1922). Bolton (1991) formalized this idea in the context of an experimental bargaining game between two players and assumed that $U_i(x_i, x_j) = u_i(x_i, x_i/x_j)$, where $u(\cdot, \cdot)$ is strictly increasing in its first argument and where the partial derivative with respect to x_i/x_j is strictly positive for $x_i < x_j$ and equal to 0 for $x_i \geq x_j$. Thus, agent i suffers if she gets less than player j, but she does not care about player j if she is better off herself. Note that this utility function implies that $\partial U_i/\partial x_j \leq 0$, just the opposite of altruism. Hence, whereas this utility function is consistent with the behavior in the bargaining games considered by Bolton, it fails to explain

---

[11] Note that Charness and Rabin do not normalize payoffs with respect to N. Thus, if the group size changes, and the parameters δ and γ are assumed to be constant, the importance of the maximin term in relation to the player's own material payoff changes.

[12] However, even in these games, altruism has some implausible implications. For example, in a public good context, altruism implies that if the government provides part of the public good (financed by taxes), then every dollar provided by the government "crowds out" one dollar of private, voluntary contributions. This "neutrality property" holds quite generally (Bernheim, 1986). However, it is in contrast to the empirical evidence reporting that the actual crowding out is rather small. This has led some researchers to include the pleasure of giving (a "warm glow effect") in the utility function (Andreoni, 1989).

giving in DGs, GEGs, and TGs or voluntary contributions in public PGGs. The same problem arises in the envy-approach of Kirchsteiger (1994).

3.1.3. Inequity Aversion

The preceding approaches assumed that utility is either monotonically increasing or monotonically decreasing in the well-being of other players. Fehr and Schmidt (1999) assume that a player is altruistic toward other players if their material payoffs are below an equitable benchmark, but she feels envy when the material payoffs of the other players exceed this level.[13] In most experiments, it is natural to assume that an equitable allocation is an equal monetary payoff for all players. Fehr and Schmidt consider the simplest utility function capturing this idea.

$$U_i(x_1, \ldots, x_N) = x_i - [\alpha_i/(N-1)] \max \sum_{j \neq i} \{x_j - x_i, 0\}$$

$$- [\beta_i/(N-1)] \max \sum_{j \neq i} \{x_i - x_j, 0\}.$$

with $\beta_i \leq \alpha_i$ and $\beta_i \leq 1$. Note that $\partial U_i / \partial x_j \geq 0$ if and only if $x_i \geq x_j$. Note also that the disutility from inequality is larger if another person is better off than player i than if another person is worse off ($\alpha_i \geq \beta_i$).

This utility function can rationalize positive *and* negative actions toward other players. It is consistent with giving in DGs, GEGs, and TGs, *and* with the rejection of low offers in UGs. It can also explain voluntary contributions in PGGs *and* the costly punishment of free riders.

A second important ingredient of this model is the assumption that individuals are heterogeneous. If all people were alike, it would be difficult to explain why we observe that people sometimes resist "unfair" outcomes or manage to cooperate even though it is a dominant strategy for a selfish person not to do so, whereas in other environments fairness concerns or the desire to cooperate do not seem to have much of an effect. Fehr and Schmidt show that the interaction of the distribution of types with the strategic environment explains why, in some situations, very unequal outcomes are obtained, whereas in other situations very egalitarian outcomes prevail. For example, in certain competitive environments (see, e.g., the UG with Proposer competition in Section 5.1), even a population that consists of *only* very fair types (high αs and βs) cannot prevent very uneven outcomes. The reason is that none of the inequity-averse players can enforce a more equitable outcome through her own actions. In contrast, in a PGG with punishment, a small fraction of inequity-averse players is sufficient to threaten credibly that free riders will be punished, which induces selfish players to contribute to the public good.

---

[13] Daughety (1994) and Fehr et al. (1998) also assume that a player values the payoff of reference agents positively, if she is relatively better off, whereas she values the others' payoff negatively, if she is relatively worse off.

Using data that are available from many experiments on the UG, Fehr and Schmidt calibrate the distribution of α and β in the population. Keeping this distribution constant, they show that their model yields quantitatively accurate predictions across many bargaining, market, and cooperation games.[14]

Neilson (2000) provides an axiomatic characterization of the Fehr and Schmidt (1999) model of inequity aversion. He introduces the axiom of "self-referent separability," which requires that if the payoff differences between player i and any subset of all other players remain constant, then the preferences of player i should not be affected by the magnitude of these differences. Neilson shows that this axiom is equivalent to having a utility function that is additively separable in the individual's own material payoff and the payoff differences to his opponents, which is an essential feature of the Fehr–Schmidt model. Neilson also offers a full axiomatic characterization of the more specific functional form used by Fehr and Schmidt.

Bolton and Ockenfels (2000) independently developed a similar model of inequity aversion. They also show that their model can explain a wide variety of seemingly puzzling evidence (e.g., giving in DGs and GEGs and rejections in UGs). In their model, the utility function is given by

$$U_i = U_i(x_i, \sigma_i),$$

where

$$\sigma_i = \begin{cases} \frac{x_i}{\sum_{j=1}^{N} x_j} & \text{if} \quad \sum_{j=1}^{N} x_j \neq 0 \\ \frac{1}{N} & \text{if} \quad \sum_{j=1}^{N} x_j = 0. \end{cases}$$

For any given σ_i, the utility function is assumed to be weakly increasing and concave in player i's own material payoff x_i. Furthermore, for any given x_i, the utility function is strictly concave in player i's share of total income, σ_i, and obtains a maximum at $\sigma_i = 1/N$.[15] Bolton and Ockenfels do not pin down a

---

[14] One drawback of the piecewise linear utility function used by Fehr and Schmidt is that it implies corner solutions for some games where interior solutions are frequently observed. For example, in the DG, a decision maker with a Fehr-Schmidt utility function would either give nothing (if her $\beta < 0.5$) or share the pie equally (if $\beta > 0.5$). Giving away a fraction that is strictly in between 0 and 0.5 is optimal only in the nongeneric case, where $\beta = 0.5$. However, this problem can be avoided by assuming nonlinear inequity aversion.

[15] This specification of the utility function has the disadvantage that it is not independent of a shift in payoffs. Consider, for example, a DG in which the dictator has to divide X dollars. Note that this is a constant sum game, because $x_1 + x_2 \equiv X$. If we reduce the sum of payoffs by X (i.e., if the dictator can take away money from her opponent or give to him out of her own pocket), then $x_1 + x_2 = 0$ for any decision of the dictator and thus we always have $\sigma_1 = \sigma_2 = 1/2$. Therefore, the theory makes the implausible prediction that, in contrast to the game where $x_1 + x_2 = X > 0$, *all* dictators should take as much money from their opponent as possible. A related problem has been noted by Camerer (1999, p. 61). Suppose that the UG is modified as follows: If the Responder rejects a proposal, the Proposer receives a small amount $\varepsilon > 0$ while the Responder receives zero. In this game, the rejection of a *positive* offer implies $\sigma = 0$, whereas acceptance implies $\sigma > 0$. Thus, the Responder never rejects any positive offer, no matter how small $\varepsilon > 0$.

specific functional form, so their utility function is more flexible. However, this also makes it more difficult to get closed-form solutions and quantitative predictions for the outcomes of many experiments. It also imposes less discipline on the researcher not to adjust the utility function to a specific set of data.

For two-player games, Fehr and Schmidt and Bolton and Ockenfels often yield qualitatively similar results. With more than two players, there are some interesting differences. In this case, Fehr and Schmidt assume that a player compares herself with each of her opponents separately. This implies that her behavior toward an opponent depends on the income difference toward this person. In contrast, Bolton and Ockenfels assume that the decision maker is not concerned about each individual opponent, but only about the average income of all players. Thus, whether $\partial U_i / \partial x_j$ is positive or negative in the Bolton–Ockenfels model does not depend on j's relative position toward i, but rather on how well i does, compared with the average. If x_i is below the average, then i would like to reduce j's income even if j has a much lower income than i herself. On the other hand, if i is doing better than the average, then she is prepared to give to j even if j is much better off than i.[16]

3.1.4. Altruism and Spitefulness

Levine (1998) offers a different solution to explain giving in some games and punishing in others. Consider the utility function

$$U_i = x_i + \sum_{j \neq i} x_j (a_i + \lambda a_j)/(1 + \lambda),$$

where $0 \leq \lambda \leq 1$ and $-1 < a_i < 1$ for all $i \in \{1, \ldots, N\}$. Suppose first that $\lambda = 0$. In this case, the utility function reduces to $U_i = x_i + a_i \sum_{j \neq i} x_j$. If $a_i > 0$, then person i is an altruist who wants to promote the well-being of other people; if $a_i < 0$, then player i is spiteful. Although this utility function would be able to explain why some people contribute in PGGs and why some (other) people reject positive offers in the UG, it cannot explain why the same person who is altruistic in one setting is spiteful in another. To deal with this problem, suppose that $\lambda > 0$. In this case, an altruistic player i (with $a_i > 0$) feels more altruistic toward another altruist than toward a spiteful person. In fact, if $-\lambda a_j > a_i$, player i may behave spitefully herself. In most experiments, where there is anonymous interaction, the players do not know the parameter a_j of their opponents and have to form beliefs about them. Thus, any sequential game becomes a signaling game in which beliefs about the other players' types are crucially important to determine optimal strategies. This may give rise to a multiplicity of signaling equilibria.

Levine uses the data from the UG to calibrate the distribution of a and to estimate λ (which is assumed to be the same for all players). He shows that,

---

[16] See Camerer (1999) and Section 4.1 for a more extensive comparison of these two approaches.

with these parameters, the model can reasonably fit the data on centipete games, market games, and PGGs. However, because $a_i < 1$, the model cannot explain positive giving in the dictator game.

3.2.   Models of Intention-Based Reciprocity

Models of social preferences share a common weakness. They assume that players are concerned only about the distributional consequences of their acts but not about the intentions that lead their opponents to choose these acts. To see that this may be a problem, consider the following two "mini-UGs" in which the strategy set of the Proposer is restricted. In the first condition, the Proposer can choose between a 50:50 and an 80:20 split. In the second condition, the Proposer must choose between an 80:20 and a 20:80 division of the pie. All theories that look only at the distributional consequences must predict that, if a Responder rejects the 80:20 split in the first condition, then she must also reject this offer in the second condition. However, in the second condition, a fair division of the pie was not feasible, and so the Responder may be more inclined to accept this offer, compared with the first treatment in which the Proposer could have split the pie evenly, but chose not to do so. In fact, Falk, Fehr, and Fischbacher (2000a) report that the 80:20 split is rejected significantly less often under the second condition.[17] This is inconsistent with any theory of social preferences that rely only on preferences over income distributions.

3.2.1.   Fairness Equilibrium

In a pioneering article, Rabin (1993) starts from the observation that our behavior is often a reaction to the (expected) *intentions* of other people. If we feel that another person has been kind to us, we often have a desire to be kind as well. If we feel that somebody wanted to hurt us, we often have the desire to retaliate, even if this is personally costly.

To model intentions explicitly, Rabin departs from traditional game theory and adopts the concept of "psychological game theory" that had been introduced by Geanakoplos, Pearce, and Stacchetti (1989). In psychological game theory, utilities depend not only on terminal-node payoffs, but also on players' beliefs. Rabin restricts attention to two-player, normal-form games. Let A_1 and A_2 denote the (mixed) strategy sets for players 1 and 2, respectively, and let $x_i: A_1 \times A_2 \rightarrow \mathbb{R}$ be player i's material payoff function.

---

[17] This criticism does not necessarily apply to Levine (1998). In his model, offering 80:20 may be interpreted as a signal that the Proposer is spiteful if the 50:50 split was available, and may be differently interpreted if the 50:50 split was not available. However, if a player knows the type of her opponent, her behavior is independent of what the opponent does to her and of why he does it to her.

We now have to define (hierarchies of) beliefs over strategies. Let $a_i \in A_i$ denote a strategy of player i. When i chooses her strategy, she must have some belief about the strategy to be chosen by player j. In all of the following $i \in \{1, 2\}$ and $j = 3 - i$. Let b_j denote player i's belief about what player j is going to do. Furthermore, to rationalize her expectation b_j, player i must have some belief about what player j believes that player i is going to do. This belief about beliefs is denoted by c_i. The hierarchy of beliefs could be continued ad infinitum, but the first two levels of beliefs are sufficient to define reciprocal preferences.

Rabin starts with a "kindness function," $f_i(a_i, b_j)$, which measures how kind player i is to player j. If player i believes that her opponent chooses strategy b_j, then she chooses effectively her opponent's payoff out of the set $[x_j^l(b_j), x_j^h(b_j)]$, where $x_j^l(b_j)(x_j^h(b_j))$ is the lowest (highest) payoff of player j that can be induced by player i if j chooses b_j. According to Rabin, a "fair" or "equitable" payoff for player j, $x_j^f(b_j)$, is just the average of the lowest and highest payoffs (excluding Pareto-dominated payoffs, however). Note that this "fair" payoff is independent of the payoff of player i. The kindness of player i toward player j is measured by the difference between the actual payoff she gives to player j and the "fair" payoff, relative to the whole range of feasible payoffs:[18]

$$f_i(a_i, b_j) = \left[x_j(b_j, a_i) - x_j^f(b_j) \right] / \left[x_j^h(b_j) - x_j^l(b_j) \right],$$

with $j = 3 - i$ and $f_i(a_i, b_j) = 0$, if $x_j^h(b_j) - x_j^l(b_j) = 0$. Note that $f_i(a_i, b_j) > 0$ if and only if player i gives player j more than the "fair" payoff.

Finally, we have to define player i's belief about how kindly she is being treated by player j. This is defined in exactly the same manner, but beliefs have to move up one level. Thus, if player i believes that player j chooses b_j and if she believes that player j believes that i chooses c_i, then player i perceives player j's kindness as given by

$$f_j'(b_j, c_i) \equiv \left[x_i(c_i, b_j) - x_i^f(c_i) \right] / \left[x_i^h(c_i) - x_i^l(c_i) \right],$$

with $j = 3 - i$ and $f_j(b_j, c_i) = 0$, if $x_i^h(c_i) - x_i^l(c_i) = 0$. These kindness functions can now be used to define a player's utility function:

$$U_i(a, b_j, c_i) = x_i(a, b_j) + f_j'(b_j, c_i)[1 + f_i(a_i, b_j)],$$

where $a = (a_1, a_2)$. Note that if player j is perceived to be unkind ($f_j'(\cdot) < 0$), player i wants to be as unkind as possible, too. On the other hand, if $f_j'(\cdot)$ is positive, player i gets some additional utility from being kind to player j as

---

[18] A disturbing feature of Rabin's formulation is that he excludes Pareto-dominated payoffs in the definition of the "fair" payoff, but not in the denominator of the kindness term. Thus, adding a Pareto-dominated strategy for player j would not affect the fair payoff, but it would reduce the kindness term.

well. Note also that the kindness terms have no dimension and that they must lie in the interval $[-1, 0.5]$. Thus, the utility function is sensitive to positive affine transformations. Furthermore, the kindness term becomes less and less important the higher the material payoffs are.

A "fairness equilibrium" is an equilibrium in a psychological game with these payoff functions [i.e., a pair of strategies (a_1, a_2) that are mutually best responses to each other and a set of rational expectations $b = (b_1, b_2)$ and $c = (c_1, c_2)$ that are consistent with equilibrium play].

Rabin's theory is important because it was the first contribution that made the notion of reciprocity precise and explored the consequences of reciprocal behavior. The model provides several interesting insights, but it is not well suited for predictive purposes. It is consistent with rejections in the UG, but there exist many other unreasonable equilibria, including equilibria in which the Responder receives more than 50 percent of the pie. The multiplicity of equilibria is a general feature of Rabin's model. If material payoffs are sufficiently small so that psychological payoffs matter, then there are always multiple equilibria. In particular, there is one equilibrium in which both players are nice to each other and one in which they are nasty. Both equilibria are supported by self-fulfilling prophecies, so it is difficult to predict which equilibrium is going to be played.

The theory also predicts that players do not undertake kind actions unless others have shown their kind intentions. Suppose, for example, that in the prisoner's dilemma, player 2 has no choice but is forced to cooperate. If player 1 knows this, then – according to Rabin's theory – she will interpret player 2's cooperation as "neutral" ($f_2'(\cdot) = 0$). Thus, she will look at only her material payoffs and will defect. This contrasts with models of inequity aversion in which player 2 would cooperate, irrespective of the reason for player 1's cooperation. We will discuss the experimental evidence that can be used to discriminate between the different approaches in Section 4.

3.2.2.   *Intentions in Sequential Games*

Rabin's theory has been defined only for two-person, normal-form games. If the theory is applied to the normal form of simple sequential games, some very implausible equilibria may arise. For example, in the sequential prisoner's dilemma, unconditional cooperation of the second player is part of a "fairness" equilibrium. The reason is that Rabin's equilibrium notion does not force player 2 to behave optimally off the equilibrium path.

In a subsequent paper, Dufwenberg and Kirchsteiger (1998) generalized Rabin's theory to N-person extensive form games for which they introduce the notion of a "Sequential Reciprocity Equilibrium" (SRE). The main innovation is to keep track of beliefs about intentions as the game evolves. In particular, it has to be specified how beliefs about intentions are formed off the equilibrium path. Given this system of beliefs, strategies have to form a fairness equilibrium in every proper subgame.[19] Applying their model to several examples, Dufwenberg and Kirchsteiger show that *conditional* cooperation in the prisoner's dilemma is an SRE. They also show that it can be an SRE in the UG in which the Proposer makes an offer that is rejected by the Responder with certainty. This is an equilibrium because both players believe that the other party wants to hurt them. However, even in these extremely simple sequential games, the equilibrium analysis is fairly complex, and there are typically many equilibria with different equilibrium outcomes due to different self-fulfilling beliefs about intentions.

3.2.3. Merging Intentions and Social Preferences

Falk and Fischbacher (1999) also generalize Rabin (1993). They consider N-person extensive form games and allow for the possibility of incomplete information. Furthermore, they measure "kindness" in terms of inequity aversion. A strategy of player j is perceived to be kind by player i if it gives rise to a payoff for player i that is higher than the payoff of player j. Note that this is fundamentally different from Rabin and Dufwenberg and Kirchsteiger, who define "kindness" in relation to the feasible payoffs of player i and not in relation to the payoff that player j gets. Furthermore, Falk and Fischbacher distinguish whether an unequal distribution could have been altered by player j or whether player j was a "dummy player" who is unable to affect the distribution by his actions. In the former case, the kindness term gets a higher weight than in the latter. However, even if player j is a dummy player who has no choice to make, the kindness term (which now reflects pure inequity aversion) gets a positive weight. Thus, Falk and Fischbacher merge intention-based reciprocity and inequity aversion.

Their model is quite complex. At every node where player i has to move, she has to evaluate the kindness of player j that depends on the expected payoff difference between the two players and on what player j could have done about this difference. This "kindness term" is multiplied by a "reciprocation term," which is positive if player i is kind to player j and negative if i is unkind. The product is further multiplied by an individual reciprocity parameter that measures the weight of player i's desire to reciprocate, compared with his

---

[19] Dufwenberg and Kirchsteiger also suggest several other deviations from Rabin's model. In particular, they measure kindness "in proportion to the size of the gift" (i.e., in monetary units). This has the advantage that reciprocity does not disappear as the stakes become larger, but it also implies that the kindness term in the utility function has the dimension of "money squared," which again makes the utility function sensitive to linear transformations. Furthermore, they define "inefficient strategies" (which play an important role in the definition of the kindness term) as strategies that yield a weakly lower payoff for all players than some other strategy for all subgames. Rabin (1993) defines inefficient strategies as those that yield weakly less on the equilibrium path. However, with more than two players in Dufwenberg and Kirchsteiger (1998), the problem arises that an additional dummy player may render an inefficient strategy efficient and might thus affect the size of the kindness term.

desire to get a higher material payoff. These preferences, together with the underlying game form, define a psychological game à la Geanakoplos et al. (1989). A subgame perfect psychological Nash equilibrium of this game is called a "reciprocity equilibrium."

Falk and Fischbacher show that there are parameter constellations for which their model is consistent with the stylized facts of the UG, the GEG, the DG, the PGG, and the prisoner's dilemma game. Furthermore, there are parameter constellations that can explain the difference in outcomes if one player moves intentionally and if she is a dummy player. Because their model contains variants of a pure intention-based reciprocity model (e.g., Rabin) and a pure inequity aversion model (e.g., Fehr and Schmidt or Bolton and Ockenfels) as special cases, it is possible to get a better fit of the data, but at a significant cost in terms of the complexity of the model.

Another attempt to combine social preferences with intention-based reciprocity is due to Charness and Rabin (2000). We described their model of quasi-maximin preferences in Section 3.1.1. In a second step, they augment these preferences by introducing a demerit profile $\rho \equiv (\rho_1, \ldots, \rho_N)$, where $\rho_i \in [0, 1]$ is a measure of how much player i deserves from the point of view of all other players. The smaller the ρ_i, the more does player i count in the utility function of the other players. Given a demerit profile ρ, player i's utility function is given by

$$U_i(x_1, x_2, \ldots, x_N \mid \rho) = (1 - \gamma)x_i + \gamma[\delta \cdot \min\{x_i, \min_{j \neq i}\{x_j + d\rho_j\}\}$$
$$+ (1 - \delta) \cdot (x_i + \sum_{j \neq i} \max\{1 - k\rho_j, 0\} \cdot x_j) - f \sum_{j \neq i} \rho_j x_j],$$

where $d, k, f \geq 0$ are three new parameters of the model. If $d = k = f = 0$, this boils down to the quasi-maximin preferences described previously. If d and k are large, then player i does not want to promote the well-being of player j. If f is large, player i may actually want to hurt player j.

The crucial step is to endogenize the demerit profile ρ. Charness and Rabin do this by comparing player j's strategy to an unanimously agreed-upon, exogenously given "selfless standard" of behavior. The more player j falls short of this standard, the higher is his demerit factor ρ_j.

A "reciprocal fairness equilibrium" (RFE) is a strategy profile and a demerit profile such that each player is maximizing his utility function given other players' strategies and given the demerit profile that is itself consistent with the profile of strategies. This definition implicitly corresponds to a Nash equilibrium of a psychological game as defined by Geanakoplos et al. (1989).

The notion of RFE has several drawbacks that make it almost impossible to use it for the analysis of even the simplest experimental games. First of all, the model is incomplete because preferences are defined only in equilibrium (i.e., for an equilibrium demerit profile ρ), and it is unclear how to evaluate outcomes out of equilibrium or if there are multiple equilibria. Second, it requires that all players have the same utility functions and agree on a "quasi-maximin" social welfare function to determine the demerit profile ρ. Finally, the model is so complicated and involves so many free parameters that it would be very difficult to test it empirically.

Charness and Rabin show that if the "selfless standard" is sufficiently small, then every RFE corresponds to a Nash equilibrium of the game in which players simply maximize their quasi-maximin utility functions. Therefore, in the analysis of the experimental evidence, they restrict attention to the much simpler model of quasi-maximin preferences that we discussed in Section 3.1.1.

3.3. Axiomatic Approaches

The models considered so far assume very specific utility functions that are defined either on (lotteries over) material payoff vectors and/or on beliefs about other players' strategies and other players' beliefs. These utility functions are based on psychological plausibility, yet most of them lack an axiomatic foundation. Segal and Sobel (1999) take the opposite approach and ask what kind of axioms generate preferences that can reflect fairness and reciprocity.

Their starting point is to assume that players have preferences over strategy profiles rather than over material allocations. Consider a given two-player game and let Σ_i, $i \in \{1, 2\}$, denote the space of (mixed) strategies of player i. For any strategy profile $(\sigma_1, \sigma_2) \in \Sigma \times \Sigma_1$, let $v_i(\sigma_1, \sigma_2)$ denote player i's material payoff function, assuming that these "selfish preferences" satisfy the von Neumann–Morgenstern axioms. However, the actual preferences of player i are given by a preference relation σ_i, σ_j over her own strategies. Note that this preference relation depends on the strategy chosen by player j. Segal and Sobel show that if the preference relation σ_i, σ_j satisfies the independence axiom and if, for a given σ_j, player i prefers to get a higher material payoff for herself if the payoff of player j is held constant (self-interest), then the preferences σ_i, σ_j over Σ_i can be represented by a utility function of the form[20]

$$u_i(\sigma_i, \sigma_j) = v_i(\sigma_i, \sigma_j) + a_i, \sigma_j v_j(\sigma_i, \sigma_j).$$

In standard game theory, $a_i, \sigma_j \equiv 0$. Positive values of this coefficient mean that player i has altruistic preferences, negative values of a_i, σ_j mean that she is spiteful.

Note that the coefficient a_i, σ_j depends on σ_j. Therefore, whether a player is altruistic or spiteful may depend on the strategy chosen by her opponent, so there is scope to model reciprocity. To do so, Segal and Sobel introduce an additional axiom, called "reciprocal altruism." This axiom requires that, when player j chooses a strategy σ_j that player i likes better than some other strategy σ_j', then player i prefers strategies that give a higher payoff to player j. Segal and Sobel show that this axiom implies that the coefficient a_i, σ_j varies with

---

[20] The construction resembles that of Harsanyi's (1955) "utilitarian" social welfare function $\Sigma \alpha_i u_i$. Note, however, that Harsanyi's axiom of Pareto efficiency is stronger than the axiom of self-interest used here. Therefore, the a_i, σ_j in Segal and Sobel may be negative.

σ_j such that (other things being equal) the coefficient increases if and only if player j chooses a "nicer" strategy.

The models of social preferences that we discussed at the beginning of this chapter – in particular the models of altruism, relative income, inequity aversion, quasi-maximin preferences, and altruism and spitefulness – can all be seen as special cases of a Segal–Sobel utility function. Segal and Sobel can also capture some, but not all, aspects of intention-based reciprocity. For example, in Rabin's (1993) model, a player's utility depended not only on the strategy chosen by her opponent, but also on why he has chosen this strategy. This can be illustrated in the "Battle of the Sexes" game. Player 1 may go to boxing, because she expects player 2 to go to boxing, too (which is kind of player 2, given that he believes player 1 to go to boxing). Yet, she may also go to boxing, because she expects player 2 to go to ballet (which is unkind of player 2 if he believes player 1 to go to boxing) and which is punished by the boxing strategy of player 1. This effect cannot be captured by Segal and Sobel, because in their framework preferences are defined on strategies only.

4. DISCRIMINATING BETWEEN THEORIES OF FAIRNESS

Most theories discussed in Section 3 have been developed during the last few years, and the evidence to discriminate between these theories is still limited. As we will show, however, the available data do exhibit some clear qualitative regularities that give a first indication of the advantages and disadvantages of the different theories.[21]

4.1.   Who Are the Relevant Reference Actors?

All theories of fairness and reciprocity are based on the idea that actors compare themselves with a set of reference actors. To whom do people compare themselves? In bilateral interactions, there is no ambiguity about who the relevant reference actor is. In multiperson interactions, however, the answer is less clear. Most of the theories that are applicable in the N-person context assume that players make comparisons with all other $N - 1$ players in the game. The only exemption is the theory of Bolton and Ockenfels (BO). They assume that players compare themselves only with the "average" player in the game and do not care about inequities between the other players. In this regard, the BO approach is inspired by the data of Selten and Ockenfels (1998) and Güth and van Damme (1998), which seem to suggest that actors do not care for inequities among the other reference agents. It would greatly simplify matters if this aspect of the BO theory were correct.

---

[21] This section rests to a large extent on joint work of one of the authors with Armin Falk and Urs Fischbacher (Falk, Fehr, and Fischbacher, 2000a, 2000b, henceforth FFF). In particular, the organization of this section according to the questions herein and many of the empirical results emerged from this joint project.

One problem with this aspect of the BO approach is that it renders the theory unable to explain the punishment pattern in the PGG with punishment. Remember that, in this experiment, the assignment of one punishment point reduces the income of the punished member by 3 points. The theory of BO predicts that punishing subjects are indifferent between punishing a free rider and punishing a cooperator. All that matters is whether punishment brings the income of the punishing subject closer to the average income in the group and, for this purpose, the punishment of a cooperator is equally good as the punishment of a defector. Yet, in contrast to this indifference prediction, the cooperators predominantly punish the defectors.

To further test the BO model, Fehr and Fischbacher (2000) conducted the following Third-Party Punishment Game. There are three players: A, B, and C. Player A is endowed with 100 experimental currency units and must decide how much of the 100 units to give to B, who has no endowment. Player B is just a dummy player and has no decision power. Player C has an endowment of 50 units and can spend this money on the punishment of A after he observes how much A gave to B. For any money unit player C spends on punishment, the payoff of player A is reduced by 3 units.[22] Note that without punishment, player C is certain to get her fair share of the total surplus (50 of 150 units). Therefore, BO predict that C will never punish. In contrast to this prediction, player A is, however, punished a lot. The less player A gives to B, the more C punishes A. For example, if A gives nothing, his income is reduced by roughly 30 percent. This indicates that many players do care about inequities among other players. Further support for this hypothesis comes from Charness and Rabin (2000), who offered player C the choice between payoff allocations (575, 575, 575) and (900, 300, 600). Because both allocations give player C the fair share of one-third of the surplus, BO predict that player C will choose the second allocation that gives him a higher absolute payoff. However, 54 percent of the subjects preferred the first allocation. Note that the self-interest hypothesis also predicts the second allocation, so one cannot conclude that the other 46 percent of the subjects have BO preferences. A recent paper by Zizzo and Oswald (2000) also strongly suggests that subjects care about the inequities among the set of reference agents.

It is important to note that theories in which fair-minded subjects have multiple reference agents do not necessarily imply that fair subjects take actions in favor of *all* other reference agents. To illustrate this, consider the following three-person UG (Güth and van Damme, 1998). In this game, there is a Proposer, a Responder who can reject or accept the proposal, and a passive Receiver who can do nothing but collect the amount of money allocated to him. The Proposer proposes an allocation (x_1, x_2, x_3), where x_1 is the Proposer's payoff, x_2 the Responder's payoff, and x_3 the Receiver's payoff. If the Responder rejects, all three players get nothing; otherwise, the proposed allocation is implemented.

---

[22] In the experimental instructions, the value-laden term "punishment" was not used. The punishment option of player C was described in neutral terms by telling subjects that player C could "assign points" to player A that reduced the incomes of A and C in the way described previously.

In this game, the Proposer allocates substantial fractions of the surplus to the Responder, but little or nothing to the Receiver. Moreover, Güth and van Damme (p. 230) report that, "there is not a single rejection that can clearly be attributed to a low share for the dummy (i.e., the Receiver, FS)." BO take this as evidence in favor of their approach because the Proposer and the Responder apparently do not take the Receiver's interest into account. However, this conclusion is premature, because it is easy to show that approaches with multiple reference agents are fully consistent with the Güth and van Damme data. The point can be demonstrated in the context of the Fehr–Schmidt model. Assume for simplicity that the Proposer makes an offer of $x_1 = x_2 = x$, whereas the Receiver gets $x_3 < x$. It is easy to show that a Responder with FS preferences will never (!) reject such an allocation, even if $x_3 = 0$ and even if he is very fair-minded (i.e., has a high β-coefficient). To see this, note that the utility of the Responder if he accepts is given by $U_2 = x - (\beta/2)(x - x_3)$, which is positive for all $\beta \leq 1$ and thus higher than the rejection payoff of zero. A similar calculation shows that it takes implausibly high β-values to induce a Proposer to take the interests of the Receiver into account.[23]

4.2.   Equality Versus Efficiency

Many models of fairness are based on the definition of a fair or equitable outcome to which people compare the available payoff allocations. In experimental games, a natural first approximation for the relevant reference outcome is the equality of material payoffs. The quasi-maximin theory of Charness and Rabin assumes instead that subjects care for the total surplus accruing to the group. A natural way to study whether there are subjects who want to maximize the total surplus is to construct experiments in which the predictions of both theories of inequality aversion (BO and FS) are in conflict with surplus maximization. This has been done by Bolle and Kritikos (1998), Andreoni and Miller (2000), Andreoni and Vesterlund (2001). Charness and Rabin (2000), Cox (2000), and Güth, Kliemt, and Ockenfels (2000). Except for the Güth et al. paper, these papers indicate that, in DG situations a nonnegligible fraction of the subjects is willing to give up some of their own money to increase total surplus, even if this implies that they generate inequality that is to their disadvantage. Andreoni and Miller and Andreoni and Vesterlund, for example, conducted DGs with varying prices for transferring money to the Receiver. In some conditions, the Allocator had to give up less than a dollar to give the Receiver a dollar; in some conditions, the exchange ratio was 1:1, and in some other conditions the Allocator had to give up more than one dollar. In the usual DGs the exchange

---

[23] The Proposer's utility is given by $U_1 = x_1 - (\beta/2)[(x_1 - x_2) + (x_1 - x_3)]$. If we normalize the surplus to one and take into account that $x_1 + x_2 + x_3 = 1$, $U_1 = (\beta/2) + (3/2)x_1[(2/3) - \beta]$; thus, the marginal utility of x_1 is positive unless β exceeds 2/3. This means that Proposers with $\beta < 2/3$ will give the Responders just enough to prevent rejection. Because the Responders neglect the interests of the Receivers, nothing is given to the Receivers.

ratio is 1:1, and there are virtually no cases in which an Allocator transfers more than 50 percent of the surplus. In contrast, in DGs with an exchange ratio of 1 : 3 (or 1 : 2), a nonnegligible number of subjects makes transfers such that they end up with less money than the Receiver. This contradicts BO, FS, and Falk and Fischbacher because in these models fair subjects never take actions that give the other party more than they get. It is, however, consistent with altruistic preferences or quasi-maximin preferences.

What is the relative importance of this kind of behavior? Andreoni and Vesterlund are able to classify subjects in three distinct classes. They report that 44 percent of their subjects ($N = 141$) are completely selfish, 35 percent exhibit egalitarian preferences (i.e., they tend to equalize payoffs), and 21 percent of the subjects can be classified as surplus maximizers. Charness and Rabin report similar results with regard to the fraction of egalitarian subjects in a simple DG, where the Allocator had to choose between (own, other) allocations of (400, 400) and (400, 750). Thirty-one percent of the subjects preferred the egalitarian and 69 percent the surplus-maximizing allocation. Among the 69 percent, there may, however, also be many selfish subjects who no longer choose the surplus-maximizing allocation when this decreases their payoff only slightly. This is suggested by the DG where the Allocator had to choose between (400, 400) and (375, 750). Here, only 49 percent of surplus-maximizing choices were observed. Charness and Rabin also present questionnaire evidence indicating that, when the income disparities are greater, the egalitarian motive gains weight at the cost of the surplus maximization motive. When the Allocator faces a choice between (400, 400) and (400, 2,000), 62 percent prefer the egalitarian allocation.

The evidence cited in the described papers indicates that surplus maximization is a relevant motive *in DGs*. This motive has not been included in the prevailing models of inequity aversion, but it would be straightforward to do this. It should also be remembered that *any* positive transfer in DGs is incompatible with intention-based reciprocity models, *irrespective of the exchange rate*. We would like to stress, however, that the DG is different from many economically important games and real-life situations, because in economic interactions it is rarely the case that one player is at the complete mercy of another player. It may well be that, in situations where *both* players have some power to affect the outcome, the surplus maximization motive is less important than in DGs. The gift exchange experiments by Fehr et al. (1993, 1998) are telling in this regard because they embed a situation that is like a DG into an environment with competitive and strategic elements.

These experiments exhibit a competitive element because the GEG is embedded into a competitive experimental market. The experiments also exhibit a strategic element because the Proposers are wage setters and have to take into account the likely effort responses of the Responders. Yet, once the Responder has accepted a wage offer, the experiments are similar to a DG because, for a given wage, the Responder essentially determines the income distribution and the total surplus by his choice of the effort level. The gift exchange experiments are an ideal environment to check the robustness of the surplus maximization motive, because an increase in the effort cost by one unit increases, on average, the total surplus by five units. Therefore, the maximal feasible effort level is, in general, also the surplus-maximizing effort level. If surplus maximization is a robust motive capable of overturning inequity aversion, one would expect that many Responders choose effort levels that give the Proposer a higher monetary payoff than the Responder.[24] Moreover, surplus maximization also means that we should *not* observe a positive correlation between effort and wages because, for a given wage, the maximum feasible effort always maximizes the total surplus.[25]

However, neither of these implications is supported by the data. Effort levels that give the Proposer a higher payoff than the Responder are virtually nonexistent. In the overwhelming majority of the cases effort is substantially below the maximally feasible level, and in less than 2 percent of the cases the Proposer earns a higher payoff than the Responder.[26] Moreover, almost all subjects who regularly chose nonminimal effort levels exhibited a reciprocal effort–wage relation. These numbers are in sharp contrast to the 49 percent of the Allocators in Charness and Rabin who preferred the (375, 750) allocation over the (400, 400) allocation. One reason for the difference across studies is perhaps the fact that it was much cheaper to increase the surplus in the Charness–Rabin example. Although the surplus increases in the gift exchange experiments on average by five units, if the Responder sacrifices one payoff unit, the surplus increases by 14 units per payoff unit sacrificed in the Charness–Rabin case. This suggests that surplus maximization gives rise to a violation of the equality constraint only if surplus increases are extremely cheap. A second reason for the behavioral difference may be that, when both players have some power to affect the outcome, the motive to increase the surplus is quickly crowded out by other considerations. This reason is quite plausible, insofar as the outcomes in DGs themselves are notoriously nonrobust.

Although the experimental results on UGs, GEGs, or PGGs are fairly robust, the DG seems to be a rather fragile situation in which minor factors can have large effects. Cox (2000), for example, reports that, in his DGs, *100 percent* of all subjects transferred positive amounts.[27] This result contrasts sharply with many other games, including the games in Charness and Rabin and many other DGs. To indicate the other extreme, Hoffman, McCabe, Shachat, and Smith

---

[24] The Responder's effort level may, of course, also be affected by the intentions of the Proposer. For example, paying a high wage may signal fair intentions that may increase the effort level. Yet, because this tends to raise effort levels, we would have even stronger evidence against the surplus maximization hypothesis, if we observe little or no effort choices that give the Proposer a higher payoff than the Responder.

[25] There are degenerate cases in which this is not true.

[26] The total number of effort choices is $N = 480$ in these experiments (i.e., the results are not an artifact of a low number of observations).

[27] In Cox's experiment, both players had an endowment of 10 and the Allocator could transfer his endowment to the Receiver where the transferred amount was tripled by the experimenter.

(1994), Eichenberger and Oberholzer-Gee (1998), and List and Cherry (2000) report on DGs with extremely low transfers.[28] Likewise, in the Impunity Game of Bolton and Zwick (1995), which is very close but not identical to a DG, the vast majority of Proposers did not shy away from making very unfair offers. The Impunity Game differs from the DG only insofar as the Responder can reject an offer; however, the rejection destroys only the Responder's, but not the Proposer's, payoff. The notorious nonrobustness of outcomes in situations resembling the DG indicates that one should be very careful in generalizing the results found in these situations to other games. Testing theories of social preferences in DGs is a bit like testing the law of gravity with a table tennis ball. In both situations, minor unobserved distortions can have large effects. Therefore, we believe that it is necessary to show that the same motivational forces that are inferred from DGs are also behaviorally relevant in economically more important games. One way to do this is to apply the theories that have been constructed on the basis of DG experiments to predict outcomes in other games. With the exemption of Andreoni and Miller (2000), this has not yet been done.

Andreoni and Miller (2000) estimate utility functions based on the results of their DG experiments and use them to predict cooperation behavior in a standard PGG. They predict behavior in period 1 of these games, in which cooperation is often quite high, rather well. However, their predictions are far away from final period outcomes, where cooperation is typically very low. In our view, the low cooperation rates in the final period of repeated PGGs constitutes a strong challenge for models that rely exclusively on altruistic or surplus-maximizing preferences. Why should a subject with a stable preference for the payoff of others or the payoff of the whole group contribute much less in the final period, compared with the first period? Models of inequity aversion and intention-based or type-based reciprocity models provide a plausible explanation for this behavior. All of these models predict that fair subjects make their cooperation contingent on the cooperation of others. Thus, if the fair subjects realize that there are sufficiently many selfish decisions in the course of a PGG experiment, they cease to cooperate as well.

4.3. Revenge Versus Inequity Reduction

Subjects with altruistic and quasi-maximin preferences do not take actions that reduce other subjects' payoffs. Yet, this is frequently observed in many important games. Models of inequity aversion account for this by assuming that the payoff reduction is motivated by a desire to reduce disadvantageous inequality. In intention-based reciprocity models and in Levine (1998), subjects punish

---

[28] In Eichenberger and Oberholzer-Gee (1998), almost 90 percent of the subjects gave nothing. In Hoffman et al. (1994), 64 percent gave nothing, and 19 percent gave between 1 percent and 10 percent. In List and Cherry, subjects earned their endowment in a quiz. Then they played the DG. Roughly 90 percent of the Allocators transferred nothing to the Receivers.

if they observe an action that is perceived to be unfair or that reveals that the opponent is spiteful. In these models, players want to reduce the opponent's payoff irrespective of whether they are better or worse off than the opponent, and irrespective of whether they can change income shares or income differences. Furthermore, intention-based theories predict that, in games in which no intention can be expressed, there will be no punishment. Therefore, a clean way to test for the relevance of intentions is to conduct control treatments in which choices are made through a random device or through some neutral and disinterested third party.

Blount (1995) was the first who applied this idea to the UG. Blount compared the rejection rate in the usual UG to the rejection rates in UGs in which either a computer generated a random offer or a third party made the offer. Because, in the random offer condition and the third-party condition, a low offer cannot be attributed to the greedy intentions of the Proposer, intention-based theories predict a rejection rate of zero in these conditions, whereas theories of inequity aversion still allow for positive rejection rates. Levine's theory is also consistent with positive rejection rates in these conditions, but his theory predicts a decrease in the rejection rate relative to the usual condition, because low offers made by humans reveal that the type who made the offer is spiteful, which can trigger a spiteful response. Blount, indeed, observes a significant and substantial reduction in the acceptance thresholds of the Responders in the random offer condition, but not in the third-party condition. Thus, the result of the random offer condition is consistent with intention- and type-based models, whereas the result of the third-party condition is inconsistent with the motives captured by these models. Yet, these puzzling results may be from some problematic features in Bount's experiments.[29] Subsequently, Offermann (1999) and FFF (2000b) conducted further experiments with computerized offers, but without the other worrisome features in Blount. In particular, in these experiments, the Responders knew that a rejection affects the payoff of a real, human "Proposer." Offerman finds that subjects are 67 percent more likely to reduce the opponent's payoff when the opponent made an intentional hurtful choice, compared with a situation in which a computer made the hurtful choice.

FFF (2000b) conducted an experiment – invented by Abbink, Irlenbusch, and Renner (2000) – that simultaneously allows for the examination of positive and negative reciprocity. In this game, player A can give player B any integer amount of money $g \in [0, 6]$ or, alternatively, she can take away from player B any integer amount of money $t \in [1, 6]$. In case of $g > 0$, the experimenter triples g so that player B receives $3g$. If player A takes away t, player A gets

---

[29] Blount's results may be affected by the fact that subjects (in two of three treatments) had to make decisions as a Proposer *and* as a Responder before they knew their actual roles. After subjects had made their decisions in both roles, the role for which they received payments was determined randomly. In one of Blount's treatments, deception was involved. Subjects believed that there were Proposers, although in fact the experimenters made the proposals. All subjects in this condition were "randomly" assigned to the responder role. In this treatment, subjects also were not paid according to their decisions, but they received a flat fee instead.

t and player B loses t. After player B observes g or t, she can pay player A an integer reward $r \in [0, 18]$ or she can reduce player A's income by making an investment $i \in [1, 6]$. A reward transfers one money unit from player B to player A. An investment i costs player B exactly i, but reduces player A's income by $3i$. This game was played in a random choice condition and in a human choice condition. It turns out that when the choices are made by a human player A, player B invests significantly more into payoff reductions for all $t \in [1, 6]$. However, as in Blount and Offerman, payoff reductions also occur when the computer makes a hurtful choice.

Kagel, Kim, and Moser (1996) provide further support that intentions play a role for payoff-reducing behavior. In their experiments, subjects bargained over 100 chips in a UG. They conducted several treatments that varied the money value of the chips and the information provided about the money value. For example, in one treatment, the Proposers received three times more money per chip than the Responders (i.e., the equal money split requires that the Responders receive 75 chips). If the Responders know that the Proposers know the different money values of the chips they reject, unequal money splits much more frequently than if the Responders know that the Proposers do *not* know the different money values of the chips. Thus, knowingly unequal proposals were rejected at higher rates than unintentional unequal proposals.

Another way to test for the relevance of intention-based or type-based punishments is to examine situations in which the subjects cannot increase their relative share or decrease payoff differences. FFF (2000a) report the results of UGs and PGGs with punishment that have this feature. In the first (standard) treatment of the UG, the Proposers could propose a $(5, 5)$ or an $(8, 2)$ split of the surplus (the first number represents the Proposer's payoff). In case of rejection, both players received zero. In the second treatment, the Proposers had the same options, but a rejection now meant that the payoff was reduced for both players by two units. The BO model, as well as the FS model, predict, therefore, that there will be no rejections in the second treatment, whereas intention-based and type-based models predict that punishments will occur. It turns out that the rejection rate of the $(8, 2)$ offer is 56 percent in the first and 19 percent in the second treatment. Thus, roughly one-third (19/57) of the rejections are consistent with a pure taste for punishment, as conceptualized in intention- and type-based models.[30]

FFF (2000a) also report the results of PGGs with punishment in which the punishing subjects could not change the payoff difference between themselves and the punished subject. In one of their treatments, subjects had to pay one money unit to reduce the payoff of another group member by one unit. Thus, BO and FS both predict that there will be no punishment at all in this condition.

---

[30] Ahlert, Crüger, and Güth (1999) also report a significant amount of punishment in UGs, in which the Responders cannot change the payoff difference. However, because they do not have a control treatment, it is not possible to say something about the relative importance of this kind of punishment.

In a second treatment, investing one unit into punishment reduced the payoff of the punished group member by three units.

FFF report that 51 percent of all subjects ($N = 93$) cooperate, which is still compatible with both BO and FS. However, another 51 percent of all cooperators punish the defectors. They invest, on average, 4.8 money units into punishment. Thus, 25 percent of the subjects punish free-riding, which is incompatible with BO and FS. To evaluate the relative importance of this amount of punishment, we have to compare these results with the results of the second condition. In the second condition, 61 percent of all subjects ($N = 120$) cooperate, and 59 percent of them punish the defectors (by imposing a punishment of 5.7 on average). Thus, the overall percentage of subjects who punish the defectors in the second condition is 36 percent. This suggests that a rather large fraction (i.e., 25/36) of the overall amount of punishment is not consistent with BO and FS.

Taken together, the evidence from Blount (1995), Offerman (1999), and FFF (2000b) indicates that the motive to punish unfair intentions or unfair types plays an important role. Although the evidence provided by the initial study of Blount was mixed, the subsequent studies indicate a clear role of these motives. However, the evidence also suggests that inequity aversion plays an additional, nonnegligible role. The evidence from the experiments in FFF (2000a) suggests that many subjects who reduce the payoff of other players do not have the desire to change the equitability of the payoff allocation. Instead, a large fraction of these subjects seems to be driven by the desire to punish (i.e., a desire to hurt the other player). It is worthwhile to point out that this desire to hurt the other players, although consistent with intention- and type-based models of reciprocity, does not necessarily constitute evidence in favor of these models. The reason is that the desire to reduce the payoff of other players may also be triggered by an unfair payoff allocation per se.[31]

4.4.   Does Kindness Trigger Rewards?

Do intention- and type-based theories of fairness do equally well in the domain of rewarding behavior? Evidence in this domain is much more mixed. Some experimental results suggest that rewarding behavior is almost unaffected by these motives. Other results indicate some minor role, and only one paper finds an unambiguous positive effect of intention- or type-based reciprocity.

---

[31] Assume that fair subjects have the following utility function: $u_i = x_i + \alpha_i [1/(n-1)]$ $\times [\sum_{j \neq i} \beta(x_i - x_j)v(x_j)]$, where α_i measures the strength of player i's nonpecuniary preference, and $v(\pi_j)$ is an increasing function of player j's material payoff. $\beta(x_i - x_j)$ is positive, if $x_i - x_j > 0$ and negative if $x_i - x_j < 0$. Thus, a state of inequality triggers the desire to reduce or increase the other players' payoff. In this regard, the utility function is similar to the preference assumption in FS. Yet, in contrast to FS, the aim of player i is no longer the reduction of the payoff difference. Instead, player i just wants to reduce or increase the other player's payoff, depending on the sign of β.

Intention-based theories predict that people are generous only if they have been treated kindly (i.e., if the first mover has signaled a fair intention). Levine's theory is similar in this regard, because generous actions are more likely if the first mover reveals that she is an altruistic type. However, in contrast to the intention-based approaches, Levine's approach is also compatible with unconditional giving, *if it is sufficiently surplus-enhancing.*

Neither intention- nor type-based reciprocity can explain positive transfers in the DG. Moreover, Charness (1996), Bolton, Brandts, and Ockenfels (1998), Offerman (1999), Cox (2000), and Charness and Rabin (2000) provide further evidence that intentions do not play a big role for rewarding behavior. Charness (1996) conducted GEGs in a random choice condition and a human choice condition. Intention-based theories predict that, in the random choice condition, the Responders will not put forward more than the minimal effort level irrespective of the wage level, because high wage offers are due to chance and not to kind intentions. In the human choice condition, higher wages indicate a higher degree of kindness and, therefore, a positive correlation between wages and effort is predicted. Levine's theory allows, in principle, for a positive correlation between wages and effort in both conditions, because an increase in effort benefits the Proposer much more than they cost the Responder. However, the correlation should be much stronger in the human choice condition because of the type-revealing effect of high wages. Charness finds a significantly positive correlation in the random choice condition. In the human choice condition, effort is only slightly lower at low wages and equally high at high wages. This indicates, if anything, only a minor role for intention- and type-driven behavior. The best interpretation is probably that inequity aversion or quasi-maximin preferences induce nonminimal effort levels in this setting. In addition, negative reciprocity kicks in at low wages that explain the lower effort levels in the human choice condition.

Cox (2000) tries to isolate rewarding responses in the context of a TG by using a related DG as a control condition. In the TG, Cox observes a baseline level of Responder transfers back to the Proposer. To isolate the relevance of intention-driven responses, he conducts a DG in which the distribution of endowments is identical to the distribution of material payoffs after the Proposers' choices in the TG. Thus, both in the TG and in the DG, the Responders face exactly the same distributions of material payoffs; but, in the TG, this distribution has been caused intentionally by the Proposers, whereas in the DG the distribution is predetermined by the experimenter. In Cox's DG, the motive of rewarding kindness can, therefore, play no role, and intention-based theories, as well as Levine's theory, predict that Responders transfer nothing back. If one takes into account that some transfers in the DG are driven by inequity aversion or quasi-maximin preferences, the difference between the transfers in the DG and the transfers in the TG measure the relevance of intention- or type-based theories. Cox's results indicate that these theories play only a minor or no role in this context. In one condition, there is no difference in transfers between the TG and the DG, and, in another condition, transfers in the DG are lower by only one-third.

The strongest evidence against the role of intentions comes from Bolton, Brandts, and Ockenfels (1998). They conducted sequential social dilemma experiments that are akin to a sequentially played prisoner's dilemma. In one condition, the first movers could make a kind choice relative to a baseline choice. The kind choice implied that – for any choice of the second mover – the payoff of the second mover increased by 400 units at a cost of 100 for the first mover. Then, the second mover could take costly actions to reward the first mover. In a control condition, the first mover could make only the baseline choice (i.e., he could not express any kind intentions). Second movers reward the first movers even more in this control condition. Although this difference is not significant, the results clearly suggest that intention-driven rewards play no role in this experiment.

The strongest evidence in favor of intentions comes from the moonlighting game of FFF (2000b) described in the previous subsection. FFF find that, for *all* positive transfers of player A, player B sends back significantly more money in the human choice condition. Moreover, the difference between the rewards in the human choice condition and the random choice condition are also quantitatively important. A recent paper by McCabe, Rigdon, and Smith (2000) also reports evidence in favor of intention-driven positive reciprocity. They show that, after a nice choice of the first mover, two-thirds of the second movers make nice choices, too; whereas if the first mover is forced to make the nice choice, only one-third of the second movers make the nice choice.

In the absence of the evidence provided by FFF and McCabe et al., one would have to conclude that the motive to reward good intentions or fair types is (at best) of minor importance. However, in view of the relatively strong results in the final two papers, it seems wise to be more cautious and to wait for further evidence. Nevertheless, the bulk of the evidence suggests that inequity aversion and efficiency-seeking are more important than intention- or type-based reciprocity in the domain of kind behavior.

4.5. Summary and Outlook

Although most fairness models discussed in Section 3 are just a few years old, the discussion in this section shows that there is already a fair amount of evidence that sheds light on the relative performance of the different models. This indicates a quick and healthy interaction between experimental research and the development of new theories. The initial experimental results discussed in Section 2 gave rise to a number of new theories, which, in turn, have again been quickly subjected to careful and rigorous empirical testing. Although these tests have not yet led to conclusive results regarding the relative importance of the different motives, many important and interesting insights have been obtained. In our view, the main results can be summarized as follows:

1. Evidence from the Third-Party Punishment Game and the PGG with punishment indicates that many subjects do compare themselves with

other people in the group and not just to the group as a whole or to the group average.

2. There is a nonnegligible number of subjects in DGs whose behavior is consistent with surplus maximization. However, the relative quantitative importance of this motive in economically relevant settings has yet to be determined, and surplus maximization alone cannot account for many robust regularities in other games.

3. Pure revenge, as captured by reciprocity models, is an important motive for payoff-reducing behavior. In some games, like the PGG with punishment, it seems to be the dominant source of payoff-reducing behavior. Because pure equity models do not capture this motive, they cannot explain a significant amount of payoff-reducing behavior.

4. In the domain of kind behavior, the motives captured by intention- or type-based models of fairness seem to be less important than in the domain of payoff-reducing behavior. Several studies indicate that inequity aversion or quasi-maximin preferences play a more important role here.

Which model of fairness does best in the light of the data, and which one should be used in applications to economically important phenomena? We believe that it is too early to give a conclusive answer to these questions. There is a large amount of heterogeneity at the individual level, and any model of fairness has difficulties in explaining the full diversity of the experimental observations. The evidence suggests, however, some tentative answers to these questions. In our view, the most important heterogeneity is the one between purely selfish subjects and fair-minded subjects. The success of the BO model and the FS model in explaining a large variety of data from bargaining, cooperation, and market games is partly from this recognition. Within the class of these equity models, the evidence suggests that the FS model does better. In particular, the experiments discussed in Section 4.1 indicate that people do not compare themselves with the group as a whole, but rather with other individuals in the group. The group average is less compelling as a yardstick to measure equity than differences in individual payoffs.

However, the FS model clearly does not recognize the full heterogeneity within the class of fair-minded individuals. Section 4.4 makes it clear that an important part of payoff-reducing behavior is not driven by the desire to reduce payoff differences, but by the desire to reduce the payoff of those who take unfair actions or reveal themselves as unfair types. The model therefore underestimates the amount of punishing behavior in situations where the cost of punishment is relatively high, compared with the payoff reductions that can be achieved by punishing. Fairness models that are exclusively based on intentions (Rabin 1993; Dufwenberg and Kirchsteiger 1998) can, in principle, account for this type of punishment. Yet, these models have other undesirable features, including multiple, and very counterintuitive, equilibria in many games and a very high degree of complexity that is from the use of psychological game theory. The same has to be said about the intention-based theory of Charness and Rabin (2000). Falk and Fischbacher (1999) are not plagued by the multiple equilibrium problem as much as the pure intention models. This is because they incorporate equity as a global reference standard. Their model shares, however, the complexity costs of psychological game theory.

Even though none of the available theories can take into account the full complexity of motives at the individual level, some theories may allow for better approximations than others. The evidence presented in Section 2 shows clearly that there are many important economic problems for which the self-interest theory is unambiguously, and in a quantitatively important way, refuted. The recent papers by BO and FS show that one can account for the bulk of this evidence by models that explicitly take into account that there are selfish and fair-minded individuals. Although we believe that it is desirable to tackle the heterogeneity within the class of fair-minded subjects in parsimonious and tractable models, we also believe that the heterogeneity between selfish and fair types is more important. In fact, in the following section, we will show that the FS model provides surprisingly good qualitative and quantitative predictions in important economic domains. Thus, even if we do not yet have a fully satisfactory model of fair behavior, one can probably go a long way with simple models that take into account the interaction between selfish and fair types.

5.   ECONOMIC APPLICATIONS

5.1.   Competition and Fairness – When Does Fairness Matter?

The self-interest model fails to explain the experimental evidence in many games in which only a few players interact, but it is very successful in explaining the outcome of competitive markets. It is a well-established experimental fact that, in a broad class of market games, prices converge to the competitive equilibrium.[32] This result holds even if the resulting allocation is very unfair by any notion of fairness. Thus, the question arises: If so many people resist unfair outcomes in, say, the UG, why don't they behave the same way when there is competition among the players?

To answer this question, consider the following UG with Proposer competition, which was conducted by Roth, Prasnikar, Okuno-Fujiwara, and Zamir (1991) in four different countries. There are $n - 1$ Proposers who simultaneously offer a share $s_i \in [0, 1]$, $i \in \{1, \ldots, n - 1\}$, to one Responder. The Responder can either accept or reject the highest offer $s^{\max} = \max_i \{s_i\}$. If there are several Proposers who offered $s^{\max}$, one of them is selected at random with equal probability. If the Responder accepts $s^{\max}$, her monetary payoff is $s^{\max}$ and the successful Proposer earns $1 - s^{\max}$, whereas all the other Proposers get 0. If the Responder rejects, everybody gets a payoff of 0.

---

[32] See, e.g., Smith (1962) and Davis and Holt (1993).

The prediction of the self-interest model is straightforward: All Proposers will offer $s = 1$, which is accepted by the Responder. Hence, all Proposers get a payoff of 0 and the monopolistic Responder captures the entire surplus. This outcome is clearly very unfair, but it describes precisely what happened in the experiments. After a few periods of adaptation, s^{max} was very close to 1, and all the surplus was captured by the Responder.[33]

This result is remarkable. It does not seem to be more fair that one side of the market gets all of the surplus in this setting than in the standard UG. Why do the Proposers let the Responder get away with it? The reason is that, in this strategic setting, preferences for fairness or reciprocity cannot have any effect. To see this, suppose that each of the Proposers strongly dislikes to get less than the Responder. Consider Proposer i and let $s' = \max_{j \neq i} \{s_j\}$ be the highest offer made by his fellow Proposers. If Proposer i offers $s_i < s'$, then his offer has no effect and he will get a monetary payoff of 0 with certainty. Furthermore, he cannot prevent that the Responder gets s' and that one of the other Proposers gets $1 - s'$; so, he will suffer from getting less than these two. However, if he offers a little bit more than s', say $s' + \varepsilon$, then he will win the competition, get a positive monetary payoff, and reduce the inequality between himself and the Responder. Hence, he should try to overbid his competitors. This process drives the share that is offered by the Proposers up to 1. There is nothing the Proposers can do about it, even if all of them have a strong preference for fairness. We prove this result formally in Fehr and Schmidt (1999) for the case of inequity-averse players, but the same result is also predicted by the approaches of Levine (1998) and Bolton and Ockenfels (2000).

Does this mean that sufficiently strong competition will always wipe out the impact of fairness? The answer to this question is negative, because fairness matters much more in market games in which the execution of contracts cannot be completely determined at the stage where the parties conclude the contracts. Labor markets are a good example. A labor contract is highly incomplete, because it cannot enforce the level of effort provided by the employee who chooses his effort level after the contract has been signed. These contractual features are captured by the GEG in an experimental setting.

When the GEG is embedded into a competitive experimental market [e.g., in Fehr et al. (1993, 1998)], wages are systematically higher than the competitive equilibrium wage predicted by the self-interest model. There is also no tendency for wages to decrease over time. The reason for this stable wage premium is the effort behavior of the Responders: On average, effort levels are increasing with wages that provide an incentive for the firms to pay a wage premium. If,

---

[33] The experiments were conducted in Israel, Japan, Slovenia, and the United States. In all experiments, there were nine Proposers and one responder. Roth et al. also conducted the standard UG with one Proposer in these four countries. They did find some small (but statistically significant) differences between countries in the standard UG, which may be attributed to cultural differences. However, there are no statistically significant differences between countries for the UG with Proposer competition.

however, the effort level is fixed exogenously by the experimenter, the firms do not shy away from pushing down wages to the competitive level. FS and BO can explain this pattern in a straightforward manner. When effort is endogenous, inequity-averse Responders respond to high wages with high effort levels to prevent an unequal distribution of the surplus from trade. This induces all firms (including purely selfish ones) to pay a wage premium because it is profitable to do so. When effort is exogenous, this mechanism does not work, and competition drives down wages to the competitive level.

5.2.   Endogenous Incomplete Contracts

If fairness concerns affect the behavior of economic agents in so many situations, then it should also be taken into account in the design of incentive schemes. Surprisingly, hardly any theoretical and very little empirical or experimental work has been done to study the impact of fairness on incentive provision. Standard contract theory neglects this issue and assumes that all agents are interested only in their own material payoffs. Over the past two decades, this theory has been highly successful in solving fairly complicated contractual problems and in designing very sophisticated mechanisms and incentive schemes. This gave rise to many important and fascinating insights, and the methods developed there have been applied in almost all areas of economics. However, standard contract theory still finds it difficult to explain the simplicity and incompleteness of many contracts that we observe in the real world. In particular, it cannot explain why the parties' monetary payoffs are often not tied to measures of performance that would be available at a relatively small cost. For example, the salary of a teacher or a university professor is rarely contingent on students' test scores, teaching ratings, or citations. These performance measures are readily available and easily verifiable, so one has to conclude that these contracts are deliberately left incomplete.[34]

In a recent paper, Fehr, Klein, and Schmidt (2000) take a fresh look at contractual incompleteness by taking concerns for fairness and reciprocity into account. They report on several simple principal–agent experiments in which the principal was given a choice whether to offer a "complete" contract or a less complete one. In the first experimental design, an agent had to pick an effort level

---

[34] The literature on incomplete contracts acknowledges contractual incompleteness, but most of this literature simply assumes that no long-term contingent contracts are feasible and does not attempt to explain this premise. See, for example, Grossman and Hart (1986) or Hart and Moore (1990) and Section 5.3. There is a small literature on endogenous incomplete contracts. Some papers in this literature [e.g., Aghion, Dewatripont, and Rey (1994), Nöldeke and Schmidt (1995), or Edlin and Reichelstein (1996)] show that, in some situations, a properly designed incomplete contract can implement the first best, so, there is no need to write a more complete contract. Some other papers [e.g., Che and Hausch (1998), Hart and Moore (1999), and Segal (1999)] show that, although an incomplete contract does not implement the first best, a more complete contract is of no value to the parties because it is impossible to get closer to the efficiency frontier.

between 1 and 10 (at a monetary cost to herself) that is perfectly observed by a principal and can be verified (at a small fixed cost) to the courts. The principal can try to induce the agent to spend effort by imposing a fine on the agent that is enforced by the courts if she works too little. However, the fine is bounded above so that the highest implementable effort level ($e^* = 4$) falls short of the first-best efficient action ($e^{FB} = 10$). In this contractual environment, principal–agent theory predicts that the principal should use the maximal fine to induce the agent to choose $e^* = 4$, and that he should offer a fixed wage that holds the agent down to her reservation utility. If the agent complies with the contract, the principal can capture roughly 30 percent of the first-best surplus for himself, while the agent gets nothing.

There are two alternatives to this "incentive contract." In one treatment, the principal could choose to offer a "trust contract" that does without a fine and simply pays a generous fixed wage up front to the agent asking her to reciprocate by spending a higher level of effort. However, effort cannot be enforced with this contract. In a second treatment, the principal could offer a "bonus contract," which specifies a fixed wage, a desired level of effort, and an announced bonus payment if the effort is to the principal's satisfaction. However, both parties know that the bonus cannot be enforced and is left at the discretion of the principal. The trust and the bonus contract are clearly less complete than the incentive contract. Because the experiments carefully rule out any repeated interactions between the parties, both types of contracts are, according to standard principal–agent theory, doomed to fail. Given the fixed wage, a pure self-interested agent will not spend any effort. Similarly, a principal who is interested only in his own income will never pay a bonus, so a rational agent should never put in any effort.

If concerns for fairness and reciprocity are taken into account, the predictions are less clear cut. Consider again the optimal incentive contract (as suggested by principal–agent theory). This contract aims at a rather unfair distribution of the surplus. If the agent is concerned about this, there are two ways how she could punish the principal. First, as in a UG, she could simply reject the contract, in which case both parties get a payoff of 0. A second, and more interesting, punishment strategy is to accept the contract and to shirk. Note that, if the incentive compatibility constraint is just binding, then the cost of shirking to the agent is zero and independent of the fixed wage offered by the principal. Thus, if the principal offers a somewhat higher wage that gives a positive (but still "unfair") share of the surplus to the agent, the agent can punish the principal by accepting the wage and shirking (at zero cost to herself). Hence, concerns for fairness and reciprocity suggest that the principal has to offer a fairly generous wage to get the agent to accept and to work, which makes the incentive contract less attractive.

On the other hand, concerns for fairness and reciprocity improve the performance of trust and bonus contracts. A fair agent will reciprocate to a generous wage offer in a trust contract by putting in a higher effort level voluntarily. Similarly, a fair principal will reciprocate to a high effort level by paying a generous bonus, making it worth the agent's while to spend more effort. Unfortunately, however, on such a general level, it is impossible to make any clear-cut predictions about the relative performance of the three types of contracts. Is the incentive contract going to be outperformed by the trust and/or the bonus contract? Is the bonus contract induced at a higher level of effort than the trust contract or the other way round?

To obtain quantitative predictions for the experiments, Fehr et al. (2000) apply the model of inequity aversion by Fehr and Schmidt (1999) to this moral hazard problem. Most other models of fairness or intention-based reciprocity would probably yield similar results, and we want to stress that these experiments were not designed to discriminate between different notions of fairness. The main advantage of our model of inequity aversion is just its simplicity, which makes it straightforward to apply to these games. However, Fehr et al. (2000) have to make a few additional assumptions. In particular, they assume for simplicity that there are only two types of subjects, "selfish" players who are interested only in their own material payoffs, and "fair" players who are willing to give up their own resources to achieve a more equal payoff distribution. Furthermore, in rough accordance with the experimental results of many UGs and DGs, they assume that 60 percent of the population are selfish and 40 percent are fair.

With these assumptions it is a straightforward exercise to analyze the different types of contracts and obtain the following predictions:

1. *Trust Contracts:* Fair agents will reciprocate to high wage offers by putting in an effort level that equalizes payoffs, whereas selfish agents will choose the minimum effort level of 1. Thus, a higher wage offer will, on average, induce a higher level of effort. However, it can be shown that if less than two-thirds of all agents are fair, paying a higher wage does not raise the principal's expected profit. Therefore, with 40 percent fair agents, the trust contract is not going to work.

2. *Incentive Contracts:* For the same reason as in the trust contract, it does not pay for the principals to elicit higher average effort levels by paying generous wages. Thus, both selfish and fair principals impose the highest possible fine to induce the agent to choose $e = 4$. However, whereas the fair principals share the surplus arising from $e = 4$ equally with the agent, selfish principals propose unfair contracts that give them the whole surplus. They anticipate that the fair agents reject these contracts; but, because the 60 percent selfish agents accept these contracts, this strategy is still profitable.

3. *Bonus Contracts:* Selfish principals always pay a bonus of zero, but fair principals pay a bonus that divides the surplus equally between the principal and the agent. Therefore, the bonus is on average increasing with the agent's effort. Moreover, the relation between the effort and the average bonus is sufficiently steep to induce a selfish agent to

put it an effort level of 7. However, the fair agent chooses an effort level of only 1 or 2 (depending on the fixed wage). The reason for this surprising result is that the fair agent is concerned not only about her expected monetary payoff, but that she suffers in addition from the inequality that arises if a selfish principal does not pay the bonus. Nevertheless, on average, the bonus contract implements a higher level of effort ($e = 5.2$) and yields a higher payoff for the principal than both the incentive contract and the trust contract.[35]

What are the experimental results? Each experiment had 10 periods, in which each principal was matched randomly and anonymously with a different agent. In the first treatment, in which principals could choose between a trust and an incentive contract, roughly 50 percent of the principals chose a trust contract and 50 percent chose an incentive contract in period 1. However, the fraction of incentive contracts rose quickly and, after period 5, roughly 80 percent of all contractual choices were incentive contracts. Those principals who offered a trust contract paid generous wages, to which some agents reciprocated by putting in a high effort level. However, in 64 percent of all trust contracts, the agents chose $e = 1$. Thus, on average, principals incurred considerable losses when they proposed trust contracts. The incentive contracts did better, but they did much less well than predicted by standard principal–agent theory. They also did less well than predicted by the model of inequity aversion. The reason is that, at the beginning, many principals offered incentive contracts with fairly high wages that were not incentive-compatible. In these cases, 62 percent of the agents shirked, imposing considerable losses on principals. On the other hand, those principals who offered incentive-compatible incentive contracts with low wages did fairly well. Principals learned to properly design incentive contracts over time. The fraction of incentive-compatible contracts increased from only 10 percent in period 1 to 64 percent in period 10.

In the second treatment, the principal had to choose between a bonus contract and an incentive contract. From the very beginning, the bonus contract was much more popular than the incentive contract and accounted for roughly 90 percent of all contractual choices. Many principals did not pay a bonus, but a significant fraction reciprocated generously to higher effort levels. The average bonus was, therefore, strongly increasing in the effort level, which made it worthwhile for the agents to put forward rather high effort levels. The average effort level was 5.2, which is significantly higher than the average effort of 2.5 induced by

---

[35] The analysis of the bonus contract is complicated by the fact that the principal has to move twice. He offers the terms of the contract at the first stage of the game, and he has to choose his bonus payment at the last stage. Thus, his contract offer may reveal some information about his type. However, it can be shown that there is no separating equilibrium in this game and that all pooling equilibria have the properties described previously. Furthermore, if we assume that a higher wage offer is not interpreted by the agent as a signal that she faces the selfish principal with a higher probability, then there is a unique pooling equilibrium. See Fehr et al. (2000).

incentive contracts. The bonus contract not only is more efficient than the incentive contract, it also yields on average a much higher payoff to the principal and a moderately higher payoff to the agent. These results are clearly inconsistent with the self-interest model, whereas the model of inequity aversion explains them surprisingly well.[36]

Our experiments demonstrate that quite powerful incentives can be given by a very incomplete bonus contract. The bonus contract relies on reciprocal fairness as an enforcement device. It does better than the more complete incentive contracts *because* it is incomplete and thus leaves more freedom to the parties to reciprocate. This enforcement mechanism is not perfect and, depending on the payoff structure and the fraction of reciprocal types in the population, it can fail. In fact, we have seen that the trust contract – in which the principal has to pay, in advance, the "bonus" unconditionally – is not viable in the set up of our experiments. Yet, the performance of the bonus contract suggests that the effect of reciprocal fairness, which has been neglected in contract theory so far, is important for optimal contractual design and should be taken into account.

5.3.   The Optimal Allocation of Ownership Rights

Consider two parties, A and B, who are engaged in a joint project (a "firm") to which they have to make some relationship-specific investments today to generate a joint surplus in the future. An important question that has received considerable attention in recent years is who should own the firm. In a seminal paper, Grossman and Hart (1986) argue that ownership rights allocate residual rights of control on the physical assets that are required to generate the surplus. For example, if A owns the firm, then he will have a stronger bargaining position than B in the renegotiation game in which the surplus between the two parties is shared ex post, because he can exclude B from using the assets that make B's relationship-specific investment less productive. Grossman and Hart show that there is no ownership structure that implements first-best investments, but some ownership structures do better than others, and there is a unique second-best optimal allocation of ownership rights.

---

[36] In a second experimental design, Fehr et al. (2000) consider a multitask principal–agent model inspired by Holmström and Milgrom (1991). In this experiment, the agents have to choose two separate effort levels ("tasks"), e_1 and e_2, both of which are observable by the principal, but only e_1 is verifiable and can be contracted on. The principal can choose between a piece-rate contract that rewards the agent for his effort spent on task 1 and a bonus contract that announces a voluntary bonus payment if the agent's effort on both tasks is to the principal's satisfaction. The overwhelming majority of principals opted for the bonus contract, which induced the agents to spend, on average, a considerable amount of effort and to allocate total effort efficiently across tasks. Those principals that chose a piece-rate contract induced the agents to concentrate all of their total efforts on task 1, which is very inefficient. Again, these results are inconsistent with the self-interest model, but they can be nicely explained by the Fehr–Schmidt model of inequity aversion.

A common feature of most incomplete contract models is that joint ownership cannot be optimal.[37] This result is at odds with the fact that there are many jointly owned companies, partnerships, or joint ventures. Furthermore, the argument neglects that reciprocal fairness may be an important enforcement mechanism to induce the involved parties to invest more under joint ownership than otherwise predicted. To test this hypothesis, Fehr, Kremhelmer, and Schmidt (2000) conducted a series of experiments on the optimal allocation of ownership rights. The experimental game is a grossly simplified version of Grossman and Hart (1986): There are two parties, A and B, who have to make investments, $a, b \in \{1, \ldots, 10\}$, respectively, to generate a joint surplus $v(a, b)$. Investments are sequential: B has to invest first; his investment level b is observed by A, who has to invest thereafter. We consider two possible ownership structures: Under A ownership, A hires B as an employee and pays her a fixed wage w. In this case, monetary payoffs are $v(a, b) - w - a$ for A and $w - b$ for B. Under joint ownership, each party gets half of the gross surplus minus his or her investment cost [i.e., $0.5v(a, b) - a$ for A and $0.5v(a, b) - b$ for B]. The gross profit function has been chosen such that maximal investments are efficient (i.e., $a^{\text{FB}} = b^{\text{FB}} = 10$), but if each party gets only 50 percent of the marginal return of their investments, then it is a dominant strategy for a purely self-interested player to choose the minimum level of investment, $\underline{a} = \underline{b} = 1$. Finally, in the first stage of the game, A can decide whether to be the sole owner of the firm and make a wage offer to B, or whether to have joint ownership.

The prediction of the self-interest model is straightforward. Under A ownership, B has no incentive to invest and will choose $b = 1$. On the other hand, A is a full residual claimant on the margin, so she will invest efficiently. Under joint ownership, each party gets only 50 percent of the marginal return, which is not sufficient to induce any investments. Hence, in this case, B's optimal investment level is unchanged, but A's investment level is reduced to $\underline{a} = 1$. Thus, A ownership outperforms joint ownership, and A should hire B as an employee.

In the experiments, just the opposite happened. Party A chose joint ownership in more than 80 percent (187 of 230) of all observations and gave away 50 percent of the gross return to B. Moreover, the fraction of joint ownership contracts increased from 74 percent in the first two periods to 89 percent in the

---

[37] To see this note that, in the renegotiation game in which the surplus is shared, each party gets its reservation utility plus a fixed fraction (50 percent, say) of the joint surplus in excess of the sum of the reservation utilities. Now, consider A ownership. If A invests, then his investment increases not only the joint surplus, but also his reservation utility (i.e., what he could get out of the firm without B's collaboration). On the other hand, if B invests, then her investment increases only the joint surplus, but it does not improve her reservation utility. The reason is that the investment requires access to the firm to be productive. Hence, without the firm, B's investment is useless. This is why A will invest more than B under A ownership. Consider now joint ownership. If both parties own the firm jointly, then each of them can prevent the other from using the assets. Hence, neither A's nor B's investment affects their respective reservation utilities. Therefore, A's investment incentives are reduced, whereas B's investment incentives do not improve. Hence, joint ownership is inferior.

last two periods. With joint ownership, B players chose on average an investment level of 8.9, and A responded with an investment of 6.5 (on average). On the other hand, if A ownership was chosen and A hired B as an employee, B's average investment was only 1.3, whereas all A players chose an investment level of 10. Furthermore A players earned much more on average if they chose joint ownership rather than A ownership.

These results are inconsistent with the self-interest model, but it is straightforward to explain them with concerns for fairness. Applying the Fehr and Schmidt (1999) model of inequity aversion gives again fairly accurate quantitative predictions. Thus, the experimental results and the theoretical analysis suggest that joint ownership may do better than A ownership, because it offers more scope for reciprocal behavior. Subjects seem to understand this and predominantly choose this ownership structure.

6. CONCLUSIONS

The self-interest model has been very successful in explaining individual behavior on competitive markets, but it is unambiguously refuted in many situations in which individuals interact strategically. The experimental evidence on, for example, UGs, DGs, GEGs, and PGGs demonstrates unambiguously not only that many people are maximizing their own material payoffs, but also that they are concerned about social comparisons, fairness, and the desire to reciprocate.

We have reviewed several models that try to take these concerns explicitly into account. A general lesson to be drawn from these models is that the assumption that some people are fair-minded and have the desire to reciprocate does not imply that these people will always behave "fairly." In some environments (e.g., in competitive markets or in PGGs without punishment), fair-minded actors will often behave as if they are purely self-interested. Likewise, a purely self-interested person may often behave as if he is strongly concerned about fairness (e.g., the Proposers who make fair proposals in the UG or generous wage offers in the GEG). Thus, the behavior of fair-minded and purely self-interested actors depends on the strategic environment in which they interact and on their beliefs about the fairness of their opponents. The analysis of this behavior is not trivial, and it is helpful to develop theoretical tools to better understand what we observe.

Some of the models reviewed focus solely on preferences over income distributions and ignore the fact that people often care about the intentions behind the actions of their opponents. Some other papers focus only on intention-based or type-based reciprocity and ignore the fact that some people are bothered by unfair distributions, even if their opponent could not do anything about it. It seems natural to try to combine these two motivations in a single model as has been done by Falk and Fischbacher (1998) and Charness and Rabin (2000). However, we believe that the cost of doing so is high. These models are rather complicated; they rely on psychological game theory, and it is difficult to apply them even to very simple experimental games. Moreover, Charness and Rabin, in particular, are plagued with multiple equilibria and have much more free parameters than all the other models. On the other hand, simple models of social preferences – for example, Bolton and Ockenfels' (2000) ERC model or our own (1999) model of inequity aversion – fit the data on large classes of games fairly well. They use standard game theory, they have fewer parameters to be estimated, and it is fairly straightforward to get clear-cut qualitative and quantitative predictions.

The main advantage of these simple models is that they can easily be applied to other fields in economics. For more than 20 years, experimental economists concentrated on simple experimental games to better understand what drives economic behavior. However, very few of the insights that have been gained had any impact on how economists interpret the world. We feel that it is now time to change this. Many phenomena in situations in which people interact strategically cannot be understood by relying on the self-interest model alone. Our examples from contract theory and the theory of property rights illustrate that models of reciprocal fairness can be fruitfully applied to important and interesting economic questions, yielding predictions that are much closer to what we observe in many situations of the real world and in carefully controlled experiments than the predictions of the self-interest model. There are many other areas in which fairness models are likely to generate interesting new insights – be it the functioning of labor markets or questions of political economy or be it the design of optimal mechanisms or questions of compliance with organizational rules and the law.

We hope that this is just the beginning. There is no shortage of important questions to which the newly developed tools and insights can be applied.

ACKNOWLEDGMENTS

We thank Glenn Ellison for many helpful comments and suggestions, and Alexander Klein and Susanne Kremhelmer for excellent research assistance. Part of this research was conducted while Klaus M. Schmidt visited Stanford University, and he thanks the Economics Department for its great hospitality. Financial support by Deutsche Forschungsgemeinschaft through Grant SCHM-1196/4-1 is gratefully acknowledged. Ernst Fehr also gratefully acknowledges support from the Swiss National Science Foundation (Project No. 1214-05100.97), the Network on the Evolution of Preferences and Social Norms of the MacArthur Foundation, and the EU-TMR Research Network ENDEAR (FMRX-CTP98-0238).

References

Abbink, K., B. Irlenbusch, and E. Renner (2000), "The Moonlighting Game: An Experimental Study on Reciprocity and Retribution," *Journal of Economic Behavior and Organization*, 42, 265–277.

Agell, J. and P. Lundborg (1995), "Theories of Pay and Unemployment: Survey Evidence from Swedish Manufacturing Firms," *Scandinavian Journal of Economics*, 97, 295–308.

Aghion, P., M. Dewatripont, and P. Rey (1994), "Renegotiation Design with Unverifiable Information," *Econometrica*, 62, 257–282.

Ahlert, M., A. Crüger, and W. Güth (1999), "An Experimental Analysis of Equal Punishment Games," mimeo, University of Halle-Wittenberg.

Alm, J., I. Sanchez, and A. de Juan (1995), "Economic and Noneconomic Factors in Tax Compliance," *Kyklos*, 48, 3–18.

Andreoni, J. (1989), "Giving with Impure Altruism: Applications to Charity and Ricardian Equivalence," *Journal of Political Economy*, 97, 1447–1458.

Andreoni, J., B. Erard, and J. Feinstein (1998), "Tax Compliance," *Journal of Economic Literature*, 36, 818–860.

Andreoni, J. and J. Miller (1993), "Rational Cooperation in the Finitely Repeated Prisoner's Dilemma: Experimental Evidence," *Economic Journal*, 103, 570–585.

Andreoni, J. and J. Miller (2000), "Giving According to GARP: An Experimental Test of the Rationality of Altruism," mimeo, University of Wisconsin and Carnegie Mellon University.

Andreoni, J. and H. Varian (1999), "Preplay Contracting in the Prisoner's Dilemma," *Proceedings of the National Academy of Sciences USA*, 96, 10933–10938.

Andreoni, J. and L. Vesterlund, "Which Is the Fair Sex? Gender Differences in Altruism," *Quarterly Journal of Economics*, 116, 293–312.

Arrow, K. J. (1981), "Optimal and Voluntary Income Redistribution," in *Economic Welfare and the Economics of Soviet Socialism: Essays in Honor of Abram Bergson*, (ed. by S. Rosenfield), Cambridge, UK: Cambridge University Press.

Becker, G. S. (1974), "A Theory of Social Interactions," *Journal of Political Economy*, 82, 1063–1093.

Berg, J., J. Dickhaut, and K. McCabe (1995), "Trust, Reciprocity and Social History," *Games and Economic Behavior*, 10, 122–142.

Bernheim, B. D. (1986), "On the Voluntary and Involuntary Provision of Public Goods," *American Economic Review*, 76, 789–793.

Bewley, T. (1999), *Why Wages Don't Fall During a Recession*. Cambridge, MA: Harvard University Press.

Binmore, K. (1998), *Game Theory and the Social Contract: Just Playing*. Cambridge, MA: MIT Press.

Binmore, K., J. Gale, and L. Samuelson (1995), "Learning to Be Imperfect: The Ultimatum Game," *Games and Economic Behavior*, 8, 56–90.

Blount, S. (1995), "When Social Outcomes Aren't Fair: The Effect of Causal Attributions on Preferences," *Organizational Behavior and Human Decision Processes*, 43, 131–144.

Bolle, F. and A. Kritikos (1998), "Self-Centered Inequality Aversion Versus Reciprocity and Altruism," mimeo, Europa-Universität Viadrina.

Bolton, G. E. (1991), "A Comparative Model of Bargaining: Theory and Evidence," *American Economic Review*, 81, 1096–1136.

Bolton, G. E., J. Brandts, and A. Ockenfels (1998), "Measuring Motivations for the Reciprocal Responses Observed in a Simple Dilemma Game," *Experimental Economics*, 3, 207–221.

Bolton, G. E. and A. Ockenfels (2000), "A Theory of Equity, Reciprocity, and Competition," *American Economic Review*, 100, 166–193.

Bolton, G. and R. Zwick (1995), "Anonymity Versus Punishment in Ultimatum Bargaining," *Games and Economic Behavior*, 10, 95–121.

Bowles, S. and H. Gintis (1999), "The Evolution of Strong Reciprocity," mimeo, University of Massachusetts at Amherst.

Bowles, S. and H. Gintis (2000), "Reciprocity, Self-Interest, and the Welfare State," *Nordic Journal of Political Economy*, 26, 33–53.

Brandts, J. and G. Charness (1999), "Gift-Exchange with Excess Supply and Excess Demand," mimeo, Universitat Pompeu Fabra, Barcelona.

Camerer, C. F. (1999), "Social Preferences in Dictator, Ultimatum and Trust Games," mimeo, California Institute of Technology.

Camerer, C. F. and R. H. Thaler (1995), "Ultimatums, Dictators and Manners," *Journal of Economic Perspectives*, 9, 209–219.

Cameron, L. A. (1999), "Raising the Stakes in the Ultimatum Game: Experimental Evidence from Indonesia." *Economic Inquiry*, 37(1), 47–59.

Carpenter, J. P. (2000), "Punishing Free-Riders: The Role of Monitoring – Group Size, Second-Order Free-Riding and Coordination," mimeo, Middlebury College.

Chamberlin, E. H. (1948), "An Experimental Imperfect Market," *Journal of Political Economy*, 56, 95–108.

Charness, G. (1996), "Attribution and Reciprocity in a Labor Market: An Experimental Investigation," mimeo, University of California at Berkeley.

Charness, G. (2000), "Responsibility and Effort in an Experimental Labor Market," *Journal of Economic Behavior and Organization*, 42, 375–384.

Charness, G. and M. Rabin (2000), "Social Preferences: Some Simple Tests and a New Model," mimeo, University of California at Berkeley.

Che, Y.-K. and D. B. Hausch (1999), "Cooperative Investments and the Value of Contracting." *American Economic Review*, 89(1), 125–147.

Cooper, D. J. and C. K. Stockman (1999), "Fairness, Learning, and Constructive Preferences: An Experimental Investigation," mimeo, Case Western Reserve University.

Costa-Gomes, M. and K. G. Zauner (1999), "Learning, Non-equilibrium Beliefs, and Non-Pecuniary Payoff Uncertainty in an Experimental Game," mimeo, Harvard Business School.

Cox, J. C. (2000), "Trust and Reciprocity: Implications of Game Triads and Social Contexts," mimeo, University of Arizona at Tucson.

Croson, R. T. A. (1999), "Theories of Altruism and Reciprocity: Evidence from Linear Public Goods Games," Discussion Paper, Wharton School, University of Pennsylvania.

Daughety, A. (1994), "Socially-Influenced Choice: Equity Considerations in Models of Consumer Choice and in Games," mimeo, University of Iowa.

Davis, D. and C. Holt (1993), *Experimental Economics*. Princeton, NJ: Princeton University Press.

Dawes, R. M. and R. Thaler (1988), "Cooperation," *Journal of Economic Perspectives*, 2, 187–197.

Dufwenberg, M. and G. Kirchsteiger (1998), "A Theory of Sequential Reciprocity," Discussion Paper, CENTER, Tilburg University.

Edlin, A. S. and S. Reichelstein (1996), "Holdups, Standard Breach Remedies, and Optimal Investment," *American Economic Review*, 86(3), 478–501.

Eichenberger, R. and F. Oberholzer-Gee (1998), "Focus Effects in Dictator Game Experiments," mimeo, University of Pennsylvania.

Ellingsen, T. and M. Johannesson (2000), "Is There a Hold-up Problem? Stockholm School of Economics," Working Paper 357.

Encyclopaedia Britannica (1998), *The New Encyclopaedia Britannica*, Volume 1, (15th ed.), London, *Encyclopaedia Britannica*.

Fahr, R. and B. Irlenbusch (2000), "Fairness as a Constraint on Trust in Reciprocity: Earned Property Rights in a Reciprocal Exchange Experiment," *Economics Letters*, 66, 275–282.

Falk, A. E. Fehr, and U. Fischbacher (2000a), "Informal Sanctions, Institute for Empirical Research in Economics," University of Zurich, Working Paper 59.

Falk, A., E. Fehr, and U. Fischbacher (2000b), "Testing Theories of Fairness–Intentions Matter," Institute for Empirical Research in Economics, University of Zurich, Working Paper 63.

Falk, A., E. Fehr, and U. Fischbacher (2000c), "Appropriating the Commons, Institute for Empirical Research in Economics," University of Zurich, Working Paper 55.

Falk, A. and U. Fischbacher (1999), "A Theory of Reciprocity, Institute for Empirical Research in Economics," University of Zurich, Working Paper 6.

Falk, A., S. Gächter, and J. Kovács (1999), "Intrinsic Motivation and Extrinsic Incentives in a Repeated Game with Incomplete Contracts," *Journal of Economic Psychology*, 20, 251–284.

Fehr, E. and A. Falk (1999), "Wage Rigidity in a Competitive Incomplete Contract Market," *Journal of Political Economy*, 107, 106–134.

Fehr, E. and U. Fischbacher (2000), "Third Party Punishment," mimeo, University of Zürich.

Fehr, E. and S. Gächter (2000), "Cooperation and Punishment in Public Goods Experiments," *American Economic Review*, 90, 980–994.

Fehr, E., S. Gächter, and G. Kirchsteiger (1997), "Reciprocity as a Contract Enforcement Device," *Econometrica*, 65, 833–860.

Fehr, E., G. Kirchsteiger, and A. Riedl (1993), "Does Fairness Prevent Market Clearing? An Experimental Investigation," *Quarterly Journal of Economics*, 108, 437–460.

Fehr, E., G. Kirchsteiger, and A. Riedl (1998), "Gift Exchange and Reciprocity in Competitive Experimental Markets," *European Economic Review*, 42, 1–34.

Fehr, E., A. Klein, and K. M. Schmidt (2000), "Endogenous Incomplete Contracts," mimeo, University of Munich.

Fehr, E., S. Kremhelmer, and K. M. Schmidt (2000), "Fairness and the Optimal Allocation of Property Rights," mimeo, University of Munich.

Fehr, E. and K. M. Schmidt (1999), "A Theory of Fairness, Competition and Co-operation." *Quarterly Journal of Economics*, 114, 817–868.

Fehr, E. and E. Tougareva (1995), "Do High Monetary Stakes Remove Reciprocal Fairness? Experimental Evidence from Russia," mimeo, Institute for Empirical Economic Research, University of Zurich.

Fischbacher, U., S. Gächter, and E. Fehr (1999), "Are People Conditionally Cooperative? Evidence from a Public Goods Experiment," Working Paper 16, Institute for Empirical Research in Economics, University of Zurich.

Forsythe, R. L., J. Horowitz, N. E. Savin, and M. Sefton (1994), "Fairness in Simple Bargaining Games," *Games and Economic Behavior*, 6, 347–369.

Frey, B. and H. Weck-Hannemann (1984), "The Hidden Economy as an 'Unobserved' Variable," *European Economic Review*, 26, 33–53.

Gächter, S. and A. Falk (1999), "Reputation or Reciprocity?" Working Paper 19, Institute for Empirical Research in Economics, University of Zürich.

Geanakoplos, J., D. Pearce, and E. Stacchetti (1989), "Psychological Games and Sequential Rationality," *Games and Economic Behavior*, 1, 60–79.

Gintis, H. (2000), "Strong Reciprocity and Human Sociality," *Journal of Theoretical Biology*, 206, 169–179.

Greenberg, J. (1990), "Employee Theft as a Reaction to Underpayment Inequity: The Hidden Cost of Pay Cuts," *Journal of Applied Psychology*, 75, 561–568.

Grossman, S. and O. Hart (1986), "An Analysis of the Principal–Agent Problem," *Econometrica*, 51, 7–45.

Güth, W., H. Kliemt, and A. Ockenfels (2000), "Fairness Versus Efficiency – An Experimental Study of Mutual Gift-Giving," mimeo, Humboldt University of Berlin.

Güth, W., R. Schmittberger, and B. Schwarze (1982), "An Experimental Analysis of Ultimatium Bargaining," *Journal of Economic Behavior and Organization*, 3, 367–388.

Güth, W. and E. van Damme (1998), "Information, Strategic Behavior and Fairness in Ultimatum Bargaining: An Experimental Study," *Journal of Mathematical Psychology*, 42, 227–247.

Hannan, L., J. Kagel, and D. Moser (1999), "Partial Gift Exchange in Experimental Labor Markets: Impact of Subject Population Differences, Productivity Differences and Effort Requests on Behavior," mimeo, University of Pittsburgh.

Harsanyi, J. (1955), "Cardinal Welfare, Individualistic Ethics, and Interpersonal Comparisons of Utility," *Journal of Political Economy*, 63, 309–321.

Hart, O. and J. Moore (1990), "Property Rights and the Nature of the Firm," *Journal of Political Economy*, 98, 1119–1158.

Hart, O. and J. Moore (1999), "Foundations of Incomplete Contracts," *Review of Economic Studies*, 66, 115–138.

Hoffman, E., K. McCabe, K. Shachat, and V. Smith (1994), "Preferences, Property Rights, and Anonymity in Bargaining Games," *Games and Economic Behavior*, 7, 346–380.

Hoffman, E., K. McCabe, and V. Smith (1996), "On Expectations and Monetary Stakes in Ultimatum Games," *International Journal of Game Theory*, 25, 289–301.

Holmström, B. and P. Milgrom (1991), "Multi-Task Principal-Agent Analyses." *Journal of Law, Economics, and Organization*, 7, 24–52.

Isaac, M. R., J. M. Walker, A. W. Williams (1994), "Group Size and the Voluntary Provision of Public Goods," *Journal of Public Economics*, 54, 1–36.

Kagel, J. H, C. Kim, and D. Moser (1996), "Fairness in Ultimatum Games with Asymmetric Information and Asymmetric Payoffs," *Games and Economic Behavior*, 13, 100–110.

Kahneman, D., J. L. Knetsch, and R. Thaler (1986), "Fairness as a Constraint on Profit Seeking: Entitlements in the Market," *American Economic Review*, 76, 728–741.

Kirchsteiger, G. (1994), "The Role of Envy in Ultimatum Games," *Journal of Economic Behavior and Organization*, 25, 373–389.

Ledyard, J. (1995), "Public Goods: A Survey of Experimental Research," Chapter 2, in *Handbook of Experimental Economics*, (ed. by A. Roth and J. Kagel), Princeton, NJ: Princeton University Press.

Levine, D. (1998), "Modeling Altruism and Spitefulness in Experiments," *Review of Economic Dynamics*, 1, 593–622.

Lind, A. and T. Tyler (1988) *The Social Psychology of Procedural Justice*. New York: Plenum Press.

List, J. and T. Cherry (2000), "Examining the Role of Fairness in Bargaining Games," mimeo, University of Arizona at Tucson.

McCabe, K., M. Rigdon, and V. Smith (2000), "Positive Reciprocity and Intentions in Trust Games," mimeo, University of Arizona at Tucson.

Miller, S. (1997), "Strategienuntersuchung zum Investitionsspiel von Berg," Dickhaut, McCabe, Diploma Thesis, University of Bonn.

Neilson, W. (2000), "An Axiomatic Characterization of the Fehr-Schmidt Model of Inequity Aversion," mimeo, Department of Economics, Texas A&M University.

Nöldeke, G. and K. M. Schmidt (1995), "Option Contracts and Renegotiation: A Solution to the Hold-Up Problem," *Rand Journal of Economics*, 26, 163–179.

Offerman, T. (1999), "Hurting Hurts More Than Helping Helps: The Role of the Self-serving Bias," mimeo, University of Amsterdam.

Ostrom, E. (1990), *Governing the Commons – The Evolution of Institutions for Collective Action*. New York: Cambridge University Press.

Ostrom, E. (2000), "Collective Action and the Evolution of Social Norms," *Journal of Economic Perspectives*, 14, 137–158.

Rabin, M. (1993), "Incorporating Fairness into Game Theory and Economics," *American Economic Review*, 83(5), 1281–1302.

Roth, A. E. (1995), "Bargaining Experiments," in *Handbook of Experimental Economics*, (ed. by J. Kagel and A. Roth) Princeton, NJ: Princeton University Press.

Roth, A. E. and I. Erev (1995), "Learning in Extensive-Form Games: Experimental Data and Simple Dynamic Models in the Intermediate Term," *Games and Economic Behavior*, 8, 164–212.

Roth, A. E., M. W. K. Malouf, and J. K. Murningham (1981), "Sociological Versus Strategic Factors in Bargaining," *Journal of Economic Behavior and Organization*, 2, 153–177.

Roth, A. E., V. Prasnikar, M. Okuno-Fujiwara, and S. Zamir (1991), "Bargaining and Market Behavior in Jerusalem, Ljubljana, Pittsburgh, and Tokyo: An Experimental Study," *American Economic Review*, 81, 1068–1095.

Samuelson, P. A. (1993), "Altruism as a Problem Involving Group Versus Individual Selection in Economics and Biology," *American Economic Review*, 83, 143–148.

Segal, I. (1999), "Complexity and Renegotiation: A Foundation for Incomplete Contracts," *Review of Economic Studies*, 66(1), 57–82.

Segal, U. and J. Sobel (1999), "Tit for Tat: Foundations of Preferences for Reciprocity in Strategic Settings," mimeo, University of California at San Diego.

Seidl, C. and S. Traub (1999), "Taxpayers' Attitudes, Behavior, and Perceptions of Fairness in Taxation," mimeo, Institut für Finanzwissenschaft und Sozialpolitik, University of Kiel.

Selten, R. and A. Ockenfels (1998), "An Experimental Solidarity Game," *Journal of Economic Behavior and Organization*, 34, 517–539.

Sen, A. (1995), "Moral Codes and Economic Success," in *Market Capitalism and Moral Values* (ed. by C. S. Britten and A. Hamlin), Aldershot, UK: Edward Elgar.

Sethi, R. and E. Somananthan (2001), "Preference Evolution and Reciprocity," *Journal of Economic Theory*, 97, 273–297.

Sethi, R. and E. Somananthan (2000), "Understanding Reciprocity," mimeo, Columbia University.

Slonim, R. and A. E. Roth (1997), "Financial Incentives and Learning in Ultimatum and Market Games: An Experiment in the Slovak Republic," *Econometrica*, 65, 569–596.

Smith, A. (1759), *The Theory of Moral Sentiments*. Indianapolis, IN: Liberty Fund (reprinted 1982).

Smith, V. L. (1962), "An Experimental Study of Competitive Market Behavior," *Journal of Political Economy*, 70, 111–137.

Sonnemans, J., A. Schram, and T. Offerman (1999), "Strategic Behavior in Public Good Games–When Partners Drift Apart," *Economics Letters*, 62, 35–41.

Suleiman, R. (1996), "Expectations and Fairness in a Modified Ultimatum Game," *Journal of Economic Psychology*, 17, 531–554.

Veblen, T. (1922), *The Theory of the Leisure Class–An Economic Study of Institutions*. London: George Allen and Unwin (first published 1899).

Zajac, E. (1995), *"Political Economy of Fairness,"* Cambridge, MA: MIT Press.

Zizzo, D. and A. Oswald (2000), "Are People Willing to Pay to Reduce Others' Income?" mimeo, Oxford University.

CHAPTER 7

Hyberbolic Discounting and Consumption

Christopher Harris and David Laibson

1. INTRODUCTION

Robert Strotz (1956) first suggested that people are more impatient when they make short-run trade-offs than when they make long-run trade-offs.[1] Virtually every experimental study on time preference has supported Strotz's conjecture.[2] When two rewards are both far away in time, decision-makers act relatively patiently (e.g., I prefer two apples in 101 days, rather than one apple in 100 days). But when both rewards are brought forward in time, preferences exhibit a reversal, reflecting more impatience (e.g., I prefer one apple right now, rather than two apples tomorrow).[3]

Such reversals should be well understood by everyone who makes far-sighted New Year's resolutions and later backtracks. We promise ourselves to exercise, diet, and quit smoking, but often postpone those virtuous behaviors when the moment arrives to make the required sacrifices. Looking to the long run, we wish to act patiently, but the desire for instant gratification frequently overwhelms our good intentions.

The contrast between long-run patience and short-run impatience has been modeled with discount functions that take an approximately hyperbolic form (Ainslie, 1992, Loewenstein and Prelec 1992, Laibson, 1997a). Such preferences imply that the instantaneous discount rate declines as the horizon increases. This pattern of discounting sets up a conflict between today's preferences and the preferences that will be held in the future. From the perspective of period 0, the discount rate between two distant periods, t and $t + 1$, is a long-term low discount rate. However, from the perspective of period t, the discount rate between t and $t + 1$ is a short-term high discount rate.

Hyperbolic consumers will report a gap between what they feel they should save and what they actually save. Prescriptive saving rates will lie above actual

---

[1] Some of Strotz's insights are anticipated by Ramsey (1928).

[2] See Ainslie (1992) and Frederick, Loewenstein, and O'Donoghue (2001) for reviews of the evidence for and against hyperbolic discounting.

[3] This example is from Thaler (1981).

savings rates, because short-run preferences for instantaneous gratification will undermine the consumer's desire to implement long-run patient plans. However, the hyperbolic consumer is not doomed to retire in poverty. Illiquid assets can help the hyperbolic consumer lock in the patient, welfare-enhancing course of action. Hence, the availability of illiquid assets becomes a critical determinant of household savings and welfare. However, too much illiquidity can be problematic. Consumers face substantial uninsurable labor-income risk, and need to use liquid assets to smooth their consumption. Hyperbolic agents seek an investment portfolio that strikes the right balance between commitment and flexibility.

In this paper, we review and extend the literature on hyperbolic discounting and consumption. We begin our analysis of hyperbolic consumers by describing an infinite-horizon consumption problem with a single liquid asset. Using this tractable problem, we characterize equilibrium behavior. We prove a new equilibrium uniqueness theorem, characterize some properties of the consumption function, and illustrate additional properties of the consumption function with numerical simulations. We show that hyperbolic consumption functions may exhibit pathologies like discontinuities, nonmonotonicities, and concavity violations. We analyze the comparative statics of these pathologies. The pathologies are exacerbated as hyperbolicity increases, risk aversion falls, and income uncertainty falls. We also show that these pathologies do not arise when the model parameters are calibrated at empirically sensible benchmark values. Finally, we review our earlier results on the Euler relation characterizing the equilibrium path (Harris and Laibson, 2001a).

We then discuss simulations of savings and asset allocation choices of households who face a *life cycle* problem with liquid assets, liquid liabilities, and illiquid assets (Angeletos, Laibson, Repetto, Tobacman, and Weinberg 2001a; hereafter ALRTW). These life cycle simulations are used to compare the behavior of hyperbolic households and exponential households. Both the exponential and hyperbolic households are calibrated to hold levels of preretirement wealth that match observed levels of wealth reported in the Survey of Consumer Finances (SCF). Despite the fact that this calibration imposes identical levels of total wealth for hyperbolics and exponentials, numerous differences arise.

First, the hyperbolic households invest comparatively little of their wealth in liquid assets. They hold relatively low levels of liquid wealth measured either as a fraction of labor income or as a share of total wealth. Analogously, hyperbolic households also borrow more aggressively in the revolving credit market (i.e., on credit cards). The low levels of liquid wealth and high rates of credit card borrowing generated by hyperbolic simulations match empirical measures from the SCF much better than the results of exponential simulations.

Because the hyperbolic households have low levels of liquid assets and high levels of debt, they are unable to smooth their consumption paths in the presence of predictable changes in income. Calibrated hyperbolic simulations display substantial comovement between consumption and predictable income growth, matching empirical measures of comovement from the Panel Study of

its analytical tractability.[7] Figure 7.1 plots the particular parameterization of the quasi-hyperbolic discount function used in our simulations: $\beta = 0.7$ and $\delta = 0.957$. Using annual periods, these parameter values roughly match experimentally measured discounting patterns. Delaying an immediate reward by a year reduces the value of that reward by approximately 40 percent $\approx 1 - \beta\delta$. By contrast, delaying a distant reward by an additional year reduces the value of that reward by a relatively small percentage: $1 - \delta$.[8]

All forms of hyperbolic preferences induce dynamic inconsistency. Consider the discrete-time quasi-hyperbolic function. The discount factor between adjacent periods t and $t + 1$ represents the weight placed on utils at time $t + 1$ relative to the weight placed on utils at time t. From the perspective of self t, the discount factor between periods t and $t + 1$ is $\beta\delta$, but the discount factor that applies between any two later periods is δ. Because we take β to be less than one, this implies a short-term discount factor that is less than the long-term discount factor.[9] From the perspective of self $t + 1$, $\beta\delta$ is the relevant discount factor between periods $t + 1$ and $t + 2$. Hence, self t and self $t + 1$ disagree about the desired level of patience that should be used to trade off rewards in periods $t + 1$ and $t + 2$.

Because of this dynamic inconsistency, the hyperbolic consumer is involved in a decision that has intrapersonal strategic dimensions. Early selves would like to commit later selves to honor the preferences of those early selves. Later selves do their best to maximize their own interests. Economists have modeled this situation as an intrapersonal game played among the consumer's temporally situated selves (Strotz, 1956). Recently, hyperbolic discount functions have been used to explain a wide range of anomalous economic choices, including procrastination, contract design, drug addiction, self-deception, retirement timing, and undersaving.[10] We focus here on the implications for life cycle savings decisions.

In the sections that follow, we analyze the "sophisticated" version of the hyperbolic model. Sophisticated hyperbolic consumers correctly predict that later selves will not honor the preferences of early selves. By contrast, "naive" consumers make current choices under the false belief that later selves will act in the interests of the current self. The assumption of naivete was first proposed

---

[7] The quasi-hyperbolic discount function is "hyperbolic" only in the sense that it captures the key qualitative property of the hyperbolic functions: a faster rate of decline in the short run than in the long run. Laibson (1997a) adopted the phrase "quasi-hyperbolic" to emphasize the connection to the hyperbolic-discounting literature in psychology (Ainslie 1992). O'Donoghue and Rabin (1999a) call these preferences "present biased." Krusell and Smith (2000a) call these preferences "quasi-geometric."

[8] See Ainslie (1992) and Frederick et al. (2000).

[9] Note that a discount factor, say θ, is inversely related to the discount rate, $-\ln\theta$.

[10] For example, see Akerlof (1991), Laibson (1994, 1996, 1997a), Barro (1997), Diamond and Koszegi (1998), O'Donoghue and Rabin (1999a, 1999b, 2000), Benabou and Tirole (2000), Brocas and Carrillo (2000, 2001), Carrillo and Dewatripont (2000), Carrillo and Marriotti (2000), Della Vigna and Paserman (2000), Della Vigna and Malmendier (2001), Gruber and Koszegi (2001), and Krusell et al. (2000a, 2000b).

by Strotz (1956), and has since been carefully studied by Akerlof (1991) and O'Donoghue and Rabin (1999a, 1999b, 2000). We return to a discussion of naifs in Section 9.

3. THE CONSUMPTION PROBLEM

Our benchmark model adopts the technological assumptions of standard "buffer-stock" consumption models like those originally developed by Deaton (1991) and Carroll (1992, 1997). These authors assume stochastic labor income and incomplete markets – consumers cannot borrow against uncertain future labor income. In this section, we consider a stripped-down stationary version of the standard buffer-stock model. In Section 8, we discuss a more complex life cycle model, with a richer set of institutional assumptions.

Our modeling assumptions for the stripped-down model divide naturally into four parts: the standard assumptions from the buffer-stock literature; the assumptions that make our model qualitatively hyperbolic; our equilibrium concept; and the technical assumptions that allow us to derive the Hyperbolic Euler Relation. We discuss the first three sets of assumptions herein. The fourth set of assumptions is presented in Section 4.1.

3.1. Buffer-Stock Assumptions

During period t, the consumer has cash on hand $x_t \geq 0$. She chooses a consumption level $c_t \in [0, x_t]$, which rules out borrowing. Whatever the consumer does not spend is saved, $s_t = x_t - c_t \in [0, x_t]$. The gross return on her savings is fixed, $R \geq 0$, and next period she receives labor income $y_{t+1} \geq 0$. Cash on hand during period $t + 1$ is, therefore, $x_{t+1} = R(x_t - c_t) + y_{t+1}$. Labor income is independently and identically distributed over time with density f.

The consumer cannot sell her uncertain stream of future labor-income payments, because of moral hazard and adverse selection, or because of prohibitions against indenturing. In other words, there is no asset market for labor.

3.2. Hyperbolic Preferences

We model an individual as a sequence of autonomous temporal selves. These selves are indexed by the respective periods, $t = 0, 1, 2, \ldots$, in which they control the consumption choice. Self t receives payoff

$$E_t \left[U(c_t) + \beta \sum_{i=1}^{\infty} \delta^i U(c_{t+i}) \right], \tag{3.1}$$

where $\beta \in [0, 1]$, $\delta \in [0, 1)$, and $U : [0, +\infty) \rightarrow [-\infty, +\infty)$. Our model nests the standard case of exponential discounting: $\beta = 1, 0 \leq \delta < 1$. Our model also nests the quasi-hyperbolic case: $\beta < 1, 0 \leq \delta < 1$.

3.3.   Equilibrium

We analyze the set of perfect equilibria in stationary Markov strategies of the intrapersonal game with players (or selves) indexed by the non-negative integers. Because income is iid., the only state variable is cash on hand x_t. We therefore restrict attention to consumption strategies C that depend only on x_t.

4.   EXISTENCE AND UNIQUENESS

This technical discussion can be skipped by readers interested primarily in applications. Such readers may wish to move immediately to Section 5.

4.1.   Technical Assumptions

We make the following technical assumptions:

U1 U has domain $[0, +\infty)$ and range $[-\infty, +\infty)$

U2 U is twice continuously differentiable on $(0, +\infty)$

U3 $U' > 0$ on $(0, +\infty)$

U4 there exist $0 < \underline{\rho} \leq \bar{\rho} < +\infty$ such that $\underline{\rho} \leq -cU''(c)/U'(c) \leq \bar{\rho}$ for all $c \in (0, +\infty)$

F1 f has domain $(0, +\infty)$ and range $[0, +\infty)$

F2 f is twice continuously differentiable

F3 there exist $0 < \underline{y} < \bar{y} < +\infty$ such that $f(y) = 0$ for all $y \notin [\underline{y}, \bar{y}]$

D $\max\{\delta, \delta R^{1-\rho}\} < 1$

Assumptions U1–U4 could be summarized by saying that U has bounded relative risk aversion. They are automatically satisfied if U has constant relative risk aversion. Assumptions F1–F3 could be summarized by saying that f is smooth, that the support of f is compact, and that 0 does not lie in the support of f. Assumption D ensures that the expected present discounted value of the consumer's utility stream is always well defined. Further discussion of these assumptions can be found in Harris and Laibson (2001a).

4.2.   The Bellman Equation of the Hyperbolic Consumer

The intrapersonal game of the hyperbolic consumer can be approached recursively as follows. Suppose that self t has current-value function W_t and continuation value function V_t, and suppose that self $t + 1$ has consumption function C_{t+1} and current-value function W_{t+1}. Then, it follows from the Envelope theorem that

$$U'(C_{t+1}(x_{t+1})) = W'_{t+1}(x_{t+1}). \tag{4.1}$$

Next, it follows from the definition of W_{t+1} and V_t that

$$\beta V_t(x_{t+1}) = W_{t+1}(x_{t+1}) - (1 - \beta)U(C_{t+1}(x_{t+1})). \tag{4.2}$$

Finally, it follows from the definition of W_t that

$$W_t(x_t) = \max_{c\in[0,x_t]} U(c) + \beta\delta \int V_t(R(x_t - c) + y)f(y)dy. \qquad (4.3)$$

Hence,

$$W_t(x_t) = \max_{c\in[0,x_t]} U(c) + \delta \int (W_{t+1} - (1-\beta)U \circ C_{t+1})$$
$$\times (R(x_t - c) + y)f(y)dy$$

[substituting for V_t in equation (4.3) using equation (4.2)]

$$= \max_{c\in[0,x_t]} U(c) + \delta \int (W_{t+1} - \varepsilon U \circ g \circ W'_{t+1})(R(x_t - c) + y)f(y)dy$$

[where $\varepsilon = 1 - \beta$ and $g = (U')^{-1}$]

$$= (\mathfrak{B}W_{t+1})(x_t),$$

say. This is the Bellman equation of the hyperbolic consumer.

4.3. The Finite-Horizon Case: Current-Value Functions

Suppose that the intrapersonal game of the hyperbolic consumer has a finite horizon $T < +\infty$. Then, in principle, the current-value functions can be shown to be unique by backward induction. Indeed, suppose for simplicity that the consumer has no bequest motive. Then, we expect $W_T = U$, $W_{T-1} = \mathfrak{B}W_T, \ldots, W_1 = \mathfrak{B}W_2$. In practice, we need to find a space of functions $\mathcal{W}$ such that, if $W_{t+1} \in \mathcal{W}$, then $W_t = \mathfrak{B}W_{t+1}$ is well defined and lies in $\mathcal{W}$. To this end, we make the following definition.

Definition 4.1. *The function* $g : (0, +\infty) \to \mathbb{R}$ *is of* **locally bounded variation** *iff there exist increasing functions* $g_+ : (0, +\infty) \to \mathbb{R}$ *and* $g_- : (0, +\infty) \to \mathbb{R}$ *such that* $g = g_+ - g_-$.

Now, let us say that two functions of locally bounded variation are equivalent iff they are equal at all points of continuity. Let $\mathcal{BV}^0_{\text{loc}}((0, +\infty))$ is the space of equivalence classes of functions of locally bounded variation, and let $\mathcal{BV}^1_{\text{loc}}((0, +\infty))$ denote the space of equivalence classes of functions W such that both W and W' are of locally bounded variation. Then, the correct choice of space for our current-value function is $\mathcal{W} = \mathcal{BV}^1_{\text{loc}}((0, +\infty))$.

To see this, note first that, if $W_{t+1} \in \mathcal{BV}^1_{\text{loc}}((0, +\infty))$, then W'_{t+1} is a function of locally bounded variation. Hence, W'_{t+1} is uniquely defined, except at a countable set of points, and $\mathfrak{B}W_{t+1}$ is uniquely defined at all points. Second, consider the operator $\mathfrak{b}_\gamma$ given by the formula

$$(\mathfrak{b}_\gamma W_{t+1})(x_t) = U(\gamma x_t) + \delta \int (W_{t+1} - \varepsilon U \circ g \circ W'_{t+1})$$
$$\times (R(1-\gamma)x_t + y)f(y)dy.$$

Then

$$\mathfrak{B}W_{t+1} = \sup_{\gamma \in [0,1]} \{\mathfrak{b}_\gamma W_{t+1}\}.$$

In other words, $\mathfrak{B}W_{t+1}$ is the upper envelope of the functions $\mathfrak{b}_\gamma W_{t+1}$. Third, note that $\mathfrak{b}_\gamma W_{t+1}$ is twice continuously differentiable. Moreover, there exists a continuous function $a : (0, +\infty) \to [0, +\infty]$ such that, for all $\gamma \in [0, 1]$,

$$|\mathfrak{b}_\gamma W_{t+1}|, |(\mathfrak{b}_\gamma W_{t+1})'|, |(\mathfrak{b}_\gamma W_{t+1})''| \le a$$

on $(0, +\infty)$. In particular, there exists a twice continuously differentiable convex function $\kappa : (0, +\infty) \to \mathbb{R}$ such that, for all $\gamma \in [0, 1]$, $\mathfrak{b}_\gamma W_{t+1} + \kappa$ is convex. Hence

$$\mathfrak{B}W_{t+1} = \sup_{\gamma \in [0,1]} \{\mathfrak{b}_\gamma W_{t+1}\} = \sup_{\gamma \in [0,1]} \{\mathfrak{b}_\gamma W_{t+1} + \kappa\} - \kappa.$$

In other words, $\mathfrak{B}W_{t+1}$ is the difference of two convex functions. In light of the following result, this is exactly what we need.

Proposition 4.2. *Suppose that* $W : (0, +\infty) \to \mathbb{R}$. *Then,* $W \in \mathcal{BV}^1_{\text{loc}}((0, +\infty))$ *iff* W *is the difference of two convex functions.*

4.4.   The Finite-Horizon Case: Consumption Functions

Suppose, again, that the intrapersonal game of the hyperbolic consumer has a finite horizon $T < +\infty$ and that the consumer has no bequest motive. Then, the consumption function of self T is unique and is given by the formula

$$C_T(x_T) = x_T;$$

and, for all $1 \le t \le T - 1$, the consumption function of self t is any function such that

$$C_t(x_t) \in \underset{c \in [0,x_t]}{\operatorname{argmax}} U(c) + \delta \int (W_{t+1} - \varepsilon U \circ g \circ W'_{t+1})$$
$$\times (R(x_t - c) + y) f(y) dy$$

for all $x_t \in [0, +\infty)$.

Now, $C_t = g \circ W'_t$ is uniquely defined and continuous, except on a countable set of points. Because this set of points has measure zero, it is encountered with probability zero. It follows that any two consumption functions of self t are observationally equivalent. By the same token, any two equilibria are observationally equivalent. This uniqueness claim can be made precise by viewing consumption functions as elements of the space $\mathcal{BV}^0_{\text{loc}}((0, +\infty))$.

4.5.   The Infinite-Horizon Case: Existence

To establish existence in the finite-horizon case, we showed that the Bellman operator $\mathfrak{B}$ was a self-map of the space $BV^1_{\text{loc}}((0, +\infty))$. To establish existence in the infinite-horizon case, we need to strengthen this result by showing that there is a nonempty compact convex subset $\mathcal{K}$ of $BV^1_{\text{loc}}((0, +\infty))$, such that $\mathfrak{B}$ is a self-map of $\mathcal{K}$.

Define $\underline{V} : [0, +\infty) \to [-\infty, +\infty)$ by the formula

$$\underline{V}(x) = U(x) + \frac{\delta}{1 - \delta} \int U(y) f(y) dy,$$

define $\bar{V} : [0, +\infty) \to [-\infty, +\infty)$ by the formula

$$\bar{V}(x) = U(x) + \sum_{t=1}^{\infty} \delta^t U\left(\sum_{s=0}^{t+1} R^s y + R^t x \right),$$

and, for all Borel measurable $V \in [\underline{V}, \bar{V}]$, define $\mathfrak{W}V : [0, +\infty) \to [-\infty, +\infty)$ by the formula

$$(\mathfrak{W}V)(x) = \max_{\gamma \in [0,1]} \left\{ U(\gamma x) + \beta \delta \int V(R(1 - \gamma)x + y) f(y) dy \right\}.$$

Finally, put $\underline{V}^- = -(\underline{V} \wedge 0)$ and $\bar{V}^+ = +(\bar{V} \vee 0)$, define $N_1 : [0, +\infty) \to [0, +\infty)$ by the formula $N_1(x) = \underline{V}^-(y) \vee \bar{V}^+(Rx + \bar{y})$, and define $N_2 : [0, +\infty) \to [0, +\infty)$ by the formula $N_2(x) = U'(x)/x \vee N_1(x)$. Then:

Theorem 4.3 [Global Regularity]. *There exist* $K > 0$ *such that, for all* $V \in [\underline{V}, \bar{V}]$,

1. $(1 - \beta)U + \beta\underline{V} \leq \mathfrak{W}V \leq (1 - \beta)U + \beta\bar{V}$,
2. $U' \leq (\mathfrak{W}V)' \leq U' \vee (KN_1)$, *and*
3. $(\mathfrak{W}V)'' \geq -KN_2$

on $(0, +\infty)$.

The required set $\mathcal{K}$ is then simply the set of $W \in BV^1_{\text{loc}}((0, +\infty))$ that satisfy the three estimates in this theorem.

4.6.   The Infinite-Horizon Case: Uniqueness

To establish uniqueness in the infinite-horizon case, we begin by showing that, no matter what the initial cash on hand of the consumer, there exists a finite interval from which the dynamics of wealth never exit.

Theorem 4.4. [Absorbing Interval]. *Suppose that* $\delta R < 1$. *Then, for all* $x_0 \in [0, +\infty)$, *there exists* $\bar{\beta}_1 \in [0, 1)$ *and* $\bar{X} \in [x_0, +\infty)$ *such that, for all* $\beta \in$

$[\bar{\beta}_1, 1]$ *and all equilibria C of the infinite-horizon model,*

$$R(x - C(x)) + y \in [\underline{y}, \bar{X}]$$

for all $x \in [0, \bar{X}]$ *and all* $y \in [\underline{y}, \bar{y}]$.

We are now in a position to prove uniqueness.

Theorem 4.5. [Uniqueness]. *Suppose that* $\delta R < 1$, *and that U is three times continuously differentiable on* $(0, +\infty)$. *Then, for all* $x_0 \in [0, +\infty)$, *there exists* $\bar{\beta}_2 \in [0, 1)$ *and* $\bar{X} \in [x_0, +\infty)$ *such that, for all* $\beta \in [\bar{\beta}_2, 1]$, *equilibrium is unique on* $[0, \bar{X}]$.

Notice that Theorem 4.5 is a local uniqueness theorem: the critical value $\bar{\beta}_2$ will in general depend on x_0. Local uniqueness is, however, all that we need: if initial cash on hand is x_0 and $\beta \in [\bar{\beta}_2, 1]$, then levels of cash on hand outside the interval $[0, \bar{X}]$ will not be observed in any equilibrium. We do not know whether theorem 4.5 has a global analog.

Proof. See the Appendix.   ■

4.7.   The Finite-Horizon Case: Robustness

By combining our existence and uniqueness results for the finite-horizon case with our regularity results, we can show that the equilibrium of the finite-horizon model depends continuously on the parameters U, f, β, and δ. This leaves one parameter unaccounted for: T. This parameter plays an important role in empirical applications. For example, simulations of calibrated life cycle models usually proceed by truncating the life cycle at some point. It is therefore crucial to verify that the equilibrium of the chosen model is robust with respect to the horizon chosen for the model.

The simplest way to establish robustness would be to show that there is a unique equilibrium of the infinite-horizon model. If we could show this, then it would follow at once from our regularity results that this equilibrium depended continuously on T. More precisely, note that T is chosen from the space $\mathbb{N} \cup \{\infty\}$. All the points of this space are isolated except for the point ∞, which is an accumulation point. By saying that the equilibrium depends continuously on T, we therefore mean that there is a unique equilibrium when $T = \infty$ and, for all $\eta > 0$, there exists a $T_0 < \infty$ such that, for all $T > T_0$, the equilibrium of the model with horizon T is within η of the equilibrium of the model with horizon ∞. In other words, the choice of horizon for the model makes very little difference to the equilibrium, provided that this horizon is sufficiently far into the future.

Unfortunately, the proof of theorem 4.5 shows only that, if β is sufficiently close to 1, then there is a unique *stationary* equilibrium of the model. This leaves open two possibilities. First, there may be more than one stationary equilibrium if β is not close to 1. Second, there may be nonstationary equilibria. It may be very difficult to make progress with the first possibility: Although it may be possible to identify other regions of parameter space in which there is a unique stationary equilibrium, it may not be true that there is a unique equilibrium for all choices of the parameters. After all, we are analyzing a game. It may, however, be possible to make progress with the second possibility: what is needed here is a proof that the Bellman operator is a contraction mapping. The proof of Theorem 4.5 falls short of this goal: it shows only that the Bellman operator is a contraction mapping when confined to the set of current-value functions of stationary equilibria.

Nonetheless, the available evidence suggests that life cycle simulations are probably robust to the choice of horizon provided that β is sufficiently close to 1.

5. GENERALIZED EULER EQUATION

In this section, we discuss the hyperbolic analog of the standard Euler Relation.[11]

5.1. Heuristic Derivation of the Hyperbolic Euler Relation

Suppose that C is an equilibrium consumption function. Adopt the perspective of self t. Because all future selves use the consumption function C, and because self t uses the same discount factor δ from period $t + 1$ onward, her continuation-value function V solves the recursive equation

$$V(x_{t+1}) = U(C(x_{t+1})) + E_{t+1}[\delta V(R(x_{t+1} - C(x_{t+1})) + y_{t+2})].$$
(5.1)

Note that $V(x_{t+1})$ is the expectation, conditional on x_{t+1}, of the present discounted value of the utility stream that starts in period $t + 1$.

Self t uses discount factor $\beta\delta$ at time t. Her current-value function W therefore solves the equation

$$W(x_t) = U(C(x_t)) + E_t[\beta\delta V(R(x_t - C(x_t)) + y_{t+1})].$$
(5.2)

Moreover

$$C(x_t) \in \operatorname*{argmax}_{c \in [0, x_t]} U(c) + E_t[\beta\delta V(R(x_t - c) + y_{t+1})],$$
(5.3)

because consumption is chosen by the current self.

The first-order condition associated with (5.3) implies that

$$U'(C(x_t)) \geq E_t[R\beta\delta V'(R(x_t - C(x_t)) + y_{t+1})],$$
(5.4)

with equality if $C(x_t) < x_t$. The first-order condition and envelope theorem together imply that the shadow value of cash on hand equals the marginal

---

[11] The material from this section was first published in Harris and Laibson (2001).

utility of consumption:

$$W'(x_t) = U'(C(x_t)).\tag{5.5}$$

Finally, V and W are linked by the equation

$$\beta V(x_{t+1}) = W(x_{t+1}) - (1 - \beta)U(C(x_{t+1})).\tag{5.6}$$

These expressions can be combined to yield the Strong Hyperbolic Euler Relation. Indeed, we have

$$U'(C(x_t)) \geq E_t[R\beta\delta V'(R(x_t - C(x_t)) + y_{t+1})]$$

[this is just the first-order condition (5.4)]

$$= E_t[R\delta(W'(x_{t+1}) - (1 - \beta)U'(C(x_{t+1}))C'(x_{t+1}))]$$

[differentiating equation (5.6) with respect to x_{t+1} and substituting in]

$$= E_t[R\delta(U'(C(x_{t+1})) - (1 - \beta)U'(C(x_{t+1}))C'(x_{t+1}))]$$

[from the analog of equation (5.5) for self $t + 1$]. Rearranging yields

$$U'(C(x_t)) \geq E_t[R(C'(x_{t+1})\beta\delta + (1 - C'(x_{t+1}))\delta)U'(C(x_{t+1}))],\tag{5.7}$$

with equality if $c < x_t$. This is the Hyperbolic Euler Relation.

When $\beta = 1$, this relation reduces to the well-known Exponential Euler Relation

$$U'(C(x_t)) \geq E_t[R\delta U'(C(x_{t+1}))].$$

Intuitively, the marginal utility of consuming an additional dollar today, $U'(C_t)$, must equal the marginal utility of saving that dollar. A saved dollar grows to R dollars by next year. Utilities next period are discounted with factor δ. Hence, the value of today's marginal savings is given by $E_t[R\delta U'(C_{t+1})]$. The expectation operator integrates over uncertain future consumption.

The difference between the Hyperbolic Euler Relation and the Exponential Euler Relation is that, in the former, the constant exponential discount factor, δ, is replaced by the effective discount factor, namely

$$C'(x_{t+1})\beta\delta + (1 - C'(x_{t+1}))\delta.$$

This effective discount factor is a weighted average of the short-run discount factor $\beta\delta$ and the long-run discount factor δ. The respective weights are $C'(x_{t+1})$, the marginal propensity to consume out of liquid wealth, and $(1 - C'(x_{t+1}))$, the marginal propensity to consume out of liquid wealth. Because $\beta < 1$, the effective discount factor is stochastic and endogenous to the model.

In the sophisticated hyperbolic model, the effective discount factor is negatively related to the future marginal propensity to consume (MPC). To gain intuition for this effect, consider a consumer at time 0 who is thinking about saving a marginal dollar for the future. The consumer at time zero – "self 0" – expects future selves to overconsume relative to the consumption rate that self 0 prefers those future selves to implement. Hence, on the equilibrium path, self 0 values marginal saving more than marginal consumption at any future time period. From self 0's perspective, therefore, it matters how a marginal unit of wealth at time period 1 will be divided between savings and consumption by self 1. Self 1's MPC determines this division. Because self 0 values marginal saving more than marginal consumption at time period 1, self 0 values the future less the higher the expected MPC at time period 1.

The effective discount factor in the Hyperbolic Euler Relation varies significantly with cash on hand. Consumers who expect to have low levels of future cash on hand will expect $C'(x_{t+1})$ to be close to one,[12] implying that the effective discount factor will approximately equal $\beta\delta$. Assuming that periods are annual with a standard calibration of $\beta = 0.7$ and $\delta = 0.95$, the effective discount rate would be $-\ln(0.7 \times 0.95) = 0.41$. By contrast, consumers with high levels of future cash on hand will expect $C'(x_{t+1})$ to be close to zero,[13] implying that the effective discount factor will approximately equal δ. In this case, the effective discount rate will be $-\ln(0.95) = 0.05$. The simulations reported below confirm these claims about the shape of C.

5.2. Exact Derivation

If the consumption function is discontinuous, then the derivation of the Hyperbolic Euler Relation is not valid. However, the consumption function is always of locally bounded variation. This property can be used to derive a weaker version of the Hyperbolic Euler Relation. This weaker version reduces to the Hyperbolic Euler Relation if the consumption function is Lipschitz-continuous. Moreover, it can be shown that the consumption function is indeed Lipschitz-continuous when β is sufficiently close to 1 (Harris and Laibson 2001a).

6. NUMERICAL SOLUTION AND CALIBRATION OF THE MODEL

We complement our theoretical analysis with numerical simulations. Numerical results help to build intuition and provide quantitative assessment of qualitative effects. In this section, we describe our strategy for simulating the one-asset, infinite-horizon model. The same broad strategy applies to the institutionally richer simulations that we describe in Section 8.

We calibrate our stripped-down model with the same parameter values used by ALRTW (2001a). Specifically, $\rho = 2$, $\beta = 0.7$, $\delta = 0.9571$, and $R = 1.0375$.[14]

---

[12] Low levels of cash on hand imply that the agent is liquidity-constrained. Hence, low levels of cash on hand imply a high MPC.

[13] When the agent is not liquidity-constrained, marginal consumption is approximately equal to the annuity value of marginal increments of wealth. Hence, the local slope of the consumption function is close to the real interest rate.

[14] ALRTW choose all of these parameters ex ante, except δ. Then, δ is chosen so that the simulated data match the empirical median wealth to income ratio of 50- to 59-year-old household heads. ALRTW also use this method to infer the preferences of exponential consumers ($\beta = 1$). They find that $\delta_{\text{exponential}} = .9437$.

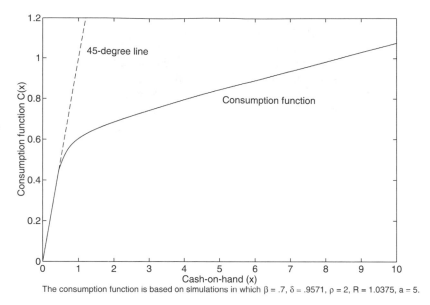

The consumption function is based on simulations in which β = .7, δ = .9571, ρ = 2, R = 1.0375, a = 5.

Figure 7.2. Calibrated consumption function.

To capture labor-income uncertainty, we adopt a shifted symmetric Beta density with support $[\varepsilon, 1 + \varepsilon]$:

$$f(Y) \propto (Y - \varepsilon)^{(a-1)}(1 + \varepsilon - Y)^{(a-1)},$$

where $a > 0$ and ε is positive, but close to zero. Hence, Y has mean $\frac{1}{2} + \varepsilon$. If $a > 1$, the density is bell-shaped and continuous on $\mathbb{R}$. Moreover, if $a > 3$, then the density is twice continuously differentiable, and therefore satisfies the regularity conditions of Section 4.

We set $a = 5$, implying that $\sigma(Y)/Y = 0.30$. This value is comparable with the value of $\sigma(Y)/Y$ implied by standard income processes estimated from the Panel Study of Income Dynamics. For example, ALRTW estimate a process for $\ln Y$ that has two components: an AR(1) process and iid. noise.[15] Their empirically estimated process implies $\sigma(Y)/Y = 0.32$.[16]

Figure 7.2 reports the equilibrium consumption function generated by our infinite-horizon, one-asset simulation.[17] The function is continuous, monotonic,

---

[15] Specifically, $\ln Y_t = $ [household fixed effects] $+$ [polynomial in age] $+ u_t + \eta_t$ where $u_t = \alpha u_{t-1} + \varepsilon_t$, and η_t and ε_t are white noise.

[16] This is an unconditional normalized standard deviation. The empirical conditional normalized standard deviation, $\sqrt{E_{t-1}(Y_t - \bar{Y}_t)^2}/Y$, is .23.

[17] To simulate our model numerically, we adopt a numerical solution algorithm that does not interpolate between points in the state space. Specifically, our algorithm discretizes the state space and forces the consumer to make choices that keep the state variables on the discrete partition. We believe that our algorithm successfully approximates the behavior that would arise in a continuous state space. Most importantly, we find that once our partition is made sufficiently fine, further refinement has no effect on our simulation results.

and concave. It appears smooth, except for the point at which the liquidity constraint begins to bind. In the next section, we identify cases in which these regularity properties cease to hold.

7. PROPERTIES OF THE CONSUMPTION FUNCTION

The consumption function in Figure 7.2 is continuous, monotonic, and concave. However, hyperbolic consumption functions need not have these desirable properties (Laibson, 1997b, Morris and Postlewaite, 1997, O'Donoghue and Rabin, 1999a, Harris and Laibson, 2001a, and Krusell and Smith, 2000). In this section we characterize the general properties of the hyperbolic consumption function. We first discuss the kinds of pathologies that can arise. We then discuss the regularity conditions that eliminate these pathologies.

7.1. Pathologies: Violations of Continuity, Monotonicity, and Concavity

To develop intuition for the existence of hyperbolic pathologies, we consider a finite-horizon version of the model of Section 3.[18] We assume that the stream of income is deterministic. We apply backward induction arguments to solve for the equilibrium policies.

First, consider the strategy of self T. Trivially, self T sets $c_T = x_T$. Self T consumes all available cash on hand.

Now, consider the problem of self $T - 1$. Self $T - 1$ knows that any resources left to self T will be consumed by self T. So, self $T - 1$ chooses c_{T-1} to maximize

$$U(c_{T-1}) + \beta\delta U(c_T)$$

subject to the constraints

$$x_T = R(x_{T-1} - c_{T-1}) + y_T,$$
$$c_{T-1} \leq x_{T-1},$$
$$c_T = x_T.$$

The first constraint is the dynamic budget constraint. The second constraint is the liquidity constraint. The third constraint reflects the equilibrium strategy of self T.

Given this problem, it is straightforward to show that, when the liquidity constraint does not bind, self $T - 1$ picks c_{T-1} such that

$$U'(c_{T-1}) = \beta\delta R U'(R \cdot (x_{T-1} - c_{T-1}) + y_T).$$

When the liquidity constraint binds, self $T - 1$ sets $c_{T-1} = x_{T-1}$. Represent self $T - 1$'s equilibrium policy function as $C_{T-1}(x_{T-1})$.

---

[18] See Laibson (1997b) for the original version of this example.

Now, consider the problem of self $T - 2$. Self $T - 2$ chooses c_{T-2} to maximize

$$U(c_{T-2}) + \beta\delta U(c_{T-1}) + \beta\delta^2 U(c_T),$$

subject to the constraints

$$x_{T-1} = R(x_{T-2} - c_{T-2}) + y_{T-1}, \quad c_{T-2} \leq x_{T-2},$$

$$c_{T-1} = C_{T-1}(x_{T-1}),$$

$$c_T = x_T.$$

The first constraint is the dynamic budget constraint. The second constraint is the liquidity constraint. The third and fourth constraints represent the strategies of selves $T - 1$ and T.

To develop intuition for the optimal policy of self $T - 2$, consider the continuation value function of self $T - 2$,

$$V_{T-1}(x_{T-1}) = u(C_{T-1}(x_{T-1})) + \delta u(R(x_{T-1} - C_T(x_{T-1})) + y_T).$$

From self $T - 2$'s perspective, wealth at time $T - 1$ has a value $\beta\delta V_{T-1}(x_{T-1})$. There exists a threshold wealth level $x_{T-1} = \hat{x}$ at which the liquidity constraint for self $T - 1$ ceases to bind. In the region to the left of $\hat{x}$, all marginal wealth is consumed in period $T - 1$, implying

$$V'_{T-1}(\hat{x}-) = U'(C_{T-1}(\hat{x})).$$

In the region to the right of $\hat{x}$, some marginal wealth is passed on to period T, implying

$$V'_{T-1}(\hat{x}+) = C'_{T-1}(\hat{x}) \cdot U'(C_{T-1}(\hat{x})) + \delta R(1 - C'_{T-1}(\hat{x}))U'(C_T(\hat{x})).$$

Note that at $x_{T-1} = \hat{x}$, self $T - 1$ is indifferent between marginal consumption in period $T - 1$, and marginal consumption in period T. So,

$$U'(C_{T-1}(\hat{x})) = R\beta\delta U'(C_T(\hat{x})).$$

Substituting this relationship into the previous expression yields

$$V'_{T-1}(\hat{x}+) = \left[C'_{T-1}(\hat{x}) + \frac{1}{\beta}(1 - C'_{T-1}(\hat{x}))\right]U'(C_{T-1}(\hat{x}))$$

$$> U'(C_{T-1}(\hat{x})) = V'_{T-1}(\hat{x}-).$$

Hence the continuation value function V_{T-1} has a kink at $x_{T-1} = \hat{x}$. At this point, the *slope* of the value function discretely rises.

This kink implies that the equilibrium consumption function of self $T - 2$ will have a downward discontinuity. To understand why, note that self $T - 2$ will never select a value of $c_{T-2} > 0$, such that $R(x_{T-2} - c_{T-2}) + y_{T+1} = x_{T-1} = \hat{x}$. If $x_{T-1} = \hat{x}$ *did* hold, self $T - 2$ could raise her welfare by either cutting or raising consumption. If

$$U'(c_{T-2}) < \beta\delta R V'_{T-1}(\hat{x}+),$$

self $T - 2$ could increase welfare by cutting consumption – with marginal cost

$U'(c_{T-2})$ – and raising saving – with marginal benefit $\beta\delta RV'_{T-1}(\hat{x}+)$. If

$$U'(c_{T-2}) \geq \beta\delta RV'_{T-1}(\hat{x}+),$$

self $T-2$ could increase welfare by raising consumption – with marginal benefit $U'(c_{T-2})$ – and lowering saving – with marginal cost $\beta\delta RV'_{T-1}(\hat{x}-) < \beta\delta RV'_{T-1}(\hat{x}+) \leq U'(c_{T-2})$.

Self $T-2$ makes equilibrium choices that avoid the region of low-continuation marginal utilities – in the neighborhood to the left of $x_{T-1} = \hat{x}$ – by jumping to the region of high-continuation marginal utilities to the right of $x_{T-1} = \hat{x}$. This avoidance can be achieved only with an equilibrium consumption function that has a discrete downward discontinuity. Figure 7.3 plots the equilibrium consumption functions for selves $T-2$, $T-1$, and T for the case in which the instantaneous utility function is isoelastic and $y_t = 1$ for all t.

Intuitively, the pathology described here arises because of a special kind of strategic interaction. Self $T-2$'s consumption function discontinuously declines because self $T-2$ has an incentive to push self $T-1$ over the wealth threshold $\hat{x}$ at which self $T-1$ has a kink in its consumption function. Self $T-2$ is willing to discretely cut its own consumption to push $T-1$ over the $\hat{x}$ threshold, because the marginal returns to the right of $\hat{x}$ are greater than the marginal returns to the left of $\hat{x}$ *from self $T-2$'s perspective*.

If this example was extended another period, we could also demonstrate that the optimal choices of self $T-3$ will violate the Hyperbolic Euler Equation. Finally, all of these pathologies would continue to arise, even if a small amount of smooth noise was added to the income process.

7.2. Sufficient Conditions for Continuity, Monotonicity, and Concavity of the Consumption Function

The previous subsection provides an example of the kinds of pathologies that can arise in hyperbolic models. However, these pathologies do *not* arise when the model is calibrated with empirically sensible parameter values (see Figure 7.2). In this section, we identify the parameter regions that generate the pathologies.

First, when β is close to one, the discontinuities and nonmonotonicities vanish. Harris and Laibson (2001a) prove this claim formally. Intuitively, when β is close to one, the hyperbolic consumption function converges to the exponential consumption function, which is continuous and monotonic.[19] Likewise, when β is close to one, the hyperbolic consumption function matches the concavity of the exponential consumption function. Carroll and Kimball (1996) provide sufficient conditions for exponential concavity (U in the HARA class), although they do not handle the case of binding liquidity constraints.

Figure 7.4 graphically demonstrates the comparative static on β. We plot the consumption functions generated by β values $\{0.1, 0.2, 0.3, \ldots, 0.7\}$.[20] The consumption functions are vertically shifted so they do not overlap. Recall

---

[19] All of the convergence results apply to an absorbing interval of x values. See Section 4 for a definition and discussion of such absorbing intervals.

[20] We adopt the baseline parameter values $a = 5$, $\delta = .0571$, $\rho = 2$, $R = 1.0375$.

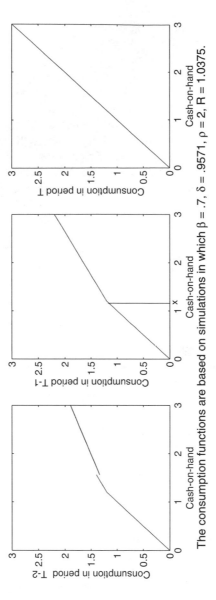

Figure 7.3. Consumption functions in periods $T - 2$, $T - 1$, and T.

The consumption functions are based on simulations in which $\beta = .7$, $\delta = .9571$, $\rho = 2$, $R = 1.0375$.

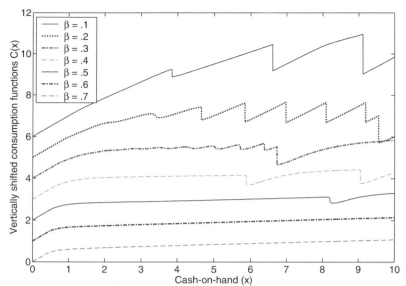

The consumption functions are based on simulations in which δ = .9571, ρ = 2, R = 1.0375, a = 5.

Figure 7.4. Variation in β.

that $\beta = 0.7$ corresponds to our benchmark calibration. As β falls below 0.4, the consumption function becomes increasingly irregular. However, regularity returns as β falls to zero: in a neighborhood of $\beta = 0$, the consumption function coincides with the 45 degree line.

Pathologies are also controlled by the curvature of the consumption function. Our simulation results imply that increasing ρ eliminates irregularities. Figure 7.5 graphically demonstrates the comparative static on ρ. We plot the consumption functions generated by ρ values $\{0.5, 0.75, 1, 1.25\}$.[21] The consumption functions are again vertically shifted. Recall that $\rho = 2$ corresponds to our benchmark calibration. As ρ falls below 1.25, the consumption function becomes increasingly irregular. The irregularities increase as ρ falls, because low curvature augments the feedback effects that engender the irregularities. Specifically, when the utility function is relatively less bowed, it is relatively less costly to strategically cut consumption today to push future selves over critical wealth thresholds.

Finally, decreasing the variance of the income process increases the degree of irregularity. Figure 7.6 graphically demonstrates the comparative static on a. We plot the consumption functions generated by a values $\{25, 50, 100, 200, 400\}$.[22] These a values correspond to $\sigma(Y)/Y$ values of $\{0.14, 0.10, 0.07, 0.05, 0.04, 0.03\}$. Recall that $a = 5$ (i.e., $\sigma(Y)/Y = 0.30$) corresponds to our benchmark calibration. As a rises above 25 (i.e., $\sigma(Y)/Y$ falls below 0.14),

[21] We adopt the baseline parameter values $a = 5$, $\beta = .7$, $\delta = .9571$, $R = 1.0375$.
[22] We adopt the baseline parameter values $\beta = .7$, $\delta = .9571$, $\rho = 2$, $R = 1.0375$.

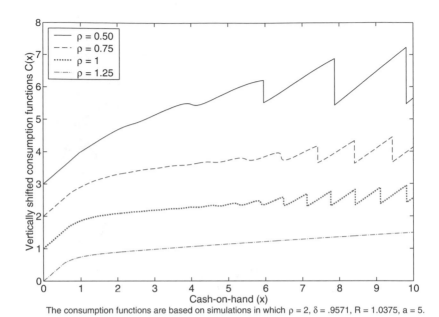

The consumption functions are based on simulations in which $\rho = 2$, $\delta = .9571$, R = 1.0375, a = 5.

Figure 7.5. Variation in the coefficient of relative risk aversion (ρ).

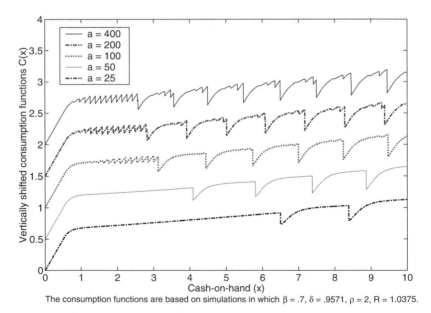

The consumption functions are based on simulations in which $\beta = .7$, $\delta = .9571$, $\rho = 2$, R = 1.0375.

Figure 7.6. Variation in income uncertainty (a).

the consumption function becomes increasingly irregular. The irregularities increase as a increases, because high a values correspond to low levels of income volatility. Low volatility makes it easier for early selves to predict future wealth levels, and to strategically push later selves over critical wealth thresholds.

In summary, irregularities vanish when β is close to one, risk aversion is high, and uncertainty is high. At the benchmark calibration, the pathologies do not arise. Moreover, our model omits some sources of uncertainty that would only reinforce the regularity of our benchmark consumption functions. For example, our model omits shocks to preferences and asset return uncertainty.[23]

8. CONSUMPTION APPLICATIONS

A series of papers have analyzed the positive and normative implications of the hyperbolic buffer-stock model: Laibson, Repetto, and Tobacman (1998, 2000) [hereafter LRT] and ALRTW (2001a, 2001b). These papers extend the precautionary saving models pioneered by Zeldes (1989b), Deaton (1991), and Carroll (1992, 1997).[24] We will focus our discussion on the work of LRT (2000) and ALRTW (2001a).

The ALRTW model incorporates most of the features of previous life cycle simulation models and adds new features, including credit cards, time-varying household size, and illiquid assets. We summarize the key features of the ALRTW model herein. A more general version of the model, and a complete description of the calibration, appear in LRT.[25]

8.1.   Model Summary

Households are divided into three levels of educational attainment. We discuss simulation results only for the largest group, households whose head has only a high school degree (roughly half of U.S. households). The simulations have been replicated for households in other educational categories, and the conclusions are quantitatively similar (see LRT).

Households face a time-varying, exogenous hazard rate of survival. Households live for a maximum of 90 periods, beginning economic life at age 20 and retiring at age 63. The retirement age is calibrated to match reported retirement ages from the PSID. Household composition – number of adults and nonadults – varies exogenously over the life cycle (also calibrated to match the PSID).

Log income, $\ln Y_{it}$, is modeled as the sum of a polynomial in age and two stochastic components: an autocorrelated component and an iid. component.

---

[23] Asset return uncertainty has an advantage over labor-income uncertainty, because the volatility generated by noisy returns scales up with the level of wealth. With sufficient asset uncertainty, it should be possible to establish that regularity applies to the entire domain of cash on hand, instead of just an absorbing interval.

[24] See, also, Engen, Gale, and Scholz (1994), Hubbard, Skinner, and Zeldes (1994, 1995), and Gourinchas and Parker (1999).

[25] This more general model allows consumers to declare bankruptcy and allows the consumer to borrow against illiquid collateral (e.g., mortgages on housing).

Different processes are estimated during the working life and during retirement (using the PSID).

Households may hold liquid assets, X_t, and illiquid assets, Z_t. Because labor income is liquid wealth, $X_t + Y_t$ represents total liquid asset holdings at the beginning of period t. Credit card borrowing is modeled as a negative value for X_t. Credit card borrowing must not exceed a credit limit equal to some fraction of current (average) income. Specifically, $X_t \geq -\lambda \cdot \bar{Y}_t$, where $\bar{Y}_t$ is cohort average income at age t, and $\lambda = 0.30$ (calibrated from the 1995 SCF). The real after-tax interest rate on liquid assets is 3.75 percent. The real interest rate on credit card loans is 11.75 percent, two percentage points *below* the mean debt-weighted real interest rate reported by the Federal Reserve Board. This low value is chosen to capture implicitly the effect of bankruptcy. Actual annual bankruptcy rates of roughly 1 percent per year imply that the effective interest rate is at least one percentage point below the observed interest rate.

The illiquid asset generates consumption flows equal to 5 percent of the value of the asset ($Z_t \geq 0$). Hence, the holding return on illiquid assets is considerably higher than the return on other assets. However, the illiquid asset can be sold only with a transaction cost.

Households have isoelastic preferences with a coefficient of relative risk aversion of $\rho = 2$. Self t has instantaneous payoff function

$$u(C_t, Z_t, n_t) = n_t \cdot \frac{\left(\dfrac{C_t + \gamma Z_t}{n_t}\right)^{1-\rho} - 1}{1 - \rho}.$$

Note that γZ_t represents the consumption flow generated by Z_t ($\gamma = 0.05$), and n_t is the effective household size, $n_t = ([\text{no. adults}_t] + 0.4[\text{no. of children}_t])$.

Households have either an exponential discount function ($\delta^t_{\text{exponential}}$) or a quasi hyperbolic discount function ($\beta\delta^t_{\text{hyperbolic}}$, with $\beta = 0.7$). ALRTW assume that the economy is populated either exclusively by exponential households or exclusively by hyperbolic households. ALRTW pick $\delta_{\text{exponential}}$ and $\delta_{\text{hyperbolic}}$ to match empirical levels of retirement saving. Specifically, $\delta_{\text{exponential}}$ is picked so that the exponential simulations generate a median wealth to income ratio of 3.2, for individuals between ages 50 and 59. The median of 3.2 is calibrated from the SCF.[26] The hyperbolic discount factor, $\delta_{\text{hyperbolic}}$, is also picked to match the empirical median of 3.2.[27]

The discount factors that replicate the SCF wealth to income ratio are .9437 for the exponential model and .9571 for the hyperbolic model. Because hyperbolic consumers have two sources of discounting – β and δ – the hyperbolic

---

[26] Wealth does not include social security wealth and other defined benefit pensions, which are already built into the model in the form of postretirement "labor income."

[27] For calibration purposes, total wealth is measured as $X + Z + (Y/24)$, where X represents liquid assets (excluding current labor income), Z represents illiquid assets, and Y represents annual after-tax labor income. The $Y/24$ is included to reflect average cash inventories used for (continuous) consumption out of labor income. If labor income is paid in equal monthly installments, $Y/12$, and consumption is smoothly spread over time, then average cash inventories will be $Y/24$.

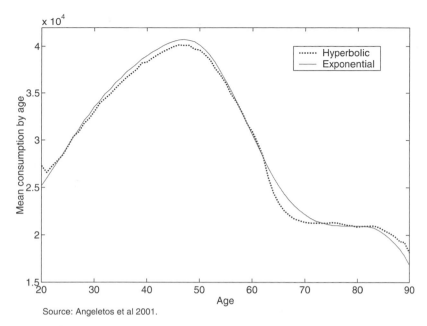

Source: Angeletos et al 2001.

Figure 7.7. Simulated mean consumption profiles of hyperbolic and exponential households.

δs lie above the exponential δs. Recall that the hyperbolic and exponential discount functions are calibrated to generate the same amount of preretirement wealth accumulation. In this manner, the calibrations "equalize" the underlying willingness to save between the exponential and hyperbolic consumers. The calibrated long term discount factors are sensible when compared with discount factors that have been used in similar exercises by other authors. Finally, note that these discount factors do not include mortality effects, which reduce the respective discount factors by an additional 1 percent on average per year.

8.2.   Simulation Results of ALRTW

Calibrated hyperbolic simulations – $\beta = 0.7$, $\delta = 0.957$ – generate life cycle consumption profiles that closely match the life cycle consumption profiles generated by calibrated exponential simulations – $\beta = 1$, $\delta = 0.944$. For example, Figure 7.7 compares hyperbolic and exponential consumption means over the life cycle. These two hump-shaped profiles are very similar.[28] The only differences arise around retirement and at the very beginning and end of life. At the beginning of life, hyperbolic consumers go on a credit card–financed spending spree,[29] leading to higher consumption than the exponentials. Around

---

[28] The consumption profiles roughly track the mean labor-income profile. This low-frequency comovement is driven by two factors. First, low income early in life holds down consumption, because consumers do not have large credit lines. Second, consumption needs peak in midlife, when the number of adult-equivalent dependents peaks at age 47.

[29] See Gourinchas and Parker (1999) for empirical evidence on the early life consumption boom.

retirement, hyperbolic consumption falls more steeply than exponential consumption, because hyperbolic households have most of their wealth in illiquid assets, which they cannot cost-effectively sell to smooth consumption. At the end of life, hyperbolic consumers have more illiquid assets to sell, slowing down the late-life collapse in consumption.

The total wealth profiles of hyperbolics and exponentials are also similar. This correspondence is not surprising, because the hyperbolic and exponential simulations are each calibrated to match the observed level of retirement wealth accumulation in the SCF. However, the two models generate very different simulated allocations across liquid and illiquid assets. Just before retirement (age 63), the average liquid asset holding of the simulated hyperbolics households is only about $10,000, whereas the exponential households have accumulated more than $45,000 in liquid wealth (1990 dollars).[30] Hyperbolics end up holding relatively little liquid wealth, because liquidity tends to be splurged to satisfy the hyperbolic taste for instant gratification. Both naive and sophisticated hyperbolics will quickly spend whatever liquidity is at their disposal.

By contrast, hyperbolics hold much more *illiquid* wealth than their exponential counterparts. Just before retirement, the average illiquid asset holding of the simulated hyperbolics is $175,000, compared with $130,000 for the exponentials. Hyperbolics are more willing to hold illiquid wealth for two reasons. First, sophisticated hyperbolics (like the hyperbolics in these simulations) view illiquid assets as a commitment device, which they value because it prevents later selves from splurging saved wealth too quickly. Second, illiquid assets are particularly valuable to hyperbolics (both naifs and sophisticates), because hyperbolics have lower long-run discount rates than exponentials. Hence, hyperbolics place relatively greater value on the long-run stream of payoffs associated with illiquid assets.[31] Hyperbolics and exponentials dislike illiquidity for the standard reason that illiquid assets cannot be used to buffer income shocks. But, this cost of illiquidity is partially offset for hyperbolics for the two reasons described: hyperbolics value commitment and hyperbolics more highly value the long-run dividends of illiquid assets. Hence, on net, illiquidity is less costly for a hyperbolic than for an exponential consumer.

To evaluate empirically the asset allocation predictions of the hyperbolic and exponential models, ALRTW compare the simulated results to survey evidence from the SCF. For example, ALRTW analyze the percentage of households that have at least 1 month of liquid wealth on hand. On average, 73 percent of simulated exponential households hold liquid assets greater than 1 month of labor income. The analogous number for hyperbolics is only 40 percent. For comparison, 42 percent of households in the SCF hold liquid financial assets greater than 1 month of labor income.

---

[30] For the purposes of the analysis in this subsection, simulated liquid assets are measured as $X^+ + (Y/24)$, where X^+ represents positive holdings of liquid assets (excluding current labor income).

[31] The long-run discount rate of a hyperbolic consumer, $-\ln(\delta_{\text{hyperbolic}}) = -\ln(.957) = .044$, is calibrated to lie below the long-run discount rate of an exponential consumer, $-\ln(\delta_{\text{exponential}}) = -\ln(.944) = .058$.

ALRTW also evaluate the models by analyzing the simulated quantity of liquid assets as a share of total assets. In the SCF, the average liquid wealth share is only 8 percent and neither the exponential nor hyperbolic simulations match this number, although the hyperbolic simulations are a bit closer to the mark. The average liquid wealth share for simulated hyperbolic households is 31 percent. The analogous exponential liquid wealth share is 50 percent.

Revolving credit – e.g., credit card borrowing – represents another important form of liquidity. Low levels of liquid assets are naturally associated with high levels of credit card debt. ALRTW contrast exponential and hyperbolic consumers by comparing their simulated propensities to borrow on credit cards.[32] At any point in time 51 percent of hyperbolic consumers borrow on their credit cards, compared with only 19 percent of exponentials. In the 1995 SCF, 70 percent of households with credit cards report that they did not fully pay their credit card bill the last time that they mailed in a payment. Hyperbolic simulations come much closer to matching these self-reports. Likewise, the simulated hyperbolic consumers borrow much more on average than the simulated exponential consumers. On average, simulated exponential households owe $900 of interest-paying credit card debt, *including* the households with no debt. By contrast, simulated hyperbolic households owe $3,400 of credit card debt. The actual amount of credit card debt owed per household with a credit card is approximately $4,600 (*including* households with no debt, but *excluding* the float).[33]

Euler Equation tests have played a critical role in the empirical consumption literature since the work of Hall (1978). Many of the papers in this literature have asked whether lagged information predicts current consumption growth. In particular, many authors have tried to determine whether predictable changes in income predict changes in consumption:

$$\Delta \ln(C_{it}) = \alpha E_{t-1} \Delta \ln(Y_{it}) + X_{it}\beta + \varepsilon_{it}. \tag{8.1}$$

Here X_{it} is a vector of control variables. The standard consumption model (without liquidity constraints) predicts $\alpha = 0$; the marginal propensity to consume out of predictable changes in income should be zero. By contrast, empirical estimates of α lie above 0, with "consensus estimates" around $\alpha = 0.2$.[34]

ALRTW estimate the standard comovement regression using *simulated* data. For the hyperbolic simulations, the coefficient on $E_{t-1} \Delta \ln(Y_{it})$ is $\alpha = 0.17$.

---

[32] See LRT (2000) for a much more detailed analysis of credit card borrowing.

[33] This average balance includes households in all education categories. It is calculated on the basis of aggregate information reported by the Federal Reserve. This figure is consistent with values from a proprietary account-level data set assembled by David Gross and Nicholas Souleles (1999a, 1999b, 2000). See LRT (2000).

[34] For example, Hall and Mishkin (1982) report a statistically significant coefficient of .200, Hayashi (1985) reports a significant coefficient of .158, Altonji and Siow (1987) report an insignificant coefficient of .091, Attanasio and Weber (1993) report an insignificant coefficient of .119, Attanasio and Weber (1995) report an insignificant coefficient of .100, Shea (1995) reports a marginally significant coefficient of .888, Lusardi (1996) reports a significant coefficient of .368, Souleles (1999) reports a significant coefficient of .344, and ALRTW (2000) report a significant coefficient of .285. See Deaton (1992) and Browning and Lusardi (1996) for a discussion of the excess sensitivity literature.

By contrast, the exponential simulations generate a value of $\alpha = 0.03$. Hyperbolic consumers hold more of their wealth in illiquid form than exponentials. So, hyperbolics are more likely to hit liquidity constraints, raising their marginal propensity to consume out of predictable changes in income.

The hyperbolic simulations also predict income-consumption comovement around retirement. Banks, Blundell, and Tanner (1998) and Bernheim, Skinner, and Weinberg (1997) argue that consumption anomalously falls during the mid-1960s, at the same time that workers are retiring and labor income is falling. ALRTW estimate the following regression to explore the consumption drop at retirement:

$$\Delta \ln(C_{it}) = I_{it}^{\text{RETIRE}}\gamma + X_{it}\beta + \varepsilon_{it}.$$

Here I_{it}^{RETIRE} is a set of dummy variables that take the value of one in periods $t-1$, t, $t+1$, and $t+2$ if period t is the age of retirement; and X_{it} is a vector of control variables. Summing the coefficients on the four dummy variables (and switching signs) generates an estimate of the "excess" drop in consumption around retirement. Estimating these coefficients from the PSID yields a statistically significant excess drop of 11.6 percent around retirement. The analogous drop for simulated hyperbolic consumers is 14.5 percent, whereas the drop for simulated exponential consumers is only 3.0 percent. Hyperbolic consumers hold relatively little liquid wealth. A drop in income at retirement translates into a substantial drop in consumption, even though retirement is an exogenous, completely predictable event.

All in all, the hyperbolic model consistently does a better job of approximating the data. Table 7.1 draws these findings together.

9. NAIFS VERSUS SOPHISTICATES

Until now, we have considered the case in which early selves hold correct expectations about the preferences and behavior of later selves. Early selves anticipate that later selves will fail to maximize the patient long-run interests of early selves. When early selves hold such correct expectations, they are referred to as sophisticates (Strotz, 1956).

Table 7.1.

	Hyperbolic	Exponential	Data
% with $\frac{\text{liquid}}{Y} > \frac{1}{12}$	40%	73%	42%
Mean $\frac{\text{liquid assets}}{\text{liquid} + \text{illiquid assets}}$	0.39	0.50	0.08
% borrowing on "Visa"	51%	19%	70%
Mean borrowing	$3,400	$900	$4,600
$C - Y$ comovement	0.17	0.03	≈0.20
% C drop at retirement	14.5%	3.0%	11.6%

Source: ALRTW (2001b).

However, it is reasonable to imagine that early selves might mistakenly expect later selves to follow through on the early selves' best intentions. This is the naive case, discussed by Strotz (1956), Akerlof (1991), and O'Donoghue and Rabin (1999a, 1999b, 2000). Such naifs have optimistic forecasts in the sense that they believe that future selves will carry out the wishes of the current self. Under this belief, the current self constructs the sequence of actions that maximizes the preferences of the current self. The current self then implements the first action in that sequence, expecting future selves to implement the remaining actions. Instead, those future selves conduct their own optimization and therefore implement actions in conflict with the patient behavior anticipated by prior selves.

In some cases, the behavior of naive hyperbolics is very close to the behavior of sophisticated hyperbolics. For example, ALRTW have replicated their calibration and analysis under the assumption that hyperbolic consumers are naive. They find that the naive hyperbolics act effectively the same as the sophisticated hyperbolics discussed above. Hence, for the consumption applications in this paper, it does not matter whether we assume that hyperbolics are naive or sophisticated.

However, this rough equivalence does not generally hold. Ted O'Donoghue and Matthew Rabin (1999a, 1999b, 2000) have written a series of papers that examine the differences between naifs and sophisticates, developing examples where naifs and sophisticates behave in radically different ways. Their most recent paper explores the issue of retirement saving. They show that naive hyperbolics may perpetually postpone asset reallocation decisions, generating sizeable welfare costs. Each one-period postponement seems optimal, because the naif mistakenly expects some future self to undertake the reallocation.

Naifs models do not exhibit any of the pathologies that we have discussed (e.g., nonmonotonic consumption functions). If consumers do not recognize that their own preferences are dynamically inconsistent, they will not have any incentive to act strategically vis-à-vis their own future selves. However, this solution to the pathology problem requires that consumers be completely naive about their own future preferences. Any partial knowledge of future dynamic inconsistency reinstates the pathologies.

O'Donoghue and Rabin (2000) also propose an intermediate model in which decision-makers partially recognize their propensity to be hyperbolic in the future. Specifically, in this intermediate model, the actor believes that future selves will have a β value equal to $\hat{\beta}$. Sophisticates hold correct expectations about the future value of β, so $\hat{\beta} = \beta$. Naifs incorrectly believe that future selves will hold preferences consistent with the long-run interests of the current self, implying $\hat{\beta} = 1$. Partial naifs lie between these extremes, so $\beta < \hat{\beta} < 1$.

10. NORMATIVE ANALYSIS
AND POLICY IMPLICATIONS

Welfare and policy analysis can be problematic in hyperbolic models. The crux of the difficulty is the lack of a clear welfare criterion.

The most traditional perspective has been adopted by Phelps and Pollak (1968) and Laibson (1996, 1997a). These authors take the multiple self framework literally, and simply apply the Pareto criterion for welfare analysis. If one allocation makes all selves as least as well off as another allocation, then the former allocation Pareto dominates the latter allocation. Even this very strong welfare criterion opens the door to interesting welfare analysis. It is typically the case that the equilibrium allocation in a hyperbolic model is Pareto-inferior to other feasible allocations that will not arise in equilibrium. These Pareto-dominant allocations can be attained only with a commitment technology. We turn to such commitment technologies (and the corresponding policies that support them) in the next subsection.

O'Donoghue and Rabin adopt a different approach to welfare analysis. They argue that the right welfare perspective is the long-run perspective. Specifically, they rank allocations using the welfare of an agent with no hyperbolicity (i.e., $\beta = 1$). In the long-run, all selves discount exponentially. So, all past selves want future selves to discount exponentially. In this sense, $\beta = 1$ is the right discounting assumption if we adopt the preferences of some "earlier" self (say at birth). Another way to motivate this welfare criterion is to ask what discount function you would advise someone else to use. Typically, we urge others to act patiently, suggesting that we normatively discourage short-run impulsivity. In the language of these models, this advice recommends $\beta = 1$.

Recently, Caplin, and Leahy (2000) have suggested another criterion. They take the multiple self framework literally and suggest a utilitarian approach. Specifically, they argue that a sensible welfare criterion would weight the welfare of all of the selves. This approach produces challenging implications. Specifically, if later selves get roughly the same weight as early selves, then late consumption should matter much more than early consumption. To see why, consider the following two-period example. Self 1 cares about periods 1 and 2 (with equal weights). Self 2 cares only about period 2. Then period 2 should get twice the weight of period 1 in the social planner's welfare function. Late consumption benefits both selves, whereas early consumption benefits only self 1.

At the moment, there is no consensus framework for measuring welfare in multiple self models. However, the different approaches reviewed herein usually give similar answers to policy questions. All of the competing welfare criteria imply that equilibrium allocations in economies without commitment typically generate savings rates that are too low (i.e., higher savings allocations would improve social welfare). This implication follows almost immediately once one adopts a welfare criterion in which $\beta = 1$ (O'Donoghue and Rabin) or once one adopts the utilitarian perspective of Caplin and Leahy. Equilibrium allocations also tend to be Pareto-inferior because the static gains of high consumption rates in the short run (gains to the current self) tend to be overwhelmed by the dynamic losses of low savings rates in the long-run steady state (dynamic losses to the expected utility of the current self). Recall that hyperbolic consumers have low long-run discount rates. Hence, the long-run outcomes matter a great deal to the welfare of the current hyperbolic consumer (Laibson 1996). A commitment to a savings rate slightly above the equilibrium savings rate will raise the welfare of all selves.

10.1. The Value of Commitment

Sophisticated hyperbolic consumers are motivated to choose policies that commit the behavior of future selves. Moreover, such commitment devices can raise the welfare of all selves if the commitment locks in patient long-run behavior. Even naive consumers will benefit from commitment, although they will not appreciate these benefits at the time they are being locked into a patient behavioral regime. However, these naive agents may not mind such commitments (ex ante), because they incorrectly expect future selves to act patiently anyway.

In a world of sophisticated hyperbolic consumers, the social planner's goal is to make commitment possible, rather than imposing it on consumers.[35] Sophisticated consumers understand the value of commitment and will adopt such commitments when it is in their interest. Hence, a 401(k), which is voluntary, might be viewed as a useful commitment device for a sophisticated hyperbolic consumer.[36] Laibson (1996) and LRT (1998) measure the welfare consequences of providing voluntary commitment technologies, like 401(k)'s, to sophisticated hyperbolic consumers.

By contrast, in a world of unsophisticated consumers (i.e., naifs), a benevolent government may want to impose commitment on consumers.[37] Social security, with its universal coverage and illiquid "balances," can be viewed as such a commitment.

11. EXTENSIONS

11.1. Asset Uncertainty

Our simulation results reported in Section 7 demonstrate that hyperbolic consumption functions become less irregular as more noise is added to the model. The analysis in Section 7 explores the case in which the noise comes from stochastic labor income. Another natural source of noise is the asset return process. In the analysis, we assumed that the asset return process was deterministic.

Incorporating random returns into the model will generate four likely benefits. First, when pathologies (e.g., nonmonotonic consumption functions) do arise, those pathologies will probably be less pronounced when asset returns are stochastic. Second, pathologies will be less likely to arise in the first place.

---

[35] Commitment technologies typically make all selves better off.

[36] 401(k)'s are defined contribution pension accounts available in most U. S. firms. These accounts have a penalty for "early" withdrawal (e.g., before age $59\frac{1}{2}$).

[37] Naturally, there are excellent reasons to be wary of activist governments. Much political activity is directed toward rent seeking. Moreover, even a benevolent social planner needs to worry about the disincentives and distortions that arise when well-intentioned politicians tax productive activities to pay for new social programs.

Third, once asset return variability is added to the model, we may be able to prove more general theorems. For example, *without* asset return variability, we can show that, as $\beta \to 1$, the consumption function becomes monotonic and continuous on an absorbing interval of cash on hand. An absorbing interval is a range of cash-on-hand values that, in equilibrium, the consumer will never leave. With asset return variability, we conjecture that we will be able to show that, as $\beta \to 1$, the consumption function becomes monotonic and continuous on the *entire* state space. This more general theorem reflects the fact that asset return uncertainty scales up with financial wealth, in contrast to labor income uncertainty that does not scale with financial wealth. Finally, adding asset uncertainty will enable us to model multiasset state spaces as long as each asset has some idiosyncratic variability. In this setting, we expect to be able to prove the existence, uniqueness, and regularity of equilibria using variants of the techniques developed in Harris and Laibson (2001a).

11.2.   Continuous-Time Hyperbolic Models

Continuous-time modeling provides a more robust way of eliminating pathologies like nonmonotonic consumption functions (Harris and Laibson, 2001b). To motivate the continuous-time formalism, recall the discrete time set-up. In the standard discrete-time formulation of quasi-hyperbolic preferences, the present consists of the single period t. The future consists of periods $t + 1, t + 2, \ldots$. A period n steps into the future is discounted with factor δ^n, and an additional discount factor β is applied to all periods except the present.

This model can be generalized in two ways. First, the present can last for any number of periods $T_t \in \{1, 2 \ldots\}$. Second, T_t can be random. The preferences in equation (11.1) are a natural continuous-time analog of this more general formulation. Specifically, the preferences of self t are given by

$$
E_t \left[\int_t^{t+T_t} e^{-\gamma(s-t)} U(c(s)) ds + \alpha \int_{t+T_t}^{+\infty} e^{-\gamma(s-t)} U(c(s)) ds \right], \quad (11.1)
$$

where $\gamma \in (0, +\infty)$, $\alpha \in (0, 1]$, $U : (0, +\infty) \to \mathbb{R}$, and T_t is distributed exponentially with parameter $\lambda \in [0, +\infty)$. In other words, self t uses a stochastic discount function, namely

$$
D_\lambda(t, s) = \begin{cases} e^{-\gamma(s-t)} & \text{if} \quad s \leq t + T_t \\ \alpha e^{-\gamma(s-t)} & \text{if} \quad s > t + T_t \end{cases}.
$$

This stochastic discount function decays exponentially at rate γ up to time $t + T_t$, drops discontinuously at $t + T_t$ to a fraction α of its level just prior to $t + T_t$, and decays exponentially at rate γ thereafter. Figure 7.8 plots a single realization of this discount function, with $t = 0$ and $T_t = 3.4$. Figure 7.9 plots the expected value of the discount function, namely

$$
E_t D_\lambda(t, s) = e^{-\lambda(s-t)} e^{-\gamma(s-t)} + (1 - e^{-\lambda(s-t)}) \alpha e^{-\gamma(s-t)},
$$

for $\lambda \in \{0, 0.1, 1, 10, \infty\}$.

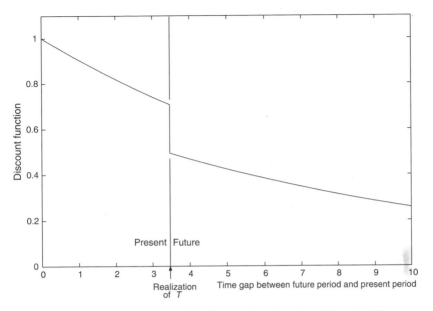

Figure 7.8. Realization of the discount function ($\alpha = 0.7$, $\gamma = 0.1$).

This continuous-time formalization is close to the deterministic functions used in Barro (1999) and Luttmer and Mariotti (2000). However, Harris and Laibson (2001b) assume that T_t is stochastic. The stochastic transition with constant hazard rate reduces the problem to a system of two differential equations that characterize present and future value functions.

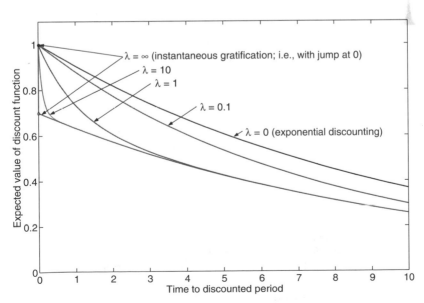

Figure 7.9. Expected value of the discount function for $\lambda \in \{0, 0.1, 1, 10, \infty\}$.

When $\lambda = 0$, the discount function is equivalent to a standard exponential discount function. As $\lambda \to \infty$, the discount function converges to a jump function, namely

$$D_\infty(t, s) = \begin{cases} 1 & \text{if } s = t \\ \alpha e^{-\gamma(s-t)} & \text{if } s > t \end{cases}.$$

This limit case is both analytically tractable and psychologically relevant. In this "instantaneous gratification" case, the present is vanishingly short. Individuals prefer consumption in the present instant discretely more than consumption in the momentarily delayed future. The lessons from this model carry over, by continuity, to the neighborhood of models in which the present is short, but not precisely instantaneous (i.e., λ large).

The instantaneous gratification model, which is dynamically *inconsistent*, shares the same value function as a related dynamically *consistent* optimization problem with a wealth-contingent utility function. Using this partial equivalence, Harris and Laibson (2001b) prove that the hyperbolic equilibrium exists and is unique. The associated equilibrium consumption functions are continuous and monotonic in wealth. The monotonicity property relies on the condition that the long-run discount rate is weakly greater than the interest rate. For this case, all of the pathological properties of discrete-time hyperbolic models are eliminated.

12. CONCLUSIONS

We have characterized the consumption behavior of hyperbolic consumers. The hyperbolic model provides two payoffs. First, it provides an analytically tractable, parsimonious foundation with which to analyze self-control problems. Second, it is easily calibrated, providing precise numerical predictions that can be empirically evaluated in competition with mainstream models. We have shown that the hyperbolic model successfully matches empirical observations on household balance sheets and consumption choices.

Relative to exponential households, hyperbolic households hold low levels of liquid wealth measured either as a fraction of labor income or as a share of total wealth. Hyperbolic households borrow more aggressively in the revolving credit market (i.e., on credit cards), but they save more actively in illiquid assets. Because the hyperbolic households have low levels of liquid assets and high levels of credit card debt, they are unable to smooth their consumption paths in the presence of predictable changes in income. Calibrated hyperbolic simulations explain observed levels of consumption-income comovement and the drop in consumption at retirement. Calibrated hyperbolic simulations generate "excess sensitivity" coefficients of approximately 0.20, very close to empirical coefficients estimated from household data.

More generally, the hyperbolic model provides a good formal foundation for the study of self-defeating behaviors. Economists usually assume that rational agents will act in their own interests. Hyperbolic agents may hold rational expectations, but they will rarely make efficient choices. Puzzling and important self-defeating behaviors like undersaving, overeating, and procrastination lose some of their mystery when analyzed with the hyperbolic model.

ACKNOWLEDGMENTS

We thank Glenn Ellison for numerous helpful suggestions. We also thank George-Marios Angeletos, Andrea Repetto, Jeremy Tobacman, and Stephen Weinberg, whose ideas and work are reflected in this paper. Laura Serban provided outstanding research assistance. David Laibson acknowledges financial support from the National Science Foundation (SBR-9510985), the Olin Foundation, the National Institute on Aging (R01-AG-1665), and the MacArthur Foundation.

APPENDIX
PROOF OF THEOREM 4.5

Fix $x_0 \in [0, +\infty)$. Suppose that W_1 and W_2 are two equilibrium current-value functions, and let S_1 and S_2 be the associated saving functions. Put $h = U \circ g$. Then,

$$\begin{aligned}
(\mathcal{B}W_1)(x) &= U(x - S_1(x)) + \delta \int (W_1 - \varepsilon h \circ W_1')(RS_1(x) + y) f(y) dy \\
&= U(x - S_1(x)) + \delta \int (W_2 - \varepsilon h \circ W_2')(RS_1(x) + y) f(y) dy \\
&\quad + \delta \int (W_1 - W_2)(RS_1(x) + y) f(y) dy \\
&\quad - \varepsilon \delta \int (h \circ W_1' - h \circ W_2')(RS_1(x) + y) f(y) dy \\
&\leq (\mathcal{B}W_2)(x) + \delta \int (W_1 - W_2)(RS_1(x) + y) f(y) dy \\
&\quad - \varepsilon \delta \int (h \circ W_1' - h \circ W_2')(RS_1(x) + y) f(y) dy.
\end{aligned}$$

Hence, to obtain an upper bound for $(\mathcal{B}W_1)(x) - (\mathcal{B}W_2)(x)$, it suffices to estimate the expressions

$$\int (W_1 - W_2)(RS_1(x) + y) f(y) dy \tag{A.1}$$

and

$$\int (h \circ W_1' - h \circ W_2')(RS_1(x) + y) f(y) dy. \tag{A.2}$$

In doing so, we shall make use of the estimates of Theorem 4.3 that apply to W_1 and W_2. In particular, the constant K and the functions N_1 and N_2 used herein are taken from that theorem.

Expression (A.1) is easy to estimate. Because S_1 is an equilibrium-saving function, $RS_1(x) + y \in [\underline{y}, \bar{X}]$ for all $x \in [\underline{y}, \bar{X}]$ and all $y \in [\underline{y}, \bar{y}]$. Hence

$$\left| \int (W_1 - W_2)(RS_1(x) + y)f(y)dy \right| \leq \|W_1 - W_2\|_{c([\underline{y}, \bar{X}])}$$

for all $x \in [\underline{y}, \bar{X}]$, where

$$\|W_1 - W_2\|_{c([\underline{y}, \bar{X}])} = \sup_{x \in [\underline{y}, \bar{X}]} |W_1(x) - W_2(x)|.$$

Expression (A.2) requires more care. Put

$$W'_\phi(x) = (1 - \phi)W'_1(x) + \phi W'_2(x).$$

Then

$$h(W'_2(x)) - h(W'_1(x)) = \int_0^1 ((W'_2 - W'_1)h' \circ W'_\phi)(x)d\phi$$

and

$$\int (h \circ W'_2 - h \circ W'_1)(RS_1(x) + y)f(y)dy$$

$$= \int \left(\int_0^1 ((W'_2 - W'_1)h' \circ W'_\phi)(RS_1(x) + y)f(y)d\phi \right)dy$$

$$= \int_0^1 \left(\int ((W'_2 - W'_1)h' \circ W'_\phi)(RS_1(x) + y)f(y)dy \right)d\phi.$$

Moreover,

$$\int ((W'_2 - W'_1)h' \circ W'_\phi)(RS_1(x) + y)f(y)dy$$

$$= -\int ((W_2 - W_1)h' \circ W'_\phi)(RS_1(x) + y)f'(y)dy$$

$$-\int ((W_2 - W_1)h'' \circ W'_\phi)(RS_1(x) + y)f(y)W''_\phi(RS_1(x) + dy)$$

(on integrating by parts). Hence, to estimate expression (A.2), we need to estimate the expressions

$$\int ((W_2 - W_1)h' \circ W'_\phi)(RS_1(x) + y)f'(y)dy \tag{A.3}$$

and

$$\int ((W_2 - W_1)h'' \circ W'_\phi)(RS_1(x) + y)f(y)W''_\phi(RS_1(x) + dy). \tag{A.4}$$

Expression (A.3) can be estimated as follows. First, note that, because S_1 is an equilibrium-saving function, $RS_1(x) + y \in [\underline{y}, \bar{X}]$ for all $x \in [\underline{y}, \bar{X}]$ and all

$y \in [\underline{y}, \bar{y}]$. Second, put

$$\underline{\lambda} = \min_{x \in [\underline{y}, \bar{X}]} U'(x) \text{ and } \bar{\lambda} = \max_{x \in [\underline{y}, \bar{X}]} U'(x) \vee N_1(x).$$

Third, note that, because $W'_\phi \in [U', U' \vee N_1]$ for all $\phi \in [0, 1]$, $W'_\phi \in [\underline{\lambda}, \bar{\lambda}]$ for all $\phi \in [0, 1]$. Hence,

$$\left| \int ((W_2 - W_1)h' \circ W'_\phi)(RS_1(x) + y)f'(y)dy \right|$$

$$\leq \|W_1 - W_2\|_{c([\underline{y}, \bar{X}])} \|h'\|_{c([\underline{\lambda}, \bar{\lambda}])} \|f'\|_{c([\underline{y}, \bar{y}])}(\bar{y} - \underline{y})$$

for all $x \in [\underline{y}, \bar{X}]$.

Expression (A.4) can be estimated as follows. First, as in the case of expression (A.3), we have

$$\left| \int ((W_2 - W_1)h'' \circ W'_\phi)(RS_1(x) + y)f(y)W''_\phi(RS_1(x) + dy) \right|$$

$$\leq \|W_1 - W_2\|_{c([\underline{y}, \bar{X}])} \|h''\|_{c([\underline{\lambda}, \bar{\lambda}])} \|f\|_{c([\underline{y}, \bar{y}])} \|W''_\phi\|_{\tau v([\underline{y}, \bar{X}])}$$

for all $x \in [\underline{y}, \bar{X}]$, where $\|W''_\phi\|_{\tau v([\underline{y}, \bar{X}])}$ denotes the total variation of the measure W''_ϕ on the interval $[\underline{y}, \bar{X}]$. Second, put

$$\mu(dx) = K N_2(x)\, dx \quad \text{and} \quad \tilde{W}''_\phi(dx) = W''_\phi(dx) + \mu(dx).$$

Then,

$$\|W''_\phi\|_{\tau v([\underline{y}, \bar{X}])} = \|\tilde{W}''_\phi - \mu\|_{\tau v([\underline{y}, \bar{X}])} \leq \|\tilde{W}''_\phi\|_{\tau v([\underline{y}, \bar{X}])} + \|\mu\|_{\tau v([\underline{y}, \bar{X}])}$$

$$= \int_{[\underline{y}, \bar{X}]} \tilde{W}''_\phi(dx) + \int_{[\underline{y}, \bar{X}]} \mu(dx)$$

$$= \int_{[\underline{y}, \bar{X}]} W''_\phi(dx) + 2 \int_{[\underline{y}, \bar{X}]} \mu(dx)$$

(because $\tilde{W}''_\phi$ and μ are both positive measures, and by definition of $\tilde{W}''_\phi$)

$$= W'_\phi(\bar{X}+) - W'_\phi(\underline{y}-) + 2 \int_{[\underline{y}, \bar{X}]} K N_2(x)\, dx$$

$$\leq \bar{\lambda} - \underline{\lambda} + 2 \int_{[\underline{y}, \bar{X}]} K N_2(x)\, dx.$$

Combining our estimates for expressions (A.1), (A.3) and (A.4), we obtain

$$(\mathfrak{B}W_1)(x) - (\mathfrak{B}W_2)(x) \leq \delta \|W_1 - W_2\|_{c([\underline{y}, \bar{X}])}$$

$$+ \varepsilon\delta \|W_1 - W_2\|_{c([\underline{y}, \bar{X}])} \|h'\|_{c([\underline{\lambda}, \bar{\lambda}])} \|f'\|_{c([\underline{y}, \bar{y}])}(\bar{y} - \underline{y})$$

$$+ \varepsilon\delta \|W_1 - W_2\|_{c([\underline{y}, \bar{X}])} \|h''\|_{c([\underline{\lambda}, \bar{\lambda}])} \|f\|_{c([\underline{y}, \bar{y}])}$$

$$\times \left(\bar{\lambda} - \underline{\lambda} + 2 \int_{[\underline{y}, \bar{X}]} K N_2(x)\, dx \right)$$

294   **Harris and Laibson**

for all $x \in [\underline{y}, \bar{X}]$. Combining this estimate with the analogous estimate for $(\mathfrak{B}W_2)(x) - (\mathfrak{B}W_1)(x)$, we obtain

$$\|\mathfrak{B}W_1 - \mathfrak{B}W_2\|_{c([\underline{y},\bar{X}])} \leq \delta(1 + \varepsilon L)\|W_1 - W_2\|_{c([\underline{y},\bar{X}])},$$

where

$$L = \|h'\|_{c([\underline{\lambda},\bar{\lambda}])}\|f'\|_{c([\underline{y},\bar{y}])}(\bar{y} - \underline{y})$$

$$+ \|h''\|_{c([\underline{\lambda},\bar{\lambda}])}\|f\|_{c([\underline{y},\bar{y}])}\left(\bar{\lambda} - \underline{\lambda} + 2\int_{[\underline{y},\bar{X}]} K N_2(x)\, dx\right).$$

It follows that, if

$$\varepsilon < \min\left\{1 - \bar{\beta}_1, \frac{1 - \delta}{\delta L}\right\},$$

then $\|\mathfrak{B}W_1 - \mathfrak{B}W_2\|_{c([\underline{y},\bar{X}])} = 0$. In other words, W_1 and W_2 coincide on $[\underline{y}, \bar{X}]$.

■

References

Ainslie, G. (1992), *Picoeconomics*. Cambridge UK: Cambridge University Press.

Akerlof, G. A. (1991), "Procrastination and Obedience," *American Economic Review (Papers and Proceedings)*, 81, 1–19.

Altonji, J. and A. Siow (1987), "Testing the Response of Consumption to Income Changes with (Noisy) Panel Data," *Quarterly Journal of Economics*, 102(2), 293–328.

Angeletos, G.-M., D. Laibson, A. Repetto, J. Tobacman, and S. Weinberg (2001a), "The Hyperbolic Buffer Stock Model: Calibration, Simulation, and Empirical Evaluation National Bureau of Economic Research," Working Paper.

Angeletos, G.-M., D. Laibson, A. Repetto, J. Tobacman, and S. Weinberg (2001b), "The Hyperbolic Consumption Model: Calibration, Simulation, and Empirical Evaluation," *Journal of Economic Perspectives*, 15, 47–68.

Attanasio, O. (1999), "Consumption," in *Handbook of Macroeconomics*, (ed. by J. Taylor and M. Woodford), Amsterdam: North-Holland.

Attanasio, O. and G. Weber (1993), "Consumption Growth, the Interest Rate, and Aggregation," *Review of Economic Studies*, 60(3), 631–649.

Attanasio, O. and G. Weber (1995), "Is Consumption Growth Consistent with Intertemporal Optimization? Evidence from the Consumer Expenditure Survey," *Journal of Political Economy*, 103(6), 1121–1157.

Banks, J., R. Blundell, and S. Tanner (1998), "Is There a Retirement Puzzle?" *American Economic Review*, 88(4), 769–788.

Barro, R. (1999), "Laibson Meets Ramsey in the Neoclassical Growth Model," *Quarterly Journal of Economics*, 114(4), 1125–1152.

Benabou, R. and J. Tirole (2000), "Willpower and Personal Rules," mimeo.

Bernheim, B. D., J. Skinner, and S. Weinberg (1997), "What Accounts for the Variation in Retirement Wealth among U.S. Households?" Working Paper 6227. Cambridge, MA: National Bureau of Economic Research.

Blundell, R., M. Browning, and C. Meghir (1994), "Consumer Demand and the Life-Cycle Allocation of Household Expenditures," *Review of Economic Studies*, 61, 57–80.

Brocas, I. and J. Carrillo (2000), "The Value of Information when Preferences are Dynamically Inconsistent," *European Economic Review*, 44, 1104–1115.

Brocas, I. and J. Carrillo (2001), "Rush and Procrastination under Hyperbolic Discounting and Interdependent Activities," *Journal of Risk and Uncertainty*, 22, 141–164.

Browning, M. and A. Lusardi (1996), "Household Saving: Micro Theories and Micro Facts," *Journal of Economic Literature*, 32, 1797–1855.

Carrillo, J. and M. Dewatripont (2000), "Promises, promises, . . . ," mimeo.

Carrillo, J. and T. Mariotti (2000), "Strategic Ignorance as a Self-Disciplining Device," *Review of Economic Studies*, 67, 529–544.

Carroll, C. D. (1992), "The Buffer Stock Theory of Saving: Some Macroeconomic Evidence," *Brookings Papers on Economic Activity*, 2, 61–156.

Carroll, C. D. (1997), "Buffer-Stock Saving and the Life Cycle/Permanent Income Hypothesis," *Quarterly Journal of Economics*, 112, 1–57.

Carroll, C. D. and M. Kimball (1996), "On the Concavity of the Consumption Function," *Econometrica*, 64(4), 981–992.

Chung, S.-H. and R. J. Herrnstein (1961), "Relative and Absolute Strengths of Response as a Function of Frequency of Reinforcement," *Journal of the Experimental Analysis of Animal Behavior*, 4, 267–272.

Deaton, A. (1991), "Saving and Liquidity Constraints," *Econometrica*, 59, 1221–1248.

Della Vigna, S. and U. Malmendier (2001), "Long Term Contracts and Self Control," mimeo.

Della Vigna, S. and D. Paserman (2000), "Job Search and Hyperbolic Discounting," mimeo.

Diamond, P. and B. Koszegi (1998), "Hyperbolic Discounting and Retirement," mimeo, MIT.

Engen, E., W. Gale, and J. K. Scholz (1994), "Do Saving Incentives Work," *Brookings Papers on Economic Activity*, 1, 85–180.

Frederick, S., G. Loewenstein, and E. O'Donoghue (2001), "Time Discounting: A Critical Review," mimeo.

Gourinchas, P.-O. and J. Parker (1999), "Consumption over the Life-Cycle," mimeo.

Gross, D. and N. Souleles (1999a), "An Empirical Analysis of Personal Bankruptcy and Delinquency," Mimeo.

Gross, D. and N. Souleles (1999b), "How Do People Use Credit Cards?" mimeo.

Gross, D. and N. Souleles (2000), "Consumer Response to Changes in Credit Supply: Evidence from Credit Card Data," mimeo.

Gruber, J. and B. Koszegi (2001), "Is Addiction 'Rational'?: Theory and Evidence," *Quarterly Journal of Economics*, 116, 1261–1303.

Hall, R. E. (1978), "Stochastic Implications of the Life Cycle–Permanent Income Hypothesis: Theory and Evidence," *Journal of Political Economy*, 86(6), 971–987.

Hall, R. E. and F. S. Mishkin (1982), "The Sensitivity of Consumption to Transitory Income: Estimates from Panel Data on Households," *Econometrica*, 50(2), 461–481.

Harris, C. and D. Laibson (2001a), "Dynamic Choices of Hyperbolic Consumers," *Econometrica*, 69, 935–957.

Harris, C. and D. Laibson (2001b), "Instantaneous Gratification," mimeo.

Hayashi, F. (1985), "The Permanent Income Hypothesis and Consumption Durability: Analysis Based on Japanese Panel Data," *Quarterly Journal of Economics*, 100(4), 1083–1113.

Hubbard, G., J. Skinner, and S. Zeldes (1994), "The Importance of Precautionary Motives in Explaining Individual and Aggregate Saving," *Carnegie–Rochester Conference Series on Public Policy*, 40, 59–125.

Hubbard, G., J. Skinner, and S. Zeldes (1995), "Precautionary Saving and Social Insurance," *Journal of Political Economy*, 103, 360–399.

King, G. R. and A. W. Logue (1987), "Choice in a Self-Control Paradigm with Human Subjects: Effects of Changeover Delay Duration," *Learning and Motivation*, 18, 421–438.

Kirby, K. N. (1997), "Bidding on the Future: Evidence Against Normative Discounting of Delayed Rewards," *Journal of Experimental Psychology*, 126, 54–70.

Kirby, K. and R. J. Herrnstein (1995), "Preference Reversals Due to Myopic Discounting of Delayed Reward," *Psychological Science*, 6(2), 83–89.

Kirby, K. and N. N. Marakovic (1995), "Modeling Myopic Decisions: Evidence for Hyperbolic Delay-Discounting within Subjects and Amounts," *Organizational Behavior and Human Decision Processes*, 64(1), 22–30.

Kirby, K. and N. N. Marakovic (1996), "Delayed-Discounting Probabilistic Rewards Rates Decrease as Amounts Increase," *Psychonomic Bulletin and Review*, 3(1), 100–104.

Krusell, P. and A. Smith (2000), "Consumption and Savings Decisions with Quasi-Geometric Discounting," mimeo.

Krusell, P., B. Kuruscu, and A. Smith (2000a), "Equilibrium Welfare and Government Policy with Quasi-Geometric Discounting," mimeo.

Krusell, P., B. Kuruscu, and A. Smith (2000b), "Asset Pricing with Quasi-Geometric Discounting," mimeo.

Laibson, D. I. (1994), "Self-Control and Savings," Ph.D. Dissertation, Massachusetts Institute of Technology.

Laibson, D. I. (1996), "Hyperbolic Discounting, Undersaving, and Savings Policy," Working Paper 5635, Cambridge, MA: National Bureau of Economic Research.

Laibson, D. I. (1997a), "Golden Eggs and Hyperbolic Discounting," *Quarterly Journal of Economics*, 112(2), 443–478.

Laibson, D. I. (1997b), "Hyperbolic Discount Functions and Time Preference Heterogeneity," mimeo, Harvard University.

Laibson, D. I. (1998), "Comments on Personal Retirement Saving Programs and Asset Accumulation," by James M. Poterba, Steven F. Venti, and David A. Wise, in *Studies in the Economics of Aging*, (ed. by David A. Wise), Chicago: NBER and the University of Chicago Press, 106–124.

Laibson, D. I., A. Repetto, and J. Tobacman (1998), "Self-Control and Saving for Retirement," *Brookings Papers on Economic Activity*, 1, 91–196.

Laibson, D. I., A. Repetto, and J. Tobacman (2000), "A Debt Puzzle," mimeo.

Loewenstein, G. and D. Prelec (1992), "Anomalies in Intertemporal Choice: Evidence and an Interpretation," *Quarterly Journal of Economics*, 97, 573–598.

Lusardi, A. (1996), "Permanent Income, Current Income, and Consumption; Evidence from Two Panel Data Sets," *Journal of Business and Economic Statistics*, 14, 81–90.

Luttmer, E. and T. Mariotti (2000), "Subjective Discount Factors," mimeo.

Millar, A. and D. J. Navarick (1984), "Self-Control and Choice in Humans: Effects of Video Game Playing as a Positive Reinforcer," *Learning and Motivation*, 15, 203–218.

Morris, S. and A. Postlewaite (1997), "Observational Implications of Nonexponential Discounting," mimeo.

Mulligan, C. (1997), "A Logical Economist's Argument Against Hyperbolic Discounting," mimeo, University of Chicago.

Navarick, D. J. (1982), "Negative Reinforcement and Choice in Humans," *Learning and Motivation*, 13, 361–377.

O'Donoghue, T. and M. Rabin (1999a), "Doing It Now or Later," *American Economic Review*, 89(1), 103–124.

O'Donoghue, T. and M. Rabin (1999b), "Incentives for Procrastinators," *Quarterly Journal of Economics*, 114(3), 769–816.

O'Donoghue, T. and M. Rabin (2000), "Choice and Procrastination," Working Paper.

Parker, J. A. (1999), "The Reaction of Household Consumption to Predictable Changes in Social Security Taxes," *American Economic Review*, 89, 959–973.

Phelps, E. S. and R. A. Pollak (1968), "On Second-Best National Saving and Game-Equilibrium Growth," *Review of Economic Studies*, 35, 185–199.

Ramsey, F. (1928), "A Mathematical Theory of Saving," *Economic Journal*, December, 38, 543–559.

Rankin, D. M. (1993), "How to Get Ready for Retirement: Save, Save, Save," *New York Times*, March 13, 33.

Read, D., G. Loewenstein, S. Kalyanaraman, and A. Bivolaru (1996), "Mixing Virtue and Vice: The Combined Effects of Hyperbolic Discounting and Diversification," Working Paper, Carnegie Mellon University.

Runkle, D. (1991), "Liquidity Constraints and the Permanent-Income Hypothesis: Evidence from Panel Data," *Journal of Monetary Economics*, 27(1), 73–98.

Shapiro, M. D. and J. Slemrod (1995), "Consumer Response to the Timing of Income: Evidence from a Change in Tax Withholding," *American Economic Review*, 85(1), 274–283.

Shea, J. (1995), "Union Contracts and the Life-Cycle/Permanent Income Hypothesis," *American Economic Review*, 85(1), 186–200.

Simmons Market Research Bureau (1996), *The 1996 Study of Media and Markets*. New York.

Souleles, N. (1999), "The Response of Household Consumption to Income Tax Refunds," *American Economic Review*, 89, 947–958.

Strotz, R. H. (1956), "Myopia and Inconsistency in Dynamic Utility Maximization," *Review of Economic Studies*, 23, 165–180.

Thaler, R. H. (1981), "Some Empirical Evidence on Dynamic Inconsistency," *Economics Letters*, 8, 201–207.

Thaler, R. H. (1992), "Saving, Fungibility, and Mental Accounts," in *The Winner's Curse*, Princeton, NJ: Princeton University Press, 107–121.

Thaler, R. H. and H. M. Shefrin (1981), "An Economic Theory of Self-Control," *Journal of Political Economy*, 89, 392–410.

Zeldes, S. P. (1989a), "Consumption and Liquidity Constraints: An Empirical Investigation," *Journal of Political Economy*, 97(2), 305–346.

Zeldes, S. P. (1989b), "Optimal Consumption with Stochastic Income: Deviations from Certainty Equivalence," *Quarterly Journal of Economics*, 104(2), 275–298.

A Discussion of the Papers
by Ernst Fehr and Klaus M. Schmidt and
by Christopher Harris and David Laibson
Glenn Ellison

It was a pleasure to serve as the discussant for this session. The authors have played a major role in developing the areas under discussion. The papers they produced for this volume are insightful and will help shape the emerging literature. The papers are excellent. I feel fortunate that my task is to comment and not to criticize.

One aspect of this session I found striking was the degree of agreement on how to define and organize a subfield of behavioral economics. In each case, the authors focus on one way in which real-world behavior departs from the standard model of rational self-interested behavior. They begin by mentioning results from a number of experiments showing systematic departures from the standard model. Although Fehr and Schmidt spend a fair amount of time distinguishing between broad classes of fairness models, both sets of authors advocate the use of simple tractable models that reflect essential features of behavior. In the final two paragraphs of the conclusions, both papers argue that behavioral economics models can add much to our understanding of important economic problems.

The similarity in the authors' perspectives makes one class of comments easy – one can look at the nice features of each subfield and suggest that the other might try to do something similar. For example, one way in which the hyperbolic discounting literature seemed ahead of the fairness literature to me is that the application to consumption is well developed theoretically and empirically to the point of being undeniably a part of macroeconomics literature. It would be nice to see work on fairness pushing as hard on a single topic and gaining acceptance within an applied community. A feature of the fairness literature I admired is the attention that has been paid to heterogeneity in fairness preferences. Although I know that behavioral economists like to work with minimal departures from rationality, I would think that large consumption data sets could provide those interested in hyperbolic discounting with ample degrees of freedom to explore models with heterogeneity in the degree of time inconsistency.

The similarity in perspective also makes it worthwhile to try to comment on whether the approach is a good one. I think it is. The one comment I would make, however, is that the "behavioral" organization of papers seems to me to have one drawback relative to the way in which most other applied papers are written. The difference I perceive in organization is that the papers focus on how a behavioral assumption can help us understand a large number of facts, rather than on the facts themselves. For example, I would regard a paper on high credit card debt as more applied and less "behavioral" if it focused narrowly on understanding credit card debt and discussed various potential explanations. The relative disadvantage of the behavioral approach is that in any paper that explains many disparate facts, one can worry that there is an implicit selection of facts consistent with the model. For example, the calibration papers discussed in Harris–Laibson did not conduct surveys of people with high credit card debt and ask them directly if they feel that they failed to foresee how quickly the debt would build up. The model "predicts" that there would be no affirmative responses, and I am sure this is not what the survey would yield. Experimental papers are similarly selective because authors must decide which experiments to conduct. Good experimentalists no doubt have a keen intuition for how experiments will turn out, and may tend to carry out only experiments in which they expect that their model will be vindicated. It seems to me that this type of criticism is harder to make of narrower applied papers – there are fewer facts to select among when one is looking at a narrow topic and the presence of competing explanations gives the authors less reason to favor any one potential explanation over the others.

As I said previously, the papers for this section are very insightful and very well done. I made a number of other specific comments at the World Congress, but I really cannot say that many of them merit being written down (especially now that the papers are in print). I therefore thought that I would devote the remainder of my time to talking more broadly about behavioral economics and its situation within the economics profession.

Behavioral economics is a potential revolution. If one judges its progress by looking at top journal publications or its success in attracting top economists, it is doing very well. In every field of economics, however, it has not yet affected how most work is done. What will be needed for the behavioral economics revolution to succeed? As an outsider, I clearly cannot offer the kind of insight based on a detailed understanding of various branches of the literature that many others could provide. Instead, I will try to approach the question as an amateur sociologist of the economics profession. There have been a number of recent successful revolutions in economic methodology (e.g., game theory and rational expectations). Behavioral economics (and other literatures like that on nonrational learning) may get valuable lessons from studying their progress.

Any such lessons, of course, will be about what makes fields take off in our profession and not necessarily about what makes research valuable.

One general thought that occurred to me on reflecting about revolutions is that the presence of interesting pure theory questions has spurred on many past revolutions. For example, I would argue that the main reason why the Folk Theorem continued to receive so much attention long after the basic principle was known was that economists enjoyed thinking and reading about cleverly constructed strategies. Franklin Fisher (1989) has criticized the finite-horizon reputation literature as an example of a literature driven by the elegance and so-phistication of the analysis. Infinite-horizon models are preferable descriptively and easily give what is probably the appropriate answer: that forming a repu-tation is possible, but will not necessarily happen. I do not want to debate the value of the reputation literature here. I just want to point out that the literature is extensive, and regardless of what people eventually conclude about the topic, it surely contributed to game theory's success. Many economists like interest-ing models, and fields that can provide them will grow. Behavioral economists who want their field to grow should not overlook this aspect of our profes-sion. As a theorist, I really enjoyed reading Harris and Laibson's discussion of the pathological properties of some hyperbolic models, and was intrigued by Fehr and Schmidt's comment that workers who care more about fairness will shirk more in their contracting game. Undoubtedly, there are many other similar opportunities.

In thinking about the theory/empirical divide, another thought that occurred to me (and here I am less confident in my casual empiricism) is that positive empirical evidence was not really a part of the takeoff of past revolutions. Em-pirical puzzles or shortcomings of the previous literature seem sometimes to be important. For example, the rational expectations revolution in macroeco-nomics was surely spurred by empirical evidence on the Phillips curve. The success of a new literature investigating failures of the old, however, seems not to be wrapped up with empirically demonstrating the superiority of new ideas. In the case of information economics, for example, the attention that Akerlof's (1970) lemons model and Spence's (1973) job market signaling model attracted was not due to any demonstration that a set of car prices or educational attain-ments were well understood using the models. In industrial organization, the game-theoretic literature exploded, whereas the empirical examination of such models proceeded at a much more leisurely pace. It seems that initial bursts of applied theory work have transformed fields and made them accepted long before any convincing empirical evidence is available. I would conclude that if behavioral economists want their revolution to occur, they might be well served to focus on producing applied theory papers that economists in various fields will want to teach their students.

There are other ways in which behavioral economists seem to be taking a different approach from past revolutions. They are spending much more time developing experimental support for their assumptions. They seem to spend much more time highlighting contrasts with the existing literature than did participants in earlier revolutions. [For example, Spence (1973) has only two references and Milgrom and Roberts (1982) only mention the decades-long legal and economic debates on predation in the first paragraph.] It seems hard to say, however, whether the leaders of previous revolutions would have taken advantage of experiments had they been easier to conduct, or if they would have been forced to write differently had they faced today's review process.

To conclude, I would like to come back to a question I have carefully avoided. Should behavioral economists follow the advice I've given? My observations only concerned what seems to make economic revolutions successful, not what work should be valued. Personally, I like pure theory and think that one of the nice features of academia is that we can stop to think about interesting issues that arise. I am happy that the profession seems to value such work. Personally, I also firmly believe that empirical work that helps us assess the applicability of new (and old theories) is extremely important. For example, I regard the work that Laibson and coauthors are carrying out on consumption as perhaps the most valuable work in the field. Thus, I would like to say that, while studying the progress of past revolutions may provide behavioral economists with valuable insights into how they can succeed, I hope that they do not pay too much attention to this and let a preoccupation with success get in the way of doing important work.

References

Akerlof, G. A. (1970), "The Market for 'Lemons': Quality Uncertainty and the Market Mechanism," *Quarterly Journal of Economics*, 84, 488–500.

Fisher, F. M. (1989), "Games Economists Play," *Rand Journal of Economics*, 20, 113–124.

Milgrom, P. R. and J. Roberts (1982), "Predation, Reputation and Entry Deterrence," *Journal of Economic Theory*, 27, 280–312.

Spence, A. M. (1973), "Job Market Signalling," *Quarterly Journal of Economics*, 87, 355–374.

CHAPTER 8

Agglomeration and Market Interaction
Masahisa Fujita and Jacques-François Thisse

1. INTRODUCTION

The most salient feature of the spatial economy is *the presence of a large variety of economic agglomerations*. Our purpose is to review some of the main explanations of this universal phenomenon, as they are proposed in urban economics and modern economic geography. Because of space constraints, we restrict ourselves to the most recent contributions, referring the reader to our forthcoming book for a more complete description of the state of the art.

Although using agglomeration as a generic term is convenient at a certain level of abstraction, it should be clear that the concept of economic agglomeration refers to very distinct real-world situations. At one extreme lies the core-periphery structure corresponding to North-South dualism. For example, Hall and Jones (1999) observe that high-income nations are clustered in small industrial cores in the Northern Hemisphere, whereas productivity per capita steadily declines with distance from these cores.

As noted by many historians and development analysts, economic growth tends to be localized. This is especially well illustrated by the rapid growth of East Asia during the last few decades. We view East Asia as comprising Japan and nine other countries, that is, Republic of Korea, Taiwan, Hong Kong, Singapore, Philippines, Thailand, Malaysia, Indonesia, and China. In 1990, the total population of East Asia was approximately 1.6 billion. With only 3.5 percent of the total area and 7.9 percent of the total population, Japan accounted for 72 percent of the gross domestic product (GDP) and 67 percent of the manufacturing GDP of East Asia. In Japan itself, the economy is very much dominated by its core regions formed by the five prefectures containing the three major metropolitan areas of Japan: Tokyo and Kanagawa prefectures, Aichi prefecture (containing Nagoya MA), and Osaka and Hyogo prefectures. These regions account for only 5.2 percent of the area of Japan, but for 33 percent of its population, 40 percent of its GDP, and 31 percent of its manufacturing employment. Hence, for the whole of East Asia, the Japanese core regions with a mere 0.18 percent of the total area accounted for 29 percent of East Asia's GDP.

Strong regional disparities within the same country imply the existence of agglomerations at another spatial scale. For example, in Korea, the capital region (Seoul and Kyungki Province), which has an area corresponding to 11.8 percent of the country and 45.3 percent of the population, produces 46.2 percent of the GDP. In France, the contrast is even greater: the Ile-de-France (the metropolitan area of Paris), which accounts for 2.2 percent of the area of the country and 18.9 percent of its population, produces 30 percent of its GDP. Inside the Ile-de-France, only 12 percent of the available land is used for housing, plants, and roads, with the remaining land being devoted to agricultural, forestry, or natural activities.

Regional agglomeration is also reflected in large varieties of cities, as shown by the stability of the urban hierarchy within most countries. Cities themselves may be specialized in a very small number of industries, as are many medium-sized American cities. However, large metropolises like Paris, New York, or Tokyo are highly diversified in that they nest a large variety of industries, which are not related through direct linkages. Industrial districts involving firms with strong technological and/or informational linkages (e.g., the Silicon Valley or Italian districts engaged in more traditional activities), as well as factory towns (e.g., Toyota City), manifest various types of local specialization. Therefore, it appears that highly diverse size/activity arrangements exist at the regional and urban levels.

Although the sources are dispersed, not always trustworthy, and hardly comparable, data clearly converge to show the existence of an urban revolution. In Europe, the proportion of the population living in cities increased very slowly from 10 percent in 1300 to 12 percent in 1800. It was approximately 20 percent in 1850, 38 percent in 1900, 52 percent in 1950, and is close to 75 percent nowadays, thus showing an explosive growth in the urban population. In the United States, the rate of urbanization increased from 5 percent in 1800 to more than 60 percent in 1950 and is now near 77 percent. In Japan, the rate of urbanization was about 15 percent in 1800, 50 percent in 1950, and is now about 78 percent. The proportion of the urban population in the world increased from 30 percent in 1950 to 45 percent in 1995 and should exceed 50 percent in 2005. Furthermore, concentration in very big cities keeps rising. In 1950, only two cities had populations above 10 million: New York and Greater London. In 1995, 15 cities belonged to this category. The largest one, Tokyo, with more than 26 million, exceeds the second one, New York, by 10 million. In 2025, 26 megacities will exceed 10 million.

Economists must explain *why firms and households concentrate in large metropolitan areas*, whereas empirical evidence suggests that the cost of living in such areas is typically higher than in smaller urban areas (Richardson, 1987). Or, as Lucas (1988, p. 39) put it in a neat way: "What can people be paying Manhattan or downtown Chicago rents for, if not for being near other people?" But Lucas did not explain why people want, or need, to be near other people.

The increasing availability of high-speed transportation infrastructure and the fast-growing development of new informational technologies might suggest that our economies enter an age that would culminate in the "death of distance." If so, locational difference would gradually fade because agglomeration forces would be vanishing. In other words, cities would become a thing of the past. Matters are not that simple, however, because the opposite trend may as well happen.[1] Indeed, one of the general principles that will come out from our analysis is that the relationship between the decrease in transport costs and the degree of agglomeration of economic activities is not that expected by many analysts: *agglomeration happens provided that transport costs are below some critical threshold*, although further decreases may yield dispersion of some activities due to factor price differentials.[2] In addition, technological progress brings about new types of innovative activities that benefit most from being agglomerated and, therefore, tend to arise in developed areas (Audretsch and Feldman, 1996). Consequently, the wealth or poverty of people seems to be more and more related to the existence of prosperous and competitive clusters of specific industries, as well as to the presence of large and diversified metropolitan areas.

The recent attitude taken in several institutional bodies and media seems to support this view. For example, in its *Entering the 21st Century: World Development Report 1999/2000*, the World Bank stresses the importance of economic agglomerations and cities for boosting growth and escaping from the poverty trap. Another example of this increasing awareness of the relevance of cities in modern economies can be found in *The Economist* (1995, p. 18):

> The liberalization of world trade and the influence of regional trading groups such as NAFTA and the EU will not only reduce the powers of national governments, but also increase those of cities. This is because an open trading system will have the effect of making national economies converge, thus evening out the competitive advantage of countries, while leaving those of cities largely untouched. So in the future, the arenas in which companies will compete may be cities rather than countries.

The remainder of this paper is organized as follows. In Section 2, we show why the competitive framework can hardly be the foundation for the economics of agglomeration. We then briefly review the alternative modeling strategies. In the hope to make our paper accessible to a broad audience, Section 3 presents in detail the two (specific) models that have been used so far to study the spatial distribution of economic activities. Several extensions of these models

---

[1] For example, recent studies show that, in the United States, 86 percent of net delivery capacity is concentrated in the 20 largest cities. This suggests that the United States is quickly becoming a country of digital haves and have-nots, with many small businesses unable to compete, and minority neighborhoods and rural areas getting left out.

[2] Transportation (or transfer) costs are broadly defined to include all the factors that drive a wedge between prices at different locations, such as shipping costs per se, tariff and nontariff barriers to trade, different product standards, difficulty of communication, and cultural differences.

are discussed in Section 4. Section 5 concludes with some suggestions for further research and policy implications.

2. MODELING STRATEGIES OF ECONOMIC AGGLOMERATIONS

As a start, it is natural to ask the following question: to what extent is the competitive paradigm useful in understanding the main features of the economic landscape? The general competitive equilibrium model is indeed the benchmark used by economists when they want to study the market properties of an economic issue. Before proceeding, we should remind the reader that the essence of this model is that all trades are impersonal: when making their production or consumption decisions, economic agents need to know the price system only, which they take as given. At a competitive equilibrium, prices provide firms and consumers with all the information they must know to maximize their profit and their utility.

The most elegant and general model of a competitive economy is undoubtedly that developed by Arrow and Debreu. In this model, a commodity is defined not only by its physical characteristics, but also by the place it is made available. This implies that the same good traded at different places is treated as different economic commodities. Within this framework, choosing a location is part of choosing commodities. This approach integrates spatial interdependence of markets into general equilibrium in the same way as other forms of interdependence. Thus, the Arrow–Debreu model seems to obviate the need for a theory specific to the spatial context.

Unfortunately, as will be seen later, *the competitive model cannot generate economic agglomerations without assuming strong spatial inhomogeneities.* More precisely, we follow Starrett (1978) and show that introducing a homogeneous space (in a sense that will be made precise below) in the Arrow–Debreu model implies that *total transport costs in the economy must be zero at any spatial competitive equilibrium*, and thus trade and cities cannot arise in equilibrium. In other words, the competitive model per se cannot be used as the foundation for the study of a spatial economy because we are interested in identifying purely economic mechanisms leading agents to agglomerate in a featureless plain.[3] This is because we concur with Hoover (1948, p. 3) for whom:

> Even in the absence of any initial differentiation at all, *i.e.*, if natural resources were distributed uniformly over the globe, patterns of specialization and concentration of activities would inevitably appear in response to economic, social, and political principles.

---

[3] Ellickson and Zame (1994) disagree with this claim and argue that the introduction of moving costs in a dynamic setting may be sufficient to save the competitive paradigm. To the best of our knowledge, however, the implications of their approach have not yet been fully worked out.

2.1.   Breakdown of the Competitive Price Mechanism in a Homogeneous Spatial Economy

The economy is formed by agents (firms and households) and by commodities (goods and services). A firm is characterized by a set of production plans, with each production plan describing a possible input–output relation. A household is identified by a relation of preference, by a bundle of initial resources, and by shares in firms' profits. A competitive equilibrium is then described by a price system (one price per commodity), a production plan for each firm, and a consumption bundle for each household that satisfies the following conditions: at the prevailing prices (i) supply equals demand for each commodity; (ii) each firm maximizes its profit subject to its production set; and (iii) each household maximizes her utility under her budget constraint defined by the value of her initial endowment and her shares in firms' profits. In other words, all markets clear while each agent chooses her most preferred action at the equilibrium prices.

Space involves a finite number of locations. Transportation within each location is costless, but shipping goods from one location to another requires the use of resources. Without loss of generality, transportation between any two locations is performed by a profit-maximizing carrier who purchases goods in a location at the market prices prevailing in this location and sells them in the other location at the corresponding market prices, while using goods and land in each location as inputs.

A typical firm produces in a small number of places. Likewise, a household has a very small number of residences. For simplicity, we therefore assume that each firm (each household) chooses a single location and engages in production (consumption) activities there. However, firms and households are free to choose any location they want (the industry is footloose). For expositional convenience, we distinguish explicitly prices and goods by their location. Given this convention, space is said to be *homogeneous* when (i) the utility function and the consumption set are the same regardless of the location in which the household resides, and (ii) the production set of a firm is independent of the location elected by this firm. In other words, consumers and producers have no intrinsic preferences for one location over others. In this context, the following unsuspected result, which we call the *Spatial Impossibility Theorem*, has been proven by Starrett (1978).

Theorem 2.1. *Consider an economy with a finite number of agents and locations. If space is homogeneous, transport is costly, and preferences are locally nonsatiated, then there is no competitive equilibrium involving transportation.*

What does it mean? If economic activities are perfectly divisible, a competitive equilibrium exists and is such that each location operates as an autarky. For example, when households are identical, locations have the same relative prices and the same production structure (backyard capitalism). This is hardly a surprising outcome because, by assumption, there is no reason for economic agents to distinguish among locations and each activity can operate at an arbitrarily small level. Firms and households thus succeed in reducing transport costs at their absolute minimum, namely zero.

However, as observed by Starrett (1978, p. 27), when economic activities are *not* perfectly divisible, the transport of some goods between some places becomes unavoidable:

> ... as long as there are some indivisibilities in the system (so that individual operations must take up space) then a sufficiently complicated set of interrelated activities will generate transport costs (Starrett 1978, p. 27).

In this case, the Spatial Impossibility Theorem tells us that no competitive equilibrium exists.

This is clearly a surprising result that requires more explanations. For simplicity, we restrict ourselves to the case of two locations, A and B. When both locations are not in autarky, one should keep in mind that the price system must do two different jobs simultaneously: (i) *to support trade between locations* (while clearing the markets in each location) and (ii) *to prevent firms and households from relocating*. The Spatial Impossibility Theorem says that, in the case of a homogeneous space, it is impossible to hit two birds with one stone: the price gradients supporting trade bear wrong signals from the viewpoint of locational stability. Indeed, if a set of goods is exported from A to B, then the associated positive price gradients induce producers located in A (who seek a higher revenue) to relocate in B, whereas location B's buyers (who seek lower prices) want to relocate in A. Likewise, the export of another set of goods from B to A encourages such "cross-relocation." The land rent differential between the two locations can discourage the relocation in one direction only. Hence, as long as trade occurs at positive costs, some agents always want to relocate.

To ascertain the fundamental cause for this nonexistence, it is helpful to illustrate the difficulty encountered by using a standard diagram approach. Depicting the whole trade pattern between two locations would require a diagram with six dimensions (two tradable goods and land at each location), which is a task beyond our capability. Thus, we focus on a two-dimensional subspace of the whole pattern by considering the production of good i only, which is traded between A and B, while keeping the other elements fixed. Because the same physical good available at two distinct locations corresponds to two different commodities, this is equivalent to studying the production possibility frontier between two different economic goods.

Suppose that, at most, one unit of good i is produced by one firm at either location using a fixed bundle of inputs. For simplicity, the cost of these inputs is assumed to be the same in both locations. The good is shipped according to an iceberg technology: when x_i units of the good are moved between A and B, only a fraction x_i / Υ arrives at its destination, with $\Upsilon > 1$, whereas the rest melts away en route (Samuelson, 1983). In this context, if the firm is located in

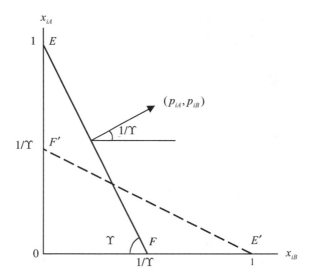

Figure 8.1. The set of feasible allocations in a homogeneous space.

A, then the output is represented by point E on the vertical axis in Figure 8.1; if the entire output is shipped to B, then the fraction $1/\Upsilon$ arrives at B, which is denoted by point F on the horizontal axis. Hence, when the firm is at A, the set of feasible allocations of the output between the two locations is given by the triangle OEF. Space being homogeneous, if the firm locates at B, the set of feasible allocations between the two places is now given by the triangle $OE'F'$. Hence, when the firm is not located, the set of feasible allocations is given by the union of the two triangles. Let the firm be set up at A and assume that the demand conditions are such that good i is consumed in both locations so that trade occurs. Then, to support any feasible trade pattern, represented by an interior point of the segment EF, the price vector (p_{iA}, p_{iB}) must be such that $p_{iA}/p_{iB} = 1/\Upsilon$, as shown in Figure 8.1. However, under these prices, it is clear that the firm can obtain a strictly higher profit by locating in B and choosing the production plan E' in Figure 8.1. This implies that there is no competitive price system that can support both the existence of trade and a profit-maximizing location for the firm.

This difficulty arises from the nonconvexity of the set of feasible allocations. If transportation was costless, the set of feasible allocations would be given by the triangle OEE' in Figure 8.1, which is convex. In this case, the firm would face no incentive to relocate. Similarly, if the firm's production activity was perfectly divisible, this set would again be equal to the triangle OEE', and no difficulty would arise.

Therefore, even though the individual land consumption is endogenous, we may conclude that *the fundamental reason for the Spatial Impossibility Theorem is the nonconvexity of the set of feasible allocations caused by the existence of positive transport costs and the fact that agents have an address in space.*

Some remarks are still in order. First, we have assumed that each firm locates in a single region. The theorem could be generalized to permit firms to run distinct plants, one plant per location because each plant amounts to a separate firm in the competitive setting (Koopmans, 1957). Second, we have considered a closed economy. The theorem can be readily extended to allow for trade with the rest of the world provided that each location has the same access to the world markets to satisfy the assumption of a homogeneous space. Third, the size of the economy is immaterial for the Spatial Impossibility Theorem to hold in that assuming a "large economy," in which competitive equilibria often emerge as the outcome generated by several institutional mechanisms, does not affect the result because the value of total transport costs within the economy rises when agents are replicated. Last, the following result sheds extra light on the meaning of the Spatial Impossibility Theorem (Fujita and Thisse, 2002).

Corollary 2.2. *If there exists a competitive equilibrium in a spatial economy with a homogeneous space, then the land rent must be the same in all locations.*

This result has the following fundamental implication for us: *in a homogeneous space, the competitive price mechanism is unable to explain why the land rent is higher in an economic agglomeration* (such as a city, a central business district, or an industrial cluster) *than in the surrounding area*. This clearly shows the limits of the competitive paradigm for studying the agglomeration of firms and households.

2.2.   What Are the Alternative Modeling Strategies?

Thus, if we want to understand something about the spatial distribution of economic activities and, in particular, the formation of major economic agglomerations as well as regional specialization and trade, the Spatial Impossibility Theorem tells us that we must make at least one of the following three assumptions:

   (i) space is heterogeneous (as in the neoclassical theory of international trade)
  (ii) externalities in production and consumption exist (as in urban economic)
 (iii) markets are imperfectly competitive (as in the so-called "new" economic geography).

Of course, in reality, economic spaces are the outcome of different combinations of these three agglomeration forces. However, it is convenient here to distinguish them to figure out what are the effects of each one of them.

   A. Comparative advantage models. The heterogeneity of space introduces the uneven distribution of immobile resources (such as mineral deposits or some production factors) and amenities

Indeed, being negligible to the market, each firm behaves as a monopolist on her residual demand, which makes it indifferent between using price or quantity as a strategy.

3.1.   The Framework

We consider a $2 \times 2 \times 2$ setting. The economic space is made of two regions (A and B). The economy has two sectors, the modern sector ($\mathbb{M}$) and the traditional sector ($\mathbb{T}$). There are two production factors, the high-skilled workers (H) and the low-skilled workers (L). The $\mathbb{M}$-sector produces a continuum of varieties of a horizontally differentiated product under increasing returns, using H as the only input. The $\mathbb{T}$-sector produces a homogeneous good under constant returns, using unskilled labor L as the only input.

The economy is endowed with L unskilled workers and with H skilled workers (labor dualism). The skilled workers are perfectly mobile between regions, whereas the unskilled workers are immobile. This extreme assumption is justified because the skilled are more mobile than the unskilled over long distances (SOPEMI 1998). Finally, the unskilled workers are equally distributed between the two regions, and thus regions are a priori symmetric.

The technology in the $\mathbb{T}$-sector is such that one unit of output requires one unit of L. The output of the $\mathbb{T}$-sector is costlessly traded between any two regions and is chosen as the numéraire so that $p^{\mathbb{T}} = 1$. Hence, the wage of the unskilled workers is also equal to 1 in both regions. Each variety of the $\mathbb{M}$-sector is produced according to the same technology such that the production of the quantity $q(i)$ requires $l(i)$ units of skilled labor given by

$$l(i) = f + cq(i), \tag{3.1}$$

in which f and c are, respectively, the fixed and marginal labor requirements. Because there are increasing returns but no scope economies, each variety is produced by a single firm. This is because, due to the consumers' preference for variety, any firm obtains a higher share of the market by producing a differentiated variety than by replicating an existing one.

The market equilibrium is the outcome of the interplay between a dispersion force and an agglomeration force. The centrifugal force is very simple. It lies in two sources: (i) the spatial immobility of the unskilled whose demands for the manufactured good are to be met and (ii) the fiercer competition that arises when firms locate back to back (d'Aspremont, Gabszewicz, and Thisse, 1979). The centripetal force is more involved. If a larger number of firms is located in one region, the number of varieties locally produced is also larger. This in turn induces some skilled living in the smaller region to move toward the larger region in which they may enjoy a higher standard of living. The resulting increase in the numbers of consumers creates a larger demand for the differentiated good which, therefore, leads additional firms to locate in this region. This implies the availability of more varieties in the region in question, but less in the others because there are scale economies at the firm's level. Consequently, as noted by

Krugman (1991a, p. 486), there is *circular causation* in the manner of Myrdal, because these two effects reinforce each other: "manufactures production will tend to concentrate where there is a large market, but the market will be large where manufactures production is concentrated."

Let λ be the fraction of skilled residing in region A and denote by $v_r(\lambda)$ the indirect utility a skilled worker enjoys in region $r = A, B$ when the spatial distribution of skilled is $(\lambda, 1 - \lambda)$. A *spatial equilibrium* arises at $\lambda \in (0, 1)$ when

$$\Delta v(\lambda) \equiv v_A(\lambda) - v_B(\lambda) = 0,$$

at $\lambda = 0$ when $\Delta v(0) \leq 0$, or at $\lambda = 1$ when $\Delta v(1) \geq 0$. Such an equilibrium always exists when $v_r(\lambda)$ is a continuous function of λ. However, this equilibrium is not necessarily unique. Stability is then used to eliminate some of them. The stability of such an equilibrium is studied with respect to the following equation of motion:[5]

$$\dot{\lambda} = \lambda \Delta v(\lambda)(1 - \lambda). \tag{3.2}$$

If $\Delta v(\lambda)$ is positive and $\lambda \in (0, 1)$, workers move from B to A; if it is negative, they go in the opposite direction. Clearly, any spatial equilibrium is such that $\dot{\lambda} = 0$. A spatial equilibrium is *stable* if, for any marginal deviation of the population distribution from the equilibrium, the equation of motion brings the distribution of skilled workers back to the original one.[6] We assume that local labor markets adjust instantaneously when some skilled workers move from one region to the other. More precisely, the number of firms in each region must be such that the labor market-clearing conditions (3.12) and (3.22) remain valid for the new distribution of workers. Wages are then adjusted in each region for each firm to earn zero profits in any region having skilled workers, because the skilled move according to the utility differential.

3.2. A Model with CES Utility and Iceberg Transport Costs

Although consumption takes place in a specific region, it is notationally convenient to describe preferences without explicitly referring to any particular region. Preferences are identical across all workers and described by a Cobb–Douglas utility:

$$u = Q^\mu T^{1-\mu}/\mu^\mu (1 - \mu)^{1-\mu}, \qquad 0 < \mu < 1, \tag{3.3}$$

---

[5] This dynamic implies that the equilibrium is reached for $t \to \infty$. One could alternately use the dynamic system proposed by Tabuchi (1986) in which the corner solutions $\lambda = 0$ and $\lambda = 1$ are reached within finite times. The difference becomes critical when the economy exhibits different equilibrium patterns over time.

[6] Note that (3.2) provides one more justification for working with a continuum of agents: this modeling strategy allows one to respect the integer nature of an agent's location (her address) while describing the evolution of the regional share of production by means of a differential equation.

where Q stands for an index of the consumption of the modern sector varieties, and T is the consumption of the output of the traditional sector. Because the modern sector provides a continuum of varieties of size M, the index Q is given by

$$Q = \left[\int_0^M q(i)^\rho di \right]^{1/\rho} \qquad 0 < \rho < 1, \qquad (3.4)$$

where $q(i)$ represents the consumption of variety $i \in [0, M]$. Hence, each consumer displays a *preference for variety*. In (3.4), the parameter ρ stands for the inverse of the intensity of love for variety over the differentiated product. When ρ is close to 1, varieties are close to perfect substitutes; when ρ decreases, the desire to spread consumption over all varieties increases. If $\sigma \equiv 1/(1 - \rho)$, then σ is the elasticity of substitution between any two varieties. Because there is a continuum of firms, each firm is negligible and the interactions between any two firms are zero, but aggregate market conditions of some kind (e.g., the average price across firms) affect any single firm. This provides a setting in which firms are not competitive (in the classic economic sense of having infinite demand elasticity), but at the same time they have no strategic interactions with one another [see (3.5)].

If y denotes the consumer income and $p(i)$ the price of variety i, then the demand functions are

$$q(i) = \mu y p(i)^{-\sigma} P^{\sigma-1} \qquad i \in [0, M], \qquad (3.5)$$

where P is the price index of the differentiated product given by

$$P \equiv \left[\int_0^M p(i)^{-(\sigma-1)} di \right]^{-1/(\sigma-1)}. \qquad (3.6)$$

The corresponding indirect utility function is

$$v = y P^{-\mu}. \qquad (3.7)$$

Without loss of generality, we choose the unit of skilled labor such that $c = 1$ in (3.1). The output of the $\mathbb{M}$-sector is shipped at a positive cost according to the "iceberg" technology: When one unit of the differentiated product is moved from region r to region s, only a fraction $1/\Upsilon$ arrives at its destination with $\Upsilon > 1$. Because mill and discriminatory pricing can be shown to be equivalent in the present setting, we may use the mill pricing interpretation in what follows. When variety i is sold in region r at the mill price $p_r(i)$, the price $p_{rs}(i)$ paid by a consumer located in region s ($\neq r$) is

$$p_{rs}(i) = p_r(i)\Upsilon.$$

If the distribution of firms is (M_r, M_s), using (3.6) the price index P_r in region r

is then given by

$$P_r = \left\{ \int_0^{M_r} p_r(i)^{-(\sigma-1)}di + \Upsilon^{-(\sigma-1)} \int_0^{M_s} p_s(i)^{-(\sigma-1)}di \right\}^{-1/(\sigma-1)},$$

(3.8)

which clearly depends on the spatial distribution of firms, as well as the level of transport costs.

Let w_r denote the wage rate of a skilled worker living in region r. Because there is free entry and exit and, therefore, zero profit in equilibrium, the income of region r is

$$Y_r = \lambda_r H w_r + L/2 \qquad r = A, B,$$

(3.9)

where λ_r is the share of skilled workers residing in region r.

Using (3.5), the total demand of the firm producing variety i and located in region r is

$$q_r(i) = \mu p_r(i)^{-\sigma} Y_r (P_r)^{\sigma-1} + \mu p_r(i)^{-\sigma} Y_s \Upsilon^{-(\sigma-1)} (P_s)^{\sigma-1}.$$

(3.10)

Because each firm has a negligible impact on the market, it may accurately neglect the impact of a price change over consumers' income (Y_r) and other firms' prices, hence on the regional price indexes (P_r). Consequently, (3.10) implies that, regardless of the spatial distribution of consumers, each firm faces an isoelastic demand. This very convenient property depends crucially on the assumption of an iceberg transport cost, which affects here the level of demand but not its elasticity.

The profit function of a firm in r is

$$\pi_r(i) = [p_r(i) - w_r]q_r(i) - w_r f.$$

Because varieties are equally weighted in the utility function, the equilibrium price is the same across all firms located in region r. Solving the first-order condition yields the common equilibrium price

$$p_r^* = \frac{w_r}{\rho}.$$

(3.11)

Substituting p_r^* into $\pi_r(i)$ leads to

$$\pi_r = \frac{w_r}{\sigma - 1}[q_r - (\sigma - 1)f].$$

Under free entry, profits are zero so that the equilibrium output of a firm is given by $q_r^* = (\sigma - 1)f$, which is independent of the spatial distribution of demand. As a result, in equilibrium, a firm's labor requirement is a constant given by $l^* = \sigma f$, and thus the total number of firms in the $\mathbb{M}$-sector is equal to $H/\sigma f$. The corresponding distribution of firms

$$M_r = \lambda_r H/\sigma f \qquad r = A, B$$

(3.12)

depends only on the distribution of the skilled workers. Hence, the model allows for studying the spatial distribution of the modern sector but not for its size.

Introducing the equilibrium prices (3.11) and substituting (3.12) for M_r in the regional price index (3.8) gives

$$P_r = \kappa_1 \big[\lambda_r w_r^{-(\sigma-1)} + \lambda_s (w_s \Upsilon)^{-(\sigma-1)} \big]^{-1/(\sigma-1)}, \tag{3.13}$$

where κ_1 is a positive constant.

Finally, we consider the labor market-clearing conditions for a given distribution of workers. The wage prevailing in region r is the highest wage that firms located there can pay under the nonnegative profit constraint. For that, we evaluate the demand (3.10) as a function of the wage through the equilibrium price (3.11):

$$q_r(w_r) = \mu (w_r/\rho)^{-\sigma} \left(Y_r P_r^{\sigma-1} + Y_s \Upsilon^{-(\sigma-1)} P_s^{\sigma-1} \right).$$

Because this expression is equal to $(\sigma - 1)f$ when profits are zero, we obtain the following implicit expression for the zero-profit wages:

$$w_r^* = \kappa_2 \big(Y_r P_r^{\sigma-1} + Y_s \Upsilon^{-(\sigma-1)} P_s^{\sigma-1} \big)^{1/\sigma}, \tag{3.14}$$

where κ_2 is a positive constant. Clearly, w_r^* is the *equilibrium wage* in region r when $\lambda_r > 0$. Substituting (3.9) for Y_r in the indirect utility (3.7), we obtain the *real wage* as follows:

$$v_r = \omega_r = \frac{w_r^*}{P_r^\mu} \qquad r = A, B. \tag{3.15}$$

Finally, the Walras law implies that the traditional sector market is in equilibrium provided that the equilibrium conditions noted previously are satisfied.

Summarizing the foregoing developments, the basic equations for our economy are given by (3.9), (3.13), (3.14), and (3.15). From now on, set $\lambda_A = \lambda$ and $\lambda_B = (1 - \lambda)$.

3.2.1.   The Core-Periphery Structure

Suppose that the modern sector is concentrated in one region, say region A, so that $\lambda = 1$. We wish to determine conditions under which the real wage a skilled worker may obtain in region B does not exceed the real wage she gets in region A.

Setting $\lambda = 1$ in (3.9), (3.13), (3.14), and (3.15), we get

$$\frac{\omega_B}{\omega_A} = \left(\frac{1+\mu}{2} \Upsilon^{-\sigma(\mu+\rho)} + \frac{1-\mu}{2} \Upsilon^{-\sigma(\mu-\rho)} \right)^{1/\sigma}. \tag{3.16}$$

The first term in the right-hand side of (3.16) is always decreasing in Υ. Therefore, if $\mu \geq \rho$, the second term is also decreasing so that the ratio ω_B/ω_A always decreases with Υ, thus implying that $\omega_B < \omega_A$ for all $\Upsilon > 1$. This

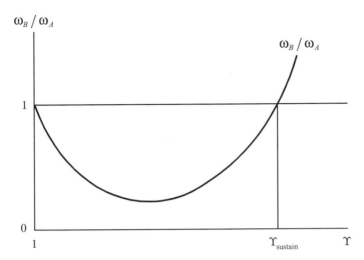

Figure 8.2. Determination of the sustain point.

means that the core-periphery structure is a stable equilibrium for all $\Upsilon > 1$. When

$$\mu \geq \rho, \tag{3.17}$$

varieties are so differentiated that firms' demands are not very sensitive to differences in transportation costs, thus making the agglomeration force very strong.

More interesting is the case in which

$$\mu < \rho; \tag{3.18}$$

that is, varieties are not very differentiated so that firms' demands are sufficiently elastic for the agglomeration force to be weak. If (3.18) holds, $\Upsilon^{-\mu\sigma+\sigma-1}$ goes to infinity when $\Upsilon \to \infty$ and the ratio ω_B/ω_A is as depicted in Figure 8.2.

In this case, there exists a single value $\Upsilon_{\text{sustain}} > 1$ such that $\omega_B/\omega_A = 1$. Hence, the agglomeration is a stable equilibrium for any $\Upsilon \leq \Upsilon_{\text{sustain}}$. This occurs because firms can enjoy all the benefits of agglomeration without losing much of their business in the other region. Such a point is called the *sustain point* because, once firms are fully agglomerated, they stay so for all smaller values of Υ. On the other hand, when transportation costs are sufficiently high ($\Upsilon > \Upsilon_{\text{sustain}}$), firms lose much on their exports, and thus the core-periphery structure is no longer an equilibrium.

Summarizing this discussion, we obtain:

Proposition 3.1. *Consider a two-region economy.*

  (i) *If $\mu \geq \rho$, then the core-periphery structure is always a stable equilibrium.*

(ii) If $\mu < \rho$, then there exists a unique solution $\Upsilon_{\text{sustain}} > 1$ to the equation

$$\frac{1+\mu}{2}\Upsilon^{-\sigma(\mu+\rho)} + \frac{1-\mu}{2}\Upsilon^{-\sigma(\mu-\rho)} = 1,$$

such that the core-periphery structure is a stable equilibrium for any $\Upsilon \leq \Upsilon_{\text{sustain}}$.

Interestingly, this proposition provides formal support to the claim made by Kaldor (1970, p. 241) more than 30 years ago:

> When trade is opened up between them, the region with the more developed industry will be able to supply the need of the agricultural area of the other region on more favourable terms: with the result that the industrial centre of the second region will lose its market and will tend to be eliminated.

3.2.2. The Symmetric Structure

Proposition 3 suggests that the modern sector is geographically dispersed when transportation costs are high, at least when (3.18) holds. To check this, we consider the symmetric configuration ($\lambda = 1/2$). In this case, for a given Υ, the symmetric equilibrium is stable (unstable) if the slope of $\Delta\omega(\lambda)$ is negative (positive) at $\lambda = 1/2$. Checking this condition requires fairly long calculations using all the equilibrium conditions. However, Fujita, Krugman, and Venables (1999) have shown the following results. First, when (3.18) does not hold, the symmetric equilibrium is always unstable. Second, when (3.18) holds, this equilibrium is stable (unstable) if Υ is larger (smaller) than some threshold value Υ_{break} given by

$$\Upsilon_{\text{break}} = \left[\frac{(\rho+\mu)(1+\mu)}{(\rho-\mu)(1-\mu)}\right]^{1/(\sigma-1)}, \tag{3.19}$$

which is clearly larger than one. This is called the *break point* because symmetry between the two regions is no longer a stable equilibrium for lower values of Υ. It is interesting to note that Υ_{break} depends on the same parameters as $\Upsilon_{\text{sustain}}$. It is immediate from (3.19) that Υ_{break} is increasing with the share of the modern sector (μ) and with the degree of product differentiation ($1/\rho$).

Because $\Upsilon_{\text{break}} < \Upsilon_{\text{sustain}}$ can be shown to hold,[7] there exists a domain of parameters over which there is multiplicity of equilibria, namely agglomeration and dispersion, as depicted in Figure 8.3. More precisely, when $\Upsilon > \Upsilon_{\text{sustain}}$, the economy necessarily involves dispersion. When $\Upsilon < \Upsilon_{\text{break}}$, agglomeration always arises, the winning region depending on the initial conditions. Finally, when $\Upsilon_{\text{break}} \leq \Upsilon \leq \Upsilon_{\text{sustain}}$, both agglomeration and dispersion are stable equilibria. In this domain, the economy displays some hysteresis because dispersion (agglomeration) still prevails when transport costs rise above the sustain point

---

[7] See Neary (2001) for a proof.

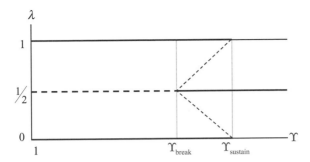

Figure 8.3. Bifurcation diagram for the core-periphery model.

(fall below the break point) while staying below the break point (above the sustain point).

Summarizing these results, when transportation costs are sufficiently low, all manufacturers are concentrated in a single region that becomes the core of the economy, whereas the other region, called the periphery, supplies only the traditional good. Firms in the modern sector are able to exploit increasing returns by selling more in the large market without losing much business in the small market. For exactly the opposite reason, the economy displays a symmetric regional pattern of production when transportation costs are large. Hence, this model allows for *the possibility of divergence between regions*, whereas the neoclassical model, based on constant returns and perfect competition in the two sectors, would predict symmetry only.

3.3.   A Linear Model of Core-Periphery

The conclusions derived in Section 3.2 are very important for the space economy. This is why it is crucial to know how they depend on the specificities of the framework used. The use of both the CES utility and iceberg cost leads to a convenient setting in which demands have a constant elasticity. However, such a result conflicts with research in spatial pricing theory in which demand elasticity is shown to vary with distance. Moreover, if using the iceberg cost is able to capture the fact that shipping is resource-consuming, such a modeling option implies that any increase in the mill price is accompanied by a proportional increase in transport cost, which seems unrealistic. Last, although models of the type considered in the foregoing are based on very specific assumptions, they are often beyond the reach of analytical resolution.

The setting considered here, which has been developed by Ottaviano, Tabuchi, and Thisse (2002), is very similar to that used in Section 3.2. However, there are two major differences. First, the output of the M-sector is traded at a cost of τ units of the numéraire per unit shipped between regions. This characteristic agrees more with reality, as well as with location theory, than the iceberg technology does. Second, preferences are given by a quasi-linear utility encapsulating a quadratic subutility instead of a Cobb–Douglas preference on the homogeneous and differentiated goods with CES subutility. These two specifications correspond to rather extreme cases: the former assumes an infinite elasticity of substitution between the differentiated product and the numéraire, the latter a unit elasticity. Moreover, firms' demands are linear and not isoelastic. Despite such major differences in settings, we will see that conclusions are qualitatively the same in the two models, thus suggesting that they hold for a whole class of models.

3.3.1.   A Model with Quadratic Utility and Linear Transport Costs

Preferences are identical across individuals and described by a quasi-linear utility with a quadratic subutility that is supposed to be symmetric in all varieties:

$$u(q_0; q(i), i \in [0, M]) = \alpha \int_0^M q(i)\,di - (\beta - \delta) \int_0^M [q(i)]^2\,di$$

$$- \delta \left[\int_0^M q(i)\,di \right]^2 + q_0, \tag{3.20}$$

where $q(i)$ is the quantity of variety $i \in [0, M]$ and q_0 the quantity of a homogeneous good chosen as the numéraire. The parameters in (3.20) are such that $\alpha > 0$ and $\beta > \delta > 0$. In this expression, α expresses the intensity of preferences for the differentiated product, whereas $\beta > \delta$ means that consumers' preferences exhibit love of variety. Finally, for a given value of β, the parameter δ expresses the substitutability between varieties: the higher δ, the closer substitutes the varieties.

Admittedly, a quasi-linear utility abstracts from general equilibrium income effects and gives the corresponding framework a fairly strong partial equilibrium flavor. However, it does not remove the interaction between product and labor markets, thus allowing us to develop a full-fledged model of agglomeration formation, independently of the relative size of the manufacturing sector.

Any individual is endowed with one unit of labor (of type H or L) and $\overline{q}_0 > 0$ units of the numéraire. Her budget constraint can then be written as follows:

$$\int_0^M p(i)q(i)\,di + q_0 = y + \overline{q}_0,$$

where y is the individual's labor income and $p(i)$ the price of variety i. The initial endowment $\overline{q}_0$ is supposed to be large enough for the residual consumption of the numéraire to be strictly positive for each individual. Hence, individual demand $q(i)$ for variety i is given by

$$q(i) = a - (b + dM)\,p(i) + dP, \tag{3.21}$$

where

$$P \equiv \int_0^M p(i)\,di,$$

which can be interpreted as the price index in the modern sector, whereas $a \equiv 2\alpha/[(\beta + (M-1)\delta]$, $b \equiv 1/[\beta + (M-1)\delta]$, and $d \equiv \delta/(\beta - \delta)[\beta + (M-1)\delta]$.

Finally, each variety can be traded at a positive cost of τ units of the numéraire for each unit transported from one region to the other, regardless of the variety. The technologies are the same as in Section 3.1, but, for simplicity, c is set equal to zero in (3.1).

Labor market clearing implies that the number of firms belonging to the $\mathbb{M}$-sector in region r is

$$M_r = \lambda_r H/f. \tag{3.22}$$

Consequently, the total number of firms in the economy is constant and equal to $M = H/f$.

Discriminatory and mill pricing are no longer equivalent in this model. In the sequel, we focus on discriminatory pricing, because this policy endows firms with flexibility in their price choice, something that could affect the process of agglomeration. This means that each firm sets a delivered price specific to each region. Hence, the profit function of a firm located in region r is as follows:

$$\pi_r = p_{rr}q_{rr}(p_{rr})(L/2 + \lambda_r H) + (p_{rs} - \tau)q_{rs}(p_{rs})(L/2 + \lambda_s H) - fw_r.$$

To illustrate the type of interaction that characterizes this model of monopolistic competition, we describe how the equilibrium prices are determined. Each firm i in region r maximizes its profit π_r, assuming accurately that its price choice has no impact on the regional price indices

$$P_r \equiv \int_0^{M_r} p_{rr}(i)di + \int_0^{M_s} p_{sr}(i)di \qquad s \neq r.$$

Because, by symmetry, the prices selected by the firms located within the same region are identical, the result is denoted by $p_{rr}^*(P_r)$ and $p_{rs}^*(P_s)$. Clearly, it must be that

$$M_r p_{rr}^*(P_r) + M_s p_{sr}^*(P_r) = P_r.$$

Given (3.22), it is then readily verified that the equilibrium prices are as follows:

$$p_{rr}^* = \frac{1}{2}\frac{2a + \tau d\lambda_s M}{2b + dM}, \tag{3.23}$$

$$p_{rs}^* = p_{ss} + \frac{\tau}{2}. \tag{3.24}$$

Clearly, these prices depend directly on the firms' distribution. In particular, p_{rr}^* decreases with the number of firms in region r and increases with the degree of product differentiation when τ is sufficiently small for the demands of the imported varieties to be positive. These results agree with what we know from standard models of product differentiation.

It is easy to check that the equilibrium operating profits earned in each market by a firm established in r are as follows:

$$\pi_{rr}^* = (b + dM)(p_{rr}^*)^2(L/2 + \lambda_r H),$$
$$\pi_{rs}^* = (b + dM)(p_{rs}^* - \tau)^2(L/2 + \lambda_s H).$$

Increasing λ_r has two opposite effects on π_{rr}^*. First, as λ_r rises, the equilibrium price (3.23) falls as well as the quantity of each variety bought by each consumer living in region r. However, the total population of consumers residing in this region is now larger so that the profits made by a firm located in r on local sales may increase. What is at work here is *a global demand effect due to the increase in the local population that may compensate firms for the adverse price effect, as well as for the decrease in each worker's individual demand.*

Entry and exit are free so that profits are zero in equilibrium. Hence, (3.22) implies that any change in the population of workers located in one region must be accompanied by a corresponding change in the number of firms. The equilibrium wage rates w_r^* of the skilled are obtained from the zero-profit condition evaluated at the equilibrium prices: $w_r^*(\lambda_r) = (\pi_{rr}^* + \pi_{rs}^*)/f$.

3.3.2. The Debate Agglomeration Vs. Dispersion Revisited

The indirect utility differential $\Delta v(\lambda)$ is obtained by plugging the equilibrium prices (3.23)–(3.24) and the equilibrium wages $w_r^*(\lambda)$ into the indirect utility associated with (3.20):

$$\Delta v(\lambda) \equiv v_A(\lambda) - v_B(\lambda) = C^*\tau(\tau^* - \tau)(\lambda - 1/2), \qquad (3.25)$$

where C^* is a positive constant and

$$\tau^* \equiv \frac{4af(3bf + 2dH)}{2bf(3bf + 3dH + dL) + d^2H(L + H)} > 0. \qquad (3.26)$$

It follows immediately from (3.25) that $\lambda = 1/2$ is always an equilibrium. Moreover, because $\Delta v(\lambda)$ is linear in λ and $C^* > 0$, for $\lambda \neq 1/2$ the indirect utility differential always has the same sign as $\lambda - 1/2$ if and only if $\tau < \tau^*$; if $\tau > \tau^*$, it has the opposite sign. In particular, *when there are no increasing returns in the manufacturing sector* ($f = 0$), the coefficient of $(\lambda - 1/2)$ is always negative because $\tau^* = 0$, and thus *dispersion is the only (stable) equilibrium*. This shows once more the importance of increasing returns for the possible emergence of an agglomeration.[8] The same holds for product differentiation, because τ^* becomes arbitrarily small when varieties become less and less differentiated ($d \to \infty$).

---

[8] Sonnenschein (1982) shows, a contrario, a related result: if the initial distribution of firms is uneven along a given circle, then the spatial adjustment of firms in the direction of higher profit leads the economy toward a uniform long-run equilibrium, each local economy being perfectly competitive.

It remains to determine when τ^* is sufficiently low for all demands to be positive at the equilibrium prices. This is so if and only if

$$L/H > \frac{6b^2 f^2 + 8bdf H + 3d^2 H^2}{dH(2bf + dH)}. \qquad (3.27)$$

The inequality (3.27) means that the population of unskilled is large relative to the population of skilled. When (3.27) does not hold, the coefficient of $(\lambda - 1/2)$ in (3.25) is always positive for all transport costs that allow for interregional trade. In this case, the advantages of having a large home market always dominate the disadvantages incurred while supplying a distant periphery. The condition (3.18) plays a role similar to (3.17).

More interesting is the case when (3.27) holds. Although the size of the industrial sector is captured here through the relative population size L/H and not through its share in consumption, the intuition is similar: the ratio L/H must be sufficiently large for the economy to display different types of equilibria according to the value of τ. This result does not depend on the expenditure share on the manufacturing sector because of the absence of general equilibrium income effects: small or large sectors in terms of expenditure share are agglomerated when τ is small enough.

Finally, stability is studied using (3.2). When $\tau > \tau^*$, it is straightforward to see that the symmetric configuration is the only stable equilibrium. In contrast, when $\tau < \tau^*$, the symmetric equilibrium becomes unstable and workers agglomerate in region r provided that the initial fraction of workers residing in this region exceeds $1/2$. In other words, agglomeration arises when the transport cost is low enough.

Proposition 3.2. *Consider a two-region economy with segmented markets.*

(i) *When (3.27) does not hold, the core-periphery structure is the only stable equilibrium under trade.*

(ii) *When (3.27) is satisfied, we have: for any $\tau > \tau^*$ the symmetric configuration is the only stable equilibrium with trade; for any $\tau < \tau^*$ the core-periphery pattern is the unique stable equilibrium; for $\tau = \tau^*$ any configuration is an equilibrium.*

Because (3.25) is linear in λ, the break point and the sustain point are the same, and thus history alone matters for the selection of the agglomerated outcome.

Looking at the threshold value τ^* as given by (3.26), we first observe that τ^* increases with the degree of product differentiation (d falls) when (3.27) holds. This is intuitively plausible because the agglomeration process is driven by the mobility of the skilled workers, whence their population must be sufficiently large for product differentiation to act as an agglomeration force. Second, higher fixed costs leads to a smaller number of firms/varieties. Still, it is readily verified that τ^* also increases when increasing returns become stronger (f rises) when

(3.27) holds. In other words, the agglomeration of the modern sector is more likely, the stronger are the increasing returns at the firm's level. Last, τ^* increases when the number of unskilled (L) decreases because the dispersion force is weaker.

Both models studied in this section yield similar results, suggesting that the core-periphery structure is robust against alternative specifications. Each model has its own merit. The former allows for income effects and the latter for a finer description of the role played by the key parameters of the economy. As will be seen later, both have been used in various extensions of the core-periphery model.

4.   FURTHER TOPICS IN ECONOMIC GEOGRAPHY

In this section, we present an abbreviated version of a few recent contributions. The interested reader will find the models at greater length in the corresponding references.

4.1.   On a ∩-Shaped Relationship Between Agglomeration and Transport Costs

The assumption of zero transport costs for the homogeneous good is not innocuous. Indeed, introducing positive transport costs for this good leads to some fundamental changes in the results presented previously. To permit trade of the traditional good even at the symmetric configuration, we assume that this good is differentiated too (e.g., oranges in A and apples in B). Thus, T as it appears in (3.3) is now given by

$$T = \left(T_A^\eta + T_B^\eta\right)^{1/\eta},$$

where $0 < \eta < 1$. The numéraire is given by the traditional good in one of the two regions. As shown by Fujita et al. (1999), the bifurcation diagram given in Figure 8.3 changes and is now as in Figure 8.4. To make things simple, we consider a fixed value for the transport costs of the traditional good and, as before, we concentrate on a decrease in the transport costs in the modern sector. When these costs are high, the symmetric configuration is the only equilibrium. Below some critical value, the core-periphery arises as before.

However, *further reductions in transport costs eventually lead to redispersion of the modern sector*. Indeed, the agglomeration of the modern sector within, say, region A generates large imports of the traditional good from region B. When transport costs in the modern sector become sufficiently low, the price indices of this good are about the same in the two regions. Then, the relative price of the traditional good in A rises because its transport cost remains unchanged. This in turn lowers region B's nominal wage, which guarantees the same utility level in both regions to the skilled. When the transport costs within the modern sector decrease sufficiently, the factor price differential becomes strong enough to induce firms to move away from A to B.

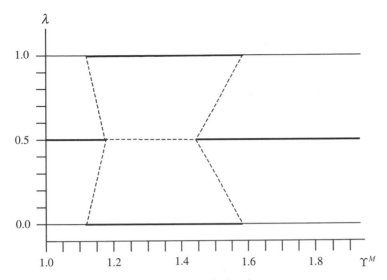

Figure 8.4. Bifurcation with positive agricultural transport costs.

Consequently, as transport costs in the modern sector keep decreasing from high to very low values, whereas transport costs in the traditional sector remain constant, the modern sector is first dispersed, then agglomerated, and redispersed, as seen in Figure 8.4. It is worth stressing that the reasons that lead to dispersion in the first and third phases are different: in the former, the modern sector is dispersed because the cost of shipping its output is high; in the latter, dispersion arises because the periphery develops some comparative advantage in terms of labor cost.

Although transport costs of both types of goods have declined since the beginning of the Industrial Revolution, what matters for the regional distribution of economic activities is not only the absolute levels of transport costs, but also their relative values across sectors (Kilkenny, 1998). For example, if both costs decrease proportionally, it can be shown that redispersion never occurs. This is not surprising because there is no force creating wage differential any more. However, if agricultural transport costs decrease at a lower pace than those of manufacturing goods, cheaper rural labor should eventually attract industrial firms, whereas the reversal in the relationship between transport costs has the opposite impact [see Fujita et al. (1999), Section 7.4 for more details].

The pattern dispersion/agglomeration/redispersion also arises as long as we consider any ingredient giving rise to factor price differentials in favor of the periphery. For example, if we assume that the agglomeration of the modern sector in one region generates higher urban costs, such as land rent and commuting costs, a sufficiently strong decrease in transport costs between regions will foster redispersion when firms located in the core region have to pay high wages to their workers. This occurs because workers must be compensated for the high urban costs associated with a large concentration of people within the same urban area (Helpman, 1998, Tabuchi, 1998, and Ottaviano et al., 2002). Another example is when all workers are immobile, whereas agglomeration of the industrial sector may arise because of technological linkages with the intermediate sector (more on this later). In this case, wage in the core region may become so high that redispersion is profitable for firms (Krugman and Venables, 1995 and Puga, 1999).

4.2.   Welfare Implications of the Core-Periphery Structure

We now wish to determine whether or not agglomeration is efficient. To this end, we assume that the planner is able (i) to assign any number of workers (or, equivalently, of firms) to a specific region and (ii) to use lump sum transfers from all workers to pay for the loss firms may incur while pricing at marginal cost. Because utilities are quasi-linear in the model of Section 3.3, a utilitarian approach may be used to evaluate the global level of welfare (Ottaviano and Thisse, 2002). Observe that no distortion arises in the total number of varieties because N is determined by the factor endowment (H) and technology (f) in the modern sector and is, therefore, the same at both the equilibrium and optimum outcomes.

Because the setting assumes transferable utility, the planner chooses λ to maximize the sum of individual indirect utilities $W(\lambda)$ (for both types of workers) in which all prices have been set equal to marginal cost. It can be shown that

$$W(\lambda) = C^o \tau (\tau^o - \tau)\lambda(\lambda - 1) + \text{constant}, \qquad (4.1)$$

where C^o is a positive constant and

$$\tau^o \equiv \frac{4af}{2bf + d(H + L)}.$$

The welfare function (4.1) is strictly concave in λ if $\tau > \tau^o$ and strictly convex if $\tau < \tau^o$. Furthermore, because the coefficients of λ^2 and of λ are the same (up to their sign), this expression always has an interior extremum at $\lambda = 1/2$. As a result, the optimal choice of the planner is determined by the sign of the coefficient of λ^2, that is, by the value of τ with respect to τ^o: if $\tau > \tau^o$, the symmetric configuration is the optimum; if $\tau < \tau^o$ any agglomerated configuration is the optimum; if $\tau = \tau^o$, the welfare level is independent of the spatial configuration.

In accordance with intuition, it is efficient to agglomerate the modern sector into a single region once transport costs are low, increasing returns are strong enough, and/or the output of this sector is sufficiently differentiated. On the other hand, the optimum is always dispersed when increasing returns vanish $(f = 0)$ and/or when varieties are close substitutes (d is large).

A simple calculation shows that $\tau^o < \tau^*$. This means that *the market yields an agglomerated configuration for a range* $(\tau^o < \tau < \tau^*)$ *of transport cost values for which it is efficient to have a dispersed pattern of activities.* In contrast, when transport costs are low $(\tau < \tau^o)$ or high $(\tau > \tau^*)$, no regional policy is required from the efficiency point of view, although equity considerations might justify such a policy when agglomeration arises. On the contrary, for intermediate values of transport costs ($\tau^o < \tau < \tau^*$), the market provides excessive agglomeration, thus justifying the need for an active regional policy to foster the dispersion of the modern sector on both the efficiency and equity grounds.[9]

This discrepancy may be explained as follows. First, workers do not internalize the negative external effects they impose on the unskilled who stay put, nor do they account for the impact of their migration decisions on the residents in their region of destination. Hence, even though the skilled have individual incentives to move, these incentives do not reflect the social value of their move. This explains why equilibrium and optimum do not necessarily coincide. Second, the individual demand elasticity is much lower at the optimum (marginal cost pricing) than at the equilibrium (Nash equilibrium pricing), and thus regional price indices are less sensitive to a decrease in τ. As a result, the fall in trade costs must be sufficiently large to make the agglomeration of workers socially desirable; this tells us why $\tau^o < \tau^*$.

4.3.   On the Impact of Forward-Looking Behavior

In the dynamics used in Section 3, workers care only about their current utility level. This is a fairly restrictive assumption to the extent that migration decisions are typically made on the grounds of current and future utility flows and costs (such as search, mismatch, and homesickness). In addition, this approach has been criticized because it is not consistent with fully rational forward-looking behavior. It is, therefore, important to determine if and how workers' expectations about the evolution of the economy may influence the process of agglomeration. In particular, we are interested in identifying the conditions under which, when initially the two regions host different numbers of skilled workers, the common belief that these workers will eventually agglomerate in the currently smaller region can reverse the historically inherited advantage of the larger region.

Formally, we want to determine the parameter conditions for which there exists an equilibrium path consistent with this belief, assuming that workers have perfect foresight (*self-fulfilling prophecy*). Somewhat different approaches have been proposed to tackle this problem, but they yield similar conclusions (Ottaviano, 1999, Baldwin, 2001, and Ottaviano et al., 2002). In what follows, we use the model of Section 3.3 because it leads to a linear dynamic system that allows for a detailed analysis of the main issues (Krugman, 1991b and Fukao and Bénabou, 1993).

Workers live indefinitely with a rate of time preference equal to $\gamma > 0$. Because we wish to focus on the sole dynamics of migration, we assume that

---

[9] Observe that the same qualitative results hold for a second-best analysis in which firms price at the Nash equilibrium while the planner controls their locations (Ottaviano and Thisse, 2002).

the consumption of the numéraire is positive for each point in time so that there is no intertemporal trade in the differentiated good. For concreteness, consider the case in which workers expect agglomeration to occur in region A, whereas region B is initially larger than A. Formally, we assume that there exists $T \geq 0$ such that, given $\lambda_0 < 1/2$,

$$\dot{\lambda}(t) > 0 \qquad t \in [0, T),$$
$$\lambda(t) = 1 \qquad t \geq T. \tag{4.2}$$

Because workers have perfect foresight, the easiest way to generate a non–bang-bang migration behavior is to assume that, when moving from one region to the other, workers incur a utility loss that depends on the rate of migration, perhaps because a migrant imposes a negative externality on the others. Specifically, we assume that the cost $CM(t)$ borne by a migrant at time t is proportional to the corresponding migration flow:

$$CM(t) \equiv \left| \frac{d\lambda(t)}{dt} \right| \bigg/ \delta, \tag{4.3}$$

where δ is a positive constant whose meaning is given herein.

For each region $r = A, B$, let us define

$$V_r(t) \equiv \int_t^T e^{-\gamma(s-t)} v_r(s)ds + e^{-\gamma(T-t)} v_A(T)/\gamma \qquad t \in [0, T), \tag{4.4}$$

where $v_r(s)$ is the instantaneous indirect utility at time s in region r. By definition, for $r = A$, $V_A(t)$ is the discounted sum of utility flows of a worker who moves from B to A at time t (i.e., today), whereas for $r = B$, $V_B(t)$ is that of a worker who currently resides in B and plans to move to A at time T. Because workers are free to choose when to immigrate, in equilibrium they must be indifferent about the time t at which they move. Hence, at any $t < T$, the following equality must hold:

$$V_A(t) - CM(t) = V_B(t) - e^{-r(T-t)} CM(T).$$

Furthermore, because no worker residing currently in B wishes to postpone his migration time beyond T, it must be that $CM(T) = 0$ (Fukao and Bénabou, 1993), and thus

$$V_A(t) - CM(t) = V_B(t) \qquad t \in [0, T).$$

Using (4.2) and (4.3), we then obtain

$$\frac{d\lambda}{dt} = \delta \Delta V \qquad t \in [0, T), \tag{4.5}$$

where $\Delta V \equiv (V_A - V_B)$, and δ can be interpreted as the speed of adjustment. This means that the private marginal cost of moving equals its private marginal benefit at any time $t < T$; of course, $\lambda(T) = 1$.

Using (4.4), we obtain the second law of motion by differentiating $V_A(t) - V_B(t)$, thus yielding

$$\frac{d\Delta V}{dt} = \gamma \Delta V - \Delta v \qquad t \in [0, T), \tag{4.6}$$

where $\Delta v \equiv v_A - v_B$ stands for the instantaneous indirect utility differential flow given by (3.25). The expression (4.6) states that the "annuity value" of being in A rather than in B (i.e., $\gamma \Delta V$) equals the "dividend" (Δv) plus the "capital gain" ($d\Delta V/dt$). As a result, because (3.25) is linear in λ, we obtain a system of two differential equations instead of one.

The system (4.5) and (4.6) always has a steady state at $(\lambda, \Delta V) = (1/2, 0)$ that corresponds to the symmetric configuration. When $\tau > \tau^*$, this steady state is globally stable. So, for the assumed belief (4.2) to be consistent with equilibrium, it must be $\tau < \tau^*$. Then, the study of the eigenvalues of the system (4.5) and (4.6) shows that two cases may arise. In the first one, when workers' migration costs are sufficiently large (δ is such that $\gamma > 2\sqrt{C\delta\tau(\tau^* - \tau)}$), the outcome of the migration dynamics is the same as the one described in Section 3.3. In other words, the equilibrium path is not consistent with (4.2), thus implying that expectations do not matter.

By contrast, when migration costs are small enough ($\gamma < 2\sqrt{C\delta\tau(\tau^* - \tau)}$), expectations may matter. More precisely, there exist two threshold values for the transport costs $\tau_1 < \tau^*/2 < \tau_2 < \tau^*$, as well as two boundary values $\lambda_1 < 1/2 < \lambda_2 < 1$ such that the equilibrium path is consistent with (4.2) if and only if $\tau \in (\tau_1, \tau_2)$ and $\lambda_0 \in [\lambda_1, \lambda_2]$. Namely, *as long as obstacles to trade take intermediate values and regions are not initially too different, the region that becomes the core is determined by workers' expectations*. This is more so either the lower the migration costs or the lower the discount rate.

4.4. The Impact of a Heterogeneous Labor Force

So far, workers have been assumed to be identical in terms of preferences. Although this assumption is fairly standard in economic modeling, it seems highly implausible that potentially mobile individuals will react in the same way to some "gap" between regions. First of all, it is well known that some people show a high degree of attachment to the region in which they were born. They will stay put even though they may guarantee to themselves higher living standards in other places. In the same spirit, lifetime considerations such as marriage, divorce, and the like play an important role in the decision to migrate. Second, regions are not similar and exhibit different natural and cultural features. Clearly, people value differently local amenities, and such differences in attitudes are known to affect the migration process.

These considerations are fundamental ingredients of the migration process and should be accounted for explicitly in workers' preferences. Even though the personal motivations may be quite diverse and, therefore, difficult to model at the individual level, it is possible to identify their aggregate impact on the

is, one may observe different outcomes from exactly the same fundamentals. The existence of multiple equilibria also helps us to understand high levels of variance of aggregates.

But, nonmarket interactions models do not just predict high levels of variance. When individuals can choose locations, the presence of these interactions often predicts segregation across space. Cities exist because of agglomeration economies that are likely to come from nonmarket complementarities.[3] Indeed, the selection of like types into the same neighborhoods is often what makes measuring social interactions quite difficult. In dynamic settings, social interactions can produce s-shaped curves that help to explain the observed time-series patterns of phenomena as disparate as telephones and women in the workplace.

The potential power of these models explains the explosion of work in this area over the past few years. In this paper, we explore the common mathematical structure of these models. Although there has been a great deal of work in this area, there has been less effort to understand the common elements between the disparate models. Instead of discussing the literature broadly, we will start with a particularly general social interactions model and examine the implications of this model. Several of the better-known models in this area can be seen as special cases of this more general model.

In this general model, the utility function includes an individual's action (or consumption), the actions of flexibly defined peer or reference groups, personal characteristics (including income), and common prices. People are arranged by social proximity, and the reference groups may include only one's closest neighbor or the entire city. One controversy in the literature is whether social interactions are best thought of as being local (i.e., people are really affected only by their closest neighbor) or global (i.e., people are affected by the average behavior of people in a large community). Our framework is sufficiently flexible to examine these extremes.

Although there are several examples in the literature that deal with discrete choice, many others deal with variables, such as education, that are more naturally thought of as continuous (e.g., Benabou, 1993, 1996, and Durlauf 1996a, 1996b). In addition, in certain contexts, the variables that we observe (e.g., out-of-wedlock births) are consequences of behavior that the agents – as opposed to the social scientist – are observing and mimicking, and this behavior may be more naturally modeled as a continuous variable. For this reason and because it is mathematically simpler, we emphasize models with continuous choices.[4]

We first examine the conditions under which for each set of exogenous parameters we obtain a unique equilibrium. A sufficient condition for a unique equilibrium is that the absolute value of the second derivative of utility with respect to one's own action is greater than the absolute value of the cross-partial derivative between one's own action and the action of the peer group. We refer to this condition as the Moderate Social Influence (MSI) condition.

---

[3] See, e.g., Krugman (1991).

[4] Some results for a model with discrete action space are derived in Section 2.4.

One, perhaps surprising, fact is that uniqueness is guaranteed by this condition, with no assumptions about the degree to which interactions are global or local.

We establish sufficient conditions for the existence of multiple equilibria. These conditions tend to be satisfied if there exists sufficient nonlinearity in the effect of peer actions on an individual's own optimal action, and not too much heterogeneity among agents. Hence, when sorting creates homogeneity, multiple equilibria are more likely.

As described previously, the main ingredient used to generate multiple equilibria in models of nonmarket interactions has been strategic complementarities. We show that strategic complementarity is *not* necessary for multiple equilibria. We present an example wherein each agent belongs to one of two groups. Individuals in each group want to differentiate themselves from the average individual in the other group in the consumption of a good. No other social interactions are present. There are multiple equilibria if the desire to differentiate is strong enough.

Even in cases with multiple equilibria, as long as there is some individual heterogeneity (generically), there will not be a continuum of equilibria. Around each equilibrium, there is an interval that contains no other equilibria. Because the model does not tell us the size of this interval, the empirical relevance of this finding may be limited. However, it does suggest that empirical approaches to estimating multiple equilibria models should focus on situations in which the different equilibria are sufficiently distinct.

Another result is that, if the MSI condition holds, and strategic complementarity prevails, there is always a well-defined social multiplier.[5] This social multiplier can be thought of as the ratio of the response of an individual action to an exogenous parameter (that affects only that person) and the (per capita) response of the entire peer group to a change in the same parameter that affects the entire peer group. In the empirical framework section of the paper, we discuss estimating this multiplier. The presence of this social multiplier implies that social interactions are generally connected with unusually high variances of aggregates. In fact, as we will argue later, it is very difficult to empirically distinguish between models with a unique equilibrium and a large social multiplier and models with multiple equilibria.

Although the results concerning uniqueness and the social multiplier are independent of the interaction structure, the same is not true for ergodicity. However, we show that if MSI prevails, shocks are independent and identically distributed across individuals, and each agent is influenced by the average action of all other agents, then the equilibrium average action for a large population is independent of the actual shocks that occur.

We do not discuss the welfare properties of equilibria. Indeed, the presence of heterogeneous individuals in our benchmark model makes it more difficult to rank equilibria. One possibility is to proceed as Brock and Durlauf (1995) and examine ex ante welfare. In general, the ranking of equilibria according to

---

[5] When the MSI condition fails to hold, the social multiplier becomes unbounded.

ex ante welfare typically depends on finer aspects of the interaction structure. We have decided not to focus on these issues here.

In the third section of the paper, we present a linear quadratic version of the social interaction model that can be used for estimation. We then discuss how different approaches to estimating the extent of social interactions fit into this framework. There are three primary approaches to estimating social interactions.

First, social interactions are estimated by looking at the covariance between individual outcomes and the average outcome of a peer group. Even in the best-case scenario, ordinary least squares coefficients based on these covariances do not yield consistent coefficient estimators of social interaction parameters. The problem occurs because peer outcomes are partially determined by the individual's outcome. Our framework suggests a correction in the univariate case for this problem. This correction will not work if unobserved individual attributes are correlated with peer attributes. This correlation can occur either because of omitted community-level characteristics or because of differential sorting into neighborhoods. The standard correction for this mutual interdependence [following Case and Katz (1991)] is to use an instrumental variables approach that relies on the exogenous characteristics of peers. This approach will successfully solve problems due to omitted community attributes, but not if there is sorting into communities. Randomized experiments offer the best chance of identifying peer effects.

The second empirical approach uses the variance of aggregates. The third empirical approach uses the logic of the multiplier. In this approach, the relationship between exogenous variables and outcomes for individuals is compared with the relationship between exogenous variables and outcomes for groups. The ratio is a measure of the size of social interactions.

All three of these approaches offer different methods of capturing social interactions and, in many cases, the estimates will be absolutely equivalent. However, all will suffer when there are omitted variables and sorting. The empirical hope is that randomization of people with peers (as in Sacerdote 2000) will help us to break this sorting. However, this randomization is rare, and if we estimate social interactions only in those cases where we have randomization, then we are likely to have only limited empirical scope for this type of work.

2. THEORETICAL MODELS OF NONMARKET INTERACTIONS

Economics has always been concerned with social interactions. Most often, economists have written about social interactions that are mediated by the market. In particular, economists have focused on the interaction that occurs when greater demand of person x for commodity z raises the price of that commodity and reduces the consumption by person y. This negative interaction lies at the core of our discipline, and when this interaction appears in our models, it tends to predict "well-behaved" systems, with unique equilibria, monotonic convergence, etc. Although negative interactions can create cycles (high demand in one period raises prices the next period) as in the case of cobweb models, they tend not to create high levels of variability.

However, as economists tried to explain more puzzling phenomena, particularly large variances over time and space, they moved to positive interaction models. The most famous early example of this move is in Keynes, whose famous "beauty contest" description of the stock market suggested the possibility of positive market-mediated interactions. One person's demand for the stock market could conceivably induce others to also purchase shares. This type of model has only recently been formalized (e.g., Froot, Scharfstein, and Stein, 1992). Several other authors have focused on different mechanisms in which we see market-mediated positive social interactions (e.g., Murphy, Shleifer, and Vishny, 1989). These models create the possibility of multiple equilibria or high levels of variability for a given set of fundamentals.

Our interest is fundamentally in nonmarket interactions. The literature on these interactions has paralleled the rise in market-mediated positive interaction models and has many similarities. Schelling (1971, 1972) pioneered the study of nonmarket interactions in economics. Following in Schelling's tradition, economists have examined the role of nonmarket interactions in a myriad of contexts.

Many of the recent papers on nonmarket interactions use random field models, also known as interactive particle systems, imported from statistical physics. In these models, one typically postulates individuals' interdependence and analyzes the macro behavior that emerges. Typical questions concern the existence and multiplicity of *macro phases* that are consistent with the postulated individual behavior. Follmer (1974) was the first paper in economics to use this framework. He modeled an economy with locally dependent preferences and examined when randomness in individual preferences will affect the aggregate, even as the number of agents grows to infinity. Brock (1993) and Blume (1993) recognized the connection of a class of interactive particle models to the economic literature on discrete choice. Brock and Durlauf (1995) develops many results on discrete choice in the presence of social interactions. Other models inspired in statistical physics start with a more explicit dynamic description on how agents' choices at a point in time are made, conditional on other agents' previous choices, and discuss the evolution of the macro behavior over time. Bak, Chen, Scheinkman, and Woodford (1993) (see also Scheinkman and Woodford, 1994) study the impact of independent sectoral shocks on aggregate fluctuations with a "sandpile" model that exhibits self-organized criticality and show that independent sectoral shocks may affect average behavior, even as the numbers of sectors grow large. Durlauf (1993) constructs a model based on local technological interactions to examine the possibility of productivity traps, in which low-productivity techniques are used, because other producers are also using low-productivity processes. Glaeser, Sacerdote, and Scheinkman (1996) use what is referred to as the *voter* model in the literature on interacting particle systems[6] to analyze the distribution of crime across American cities. Topa (1997) examines the spatial distribution of unemployment with the aid of *contact processes.*[7]

A related literature, which we do not discuss here, studies social learning.[8] In these models, agents typically learn from observing other agents and base decisions on the observed decisions of others.

Becker and Murphy (2000) present a particularly far-ranging analysis of the social interactions in economics. This volume extends Becker's (1991) earlier analysis of restaurant pricing when there are social interactions in the demand for particular restaurants. This work is particularly important because of its combination of social interactions with maximizing behavior and classic price theory. In the same vein, the work of Pesendorfer (1995) on cycles in the fashion industry examines how a monopolist would exploit the presence of nonmarket interactions.

In the remainder of this section, we develop a model of nonmarket interactions that will hopefully serve to clarify the mechanisms by which nonmarket interactions affect macro behavior. The model is self-consciously written in a fashion that makes it close to traditional economic models, although it can accommodate versions of the models that were inspired by statistical physics. We consider only a static model, although we also examine some ad hoc dynamics. On the other hand, our framework encompasses several of the examples in the literature and is written so that special cases can be used to discuss issues in the empirical evaluation of nonmarket interactions (see Section 3).[9] In the spirit of the work of Pesendorfer (1995) or Becker and Murphy (2000), we explicitly allow for the presence of prices, so that the model can be used to study the interplay between market and nonmarket interactions.

Next, we write down the details of the model. In Section 2.2, we describe some examples in the literature that fit into our framework. We present results for the case of continuous actions in Section 2.3. These results concern sufficient conditions for uniqueness or multiplicity of equilibria, the presence of a *social multiplier*, the stability of equilibria, and ergodicity. Models with discrete actions and large populations are treated in Section 2.4. At the end of this section, we give a short discussion of endogenous peer group formation.

---

[6] See, e.g., Ligget (1985).

[7] See, e.g., Ligget (1985).

[8] See, e.g., Arthur (1989), Banerjee (1992), Bikhchandani, Hirshleifer, and Welch (1992), Ellison (1993), Kirman (1993), Young (1993), Ellison and Fudenberg (1994), and Gul and Lundholm (1995).

[9] In particular, our framework is related to the pioneering work of Cooper and John (1988) on coordination failures. They study a particular version of our framework where each agent interacts with the average agent in the economy and focus on models where there is no heterogeneity across agents.

2.1. A Model of Nonmarket Interactions

We identify each agent with an integer $i = 1, \ldots, n$. Associated with each agent i are his peer, or reference, groups P_i^k, $k = 1, \ldots, K$, each one a subset of $\{1, \ldots, n\}$ that does not contain i. We allow for multiple reference groups ($K > 1$) to accommodate some of the examples that have appeared in the literature (see Example 2.5). Later, we will discuss the case where the agent chooses his reference groups, but in most of what follows, the P_i^k's are fixed. Each agent is subject to a "taste shock" θ_i, a random variable with support on a set Θ. Finally, each agent chooses an action $a \in \mathcal{A}$. Typically, the set $\mathcal{A}$ will be a finite set, *the discrete choice case,* or an interval of the real line, *the continuous choice case.* The utility of agent i depends on the action chosen by him, a_i, and the actions chosen by all other agents in his peer group. More precisely, we assume that

$$U^i = U^i \left(a_i, A_i^1, \ldots, A_i^K, \theta_i, p \right), \tag{2.1}$$

where

$$A_i^k = \sum_{j=1}^{n} \gamma_{ij}^k a_j, \tag{2.2}$$

with $\gamma_{ij}^k \geq 0$, $\gamma_{ij}^k = 0$ if $j \notin P_i^k$, $\sum_{j=1}^{n} \gamma_{ij}^k = 1$, and $p \in \Pi$ is a vector of parameters.

In other words, the utility enjoyed by agent i depends on his own chosen action, on a weighted average of the actions chosen by agents in his reference groups, on his taste shock, and on a set of parameters. We allow the utility function to vary across agents because, in some cases, we want to identify variations in the parameters θ_i explicitly with variations on income or other parameters of the problem. We also assume that the maximization problem depends only on the agent being able to observe the relevant average action of peers. In some applications, we will allow for $P_i^k = \emptyset$, for some of the agents. In this case, we may set A_i^k to be an arbitrary element of $\mathcal{A}$, and U^i to be independent of A_i^k. In many examples, each agent will have a unique reference group. In this case, we drop the superscript k and write P_i instead of P_i^1 etc.

Typically, p will be interpreted as the exogenous (per unit) price of taking action.[10] In addition, we will think of $\theta_i = (y_i, \zeta_i)$, where y_i represents income and ζ_i a shock to taste. In this case,

$$U^i \left(a_i, A_i^1, \ldots, A_i^K, \theta_i, p \right) = V \left(a_i, A_i^1, \ldots, A_i^K, \zeta_i, y_i - pa_i \right). \tag{2.3}$$

An equilibrium is defined in a straightforward way. For given vectors $\theta = (\theta_1, \ldots, \theta_n) \in \Theta^n$ and p, an equilibrium for (θ, p) is a vector $a = (a_1, \ldots, a_n)$

---

[10] One can also extend the notion of equilibrium to allow for an endogenous p.

such that, for each i,

$$a_i \in \operatorname{argmax} U^i \left(a_i, \sum_{j=1}^n \gamma_{ij}^1 a_j, \ldots, \sum_{j=1}^n \gamma_{ij}^K a_j, \theta_i, p \right). \tag{2.4}$$

This definition of equilibrium requires that, when making a decision, agent i observes A_i^k – the summary statistics of other agents' actions that affect his utility. As usual, we can interpret this equilibrium as a steady state of a dynamical system in which at each point in time, agents make a choice based on the previous choices of other agents, although additional assumptions, such as those in Proposition 2.4, are needed to guarantee that the dynamical system will converge to such a steady state.

2.2.   Some Examples

Example 2.1. *The discrete choice model of Brock and Durlauf (1995).*[11]
    Here the set $\mathcal{A} = \{-1, 1\}$, *and* $\Theta = R$. *Each agent has a single reference group, all other agents, and the weights* $\gamma_{ij} \equiv 1/(n-1)$. *This choice of reference group and weights is commonly referred to as global interactions. Let*

$$U^i(a_i, A_i, \theta) = ha_i - J(A_i - a_i)^2 + \left(\frac{1 - a_i}{2} \right) \theta_i, \tag{2.5}$$

where $h \in R$, $J > 0$. *The* θ_i*'s are assumed to be independently and identically distributed with*

$$Prob(\theta_i \le z) = \frac{1}{1 + \exp(-\nu z)},$$

for some $\nu > 0$. *h measures the preference of the average agent for one of the actions, J the desire for conformity, and* θ_i *is a shock to the utility of taking the action* $a_i = -1$. *Brock and Durlauf also consider generalized versions of this model where the* γ_{ij}*s vary, thus allowing each agent to have a distinct peer group.*

Example 2.2. *Glaeser and Scheinkman (2001).*
    The utility functions are:

$$U^i(a_i, A_i, \theta_i, p) = -\frac{1 - \beta}{2} a_i^2 - \frac{\beta}{2}(a_i - A_i)^2 + (\theta_i - p)a_i.$$

Here, $0 \le \beta \le 1$ *measures the taste for conformity. In this case,*

$$a_i = [\beta A_i + \theta_i - p]. \tag{2.6}$$

Note that, when $p = 0$, $\beta = 1$, *and the* A_i'*s are the average action of all other agents, this is a version of the Brock–Durlauf model with continuous actions.*

---

[11] A related example is in Aoki (1995).

Unfortunately, this case is very special. Equilibria exist only if $\sum_i \theta_i = 0$, and, in this case, a continuum of equilibria would exist. The model is, as we will show, much better behaved when $\beta < 1$.

In Glaeser and Scheinkman (2001), the objective was to admit both local and global interactions in the same model to try to distinguish empirically between them. This was done by allowing for two reference groups, and setting $P_i^1 = \{1, \ldots, n\} - i$, A_i^1 the average action of all other agents, $P_i^2 = \{i - 1\}$ if $i > 1$, $P_1^2 = \{n\}$, and writing

$$U^i\left(a_i, A_i^1, a_{i-1}, \theta_i, p\right) = -\frac{1 - \beta_1 - \beta_2}{2}a_i^2 - \frac{\beta_1}{2}\left(a_i - A_i^1\right)^2$$
$$- \frac{\beta_2}{2}(a_i - a_{i-1})^2 + (\theta_i - p)a_i.$$

Example 2.3. *The class of models of strategic complementarity discussed in Cooper and John (1988).*

Again the reference group of agent i is $P_i = \{1, \ldots, n\} - i$. The set $\mathcal{A}$ is an interval on the line and $A_i = 1/(n - 1)\sum a_{j\neq i}$. There is no heterogeneity and the utility of each agent is $U^i = U(a_i, A_i)$. Cooper and John (1988) examine symmetric equilibria. The classic production externality example fits in this framework. Each agent chooses an effort a_i, and the resulting output is $f(a_i, \bar{a})$. Each agent consumes his per capita output and has a utility function $u(c_i, a_i)$. Write

$$U(a_i, A_i) = u\left(f\left(a_i, \frac{(n-1)A_i + a_i}{n}\right), a_i\right).$$

Example 2.4. *A simple version of the model of Diamond (1982) on trading externalities.*

Each agents draws an e_i, which is his cost of production of a unit of the good. The e_i's are distributed independently across agents and with a distribution H and density $h > 0$, with support on a (possibly infinite) interval $[0, d]$. After a period in which the agent decides to produce or not, he is matched at random with a single other agent, and if they both have produced, they exchange the goods and each enjoys utility $u > 0$. Otherwise, if the agent has produced, he obtains utility $\theta_i \geq 0$ from the consumption of his own good. If the agent has not produced, he obtains utility 0. We assume that all agents use a cutoff policy, a level x_i such that the agent produces if and only if $e_i \leq x_i$. We set

$$a_i = H(x_i),$$

the probability that agent i will produce. Here, the reference group is again all $j \neq i$, and

$$A_i = E(a_j | j \neq i) \equiv \frac{\sum_{j \neq i} a_j}{n - 1}.$$

Hence, if he uses policy a_i, an agent has an expected utility that equals

$$U^i(a_i, A_i, \theta_i) = \int_0^{H^{-1}(a_i)} [uA_i + \theta_i(1 - A_i) - e]h(e)de.$$

Optimality requires that $x_i = \min\{uA_i + \theta_i(1 - A_i), d\}$.

Suppose first that $\theta_i \equiv 0$. A symmetric equilibrium ($a_i \equiv a$) will exist whenever there is a solution to the equation

$$a = H(ua). \tag{2.7}$$

If H is the uniform distribution in $[0, u]$, then every $a \in [0, 1]$ is a symmetric equilibrium, As we will show in Proposition 2.2, this situation is very special. For a fixed H, for almost every vector $\theta = (\theta_1, \ldots, \theta_n)$, (interior) equilibria are isolated.

Example 2.5. *A matching example that requires multiple reference groups (Pesendorfer, 1995).*

In a simple version, there are two groups, leaders (L) and followers (F), with n_L and n_F members, respectively. An individual can use one of two kinds of clothes. Buying the first one ($a = 0$) is free; buying the second ($a = 1$) costs p. Agents are matched randomly to other agents using the same clothes. Suppose the utility agent i, who is of type $t \in \{L, F\}$ and is matched to an agent of type t', is $V_i(t, t', a, p, \theta_i) = u(t, t') - ap + \theta_i a$, where θ_i is a parameter that shifts the preferences for the second kind of clothes. Assume that

$$u(L, L) - u(L, F) > p > u(F, L) - u(F, F) > 0, \tag{2.8}$$

where we have abused notation by writing $u(L, L)$ instead of $u(t, t')$ with $t \in L$ and $t' \in L$ etc. In this example, each agent has two reference groups. If $i \in L$, then $P_i^1 = L - \{i\}$ and $P_i^2 = F$. On the other hand, if $i \in F$, then $P_i^1 = L$ and $P_i^2 = F - \{i\}$.

2.3.   Equilibria with Continuous Actions

In this subsection, we derive results concerning the existence, number of equilibria, stability, and ergodicity of a basic continuous action model. We try not to rely on a specific structure of reference groups or to assume a specific weighting for each reference group. We assume that $\mathcal{A}$ is a (possibly unbounded) interval in the real line, that each U^i is at least twice continuously differentiable, and that the second partial derivative with respect to an agent's own action $U_{11}^i < 0$.[12] Each agent i has a single reference group P_i. The choice a single peer group for each agent and a scalar action is not crucial, but it substantially simplifies the notation.

---

[12] As usual, this inequality can be weakened by assuming that $U_{11}^i \leq 0$ and that at the optimal choice strict inequality holds.

We also assume that the optimal choices are interior, and hence, because $i \notin P_i$, the first-order condition may be written as

$$U_1^i(a_i, A_i, \theta_i, p) = 0. \tag{2.9}$$

Because $U_{11}^i < 0$, then $a_i = g^i(A_i, \theta_i, p)$ is well defined and

$$g_1^i(A_i, \theta_i, p) = -\frac{U_{12}^i(a_i, A_i, \theta_i, p)}{U_{11}^i(a_i, A_i, \theta_i, p)}. \tag{2.10}$$

We will write $G(a, \theta, p)$ for the function defined in $R^n \times \Theta^n \times \Pi$ given by

$$G(a, \theta, p) = \left(g^1(A_1, \theta_1, p), \ldots, g^n(A_n, \theta_n, p)\right).$$

Recall that, for given vectors $\theta = (\theta_1, \ldots, \theta_n) \in \Theta^n$ and p, an equilibrium for (θ, p) is a vector $a(\theta, p) = (a_1(\theta, p), \ldots, a_n(\theta, p))$, such that, for each i,

$$a_i(\theta, p) = g^i(A_i(a(\theta, p)), \theta_i, p). \tag{2.11}$$

Proposition 2.1 gives conditions for the existence of an equilibrium.

Proposition 2.1. *Given a pair $(\theta, p) \in \Theta^n \times \Pi$, suppose that I is a closed-bounded interval such that, for each i, $g^i(A_i, \theta_i, p) \in I$, whenever $A_i \in I$. Then, there exists at least one equilibrium $a(\theta, p) \in I^n$. In particular, an equilibrium exists if there exists an $m \in R$, with $[-m, m] \subset \overset{\circ}{A}$, and such that, for any i and $A_i \in [-m, m]$, $U_1^i(-m, A_i, \theta_i, p) \geq 0$, and $U_1^i(m, A_i, \theta_i, p) \leq 0$.*

Proof. If $a \in I^n$, because A_i is a convex combination of the entries of a, $A_i \in I$. Because $g^i(A_i, \theta_i, p) \in I$, whenever $A_i \in I$, the (continuous) function $G(\cdot, \theta, p)$ maps I^n into I^n, and therefore must have at least one fixed point. The second part of the proposition follows because $U_{11} < 0$ implies that $g^i(A_i, \theta_i, p) \in [-m, m]$, whenever $A_i \in [-m, m]$. QED ∎

Proposition 2.1 gives us sufficient conditions for the existence of an equilibrium for a given (θ, p). The typical model, however, describes a process for generating the θ_i's in the cross-section. In this case, not all pairs (θ, p) are equally interesting. The process generating the θ_i's will impose a distribution on the vector θ, and we need only to check the assumptions of Proposition 2.1 on a set of θ's that has probability one. For a fixed p, we define an *invariant interval* I as any interval such that there exists a set $\Lambda \subset \Theta^n$ with $\text{Prob}(\Lambda) = 1$, such that for each i, and for all $\theta \in \Lambda$, $g^i(A_i, \theta_i, p) \in I$, whenever $A_i \in I$. If multiple disjoint compact invariant intervals exist, multiple equilibria prevail with probability one.

It is relatively straightforward to construct models with multiple equilibria that are perturbations of models without heterogeneity.[13] Suppose that Θ is an

---

[13] A model without heterogeneity is one where all utility functions U^i and shocks θ_i are identical. We choose the normalization $\theta^i \equiv 0$. We will consider perturbations in which the utility functions are still uniform across agents, but the θ^i can differ across agents.

interval containing 0 and that $g(A, \theta)$ is a smooth function that is increasing in both coordinates. The assumption that g is increasing in θ is only a normalization. In contrast, the assumption that g is increasing in A is equivalent to $U_{12} > 0$ (i.e., an increase in the average action by the members of his reference group, increases in the marginal utility of an agent's own action). This assumption was called strategic complementarity in Bulow, Geanakoplos, and Klemperer (1985). Let x be a stable fixed point of $g(\cdot, 0)$ [i.e., $g(x, 0) = 0$ and $g_1(x, 0) < 1$]. If the interval Θ is small enough, there exists an invariant interval containing x. In particular, if a model without heterogeneity has multiple stable equilibria, the model with small noise, that is, where $\theta^i \in \Theta$, Θ a small interval, will also have multiple equilibria. The condition on invariance must hold for almost all $\theta \in \Theta$. In particular, if we have multiple *disjoint* invariant intervals and we shrink Θ, we must still have multiple disjoint invariant intervals. On the other hand, if we expand Θ, we may lose a particular invariant interval, and multiple equilibria are no longer assured. An implication of this reasoning is that when individuals are sorted into groups according to their θs, and agents do not interact across groups, then multiple equilibria are more likely to prevail. In Section, 2.5, we discuss a model where agents sort on their θs.

In this literature, strategic complementarity is the usual way to deliver the existence of multiple equilibria. The next example shows that, in contrast to the results of Cooper and John (1988), in our model, because we consider a richer structure of reference groups, strategic complementarity is *not* necessary for multiple equilibria.

Example 2.6. *This is an example to show that, in contrast to the case of purely global interactions, strategic complementarity is not a necessary condition for multiple equilibria. There are two sets of agents $\{S_1\}$ and $\{S_2\}$, and n agents in each set. For agents of a given set, the reference group consists of all the agents of the other set. If $i \in S_k$,*

$$A_i = \frac{1}{n} \sum_{j \in S_\ell} a_j,$$

$\ell \neq k$. There are two goods, and the relative price is normalized to one. Each agent has an initial income of one unit, and his objective is to maximize

$$U^i(a_i, A_i) = \log a_i + \log(1 - a_i) + \frac{\lambda}{2}(a_i - A_i)^2. \qquad (2.12)$$

Only the first good exhibits social interactions, and agents of each set want to differentiate from the agents of the other set. Provided $\lambda < 8$, $U_{11}^i < 0$. However, there is no strategic complementarity – an increase in the action of others (weakly) decreases the marginal utility of an agent's own action. We will look for equilibria with a_i constant within each set. An equilibrium of this type is described by a pair x, y of actions for each set of agents. In equilibrium *we must have:*

$$1 - 2x + \lambda x(1 - x)(x - y) = 0, \qquad\qquad (2.13)$$

$$1 - 2y + \lambda y(1 - y)(y - x) = 0. \qquad\qquad (2.14)$$

Clearly $x = y = 1/2$ is always an equilibrium. It is the unique equilibrium that is symmetric across groups. Provided $\lambda < 4$, the Jacobian associated with equations (2.13) and (2.14) is positive, which is compatible with uniqueness even if we consider asymmetric equilibria. However, whenever $\lambda > 4$, the Jacobian becomes negative and other equilibria must appear. For instance, if $\lambda = 4.04040404$, $x = .55$ and $y = .45$ is an equilibrium, and consequently so is $x = .45$ and $y = .55$. Hence, at least three equilibria are obtained, without strategic complementarity.

Proposition 2.1 gives existence conditions that are independent of the structure of the reference groups and the weights γ_{ij}'s. Also, the existence of multiple invariant intervals is independent of the structure of interactions embedded in the P_ls and γ_{ij}s, and is simply a result of the choice of an individual's action, given the "average action" of his reference group, the distribution of his taste shock, and the value of the exogenous parameter p.

In some social interaction models, such as the Diamond search model (Example 2.4), there may exist a continuum of equilibria. The next proposition shows that these situations are exceptional.

Proposition 2.2. *Suppose Θ is an open subset of R^k and that there exists a coordinate j such that $\partial U_1^i / \partial \theta_i^j \neq 0$; that is, θ_i^j has an effect in the marginal utility of the action. Then, for each fixed p, except for a subset of Θ^n of Lebesgue measure zero, the equilibria are isolated. In particular if the θ_i^j's are independently distributed with marginals that have a density with respect to the Lebesgue measure, then, for each fixed p, except for a subset of Θ^n of zero probability, the equilibria are isolated.*

Proof. For any p, consider the map $F(a, \theta) = a - G(a, \theta, p)$. The matrix of partial derivatives of F with respect to θ^j is a diagonal matrix with entry $d_{ii} \neq 0$, because $\partial U_1^i / \partial \theta_i^j \neq 0$. Hence, for each fixed p, DF has rank n, and it is a consequence of Sard's theorem (see, e.g., Mas-Colell 1985, p. 320) that, except perhaps for a subset of Θ^n of Lebesgue measure zero, F_1 has rank n. The implicit function theorem yields the result. QED   ∎

Consider again the search model discussed in Example 2.4. Suppose that $u \leq d$ and that each θ_i is in an open interval contained in $(0, d)$. Then, at any interior equilibrium, the assumptions of the Proposition are satisfied. This justifies our earlier claim that the continuum of equilibria exists when $\theta_i \equiv 0$ is exceptional. In the model discussed in Example 2.2, if $p = 0$, $\beta = 1$, and the reference group of each agent is made up by all other agents (with equal weights), then if $\sum \theta_i \neq 0$, there are no equilibria, whereas if $\sum \theta_i = 0$, there is a continuum. Again, the continuum of equilibria is exceptional. However, if $\beta < 1$, there is a unique equilibrium for any vector θ. This situation is less discontinuous than it seems. In equilibrium,

$$\frac{\sum a_i}{n} = \frac{1}{1-\beta} \frac{\sum \theta_i}{n}.$$

Hence, if we fix $\sum \theta_i \neq 0$ and drive β to 1, the average action becomes unbounded.

Although Proposition 2.2 is stated using the θ_i's as parameters, it is also true that isolated equilibria become generic if there is heterogeneity across individuals' utility functions.

One occasionally proclaimed virtue of social interaction models is that they create the possibility that multiple equilibria might exist. Proposition 2.1 gives us sufficient conditions for there to be multiple equilibria in social interactions models. One way to ensure uniqueness in this context is to place a bound on the effect of social interactions.

We will say that MSI prevails if the marginal utility of an agent's own action is more affected (in absolute value) by a change on his own action than by a change in the average action of his peers. More precisely, we say that MSI prevails if

$$\left| \frac{U_{12}^i(a_i, A_i, \theta_i, p)}{U_{11}^i(a_i, A_i, \theta_i, p)} \right| < 1. \tag{2.15}$$

From equation (2.10), the MSI condition implies

$$|g_1^i(A_i, \theta_i, p)| < 1. \tag{2.16}$$

This last condition is, in fact, weaker than inequality (2.15), because it is equivalent to inequality (2.15) when a_i is optimal, given (A_i, θ_i, p). We use only inequality (2.16), and therefore we will refer to this term as the MSI condition.

The next proposition shows that, if the MSI condition holds, there will be at most one equilibrium.[14]

Proposition 2.3. *If for a fixed (θ, p), MSI holds [that is, inequality (2.16) is verified for all i], then there exists at most one equilibrium $a(\theta, p)$.*

Proof. The matrix of partial derivatives of G with respect to a, which we denote by $G_1(a, \theta, p)$, has diagonal elements equal to 0 and, using Equation (2.10), off-diagonal elements $d_{ij} = g_1^i(A_i, \theta_i, p)\gamma_{ij}$. Also, for each i,

---

[14] Cooper and John (1988) had already remarked that an analoguous condition is sufficient for uniqueness in the context of their model.

$$\sum_{j \neq i} |d_{ij}| = |g_1^i(A_i, \theta_i, p)| \sum_{j \neq i} \gamma_{ij} = |g_1^i(A_i, \theta_i, p)| < 1.$$

It follows from the mean-value theorem that, for each (θ, p), $G(a, \theta, p) = a$ has a unique solution. QED ∎

To guarantee that uniqueness always prevails, MSI should hold for all $(\theta, p) \in \Theta^n \times \Pi$. The assumption in Proposition 2.3 is independent of the structure of interactions embedded in the P_i's and the γ_{ij}'s. An example where MSI is satisfied is when $U(a_i, A_i, \theta_i, p) = u(a_i, \theta_i, p) + w(a_i - A_i, p)$, where $u_{11} < 0$, and, for each p, $w(\cdot, p)$ is concave.

If, in addition to MSI, we assume strategic complementarity ($U_{12} > 0$), we can derive stronger results. Suppose p has a component, say p^1, such that each g^i has a positive partial derivative with respect to p^1. In equilibrium, we have, writing $F_1 = I - G_1$,

$$\frac{\partial a}{\partial p^1} = (F_1)^{-1}(a, \theta, p)\left(\frac{\partial g^1}{\partial p^1}, \dots, \frac{\partial g^n}{\partial p^1}\right)'. \tag{2.17}$$

Because F_1 has a dominant diagonal that is equal to one, we may use the Neumann expansion to write

$$(F_1)^{-1} = I + (I - F_1) + (I - F_1)^2 + \cdots. \tag{2.18}$$

Recall that all diagonal elements of $(I - F_1)$ are zero and that the off-diagonal elements are $g_1^i(A_i, \theta_i, p)\gamma_{ij} > 0$. Hence, each of the terms in this infinite series is a matrix with nonnegative entries, and

$$\frac{\partial a}{\partial p^1} = (I + H)\left(\frac{\partial g^1}{\partial p^1}, \dots, \frac{\partial g^n}{\partial p^1}\right)', \tag{2.19}$$

where H is a matrix with nonnegative elements. The nonnegativity of the matrix H means that there is a **social multiplier** (as in Becker and Murphy 2000).[15] An increase in p^1, holding all a_j's, $j \neq i$, constant, leads to a change

$$da_i = \frac{\partial g^i(A_i, \theta_i, p)}{\partial p^1} dp^1,$$

whereas, in equilibrium, that change equals

$$\left[\frac{\partial g^i(A_i, \theta_i, p)}{\partial p^1} + \sum_j H_{ij} \frac{\partial g^j(A_j, \theta_j, p)}{\partial p^1}\right] dp^1.$$

The effect of a change in p^1 on the average

$$\bar{A} \equiv \frac{\sum_i a_i}{n}$$

---

[15] Cooper and John (1988) define a similar multiplier by considering symmetric equilibria of a game.

is, in turn,

$$d\bar{A} = \frac{1}{n} \left[\sum_i \frac{(\partial g^i(A_i, \theta_i, p)}{\partial p^1} + \sum_{i,j} H_{ij} \frac{\partial g^j(A_j, \theta_j, p)}{\partial p^1} \right] dp^1.$$

This same multiplier also impacts the effect of the shocks θ_i. Differences in the sample realizations of the θ_is are amplified through the social multiplier effect.

The size of the social multiplier depends on the value of $g_1^i \equiv \partial g/\partial A_i$. If these numbers are bounded away from one, one can bound the social multiplier. However, as these numbers approach unity, the social multiplier effect gets arbitrarily large. In this case, two populations with slightly distinct realizations of the θ_is could exhibit very different average values of the actions. In the presence of unobserved heterogeneity, it may be impossible to distinguish between a large multiplier (that is, g_1 is near unity) and multiple equilibria.

Propositions 2.1 and 2.3 give us conditions for multiplicity or uniqueness. At this level of generality, it is impossible to refine these conditions. It is easy to construct examples, where $g_1 > 1$ in some range, but still only one equilibrium exists.

One common way to introduce ad hoc dynamics in social interaction models is to simply assume that, in period t, each agent chooses his action based on the choices of the agents in his reference group at time $t - 1$.[16] Such processes are not guaranteed to converge, but the next proposition shows that when MSI prevails, convergence occurs.

Let $a^t(\theta, p, a^0)$ be the solution to the difference equation

$$a^{t+1} = G(a^t, \theta, p),$$

with initial value a^0.

Proposition 2.4. *If, for a fixed (θ, p), $|g_1^i(\cdot, \theta_i, p)| < 1$, for all i, then*

$$\lim_{t \to \infty} a^t(\theta, p, a^0) = a(\theta, p).$$

Proof. For any matrix M, let $\|M\| = \max_i \sum_j |M_{ij}|$ be the matrix norm. Then, $\max_i |a_i^{t+1} - a_i(\theta, p)| \le \sup_y \|G_1(y, \theta, p)\| (\max_i |a_i^t - a_i(\theta, p)|) \le \max_i |a_i^t - a_i(\theta, p)|$ Hence, the vectors a^t stay in a bounded set B and, by assumption, $\sup_{y \in B} \|G_1(y, \theta, p)\| < 1$. Hence, $\lim_{t \to \infty} a^t(\theta, p, a^0) = a(\theta, p)$. QED ∎

One intriguing feature of social interaction models is that, in some of these models, individual shocks can determine aggregate outcomes for large groups.

---

[16] In social interaction models, ad hoc dynamics is frequently used to select among equilibria as in Young (1993, 1998) or Blume and Durlauf (1998).

In contrast to the results presented earlier, which are independent of the particular interaction structure, ergodicity depends on a more detailed description of the interactions. For instance, consider the model in Example 2.2 with $p = 0$, the θ_i's iid, $P_1 = \emptyset$, and $P_i = \{1\}$ for each $i > 1$. That is, agent 1 is a "leader" that is followed by everyone. Then, $a_1 = \theta_1$ and $a_i = \theta_i + \beta a_1$. Hence, the average action, even as $n \to \infty$, depends on the realization of θ_1, even though the assumption of Proposition 2.3 holds. Our next proposition shows that, when MSI holds, shocks are iid, and individuals' utility functions depend only on their own actions and the average action of their peer group, then, under mild technical conditions, the average action of a large population is independent of the particular realization of the shocks.

Proposition 2.5. *Suppose that*

1. *θ_i is identically and independently distributed.*
2. *U^i (and hence g^i) is independent of i.*
3. *$P_i = \{1, \ldots, i-1, i+1, \ldots, n\}$.*
4. *$\gamma_{i,j} \equiv 1/(n-1)$.*
5. *$\mathcal{A}$ is bounded.*
6. *MSI holds uniformly, that is,*

$$\sup_{A_i, \theta_i} |g_1(A_i, \theta_i, p)| < 1.$$

Let $a^n(\theta, p)$ denote the equilibrium when n agents are present and agent i receives shock θ_i. Then, there exists an $\bar{A}(p)$ such that, with probability one,

$$\lim_{n \to \infty} \sum_{i=1}^{n} \frac{a_i^n(\theta, p)}{n} = \bar{A}(p). \tag{2.20}$$

Proof. We omit the argument p from the proof. Let $A^n(\theta) = \sum_{i=1}^{n} a_i^n(\theta)/n$. The boundedness of $\mathcal{A}$ ensures that there are convergent subsequences $A^{n_k}(\theta)$. Suppose the limit of one such convergent subsequence is $A(\theta)$. Note that $|A_i^{n_k}(\theta) - A^{n_k}(\theta)| \le b/n_k$, for some constant b. Hence, for any $\epsilon > 0$, we can find K such that if $k \ge K$,

$$\left| \sum_{i=1}^{n_k} \frac{a_i^{n_k}(\theta)}{n_k} - \sum_{i-1}^{n_k} \frac{g(A(\theta), \theta_i)}{n_k} \right| = \left| \sum_{i=1}^{n_k} \frac{g(A_i^{n_k}, \theta_i)}{n_k} - \sum_{i=1}^{n_k} \frac{g(A(\theta), \theta_i)}{n_k} \right| \le \epsilon. \tag{2.21}$$

Furthermore, because the θ_i are iid and g_1 is uniformly bounded, there exists a set of probability one that can be chosen independent of A, such that,

$$\sum_{i=1}^{n} \frac{g(A, \theta_i)}{n} \to \int_{\Theta} g(A, y) dF(y),$$

where F is the distribution of each θ_i. Hence, given any $\epsilon > 0$, if k is sufficiently large,

$$\left| A^{n_k}(\theta) - \int_\Theta g(A(\theta), y) dF(y) \right| \leq \epsilon,$$

or

$$A(\theta) = \int_\Theta g(A(\theta), y) dF(y)$$

in the hypothesis of the proposition guarantees that $g(\cdot, \theta_i)$ is a contraction and, as a consequence, this last equation has at most one solution, $\bar{A}$. In particular, all convergent subsequences of the bounded sequence $A^n(\theta)$ converge to $\bar{A}$ and, hence, $A^n(\theta) \to \bar{A}$. QED. ∎

The assumptions in the proposition are sufficient, but not necessary, for ergodicity. In general, models in which shocks are i.i.d. and interactions are local tend to display ergodic behavior.

2.4. "Mean Field" Models with Large Populations and Discrete Actions

In this subsection, we will examine models with discrete action spaces (actually two possible actions), in which the utility function of the agents depends on their own action and the average action taken by the population. Much of our framework and results are inspired by the treatment by Brock and Durlauf (1995) of Example 2.1 described previously. The action space of individuals is {0, 1}. As in Brock and Durlauf, we will assume that

$$U^i = U(a_i, A, p) + (1 - a_i)\theta_i;$$

that is, the shock θ_i is the extra utility an agent obtains from taking action 0. We will assume that $U(a_i, \cdot, \cdot)$ is smooth and that the θ_i's are iid with a cdf F with continuous density f. Agents do not internalize the effect that their action has on the average action.

We also assume strategic complementarity, which in this context we take to be $U_2(1, A, p) - U_2(0, A, p) > 0$; that is, an increase in the average action increases the difference in utility between action 1 and action 0.

Given A, agent i will take action 1 if, and only if, $\theta_i \leq U(1, A, p) - U(0, A, p)$. In a large population, a fraction $F(U(1, A, p) - U(0, A, p))$ will take action 1; the remainder will take action 0.

A *mean-field equilibrium*, thereafter MFE, is an average action $\bar{A}$ such that

$$F(U(1, \bar{A}, p) - U(0, \bar{A}, p)) - \bar{A} = 0. \tag{2.22}$$

This definition of an MFE is exactly as in the Brock and Durlauf treatment of Example 2.1. The next proposition corresponds to their results concerning equilibria in that example.

Proposition 2.6. *An MFE always exists. If $0 < \bar{A} < 1$ is an equilibrium where*

$$f(U(1,\bar{A}, p) - U(0, \bar{A}, p))[U_2(1,\bar{A}, p) - U_2(0,\bar{A}, p)] > 1, \quad (2.23)$$

then there are also at least two other MFE's, one on each side of $\bar{A}$. On the other hand, if, at every MFE, $f(U(1,\bar{A}, p) - U(0,\bar{A}, p))[U_2(1,\bar{A}, p) - U_2(0,\bar{A}, p)] < 1$, there exists a single MFE.

Proof. $H(A) = F(U(1, A, p) - U(0, A, p)) - A$ satisfies $H(0) \geq 0$, and $H(1) \leq 0$ and is continuous. If inequality (2.23) holds, then $H(\bar{A}) = 0$ and $H'(\bar{A}) > 0$. QED. ∎

The first term on the left-hand side of inequality (2.23) is the density of agents that are indifferent between the two actions, when the average action is $\bar{A}$. The second term is the marginal impact of the average action on the preference for action 1 over action 0, which, by our assumption of strategic complementarity, is always > 0. This second term corresponds exactly to the intensity of social influence that played a pivoting role in determining the uniqueness of equilibrium in the model with a continuum of actions.

If there is a unique equilibrium,[17] then

$$\frac{\partial \bar{A}}{\partial p} = \frac{f(U(1,\bar{A}, p) - U(0,\bar{A}, p))[U_3(1,\bar{A}, p) - U_3(0,\bar{A}, p)]}{1 - f(U(1,\bar{A}, p) - U(0,\bar{A}, p))[U_2(1,\bar{A}, p) - U_2(0,\bar{A}, p)]}.$$

$$(2.24)$$

The numerator in this expression is exactly the average change in action, when p changes, and agents consider that the average action remains constant. The denominator is, if uniqueness prevails, positive.

As we emphasized in the model with continuous actions, there is a continuity in the multiplier effect. As the parameters of the model (U and F) approach the region of multiple equilibria, the effect of a change in p on the equilibrium average action approaches infinity.

In many examples, the distribution F satisfies:

1. Symmetry ($f(z) = h(|z|)$)
2. Monotonicity (h is decreasing)

If, in addition, the model is unbiased [$U(1, 1/2, p) = U(0, 1/2, p)$], then $A = 1/2$ is an MFE. The fulfillment of inequality (2.23) now depends on the value of $f(0)$. This illustrates the role of homogeneity of the population in producing multiple equilibria. If we consider a parameterized family of models in which the random variable $\theta_i = \sigma x_i$, where $\sigma > 0$, then $f^\sigma(0) = (1/\sigma)f^1(0)$. As $\sigma \to 0$ ($\sigma \to \infty$), inequality (2.23) must hold (resp. must reverse). In particular, if the

---

[17] In here and in what follows, we require strict uniqueness; that is, the left-hand side of inequality (2.23) is less than one.

population is homogeneous enough, multiple equilibria must prevail in the unbiased case.

These reasonings can be extended to biased models, if we assume that $[U_2(1, \cdot, p) - U_2(0, \cdot, p)]$ is bounded and bounded away from zero, and that the density f^1 is continuous and positive.[18] For, in this case, for σ large,

$$\sup_{A}\{f^{\sigma}(U(1, A, p) - U(0, A, p))[U_2(1, A, p) - U_2(0, A, p)]\} < 1.$$

$$(2.25)$$

Hence, equilibrium will be unique, if the population displays sufficient heterogeneity. On the other hand, as $\sigma \to 0$, inequality (2.25) is reversed and multiple equilibria appear.

We can derive more detailed properties if we assume, in addition to the symmetry and monotonicity properties of f, that $U_{22}(1, A, p) - U_{22}(0, A, p) \leq 0$; that is, the average action A has a diminishing marginal impact on the preference for the high action. In that case, it is easy to show that there are at most three equilibria.

2.5.   Choice of Peer Group

The mathematical structure and the empirical description of peer or reference groups vary from model to model. In several models (e.g., Benabou, 1993, Glaeser, Sacerdote, and Scheinkman, 1996, Gabszewicz and Thisse, 1996, or Mobius, 1999), the reference group is formed by geographical neighbors. To obtain more precise results, one must further specify the mathematical structure of the peer group relationship – typically assuming either that all fellow members of a given geographical unit form a reference group or that each agent's reference group is formed by a set of near-neighbors. Mobius (1999) shows that, in the context that generalizes Schelling's (1972) tipping model, the persistence of segregation depends on the particular form of the near-neighbor relationship. Glaeser, Sacerdote, and Scheinkman (1996) show that the variance of crime rates across neighborhoods or cities would be a function of the form of the near-neighbor relationship.

Kirman (1983), Kirman, Oddou, and Weber (1986), and Ioannides (1990) use random graph theory to treat the peer group relationship as random. This approach is particularly useful in deriving properties of the probable peer groups as a function of the original probability of connections. Another literature deals with individual incentives for the formation of networks (e.g., Boorman, 1975, Jackson and Wolinsky, 1996, and Bala and Goyal 2000).[19]

---

[18] An example that satisfies these conditions is the model of Brock and Durlauf described in Example 2.1. Brock and Durlauf use a slightly different state space, but once the proper translations are made, $U_2(1, A, p) - U_2(0, A, p) = kJ$ for a positive constant k and $0 < f^1(z) \leq \nu$.

[19] A related problem is the formation of coalition in games (e.g., Myerson, 1991).

One way to model peer group choice is to consider a set of neighborhoods indexed by $\ell = 1, \ldots, m$ each with n_ℓ slots with $\sum_\ell n_\ell \geq n$.[20] Every agent chooses a neighborhood to join after the realization of the θ_i's. To join neighborhood P^ℓ, one must pay q_ℓ. The peer group of agent i, if he joins neighborhood ℓ, consists of all other agents j that joined ℓ with $\gamma_{ij} = \gamma_{ij'}$ for all peers j and j'. We will denote by A^ℓ the average action taken by all agents in neighborhood ℓ. Our equilibrium notion, in this case, will parallel Tiebout's equilibrium (see, e.g., Bewley 1981).

For given vectors $\theta = (\theta_1, \ldots, \theta_n) \in \Theta^n$ and p, an equilibrium will be a set of prices $(q_1, \ldots, q_m)$, an assignment of agents to neighborhoods, and a vector of actions $a = (a_1, \ldots, a_n)$, that is, an equilibrium given the peer groups implied by the assignment, such that, if agent i is assigned to neighborhood ℓ, there is no neighborhood ℓ' such that

$$\sup_{a_i} U^i(a_i, A^{\ell'}, \theta_i, p) - q_{\ell'} > \sup_{a_i} U^i(a_i, A_i, \theta_i, p) - q_\ell. \tag{2.26}$$

In other words, in an equilibrium with endogenous peer groups, we add the additional restriction that no agent prefers to move.

To examine the structure of the peer groups that arise in equilibrium we assume, for simplicity, that the U^is are independent of i, that is, that all heterogeneity is represented in the θ_is. If an individual with a higher θ gains more utility from an increase of the average action than an individual with a lower θ, then segregation obtains in equilibrium. More precisely, if Θ is an interval $[t_0, t^0]$ of the line, and

$$V(A, \theta, p) \equiv \sup_{a_i} U(a_i, A, \theta, p)$$

satisfies

$$V(A, \theta, p) - V(A', \theta, p) > V(A, \theta', p) - V(A', \theta', p)$$

whenever $A > A'$ and $\theta > \theta'$, there exist points $t_0 = t_0 < t_1, < \cdots < t_m = t^0$ such that agent i chooses neighborhood ℓ if and only if $\theta_i \in [t_{\ell-1}, t_\ell]$ (e.g., Benabou, 1993, and Glaeser and Scheinkman, 2001). Although other equilibria exist, these are the only "stable" ones.

3. EMPIRICAL APPROACHES TO SOCIAL INTERACTIONS

The theoretical models of social interaction models discussed previously are, we believe, helpful in understanding a wide variety of important empirical

---

[20] This treatment of peer group formation is used in Benabou (1993) and Glaeser and Scheinkman (2001). However, in several cases, peer groups have no explicit fees for entry. Mailath, Samuelson, and Shaked (1996) examine the formation of peer groups when agents are matched to others from the same peer group.

regularities. In principle, large differences in outcomes between seemingly homogeneous populations, radical shifts in aggregate patterns of behavior, and spatial concentration and segregation can be understood through social interaction models. But these models are not only helpful in understanding stylized facts, they can also serve as the basis for more rigorous empirical work. In this section, we outline the empirical approaches that can be and have been used to actually measure the magnitude of social interactions.

For simplicity, in this empirical section, we focus on the linear-quadratic version of the model discussed in Example 2.2. Our decision to focus on the linear-quadratic model means that we ignore some of the more important questions in social interactions. For example, the case for place-based support to impoverished areas often hinges on a presumption that social interactions have a concave effect on outcome. Thus, if impoverished neighborhoods can be improved slightly by an exogenous program, then the social impact of this program (the social multiplier of the program) will be greater than if the program had been enacted in a more advantaged neighborhood. The case for desegregation also tends to hinge on concavity of social interactions. Classic desegregation might involve switching low human capital people from a disadvantaged neighborhood and high human capital people from a successful neighborhood. This switch will be socially advantageous if moving the low human capital people damages the skilled area less than moving the high human capital people helps the less skilled area. This will occur when social interactions operate in a concave manner.

As important as the concavity or convexity of social interactions has been, most of the work in this area has focused on estimating linear effects.[21]

To highlight certain issues that arise in the empirical analysis, we make many simplifying assumptions that help us focus on the relevant problems.[22] We will use the linear model in Example 2.2. We assume we can observe data on C, equally sized,[23] groups. All interactions occur within a group.

Rewriting equation (2.6) for the optimal action, to absorb p in the θ_i', we have

$$a_i = \beta A_i + \theta_i. \tag{3.1}$$

We will examine here a simple form of global interactions. If agent i belongs to group ℓ,

$$A_i = \frac{1}{n-1} \sum_{j \neq i} a_j,$$

---

[21] Crane (1991) is a notable exception. He searches for nonlinearities across a rich range of variables and finds some evidence for concavity in the social interactions involved in out-of-wedlock births. Reagan, Weinberg, and Yankow (2000) similarly explore nonlinearities in research on work behavior and find evidence for concavity.

[22] A recent survey of the econometrics of a class of interaction-based binary choice models, and a review of the empirical literature, can be found in Brock and Durlauf (2001).

[23] The assumption of equally sized groups is made only to save on notation.

where the sum is over the agents j in group ℓ, and n is the size of a group. We will also assume that $\theta_i = \lambda_\ell + \varepsilon_i$, where the ε_i's are assumed to be iid, mean zero λ_ℓ is a place-specific variable (perhaps price) that affects everyone in the group, and ε_i is an idiosyncratic shock that is assumed to be independent across people.

The average action within a group is

$$\frac{\sum_i a_i}{n} = \frac{\lambda_\ell}{1 - \beta} + \frac{\sum_i \varepsilon_i}{n(1 - \beta)}. \tag{3.2}$$

The optimal action of agent i is then

$$a_i = \frac{\lambda_\ell}{1 - \beta} + \frac{(n - 1 - \beta n + 2\beta)\varepsilon_i}{(n - 1 + \beta)(1 - \beta)} + \frac{\beta \sum_{j \neq i} \varepsilon_j}{(n - 1 + \beta)(1 - \beta)}. \tag{3.3}$$

The variance of actions on the whole population is

$$\mathrm{Var}(a_i) = \frac{\sigma_\lambda^2}{(1 - \beta)^2} + \sigma_\varepsilon^2 \left(1 + \left(\frac{\beta}{1 - \beta} \right)^2 \frac{3(n - 1) - 2\beta(n - 2) - \beta^2}{(n - 1 + \beta)^2} \right). \tag{3.4}$$

As $n \to \infty$, this converges to $[\sigma_\lambda^2/(1 - \beta)^2] + \sigma_\varepsilon^2$. In this case, and in the cases that are to follow, even moderate levels of n ($n = 30+$) yield results that are quite close to the asymptotic result. For example, if $n = 40$ and $\beta \leq .5$, then the bias is at most $-.05\sigma_\varepsilon^2$. Higher values of β are associated with more severe negative biases; but, when $n = 100$, a value of $\beta = .75$ (which we think of as being quite high) is associated with a bias of only $-.135\sigma_\varepsilon^2$.

3.1. Variances Across Space

The simplest, although hardly the most common, method of measuring the size of social interactions is to use the variance of a group average. The intuition of this approach stems from early work on social interactions and multiple equilibria [see, e.g., Schelling (1978), Becker (1991), or Sah (1991)]. These papers all use different social interaction models to generate multiple equilibria for a single set of parameter values.

Although multiple equilibria are often used as an informal device to explain large cross-sectional volatility, in fact this multiplicity is not needed. What produces high variation is that social interactions are associated with large differences across time and space that cannot be fully justified by fundamentals. Glaeser, Sacerdote, and Scheinkman (1996) use this intuition to create a model in which social interactions are associated with a high degree of variance across space without multiple equilibria. Empirically, it is difficult to separate out extremely high variances from multiple equilibria, but Glaeser and Scheinkman (2001) argue that for many variables high-variance models with a single equilibrium are a more parsimonious means of describing the data.

Suppose we obtain $m \leq n$ observations of members of a group. The sum of the observed actions, normalized by dividing by the square root of the number of observations, will have variance

$$\text{var}\left(\frac{\sum_i a_i}{\sqrt{m}}\right) = \frac{m\sigma_\lambda^2}{(1-\beta)^2} + \frac{\sigma_\varepsilon^2}{(1-\beta)^2}$$

$$+ (n-m)\sigma_\varepsilon^2 \frac{\beta^2(n-2) - 2\beta(n-1)}{(1-\beta)^2(n-1+\beta)^2}. \tag{3.5}$$

When $m = n$, (3.5) reduces to $[n\sigma_\lambda^2/(1-\beta)^2] + [\sigma_\varepsilon^2/(1-\beta)^2]$, which is similar to the variance formula in Glaeser, Sacerdote, and Scheinkman (1996) or Glaeser and Scheinkman (2001). Thus, if $m = n$ and $\sigma_\lambda^2 = 0$, as $n \to \infty$ the ratio of the variance of this normalized aggregate to the variance of individual actions converges to $1/(1-\beta)^2$. Alternatively, if m is fixed, then as n grows large, the aggregate variance converges to

$$\frac{m\sigma_\lambda^2}{(1-\beta)^2} + \sigma_\varepsilon^2,$$

and the ratio of the aggregate variance to the individual variance (when $\sigma_\lambda^2 = 0$) converges to one.

The practicality of this approach hinges on the extent to which σ_λ^2 is either close to zero or known.[24] As discussed previously, λ_ℓ may be nonzero either because of correlation of background factors or because there are place-specific characteristics that jointly determine the outcomes of neighbors. In some cases, researchers may know that neighbors are randomly assigned and that omitted place-specific factors are likely to be small. For example, Sacerdote (2000) looks at the case of Dartmouth freshman year roommates who are randomly assigned to one another. He finds significant evidence for social interaction effects. In other contexts [see Glaeser, Sacerdote, and Scheinkman (1996)], there may be methods of putting an upper bound on σ_λ^2 that allows the variance methodology to work. Our work found extremely high aggregate variances that seem hard to reconcile with no social interactions for reasonable levels of σ_λ^2. In particular, we estimated high levels of social interactions for petty crimes and crimes of the young. We found lower levels of social interactions for more serious crimes.

3.2.   Regressing Individual Outcomes on Group Averages

The most common methodology for estimating the size of social interactions is to regress an individual outcome on the group average. Crane (1991), discussed previously, is an early example of this approach. Case and Katz (1991) is another early paper implementing this methodology (and pioneering the instrumental variables approach discussed herein). Since these papers, there has been a torrent

---

[24] In principle, we could use variations in n across groups, and the fact that when $m = n$ the variance of the aggregates is an affine function of m to try to separately estimate σ_λ and σ_ε.

of later work using this approach, and it is the standard method of trying to measure social interactions.

We will illustrate the approach considering a univariate regression in which an individual outcome is regressed on the average outcome in that individual's peer group (not including himself). In almost all cases, researchers control for other characteristics of the subjects, but these controls would add little but complication to the formulas. The univariate ordinary least squares coefficient for a regression of an individual action on the action of his peer is

$$\frac{\text{cov}\left(a_i, \sum_{j \neq i} a_j/(m-1)\right)}{\text{Var}\left(\sum_{j \neq i} a_j/(m-1)\right)}. \tag{3.6}$$

The denominator is a transformation of (3.5), where $m - 1$ replaces $\sqrt{m}$:

$$\text{Var}\left(\frac{\sum_{j \neq i} a_j}{m-1}\right) = \frac{\sigma_\lambda^2}{(1-\beta)^2}$$
$$+ m\sigma_\varepsilon^2 \frac{[(n-1+\beta) - \beta(n-m)]^2 + \beta^2 m(n-m)}{(m-1)^2(1-\beta)^2(n-1+\beta)^2}. \tag{3.7}$$

The numerator is

$$\text{cov}\left(a_i, \frac{\sum_{j \neq i} a_j}{m-1}\right) = \frac{\sigma_\lambda^2}{(1-\beta)^2} + \beta\sigma_\varepsilon^2 \frac{(2n-2-\beta n + 2\beta)}{(1-\beta)^2(n-1+\beta)^2}. \tag{3.8}$$

When $\sigma_\lambda = 0$, then the coefficient reduces to

$$\text{coeff} = \frac{(m-1)^2}{m} \frac{2\beta(n-1) - \beta^2(n-2)}{(n-1+\beta)^2 - (n-m)[2\beta(n-1) - \beta^2(n-2)]}. \tag{3.9}$$

When $m = n$,

$$\text{coeff} = 2\beta \frac{(n-1)^2}{n(n-1+\beta)} - \beta^2 \frac{(n-1)^2}{(n-1+\beta)^2}. \tag{3.10}$$

Hence as $n \to \infty$, the coefficient converges to $2\beta - \beta^2$. Importantly, because of the reflection across individuals, the regression of an individual outcome on a group average cannot be thought of as a consistent estimate of β. However, under some conditions ($m = n$, large, $\sigma_\lambda^2 = 0$), the ordinary least squares coefficient does have an interpretation as a simple function of β.

Again, the primary complication with this methodology is the presence of correlated error terms across individuals. Some of this problem is corrected by controlling for observable individual characteristics. Indeed, the strength of this approach relative to the variance approach is that it is possible to control for observable individual attributes. However, in most cases, the unobservable characteristics are likely to be at least as important as the observable ones and are likely to have strong correlations across individuals within a given locale. Again, this correlation may also be the result of place-specific factors that affect all members of the community.

One approach to this problem is the use of randomized experiments that allocate persons into different neighborhoods. The Gautreaux experiment was an early example of a program that used government money to move people across neighborhoods. Unfortunately, the rules used to allocate people across neighborhoods are sufficiently opaque that it is hard to believe that this program really randomized neighborhoods.

The Moving to Opportunity experiment contains more explicit randomization. In that experiment, funded by the department of Housing and Urban Development, individuals from high-poverty areas were selected into three groups: a control group and two different treatment groups. Both treatment groups were given money for housing, which they used to move into low-poverty areas. By comparing the treatment and control groups, Katz, Kling, and Liebman (2001) are able to estimate the effects of neighborhood poverty without fear that the sorting of people into neighborhoods is contaminating their results. Unfortunately, they cannot tell whether their effects are the results of peers or other neighborhood attributes. As such, this work is currently the apex of work on neighborhood effects, but it cannot really tell us about the contribution of peers vs. other place-based factors. Sacerdote (2000) also uses a randomized experiment. He is able to compare people who are living in the same building, but who have different randomly assigned roommates. This work is therefore a somewhat cleaner test of peer effects.

Before randomized experiments became available, the most accepted approach for dealing with cases where $\sigma_\lambda^2 \neq 0$ was to use peer group background characteristics as instruments for peer group outcomes. Case and Katz (1991) pioneered this approach, and under some circumstances it yields valid estimates of β. To illustrate this approach, we assume that there is a parameter (x) that can be observed for all people and that is part of the individual error term (i.e., $\epsilon_i = \gamma x_i + \mu_i$). Thus, the error term can be decomposed into a term that is idiosyncratic and unobservable, and a term that is directly observable. Under the assumptions that both components of ϵ_i are orthogonal to λ_ℓ and to each other, using the formula for an instrumental variables estimator we find that

$$\frac{\text{Cov}\left(a_i, \sum_{j \neq i} x_j/(m-1)\right)}{\text{Cov}\left(\sum_{j \neq i} a_j/(m-1), \sum_{j \neq i} x_j/(m-1)\right)} = \frac{\beta}{\beta + (1-\beta)\frac{n-1}{m-1}}.$$

(3.11)

When $m = n$, this reduces to β. Thus, in principle, the instrumental variables estimator can yield consistent estimates of the social interaction term of interest.

However, as Manski (1993) stresses, the assumptions needed for this methodology may be untenable. First, the sorting of individuals across communities may mean that $\text{Cov}(x_i, \mu_j) \neq 0$ for two individuals i and j living in the same community. For example, individuals who live in high-education communities may have omitted characteristics that are unusual. Equation (3.11) is no longer valid in that case, and, in general, the instrumental variables estimator will overstate social interactions when there is sorting of this kind. Second, sorting may also mean that $\text{Cov}(x_i, \lambda_\ell) \neq 0$. Communities with people who have high schooling levels, for example, may also have better public high schools or other important community-level characteristics.

Third, the background characteristic of individual j may directly influence the outcome of person i, as well as influencing this outcome through the outcome of individual j. Many researchers consider this problem to be less important, because it occurs only when there is some level of social interaction (i.e., the background characteristic of person j influencing person i). Although this point is to some extent correct, it is also true that even a small amount of direct influence of x_j on a_i can lead to wildly inflated estimates of β, when the basic correlation of x_j and a_j is low. (Indeed, when this correlation is low, sorting can also lead to extremely high estimates of social interaction.) Because of this problem, instrumental variables estimates can often be less accurate than ordinary least squares estimates and need to be considered quite carefully, especially when the instruments are weak.

3.3.   Social Multipliers

A final approach to measuring social interactions is discussed in Glaeser and Scheinkman (2001) and Glaeser, Laibson, and Sacerdote (2000), but to our knowledge has never been really utilized. This approach is derived from a lengthier literature on social multipliers in which these multipliers are discussed in theory, but not in practice (see Schelling 1978), The basic idea is that, when social interactions exist, the impact of an exogenous increase in a variable can be quite high if this increase impacts everyone simultaneously. The effect of the increase includes not only the direct effect on individual outcomes, but also the indirect effect that works through peer influence. Thus, the impact on aggregate outcomes of an increase in an aggregate variable may be much higher than the impact on an individual outcome of an increase in an individual variable.

This idea has been used to explain how the pill may have had an extremely large effect on the amount of female education (see Goldin and Katz, 2000). Goldin and Katz argue that there is a positive complementarity across women who delay marriage that occurs because when one woman decides to delay marriage, her prospective spouse remains in the marriage market longer and is also available to marry other women. Thus, one woman's delaying marriage may increase the incentives for other women to delay marriage, and this can create a social multiplier. Berman (2000) discusses social multipliers and how they might explain how government programs appear to have massive effects on labor practices among Orthodox Jews in Israel. In principle, social multipliers might explain phenomena such as the fact that there is a much stronger connection between out-of-wedlock births and crime at the aggregate level than at the individual level (see Glaeser and Sacerdote, 1999).

In this section, we detail how social multipliers can be used in practice to estimate the size of social interactions. Again, we assume that the individual disturbance term can be decomposed into $\epsilon_i = \gamma x_i + \mu_i$, and that $m = n$. When we estimate the microregression of individual outcomes on characteristic x, when x is orthogonal to all other error terms, the estimated coefficient is

$$\text{Individual coeff} = \gamma \frac{(1 - \beta)n + (2\beta - 1)}{(1 - \beta)n - (1 - \beta)^2}. \tag{3.12}$$

This expression approaches γ as n becomes large, and for even quite modest levels of n ($n = 20$), this expression will be quite close to γ.

Our assumption that the x_i terms are orthogonal to the u_i terms is probably violated in many cases. The best justification for this assumption is expediency – interpretation of estimated coefficients becomes quite difficult when the assumption is violated. One approach, if the assumption is clearly untenable, is to use place-specific fixed effects in the estimation. This will eliminate some of the correlation between individual characteristics on unobserved heterogeneity.

An ordinary least squares regression of aggregate outcomes on aggregate x variables leads to quite a different expression. Again, assuming that the x_i terms are orthogonal to both the λ_ℓ and μ_i terms, then the coefficient from the aggregate regression is $\gamma/(1 - \beta)$.

The ratio of the individual to the aggregate coefficient is therefore

$$\text{Ratio} = \frac{(1 - \beta)n + 2\beta - 1}{n - 1 + \beta}. \tag{3.13}$$

As n grows large, this term converges to $1 - \beta$, which provides us with yet another means of estimating the degree of social interactions. Again, this estimate hinges critically on the orthogonality of the error terms, which generally means an absence of sorting. It also requires (as did the instrumental variables estimators) the assumption that the background characteristics of peers have no direct effect on outcomes.

3.4.   Reconciling the Three Approaches

Although we have put forward the three approaches as distinct ways to measure social interactions, in fact they are identical in some cases. In general, the microregression approach of regressing individual outcomes on peer outcomes (either instrumented or not) requires the most data. The primary advantage of this approach is that it creates the best opportunity to control for background characteristics. The variance approach is the least data intensive, because it generally requires only an aggregate and an individual variance. In the case of a binary variable, it requires only an aggregate variance. Of course, as Glaeser, Sacerdote, and Scheinkman (1996) illustrate, this crude measure can be improved on with more information. The social multiplier approach lies in the middle. This approach is closest to the instrumental variable approach using microdata.

ACKNOWLEDGMENTS

We thank Roland Benabou, Alberto Bisin, Avinash Dixit, Steve Durlauf, James Heckman, Ulrich Horst, and Eric Rasmusen for comments; Marcelo Pinheiro for research assistance; and the National Science Foundation for research support. We greatly benefited from detailed comments by Lars Hansen on an earlier version.

References

Aoki, M. (1995), "Economic Fluctuations with Interactive Agents: Dynamic and Stochastic Externalities," *Japanese Economic Review*, 46, 148–165.

Arthur, W. B. (1989), "Increasing Returns, Competing Technologies and Lock-in by Historical Small Events: The Dynamics of Allocation under Increasing Returns to Scale," *Economic Journal*, 99, 116–131.

Bak, P., K. Chen, J. Scheinkman, and M. Woodford (1993), "Aggregate Fluctuations from Independent Sectoral Shocks: Self-Organized Criticality in a Model of Production and Inventory Dynamics," *Ricerche Economiche*, 47, 3–30.

Bala, V. and S. Goyal (2000), "A Non-Cooperative Model of Network Formation," *Econometrica*, 68, 1181–1229.

Banerjee, A. (1992), "A Simple Model of Herd Behavior," *Quarterly Journal of Economics*, 107, 797–818.

Becker, G. (1991), "A Note on Restaurant Pricing and Other Examples of Social Influences on Price," *Journal of Political Economy*, 99(5), 1109–1116.

Becker, G. and K. M. Murphy (2000), "*Social Economics: Market Behavior in a Social Environment*," Cambridge, MA: Belknap-Harvard University Press.

Benabou, R. (1993), "Workings of a City: Location, Education, and Production," *Quarterly Journal of Economics*, 108, 619–652.

Benabou, R. (1996), "Heterogeneity, Stratification, and Growth: Macroeconomic Effects of Community Structure," *American Economic Review*, 86, 584–609.

Berman, E. (2000), "Sect, Subsidy, and Sacrifice: An Economist's View of Ultra-Orthodox Jews," *Quarterly Journal of Economics*, 15, 905–954.

Bewley, T. (1981), "A Critique of Tiebout's Theory of Local Public Expenditures," *Econometrica*, 49(3), 713–740.

Bikhchandani, S., D. Hirshleifer, and I. Welch (1992), "A Theory of Fads, Fashion, Custom, and Cultural Exchange as Information Cascades," *Journal of Political Economy*, 100, 992–1026.

Blume, L. (1993), "The Statistical Mechanics of Strategic Interaction," *Games and Economic Behavior*, 5, 387–424.

Blume, L. and S. Durlauf (1998), "Equilibrium Concepts for Social Interaction Models," Working Paper, Cornell University.

Boorman, S. (1975), "A Combinatorial Optimization Model for Transmission of Job Information through Contact Networks," *Bell Journal of Economics*, 6(1), 216–249.

Brock, W. (1993), "Pathways to Randomness in the Economy: Emergent Nonlinearity and Chaos in Economics and Finance," *Estudios Economicos*, 8(1), 3–55.

Brock, W. and S. Durlauf (1995), "Discrete Choice with Social Interactions," Working Paper, University of Wisconsin at Madison.

Brock, W. and S. Durlauf (2001), "Interactions Based Models," in *Handbook of Econometrics* (ed. by J. Heckman and E. Leamer), Amsterdam: North-Holland.

Bulow, J., J. Geanakoplos, and P. Klemperer (1985), "Multimarket Oligopoly: Strategic Substitutes and Complements," *Journal of Political Economy*, 93, 488–511.

Case, A. and L. Katz (1991), "The Company You Keep: The Effects of Family and Neighborhood on Disadvantaged Families," NBER, Working Paper 3705.

Cooper, R. and A. John (1988), "Coordinating Coordination Failures in Keynesian Models," *Quarterly Journal of Economics*, 103, 441–464.

Crane, J. (1991), "The Epidemic Theory of Ghettos and Neighborhood Effects on Dropping Out and Teenage Childbearing," *American Journal of Sociology*, 96, 1226–1259.

Diamond, P. (1982), "Aggregate Demand Management in Search Equilibrium," *Journal of Political Economy*, 90, 881–894.

Durlauf, S. (1993), "Nonergodic Economic Growth," *Review of Economic Studies*, 60, 349–366.

Durlauf, S. (1996a), "A Theory of Persistent Income Inequality," *Journal of Economic Growth*, 1, 75–93.

Durlauf, S. (1996b), "Neighborhood Feedbacks, Endogenous Stratification, and Income Inequality," in *Dynamic Disequilibrium Modeling – Proceedings of the Ninth International Symposium on Economic Theory and Econometrics*, (ed. by W. Barnett, G. Gandolfo, and C. Hillinger), Cambridge: Cambridge University Press.

Ellison, G. (1993), "Learning, Local Interaction, and Coordination," *Econometrica*, 61, 1047–1072.

Ellison, G. and D. Fudemberg (1993), "Rules of Thumb for Social Learning," *Journal of Political Economy*, 101, 612–644.

Follmer, H. (1974), "Random Economies with Many Interacting Agents," *Journal of Mathematical Economics*, 1, 51–62.

Froot, K., D. Scharfstein, and J. Stein (1992), "Herd on the Street: Informational Inefficiencies in a Market with Short-Term Speculation," *Journal of Finance*, 47, 1461–1484.

Gabszewicz, J. and J.-F. Thisse (1996), "Spatial Competition and the Location of Firms," in *Location Theory*, (ed. by R. Arnott) *Fundamentals of Pure and Applied Economics*, Vol. 5, (ed. by J. Lesourne and H. Sonnenschein), Chur, Switzerland: Harwood Academic, 1–71.

Gale, D. and H. Nikaido (1965), "The Jacobian Matrix and the Global Univalence of Mappings," *Mathematische Annalen*, 159, 81–93.

Glaeser, E., D. Laibson, and B. Sacerdote (2000), "The Economic Approach to Social Capital," Working Paper 7728, NBER.

Glaeser, E. and B. Sacerdote (1999), "Why Is There More Crime in Cities?" *Journal of Political Economy*, 107(6), 225–258.

Glaeser, E., B. Sacerdote, and J. Scheinkman (1996), "Crime and Social Interactions," *Quarterly Journal of Economics*, 111, 507–548.

Glaeser, E. and J. Scheinkman (2001), "Measuring Social Interactions," in *Social Dynamics*, (ed. by S. Durlauf and P. Young.), Cambridge, MA: MIT Press.

Goldin, C. and L. Katz (2000), "The Power of the Pill: Oral Contraceptives and Women's Career and Marriage Decisions," NBER, Working Paper 7527.

Gul, F. and R. Lundholm (1995), "Endogenous Timing and the Clustering of Agents' Decisions," *Journal of Political Economy*, 103, 1039–1066.

Ioannides, Y. (1990), "Trading Uncertainty and Market Structure," *International Economic Review*, 31, 619–638.

Jackson, M. and A. Wolinsky (1996), "A Strategic Model of Economic and Social Networks," *Journal of Economic Theory*, 71(1), 44–74.

Katz, L., A. Kling, and J. Liebman (2001), "Moving to Opportunity in Boston: Early Results of a Randomized Mobility Experiment," *Quarterly Journal of Economics*, 106, 607–654.

Kirman, A. (1993), "Ants, Rationality, and Recruitment," *Quarterly Journal of Economics*, 93, 137–156.

Kirman, A. (1983), "Communication in Markets: A Suggested Approach," *Economics Letters*, 12, 1–5.

Kirman, A., C. Oddou, and S. Weber (1986), "Stochastic Communication and Opportunities in Baltimore: Early Evidence," Working Paper, Joint Center for Poverty Research, Northwestern University.

Krugman, P. (1991), *"Geography and Trade,"* Cambridge, MA: MIT Press.

Ligget, T. (1985), *Interacting Particle Systems*, New York: Springer-Verlag.

Mailath, G., L. Samuelson, and A. Shaked (1996), "Evolution and Endogenous Interactions," Working Paper, Social Systems Research Institute, University of Wisconsin at Madison.

Manski, C. (1993), "Identification of Endogenous Social Effects: The Reflection Problem," *Review of Economic Studies*, 60, 531–542.

Mas-Colell, A. (1985), "The Theory of General Economic Equilibrium: A Differentiable Approach," Cambridge: Cambridge University Press.

McKenzie, L. W. (1960), "Matrices with Dominant Diagonals and Economic Theory," in *Mathematical Methods in the Social Sciences, 1959*, Stanford, CA: Stanford University Press.

Mobius, M. (1999), "The Formation of Ghettos as a Local Interaction Phenomenon," Working Paper, Massachusetts Institute of Technology.

Murphy, K., A. Shleifer, and R. Vishny (1989), "Industrialization and the Big Push," *Journal of Political Economy*, 97(5), 1003–1026.

Myerson, R. (1991), *Game Theory: Analysis of Conflict.* Cambridge, MA: Harvard University Press.

Pesendorfer, W. (1995), "Design Innovation and Fashion Cycles," *The American Economic Review*, 85(4), 771–792.

Reagan, P, B. Weinberg, and J. Yankow (2000), "Do Neighborhoods Affect Work Behavior?" Evidence from the NLSY 79 Working Paper, Ohio State University.

Sacerdote, B. (2000), Peer Effects with Random Assignment: Results for Dartmouth Roommates, NBER, Working Paper 7469.

Sah, R. (1991), "Social Osmosis and Crime," *Journal of Political Economy*, 99, 1272–1295.

Scheinkman, J. and M. Woodford (1994), "Self-Organized Criticality and Economic Fluctuations," *American Economic Review*, 84(2), 417–421.

Schelling, T. (1971), "Dynamic Models of Segregation," *Journal of Mathematical Sociology*, 1, 143–186.

Schelling, T. (1972), "A Process of Residential Segregation: Neighborhood Tipping," in *Racial Discrimination in Economic Life*, (ed. by A. Pascal), Lexington, MA: Lexington Books.

Schelling, T. (1978), *Micromotives and Macrobehavior*. New York: Norton.

Shiller, R. (2000), *Irrational Exuberance*. Princeton, NJ: Princeton University Press.

Topa, G. (1997), "Social Interactions, Local Spillovers and Unemployment," Working Paper, New York University.

Young, H. P. (1993), "The Evolution of Conventions," *Econometrica*, 61, 57–84.

Young, H. P. (1998), *Individual Strategy and Social Structure: An Evolutionary Theory of Institutions*. Princeton, NJ: Princeton University Press.

Index